Introduction to
Sardinia

Equidistant from the Italian mainland and the Tunisian coast, Sardinia is, in the words of D.H. Lawrence, "lost between Europe and Africa and belonging to nowhere". With its own language and distinct customs, the island boasts a fiercely independent character while remaining unmistakably and exuberantly Italian. There is nothing particularly homogenous about the place, however. As the Mediterranean's second biggest island after Sicily – though with less than a third of Sicily's population – Sardinia encompasses a range of diverse faces, from the sleek yachts of the fabled Costa Smeralda to the simple shepherd's society of the mountainous interior. The fact that you can pass from one to the other in less than an hour is part of the island's appeal.

Neither image, of course, represents more than a fragment of the whole picture. Sardinia has secluded **beaches** and rocky headlands on every coast, interspersed with dramatic cliffs and placid lagoons, while the interior is characterized by forested **mountains** and pungent expanses of wild *macchia* – all of which help to account for the rich diversity of wildlife.

Not only the island but each of its four **provinces** of Cágliari, Oristano, Sássari and Nuoro has this range, while within – or sometimes transcending – these administrative boundaries there exists a mosaic of smaller

Corsica

Bonifacio

I. La Maddalena

Santa Teresa
di Gallura

I. Caprera

Palau

Porto Cervo

I. Asinara

Arzachena

Costa
Smeralda

Punta
Falcone

Tempio
Pausania

Olbia

Golfo Aranci

Stintino

Castelsardo

Porto
Torres

Sássari

Lago del
Coghinas

Anghelu
Ruju

Chilivani

Buddusò

Posada

Capo
Caccia

Alghero

Torralba

Siniscola

Nuraghe di
Santu Antine

Nuoro

Orosei

Bosa

Cala Gonone

Macomer

Oliena

Dorgali

Mamoiada

Orgósolo

Abbasanta

Lago
Omodeo

Fonni

Sinis

Sórgono

Tonara

Désulo

Aritzo

MONTI DEL

Arbatax

Tharros

Oristano

GENNARGENTU

Tortolì

T Y R R H E N I A N S E A

Gesturi

Su Nuraxi
Barúmini

Las Plassas

Sanluri

Metres	
	1500
	1000
	500
	200
	100
	0

Iglésias

Muravera

I. di
San Pietro

Portoscuso

Carbonia

Carloforte

Cágliari

Villasimius

Calasetta
Sant'Antíoco

I. di
Sant'Antíoco

Pula

Nora

N

ITALY

Sardinia

The **Rough Guide** to

Sardinia

written and researched by

Robert Andrews

NEW YORK • LONDON • DELHI

www.roughguides.com

△ Cathedral, Sássari

△ Nuraghe Mannu, Cala Gonone

territories, each with its different traditions, dialects and historical roots – for instance Gallura, Logudoro, Sulcis and Sarrabus. At a still more local level, each village celebrates its individuality at the many flamboyant **festivals** that take place throughout the year. Ranging from rowdy medieval pageants to dignified religious processions, these festivities help to keep tradition alive in an island where the past is inescapable.

Where to go

Sardinia's lively capital, **Cágliari**, is a microcosm of Sardinia's diversity, where you'll find traces of every phase of the island's past, from the spindly statuettes of the mysterious nuraghic culture to the Roman theatre and Pisan citadel. Some of the best Roman and Carthaginian ruins stand a short journey outside town at **Nora**, one of the numerous sites which attest to Sardinia's important role in ancient times. Many of the Mediterranean powers that occupied the island were drawn to its mines, still visible throughout the regions of **Sulcis** and **Iglesiente**, west of Cágliari. Off the Sulcis coast, the islands of **Sant'Antíoco** and **San Pietro** provide more archeological remains, while the southern littoral and the Iglesiente's **Costa Verde** are among Sardinia's most scenic coasts, dotted with some prime beaches.

The island's only extensive plain, the **Campidano**, separates Iglesiente from **La Marmilla**, a hilly country holding some spectacular nuraghic sites, including Sardinia's biggest, **Su Nuraxi**. East of Cágliari, the rugged **Sarrabus** area is fringed by more acres of clean sandy beaches, with resort facilities concentrated in the towns of **Villasimius** and **Muravera**. On the western side of the island, the province of **Oristano** holds an abundance of nuraghic, Carthaginian and Roman remains, the most important of which – the ruins of **Tharros** – lie on the **Sinis peninsula**, whose lagoons and beaches form a protected habitat for aquatic birds. North of here, **Bosa** is an

Sardinia's Pisan churches

Visitors to Sardinia who have spent any time in Tuscany may be surprised to discover a whole string of Romanesque churches scattered throughout the island which would look more at home in that mainland region. The odd juxtaposition is due to the close association of Pisa with Sardinia between the eleventh and fourteenth centuries. Religious orders were introduced and architects imported, leading to the construction of churches all over the island, but with a particular concentration in the Logudoro and Anglona areas of northern Sardinia. You'll encounter the characteristic black-and-white pattern in the unlikeliest of places, sometimes in remote countryside, such as the marooned-looking Santa Trinità di Saccargia. Two of the most monumental examples, San Gavino and San Simplicio, seem lost among the quiet back streets of Porto Torres and Olbia respectively. Most of the surviving specimens are in a good state of repair, but the interiors have little in the way of decoration – which helps to preserve their murky medieval atmosphere intact.

attractive river port, crowned by an old castle and separated by a long, unspoilt stretch of rocky coast from the much busier resort of **Alghero**, which draws much of the island's tourist trade while retaining its distinctive Catalan character, the result of intense settlement five centuries ago. **Stintino**, on the island's northwestern tip, lies near some beaches of jaw-dropping beauty.

△ Elephant Rock, Castelsardo

Inland, Sardinia's second city, **Sássari**, makes a good base for touring the Pisan churches scattered throughout the Logudoro area south and east of here. On the north coast, picturesque **Castelsardo** is the chief town of **Anglona**, a region indelibly associated with the Doria family of Genoa. Bordering it, **Gallura**'s dramatically craggy interior, swathed in cork forests and *macchia*, backs onto its famously beautiful granite coastline, where the **Costa Smeralda** remains an exclusive enclave among a host of less celebrated but equally enticing stretches of rocky or sandy shore. Some of the best beaches are clustered around such centres as **Santa Teresa di Gallura** – the chief port for connections with Corsica – on Sardinia's northern tip,

△ Musicians at festival

The art of costume

In a deeply traditional society such as Sardinia's, the local **costumes** are at the heart of popular culture. Every village has its distinctive garb, often several versions, and it is this very diversity that makes the local outfits so fascinating. Apart from a few villages in the interior where they are mainly the preserve of elderly folk, the costumes are not a part of everyday wear, but are taken out on special occasions. You're most likely to come across them either at dances and musical events, when the local performers appear in all their finery, or in set-piece processions at festas.

The costumes fall into two main groups, the first of which has a gaudy, medieval flavour, including white masks, black belted tunics, white pantaloons and black knee-length boots for the men and shawls, scarlet aprons, copious lace and jewellery for women. The second group belongs to a much darker, more pagan tradition, especially prevalent in the mountainous province of Nuoro, where local events may feature characters lumbering scarily through the streets in shaggy goats' hair jackets, grotesque black masks and long horns. You'll find costumes on show in various village museums, but the most comprehensive collection is at Nuoro's ethnographic museum (see p.314).

and **Palau**, embarkation point for trips to the **Maddalena archipelago**, whose crystalline waters are also a magnet for boatloads of visitors in summer. South of here, **Olbia** is the main entry point for most of the seasonal swarms from the mainland, although it doesn't warrant an extended stay.

Below Olbia, most of Sardinia's eastern coast is largely inaccessible, the sheer cliff walls punctuated by a few developed spots such as **Cala Gonone** and by the small-scale ferry port of **Arbatax**. The huge central province of **Nuoro** occupies most of the mountainous interior, and is the best place to encounter the last authentic remnants of the island's rural culture, particularly its costumes and village festivals. If your image of Sardinia is all shaggy sheep and offbeat folklore – the kind of place depicted in films like *Padre Padrone* – then these bleak slopes and isolated villages will probably fit the bill. This is especially true in the central area known as **Barbagia**, where the sparse population is concentrated in small, insulated villages that provide an excellent opportunity to view the quiet life of the interior at first hand, and make useful bases for mountain rambles. Although Sardinia's peaks are not particularly high by European standards (no mountain exceeds 2000m), the terrain can be both awesome and forbidding, particularly in the central ring of the **Gennargentu** mountains, which are often blanketed in snow between November and March.

△ Mouflon

When to go

The best advice that can be given regarding when to visit Sardinia is to avoid the month of **August** at all costs. Travelling at this time is by no means impossible, but the negative factors include sweltering heat, crowds, increased prices, frayed tempers and scarce accommodation. June, July and September can also be oppressively hot, but there is nothing like the kind of holiday frenzy of the peak weeks. You can count on **swimming** fairly comfortably at any time between May

△ Mural, Orgosolo

△ Beach, Costa Rei

and late September, nor will you be considered excessively eccentric if you take dips during the winter months. Unless you're camping, there's much to be said for travelling in Sardinia in **winter** – the weather can be warm and clear and the tourist presence is refreshingly low-key, though the diminished daylight hours in this period can limit your freedom of movement, and you may find many facilities (including most campsites) closed. Some of the best festivals take place in **spring**, and this is also the ideal period for walking, when the countryside is at its most vibrant, the air limpid and the wildlife abundant. **Autumn** is also an inspiring time for being outdoors, especially for the gradations of colour on the forested slopes of the interior.

Average daily temperatures (°C) and monthly rainfall (mm)

	Jan	Feb	Mar	Apr	May	Jun	Jul	Aug	Sep	Oct	Nov	Dec
Cágliari (sea level)												
Av temp (°C)	10	11	12.5	14.5	18	24	25	25.5	23	18.5	14	12
Rainfall (mm)	4.4	4	3.9	3.5	3.5	0.8	0.5	0.8	3	5	6	7
Nuoro (alt 550m)												
Av temp (°C)	4	5	7	10	14	19	23	22	19	15	9	6
Rainfall (mm)	15.5	15	14	11.5	10	3.5	1.5	1.5	6	10.5	15	18

22
things not to miss

It's not possible to see everything Sardinia has to offer in one trip – and we don't suggest you try. What follows is a selective taste of the island's highlights – historic monuments, dramatic landscapes and great beaches. Arranged in five colour-coded categories, you can browse through to find the very best things to see, do and experience. All highlights have a page reference to take you straight into the guide, where you can find out more.

01 **S'Ardia horse race** Page **184** • One of the most exciting annual events on the island, in which bareback riders career recklessly around the church of Sant'Antine amid much audience participation.

02 **Boat tour to Tavolara** Page **273** • Take a boat trip to this formidable-looking wedge of rock, rising dramatically above the coast south of Olbia and with great swimming opportunities.

04 **San Gavino, Porto Torres** Page **243** • One of the island's most eminent Pisan churches, tucked in the back streets of this northern port.

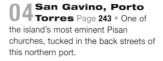

03 **Nuraghe Santu Antine** Page **256** • One of the island's most imposing *nuraghi*, occupying the plains southeast of Sássari amid a cluster of these prehistoric monuments.

05 **Bosa** Page **211** • Explore the atmospheric lanes of this quiet, riverside town overlooked by a hilltop castle, dine at its excellent restaurants or head for the enticing beaches nearby.

06 Walk to Tiscali, near Nuoro Page **322** • The climb to this nuraghic village – cunningly hidden within a huge cave in the Lanaittu valley east of Nuoro – makes a memorable half-day hike.

07 Museo Archeologico, Cágliari Page **77** • Sardinia's premier archeological collection, this well-presented display includes grinning deities, nuraghic figurines and Phoenician inscriptions from the dawn of history.

08 Inland Gallura Page **297** • Interspersed with thick groves of cork oaks, the granite rockscape of this scarcely populated mountainous zone offers unforgettable panoramas.

09 La Pelosa Page **222** • The beaches and rocky backdrop of this beauty spot are postcard-perfect, with aquamarine water and views out to the island of Asinara.

10 **Neptune's Grotto, Alghero** Page **206** • Stalagtites, stalagmites and eccentric rock formations are the highlights of a tour through the Grotta di Nettuno, a cave complex set in towering cliffs by the sea.

11 **Castelsardo old town** Page **249** • With historic churches buried among its steep lanes, and a castle/museum at its summit offering distant coastal views, this old Doria stronghold repays the uphill slog.

12 **Cágliari's old town** Page **73** • A wander through Cágliari's old citadel combines historic monuments, a warren of medieval lanes and fine views of the city and the coast.

13 **Seafood in Alghero** Page **202** • Alghero's restaurants are renowned for their fresh seafood platters, with ingredients fresh from the boat.

14 Nora Page 103 • An important centre for Phoenicians, Carthaginians and Romans for more than a thousand years, Nora's splendid seaside position and fragmentary ruins still evoke its former glory.

15 Sa Sartiglia, Oristano Page 167 • Costumed hijinks and equestrian showmanship recall the medieval roots of this boisterous festival.

16 Santissima Trinità di Saccargia Page 253 • Strikingly situated, this is one of the best preserved of the Pisan-Romanesque churches that dot northern Sardinia.

17 Tharros, Sinis Peninsula Page 173 • Founded by the Phoenicians on a promontory jutting into the sea, this historic site retains extensive evidence of the Punic and Roman settlers who followed.

18 Exploring the Costa del Sud Page **106** • Sardinia's rocky southern coast, interspersed with sandy beaches and rocky coves, is perfect for a scenic hike or cycle.

19 Ethnographic Museum, Sant'Antioco Page **112** • A visit to this lively collection offers an intriguing foray into the local culture – it's crammed with examples of craftwork, traditional tools and cooking implements.

21 Santa Cristina Page **182** • The sacred well and scattered nuraghic monuments under a canopy of centuries-old olive trees constitute one of the island's most picturesque prehistoric sites.

20 Sassari's old town Page **233** • The compact old quarter of Sardinia's second city shelters some handsome remnants from its long history, such as the Renaissance Fonte Rosello.

22 Easter celebrations Page **48** • Costumes, processions and intense drama are the main ingredients of Sardinia's various festas commemorating Easter.

Contents

Using this Rough Guide

We've tried to make this Rough Guide a good read and easy to use. The book is divided into six main sections, and you should be able to find whatever you want in one of them.

Colour section

The front colour section offers a quick tour of Sardinia. The **introduction** aims to give you a feel for the island, with suggestions on where to go. We also tell you what the weather is like and include a basic fact file. Next, our author rounds up his favourite aspects of the island in the **things not to miss** section – whether it's great scenery, amazing architecture or a special museum. Right after this comes a full **contents** list.

Basics

The Basics section covers all the **pre-departure** nitty-gritty to help you plan your trip. This is where to find out which airlines fly to your destination, what paperwork you'll need, what to do about money and insurance, about Internet access, food, security, public transport, car rental – in fact just about every piece of **general practical information** you might need.

Guide

This is the heart of the Rough Guide, divided into user-friendly .chapters, each of which covers a specific area. Every chapter starts with a list of **highlights** and an **introduction** that helps you to decide where to go, depending on your time and budget. Likewise, introductions to the various towns and smaller areas within each chapter should help you plan your itinerary. We start most town accounts with information on arrival and accommodation, followed by a tour of the sights, and finally reviews of places to eat and drink, and details of nightlife. Longer accounts also have a directory of practical listings. Each chapter concludes with **public transport** details for that region.

Contexts

Read Contexts to get a deeper understanding of what makes Sardinia tick. We include an introduction to its **history**, plus a further reading section that reviews the most important **books** relating to the island.

Language

The **Language** section gives useful guidance for speaking Italian, and pulls together all the vocabulary you might need on your trip, including a comprehensive food glossary.

Index + small print

Apart from a **full index**, which includes maps as well as places, this section covers publishing information, credits and acknowledgements, and also has our contact details in case you want to send in updates and corrections to the book – or suggestions as to how we might improve it.

Map and chapter list

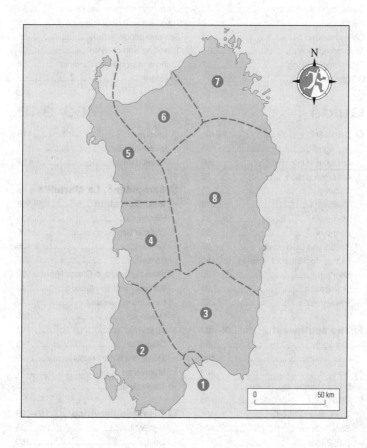

Contents

Contexts
347–365

Language
367–383

Index and small print
385–396

Map symbols

Maps are listed in the full index using coloured text.

-----	International boundary	@	Internet
--- ··	Provincial boundary	☦	Church (regional maps)
--- ---	Chapter division boundary	⌇	Gorge
═══	Highway	⌄⌄	Mountain range
═══	Main road	⌒	Cave
──	Minor road	▲	Peak
──	Unpaved road	♛	Castle
═══	Railway	⚠	Campsite
═══	River/canal	Ѱ	Spa
── ──	Ferry route	★	Bus stop
⏝	Bridge	⊠	Post office
═══	Steps	ⓘ	Tourist information
▪▪▪	Wall	♦	Places of interest
♟	Museum	⊞	Hospital
P	Parking	▮	Building
✈	Airport	✚	Church (town maps)
∴	Ruins	⬯	Stadium
ᎀ	Archeological site	▨	Park
◉	Accommodation	⊞	Cemetery
▣	Restaurant		

Basics

Basics

Getting there

Of the two ways to reach Sardinia – by air or by sea – flying is obviously the quicker, and prices often compare well with the long rail/ferry option. Even so, arriving by sea has much to recommend it, helping to give a sense of Sardinia as an island, though the ferries can get uncomfortably congested in high season.

You can fly directly from the UK either by charter flight or by a scheduled service, usually routed via the Italian mainland. Airfares always depend on the **season**, with the highest being around July and August; fares drop during the "shoulder" seasons – April to June and September to October – and you'll get the best prices during the low season, November to March (excluding Christmas and New Year, when prices are hiked up and seats are at a premium). Note also that flying on weekends is generally more expensive; the price ranges quoted below assume mid-week travel.

You can often cut costs by going through a **specialist flight agent**. This can be either a **consolidator**, who buys up blocks of tickets from the airlines and sells them at a discount, or a **discount agent**, who in addition to dealing with discounted flights may also offer special student and youth fares and a range of other travel-related services such as travel insurance, rail passes, car rentals, tours and the like. Some agents specialize in **charter flights**, which may be cheaper than anything available on a scheduled flight, but, again, departure dates are fixed and withdrawal penalties are high.

You might also consider a **package deal** from one of the tour operators listed below. Although Sardinia is not a particularly cheap package holiday destination, many operators offer rates as competitively as you could find on your own and also provide specialized tours, such as hiking or archaeology. Some agents can sell you an **open-jaw** return, flying to one airport and returning from another – a good idea if you want to make your way across the island or to Sardinia from somewhere else in Italy, and generally are no more expensive than a standard charter return.

The main Sardinian **airports** are outside the towns of Cágliari, Olbia and Alghero. Fares with Alitalia from Rome or Milan to any one of these are in the range of US\$180–300, with no student discounts available. For information on flights to Sardinia from the Italian mainland, see p.14.

Booking flights online

Many airlines and discount travel websites offer you the opportunity to book your tickets online, cutting out the costs of agents and middlemen. Good deals can often be found through discount or auction sites, as well as through the airlines' own websites.

Online booking agents and general travel sites

ⓦ **www.cheapflights.com** Bookings from the UK and Ireland. Flight deals, travel agents and links to other travel sites.

ⓦ **www.cheaptickets.com** American discount flight specialists.

ⓦ **www.ebookers.com** Low fares on an extensive selection of scheduled flights.

ⓦ **www.etn.nl/discount.htm** A US hub of discount agent web links.

ⓦ **www.expedia.com** Discount airfares, all-airline search engine and daily deals.

ⓦ **www.flyaow.com** Online air travel info and reservations site.

ⓦ **www.hotwire.com** Bookings from the US only. Last-minute savings of up to forty percent on regular published fares, though there are no refunds, transfers or changes allowed.

ⓦ **www.lastminute.com** Bookings from the UK only, offering good last-minute holiday package and flight-only deals.

ⓦ **www.priceline.co.uk** & ⓦ **www.priceline.com** Name-your-own-price websites that have deals at around forty percent off standard fares. You can't specify flight times (although you do specify dates), and the tickets are non-refundable, non-transferable and non-changeable.

ⓦ**www.smilinjack.com/airlines.htm** Lists an up-to-date compilation of airline website addresses.
ⓦ**http://travel.yahoo.com** Incorporates a lot of Rough Guide material in its coverage of destination countries and cities across the world, with information about places to eat and sleep etc.
ⓦ**www.travelshop.com.au** Australian website offering discounted flights, packages, insurance and online bookings.
ⓦ**www.travelocity.com** Destination guides and best deals for car rental, accommodation as well as fares.

Flights from the UK and Ireland

Direct flights from the UK take around two and a half hours from London, either to Olbia or Fertilia (near Alghero) in the north of the island, or Cágliari in the south.

The cheapest way to fly is by direct **charter**, though you'd be advised to book some weeks in advance in high season (Easter, July & Aug). Flight-only deals to Cágliari, Fertilia or Olbia cost from around £110–250 return in high season; outside the summer months, when flights are far less frequent, you probably won't find anything much under £200. There are daily summer departures from the various London airports (1–2 weekly in summer from Manchester), down to once or twice a week in the winter.

These flights are available from the numerous specialist **agencies** (see p.11) that deal with charter flights. If you're prepared to book at the last minute, you might find some very good deals, though seat availability is limited – if you're committed to certain dates, book ahead. Apart from the agencies, other places to check for budget flights are the classified sections in the weekend newspapers and *Time Out* magazine. It's also well worth checking out the **low cost** airline Ryanair which flies direct to Alghero from £110 return (including taxes), though you're limited to flying from Stansted airport. It may also be worth looking at cheap flights to **other Italian destinations**: Fiumicino, Rome's main airport, is only about four hours by fast ferry from Olbia, for example.

You'll pay £105–200 for the only direct **scheduled flight** through Meridiana, which flies on Tuesdays and Saturdays from London Gatwick to Olbia between April and October. Book well ahead in the high season (mid-April to mid-Sept). Flights with Alitalia to Cágliari are more expensive and routed via Italian mainland airports (usually Milan or Rome), which could mean a total journey time of anything up to five hours if you have to wait for a connecting internal flight (flight time from the mainland to Sardinia is about one hour); fares are in the region of £270 in high season. However, scheduled services to the mainland are very frequent (several times daily), though almost all are from one of the London airports. British Airways fly daily from Heathrow, Gatwick and Manchester, Alitalia fly daily from Heathrow, Gatwick via Rome or Milan for around £120–160 return in low season, rising to £250–300 in high season. The cheapest scheduled tickets normally come with certain restrictions. Usually your trip has to include a Saturday night away, and any changes to your ticket incur an additional fee; tickets are also rarely valid for longer than one month.

The cheapest current high-season return fares **from Dublin** to Cágliari (booked at least seven days in advance) are around €480 return; it makes more sense to get to London and then catch a Sardinia-bound plane from there. There are numerous daily flights to London with Ryanair, Aer Lingus, British Airways and British Midland, costing from around €50 for a return to Gatwick, Luton or Stansted, though there are plenty of discounts.

Most airlines now offer direct phone- or internet booking, with many of the **low-cost** operators operating a **ticketless** system; you are given a reference number with which to check in at the airport.

Airlines in the UK and Ireland

Aer Lingus UK ☎0845/084 4444, Republic of Ireland ☎0818/365 000, ⓦwww.aerlingus.ie.
Alitalia UK ☎0870/544 8259, Republic of Ireland ☎01/677 5171, ⓦwww.alitalia.co.uk.
British Airways UK ☎0870/850 9850, Republic of Ireland ☎1800/626 747, ⓦwww.ba.com.
British Midland UK ☎0870/607 0555, Republic of Ireland ☎01/407 3036, ⓦwww.flybmi.com.

Ryanair UK ☎0871/246 0000, Republic of Ireland
☎0818/303 030, ⓦwww.ryanair.com.

Flight and travel agents in the UK and Ireland

Co-op Travel Care UK ☎0870/112 0085,
ⓦwww.travelcareonline.com. Flights to Cágliari.
Flightbookers UK ☎0870/010 7000,
ⓦwww.ebookers.com. Low fares on an extensive
selection of scheduled flights.
Impulse Flights UK ☎0870/888 0228,
ⓦwww.magictravelgroup.co.uk. Sardinia charter
flights from the Magic of Italy group.
Lee Travel Republic of Ireland ☎021/427 7111,
ⓦwww.leetravel.ie. Flights and holidays to Italy.
North South Travel UK ☎01245/608 291,
ⓦwww.northsouthtravel.co.uk. Friendly,
competitive travel agency, offering discounted fares
worldwide – profits are used to support projects in
the developing world, especially the promotion of
sustainable tourism.
STA Travel UK ☎0870/1600 599,
ⓦwww.statravel.co.uk. Worldwide specialists in
low-cost flights and tours for students and under-
26s, though other customers welcome.
Trailfinders UK ☎020/7937 1234
ⓦwww.trailfinders.co.uk Republic of Ireland
☎01/677 7888, ⓦwww.trailfinders.ie. One of the
best-informed and most efficient agents for
independent travellers.
usit NOW Dublin ☎01/602 1600, Belfast
☎028/9032 7111, ⓦwww.usitnow.ie. Student and
youth specialists for flights and trains.

Package holidays

If you don't want to move around much, it's
always worth looking at **travel-plus-
accommodation** package holidays. Many
companies offer travel at rates as competitive as any you could find on your own, and
any travel agent can fill you in on all the latest offers. Most packages are to Alghero
and Stintino in the northwest of the island,
Santa Teresa di Gallura and the Costa
Smeralda region in the northeast, Santa
Margherita di Pula in the southwest, and the
area around Villasimius in the southeast.

It's obviously cheapest to go out of season
– something to be recommended anyway,
as the resorts and sights are much less
crowded, and the sea is often warm enough
to bathe in as early as Easter and as late as
October.

Should you want to rent a car in Sardinia,
it's well worth checking with the package
company before you leave, as some **fly-
drive deals** work out very cheaply. See
p.31–32 for car-rental details.

Package holiday operators

Citalia ☎020/8686 0677, ⓦwww.citalia.co.uk.
Packages in the poshest places, including the Costa
Smeralda, Santa Margherita di Pula and Villasimius,
between May and September, with prices starting
from about £740 per person per week, more than
double that in August. It's worth checking for special
offers; car rental is also laid on.
Interhome ☎020/8891 1294,
ⓦwww.interhome.co.uk. Holiday homes throughout
Sardinia, including apartments in Torre dei Corsari
and Santa Teresa di Gallura for four people at around
£630 in peak season.
Italiatour ☎01883/621 900,
ⓦwww.italiatour.co.uk. Hotel accommodation in the
Santa Margherita di Pula and Villasimius area
between May and September from £600 per person
per week.
Magic of Italy ☎08708/880 222,
ⓦwww.magictravelgroup.co.uk. Packages
throughout the island, including hotels, apartments
and farm accommodation, two-centre holidays, or
just fly-drive deals.
Sardatur ☎020/7242 2455, ⓦwww
.Sardinia-holidays.co.uk. Hotels and self-catering
villas and apartments in the Santa Margherita di Pula
area, the Costa Smeralda and Alghero, plus a fly-
drive option where you can choose different lodgings
all over the island.
Voyages Ilena ☎020/7924 4440, ⓦwww
.voyagesilena.co.uk. Villas, apartments and hotels in
the prime holiday areas of northeast Sardinia, Alghero
and around, and the southwest and southeast.

Specialist tours

There are increasing numbers of **specialist
holiday operators** dealing with Sardinia,
mostly offering walking tours, but also climbing, cycling and diving holidays. These don't
come cheaply: accommodation, food, local
transport and the services of a guide are
nearly always included, and a week's half-
board holiday can cost from £800 per person, full-board as much as £1400.

Specialist tour operators

Alternative Travel Group ☎01865/315 678,
ⓦwww.atg-oxford.co.uk. Inclusive eight-day

walking holidays (May & Oct) in the mountains around Oliena, near Nuoro; expensive (around £1395, excluding flights) but well organized.
Headwater ☎01606/720 033, ⓦwww .headwater.com. Walking holidays in the Maddalena islands and between Aritzo, in the Barbagia region, and the east-coast resort of Cala Gonone (respectively around £740 and £1100 in high season, including flights Gatwick–Olbia).
Saddle Skedaddle ☎0191/265 1110, ⓦwww.skedaddle.co.uk. Short breaks (Fri–Tues; £345) and week-long cycles across the island (£645–725), on-road and off-road; prices include everything apart from flights
Tabona & Walford ☎020/8706 015, ⓦwww .tabonaandwalford.com. Eight-day coastal and mountain walking trips (May); £1200 excluding flights. Also bespoke tours.

Flights from the US and Canada

Although there are no direct flights from the **USA** to Sardinia, you can fly to the Italian mainland from a number of cities. The main points of entry are Rome and Milan, from either of which there are plenty of connecting flights to Sardinia. It might be a good idea to take advantage of the wide choice of well-priced flights available from all over North America to various **European cities** (particularly in Britain or Germany), as there's a greater range of options for reaching Sardinia from there. **Flying** is the most straightforward way to get from Britain to Sardinia, and prices are competitive; see p.10 for full details.

Alitalia, the Italian national airline, offers the widest choice of routes between the USA and Italy, flying direct every day from New York, Boston, Miami, Chicago and Los Angeles to Milan and Rome. As for **American-based airlines**, Delta Airlines flies daily from New York non-stop, and also from Chicago and Los Angeles to Rome and Milan with stopovers in either New York or a European city; TWA flies daily from LA and Chicago via New York to Milan and Rome; American Airlines flies daily direct to Milan from Chicago and Miami; and Continental flies daily from Newark to Rome and Milan.

If you want to **stop over in Europe**, it's worth considering one of the European airlines with services to Italy, including: Air France (via Paris); British Airways (via

London); Iberia (via Madrid); Icelandair (via Luxembourg); KLM/Northwest (via Amsterdam); Lufthansa (via Frankfurt or Münich); and SAS (via Copenhagen) – all of which have services to at least Rome and Milan. Direct flights to Italy take around nine hours from New York or Boston, twelve hours from Chicago, and fifteen hours from Los Angeles; for the **connection to Sardinia** add on another hour or two, depending on the service, plus any time spent waiting for the connection itself.

The basic round-trip **fares to Rome or Milan** vary little between airlines, though it's always worth asking about special promotions. Generally, the cheapest round-trip fare, travelling midweek in low season, starts at around US$590 from New York or Boston to Rome, rising to around US$700 during the shoulder season, and to about US$850 during the summer. Flights from LA work out about US$200 on top of these round-trip fares; from Miami and Chicago, add on about US$100.

The only airlines to fly direct to Italy **from Canada** are Alitalia, which flies daily from Toronto and Montréal to Rome or Milan and Canadian Airlines, which flies to Rome from Toronto and Montréal for around CAN$950 in low season and CAN$1200 in high season, plus connecting flights to Sardinia. Note that these prices do not include taxes. Flights to Italy take around nine hours from the eastern Canadian cities, fifteen hours from the west.

Airlines in North America

Air Canada ☎1-888/247-2262, ⓦwww.aircanada.ca.
Air France US ☎1-800/237-2747, Canada ☎1-800/667-2747, ⓦwww.airfrance.com.
Alitalia US ☎1-800/223-5730, Canada ☎1-800/361-8336, ⓦwww.alitalia.com.
American Airlines ☎1-800/433-7300, ⓦwww.aa.com.
British Airways US ☎1-800/247-9297, Canada ☎1-800/AIRWAYS or ☎416-250 0880, ⓦwww.britishairways.com.
Continental Airlines US ☎1-800/523-3273, international ☎1-800/231-0856, ⓦwww.continental.com.
Delta Air Lines Domestic ☎1-800/221-1212, international ☎1-800/241-4141, ⓦwww.delta.com.

Iberia ☎1-800/772-4642, ⓦwww.iberia.com.
KLM/Northwest Airlines ☎1-800/447-4747,
ⓦwww.klm.com.
Swiss ☎1-877/359-7947, ⓦwww.swiss.com.

Discount travel companies in North America

Air Brokers International ☎1-800/883-3273,
ⓦwww.airbrokers.com. Consolidator and specialist
in round-the-world tickets.
Airtech ☎1-877/247-8324 or 212/219-7000,
ⓦwww.airtech.com. Standby seat broker; also
deals in consolidator fares and courier flights.
Council Travel ☎1-800/2COUNCIL,
ⓦwww.counciltravel.com. Nationwide organization
that mostly specializes in student/budget travel.
Flights from the US only.
Educational Travel Center ☎1-800/747-5551
or 608/256-5551, ⓦwww.edtrav.com.
Student/youth discount agent.
STA Travel US ☎1-800/781-4040, Canada
1-888/427-5639, ⓦwww.sta-travel.com. Worldwide
specialists in independent travel; also student IDs,
travel insurance, car rental, rail passes, etc.
Student Flights ☎1-800/255-8000 or 480/951-
1177, ⓦwww.isecard.com. Student/youth fares,
student IDs.
Travel Cuts Canada ☎1-800/667-2887,
US ☎1-866/246-9762; ⓦwww.travelcuts.com.
Canadian student-travel organization.
Worldtek Travel ☎1-800/243-1723,
ⓦwww.worldtek.com. Discount travel agency.

Packages and organized tours

There are dozens of companies operating
group travel and **tours** in Italy, ranging from
full-blown luxury escorted tours to small
groups sticking to specialized itineraries.
However, specifically Sardinian options are
less common, though the agencies listed
below usually offer tours at least partly
based on the island. If you're happy to stay
in one (or two) places, you can also, of
course, simply book a hotel-plus-flight deal,
or, if you're keener to self-cater, rent a villa or
a farmhouse for a week or two. Prices vary
wildly, so check what you're getting for your
money – many don't include the cost of the
air fare. Reckon on paying at least
US$1500/Can$2250 for a ten-day touring
vacation without flight, and up to as much as
US$5000/Can$7500 for a fourteen-day
escorted specialist package with flight.

Tour operators

Amelia International ☎1-800/742-4591,
ⓦwww.ameliainternational.com. Small group
escorted tours and customized packages.
CIT Tours ☎1-800/CIT-TOUR, Toronto
☎1-800/387-0711, Montréal ☎1-8000/351-
7799, ⓦwww.cittours-canada.com. Specializes
exclusively in tours to Italy and sells Italian rail
passes.
Geographic Expeditions ☎1-800/777-8183 or
415/922-0448, ⓦwww.geoex.com. Ten-day hiking
and kayaking trip in Sardinia for around $3000.
Italiatour US ☎1-800/845-3365, Canada
☎888/515-5345 ⓦwww.italiatourusa.com. In
conjunction with Alitalia, offers fly-drive tours, and
escorted and individual programs.

Flights from Australia and New Zealand

There are no direct flights from Australia and
New Zealand to Sardinia, although many airlines fly to Rome or Milan, from where it's
easy to pick up a connecting flight. However,
if you're visiting Sardinia as part of a wider
European trip, you could head first for the
UK, as there are plenty of options to Sardinia
once there (see p.10). Some airlines offer
discounted Italian tour packages or deals on
accommodation and car rentals.

The only direct flights from **Australia** to
Italy are with Alitalia and British Airways,
though you can reach Rome or Milan with a
host of other airlines; the cheapest fares are
usually with Garuda or Thai Airways. Reckon
on paying anything from AS$1500 to
AS$2500 in high season; the best deals
from New Zealand work out at NZ$2000 in
low season, rising to around NZ$3200.

Airlines

Alitalia Australia ☎02/9244 2400,
ⓦwww.alitalia.com.
British Airways Australia ☎1300/767 177,
New Zealand ☎0800/274 847,
ⓦwww.britishairways.com.
Cathay Pacific Australia ☎13 17 47,
ⓦwww.cathaypacific.com/au; New Zealand
☎09/379 0861 or 0508/800 454,
ⓦwww.cathaypacific.com/nz.
Garuda Indonesia Australia ☎1300/365 330,
New Zealand ☎09/366 1862, ⓦwww
.garuda-indonesia.com.

Japan Airlines Australia ☎02/9272 1111, New Zealand ☎09/379 9906, ⓦwww.japanair.com.
KLM/Northwest Airlines Australia ☎1300/303 747, ⓦwww.klm.com/au_en, New Zealand ☎09/309 1782, ⓦwww.klm.com/nz_en.
Lufthansa Australia ☎1300/655 727, New Zealand ☎0800/945 220, ⓦwww.lufthansa.com.
Malaysia Airlines Australia ☎13 26 27, New Zealand ☎0800/777 747, ⓦwww.malaysiaairlines.com.my.
Qantas Australia ☎13 13 13, ⓦwww.qantas.com.au; New Zealand ☎0800/808 767, ⓦwww.qantas.co.nz.
Singapore Airlines Australia ☎13 10 11, New Zealand ☎0800/808 909, ⓦwww.singaporeair.com.
Thai Airways Australia ☎1300/651 960, New Zealand ☎09/377 0268, ⓦwww.thaiair.com.

Travel agents

Budget Travel New Zealand ☎0800/808 040, ⓦwww.budgettravel.com. Discount flights and holiday specialists.
Flight Centre Australia ☎13 31 33 or 02/9235 3522, ⓦwww.flightcentre.com.au; New Zealand ☎0800/243 544 or 09/358 4310, ⓦwww.flightcentre.co.nz. Discount international air fares and holiday packages.
Northern Gateway Australia ☎1800/813 288, ⓦwww.northerngateway.com.au. RTW fares and European flights.
STA Travel Australia ☎1300/733 035, ⓦwww.statravel.com.au; New Zealand ☎0508/782 872, ⓦwww.statravel.co.nz. Worldwide specialists in low-cost flights and tours for students and under-26s.
Student Uni Travel Australia ☎02/9232 8444, ⓦwww.sut.com.au; New Zealand ☎09/379 4224, ⓦwww.sut.co.nz. Good deals for students.
Trailfinders Australia ☎02/9247 7666, ⓦwww.trailfinders.com.au. One of the best-informed and most efficient agents for independent travellers.
travel.com.au and **travel.co.nz** Australia ☎1300/130 482 or 02/9249 5444, ⓦwww.travel.com.au; New Zealand ☎0800/468 332, ⓦwww.travel.co.nz. Comprehensive online travel company.

Specialist tour operators

Abercrombie & Kent Australia ☎03/9536 1800 or 1300/851 800, New Zealand ☎0800/441 638, ⓦwww.abercrombiekent.com.au. Upmarket cruises calling at Sardinia and Sicily.

Flights from the Italian mainland

Most flights to Sardinia start from the Italian **mainland**, connecting all three of Sardinia's major airports – Fertilia (for Alghero), Olbia and Cágliari – with Rome, Bologna and Milan. The most frequent flights are between Rome and Cágliari (at least 10 daily), and **Cágliari** also has flights from Genoa (1–2 daily); Naples (1 daily); Turin (1 daily); Venice (2–3 daily) and Verona (1 daily). There are also regular flights to Cágliari from Palermo, Pisa and Olbia. There are at least three arrivals daily from Rome and Milan to **Olbia**, two from Bologna and one from Pisa; **Fertilia** has at least four from Rome and three from Milan.

The main **carriers** are Alitalia (ⓦwww.alitalia.it) and Meridiana (ⓦwww.meridiana.it); other lines are Alpi Eagles (from Venice and Verona) and Air Dolomiti (from Genoa). Flight time is about one hour from Rome to Cágliari and about seventy minutes from Milan to Fertilia. Fares vary seasonally and according to how far in advance you book: the cheapest fares are between Rome and Olbia, from about €75 one-way. Purchasing the tickets in Italy – either from a travel agent or direct from the airline – is usually cheaper than buying from abroad.

Overland from the UK and Ireland

The **overland route** to one of the embarkation ports for Sardinia may prove quite a laborious experience, whether you do it by coach, train or your own transport. Obviously, you can choose to do the journey at a more leisurely pace, or speed down through France as quickly as possible, in which case it can turn out to be quite an endurance test.

By rail from the UK and Ireland

Travelling **by train** to Sardinia won't save you much money, but allows you the possibility of breaking your journey. The journey from London across the Channel by ferry, through France to the nearest ports of Marseille, Genoa and Livorno takes a minimum of nine hours, including at least one change of trains, depending on which of the three possible routes you take.

Fares vary according to the route taken, but the ordinary second-class **return fare** on the fastest route (using Eurostar via Paris) to Genoa will cost you £240, to Livorno £260, and to Marseille around £110; all tickets are valid for two months and should be booked at least one week ahead. If you qualify, ask about discounts for the under-26s. Using slower trains and the ferry crossings doesn't lower the cost significantly.

The **Eurostar** passenger train goes from Waterloo International in London to Paris (3hr) and Brussels (2hr 40min) via Ashford in Kent (1hr from London) and the Channel Tunnel. Eurostar passengers must change stations in Paris, which means a metro journey from the Gare du Nord to the Gare de Bercy. The cheapest return ticket to Paris is currently £79, though restrictions apply. You can get through-ticketing – including the tube journey to Waterloo International – from Eurostar (see below), from most travel agents or from mainline train stations in Britain; typical add-on prices for a return ticket to Paris from Edinburgh or Glasgow is £30, from Manchester £20 and Birmingham £13.50. Note that Inter-Rail passes give discounts on the Eurostar service.

Details on all international rail tickets and passes are best obtained through the Internet or by contacting the agents listed below. Don't expect much help from travel agents on planning routes or the Italian State Railway office to answer the phone. All of these prices apply to the slower ferry crossing from Dover or Folkestone.

If you're planning to make Sardinia part of a longer European trip, it might be worth investing in a **rail pass** – the **InterRail** and **Eurail** passes offer a month's unlimited rail travel throughout Europe, but note that they must be bought before leaving home. See "Getting Around" (p.27) for details of all rail passes available, including those for use solely on the Italian state network.

Rail contacts

Eurostar UK ☏ 0870/160 6600,
ⓦ www.eurostar.com.
Italian State Railways UK ☏ 020/7724 0011,
ⓦ www.trenitalia.com.

Northern Ireland Railways UK ☏ 028/9024 2420, ⓦ www.nirailways.co.uk. Sells InterRail passes.
Rail Europe ☏ 08705/848 848, ⓦ www.raileurope.co.uk. Eurostar, InterRail and Euro-Domino passes.

By bus from the UK and Ireland

You can travel to Sardinia by **bus** as far as the ferry crossing at Marseille and Toulon using National Express Eurolines from London. At the time of writing, a daily service departs from Victoria Coach Station at 6.30pm, arriving at Marseille the next day at 2pm local time, and at Toulon an hour later (return trip £105, £69 if booked fifteen days in advance; children half-price). Buses use the Channel ferry crossing, which is included in the price.

Bus contacts in the UK and Ireland

Busabout UK ☏ 020/7950 1661,
ⓦ www.busabout.com. Busabout runs from April to October, taking in fifty European cities, with add-on connections to 35 more, plus a link to London and through tickets from elsewhere in Britain and Ireland. Flexipasses, available from the company or any international branch of STA, allow seven days' travel within one month, twelve days' travel within two months, sixteen days' travel within three months, etc; consecutive passes allow from two weeks to three months' travel. Prices start at £219.
Eurolines UK ☏ 0870/514 3219, Republic of Ireland ☏ 01/836 6111, ⓦ www.eurolines.co.uk. Tickets can also be purchased from any Eurolines or National Express agent (☏ 0870/580 8080, ⓦ www.nationalexpress.com).

By car and ferry from the UK and Ireland

If you're travelling with your **own vehicle**, the best cross-Channel options for most drivers will be the standard ferry/hovercraft links between Dover and Calais/Ostend or Newhaven and Dieppe. Crossing using Eurotunnel (24-hour service, departures every 15min at peak periods) will speed up the initial part of the journey.

Something to bear in mind when calculating driving costs is that **motorway tolls** can add up to another £60 per car driving from Calais to Genoa. Driving in Italy is more expensive than just about anywhere else in Europe, with relatively high fuel prices and rental charges.

Ferries to Sardinia from France and Italy

From the Italian mainland

Tirrenia run most of the services to Sardinia from the Italian mainland and from Palermo and Trápani in Sicily. The **prices** given are the cheapest one-way, high-season fares for reclining chair or deck class. Berths in shared cabins cost about €20 more. Car fares given here are for vehicles less than 3.5 or 4m in length; reckon on another €15–20 for cars longer than this.

Ferries (*Traghetti*) From Italy

Route	Company	Frequency	Length of crossing	Single passenger	Car fare
Civitavecchia–Arbatax	Tirrenia	2 weekly	10hr 30min	€28.50	€72
Civitavecchia–Cágliari	Tirrenia	1 daily	14hr 30min–17hr	€33.50	€95.50
Civitavecchia–Golfo Aranci	Sardinia	1–2 daily (June–Sept)	7–10hr	€20–57	€42.50–90.50
Civitavecchia–Olbia	Tirrenia	1 daily	8hr	€19.50	€87.50
Civitavecchia –Olbia	Moby	5–7 weekly (April–Sept)	5hr	€55.50	€117.50
Genoa–Arbatax	Tirrenia	2 weekly	14–19hr	€42	€95
Genoa–Cágliari	Tirrenia	2 weekly (mid-June to Aug)	20hr	€48.50	€77.50
Genoa–Olbia	Grandi Navi Veloci	1 daily (early June to late Sept)	8–10hr	€38–77	€79–129
Genoa –Olbia	Moby	5–7 weekly (June to mid-Sept)	5hr	€58	€115
Genoa–Olbia	Tirrenia	3–10 weekly	8–13hr 15min	€40.50–53.50	€95.50–103
Genoa–Palau	Enermar	1–4 weekly (mid-April to Sept)	12hr	€40–64	€66–121
Genoa–Porto Torres	Grandi Navi Veloci	6–8 weekly	11hr	€43–74	€97–129
Genoa–Porto Torres	Tirrenia	1–2 daily	8–10hr	€40.50–53.50	€95.50–103
Livorno–Golfo Aranci	Sardinia Ferries	4–8 weekly (April–Oct)	8–10hr	€23.50–50.50	€40.50–116.50
Livorno –Cágliari	Linee dei Golfi	1 weekly	7hr	€28–39	€37–87
Livorno–Olbia	Moby	6–21 weekly (March–Jan)	9–12hr	€49	€112.50

Route	Company	Frequency	Length of crossing	Single passenger	Car fare
Livorno–Olbia	Linee dei Golfi	3–6 weekly	11hr	€27.50–38.50	€36.50–86.50
Napoli–Cágliari	Tirrenia	1–2 weekly	16hr 15min	€32.50	e€80.50
Palermo–Cágliari	Tirrenia	1 weekly	13hr 30min	€32.50	€78
Piombino–Olbia	Linee dei Golfi	9–16 weekly	8–9hr	€18.50–37	€37.50–81.50
Trápani–Cágliari	Tirrenia	1 weekly	11hr 30min	€32.50	€78

"Fast" or "express" ferries (*mezzi veloci/unità veloci*)

Daytime crossings take the shortest time. Fares vary according to season and speed of mezzo veloce.

Civitavecchia–Golfo Aranci	Sardinia Ferries	5–14 weekly (mid-April to Sept)	3hr 50min	€33–57	€46.50–119.50
Civitavecchia–Olbia	Tirrenia	1–4 daily (June to early Sept)	4–6hr	€39.50–49	€90.50–101
Fiumicino–Arbatax	Tirrenia	2 weekly (mid-July to Aug)	4hr 45min	€48	€85.50
Fiumicino–Golfo Aranci	Tirrenia	2–3 daily (mid-June to early Sept)	3hr 30min	€47	€99
Genoa–Palau	Tris	1 daily (July–Aug)	5hr 30min	€52.50–92.50	€74.50–102.50
Livorno–Golfo Aranci	Sardinia Ferries	5 weekly (June–Sept)	6hr	€29.50–58.50	€64–116.50

From the French mainland and Corsica

In summer, you could cross to Bastia, Corsica, with Corsica Ferries (from Savona or Livorno) or Moby (from Genoa or Livorno), then make your way down to Bonifacio (178km), from where it's a short crossing to Sardinia. Note that there are also irregular seasonal crossings from Porto Vecchio in Corsica, and that the year-round ferry from Trápani (Sicily) starts in Tunis.

Bonifacio (Corsica)–Santa Teresa di Gallura	Moby	4–10 dailly (April–Sept)	50min	€15	€44.50
Bonifacio (Corsica)–Santa Teresa di Gallura	Saremar	2–4 daily	1hr	€12	€29.50
Marseille–Porto Torres	SNCM	2–4 weekly	12–16hr	€48	€84

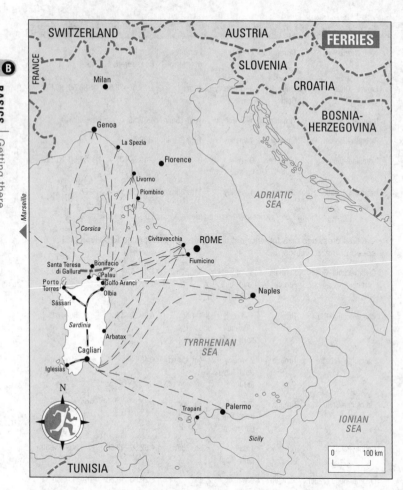

By ferry from the Italian mainland and France

From the Italian mainland, the shortest **ferry crossing** to Sardinia is by "Fast Ferry" or "Express Ferry" from Genoa, Civitavecchia and Fiumicino, though these only run during the summer months. Considerably cheaper regular ferries run year-round from these and other mainland Italian and Sicilian ports, and there are also direct SNCM ferries from Marseille and (occasionally) Toulon in France. Marseille, Toulon and Nice also have regular connections with Corsica, from whose southern tip there are frequent ferry links to Sardinia, providing you with an interesting exercise in comparing and contrasting the two islands.

UK agents for Italian ferries

Corsica Ferries c/o Viamare, Graphic House, 2 Sumatra Rd, London NW6 1PU ☎020/7431 4560 or 0870/410 6040, ⓦwww.viamare.com.

Grandi Navi Veloci c/o Viamare (see above), ⓦwww.gnv.it.

Moby Lines c/o Viamare (see above), ⓦwww.mobylines.it.

SNCM c/o Southern Ferries, 179 Piccadilly, London W1V 9DB ☎020/7491 4968, ⓦwww.sncm.fr.

Tirrenia Line c/o SMS, 40–42 Kenway Rd, London SW5 0RA ☎ 020/7373 6548, ⓦ www.tirrenia.it.

Any travel agent can provide up-to-date cross-Channel schedules and make advance bookings (essential in high season if you're driving). For the Italian crossings, contact the companies or their agents; more details on all these routes are given in the box on p.16–17. In the low season, watch out for **special offers** on the Italian ferries if you're buying a return ticket on your outward journey; check with the agent.

Cross-channel ferry companies

Brittany Ferries UK ☎ 0870/536 0360, Republic of Ireland ☎ 021/427 7801, ⓦ www .brittanyferries.co.uk. Poole to Cherbourg; Portsmouth to Caen and St Malo; Plymouth to Roscoff and to Santander (March–Nov/Dec); Cork to Roscoff (March–Oct only).

Eurotunnel UK ☎ 0870/535 3535, ⓦ www3.eurotunnel.com.

Hoverspeed UK ☎ 0870/240 8070, ⓦ www.hoverspeed.com. Twenty-four daily departures. Dover to Calais and Ostend; Newhaven to Dieppe.

Irish Ferries UK ☎ 0870/517 1717, Northern Ireland ☎ 0800/018 2211, Republic of Ireland ☎ 1890/313 131, ⓦ www.irishferries.com. Services from Rosslare to Cherbourg and Roscoff run from March to Sept.

P&O Ferries UK ☎ 0870/520 2020, ⓦ www.poferries.com. Dover to Calais; Portsmouth to Cherbourg and Le Havre.

Sea France ☎ 0870/571 1711, ⓦ www.seafrance.com. Dover to Calais.

Red tape and visas

British, Irish and other EU citizens can enter Sardinia and stay as long as they like on production of a valid passport. Citizens of the United States, Canada, Australia and New Zealand also need only a valid passport, but are limited to stays of three months. All other nationals should consult the relevant embassies about visa requirements.

Legally, you're required to **register** with the police within three days of entering Italy, though if you're staying at a hotel this will be done for you. Although the police in some towns have become more punctilious about this, most would still be amazed at any attempt to register yourself down at the local police station while on holiday. However, if you're going to be living here for a while, you'd be advised to obtain the necessary *permesso di soggiorno* (permit). For more on living and working in Italy see p.58.

Italian embassies and consulates abroad

Australia 12 Grey St, Deakin, Canberra, ACT 2600 ☎ 02/6273 3333, ⓦ www.ambitalia.org.au. Consulates in Melbourne (☎ 03/9867 5744) and Sydney (☎ 02/9392 7900).

Canada 275 Slater St, Ottawa, ON K1P 5H9 ☎ 613/232-2401, ⓦ www.italyincanada.com. Consulates in Montréal (☎ 514/849-8351) and Toronto (☎ 416/977-1566).

Ireland 63–65 Northumberland Rd, Dublin ☎ 01/660 1744, ⓦ www.italianembassy.ie.

New Zealand 34–38 Grant Rd, PO Box 463, Thorndon, Wellington ☎ 04/473 5339, ⓦ www.italy-embassy.org.nz.

UK 14 Three Kings Yard, London W1Y 2EH ☎ 020/7312 2200, ⓦ www.embitaly.org.uk. Consulates in Edinburgh (☎ 0131/226 3631) and Manchester (☎ 0161/236 9024).

USA 3000 Whitehaven St NW, Washington DC 20008, ☎ 202/612-4400, ⓦ www.italyemb.org. Consulates in Chicago (☎ 312/467-1550), New York (☎ 212/737-9100) and San Francisco (☎ 415/931-4924).

Information, websites and maps

Before you leave, it's worth calling the Italian State Tourist Office (ENIT) for a selection of maps and brochures – though much of it can easily be picked up later in Sardinia. It's worth grabbing any accommodation listings and town plans they may have for the area you're interested in, as well as a camping brochure.

Tourist Offices

The main Sardinian tourist organization is **ESIT** (*Ente Sardo Industrie Turistiche*), with an information office in Cágliari. Most Sardinian towns and the three principal airports have a **tourist office**: either an APT or EPT (*Azienda Promozione Turistica/Ente Provinciale per il Turismo*), a provincial branch of the state organization, or an AAST (*Azienda Autónoma di Soggiorno e Turismo*), a smaller local outfit. When there isn't either an APT/EPT or AAST, there will sometimes be a **Pro Loco** office, run by the town hall, which may have much the same kind of information, though these generally keep much shorter hours. All of these vary in usefulness, and away from the main cities and tourist areas the staff aren't likely to speak English. However, you should always be able at least to get a free town plan, accommodation lists and a local listings booklet in Italian, and some offices will reserve you a room and sell tickets for performances in, for example, some archeological sites and seats at festas. You will also see unofficial **independent tourist offices** in some places, offering a host of other services such as car hire, apartment rental, excursions etc, as well as dispensing lots of free information.

Summer **opening hours** are usually Monday to Friday 9am to 1pm and 4 to 7pm, Saturday 9am to 1pm, but check the guide for more details. If the tourist office isn't open and all else fails, the local telephone office and most bars with phones carry a copy of the local telephone directory and yellow pages (*Págine Gialle*), with addresses and numbers of most of the organizations you're likely to want to know about. There's also an island-wide, toll-free telephone service (☎800/013 153), giving tourist information during office hours.

Italian State Tourist offices

Australia Level 26, 44 Market St, Sydney NSW 2000, ☎02/9962 1666, ✉enitour@ihug.com.au.
Canada 175 Bloor St East, Suite 907, South Tower, Toronto ON M4W 3R8 ☎416/925-4882, ⓦwww.italiantourism.com.
Ireland Italian Embassy, 63 Northumberland Rd, Dublin 4, ☎01/660 1744.
New Zealand Italian Embassy, 34 Grant Rd, Thorndon, Wellington ☎04/473 5339.
UK 1 Princes St, London W1B 2AY ☎020/7408 1254; brochure requests ☎0900/1600 280, ⓦwww.enit.it.
US 630 Fifth Ave, Suite 1565, New York, NY 10111 ☎212/245-5618, brochure requests ☎212/245-4822; 500 North Michigan Ave, Suite 2240, Chicago, Illinois 60611 ☎312/644-0996, brochure requests ☎312/644-0990; 12400 Wilshire Blvd, Suite 550, Los Angeles, CA 90025 ☎310/820-1898, brochure requests ☎310/820-0098.

Useful websites

Sardinian **websites** have proliferated in recent years and provide a wealth of information, though some are out of date; we've listed some useful ones here.

General sites

ⓦ**www.beniculturali.it** Italian Ministry for Arts and the Environment, with details of museums, exhibitions and performances.
ⓦ**www.bikesardegna.it** Bike itineraries throughout the island, with detailed route descriptions, mainly in Italian at present.
ⓦ**www.camping.it** Great site for campers, covering virtually every campsite in Italy.
ⓦ**www.enit.it** Italian State Tourist Board, with plenty of regional information.
ⓦ**www.eurocamping.net** Useful information on campsites throughout Europe, including Sardinia.

@ www.italyintour.com Good for a small selection of hotels & B&Bs in Sardinia, last-minute booking bargains as well as general background and itineraries, though may be out of date.

@ www.lanuovasardegna.it Online local newspaper, with news, weather and timetables (in Italian).

@ www.marenostrum.it Good general site with plenty of information, articles and links, plus lists of specialized operators for climbing, riding, diving and other watersports.

@ www.museionline.it Links to museum and exhibition sites, dates and events.

@ www.paginegialle.it Italian yellow pages online.

@ www.regione.sardegna.it Official tourist website for the whole island.

@ www.sardegnaonline.it Has some general travel information, but it's a bit untidy and awkward to use.

@ www.sardiniaforyou.com "Online travel agency" with general information on the island, details on a few specific accommodation options, and good links.

@ www.sardinia.net Routes and itineraries, plus articles on culture and history, but limited information on hotels and campsites. Numerous links to other useful websites.

@ www.sardiniatravel.it Articles, itineraries, weather information and material on accommodation, with numerous links.

Regional Information

@ www.provincia.nuoro.it General information on the province of Nuoro, in central Sardinia.

@ www.infoalghero.it Wide-ranging site, giving copious background and specific information on the resort of Alghero and around.

@ www.inforistano.it As above, but for the Oristano area.

Transport and schedules

@ www.airone.com Routes and schedules for the airline Airone.

@ www.alitalia.it Alitalia schedhules from the mainland.

@ www.arst.sardegna.it Timetables and fares for the island-wide bus service.

@ www.ferroviemeridionalisarde.it Trains and buses covering Cágliari and Sardinia's southwest.

@ www.ferroviesardegna.it Timetables and fares for trains and buses of the private FdS company.

@ www.meridiana.it Meridiana airlines routes and schedules.

@ www.saremar.it Ferries linking the Sardinian mainland with San Pietro, the Maddalena Islands and Corsica.

@ www.tirrenia.it The biggest of the ferry companies serving Sardinia.

@ www.traghetti.com For all Italian ferry routes.

@ www.trenitalia.it Italian State Railways (FS) timetable information.

Maps

The best large-scale **road map** of Sardinia is published by the Touring Club Italiano (*Sardegna*, 1:200,000), usually available from the outlets listed below. Otherwise, the Automobile Club d'Italia (see "Cars" on p.31) issues a good, free 1:275,000 road map, available from the State Tourist offices, while local tourist offices in Sardinia often have road maps of varying quality to give away.

For **hiking**, you'll need at least a scale 1:100,000 map (better 1:50,000), though there's not much around – again, check with one of the specialist map shops listed below or with the Club Alpino Italiano, Via Fonseca Pimental 7, 20121 Milan ☎02.2614.1378. For specific towns, the maps in the guide should be fine for most purposes, though local tourist offices also often hand out reasonable town plans and regional maps.

In the UK and Ireland

Blackwell's Map and Travel Shop 50 Broad St, Oxford OX1 3BQ ☎01865/793 550, @ www.maps.blackwell.co.uk.

Easons Bookshop 40 O'Connell St, Dublin 1 ☎01/858 3881, @ www.eason.ie.

Heffers Map and Travel 20 Trinity St, Cambridge CB2 1TJ ☎01865/333 536, @ www.heffers.co.uk.

Hodges Figgis Bookshop 56–58 Dawson St, Dublin 2 ☎01/677 4754.

The Map Shop 30a Belvoir St, Leicester LE1 6QH ☎0116/247 1400, @ www.mapshopleicester.co.uk.

National Map Centre 22–24 Caxton St, London SW1H 0QU ☎020/7222 2466, @ www.mapsnmc.co.uk.

Newcastle Map Centre 55 Grey St, Newcastle-upon-Tyne, NE1 6EF ☎0191/261 5622.

Ordnance Survey Ireland Phoenix Park, Dublin 8 ☎01/802 5300, @ www.osi.ie.

Ordnance Survey of Northern Ireland Colby
House, Stranmillis Ct, Belfast BT9 5BJ ☎028/9025
5755, ⊛www.osni.gov.uk.
Stanfords 12–14 Long Acre, WC2E 9LP
☎020/7836 1321, ⊛www.stanfords.co.uk.
The Travel Bookshop 13–15 Blenheim Crescent,
W11 2EE ☎020/7229 5260,
⊛www.thetravelbookshop.co.uk.

In the US and Canada

Adventurous Traveler.com 102 Lake Street,
Burlington, VT 05401 ☎1-800/282-3963,
⊛www.adventuroustraveler.com.
Book Passage 51 Tamal Vista Blvd, Corte
Madera, CA 94925 ☎1-800/999-7909,
⊛www.bookpassage.com.
Distant Lands 56 S Raymond Ave, Pasadena, CA
91105 ☎1-800/310-3220,
⊛www.distantlands.com.
Elliot Bay Book Company 101 S Main St,
Seattle, WA 98104 ☎1-800/962-5311,
⊛www.elliotbaybook.com.
Globe Corner Bookstore 28 Church St,
Cambridge, MA 02138 ☎1-800/358-6013,
⊛www.globercorner.com.
Map Link 30 S La Patera Lane, Unit 5, Santa

Barbara, CA 93117 ☎1-800/962-1394,
⊛www.maplink.com.
Rand McNally US ☎1-800/333-0136,
⊛www.randmcnally.com. Around thirty stores
across the US; dial ext 2111 or check the website
for the nearest location.
The Travel Bug Bookstore 2667 W Broadway,
Vancouver V6K 2G2 ☎604/737-1122,
⊛www.swifty.com/tbug.
World of Maps 1235 Wellington St, Ottawa,
Ontario K1Y 3A3 ☎1-800/214-8524,
⊛www.worldofmaps.com.

In Australia and New Zealand

The Map Shop 6–10 Peel St, Adelaide, SA 5000
☎08/8231 2033, ⊛www.mapshop.net.au.
Mapland 372 Little Bourke St, Melbourne,
Victoria 3000 ☎03/9670 4383,
⊛www.mapland.com.au.
MapWorld 173 Gloucester St, Christchurch
☎0800/627 967 or 03/374 5399,
⊛www.mapworld.co.nz.
Perth Map Centre 900 Hay St, Perth, WA 6000
☎08/9322 5733, ⊛www.perthmap.com.au.
Specialty Maps 46 Albert St, Auckland 1001
☎09/307 2217, ⊛www.specialtymaps.co.nz.

Insurance

Even though EU health care privileges apply in Sardinia, you'd do well to take out an insurance policy before travelling to cover against theft, loss and illness or injury. Before paying for a new policy, however, it's worth checking whether you're already covered: some all-risks home insurance policies may cover your possessions when overseas, and many private medical schemes include cover when abroad. In Canada, provincial health plans usually provide partial cover for medical mishaps overseas, while holders of official student/teacher/youth cards in Canada and the US are entitled to meagre accident coverage and hospital in-patient benefits. Students will often find that their student health coverage extends during the vacations and for one term beyond the date of last enrolment.

If not already covered, you might want to contact a specialist travel insurance company, or consider the travel insurance deal we offer (see below). A typical travel insurance policy usually provides cover for the loss of baggage, tickets and – up to a certain limit – cash or cheques, as well as cancellation or curtailment of your journey. Most of them exclude so-called dangerous sports unless an extra premium is paid: in Sardinia this can mean scuba-diving, whitewater rafting, windsurfing and trekking, though probably not kayaking or jeep safaris. Many policies can be chopped and changed to exclude coverage you don't need – for example,

sickness and accident benefits can often be excluded or included at will. If you do take medical coverage, ascertain whether benefits will be paid as treatment proceeds or only after return home, and whether there is a 24-hour medical emergency number. When securing baggage cover, make sure that the per-article limit – typically under £500 – will cover your most valuable possession. If you need to make a claim, you should keep receipts for medicines and medical treatment, and in the event you have anything stolen, you must obtain an official statement from the police (*polizia* or *carabinieri*).

Rough Guides travel insurance

Rough Guide offers its own low-cost travel insurance, especially customized for our statistically low-risk readers by a leading British broker, provided by the American International Group (AIG) and registered with the British regulatory body, GISC (the General Insurance Standards Council).

There are five main Rough Guides insurance plans: **No Frills** for the bare minimum for secure travel; **Essential**, which provides decent all-round cover; **Premier** for comprehensive cover with a wide range of benefits; **Extended Stay** for cover lasting four months to a year; and **Annual multi-trip**, a cost-effective way of getting Premier cover if you travel more than once a year. Premier, Annual Multi-Trip and Extended Stay policies can be supplemented by a "Hazardous Pursuits Extension" if you plan to indulge in sports considered dangerous, such as scuba-diving or trekking.

For a **policy quote**, call the Rough Guide Insurance Line: toll-free in the UK ☏0800/015 09 06 or ☏+44 1392 314 665 from elsewhere. Alternatively, get an online quote at ⊛www.roughguides.com/insurance.

Costs, money and banks

While Sardinia isn't particularly cheap compared with some other Mediterranean holiday spots, it's still noticeably less expensive than mainland Italy. You'll find that transport, food and accommodation especially are good value, but items such as petrol, car rental and entry into some museums are quite pricey by southern European standards. Prices rise considerably July–September.

Costs

If you're watching your budget – camping, buying some of your own food in the shops and markets – you could get by on as little as £20–30/€30–40/US$30–50 a day; a more realistic **average daily budget** is around £55–70/€75–100/US$87–110 a day, including meals in restaurants, hotel accommodation and some travel costs; while on £70–90/€100–125/US$110–150 a day you could be living pretty comfortably. Most basic things are fairly inexpensive: a pizza and a beer cost around £5/€7/$8 just about everywhere, a full meal with wine around £11–18/€15–25/$17.50–28.50; buses and trains are relatively cheap, and distances between towns small; and hotel rooms in the cities start at around £29/€40/$46 a double. It's the snacks and drinks that add up: ice creams, soft drinks and coffee all cost around the same price (if not more) as at home. And if you sit down for any of these, it'll cost around thirty percent more.

Of course, these prices are subject to where and when you go. Accommodation and food in the Costa Smeralda are downright expensive, and you might eat much better at half the price in an unpretentious trattoria in a small village. On the whole, the coastal resorts are more costly, while places in the interior are relatively cheap (though don't expect much choice of places to stay and eat). In holiday areas, you'll pay more in summer for accommodation, but you can find some fantastic bargains **out of season**, when nearly all hotels and *pensioni* drop their prices. Note that for **single accommodation**, which can be hard to come by, you may find yourself paying most of the price of a double room.

Unless you're negotiating for really costly items, **bargaining** is not really on in shops, though you'll find you can get a "special price" for some rooms in cheap hotels if you're staying a few days, and that things like guided tours are negotiable, especially out of season. In **markets**, you can haggle for everything except food, indeed it's virtually *de rigueur* when dealing with craft items and the like bought from individuals – ask for *uno sconto* ("a discount"). The craftwork for sale in the official chain of shops, ISOLA (addresses in Guide), is normally fixed-price.

Youth and student discounts

On the whole, there are few benefits for students in Sardinia: it's the one place where an ISIC card is no use at all; under-18s and over-65s, on the other hand, get into museums and archeological sites free. The various official and quasi-official **youth/student ID cards** may be useful for discounts for some performances and other entry tickets, however. All full-time students are eligible for the International Student ID Card (ISIC, ⓦwww.isiccard.com), and for Americans there's also a health benefit, providing up to $3000 in emergency medical coverage and $100 a day for sixty days in the hospital, plus a 24-hour hotline to call in the event of a medical, legal or financial emergency. The card costs £7 in the UK; €12.70 in the Republic of Ireland; $22 in the USA; Can$16 in Canada; AUS$16.50 in Australia; NZ$21 in New Zealand.

You only have to be 26 or younger to qualify for the **International Youth Travel Card**, which costs US$22/£7 and carries the same benefits. Teachers qualify for the **International Teacher Card**, offering similar discounts and costing US$22, Can$16, AUS$16.50 and NZ$21. All these cards are available in the US from Council Travel, STA, Travel CUTS and, in Canada, Hostelling International (see p.13 & 36 for addresses); in Australia and New Zealand from STA or Campus Travel; and in the UK from STA.

Several other travel organizations and accommodation groups also sell their own cards, good for various discounts. A university photo ID might open some doors, but is not easily recognizable, as are the ISIC cards.

Money and banks

The main **banks** you'll see in Sardinia are the Banco di Sardegna, Banco di Sássari, and the Banca Commerciale Italiana. **Banking hours** vary slightly from town to town, but generally banks are open Monday to Friday, 8.30am–1.20pm and 3–4pm. Outside these times you can change travellers' cheques and cash at large hotels and the main airports. Some banks open on Saturday mornings as well; check the text and city Listings sections.

Cash and travellers' cheques

It's a good idea to have at least some euros for when you first arrive. You can buy euros over the counter in British banks; most American banks will need a couple of days' notice. At the time of writing, you'll get around €1.40 to the pound sterling and €1.15 to the US$. Try and get some smaller-denomination currency for bus or taxi rides from your point of disembarkation: if you don't have the right change, it's up to

you to find it – a general rule throughout Italy.

Travelling with cash has some practical advantages – you avoid paying multiple exchange fees for a start – but cash is also a liability to carry around, even if it's stored in a hotel safe, and insurance policies will only refund a limited amount if it's stolen (usually around £250), and then not until your return.

Travellers' cheques are safer but they usually incur a charge – both when you buy them and when they are cashed. The usual fee for travellers' cheque sales is one or two percent, though this fee may be waived if you buy the cheques through a bank where you have an account. It pays to get a selection of denominations. Make sure to keep the purchase agreement and a record of cheque serial numbers safe and separate from the cheques themselves. In the event that cheques are lost or stolen, the issuing company will expect you to report the loss immediately to their office in Italy; most companies claim to replace lost or stolen cheques within 24 hours.

Credit and debit cards

Credit cards are a very handy backup source of funds, and can be used either in ATMs or over the counter. Most better hotels and restaurants, and most petrol stations, stores and supermarkets in Sardinia accept Mastercard and Visa, but American Express is less common, while other cards are only rarely accepted. Remember that all cash advances are treated as loans, with interest accruing daily from the date of withdrawal; there may be a transaction fee on top of this. However, you may be able to

Currency

On January 1, 2002, Italy was one of twelve European Union countries to change over to a single currency, the **euro** (EU$). The euro is split into 100 cents. There are seven euro **notes** – in denominations of 500, 200, 100, 50, 20, 10, and 5 euros, each a different colour and size – and eight different **coin** denominations, including 2 and 1 euros, then 50, 20, 10, 5, 2, and 1 cents. Euro coins feature a common EU design on one face, but different country-specific designs on the other. No matter what the design, all euro coins and notes can be used in any of the twelve member states (Austria, Belgium, Finland, France, Germany, Greece, Ireland, Italy, Luxembourg, Portugal, Spain and The Netherlands).

make withdrawals from ATMs in Sardinia using your debit card, which is not liable to interest payments, and the flat transaction fee is usually quite small – your bank will be able to advise on this. Make sure you have a personal identification number (PIN) that's designed to work overseas.

A compromise between travellers' cheques and plastic is Visa TravelMoney, a disposable pre-paid debit card with a PIN which works in all ATMs that take Visa cards. You load up your account with funds before leaving home, and when they run out, you simply throw the card away. You can buy up to nine cards to access the same funds – useful for couples or families travelling together – and it's a good idea to buy at least one extra as a back-up in case of loss or theft (if your card is stolen in Italy, call the 24-hour toll-free customer assistance number as soon as possible: ☎800.819.014). The card is available in most countries from branches of Thomas Cook and Citicorp. For more information, check the Visa TravelMoney website at ⓦusa.visa.com/personal/cards/visa_travel_money.html.

Wiring money

Having **money wired from home** using one of the companies listed below is never convenient or cheap, and should be considered a last resort. It's also possible to have money wired directly from a bank in your home country to a bank in Sardinia: your home bank will need the address of the bank where you want to pick up the money and the address and telex number of the Rome head office, which will act as the clearing house; money wired this way normally takes two working days to arrive, and costs around £25/$40 per transaction.

Money-wiring companies

Travelers Express MoneyGram UK ☎0800/018 0104, Republic of Ireland ☎1850/205 800, US☎1-800/955-7777, Canada ☎1-800/933-3278, Australia ☎1800/230 100, New Zealand ☎0800/262 263, ⓦwww.moneygram.com.
Western Union UK ☎0800/833 833, Republic of Ireland ☎1800/395 395, US and Canada ☎1-800/325-6000, Australia ☎1800/501 500, New Zealand ☎0800/270 000, ⓦwww.westernunion.com.

Health

EU citizens can take advantage of Italy's health services under the same terms as the residents of the country. You'll need form E111, available from any main post office. The Australian Medicare system also has a reciprocal health care arrangement with Italy. However, you should also take out ordinary travel insurance – certainly if you're a non-EU citizen (see p.23 for more details).

Vaccinations are not required. However, cholera and typhoid jabs are a wise precaution if you intend to continue to North Africa – in which case, make sure you also have an up-to-date polio booster. Otherwise, Sardinia doesn't present too many health worries: the worst that's likely to happen to you is suffering from the extreme heat in summer or from an upset stomach – shellfish is the usual culprit. Tap water is perfectly

safe to drink (unless there's a sign saying "*acqua non potabile*"), though bottled water is available everywhere.

Pharmacies

An Italian pharmacist (*farmacia*) is well-qualified to give you advice on minor ailments, and to dispense prescriptions. There's generally one open all night in the bigger towns; they work on a rota system, and you should find the address of the one currently open on any *farmacia* door or listed in the local paper. Condoms (*profilático*) are available over the counter from all pharmacists and some supermarkets; the Pill (*la píllola*) is available on prescription only.

Doctors and hospitals

If you need treatment, go to a **doctor** (*médico*); every town and village has one. Ask at a pharmacy, or consult the local *Págine Gialle* (*Yellow Pages*) under *Azienda Unità Sanitaria Locale* or *Unità Sanitaria Locale*, or *Pronto Soccorso*. The *Págine Gialle* also list some specialist practitioners in fields such as acupuncture and homeopathy, the latter much more common in Italy than in many countries. If you're eligible, take your E111 with you to the doctor's: this should enable you to get free treatment and prescriptions for medicines at the local rate – about ten percent of the price of the medicine. For repeat medication, take any empty bottles or capsules with you to the doctor's – the brand names often differ.

If you get taken **seriously ill**, or involved in an accident, head for the nearest **hospital** and go to the *Pronto Soccorso* (casualty) section, or phone ☎118 and ask for "*ospedale*" or "*ambulanza*". Hospital standards don't differ significantly from other clinics in western Europe. Don't expect medical and other hospital staff to speak fluent English, however. Throughout the guide, you'll find listings for pharmacists, hospitals and emergency services in all the major cities.

Incidentally, try to avoid going to the **dentist** (*dentista*) while you're in Sardinia. These aren't covered by the *mutua* or health service, and for the smallest problem they'll make you pay through the teeth. Take local advice, or consult the local *Yellow Pages*.

If you don't have a spare pair of glasses, take a copy of your prescription with you; an **optician** (*óttico*) will be able to make you up a new pair should you lose or damage them.

Getting around

Although distances aren't especially large in Sardinia, getting around by public transport is not always easy. The rail system is slow, few buses run on Sunday, and route information can be frustratingly difficult to obtain, even from the bus and train stations themselves. On the positive side, public transport prices are among the cheapest in Europe.

Although general points are covered below, each chapter's "Travel details" section has the full picture on transport schedules and frequencies. Note that many bus services are much reduced or non-existent on Sundays.

One thing to bear in mind is that travelling by train is not the best way to see all of the island. Some stations are miles away from their towns, while much of the east and centre of Sardinia is only accessible by bus or car. Driving, biking and walking are the best modes for exploring anywhere off the beaten path, though it makes sense to use public transport for direct journeys between towns. It's useful to know that in case of strikes, there are always a small number of essential transport services guaranteed to run, though these can get packed.

As for the roads, drivers and pedestrians alike are advised to watch the traffic at all times. Driving in Sardinia is not the competitive sport that it can be in Rome, Naples or Sicily, but neither is dilatory or indecisive behaviour at the wheel or crossing roads much tolerated. Nonetheless, anyone used to negotiating mainland Italy's roads will find Sardinia a doddle, and pedestrians accustomed to being treated as human skittles will be pleasantly surprised to find that drivers actually stop at pedestrian crossings and respect red lights. Local pedestrians also respect signals, and especially in Cágliari and Sássari, where traffic is heavy and constant, you'll find it's a lot less stressful to wait with everyone else for the signal to cross.

If you're in a hurry, you can always travel around Sardinia **by plane**; flights are frequent and it's usually possible just to purchase your ticket at the airport and jump on the first flight (though prior booking is recommended).

By rail

Sardinia's **train network** connects all the major towns, though few of the intermediate stops are very useful. The main lines are operated by Italian State Railways, Ferrovie dello Stato (FS), also known as Trenitalia, and by two independent companies, Ferrovie Meridionali della Sardinia (FMS) and Ferrovie della Sardinia (FdS, also known as Ferrovie Sarde or Ferrovie Complementari Sarde). FMS runs a service between Cágliari, Iglésias and Carbónia, while FdS operates various lines: the Sássari–Alghero branch line, the Nuoro–Macomer–Bosa route, Tempio Pausania–Palau, and a couple of very limited internal routes from Cágliari. On some of these routes, steam trains (*trenino verde*) take over in summer, otherwise these smaller lines are diesel-driven, and therefore noisy and not exactly smooth. All trains can get quite full at certain times – for example, the school runs in the morning and at lunchtime. On the whole, the trains leave punctually, and arrive within ten minutes or so of the scheduled time. Smoking is not permitted on any train.

Train **tickets** can be bought from any train station; by telephone at ☎892.021 (from a land line) or ☎199.166.177 (from a mobile); online at ⓦwww.trenitalia.com, and from authorized travel agents. **Fares** are very reasonable. Tickets are charged by the kilometre; the longest trip you can make on the island, the 300km loop from Olbia to Cágliari costs less than €15 for a second-class ticket, though most of the journeys you'll make will be much shorter and cheaper. Bikes can be carried on trains marked with a bicycle symbol on the timetables for a €3.50 supplement. Note that all tickets must be validated – punched in machines scattered around the station and platforms – within six hours for distances of less than 200km, or 24 hours for distances over 200km. Failure to do this may land you with an on-the-spot fine. If you don't have time to buy a ticket, you can simply board your train and pay the conductor, though you'll be charged a *supplemento* of €5.

Timetables

As well as the boards displayed at stations ("Departures" are *Partenze*, "Arrivals" *Arrivi*, "Delayed" *In Ritardo*), a timetable is useful, even if you use it only to discover exactly how late your train is. The Sardinian routes are covered by FS's booklet, *In Treno Sardegna* (€1), issued twice-yearly and available from most main train stations. Pay attention to the timetable notes, which may specify the dates between which some services run (*Si effetua dal . . . al . . .*), or whether a service is seasonal (*periódico*), denoted by a vertical squiggle; *feriale* is the word for the Monday to Saturday service, symbolized by two crossed hammers, *festivo* means that a train runs

Useful timetable publications

The red-covered **Thomas Cook European Timetables** (available from all branches of Thomas Cook and online at ⓦwww.thomascookpublishing.com) details schedules of over 50,000 trains in Europe, as well as the times of over two hundred ferry routes and rail-connecting bus services. It's updated and issued every month; main changes are in the June edition (published end of May), with details of the summer European schedules, and October (published at the end of Sept) for the winter schedules; some have advance summer/winter timings also.

only on Sundays and holidays, with a cross as its symbol.

Rail passes

A rail pass is worth considering if you plan to travel extensively around Italy or Europe, though it's not actually a lot of help once you've arrived in Sardinia, since the rail network isn't that extensive (see p.28). The Europe-wide **InterRail** and **Eurail** passes (see p.15) give unlimited travel on the FS network, though you'll be liable for (small) supplements on the faster trains.

There's a huge array of rail passes available; some must be bought before leaving home, while others can only be bought in Italy itself. The national rail companies of many European countries also offer their own passes, most of which can be bought in advance through Rail Europe or direct from the national rail company or tourist office. Rail Europe is the umbrella company for all national and international rail purchases, and its comprehensive website (W www.raileurope.com) is the most useful source of information on which rail passes are available; it also gives all current prices.

Inter-Rail pass

These passes are only available to European residents, and you'll be asked to provide proof of residency before being allowed to buy one. They come in over-26 and (cheaper) under-26 versions, and cover 28 European countries (including Turkey and Morocco) grouped together in zones: Italy is zone G, together with Greece, Turkey and Slovenia, also covering some ferry services between Italy and Greece

The passes are available for 22 days (one zone only), or one month, and you can purchase up to three zones or a global pass covering all zones. Although InterRail passes do not include travel between Britain and the continent, InterRail Pass holders are eligible for discounts on rail travel in Britain and Northern Ireland, on cross-Channel ferries, and are also eligible for a discount on the London–Paris Eurostar service.

Euro Domino pass

Euro-Domino passes are valid on the Italian network, but they are only available to EU residents or to anyone living in Europe for at least six months prior to the date of travel. These passes are available for between three and eight days' travel within a one-month period. Adults have the option of first- or second-class travel. Currently, first-class travel works out at €139 (three days), €171 (five days) and €204 (eight days). Corresponding fares for under-26s are €89, €109 and €140. There is also a half-price child fare (age 4–11).

Eurailpasses

A **Eurailpass** is unlikely to pay for itself if you're planning to stick to Sardinia or even just Italy. The pass, which must be purchased before arrival in Europe, allows unlimited free first-class train travel in Italy and sixteen other countries and is available in increments of fifteen days, 21 days, one month, two months and three months. If you're under 26, you can save money with a **Eurailpass Youth**, which is valid for second-class travel or, if you're travelling with one or more companions, a **Eurailpass Saver**, both of which are available in the same increments as the Eurailpass. You stand a better chance of getting your money's worth out of a **Eurailpass Flexi**, which is good for ten or fifteen days' first-class travel within a two-month period. This, too, comes in under-26/second-class (**Eurailpass Youth Flexi**) and group (**Eurailpass Saver Flexi**) versions.

In addition, a scaled-down version of the Eurailpass Flexi, the **Eurail Selectpass**, is available which allows travel in specific European countries, including France and Italy, for any five-, six-, eight-, ten- or fifteen days within a two-month period. Like the Eurailpass, the Selectpass is also available in first-class, second-class youth, as well as first-class saver options for two or more travelling together.

Details of prices for all these passes can be found on W www.eurail.com, and the passes can be purchased from one of the agents listed below.

Rail contacts

In North America

CIT Rail US ☎ 1-800/CIT-TOUR or 212/730-2400, W www.cit-tours.com, Canada ☎ 1-800/361-7799,

@ www.cittours-canada.com. Eurail, Europass and Italian passes.
DER Travel US ☎ 1-888/337-7350, @ www.dertravel.com/rail. Eurail, Europass and individual country passes.
Europrail International Canada ☎ 1-888/667-9734, @ www.europrail.net. Eurail, Europass and many individual country passes.
Rail Europe US ☎ 1-877/257-2887, Canada ☎ 1-800/361-RAIL, @ www.raileurope.com/us. Official North American Eurail Pass agent; also sells Europass, multinational passes and most single-country passes.

In Australia and New Zealand

CIT World Travel Australia ☎ 02/9267 1255 or 03/9650 5510, @ www.cittravel.com.au. Eurail, Europass and Italian rail passes.
Rail Plus Australia ☎ 1300/555 003 or 03/9642 8644, @ www.railplus.com.au. Sells Eurail and Europass passes.
Trailfinders Australia ☎ 02/9247 7666, @ www.trailfinder.com.au. All Europe passes.

By bus

Sardinia is served by an extensive network of **buses** (*autobus* or *pullman*) covering almost every town and village and a good number of beaches too, though schedules can be sketchy and much reduced on Sundays. Prices and some journey times compare favourably with the trains, with a Cágliari–Sássari trip, for example, costing around €13.50, taking 3–4hr.

The main, state-run bus company, **ARST**, operates a comprehensive service covering local routes from the main cities of Cágliari, Oristano, Sássari, Nuoro and Olbia, while the biggest private company, **PANI**, runs fast daily services between these main cities with a limited number of stops in between. Other private companies stick mainly to specific areas, such as Ferrovie Meridionali della Sardegna (FMS) in the southwest and Ferrovie della Sardegna (FdS) mainly around Cágliari, Sássari and Alghero, while Olbia airport is connected by Nuragica buses to Sássari, by DePlano to Nuoro, and by Turmo to Alghero – schedules are summarized at the end of each chapter. Note that some services covering beach areas and archeological zones only operate during the summer, and that lots of services are linked to school/market requirements – sometimes meaning a frighteningly early start, last departures in the afternoon, and occasionally no buses at all during school holidays.

City **bus terminals** are all very central, and most buses make stops at the local train station – if you want the bus station, ask for the *autostazione*. **Timetables** are rarely available to be given out, but are usually posted up at the bus stops and stations. Wherever possible, you buy **tickets** before boarding, from ticket offices and local bars and tobacconists, though if everywhere is closed you can buy tickets on board (for which a small supplement may be charged). For longer hauls (and if you want to be sure of a place), it's worth buying them in advance. Bus stops are often quite difficult to track down; if you want directions, ask: *Dov'è la fermata dei pullman?* ("Where's the bus stop?") If you want to get off a bus, ask *posso scéndere?* ("Can I get off?"); "the next stop" is "*la próssima fermata*".

City buses are always cheap, usually charging a flat fare of around €0.60, and worth utilizing for quick rides across town. Invariably, you need a ticket before getting on. Buy them in bars, *tabacchi*, or from the kiosks and vendors at bus terminals and stops, and then punch them in the machine on board. Checks are occasionally made by inspectors, who can charge spot fines. Smoking is strictly prohibited.

A few bus services are operated by one of the railway companies, usually on the periphery of the rail network. These are detailed in the train timetables and in the text.

By car

Car travel across the island can be very quick as long as you follow the main roads. Minor roads can be narrow, very bendy and often confusing, though they can also be the most spectacular routes. The island has no motorways or autostradas, and therefore no tolls; instead, good dual carriageways, or **superstradas**, run for most of the way between Cágliari, Oristano, Olbia, Sássari and Nuoro. The straightest and fastest is the SS131, aka the Carlo Felice highway, named after the Savoyan king who commissioned it. Extending the length of the island, from Cágliari via Oristano and Sássari as far as

Porto Torres, this is rarely congested, though occasionally poorly lit and surfaced; beware of tricky junctions.

Other superstradas branch off east to Nuoro and Olbia, others link Cágliari with Iglésias, Carbónia and Sant'Antíoco, and Nuoro with the northeast coast. Most other roads are of the twisty variety, and the going can be slow, particularly along the coasts in summer (the SP125 running behind the Costa Smeralda between Olbia and Santa Teresa di Gallura is especially gruesome). It is Sardinia's **secondary roads** that are the most rewarding to explore, however, though these may increase your journey time, and you'll need to exercise maximum caution in negotiating their twists and turns. Try to avoid taking minor roads through the mountains after dark, not only for the greater risk (there's no illumination), but because you'll miss the often extraordinary scenery that is the main reason for using them.

At all times while driving in **rural areas**, be prepared for the unexpected appearance of a flock of sheep or panniered horse on the road. In remoter parts, there are **strade bianche**, or "white roads" – little more than rough tracks which can continue for hours, seemingly going nowhere; these can become very rocky, and should not be attempted with a low axle. Signposting on these lanes is nonexistent, and it's easy to lose one's direction. Nonetheless, they're perfect for spontaneous detours, and can lead to excellent spots for a walk or picnic, not to mention the splendid beaches often lying at the end of them.

Italy is one of the most expensive countries in Europe in which to buy **fuel**: it's around €1.10/litre for unleaded (*senza piombo*). Fuel stations are spaced at fairly regular intervals along the superstradas, and there are pumps in most towns and villages. Although most are closed 12.30–3.30pm and after 7.30pm, and often on Sunday or one other day of the week, an increasing number have self-service dispensers which take euro notes and credit cards. Make sure your notes aren't dog-eared, or the machines won't accept them. If your tank is filled before all your prepaid fuel is dispensed, you can punch a button for a receipt and ask for a refund when the station opens. All stations accept major credit cards.

For **documentation**, you need a valid driving licence and, if you are a non-EU licence holder, an international driving permit. Always contact your insurance company prior to leaving, to request cover for outside your home country. It's compulsory to carry your car documents and passport while you're driving, and you'll be required to present them if you're stopped by the police. You are also required to carry a portable triangular danger sign, available in Britain from most AA, RAC or Automobile Club d'Italia (ACI) offices, in Australia from NRMA, RACQ and RACV offices, in the US from the AAA, and in Canada from the CAA.

Rules of the road are straightforward: drive on the right; at junctions, where there's any ambiguity, give precedence to vehicles coming from the right, and observe the speed limits (50kph/30mph in built-up areas, 110kph/70mph on country roads). Note that some road customs are markedly different from what you may be used to: flashing headlights, for example, are not a signal to allow you priority, but on the contrary mean: "Look out, I'm coming!"

If you **break down**, dial ☏116 at the nearest phone and tell the operator where you are, the type of car and your registration number. The nearest office of the ACI will send someone out to fix your car, though it's not a free service, and you'll pay a further hefty bill if you need a tow. Temporary membership of ACI (Via Marsala 8, 00185 Roma; ☏803.106) gives free or discounted tows and repairs; alternatively, arrange cover with a motoring organization in your country before you leave. Any ACI office in Sardinia can tell you where to get **spare parts** for your particular car.

Car rental in Sardinia is expensive, starting from around £200/$320 per week for a Fiat Punto or Panda plus fuel, at one of the major international firms, usually less from local companies (contact details are given in the city listings). Some rental deals cost less per day, but involve an additional charge for every kilometre driven over, say, 100km. Your best plan, however, is to arrange car hire in conjunction with your flight/holiday – most travel agents or tour operators can provide details; as can the major **rental companies** (see below for numbers), which all have offices at each of the main airports. Note that choosing a smaller car is preferable both for negotiating narrow alleys and for easier parking.

Although **car crime** is rarer than in most of mainland Italy, it's prudent not to leave anything visible in the car when you leave it, including the radio. If you're taking your own vehicle, consider installing a detachable car-radio, and always depress your aerial and tuck in your wing mirrors. The main cities and ports have **garages** where you can leave your car, a safe enough option. At least the car itself is unlikely to be stolen if it's got a right-hand drive and a foreign number-plate: they're too conspicuous to be of much use to thieves.

Parking can be a real headache in Sardinia. The task of finding a space is easier in the early afternoon, when towns are quiet, or at night. At all other times, strictly enforced restrictions operate, allowing you to leave your vehicle only in designated areas – usually between blue lines. Seek out the parking attendant and buy a ticket for as long as you think you'll be parked; it's not expensive, usually around €0.50 for the first hour, €1 for every subsequent hour. If you park in a *zona di rimozione*, your car will most likely be towed away; and if you've chosen a street that turns into a market by day, you'll be stuck until it closes down.

Car rental agencies

In the UK and Ireland

Avis UK ☎0870/606 0100, ⊛www.avis.co.uk; Republic of Ireland ☎01/605 7500, ⊛www.avis.ie.
Budget UK ☎0800/181 181, ⊛www.budget.co.uk; Republic of Ireland ☎0903/277 11, ⊛www.budget.ie.
Europcar UK ☎0845/722 2525, ⊛www.europcar.co.uk; Republic of Ireland ☎01/614 2888, ⊛www.europcar.ie.
Hertz UK ☎0870/844 8844, ⊛www.hertz.co.uk; Republic of Ireland ☎01/676 7476, ⊛www.hertz.ie.
Holiday Autos UK ☎0870/400 0099, ⊛www.holidayautos.co.uk; Republic of Ireland ☎01/872 9366, ⊛www.holidayautos.ie.

National UK ☎0870/536 5365, ⊛www.nationalcar.co.uk.
Thrifty UK ☎01494/751 600, ⊛www.thrifty.co.uk; Republic of Ireland ☎1800/515 800, ⊛www.thrifty.ie.

In North America

Avis US ☎1-800/331-1084, Canada ☎1-800/272-5871, ⊛www.avis.com.
Budget US ☎1-800/527-0700, Canada ☎1-800/268.8900 ⊛www.budget.com.
Europcar US & Canada ☎1-877/940 6900, ⊛www.europcar.com,
Hertz US ☎1-800/654-3001, Canada ☎1-800/263-0600, ⊛www.hertz.com.
Holiday Autos US ☎1-800/422-7737, ⊛www.holidayautos.com.
National US and Canada ☎1-800/227-7368, ⊛www.nationalcar.com.
Thrifty US and Canada ☎1-800-THRIFTY (847-4389), ⊛www.thrifty.com.

In Australia and New Zealand

Avis Australia ☎13 63 33, ⊛www.avis.com.au, NZ ☎0800/655 111, ⊛www.avis.co.nz.
Budget Australia ☎1300/362 848, ⊛www.budget.com.au; NZ ☎09/976 2222, ⊛www.budget.co.nz.
Hertz Australia ☎13 30 39, ⊛www.hertz.com.au; NZ ☎0800/654 321, ⊛www.hertz.co.nz.
Holiday Autos Australia ☎1300/554 432, ⊛www.holidayautos.com.au; NZ ☎0800/144 040, ⊛www.holidayautos.co.nz.
National Australia ☎13 10 45, ⊛www.nationalcar.com.au; NZ ☎0800/800 115, ⊛www.nationalcar.co.nz.
Thrifty Australia ☎1300/367 227, ⊛www.thrifty.com.au; NZ ☎09/309 0111, ⊛www.thrifty.co.nz.

Motoring organizations

Australia AAA ☎02/6247 7311, ⊛www.aaa.asn.au.
Canada ☎613/247-0117, ⊛www.caa.ca.
Ireland AA Dublin ☎01/617 9988, ⊛www.aaireland.ie.
Italy TCI ☎02.852.6304, ⊛www.touringclub.it.
New Zealand AA ☎09/377 4660, ⊛www.nzaa.co.nz.
UK AA ☎0870/600 0371, ⊛www.theaa.com; RAC ☎0800/550 055, ⊛www.rac.co.uk.
USA AAA ☎1-800/AAA-HELP, ⊛www.aaa.com.

Hitchhiking

Hitchiking (*autostop*) is not widely practised in Sardinia and is not recommended as a means of getting around the island. It's definitely not something that women should do on their own, particularly in the more out-of-the-way places; also be warned that cars will sometimes stop to offer you a lift if you're standing alone at a bus stop. If you're hitching, travel in pairs, and always ask where the car is headed before you commit yourself ("*Dov'è diretto?*"). If you want to get out, say: "*Mi fa scéndere?*"

By bike

Increasing numbers of people in Sardinia are using **bicycles**, either for long-distance pedalling or for getting around locally. Most big towns have rental facilities, as do seaside resorts like Alghero and Santa Teresa di Gallura and some of the offshore islands, and bikes are also available at some hotels – check the text for details; the charge is usually around €10 per day, less out of season. If you use a bike, take care to make yourself conspicuous, especially outside towns, where the very rarity of cyclists means people won't be expecting you. Prepare too for some arduous uphill pedalling.

The roads are perfect for petrol-assisted cruising, however, and have become a favourite touring ground for squads of bikers from Germany and Switzerland. Motorbike-rental is rare, however, though most places that rent out bicycles also rent out **mopeds** and **scooters**. If you opt for one of these, remember that the smaller models are not suitable for any kind of long-distance travel, though they're ideal for buzzing around towns and beaches; expect to pay from €40 a day in high season. Crash helmets are compulsory, though you'll see many Sards just riding with one slung over one arm.

By ferry and hydrofoil

You'll use **ferries** to get to the offshore islands, from Palau for La Maddalena and Calasetta or Portovesme for San Pietro. The main companies are Enermar (℡899.200.001, ⊛www.enermar.it) and Saremar (℡199.123.199, ⊛www.saremar.it). Departures are at least hourly, there are more in high season, and summer also sees a night-time service for anyone dining out on the opposite shore, for example. All take vehicles, and if you are transporting yours it makes sense to get to the port early to be sure of a place (things can get quite congested in August, especially); some offices are only open 20min before departure. Frequencies are listed in the text and in "Travel Details" on p.127 and p.304. Saremar and Moby Lines (℡0565.9361, ⊛www.moby.it) also operate daily services between Santa Teresa di Gallura and Bonifacio in Corsica, and all seaside holiday centres offer boat tours of the coast and islands.

Accommodation

On the whole, accommodation in Sardinia is cheaper than in the rest of Italy. The main problem may be scarce availability, as the island's comparatively few hotels can be fully booked in summer. Even outside the high season, it's advisable to book as early as you can.

All types of accommodation are officially graded, their tariffs fixed by law. In tourist areas there's often a low-season and high-season price, though "high season" is a variable concept – it's usually between mid-July and mid-September. Nearly all mid- and high-range places include breakfast in the price – whether you want it or not. If you're watching your budget, youth hostels, B&Bs, private rooms and numerous campsites with bungalows or caravans to rent are all possibilities – for more on which, see below.

The prices of all lodging options should be listed in the local accommodation booklets provided by the tourist office and conspicuously posted at the premises. If the prices don't correspond, demand to know why, and don't hesitate to report infractions to the tourist office. In any case, always make sure you know exactly how much you're going to pay before you accept the room.

Hotels

Although all hotels are now officially *alberghi*, subject to the same regulations, they can be divided into distinct categories. The cheapest hotel-type accommodation is a **locanda** – basic, but on the whole clean and safe,

and nearly always corresponding to category ❶, ie under €35 for a double room without bath/shower; in some cases you'll find prices as low as €25 for a double. Similar in style, but a notch higher in comfort, the **pensione** is a small, family-run establishment, often with a trattoria attached. These are still quite common in Sardinia, but increasingly they're being superseded by the more professional **albergo**, where all rooms will have en-suite bathrooms, and there's usually a restaurant on the premises. All *alberghi* come graded with from one to five stars, which usually reflects fairly accurately the quality of the place. On average, you'll pay around £50–75/€75–100/$85–115 a night for a double room in a three-star during high season, up to €20 less in a resort at low season. Most two-stars fall into the ❸ and ❹ categories, while three-stars normally correspond to categories ❺ and ❻. In resorts – especially on the Costa Smeralda – four-star hotels can charge pretty much what they like, which means prices in categories ❼, ❽ and ❾ are the norm. Six of Sardinia's nine five-stars are here, charging seriously expensive rates. That said, there are some bargains among the luxury hotels

Accommodation price codes

The hotels, hostels and B&Bs listed in this guide have been categorized according to the price codes below, which represent the cheapest available double room in high season (Aug). Out of season, you'll usually pay a lower price than those suggested here. Most places with two or more stars include breakfast in the price. Cheaper hotels often have shared bathrooms and showers, though many also have a few en-suite rooms, for which you'll pay more – generally the next category up in price. Higher-category hotels nearly always have only en-suite rooms.

❶ under €35	❷ €35–50	❸ €50–65
❹ €65–80	❺ €80–100	❻ €100–125
❼ €125–150	❽ €150–200	❾ over €200

which remain open outside the summer season, many dropping their room rates by as much as forty percent to attract custom. In all places, it's always worth trying to negotiate a lower price than the official one in the low season, especially if you're staying more than a couple of nights (ask *c'è uno sconto per tre/quattro/cinque notti?*). When demand is high, on the other hand, many establishments require that you take half- or full-board, and there may also be a minimum stay of five or more nights. In practice, if you call on spec, you'll often be given a room for just a night or two if there's availability. In all cases, always ask to see the room and – in the cheaper places – the bathroom before you agree to stay: *posso vedere?* ("May I see?").

There are few **single rooms** available, and these are often occupied during the week by workers and commercial travellers. In high season especially, lone travellers will often pay most (if not all) the price of a double. **Three or more people** sharing a room should expect to pay around 35 percent on top of the price of a double room.

B&Bs, private rooms, apartments and agriturismi

Recent years have seen a big growth in **B&Bs** in Sardinia, mostly in towns. These can vary a lot, but are generally clean and comfortable, and set aside from the family's living quarters. Most have shared bathrooms, while others are fairly luxurious, with all the facilities you might expect in a two-star hotel, but with better breakfasts. The quality of the accommodation isn't always reflected in the price; most charge around €60 for two in high season, about €50 at other times.

Some tourist resorts, for example Alghero and Stintino, also advertise **private rooms** for rent, which often come equipped with a kitchen. Prices are highly negotiable (in the region of €15–40 per person per night), and can be very reasonable in low season. For B&Bs or rooms, ask in local bars, shops and tourist offices, and watch for "B&B" or "*cámere*" (rooms) signs. Depending on the season and location, you'll pay anything from €25–40 per person per night.

For longer-term stays in resorts, you can also rent holiday **apartments**. This can be horrendously expensive in summer – over €500 a month even for a one-bedroom place – but there are real bargains to be had in May, late-September or during the winter; ask in the local tourist office or estate agency (*agenzia immobiliare*), and keep an eye out for local advertisements.

Outside towns, you might consider a night or two in an **agriturismo**, a cottage or farmhouse offering informal dinner, bed and breakfast. Many also have various activities available, such as escorted walks and excursions, horse riding, hunting and mountain-biking. Most of these places are relatively inaccessible and remote from the bar culture of the resorts – a bonus or downside, depending on your point of view – but if you want to get close to nature, or to isolated beaches, they're ideal. Although some *agriturismi* have expanded and standardized their facilities, detracting from one of the main reasons to stay in them in the first place, others genuinely provide a face-to-face encounter with Sards and offer more authentic country cooking than most places on the tourist track – indeed, some are renowned for their cuisine. They tend to be a little pricier than B&Bs, charging from around €60 for a double room, and another €25 or so a head for a three-course dinner. Some *agriturismi* are detailed in the guide, and local tourist offices can tell you of all the suitable places in the area. Alternatively, contact one of the agriturismo associations directly: *Agriturist* ☎070.303.486; *Terranostra* ☎070.668.367; or *Turismo Verde* ☎070.373.73. Some of the websites on p.20–21 also have links to agriturismo (for example, ⓦwww.sardinia.net/agritur).

Camping

Sardinia has about ninety officially graded **campsites** dotted around its coasts and the outlying islands. There are no official sites in Sardinia's interior, though the coastal sites can be a fair walk from the sea. Facilities range from very rudimentary to the full gamut of shops, disco, pool and watersports, and many offer bungalows, caravans or cabins with cooking facilities at reasonable rates. Campers can expect to pay around €5–8 per person plus €6–10 for a pitch, while a bungalow or caravan might cost around €40–60 a night. Addresses, telephone numbers and websites are detailed in the text; try to get a look at a place on its website before deciding to stay. Months of opening are also specified – though bear in mind that these periods are very flexible, and campsites generally open or close whenever they want, depending on business. Only a handful of campsites stay open between October and April. Don't assume there will always be availability in summer: the better sites fill up quickly, so always phone first. Full details of all campsites are contained in the book *Campeggi e Villagi Turistici in Italia*, published by the Touring Club Italiano (Corso Italiano 10, 20122 Milan ☏02/852.6245) and available from bookshops, and on the comprehensive website ⓦwww.camping.it.

If you're planning to do a lot of camping, a good investment is an international camping carnet, which gives discounts at member sites. Many campsites will take it instead of making you surrender your passport during your stay, and it covers you for third-party insurance when camping. In the **UK and Ireland**, the carnet costs £4.50, and is available to members of the AA or the RAC (see p.32), or for members only from either of the following: the **Camping and Caravanning Club** (☏024/7669 4995, ⓦwww.campingandcaravanningclub.co.uk; annual membership £27.50), or the foreign touring arm of the same company, the **Carefree Travel Service** (☏024/7642 2024), which provides the international camping carnet free if you take out insurance with them; they also book ferry crossings and inspect camping sites in Europe. In the **US and Canada**, the carnet is available from home motoring organizations, or from **Family Campers and RVers** (FCRV; ☏1-800/245-9755, ⓦwww.fcrv.org). FCRV annual membership costs $25, and the carnet an additional $10.

By and large, **camping rough** in Sardinia is a non-starter: it's frowned on in the tourist areas and on the offshore islands, and regarded with outright suspicion in the interior (Sards are especially wary of the danger of forest fires). Occasional possibilities are detailed in the text; anywhere else you're likely to attract the unwelcome attention of the local police.

Hostels

Sardinia has five official Hostelling International (HI) **youth hostels**, three in the northwest of the island – in Fertilia (near Alghero), Bosa and Castelsardo – and two in the southeast, both by the sea near Muravera (one of them a campsite with bungalows). Additionally, there are a few unofficial hostels, as good if not better than the HI ones, for example at Lanusei, near Arbatax. HI hostels, of course, require membership, and while it's hardly worth joining just to use the few in Sardinia, there are perks – such as discounts on rail travel, student cards, car hire and books. Temporary membership is available for around €2.60 for a single night; six temporary membership stamps makes you a full member. Alternatively, contact your home hostelling organization (see below). Booking in advance is essential, either over the phone or on the website ⓦwww.ostellionline.org: availability is limited at all times, and in the summer months hostels are almost permanently full to capacity. Charges are around €10 for a dormitory bed, €8 for an evening meal and €1.50 for breakfast, if this is not included in the overnight rate.

Youth hostel associations

Australia ☏02/9261 1111, ⓦwww.yha.org.au.
Canada ☏1-800/663 5777, ⓦwww.hihostels.ca.
England and Wales ☏0870/770 8868, ⓦwww.yha.org.uk.
Italy ☏06.487.1152, ⓦwww.ostellionline.org.
New Zealand ☏03/379 9970, ⓦwww.yha.org.nz.
Northern Ireland ☏028/9032 4733, ⓦwww.hini.org.uk.
Republic of Ireland ☏01/830 4555, ⓦwww.irelandyha.org.
USA ☏202/783-6161, ⓦwww.hiayh.org.

Eating and drinking

Eating and drinking are refreshingly good-value in Sardinia, and the quality usually high. Often, even the most out-of-the-way village will boast somewhere you can get a good, solid lunch, while towns like Cágliari and Alghero can keep foodies happy for days. If you stay away from the few ruinously expensive places, a full meal with local wine generally costs around £15/€20/US$23 a head, though there are often much cheaper set-price menus available: see p.40 for more detailed prices.

The summary below and the food glossary in Contexts will help you find your way around supermarkets and menus, but ask to look if you're not sure what you're ordering. Also, check our lists of specialities, some of which are found in nearly every restaurant (p.380–381).

Sardinian cuisine

Historically, the twin pivots of traditional **Sardinian cuisine** were land- and sea-based local produce, and this continues to be the principal distinction today. Mutton, beef, game, boar, horsemeat and donkey are the staples of the cooking in the interior, while the coasts rely on whatever can be fished out of the sea – tuna, sea-bass and sardines all figure heavily. Add to these the basic ingredients of Italian cooking – pasta, tomato sauce, olives and fresh vegetables – and a choice of seasonal fruit and sheep's cheese. Some of the most famous Italian wines hail from Sardinia – wine was already being made on the island at the time of the Phoenicians – and a meal is often rounded off with *dolci*, traditional biscuits of almonds and honey.

The mild winters and long summers mean that **fruit and vegetables** are less seasonal than in northern Europe, and are much bigger and more impressive: strawberries appear in April, oranges are available right through the winter, and even bananas are grown on a small scale. Unusual and unexpected foods and fruit are a bonus too: prickly pears (introduced from Mexico by the Spanish), artichokes, asparagus, wild mushrooms and wafer bread are common, while foreign elements have been introduced to specific areas – couscous on the island of San Pietro, and Catalan dishes in Alghero.

Breakfasts, snacks and ice cream

Most Sardinians start the day in a bar, their **breakfast** (*prima colazione*) consisting of a milky coffee (caffelatte or cappuccino), and the ubiquitous *cornetto* – a jam-, custard- or chocolate-filled croissant, which you usually help yourself to from the counter; bigger bars and patisseries (*pasticceria*) will have more choice. Breakfast in a hotel will be a limp (and expensive) affair, usually worth avoiding, but you'll often find a truly impressive spread at B&Bs and *agriturismi*, including home-made jams, fruit and yoghurt.

At other times of the day, **rolls** (*panini*) can be pretty substantial, packed with any number of fillings. Most bars sell these, though you'll get fresher stuff by going into an *alimentari* (grocer's shop) and asking them to make you one from whatever they've got on hand: you'll pay around €3 each, depending on what and how much you choose for the filling. Bars may also offer **sandwiches** (*tramezzini*), ready-made sliced white bread sandwiches with mixed fillings – lighter and less appetizing than your average *panino*. Toasted sandwiches (*toste*) are common too: in a sandwich bar you can get whatever you like put inside them; in bars which have a sandwich toaster you're more likely to be offered a variation on cheese with ham or tomato.

Apart from sandwiches, other prepared takeaway food is pretty thin on the ground. You'll get most of the things already mentioned, plus small pizzas, portions of prepared pasta, chips, even full hot meals, in a **távola calda**, a snack bar that's at its best in the morning when everything is fresh. The bigger towns have them, often combined with normal bars, and there's sometimes one in main train stations.

You'll get more adventurous ingredients in **markets** – good bread, fruit, pizza slices and picnic food, such as cheese, salami, olives, tomatoes and salads. Some markets sell traditional takeaway food from stalls, usually things like boiled artichokes, cooked octopus, sea urchins and mussels, and *focacce* – oven-baked pastry snacks either topped with cheese and tomato, or filled with spinach, fried offal or meat. For picnics, some tinned and bottled things are worth looking out for too: sweet peppers (*peperoni*), baby squid (*calamari*), seafood salad (*insalata di mare*) and preserved vegetables. You'll find **supermarkets** in most towns; look out for the "two-for-the-price-of-one" offers on items such as tinned fish, meat, biscuits and soft drinks.

You'll probably end up with an **ice cream** (*gelato*) at some point: in summer, a cone (*un cono*) is an indispensable accessory to the evening *passeggiata*, and many people eat a dollop of ice cream in a brioche for breakfast. Most bars have a fairly good selection, but for real choice go to a **gelateria** (ice cream parlour) where the range is a tribute to the Italian imagination and flair for display. If they make their own on the premises, there'll be a sign saying *produzione propria.* You'll have to go by appearance rather than attempt to decipher their exotic names, many of which don't mean much even to Italians; you'll find it's often the basics – chocolate, lemon, strawberry and coffee – that are best. There's no trouble in identifying the finest *gelateria* in town: it's the one that draws the crowds.

Pizzas

As elsewhere in Italy, **pizza** in Sardinia comes flat and not deep-pan, and the choice of toppings is fairly limited – none of the pineapple-and-sweetcorn variations beloved of foreign pizzerias. It's also easier to find pizzas cooked in the traditional way, in wood-fired ovens (*forno a legna*), rather than squeaky-clean electric ones, so that the pizzas arrive blasted and bubbling on the surface, with a distinctive charcoal taste. However, because of the time it takes to set up and light the wood-fired ovens, these pizzas are usually only served at night, except on Sundays and in some resorts in summer.

Pizzerias, which range from a stand-up counter to a fully-fledged sit-down restaurant, on the whole sell just pizzas and drinks, usually chips, sometimes salads. A basic cheese and tomato pizza here costs around €4/£3/US$4.50, something a bit fancier between €5 and €8 (£3.50/US$6–£5.75 /US$9). To follow local custom, it's quite acceptable to cut it into slices and eat it with your hands, washing it down with a beer or Coke rather than wine. You'll also get pizzas in larger towns and tourist areas in a hybrid pizzeria-ristorante, which serves meals too and is slightly more expensive. Check our list of pizzas on p.376 for what you get on top of your dough.

Full meals: lunch and dinner

Full **meals** are much more elaborate affairs. These are generally served in a **trattoria** or a **ristorante**, though these days there's often a fine line between the two: traditionally, a trattoria is cheaper and more basic, offering good home-cooking (*cucina casalinga*), while a ristorante is more upmarket (tablecloths and waiters). The main differences you'll notice, though, are more to do with opening hours and the food on offer. In small towns and villages, a trattoria is usually best at lunch time and often only open then – there probably won't be a menu, and the waiter will simply reel off a list of what's on that day. In large towns both will be open in the evening, but you'll find more choice in a ristorante, which will always have a menu. In either, a pasta course, meat or fish, fruit and a drink, should cost around €15–30/£11–20/US$17–35 (fish pushes up the price). Watch out for signs saying *menu turístico, pranzo turístico* or *pranzo completo* – a limited set menu, including wine, which can cost as little as €15/£11/US$17, but is usually more in the region of €18–25/£13–18/US$20–30. Classier *ristoranti* will charge around €30–50/£20–36/ US$35–60 per head, including quality wine, and these are often worth going out of your way for.

Other types of eating place include those usually found in tourist resorts, that describe themselves as a trattoria-ristorante-pizzeria; távole calde, for warmed-up snacks (see p.38), spaghetterie, which specialize in pasta dishes, and birrerie – pubs with snacks and music, often the haunts of the local youth. Lastly, if you ever tire of the Sardinian diet you might try out one of the many **Chinese restaurants** which have sprouted in most large towns in the last few years – they're at least as good as the ones in Britain, and are significantly cheaper than most Italian restaurants. Many eating places close for three or four weeks in November or February.

Traditionally, a **meal** (lunch is pranzo, dinner is cena) starts with an **antipasto** (literally "before the meal"): you'll only find this in restaurants, at its best when you circle around a table and pick from a selection of cold dishes, main items including stuffed artichoke hearts, olives, salami, anchovies, seafood salad, aubergine in various guises, sardines and mixed rice. A plateful will cost around €8/£5.75/US$9. If you're moving on to pasta and a main course, however, you'll need to pace yourself.

As far as the **menu** goes, it starts with soup or pasta, **il primo**, usually costing €5–10/£3.50–7/US$5.75–11.50, and moves on to **il secondo**, the meat or fish dish, which ranges roughly €10–15/£7–11 /US$11.50–17. This course is generally served alone except for perhaps a wedge of lemon or tomato. **Vegetables** and **salads** (contorni) are ordered and served separately, and often there won't be much choice: potatoes will usually come as chips (patatine fritte), but you can also find them boiled (lesse) or roast (arroste), while salads are simply green (verde) or mixed (mista), usually with tomato. **Bread** (pane), which in Sardinia comes in a variety of forms – though rarely brown (integrale) – will be served with your meal. Used in ceremonies as well as for everyday needs, Sardinian bread can be thin and crispy or soft, floury and delicately shaped, and differs markedly from place to place.

If there's no menu, the verbal list of what's available can be a bit bewildering, but if you don't hear anything you recognize just ask for what you want: everywhere should have pasta with tomato sauce (pomodoro) or meat sauce (al ragù).

Afterwards, you'll usually get a choice of fruit (frutta), while in a ristorante, you'll probably be offered other desserts (dolci) as well. Sardinia is renowned for its almond-based sweets, though they're not always available; most restaurants will only have fresh fruit salad (macedonia) and fresh or packaged ice cream and desserts – in common with the rest of Italy, Sardinia has embraced the mass-produced, packaged sweets produced by brands such as Ranieri – tiramisù, tartufo and zuppa inglese are the most common; some of them aren't bad, but they're a poor substitute for the real thing.

It's useful to know that you don't have to order a full meal in trattorias and most restaurants. Asking for just pasta and a salad, or the main course on its own, won't outrage the waiter. Equally, asking for a dish listed as a first course as a second course, or having pasta followed by pizza (or vice versa), won't be frowned upon.

Something to watch for is **ordering fish**, which will usually be served by weight (usually per 100g, all'etto) – if you don't want the biggest one they've got, ask to see what you're going to eat and check the price first.

Vegetarian food

Some **vegetarians** might find their food principles stretched to the limit in Sardinia. If you're a borderline case, the abundance of excellent fish and shellfish and the knowledge that nearly all eggs and meat are free-range might just push you over the edge. On the whole, though, it's not that difficult if you're committed. Most pasta sauces are based on tomatoes or dairy products, and

In the guide, **telephone numbers** are only given for restaurants where it's necessary to reserve a table in advance. Outside Cágliari, Olbia and Alghero – and not always there – the staff are unlikely to speak English, so you may have to get someone to ring for you.

it's easy to pick a pizza that is meat- (and fish-) free. Most places can be persuaded to cook egg dishes or provide you with a big mixed salad.

The only real problem is one of comprehension: saying you're vegetarian (*sono vegetariano/a*) and asking if the dish has meat in it (*c'è carne dentro?*) is only half the battle: poultry and especially *prosciutto* are regarded by many waiters as barely meat at all. Better is to ask what the dish is made with (*com'è fatto?*) before you order, so that you can spot the offending "non-meaty" meat. Remember even "vegetarian" minestrone and risotto are cooked with meat stock.

If you're a **vegan**, you'll be in for a hard time, though pizzas without cheese are a good stand-by, and the fruit is excellent. Soups are usually made with a fish or meat broth. However, you'll have absolutely no success explaining to anyone why you're a vegan – an incomprehensible concept to a Sardinian.

The bill

At the end of the meal, ask for **the bill** (*il conto*). In many trattorias this doesn't amount to much more than an illegible scrap of paper, and if you want to be sure you're not being ripped off, ask to have a receipt (*una ricevuta*), something they're legally obliged to give you anyway. Nearly everywhere, you'll pay cover (*pane e coperto*), which amounts to €1–2 per person; service (*servizio*) will be added as well in most restaurants, another ten percent – though up to fifteen percent or even twenty percent in some places. If **service** is included, you won't be expected to **tip**; otherwise leave ten percent, though bear in mind that the smaller places – pizzerias and trattorias – won't expect this.

Drinks

Although Sard children are brought up on wine, there's not the same emphasis on dedicated **drinking** here as there is in Britain or America. You'll rarely see drunks in public, young people don't make a night out of getting wasted, and women especially are frowned upon if they're seen to indulge. Nonetheless, there's a wide choice of alcoholic drinks available in Sardinia, at low prices; soft drinks come in multifarious hues, thanks to the abundance of fresh fruit, and there's also mineral water and crushed ice drinks.

Coffee, tea and soft drinks

One of the most distinctive smells in a Sardinian street is the aroma of fresh **coffee**, usually wafting out of a bar (many trattorias and pizzerias don't serve hot drinks). It's always excellent: the basic choice is either small, black and very strong (espresso, or just *caffè*), or weaker, white and frothy (cappuccino), but there are other varieties, too. A caffelatte is an espresso in a big cup filled up to the top with hot milk. If you want your espresso watered down, ask for a *caffè lungo*; with a shot of alcohol – and you can

---

Meal Prices

In the accounts of any large town or city in the guide, recommended restaurants are **graded** according to the following scale:

Inexpensive: under €15	Moderate: €15–30
Expensive: €30–50	Very expensive: over €50

These prices reflect the per person cost of a **full meal** including wine and cover charge – usually consisting of pasta, main course, salad or vegetable, dessert or fruit, and coffee. Obviously, in every restaurant, you'll be able to eat for less than the upper price limit if you only have a couple of courses; and in pizzerias you'd rarely be able to spend more than €12 a head even if you wanted to. The price categories, which are based on prices in 2003, are simply intended as a guide to what you could spend if you pushed the boat out in each restaurant. (For a general idea of the cost of various meals in Sardinia, see p.39).

ask for just about anything in your coffee – is *caffè corretto*; with a drop of milk is *caffè macchiato* ("stained"). If you want to be sure of a coffee without sugar, ask for *caffé senza zúcchero*, though in most bars you serve yourself with sugar. Most places also sell decaffeinated coffee (ask for Hag, even when it isn't); while in summer you'll probably want to have your coffee cold (*caffè freddo*). In holiday centres, you might find *granita di caffè* in summer – cold coffee with crushed ice and topped with cream (*senza panna* if you prefer it without).

Tea is best in summer, when you can drink it iced (*tè freddo*) usually mixed with lemon (also available in tins with peach); it's an excellent thirst-quencher. Hot tea (*tè caldo*) comes with lemon (*con limone*) unless you ask for milk (*con latte*). **Milk** itself is drunk hot as often as cold, or you can get it with a dash of coffee (*latte macchiato*), and in a variety of flavoured drinks (*frappé*) too.

Alternatively, there are various **soft drinks** (*analcóliche*) to choose from. A **spremuta** is a fresh fruit juice, squeezed at the bar, usually orange, lemon or grapefruit. You might need to add sugar to a lemon juice (*spremuta di limone*), but orange juice (*spremuta di arancia*) is usually sweet enough on its own, especially the crimson-red variety, made from blood oranges. You can also have orange and lemon mixed (*mischiato*). A **frullato** is a fresh fruit shake, often made with more than one fruit. A **granita** (a crushed-ice drink) comes in several flavours other than coffee. Otherwise, there's the usual range of fizzy drinks and concentrated juices; Coke is prevalent, but the home-grown Italian alternative, Chinotto, is less sweet – good with a slice of lemon. **Tap water** (*acqua normale*) is drinkable everywhere and you won't pay for it in a bar. But **mineral water** (*acqua minerale*) is the usual choice, either still (*senza gas* or *naturale*) or fizzy (*con gas*, *gassata* or *frizzante*).

Beer, wines and spirits

Beer (*birra*) is usually a lager-type brew which comes in a third of a litre (*píccolo*) or two thirds of a litre (*grande*) bottles: commonest (and cheapest) are the Italian brand, Peroni, and the Sardinian Ichnussa, both of

which are fine, if a bit weak. A small (33cl) bottle of Ichnussa beer costs about €1.55 in a bar or restaurant, a larger (66cl) bottle €2.60; if this is what you want, ask for *birra nazionale*, otherwise you'll be given the more expensive imported beers, like Carlsberg and Becks. In some bars and bigger restaurants and in all *birrerias* you also have a choice of draught lager (*birra alla spina*), sold in units of 25cl (*píccola*) and 50cl (*media*), measure for measure more expensive than the bottled variety. In some places you might find so-called "dark beers" (*birra nera*, *birra rossa* or *birra scura*), which have a slightly maltier taste, and in appearance resemble stout or bitter. These are the dearest of the draught beers, though not necessarily the strongest.

With just about every meal you'll be offered **wine** (*vino*), either red (*rosso*) or white (*bianco*), labelled or local. If you're unsure and want the local stuff, ask for *vino locale*: on the whole it's fine, often served straight from the barrel in jugs or old bottles and costing as little as €4 a litre.

Bottled wine is much more expensive, though still good value; expect to pay from around €7 a bottle in a restaurant, more like €10–15 in places like Alghero. One peculiarity is that bars don't tend to serve wine **by the glass** – when they do, you'll pay around €2. A standard dry red available everywhere but mainly produced around Dorgali and the eastern regions, is Cannonau; others to watch for are Vermentino, a tangy white from Gallura; Campidano di Terralba (red and white), from Oristano province; Mandrolisai, a bitter red but smoother rosé from the Sulcis region; the fruity dry white Nuragus from the provinces of Cágliari and Oristano; Torbato, an aromatic white served chilled with fish, from around Alghero; Semidano, a dry white from the Campidano, and Monica, a strong dry red, best drunk young.

Sardinia produces good **dessert wines**, the most famous being Vernaccia, sweet or dry, honey-coloured, with a bitter-almond taste, from the Tirso river area around Oristano. If you're heading to Bosa, watch out for mellow Malvasia, also served as a table wine, and also produced around Cágliari. Sweet white Moscato comes from Cágliari, Sorso-Sénnori and Tempio

Pausánia, while the Alghero territory produces Anghelu Ruju, one of the strongest and best dessert wines, a sweet red with cherry and cinnamon aromas.

Fortified wine is fairly popular too: Martini (red or white) and Cinzano are nearly always available; Cynar (an artichoke-based sherry) and Punt'e Mes are other common aperitifs. If you ask for a Campari-Soda you'll get a ready-mixed version in a little bottle; a slice of lemon is a *spicchio di limone*; ice is *ghiaccio*.

All the usual **spirits** are on sale and known mostly by their generic names – except brandy, which you should call *cognac* or ask for by name. The best Italian brandies are Stock and Vecchia Romagna; for all other spirits, if you want the cheaper Italian stuff, again, ask for *nazionale*. A generous shot costs around €1–2. Among the **liqueurs**, favourite in Sardinia is *mirto*, made from the leaves and berries of wild myrtle, which you should drink chilled; the red is rated more highly than the white. There's also the standard selection of **amari** (literally "bitters"), an after-dinner drink served with (or instead of) coffee. It's supposed to aid digestion, and is often not bitter at all, but can taste remarkably medicinal. The favourite brand is Averna, but there are dozens of different kinds. **Other strong drinks** available are *grappa di mirto*, almost pure alcohol, from distilled myrtle husks; *Fil'e Ferru*, a fiery grappa-like concoction brewed in the interior, and, though not especially Sardinian, *sambuca* – a sticky-sweet, aniseed liqueur, traditionally served with one or more coffee beans in it and set on fire, though only tourists are likely to experience this these days.

Where to drink

Bars in Sardinia are either functional stops or social centres. You'll come to the first category for drinking on the hoof, a coffee in the morning, a quick beer or cup of tea. Social bars have tables and a greater range of snacks, and are amenable to whiling away part of a morning or afternoon, reading or people-watching. Many bars don't stay open much after 9pm, though this varies from place to place, and hours are extended in summer. As in bars throughout the Mediterranean, there are no set licensing hours and children have free access. Some have a public phone and won't object to you using that or their toilet facilities, even if you're not drinking there.

If you're just having a drink at a stand-up bar, pay first at the cash desk (*la cassa*), present your receipt (*scontrino*) to the bar person and give your order. If there's no cashier, pay either before or after being served. If you're sitting down, wait for someone to take your order, and there'll usually be a 25–35-percent service charge (shown on the price list as *távola*); you're often expected to pay the bill on being served. If you don't know how much a drink will cost, there should be a list of prices (the *listino prezzi*) behind the bar or *cassa*. When you present your receipt, it's customary to leave an extra €0.50 or so on the counter – though no one will object if you don't.

For more serious drinking, most people go out and eat as well, at a pizzeria or restaurant, and spin the meal out accordingly if they want a few more beers. Otherwise, they repair to a **birreria** (literally "beer shop"), where people go just to drink, though often they sell food too. These are where you'll find young people at night, listening to music or glued to rock videos; they're often called "pubs", although they bear little relation to their British namesakes. In tourist areas, bars and cafés (*caffè*) are more like the real European thing and they're open later, but they're more expensive than the common-or-garden bar. Other places to get a drink are an **enoteca**, a rudimentary wine bar selling cheap local wine by the glass and a **bar-pasticceria**, which sells wonderful cakes and pastries too, and a **távola calda** in a railway station always has a bar.

Communications

As a country of compulsive communicators, Italy presents no problems for staying in touch, whether by phone, mail or electronic media. Despite the ubiquity of mobile phones, public telephones are widely distributed throughout Sardinia, most villages have a post office, and Internet points are increasingly common, at least in the towns.

Mail

Post office opening hours are usually Monday–Friday 8.10am–6.40pm, Saturday 8.10am–1.20pm; smaller towns won't have a service on a Saturday and post offices everywhere close at 4pm on the last day of month, or noon if this is a Saturday. If you want stamps, you can buy them in *tabacchi* too, as well as in some gift shops in the tourist resorts. The Italian postal service is one of the slowest in Europe – if your letter is urgent, consider spending extra for the express service.

Letters can be sent **poste restante** to any main post office in Sardinia, by addressing them "Fermo Posta", followed by the name of the town. When collecting something, take your passport, and if your name doesn't turn up make sure they check under middle names and initials.

Telephones

Public **telephones**, mostly run by Telecom Italia, come in various forms, usually with clear instructions printed on them (in English, too). For the most common type, you'll need a **telephone card** (*scheda telefónica*), available for €2.50 or €5 from *tabacchi* or news stands. Note that the perforated corner of these cards must be torn off before they can be used. Bars will often have a phone you can use, though these often take coins only: look for the yellow phone symbol. Some cabins still take coins, but these are being phased out. Note that you need to insert your card or a coin even when dialling toll-free numbers (the money is refunded at the end of the call). Alternatively you could find a telephone office, which often doubles as a fax/Internet point (listed in the text in the larger towns). You can do the same at hotels, but they normally charge 25 percent more. Phone **tariffs** are among the most expensive in Europe; they're at their dearest from Monday to Friday between 8.30am and 1pm, but cheapest between 10pm and 8am Monday to Saturday and all day Sunday.

Calling home from Sardinia

You can make **international calls** from any booth that accepts cards, and from any other booth labelled "*interurbano*" or "*internationale*". One of the most convenient ways of phoning home from abroad is via a **telephone charge card** from your phone company back home. Using a PIN number, you can make calls from most hotels, public and private phones that will be charged to your account. Since most major charge cards are free to obtain, it's certainly worth getting one at least for emergencies; enquire first, though, whether your destination is

Italian phone numbers

Telephone numbers change with amazing frequency in Italy. The latest innovation has been to merge the local code with the individual number, so that it is necessary to dial the entire number wherever you are. Numbers beginning ☏800 and ☏167 are reduced tariff or free, and those beginning ☏199 and ☏848 are charged at the national rate. ☏170 will get you through to an English-speaking operator.

International telephone codes

Note that the initial zero is omitted from the area code when dialling the UK, Ireland, Australia and New Zealand from abroad.

UK international access code + 44 + city code.
Republic of Ireland international access code + 353 + city code.
USA and Canada international access code + 1 + area code.
Australia international access code + 61 + city code.
New Zealand international access code + 64 + city code.

covered, and bear in mind that rates aren't necessarily cheaper than calling from a public phone.

In **the UK and Ireland**, British Telecom (☎0800/345 144, ☒www.chargecard .bt.com) will issue free to all BT customers the BT Charge Card, which can be used in 116 countries; AT&T (dial ☎0800/890 011, then 888/641-6123 when you hear the AT&T prompt to be transferred to the Florida Call Centre, free 24 hours) has the Global Calling Card.

In the **US and Canada**, AT&T, MCI, Sprint, Canada Direct and other North American long-distance companies all enable their customers to make credit-card calls while overseas, billed to your home number. Call your company's customer service line to find out if they provide service from Italy, and if so, what the toll-free access code is.

To call **Australia and New Zealand** from overseas, telephone charge cards such as Telstra Telecard or Optus Calling Card in Australia, and Telecom NZ's Calling Card can be used to make calls abroad, which are charged back to a domestic account or credit card. Apply to Telstra (☎1800/038 000), Optus (☎1300/300 937) or Telecom NZ (☎04/801 9000).

Alternatively, use a special **international phone card** (*carta telefónica internazionale*) available in various denominations from post offices; all cardphones accept them, but before each call you need to dial the special access number and PIN number printed on the back of the card. To make a **collect/reversed charge** call (*cárico al des-tinatario*), dial ☎170 or 172, followed by the country code (see box on p.43), which will connect you to an operator in your home country. Alternatively, dial ☎800.070.606, wait for the prompt, then dial 1 for an English operator. The service also accepts credit-card and calling-card calls.

Mobile phones

Mobile phones work on the GSM European standard. You'll hardly see an Italian without one, but if you plan to join them, make sure you make the necessary arrangements with your mobile phone company before you leave. After arrival, your phone should lock onto one of the Italian frequencies – Omnitel, Wind or Tim – according to which is strongest.

Most **UK mobiles** use GSM too, which gives access to most places worldwide. For all but the very top-of-the-range packages, you'll have to inform your phone provider before going abroad to get international access switched on. You may get charged extra for this, depending on your existing package.

Unless you have a tri-band phone, it's unlikely that a mobile bought for use inside the **US** will work outside the States (and vice versa). For details of which mobiles will work outside the US, contact your service provider. Most mobiles in **Australia** and **New Zealand** use GSM, which works well in Europe.

Note that calls are expensive – they're routed via your home country – and you're also charged for part of the cost of incoming calls, as people calling you will pay the usual rate. Calls to your **message** centre can also be pricey, and you'll need to check with your company that this service will be available to you. If it is, you'll be provided with a new access code, as your home one is unlikely to work abroad.

For further information about using your phone abroad, check out ☒www

Calling Sardinia from abroad

Dial the access code ☎00 from Britain, Ireland and New Zealand or ☎0011 from Australia, Canada and the US; then 39 (for Italy); then the area code including the first zero (the major towns are listed below); and then the subscriber number. All telephone numbers listed in the Guide include the relevant area code.

Alghero ☎079
Arbatax ☎0782
Bosa ☎0785
Cágliari ☎070
Costa Smeralda ☎0789

Nuoro ☎0784
Olbia ☎0789
Oristano ☎0783
Sássari ☎079
Villasimius ☎070

.telecomsadvice.org.uk/features/using_your _mobile_abroad.htm.

Email

One of the best ways to keep in touch while travelling is to sign up for a free Internet email address that can be accessed from anywhere, for example YahooMail or Hotmail – accessible through ⊛www.yahoo.com and ⊛www.hotmail.com. Once you've set up an account, you can use these sites to pick up and send mail from any Internet point, or hotel with Internet access. Most towns in Sardinia have some kind of Internet point (and they're listed in the Guide). In smaller places, someone can usually point out a bar or office that provides this service. The usual cost is around €3 for thirty minutes.

A useful website is ⊛www.kropla.com, which gives details of how to plug your laptop in when abroad, phone country codes around the world, and information about electrical systems in different countries.

The media

Sards number among Italy's most avid readers of newspapers. You'll find the main national papers on any newsstand: *La Repubblica* is middle-to-left, with a lot of cultural coverage; *Il Corriere della Sera* is authoritative and rather conservative; *L'Unità* is the former Communist Party organ, also strong on culture; *Il Manifesto*, a more radical and readable left-wing daily, and the pink *Gazzetta dello Sport*, essential reading for the serious sports fan.

Most people, however, prefer Sardinian **local papers**, which offer non-Sards good insights into local concerns as well as being useful for transport timetables, entertainments listings, festival announcements, etc. There are two main ones: *L'Unione Sarda*, most read in Cágliari and the south of the island, and *La Nuova Sardegna*, also called "La Nuova", favoured in Sássari and the north. There is little to tell between them in terms of content, and each has local editions for each of the main towns. Note that Monday editions are almost exclusively devoted to sport, with no coverage of other events. **English-language newspapers** can be found in Cágliari, Sássari, Oristano, Nuoro, Olbia, Porto Cervo and Alghero, at the train station and the main piazza or corso, usually a day or two late.

Surprisingly, for such an outdoor society, Italians are among the most avid **TV-watchers** in the world. The three state-run channels, RAI 1, 2 and 3, have got their backs against the wall in the face of the domination of the numerous private channels by Prime Minister Berlusconi, who owns Rete 4, Canale 5 and Italia 1 – three of the biggest in the independent sector. On the whole, the output is fairly bland, with a heavy helping of soaps, sitcoms, cabaret shows and films, though the RAI channels have less advertising and mix some good reporting in among the dross. RAI 3 has the most intelligent coverage, and broadcasts Sardinian news programmes. Of the local channels, *Videolina* is most popular in Cágliari, *Sardegna Uno* in the north, *TeleSardegna* around Nuoro, and *Tele Regione* transmits everywhere. Advertising is constant on all stations.

The situation in **radio** is even more anarchic, with the FM waves crowded to the extent that you can pick up a new station just by walking down the corridor. Again, the RAI stations are generally more professional, though daytime listening is virtually undiluted non-stop dance music. RAI 3 has classical and jazz music, and afternoons devoted to themes such as Brazilian or Celtic music. Frequencies vary according to where you are, so be prepared for constant retuning.

Opening hours, public holidays and festivals

Basic hours for most shops and businesses in Sardinia are Monday to Saturday from 8 or 9am to around 1pm, and from around 4pm to 7 or 8pm, though some offices work to a more standard European 9am–5pm day. Everything, except museums, bars and restaurants, closes on Sunday, though you might find pasticcerias, and fish shops in some coastal towns, open until Sunday lunchtime.

Other disrupting factors are **national holidays** and local **saints' days** (see Festivals, overleaf). On national holidays (shown in the box), expect shops and offices to be closed, and a Sunday transport service. Local religious holidays don't generally close down shops and businesses, but accommodation space may be tight.

Churches, museums and archeological sites

The rules for visiting **churches** are much as they are all over the Mediterranean. Dress modestly, which usually means no shorts, and covered shoulders for women, and avoid wandering around during a service. Most churches open around 7 or 8am for Mass and close around 11am or noon, opening up again at 4–5pm, and closing at 7 or 8pm; smaller ones will only open for early morning and evening services; some only open on Sunday and on religious holidays. Other churches, which have become fully-fledged tourist stops, are open all day

Public Holidays

January 1 New Year's Day
January 6 Epiphany
Good Friday
Easter Monday
April 25 Liberation Day
May 1 Labour Day
August 15 Ferragosto; Assumption of the Blessed Virgin Mary
November 1 Ognissanti (All Saints)
December 8 Immaculate Conception of the Blessed Virgin Mary
December 25 Christmas Day
December 26 St Stephen's Day

every day, for example the Pisan churches of Santa Trinità di Saccárgia, near Sássari, and San Gavino, in Porto Torres. Occasionally you'll come across churches, monasteries or convents **closed for restoration** (*chiuso per restauro*). Some of these are long-term closures, though you might be able to persuade a workman or priest/curator to show you around, even if there's scaffolding everywhere.

Museums are generally open either all day or 9am–1pm and 4–8pm, 3–7pm in winter. Those that aren't open daily are most likely to be closed on Monday. **Archeological sites** are usually open daily from 9am until an hour before sunset, in practice until around 5pm in winter, 8pm in summer. The most important nuraghi (Sardinia's famous prehistoric towers) share these hours, though most of the smaller ones are open to anyone at all hours. If you need to cross private land to reach them, it's best to ask first.

Festivals and entertainment

Sardinia's festivals – *feste* or *sagre* – are high points of the island's cultural life, and excellent opportunities to view traditional costumes and dancing and to hear local music. While many are religious in origin – mostly feast days for saints having a special role for a particular locality – others are purely secular, often celebrating the harvest or simply perpetuating ancient games and competitions. These are still basically unchanged in the smaller towns and villages, though some have evolved into much larger affairs spread over three or four days, and others have been developed with an eye to tourism.

In all, masks and costumes play a prominent role, the first representing a variety of functions and traditions and injecting an eerie theatricality into the event, the second an emblem of local identity. Horses, too, are usually present, and often the main protagonists of the proceedings. Many events attract groups of singers and dancers from surrounding villages, and special food and sweets are available from stalls. Local people spend months preparing for the occasion, and they're well worth scheduling into your visit.

Sardinia has a number of *chiese novene*, remote churches open only for nine days a year when **pilgrimages** take place. The best-known of these are Sant'Antine, outside Sédilo, and San Salvatore, on the Sinis peninsula, where pilgrims gather at the beginning of July and the beginning of September respectively – both places are in Oristano province.

Aside from the festivals, there's a fair selection of cultural events happening throughout the year in Sardinia. **Concerts** and **dramatic performances** are sometimes held at outdoor venues in summer, and **films**, too, can be enjoyed under the stars. The ESIT office in Cágliari (see p.69 & 72) or any of the provincial tourist offices can tell you about forthcoming events.

Festivals

January

16–17 Sant'Antonio's (St Anthony's) day is celebrated in dozens of Sardinian villages, usually with bonfires, since the saint is supposed, Prometheus-like, to have given the gift of fire to men after he stole it from hell. The liveliest celebrations are at the villages of Abbasanta, near Oristano, and Mamoiada, Bitti, Lodè, Orosei and Lula, around Nuoro.

19–20 Among the villages commemorating **San Sebastiano**'s day are Turri and Ussana, both in Cágliari province, and Bulzi, inland from Castesardo. Again, bonfires, processions and holy singing are the order of the day, usually ending up with wine and food all round.

February

3 San Biagio's day in Gergei, near Barúmini (north of Cágliari), sees the festival of **Su Sessineddu**, named after the *sessini* – reed frames on which sweets, fruits and flowers are hung and attached to the horns of oxen. This is primarily a children's festival, which involves seeing who can scoff the most goodies before staggering home.

Carnival Traditionally, the Carnival period starts with Sant'Antonio's day on 17 January, but in practice most of the action takes place over three days climaxing on Shrove Tuesday, most often in February.

Although the occasion is intended as a prelude to the abstinence of Lent (*carne vale* = farewell to meat), most Carnival celebrations smack of paganism. Children raid their family trunks or, in richer households, buy or hire costumes to wear as fancy dress. Impressive masks are commonly worn, producing a somewhat sinister effect.

In Mamoiada, south of Nuoro, the three-day festival features music, dancing and the distribution of wine and sweets, climaxing in the ritual procession of the *issohadores* and *mamuthones* representing respectively hunters and hunted. The latter are clad in shaggy sheepskin jerkins, their faces covered in chilling black wooden masks, their backs hidden beneath dozens of sheep-bells with which they create a jangling, discordant clamour. Meanwhile the "hunters" lasso bystanders who are supposed to appease them with gifts of wine (but rarely do).

Oristano's **Sa Sartiglia** is wildly different, a medieval pageant involving much horseback racing and a jousting competition in which masked and mounted "knights" attempt to ram their swords through a hanging ring, called *sartija* – a Spanish word which gives its name to the festival. The whole three-day event is directed by the *componidori*, also white-masked and dressed in an elaborate frilly costume.

Various other strange goings-on take place during this period: a six-day festival at Bonorva, between Oristano and Sássari, includes masked processions, dances and ritual burnings of puppets; Bosa, south of Alghero, holds another six-day event, with theatrical funeral processions and costumed searches for the *Giolzi*, spirit of Carnival and sexuality; the normally taciturn mountain village of Tempio Pausánia, in Gallura, bursts into life with masks and floats as another symbolic puppet is incinerated; while frenetic horse races are held at Santu Lussurgiu, in the mountains north of Oristano.

March

March is traditionally bereft of merry-making on account of Lent, though Muravera (on the coast east of Cágliari) holds its **Sagra dell'Agrume** to mark the citrus fruit (*agrumi*) harvest. Traditional Sardinian dances are performed as peasant carts trundle through town. It's always held on a Sunday, though the date varies.

April

23 Several villages on the island celebrate **San Giorgio**'s day: Bonnanaro, south-east of Sássari, is the scene of religious processions and prayers conducted entirely in Sard; Bitti, a mountain village north of Nuoro, has a horseback procession in traditional costume and renditions of mournful shepherds' songs; and Onifai, near Orosei, holds horseback processions, dances and poetry competitions.

Easter

Usually occurring in April, **Easter** is a time of holy processions throughout the island. Most towns and villages feature events on Good Friday, when silent processions carrying a statue of Jesus on the cross file through the streets and into the main church, where the image may be ritually taken down from the cross before being laid in a coffin. On Easter Sunday, the image is again paraded through the streets, to meet a statue of the Madonna in a symbolic encounter known as *Su Incontru*, amid much celebration and gunfire. One of the most dramatic Easter celebrations takes place in Iglesias, where there are almost daily processions for a week, beginning on the Tuesday of Easter week, culminating in a re-enactment of the Passion, with all the local guilds represented. Other places with distinctive rites include Alghero; Castelsardo; Sássari; Oliena (near Nuoro), and Santu Lussurgiu (north of Oristano), where fifteenth-century Gregorian chants are sung on Good Friday.

On the first Sunday after Easter, religious processions and musical events take place in Alghero and Valledoria (near Castelsardo), and the following Sunday sees three days of events to commemorate the feast day of **Sant'Antíoco**. These are naturally most exuberant in the town named after him, but impressive celebrations are also held in Dolianova, outside Cágliari; Gavoi, in the Barbagia region southwest of Nuoro; Mogoro, south of Oristano; Ulassai, south of Lanusei on the eastern seaboard; and Villasor, northwest of Cágliari.

May

1–4 May's biggest event, if not the whole year's, is Cágliari's feast day in honour of the martyr **Sant'Efisio**. Although the festival commemorates the saint's delivery of the city from plague in 1656, in one sense it belongs to the whole island, since costumed delegations from dozens of villages throughout the island participate. Accompanied for part of the way by extravagantly decorated ox-drawn carts, the procession escorts the image of the saint through the streets of the capital, whereupon a smaller hard core of devotees continues on to Sant'Efisio's church, 40km down the coast near the ruins of Roman Nora, site of the saint's martyrdom. The journey takes the best part of two days, and that's just the outward leg. The opening and closing ceremonies are excellent opportunities to see a good selection of the island's costumes out at once.

15 Olbia's yearly extravaganza commemorates another martyr, **San Simplicio**, its patron saint, and consists of fireworks, the distribution of sweets and wine, and various games and water competitions.

Ascension Day The penultimate Sunday of May sees more costumed revelry, this time in Sássari, though without any of the religious overtones of Cágliari's festa. Many of the same costumes that appeared there can be seen at this pageant, **La Cavalcata**, which, as its name suggests, has a distinctly horsey flavour to it, culminating in grand equestrian stunts in the afternoon. The occasion originated with the successful repulse of a Muslim raid around the year 1000.

29 In the countryside outside Onanì, northeast of Nuoro, traditional Sardinian dances take place for three consecutive days and nights.

Pentecost – a movable feast fifty days after Easter – sees four days of celebration at Porto Torres, including an impressive procession carrying plaster images of the town's martyred saints from the clifftop church of Balai to the Pisan basilica of San Gavino. On the following day, the saints are transported to the sea, and there's a huge fish fry-up. One of the features of this festival is a boat-race involving teams from five of the main seaside towns on Sardinia's northern coast, and there's also a costumed parade.

Suelli, north of Cágliari, likewise has a prolonged celebration of Pentecost, beginning the Friday before, when the entire population exits from the town and spends the night in the fields gathering wood, singing songs and dancing. The wood collected gets brought into the town, and a bonfire is lit on Pentecost Sunday, amid costumed processions and games.

June

2 The island's most important **horse fair** takes place outside Santu Lussurgiu, north of Oristano, around the Romanesque church of San Leonardo.

Second Sunday Fonni, south of Nuoro, hosts a festival devoted to the "Blessed Virgin of the Martyrs" – **Beata Vérgine dei Mártiri**. Costumes and processions on horseback are the main features.

15 San Vito, outside Muravera (on the coast east of Cágliari), honours its saint with three days of spirited feasting.

24 A pre-Christian feast day marking the summer solstice coincides with **St John the Baptist's day**, and is celebrated in more than fifty villages all over Sardinia, with the usual processions, dances, songs and poetry competitions. Among the villages are Bonorva, between Oristano and Sássari; Buddusò, in the Galluran mountains between Olbia and Nuoro; Escalaplano, a mountain village between Cágliari and Lanusei; Fonni, and nearby Gavoi.

29 Ss Peter and Paul are commemorated in a score of Sardinian villages, notably Ollolai and Orgósolo, both south of Nuoro; Terralba, south of Oristano, and Villa San Pietro, on the coast south of Cágliari.

July

6–8 Locals at Sédilo, between Oristano and Nuoro, indulge their passion for horses with characteristic gusto in the three-day **S'Ardia di Costantino**, in honour of the Roman emperor (and saint) Constantine. The reckless horse-racing guarantees plenty of thrills and spills and attracts thousands of fans.

25 Orosei, on the coast east of Nuoro, stages one of the most important of the island's many **poetry competitions**, in which contestants recite or sing verses.

31 There are three days of merriment at Musei, just off the Iglesias–Cágliari road, in honour of the founder of the Jesuit order, **St Ignatius of Loyola** (Sant'Ignazio); it has all the usual festival paraphernalia, usually kicking off on the nearest Sunday to the 31st.

August

This is the month when tourists flood into the island, emigrés return for the summer, and all the resorts devote every last euro to entertainment. The high point comes in the middle of the month with Ferragosto, a national holiday celebrated more exuberantly than Christmas.

First Sunday On the first Sunday of the month, Bosa hosts various events in honour of **Santa Maria del Mare**, with an emphasis on the water, including a river procession and various water-sports.

15 Mid-August, or **Ferragosto**, is the day when villages all over Italy erupt with dazzling fireworks displays to mark the festival of the Madonna: the Assumption, or Assunta. Some of Sardinia's Ferragosto celebrations are coupled with another festival, as in Sássari's spectacular **I Candelieri**. The event – which had its origin in the fifteenth century when plague was averted by divine intervention – starts on the 14th, and takes its name from the huge candles carried through thronged streets amid delirious dancing. Each candle represents one of the city's guilds, whose traditional colours are emblazoned on the candlesticks along with the tools and symbols of the trade.

A similar festa is held in the nearby village of Nulvi, also starting on the 14th, but with just three candles (here representing shepherds, farmers and craftsmen), which are preceded by twelve monks – representing the apostles – singing medieval hymns. The Madonna herself is wheeled around town on the 15th, and there follows some sort of religious ceremony every day until the 22nd.

In Golfo Aranci, north of Olbia, the regular Ferragosto festivities are combined with a **Sagra del Pesce**, a fishing festa involving the consumption of much seafood.

Other Ferragosto events worthy of mention are held at Dorgali and Orgósolo, both in the Nuoro region, and Guasila, north of Cágliari.

Penultimate Sunday of August Nuoro's **Sagra del Redentore** includes parades and the most important of the island's costume competitions. This is the biggest of the festivals in Sardinia's mountainous Barbagia district.

29 The second, religious part of Nuoro's annual festival features a procession up to the statue of Christ the Redeemer on top of nearby Monte Ortobene. On the same day, St John the Baptist has a second holy day celebrated in several villages, notably Orotelli, west of Nuoro, and San Giovanni di Sinis, west of Oristano.

September

Formerly the first month of the year, according to the old Sardinian calendar, September marks the return to work and is the traditional time for contracts to be sealed and marriages made.

First Sunday The lagoon town of Cabras, near Oristano, re-enacts the rescue of its statue of **San Salvatore** from raiders in the sixteenth century: an army of barefoot young men dressed in white sprint the 8km from the saint's sanctuary into town with the saint borne aloft.

7–17 Santa Maria de Sauccu Two separate processions take off from Bortigali, near Macomer, to a sanctuary 10km away in the mountains, the venue for dances, picnics and poetic competitions over the next nine days.

8 The **Madonna** is venerated in Ales, a village southeast of Oristano, when her statue is brought out amid much fanfare no less than six times in three days.

Second Sunday: Nostra Signora di Regnos Altos Not for the first time in the year, the banners and bunting are strung across the narrow lanes of Bosa's old centre; once the religious formalities are out of the way, tables are laid and much food is guzzled and drink quaffed.

Last Sunday of September More than 100,000 devotees every year come to pay their tributes to **Santa Greca**, in five days of festivities at Decimomannu, outside Cágliari.

October

4 The village of Alà dei Sardi, nestled in the mountains between Nuoro and Olbia, takes to the fields and spends two days attending open-air masses, eating and feasting in honour of **St Francis**.

Last Sunday of October The **Sagra delle Castagne**, or chestnut fair, is held at Aritzo in the heart of the Barbagia mountains. The smell of the cooking nuts permeates the air around here for days.

November–December

The end of the year is a lean time for outdoor festivals, though a few saints are remembered, notably St Andrew on the last day of November.

1–2 November Tuttisanti, or All Saints Day, is a public holiday, and is followed by the **Day of the Dead**, a time of mourning observed all over the Catholic world. Families troop en masse to the local cemetery where loved ones are buried; in parts of Sardinia, the table is laid and the favourite dishes of the deceased are served up and left overnight – apparently, just the odours are enough to satisfy them.

Christmas

Christmas Eve and **Christmas Day** are not the big commercial affair they are in some countries. This is primarily a family event; fish is normally eaten on Christmas Eve, and lamb is the traditional fare on Christmas Day, followed by *panettone*, a dry, sweet cake.

Music and dance

The island's archeological remains provide spectacular settings for **concerts**, usually classical, and there are regular events by local and visiting international orchestras in the theatres at Cágliari and Sássari. The **opera** season runs from January to June, the best venues being the Teatro Cívico in Cágliari and Sássari. Smaller theatres in all the main towns and cities also have music programmes, with a season of classical music in Alghero every August and a festival of sacred **choral music** in the Pisan church of San Gavino in Porto Torres during the first week of September.

Unaccompanied harmony singing, in fact, forms a central part of Sardinia's musical tradition, and you'll come across it at many of the local festivals. Most village singing groups either belong to the *coros* (choral) or *tenores* (four-part) traditions, and the latter groups, in particular, have made quite an impact internationally in recent years. Festivals are also a good place to see **traditional instruments** being played; if you miss them there are plenty of examples to be seen in museums. Apart from drums and accordion, the most distinctive instrument is the *launeddas*, a simple, polyphonic triple pipe made from reed.

Together with an accordion, drum and guitar, the *launeddas* is the usual accompaniment to **Sardinian dancing**, a curiously twitchy spectacle, in which the feet perform a constant fast rhythm while the rest of the body remains still. The group of men and women might have to sustain the synchronized movement for a long time, exercising flawless control during the elaborate sequence – definitely worth catching if you get the chance.

There's no specific Sardinian **rock music** scene. Radio and TV are dominated by mainstream Italian chart music – mostly ballads, dance music and Europop, with a smattering of British and American hits. The island has made more impact in the field of **jazz**, contributing some big names to the Italian and European scenes – for example, the trumpeter Paolo Fresu, who has accentuated the Sard connection in his work. Some big international jazz and rock names do come to Sardinia, and, in summer especially, a few of the more enterprising local councils sponsor open-air concerts in public squares or parks.

Theatre and cinema

Regular **theatre** is popular in Sardinia. Most performances, unsurprisingly, take place in the main cities of Cágliari and Sássari, the Teatro Cívico in each place being the premier venue for mainstream works. Smaller theatres in both cities and some other towns stage more experimental material, while summer sees open-air performances in Cágliari's Anfiteatro Romano, amid the ruins of Nora and Tharros, and at Villasimius.

There are **cinemas** in most towns, though all English-language films are dubbed into Italian. An alternative in summer to the indoor movie houses are the open-air film shows that take place in some towns and tourist resorts, detailed in the text. The island of Tavolara, east of Olbia, hosts a unique **film festival** every year in mid-July, with open-air screenings of new, mainly low-budget Italian films. You can reach the island by boat from Porto San Paolo; for programmes, see the festival website: ⓦhttp://web.tin.it/cinematavolara.

Outdoor pursuits

In spite of the traditional stereotype of a holiday in Sardinia as a passive, beach-lounging affair, the island is becoming increasingly popular for its numerous possibilities for **outdoor activities**. Chief among these are hiking, riding and watersports, though there is also growing interest in such pursuits as free climbing, caving and kayaking. The island has one ski run, in the Gennargentu mountains near Fonni (see p.329–330), the season extending from December to March. Biking is described on p.33. You'll find public tennis courts in most towns and attached to hotels, with racquets sometimes available for rent.

Hiking

Walking – ie serious **hiking** – was until recently a fairly rare phenomenon in Sardinia, and there are no long-distance paths and few marked routes. Nonetheless, the island can boast some of the most magnificent walking country in Europe, including the Gorropu canyon (see p.338), Sopramonte, south of Nuoro (p.322–323), and, still further south, the Gennargentu mountains (p.328–329). But almost every part of Sardinia offers scope for serious or casual hikes, and there are scores of hiking cooperatives that will supply **guides** for walks of all levels of difficulty. Phone numbers for some of these are given in the text; others may be contacted through local tourist offices, such as that at Oliena (see p.324), which can also supply itineraries and rough maps, or else the Sardinian branch of the Associazione Italiana Guide Ambientali Escursionistiche (AIGE ⓣ0783.52.283, ⓦwww.gae.it), which has a database listing 150 guides for the whole island.

We've described some simple hikes in the guide. Remember to bring suitable footwear, headwear and a good supply of water, and to inform somebody (for example, the hotel or local tourist office) where you're heading. Longer hikes are inadvisable without an experienced guide. For maps, see p.21–22.

Riding

Horses and Sardinia have been an item for centuries, and Sards have long been acknowledged as among Italy's finest riders. There's ample evidence of this on display in the festivals featuring equestrian skills, notably in Oristano province, and in the **riding** courses and excursions available throughout the island. The largest of the riding operations is also in Oristano province, at Ala Birdi (see p.179); it organizes courses and a range of treks through pinewoods and on the nearby beaches, and can provide information on riding activities over the whole island. The Barbágia, too, provides myriad possibilities for mountain riding, for example from Su Gologone, near Oliena and Nuoro (see p.324). You'll find other stables throughout the island. Rates depend on the length of the excursion and whether or not you're part of a group.

Watersports

You'll find a full range of **watersports** available on most coasts as soon as the beaches start filling up in summer. **Scuba diving** is offered by small firms in most holiday centres, and is most popular around Alghero and the northwest, Stintino in the north, and Muravera and the eastern coast. **Water-skiing** still takes place, but has largely been supplanted by **windsurfing**, for which the favourite spot is Porto Pollo, near Palau (also the place for kite-surfing). All of these activities are often available from the bigger hotels, even for non-residents, and from some campsites. **Surfers** tend to congregate at Capo Mannu on the Sinis peninsula, near Oristano.

Sailing is another favourite summer pastime, particularly on the Costa del Sud and Costa Smeralda, and around the Maddalena archipelago. This is a high-spending pursuit in Sardinia, however, and most enthusiasts will have to make do with joining a group with a full crew to do the actual sailing. Ask at tourist offices in Olbia, Pula, Palau and Porto Cervo about companies offering these expeditions.

Crime and personal safety

Mention crime in Sardinia to most people and they think of bandits in the hills. The abduction of rich industrialists or members of their families has been the most high-profile felony practised on the island since it was found to be more lucrative than sheep-rustling, though kidnapping is now a comparatively rare event, and should not affect tourists at all. In the interior, road signs peppered with gunshot are more an indication of bored youth than anything more menacing, and the feuds which occasionally erupt between families are always "domestic" affairs, and now rarely violent.

In fact, Sardinia is one of Italy's safest regions, with a remarkably low level of violence, drunkenness and crime. Most **petty juvenile crime** is connected with drug addiction in the cities of Cágliari and Sássari. You can minimize the risk of falling victim to **muggings** or **pickpockets** by being discreet: don't flash anything of value, keep a firm hand on your camera, and carry shoulder-bags, as you'll see many Sardinian women do, slung across your body. You might consider entrusting money, credit cards and valuables to hotel managers, rather than leave them in your room, and it's wise to avoid badly lit or deserted areas at night. Confronted with a robber, your best bet is to submit meekly – panic can lead to violence, though very few tourists see anything of this.

Emergencies

- ☏ 112 for the police (Polizia or Carabinieri)
- ☏ 113 for any emergency (*emergenza*) service
- ☏ 115 for the fire brigade (*Vigili del Fuoco*)
- ☏ 116 for road assistance (*Soccorso Stradale*)
- ☏ 118 for ambulance (*Pronto Soccorso*)

The police

If the worst happens, you'll be forced to have some dealings with the **police**. In Sardinia, as in the rest of Italy, they come in many forms. The most innocuous are the **Polizia Urbana** or town police, mainly concerned with directing the traffic and punishing parking offences. The **Guardia di Finanza**, often heavily armed and racing ostentatiously through the cities in their cars, are responsible for investigating smuggling, tax evasion and other similar crimes. Most conspicuous are the **Carabinieri** and **Polizia Statale**; no one knows what distinguishes their roles, apart from the fact that the Carabinieri – usually in black uniforms – are organized along military lines and are a branch of the armed forces. They are also the butt of most of the jokes about the police, usually on the "How many Carabinieri does it take to...?" level. Each of the two forces is meant to act as a check and counterbalance to the other: a fine theory, though it results in much time-wasting and rivalry in practice.

Hopefully, you won't need to get entangled with either, but in the event of theft you'll need to report it at the headquarters of the Polizia Statale, the **Questura**; you'll find their address in the local telephone directory. if you're staying for any length of time, the Questura is also where you obtain a *permesso di soggiorno* or a **visa extension**.

In any brush with the authorities, your experience will depend on the individuals you're dealing with, though most Sard police officers – male and female – are unfailingly polite. Apart from **topless bathing** (permitted, but don't try anything more daring) and **camping rough**, don't expect a soft touch if you've been picked up for any offence, especially if it's drug-related: it's not unheard of to be stopped and searched if you're young and carrying a backpack, and there are plenty of plain-clothes police and informers on the lookout for any suspicious activity.

Drugs are generally frowned upon by everyone above a certain age, and universal hysteria about *la droga*, fuelled by the epidemic of heroin addiction that has become a serious problem for Sardinia, means that any distinction between the "hard" and "soft" variety has become blurred. Theoretically, everything is illegal above the possession of a few grams of cannabis or marijuana "for personal use", though there's no agreed definition of what this means, and anyone caught with anything can expect to have the substances confiscated and may have to undergo a body-search, while larger quantities may lead to a fine or worse. Any harder drugs found will probably result in a stint in jail, at least for as long as it takes for them to analyze the stuff, draw up reports and wait for the bureaucratic wheels to grind.

For the addresses of the nearest **foreign consulates** see p.60 – though they're unlikely to be very sympathetic or do anything more than put you in touch with a lawyer.

Travellers with disabilities

Although most Sardinians are helpful enough if presented with a specific problem, the island is hardly geared towards accommodating travellers with disabilities, although things are (slowly) improving. Many sites and monuments may pose significant obstacles for anyone with restricted mobility, while few budget or mid-range hotels have lifts, let alone ones capable of taking a wheelchair (higher-grade hotels may have some rooms adapted for use by disabled visitors).

In the medieval city centres and old villages, narrow cobbled streets, steep inclines, chaotic driving and parking are hardly conducive to a stress-free holiday either, while crossing the street in Cágliari is a trial at the best of times. That said, Sardinia presents a much less frenetic level of bustle than other areas in Italy's south, while Alghero, the most popular resort, has a highly user-friendly grid of traffic-free streets.

However, there are measures you can take to make your visit to Sardinia easier. Contacting one of the **organizations** listed below puts you in touch with a wide range of facilities and information that may prove useful. If the thought of negotiating your own way around the island proves too daunting, consider an organized **tour**: it will be more expensive than planning your own trip, but accommodation is usually in higher-category hotels, which should have at least some experience of and facilities for disabled travellers; you'll also have someone on hand who speaks Italian to help smooth the way. It's also worth consulting the lists of specialist Sardinian tour operators on p.11–12 & 14 for an assessment of specific resorts and destinations.

At all times, give the fullest information to travel agencies, insurance companies and travel companions. If your walking capabilities are limited, remember that you're likely to be covering greater distances while travelling (often over rougher terrain and in hotter temperatures) than you are used to. If you use a **wheelchair**, have it serviced before you go, and carry a repair kit.

Read your travel **insurance** small print carefully to make sure that people with a pre-existing medical condition are not excluded. Use your travel agent to make your journey simpler: airline or bus companies can cope better if they are expecting you, with a wheelchair provided at airports and staff primed to help. A **medical certificate** of your fitness to travel, provided by your doctor, is also extremely useful; some airlines or insurance companies may insist on it. Make sure that you have extra supplies of drugs – carried with you if you fly – and a prescription including the generic name in case of emergency.

Contacts for travellers with disabilities

Several organizations exist that can supply general information on travelling with disabilities. The following can help you directly or put you in touch with others in more specific fields; it's advisable to contact them early in the planning process.

In the UK

Holiday Care 7th floor, Sunley House, 4 Bedford Park, Croydon, Surrey CR0 2AP ☏0845/124 9971, minicom ☏0845/124 9976, ⓦwww .holidaycare.org. Provides free lists of accessible accommodation in places including Sardinia, and information on financial help for holidays.
Tripscope The Vassall Centre, Gill Avenue, Bristol BS16 2QQ ☏0845/7585 641, ⓦwww .tripscope.org.uk. This registered charity provides a national telephone and online information service offering free advice on UK and international transport for those with a mobility problem.

In the US and Canada

Mobility International USA PO Box 10767, Eugene, Oregon 97440 ☏541/343-1284,

@www.miusa.org. Information and referral services, access guides, tours and exchange programmes.

Society for the Advancement of Travelers with Handicaps (SATH) 347 5th Ave, New York, NY 10016 ☎212/447-7284, @www.sath.org. Non-profit educational organization that has actively represented travellers with disabilities since 1976. Articles and advice for travellers available online.

Wheels Up! ☎1-888/38-WHEELS, @www.wheelsup.com. Provides discounted airfare, tour and cruise prices for disabled travellers, also has an online newsletter on its comprehensive website.

ACROD (Australian Council for Rehabilitation of the Disabled) PO Box 60, Curtin ACT 2605; 33 Thesiger Court, Deakin ACT 2600; ☎/TTY 02/6283 3200, @www.acrod.org.au. Provides lists of travel agencies and tour operators for people with disabilities, mostly for members only.

Sex and gender issues

While Sardinia's attitudes on gender issues have more in common with the prejudices prevailing in much of the Italian south than with sophisticated cities like Rome and Milan, the regular flow of tourists through the island has helped to moderate much of the ingrained intolerance. The importance placed on good manners alone will mean that abuse and discrimination are rarely encountered.

Italy's past reputation for sexual harassment of **women** is well known and well founded. Generally, though, things have improved radically in recent years, and, while you can expect to attract occasional unwelcome attention in bars, restaurants and on the beach if you're travelling on your own or with another woman, such intrusion is increasingly rare and frowned upon. If you are pestered, however, there is unlikely to be any violent intent, and it can usually be stopped with a loud *Lasciátemi in pace!* ("Leave me alone!"), though stronger language is not advised. As a last resort, don't hesitate to approach a policeman. Obviously, travelling with men cuts out much of the more intense hassle, and perhaps the best strategy of all for a woman alone in Sardinia, where the sanctity of the family is still paramount, is to flaunt a wedding ring.

Sardinia has no openly **gay scene** outside a few scattered clubs, bars and beaches. While physical contact is fairly common – on the level of linking arms and kissing cheeks at greetings and farewells – any overt display of strong affection between members of the same sex may be met by hostility. Gays will find a more sympathetic atmosphere in the cities of Cágliari and Sássari, and in the clubs and beaches of the cosmopolitan Costa Smeralda. For general information, contact ARCI-Gay/ARCI-Lesbica, Piazza di Porta Saragozza 2, PO Box 692, 40100 Bologna ☎051.644.7054.

Contacts for gay and lesbian travellers

@www.gaytravel.co.uk Online gay and lesbian travel agent, offering good deals on all types of holiday. Also lists gay- and lesbian-friendly hotels around the world.

Madison Travel ☎01273/202 532, @www.madisontravel.co.uk. Established travel agents specializing in packages to gay- and lesbian-friendly mainstream destinations, and also to gay/lesbian destinations.

In the US and Canada

Damron ☎1-800/462-6654 or 415/255-0404, ⓦwww.damron.com. Publisher of the *Men's Travel Guide*, a pocket-sized yearbook full of listings of hotels, bars, clubs and resources for gay men; the *Women's Traveller*, which provides similar listings for lesbians; and *Damron Accommodations*, which provides detailed listings of over 1000 accommodations for gays and lesbians worldwide.

gaytravel.com ☎1-800/GAY-TRAVEL, ⓦwww.gaytravel.com. The premier site for trip planning, bookings, and general information about international gay and lesbian travel.

International Gay & Lesbian Travel Association ☎1-800/448-8550 or 954/776-2626, ⓦwww.iglta.org. Trade group that can provide a list of gay- and lesbian-owned or -friendly travel agents, accommodation and other travel businesses.

In Australia and New Zealand

Silke's Travel ☎1800/807 860 or 02/8347 2000, ⓦwww.silkes.com.au. Long-established gay and lesbian specialist, with emphasis on women's travel.

Travelling with children

Children are adored in Sardinia, and will be welcomed and catered for in bars and restaurants (though be warned that few of these are smoke-free environments). Hotels normally charge around thirty percent extra to put a bed or cot in your room, though kids pay less on trains (see p.28–29) and enter museums and other tourist sites for free. Many coastal hotels and most campsites are well-equipped for family holidays, and lay on a range of entertainments and activities for kids and parents.

Although there are few attractions designed specifically for kids (the aquarium in Alghero and Sardegna in Miniatura near Barumini are good exceptions), the island's **beaches** provide all the entertainment most kids would want, while the prehistoric nuraghi, the numerous castles and some archeological sites provide lots of fun inland. The main **hazards** when travelling with children in Sardinia are the heat and sun in summer. Sunblock can be bought at any chemist's, and bonnets or straw hats in most markets. Other risks include the possibility of stepping on sea-urchins, black or brown spiky balls that lurk on rocks and can be extremely painful when stepped on – if this happens, ask advice on how to remove the spines. Take advantage of the less intense periods – mornings and evenings – for travelling, and use the quiet of siesta time to recover flagging energy. The rhythms of the southern climate soon modify established patterns, and you'll find it more natural carrying on later into the night, past normal bedtimes. In summer, it's not unusual to see Sardinian children out at midnight, and not looking much the worse for it.

Contacts for travellers with children

In the UK and Ireland

Club Med ☎0700/258 2932, ⓦwww .clubmed.co.uk. Specializes in purpose-built holiday resorts, with kids' club, entertainment and sports facilities on site.

Mark Warner Holidays ☎0870/770 4222, ⓦwww.markwarner.co.uk. Holiday villages with children's entertainment and childcare included.

Simply Travel ☎020/8541 2200, ⓦwww .simply-travel.com. Upmarket tour company offering villas and hotels. In some destinations, they can provide qualified, English-speaking nannies to come to your villa and look after the children.

In the US

Rascals in Paradise ☏415/921-7000,

ⓦ www.rascalsinparadise.com. Can arrange scheduled and customized itineraries built around activities for kids.
Travel with Your Children ☏1-888/822-4FTT or 212/477-5524. Publishes a regular online newsletter, *Family Travel Times* (ⓦ www.familytraveltimes.com).

Living and working in Sardinia

Although Sardinia would make a fine place to set up home, the possibilities of supporting yourself on the island are limited. With one of the highest unemployment rates of all the Italian regions, there are few opportunities for finding full-time employment, and your best chance is bar work (seasonal), teaching English or nannying – au pair work is not really a viable option.

Non-EU citizens are not eligible to work in Sardinia, and even EU citizens must go through the various **bureaucratic procedures** for both working and living on the island, which primarily means obtaining a *libretto di lavoro* (work permit) and a *permesso di soggiorno* (residence permit), both available from the Questura (see p.54). For the first you must have a letter from your prospective employers saying they are prepared to take you on. For the second (which is also necessary if you want to buy a car or have a bank account in Italy) you'll need a passport, passport-sized photos and a lot of patience.

Teaching

The obvious choice is to **teach English**, for which the demand has expanded enormously in recent years. You can do this in two ways: freelance private lessons, or through a language school. **Private lessons** generally pay best, and you can charge around £5–10/€7–14/US$8–16 an hour, though there's scope for bargaining. Advertise in bars, shop windows and local newspapers, and, most importantly, get the news around by word-of-mouth that you're looking for work, emphasizing your excellent background, qualifications and experience.

An advantage of private teaching is that you can start at any time of the year (summer especially is a good time because there are schoolchildren and students who have to retake exams in September); the main disadvantage is that it can take weeks to get off the ground, and you need enough money to support you until then. The best opportunities for this kind of work are found in the tourist resorts and the bigger towns and cities.

Teaching in schools, you start earning immediately (though some schools can pay months in arrears). Teaching classes usually involves more hours per week, often in the evening, and for less per hour, though the amount you get depends on the school. For the less reputable places, you can get away without any qualifications and a bit of bluff, but you'll need to show a degree and a CELTA certificate for the more professional language schools. For these, it's best to apply in writing from Britain (look for the ads in *The Guardian* and *The Times Educational Supplement*, and contact the Italian Cultural Institute at 39 Belgrave Square, London SW1X 8NX ☏020/7235 1461), preferably before the summer, though you can also find openings in September. If you're looking on the spot, sift through the *Yellow Pages*

(*Págine Gialle*) and do the rounds on foot, asking to speak to the *direttore* or his/her secretary; don't bother to try in August when everything is closed. Strictly speaking, you could get by without any knowledge of Italian, but some definitely helps.

The best teaching jobs of all are with a university as a **lettore** (foreign language teacher), a job requiring fewer hours than the language schools and generally offering a fuller pay packet. Universities need English-language teachers in most faculties, and you should write to the individual faculties at the universities of Cágliari or Sássari (addressed to Ufficio di Personale). That said, success in obtaining a university teaching job usually depends on you knowing someone already in place – as with so many things in Sardinia.

Your chances of finding teaching work are obviously enhanced with the right qualifications: you can get a **CELTA** (Certificate in English Language Teaching to Adults) qualification before you leave home or even while you're abroad. International House has branches in many countries (including Italy), which offer the course. Strictly speaking, you don't need a degree to do the course, but you'll certainly find it easier to get a job with the degree/certificate combination. Certified by the RSA, the course is very demanding and costs about £944 for the month's full-time tuition; you'll be thrown in at the deep end and expected to teach right away. The British Council's website, ⓦwww.british council.org/work/jobs.htm, has a list of English-teaching vacancies.

Other options

If teaching's not up your street, there's the possibility of **bar/restaurant work** too – not the most lucrative of jobs, though you should make enough to keep you in Sardinia over the summer. You'll have to ask around in the resorts for this type of work, and a knowledge of Italian is essential. Women in particular might consider **domestic work** in houses: many Italians like the idea of English-speaking nannies to look after their children while speaking English to them for a few hours a day. Such posts are sometimes advertised in your home country, or else look in local newspapers and ask around while you're on the spot.

Useful publications and websites

If you're thinking of teaching English in Sardinia, visit ⓦwww.tefl.net, a general website that provides a useful introduction to the field. **Vacation Work** publishes books on summer jobs abroad and how to work your way around the world; call ☏01865/241 978, or visit ⓦwww .vacationwork.co.uk for their catalogue. **Travel magazines** like the reliable *Wanderlust* (every two months; £2.80; ⓦwww.wanderlust.co.uk) have a Job Shop section which often advertises job opportunities with tour companies. ⓦwww .studyabroad.com is a useful website with listings and links to study and work programmes worldwide.

Study and work programs

From the UK

British Council ☏020/7930 8466. Produces a free leaflet which details study opportunities abroad. The Council's Central Management Direct Teaching (☏020/7389 4931) recruits TEFL teachers for posts worldwide (check ⓦwww.britishcouncil.org/work /jobs.htm for a current list of vacancies), and its Central Bureau for International Educational and Training (☏020/7389 4004, ⓦwww.centralbureau .org.uk) enables those who already work as educators to find out about teacher development programmes abroad. It also publishes a book, *Year Between*, aimed principally at gap-year students detailing volunteer programmes, and schemes abroad.

Erasmus EU-run student exchange programme enabling students at participating universities in Britain and Ireland to study in one of 26 European countries (including Italy). Mobility grants are available for three months to a full academic year. Anyone interested should contact their university's international relations office, or check the Erasmus website ⓦeuropa.eu.int/comm/education /erasmus.html.

International House ☏020/7518 6999, ⓦwww.ihlondon.com. Head office for reputable English-teaching organization which offers TEFL training leading to the award of a Certificate in English Language Teaching to Adults (CELTA), and recruits for teaching positions in Britain and abroad.

From the US

AFS Intercultural Programs 10016 ☎1-800/876-2377 or 212/299 9000, ⓦusa.afs.org. Runs summer experiential programs aimed at fostering international understanding for teenagers and adults.
Bernan Associates ☎1-800/274-4888, ⓦwww.bernan.com. Distributes UNESCO's encyclopedic *Study Abroad*.
Experiment in International Living ☎1-800/345-2929 or 802/257-7751,

ⓦwww.usexperiment.org. Summer program for high-school students.
Harper Collins Perseus Division ☎1-800/242-7737, ⓦwww.harpercollins.com. Publishes *International Jobs: Where They Are, How to Get Them*.

From Australia

Australians Studying Abroad ☎03/9509 1955, ⓦwww.asatravinfo.com.au. Study tours focusing on art and culture.

Directory

Addresses Usually written as the street name followed by the number – eg Via Roma 69. Interno refers to the flat number – eg interno 5 (often abbreviated as int.). Always use postal codes.

Airport Tax Around £20 for British and Italian airports combined, usually included in the price of your ticket.

Beaches There are excellent beaches on every coast of Sardinia, most of them easy to find, the better-known ones indicated by brown signposts. You'll have to pay for access to the supervised beaches referred to as lidos, which offer deck chairs and parasols for a few thousand lire, with unlimited use of showers and toilets. In other places, you have to leave your vehicle in a private or council-run car park, for around €5 a day. Most beaches are free, but not always clean, especially during winter when some look like dumps; it's not worth anyone's while to clean them until the season starts at Easter. On the other hand, any beach that's remotely inaccessible should remain in a fairly pristine state. Some coasts are prone to invasions of jellyfish (*meduse*) in very warm weather. These are not dangerous, but can cause quite a sting, so take local advice.

Camping Gaz Easy enough to buy for the small portable camping stoves, either from hardware stores (*ferramenta*) or camping/sports shops. You can't carry canisters on aeroplanes.

Cigarettes The state monopoly brand – MS, jokingly referred to as Morte Sicura (Certain Death) – sell for around €2.50 for a pack of twenty, but most people tend to smoke imported brands, all of which are more expensive at around €3.30 per pack. You buy cigarettes from *tabacchi* (see p.61).

Consulates The following consular agencies can all be found at the respective embassies in Rome: Australia, Corso Trieste 25c ☎06.852 721; Canada, Via Zara 30 ☎06.445 981; UK Via XX Settembre 80a ☎06.482 5441; Ireland, Piazza Campitelli 3 ☎06.697 9121; New Zealand, Via Zara 28 ☎06.441 7171; USA, Via Veneto 121 ☎06.46 741.

Electricity The supply is 220V, though anything requiring 240V will work. Most plugs have two round pins: a travel plug is useful.

Entrance Fees The entrance fee for museums and sites is usually €2–4, although under-18s and over-60s get in free on production of documentary proof of age. Some sites insist on escorting you around, their running commentary – sometimes available in English – included in the price, and it's not expected that you hand over a tip.

Laundry There are currently no coin-operated laundrettes in Sardinia, so you'll have to use a *lavanderia*, or service-wash laundry, where items are individually charged – say €2.50 for a shirt, €3 for a skirt or trousers – and are returned a day or two later, immaculately ironed. Addresses are given in the Listings sections for cities. Although you can usually get away with it, washing clothes in your hotel room is disapproved of, and the water supply itself may be limited in summer.

Left Luggage Most bigger train stations have left luggage offices, and charge around €2.50 per bag per hour. Ask for *Il depósito bagagli*.

Public Toilets Usually found in bars and restaurants; you'll generally be allowed to use them whether you're eating and drinking or not. You'll find most places to be very clean, though it's advisable not to be without your own toilet roll.

Receipts Shops, bars and restaurants are all legally obliged to provide you with a receipt (*una ricevuta* or *uno scontrino*). Don't be surprised when it's thrust upon you, as they – and indeed you – can be fined if you don't take it.

Tabacchi These ubiquitous tobacco shops – recognizable by a sign displaying a white "T" on a black or blue background – also sell sweets, postcards and other writing equipment, stamps and sometimes bus tickets and toiletries.

Time Sardinia (and Italy) is one hour ahead of Britain, except for one week at the end of September when the time is the same. Italy is seven hours ahead of Eastern Standard Time and ten hours ahead of Pacific Time.

Water Safe to drink throughout the country, and especially prized from mountain springs. You'll find bottled mineral water is on sale everywhere.

Things to Take

Universal electric plug adaptor
Universal sink plug
Flashlight
Earplugs (for noisy hotel rooms)
High-factor sun block
Mosquito repellent
Antiseptic cream
Pocket alarm clock
Multi-purpose penknife
Needle and thread
Towel (for the beach)
Water bottle
Hat
Driving licence
Sunglasses

Guide

Guide

Cágliari

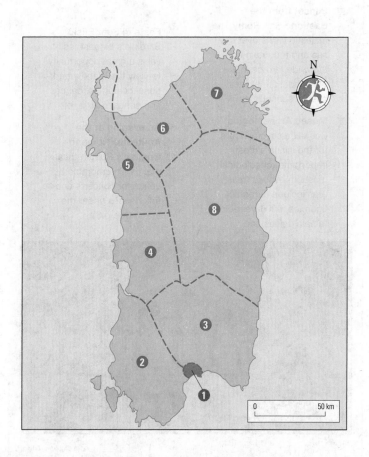

CHAPTER 1

Highlights

✻ **A meal at Quattro Mori**
The courses keep on coming at this boisterous trattoria – a fantastic introduction to the island's cuisine, with shellfish a speciality. See p.89

✻ **Sunset from the Bastione San Remy** The majestic views over city, sea and mountain from this wide terrace in the old citadel are at their best at sunset. See p.73

✻ **Museo Archeologico** Set aside several hours for the island's most important archeological museum, whose treasures include nuraghic figurines, 6000-year-old female deities and

Phoenician jewellery. See p.77

✻ **Mostra di Cere Anatomiche** A strangely beautiful waxworks collection, created in the nineteenth century for anatomy students. See p.77

✻ **Festa di Sant'Efisio** Sardinia's biggest festival is a great opportunity to view the island's traditional costumes, dances and songs. See p.82

✻ **An evening at the Anfiteatro Romano Cágliari's** Roman theatre makes a memorable venue for concerts and folk dances under the stars. See p.83

△ Cathedral, Cágliari

Cágliari

S ituated at the centre of the broad curve of the Golfo di Cágliari, backed by lagoons and surmounted by an imposing ring of medieval walls, **CÁGLIARI** is visually the most impressive of Sardinia's cities. Viewing it from the sea at the start of his Sardinian sojourn in 1921, D.H. Lawrence compared it to Jerusalem: "strange and rather wonderful, not a bit like Italy", and still today, Cágliari retains a very different identity from mainland towns of an equivalent size, not least for its less frenetic pace and unusual setting – its calm lagoons (*stagni*) the habitat of cranes, flamingos and cormorants, and with a backdrop of mountains receding down the coast.

As the island's capital since Roman times at least, Cágliari is also littered with the remains of two thousand years of history. Today, it remains Sardinia's busiest **port**, with the greatest concentration of industry. Intimidating as this may sound, Cágliari is much more than a mere administrative centre or urban sprawl, offering both chic sophistication and medieval charm in the raggle-taggle of narrow lanes crammed into its high citadel and port area. The city's old core is small and compact enough to explore on foot, in between taking in its splendid and diverse collection of museums, archeological remains and historic churches. And, should you find yourself succumbing to sightseeing fatigue, you can unwind on the enormous expanse of sandy beach at nearby Poetto.

Almost all of Cágliari's attractions are encompassed within the four oldest quarters of the city: Castello, Marina, Stampace and Villanova. You will probably

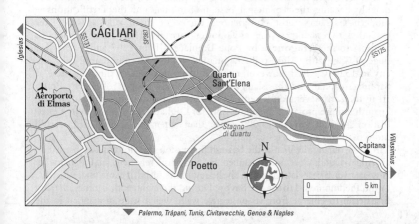

Palermo, Trápani, Tunis, Civitavecchia, Genoa & Naples

spend most time in the old citadel, **Castello**, not for its hotels – there are none – but for the city's flamboyant cathedral and best museums, not to mention the superb vistas. Beneath the citadel walls, the seafront **Marina** quarter holds most of the shops, restaurants, banks and hotels, as well as a couple of absorbing historical remains. Bounding the area to the north, the pedestrianized Via Manno – boasting some of the city's smartest boutiques as well as one of the most elegant evening promenades on the whole island – drops down to the broad, traffic-filled Largo Carlo Felice. Near the intersection of the two streets, Piazza Yenne is one of the city's favourite venues for sitting with an ice cream or a beer, while the arcaded Via Roma, forming the southern limit of Marina, is another popular spot for a coffee and pastry, looking straight across to the port.

West of Largo Carlo Felice, the **Stampace** district contains some of the city's oldest churches, and lies within a short walk of the city's best Roman remains, a theatre and a residential complex from the imperial era. While **Villanova**, the area extending east of Castello and Marina, is somewhat less picturesque, it does contain two of Sardinia's most important religious monuments, the ancient church of San Saturnino and the Santuario di Bonaria.

With Sardinia's best choice of hotels and some of its cheapest restaurants, Cágliari makes an ideal base for excursions further afield, and the town is within easy distance of all the places mentioned in the southwest of the island (Chapter 2, p.95), and the south and southeast (Chapter 3, p.129). For information on bus and train connections, as well as ferry departures, see Travel details on p.92–93.

Some history

Probably founded by the **Phoenicians**, who gave it the name of Karalis, Cágliari became a colony of the **Carthaginians** until its capture by the **Romans** in 238 BC. As an important and flourishing *municipium*, the city was one of the major trading ports in the Mediterranean, but declined with the demise of Roman power, eventually falling to the Vandals and Goths in 455 AD. After a brief Byzantine revival, it was repeatedly plundered by the **Saracens**. The threat from marauders remained so great that, during the era of the *giudicati*, the site of Santa Igia, on a lagoon to the west of the city, was preferred as a more defensible base.

Cágliari's fortunes only revived in the middle of the thirteenth century after the local *giudichessa* granted the hill behind her capital to the **Pisans**. They walled and populated it, creating the citadel now known as Castello. It quickly became their principal base in Sardinia, and the fortifications – modern Cágliari's most conspicuous legacy of Pisan rule – were later extended to encompass the city's lower quarters. The formal cession of Sardinia to the **Aragonese** by Pope Boniface VIII in 1297 and a two-year siege of Cágliari by Alfonso d'Aragona led to the Pisan withdrawal from the city in 1326. Cágliari, however, retained its position under the Aragonese as Sardinia's capital, and the island's first university was opened here by Philip III in the early seventeenth century. Even so, absorption into the ramshackle Spanish empire proved a mixed blessing for Cágliari – in 1700, the city's population stood at a mere 15,000, fewer than when the Spanish first arrived more than three centuries earlier.

In 1708, during the War of the Spanish Succession, the city was bombarded by an Anglo-Dutch fleet and occupied by a English regiment in the name of Austria; twelve years later, along with the rest of the island, it came under the rule of the Piedmontese **House of Savoy**. During the eighteenth century, the city first began to emerge from its protective walls, which were dismantled in the quarters of Stampace, Marina and Villanova, to be replaced by the broad boulevards along which the traffic rumbles today. Although Cágliari repulsed an attack by French forces in 1793, the ideas of the French Revolution were infiltrating the island in other ways. The following year, the so-called "Sardinian Revolution" broke out in Cágliari against the centralizing tendencies of the Savoyard government, and was brutally suppressed. However, the city benefitted over the following decades from the social and institutional reforms that filtered through the island under the Savoy dynasty, and, in common with the rest of the island, welcomed being integrated into the new kingdom of Italy in 1861.

During **World War II**, heavy aerial bombardment destroyed nearly half the city in February and May 1943. Many of the bomb sites have only recently been filled in, often with bold modernistic constructions which do not on the whole disrupt the harmony of the city centre. The real changes in the last twenty or thirty years have occurred on the northern outskirts of town, where new apartment blocks and businesses have mushroomed, since expansion in any other direction is restricted by the lagoons and the sea. Today, a brisk, confident city with a population of nearly a quarter of a million, Cágliari has the island's worst traffic – though without the chaos that would prevail in any mainland city of comparable size – the most engaging museums and monuments, and the broadest and most forward-looking cultural scene.

Arrival, information and getting around

Cágliari's **port** lies in the heart of the town, opposite Via Roma, the main thoroughfare; the Stazione Maríttima here has an information desk which opens to coincide with the arrival of boats. The **airport** sits beside the city's largest *stagno* (lagoon), 6km northwest of the centre: facilities include a **bank** (Mon–Fri 8.20am–1.20pm & 2.30–3.30pm, Sat 8.20am–12.30pm) with an ATM, and an **information desk** (daily 8am–8pm). A bus service to Piazza Matteotti in the town centre runs at least every ninety minutes from 6.20am until around 11pm (last departure timed for the last flight arrival), taking fifteen minutes (tickets €0.67 from the airport shop); otherwise a taxi ride costs around €15 (more after 10pm).

All ARST buses, including the airport bus, use the **bus station** on Piazza Matteotti, though PANI **buses** from Oristano and Sássari stop at the Stazione Maríttima, and FMS buses from Sulcis stop on Via Roma. Piazza Matteotti, is also the terminus for most **local buses** and is the site of the main **train station**; FdS trains from Arbatax and Mandas use the station at Piazza Repúbblica. Cágliari is not much fun to **drive** around, with often heavy traffic, narrow or one-way streets and pedestrian areas, and you'll need to pay to park almost everywhere in the central area during the hours 8.30am–1pm and 4–8pm between Monday and Saturday: €0.50 for the first hour, €1 for every subsequent hour, slightly more at the port – a parking attendant is usually hovering in the vicinity.

There's a handy tourist **information kiosk** on Piazza Matteotti (April–Sept daily 8am–8pm; Oct–March Mon–Fri 9am–6pm, Sat 9am–2pm & 3–6pm ☏070.669.255) and one in the Stazione Maríttima (daily: 9am–1.30pm & 3–6pm ☏070.668.352. There's another tourist office for Cágliari province (roughly the southern third of the island) at the far end of Via Roma, Piazza Deffenu 9 (Mon–Fri 8.30am–1pm & 3.30–5.30pm, ☏070.604.241 or toll-free ☏800.203.541), but the **main tourist office**, which dispenses information

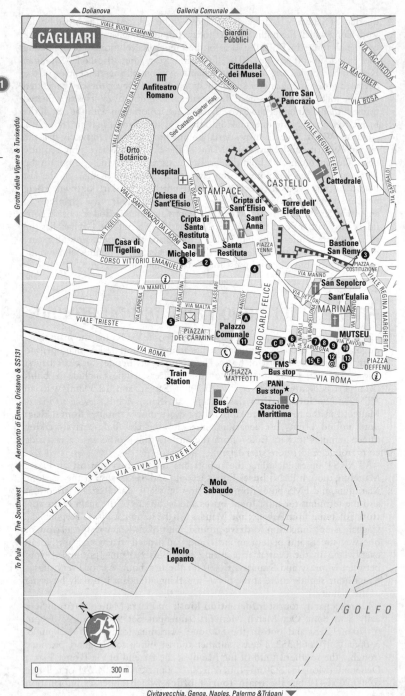

CÁGLIARI

▲ Dolianova   Galleria Comunale ▲

VIALE BUON CAMMINO

Giardini
Púbblicis

Cittadella
dei Musei

⚎ Anfiteatro
Romano

Torre San
Pancrazio

CASTELLO

Cattedrale

Orto
Botánico

Hospital

Chiesa di
Sant'Efisio

STAMPACE

Cripta di
Sant'Efisio

Torre dell'
Elefante

Cripta di
Santa
Restituta

Sant'
Anna

PIAZZA
YENNE

Bastione
San Remy ③

⚎ Casa di
Tigellio

San
Michele ①

Santa
Restituta

PIAZZA
COSTITUZIONE

② CORSO VITTORIO EMANUELE

④

San Sepolcro

VIA MANNO

Sant'Eulalia

MARINA

ⓘ

VIA MAMELI

MUTSEU

⑤

PIAZZA
DEL CÁRMINE

Ⓐ

Palazzo
Comunale
⑪

ⒸⒷ

⑥

⑦ ⑧
⑨ ⑩

Ⓒ

ⓘ

⑭ Ⓓ

★
FMS
Bus stop

⑮ Ⓔ

⑫

⑬
Ⓖ

PIAZZA
DEFFENU
ⓘ

Train
Station

ⓘ
PIAZZA
MATTEOTTI

PANI
Bus stop ★

VIA ROMA

Bus Station

Stazione
Marittima

ⓘ

VIA RIVA DI PONENTE

Molo
Sabaudo

Molo
Lepanto

GOLFO

N

0   300 m

70

Civitavecchia, Genoa, Naples, Palermo &Trápani ▼

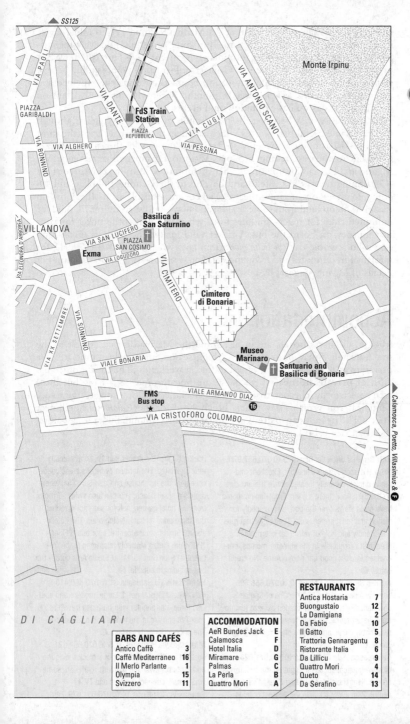

SS125

VIA PAOLI

VIA DANTE

PIAZZA
GARIBALDI

FdS Train
Station

VIA ANTONIO SCANO

VIA CUGIA

PIAZZA
REPUBBLICA

VIA ALGHERO

VIA PESSINA

VIA BONNINO

Monte Irpinu

Basilica di
San Saturnino

VILLANOVA

VIA SAN LUCIFERO

PIAZZA
SAN COSIMO

Exma

VIA LOGUDORO

VIA ELEONORA D'ARBOREA

VIA CIMITERO

Cimitero
di Bonaria

VIA XX SETTEMBRE

VIA SONNINO

VIALE BONARIA

Museo
Marinaro

Santuario and
Basilica di Bonaria

FMS
Bus stop

VIALE ARMANDO DIAZ

16

VIA CRISTOFORO COLOMBO

Calamosca, Poetto, Villasimius & F

DI CÁGLIARI

BARS AND CAFÉS

Antico Caffè	3
Caffè Mediterraneo	16
Il Merlo Parlante	1
Olympia	15
Svizzero	11

ACCOMMODATION

AeR Bundes Jack	E
Calamosca	F
Hotel Italia	D
Miramare	G
Palmas	C
La Perla	B
Quattro Mori	A

RESTAURANTS

Antica Hostaria	7
Buongustaio	12
La Damigiana	2
Da Fabio	10
Il Gatto	5
Trattoria Gennargentu	8
Ristorante Italia	6
Da Lillicu	9
Quattro Mori	4
Queto	14
Da Serafino	13

covering the whole of Sardinia, is at Via Mameli 97 (mid-Feb to mid-May & mid-Sept to mid-Oct Mon–Sat 9am–7pm, Sun 9am–2pm; mid-May to mid-Sept daily 8am–8pm; mid-Oct to mid-Feb Mon–Sat 9am–6pm ☎070.60.231 or toll-free ☎800.013.153). Any of Cágliari's information points should be able to provide an *annovario* (accommodation booklet) covering the province and may also stock *Vivi Cágliari*, a free bi-monthly sheet with the latest details on the city's sights as well as exhibitions and events.

You can easily walk between the main points of interest in Cágliari, though there are some useful **bus routes** which can help on the longer trips: the most useful is #10, running between Viale Trento to the west of the city and Piazza Garibaldi to the east, taking in Corso Vittorio Emanuele, Piazza Yenne, Via Manno and Piazza Costituzione. Other useful routes from Piazza Matteotti are #7, running up to the Castello and beyond to the Giardini Púbblici, and #8 going to the Roman amphitheatre. Tickets are available from the kiosk in Piazza Matteotti and from some *tabacchi* and news kiosks, costing €77, valid for unlimited rides for ninety minutes from when you punch the ticket for your first journey, on board the bus. A ticket valid for two hours costs €1.29, and one valid a whole day (*biglietto giornaliero*) costs €2.07. Call ☎070.20.911 for information on routes and frequencies (Mon–Fri 9am–1pm & 3–6.30pm). For details of leaving Cágliari by bus, see p.93.

Accommodation

Most of Cágliari's **hotels** are in or around the Marina district, nearest to the sea. Availability may be restricted in high season, and single rooms are at a premium at all times (though easiest to find at weekends). The tourist office has a list of **private homes** where guests are put up on a B&B basis, but these aren't necessarily cheaper than the budget choices below, nor are they very central. If you want to stay near a beach, head for the *Calamosca* hotel, near Poetto. The nearest **campsite** is at Capitana, a forty-minute bus ride east along the coast (see p.147).

AeR Bundes Jack Via Roma 75 ☎070.657.970, ✉hotel.aerbundesjack@libero.it. Excellent mid-range choice, centrally located above the arcades on the third floor (there's a lift). Front-facing rooms have great views over the port, all are solidly furnished and most are en suite. The family that runs it is friendly and helpful with local information. Breakfast is available in the summer months, otherwise there's a good bar right outside. No credit cards. ❹

Aurora Salita Santa Chiara 19 ☎070.658.625, ⓦwww.albergoaurora.3000.it. One of Cágliari's cheapest deals, housed in a faded palazzo just up from Piazza Yenne. All eight rooms are basic and reasonably clean, and they're often full. No credit cards. ❷

Calamosca Viale Calamosca ☎070.371.628, ⓦwww.hotelcalamosca.it. Right on the sea, this is an excellent choice for avoiding Cágliari's noisy centre, 2km away. It's also the nearest hotel to

Poetto, Cágliari's summer suburb, so availability may be limited. The terrace overlooks a secluded cove near the lighthouse on Capo Sant'Elia, where there's a small beach; you can also swim off rocks from the hotel garden. Ask for sea-facing rooms, the same price as back-facing ones. The hotel's about 15min from the centre: take bus "PF" or "PQ" from Piazza Matteotti, changing to the frequent #11 (on Sun #5/11) at Stadio Amsicora – the bus stops right outside. ❺

Hotel Italia Via Sardegna 31 ☎070.660.410, ✉hotelitalia@tiscalinet.it. Large, modern and soulless three-star popular with business travellers, with TVs and a/c in the rooms and a restaurant. The price includes breakfast. ❺

Miramare Via Roma 59 ☎ & ⓕ070.664.021. Located on the second floor of a block facing the port (but no views), the bathless rooms are somewhat small, but each has a/c and TV. ❷

Palmas Via Sardegna 14 ☎070.651.679. Fairly

ordinary, no-frills place, but friendly enough. Plain rooms have no view or private bathrooms, but they're quite spacious and some have in-room showers. No credit cards. **❷**

La Perla Via Sardegna 18 ℡070.669.446. Slightly more expensive and more antique than its neighbour *Palmas* (see opposite), this has quiet, clean rooms with shared facilities. No credit cards. **❷**

Quattro Mori Via Angioy 27 ℡070.668.535, ⓦwww.hotel4mori.it. The vaulted entrance of this two-star just up from Piazza Matteotti is grand enough, but the rooms are nothing special; ask to see one before booking in. All have TVs and en-suite bathrooms. **❹**

La Terrazza Via Santa Margherita 21 ℡070.668.652, ⓦwww.laterrazzahotel.com. Above a Chinese restaurant near Piazza Yenne, this place has small over-priced rooms, with or without bath, but it's an acceptable last resort if everywhere else in the centre is full. **❷**

Castello

Secure on its hill, Cágliari's **Castello** district was traditionally the seat of Sardinia's administration, aristocracy and highest ecclesiastical offices. The intricate knot of alleys visible today, accessed from various points in its thick girth of walls, has altered little since the Middle Ages, though most of the dwellings date from much later. Draped with washing strung across the balconies, many of the high blocks are run-down and don't admit much light, though the lack of fuss or traffic makes for an agreeable stroll through the long alleys of this homogenous quarter, either before or after visiting its major sights. While things get pretty ghostly at night, during the daytime there's a continuous hum of low-level activity in the antique shops, restorers' studios and watch-repairers'. Contrive an invitation into a private home, if you can; many of Castello's houses prove to be fascinating repositories of past building styles. Note that you can save yourself the steepish walk to Castello or back to the port on bus #7 from Piazza Matteotti, with a stop in Piazza Indipendenza (every 15min, or every 30min on Sun). There's also a handy lift up from the lower town, from behind Santa Chiara, above Piazza Yenne (8am–2pm & 4–10pm; free).

The most evocative entry to the district is from the monumental **Bastione San Remy** on Piazza Costituzione, the southern spur of the defensive walls, remodelled between 1899 and 1902. Its triumphal tone is diluted somewhat by the graffiti and weeds sprouting out of its walls, and by the groups of youths who collect here to make music and smoke spliffs, but it's worth the haul up the grandiose flight of steps for the broad terrace above, offering fabulous vistas over the port and the lagoons and mountains beyond. You can catch some of the best views at sunset, though it makes a good place for a pause at any time, with shady benches conducive to picnics or siestas. A flea market sets up here most Sundays.

The Torre dell'Elefante and Via Santa Croce

From the bastion, you can wander off in any direction to enter the tangled maze of Castello's steps and alleys. Leading off to the west, Via Università curves round the lower perimeter of the walls beneath the bombed-out shell of an old palazzo, past the main **university** building and the old **Seminario Tridentino**, both built in the eighteenth century. The road fetches up at the **Torre dell'Elefante**, which you can climb for the view (Tues–Sun: May–Oct 9am–1pm & 3.30–7.30pm, Nov–April 9am–4.30pm; last admissions 15min before closing; under-12s not admitted; €2). Famed local architect Giovanni Capula designed the tower in 1307, a little later than the Torre San Pancrazio

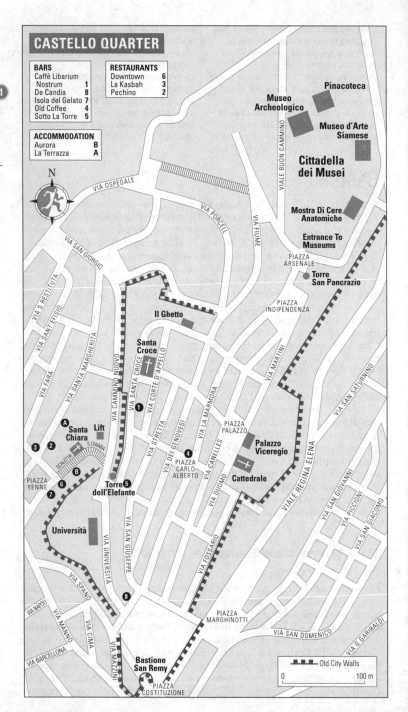

CASTELLO QUARTER

BARS
Caffè Libarium
Nostrum   **1**
De Candia   **8**
Isola del Gelato **7**
Old Coffee   **4**
Sotto La Torre   **5**

RESTAURANTS
Downtown   **6**
La Kasbah   **3**
Pechino   **2**

ACCOMMODATION
Aurora   **B**
La Terrazza   **A**

N

VIA OSPEDALE
VIA PORCELL
VIA FIUME
VIALE BUON CAMMINO

Pinacoteca

Museo Archeologico

Museo d'Arte Siamese

Cittadella dei Musei

Mostra Di Cere Anatomiche

Entrance To Museums

PIAZZA ARSENALE

Torre San Pancrazio

PIAZZA INDIPENDENZA

VIA SAN GIORGIO
VIA S RESTITUTA
VIA SANT'EFISIO
VIA FARA
VIA SANTA MARGHERITA
VIA CAMMINO NUOVO
VIA SANTA CROCE
VIA CORTE D'APPELLO
VIA STRETTA
VIA DEI GENOVESI
VIA LA MARMORA
VIA CANELLES
VIA MARTINI
VIA SAN SATURNINO
VIALE REGINA ELENA

Il Ghetto

Santa Croce

1

Santa Chiara
Lift
S CHIARA
SCALETTA

A
B
3
2
6
7

PIAZZA YENNE

Torre dell'Elefante **5**

4
PIAZZA CARLO ALBERTO

PIAZZA PALAZZO

Palazzo Viceregio

Cattedrale

VIA DUOMO
VIA FOSSARIO

Università

VIA SAN GIUSEPPE
VIA UNIVERSITÀ
VIA SPANO
VIA NAPOLI
VIA MANNO
VIA CIMA
VIA BARCELLONA
VIA MAZZINI

8

VIA SAN GIOVANNI
VIA PICCIONI
VIA SAN GIACOMO
VIA G GARIBALDI
VIA SAN DOMENICO

PIAZZA MARGHINOTTI

Bastione San Remy

PIAZZA COSTITUZIONE

▪▪▪▪ Old City Walls

0   100 m

further up the hill (see p.76–77). Both are considered masterpieces of military engineering; together they formed the main bulwarks of Cágliari's defences, hastily erected by Pisa against the Aragonese threat, and tested in the siege of the city just twelve years later. The sheer, unbattlemented walls are constructed of great blocks of off-white granite. Like the other Pisan towers, the Torre dell'Elefante has a half-finished look, with the side facing the old town completely open. If you only want to climb one of Cágliari's towers, this is the better choice, as it has access to the top terrace. At the bottom, notice the surviving gate mechanism and the spiky gate itself, menacingly poised over the entrance. A small carving of an elephant on a plinth on one side gives the tower its name.

Continuing north from the Torre dell'Elefante up **Via Santa Croce**, where bars with outdoor seating provide a great vista from the top of the city walls, you'll pass the restored **church of Santa Croce**, recently discovered to have been built on the ruins of the old synagogue following the expulsion of the Jewish community in 1492. There are no traces of the old Jewish quarter left, though it is recalled in the name of a local exhibition centre, **Il Ghetto**, further up the street at Via Santa Croce 18 (Tues–Sun: May–Sept 10.30–1pm & 6–9.30pm, Oct–April 10.30–1pm & 5–8.30pm; €2.60), converted from barracks that once housed the dragoons of Carlo Emanuele III, the eighteenth-century Savoy king of Sardinia. There is nothing relating to Cágliari's Jews within, though the temporary exhibitions can be absorbing, and the structure of the well-restored building is interesting in itself, with views over the city from a small terrace.

The Cattedrale

Following the line of walls north from the Bastione San Remy, you'll soon reach the nucleus of the Castello district – **Piazza Palazzo**, an elongated area not enhanced by its use as the quarter's main car park. The buildings which line the square are mostly eighteenth-century, though the **Cattedrale Santa Maria del Castello** (Mon–Sat 8am–12.30pm & 4–7pm, Sun 8am–1pm & 4–8pm) at one end of it has a more venerable history. Dating originally from the thirteenth century, it later, as D.H. Lawrence put it, went through "the mincing machine of the ages, and oozed out Baroque and sausagey". Nothing of this, however, is visible in the present frontage – Lawrence's sausages went back into the mincer in 1933, to be replaced by the present tidy pastiche of a typical Pisan Romanesque arcaded facade.

The **interior** shows a mixture of Gothic and Baroque elements, the ornate painted ceiling rising to a trim cupola. The nave is lined with shallow side chapels, the third on the right holding a vivid sculpture of devils being cast to hell by San Michele. The pair of massive stone **pulpits** which flank the main doors are adorned with carved reliefs showing scenes from the life of Jesus, including the *Adoration of the Magi*, the *Baptism*, the *Sermon on the Mount* and the *Last Supper*. They were originally crafted around 1160 by Guglielmo da Pisa as a single piece, which graced Pisa's cathedral for a century and a half before being presented to Cágliari, where it was divided in the seventeenth century. The same sculptor's set of lions – four fierce-looking creatures devouring their prey – adorns the steps leading up to the altar.

A copy of the church's finest painting, the fifteenth-century *Trittico di Clemente VII*, stands to the right of the altar – the original is kept elsewhere in the cathedral under more secure conditions, displayed only on August 15 and 16 (the Feast of the Assumption). The work's authorship is unknown, though it is thought to be the work of different Flemish artists at different times, and may itself be a copy of a lost painting by Rogier van der Weyden. The triptych was part of a collection of precious items stolen from the private apartments of Pope Clement VII during the sack of Rome in 1527, and brought to Cágliari by Catalan sailors, who confessed their guilt when their vessel was caught up in a fierce storm during the crossing from the mainland. The treasure was handed in to the archbishop of Cágliari, who returned it to the pope. Grateful to have recovered his other lost property, Clement subsequently presented the painting to the cathedral. Apart from the hunched, wan figure of the dead Christ in the central panel, the work depicts the Madonna and saints Anne and Margaret, the latter holding a dragon. Next to this masterpiece, you may also see the powerful *Retablo della Crocefissione*, a six-panelled polyptych attributed to Michele Cavaro (1517–84) or, more probably, to his workshop.

Of the numerous tombs crammed into the cathedral, the most important is the incredibly elaborate fifteenth-century sepulchre of Martin II of Aragon in the left transept, and those of the Savoy royal family in the densely adorned subterranean **crypt** beneath the altar. The latter includes the tombs of Marie-Josephine of Savoy, wife of Louis XVIII of France, and the infant son of Vittorio Emanuele I of Savoy and Maria-Teresa of Austria, Carlo Emanuele, who died in 1799. Little of the walls and ceiling of this low, vaulted chamber hewn directly out of the rock has been left undecorated; the carvings include work by Sicilian artists of the Sardinian saints, whose ashes were said to have been found under the church of San Saturnino (see p.84) in 1617.

The Palazzo Viceregio

The cathedral is flanked in one corner of the square by the nondescript archbishop's palace, the work of the architect Davisto in 1769. He was also responsible for the **Palazzo Viceregio**, the second building to the left of the Cattedrale, once the official palace of the Piedmontese kings of Sardinia, though rarely inhabited by them and now used for meetings of the provincial assembly. The three-storey building is also known as Palazzo Regio, though the large inscription at the top of the porticoed Neoclassical facade names it the Palazzo del Governo, above a dedication to Carolus Emanuel III (Carlo Emanuele III). The rooms are occasionally open to the public for exhibitions, though the custodian may take you up between 9am and 2pm (not Sun) if there's nothing much going on. Apart from the grandiose entrance hung with the unsmiling portraits of the Piedmontese viceroys who governed the island from here, the most sumptuous rooms are the reception rooms upstairs, adorned with low chandeliers, gilt mirrors and painted ceilings. Exhibitions held here are usually well-organized and illuminating, and worth the couple of euros entry; recent subjects include "The Phoenicians in Sardinia".

The Torre San Pancrazio

At the opposite end of Piazza Palazzo, along Via Martini, the smaller Piazza Indipendenza is overlooked by the best restored of Cágliari's fortified towers, the **Torre San Pancrazio** (Tues–Sun: May–Oct 9am–1pm & 3.30–7.30pm; Nov–April 9am–4.30pm; last admissions 15min before closing; under-12s not admitted; €2). Very similar in design to the Torre dell'Elefante (see p.73 & 75), and like that one open at one side, the tower repays the climb up four levels with magnificent views over the old town and port, extending south as far as the refinery at Sarroch and the sliver of land holding the remains of Nora (see p.103–104). The tower, which rises to 36m, dates from 1305, as attested by a marble plaque near the entrance, and was the work of the renowned Pisan-Cagliaritan military architect Giovanni Capula. It subsequently became a prison and later still an observatory, when Alberto di Lamármora, Sardinia's greatest nineteenth-century all-round scientist, placed star-gazing and cartographic instruments on its top in 1835.

The tower stands above the Porta di San Pancrazio gateway, usually busy with cars passing through Piazza dell'Arsenale, where a plaque records the brief visit made to Cágliari by the Spanish author of Don Quixote, Miguel de Cervantes, in 1573, shortly before his capture and imprisonment by Moorish pirates.

The Cittadella dei Musei

From Piazza dell'Arsenale, a fortified arched gateway gives access to the **Cittadella dei Musei**, a museum and study complex erected on the site of the former royal arsenal. The modern concrete cunningly incorporates parts of the older structure and has been softened by greenery. Foremost of the city's principal museums housed here is the **Museo Archeologico** (daily: 9am–8pm; €4, or €5 with Pinacoteca, see p.78), a must for anyone interested in Sardinia's past. The island's most important prehistoric, Phoenician, Carthaginian and Roman finds are gathered here, including jewellery and coins, busts and statues of gods and muses, and funerary items from the sites of Nora (see p.103–104), Tharros (p.173–174) and Sant'Antíoco (p.111–112). Some of the earliest finds are from the island's Bonu Ighinu culture (c. 4000–3500 BC), including, on the ground floor (showcase 1), striking sculptures of rotund **female deities**, with broad, inscrutable smiles. Elsewhere, a Phoenician bronze **statue of Hercules** highlights the strong trading links that stretched across the Mediterranean to Italy in the fourth century BC, and to Etruria and Greece before then, while a **stone tablet** almost lost by the entrance shows, in Phoenician characters, the first recorded occurrence of the name "Sardinia". The ninth- or eighth-century-BC stele, unearthed at Nora in 1773, is considered the most ancient Phoenician find in the western Mediterranean, and appears to commemorate the building of a temple erected on the arrival of the first Phoenician settlers on the island.

The museum's most absorbing pieces, however, come from Sardinia's nuraghic culture, notably a series of **bronze statuettes**, or *bronzetti*, ranging from about thirty to ninety centimetres in height, spindly and highly stylized but packed with invention and quirky humour. Representing warriors and hunters, athletes, shepherds, nursing mothers, bulls, stags and other wild animals, these figures were votive offerings, made to decorate the inside of temples, and later buried to protect them from the hands of foreign predators. You can recognize the chieftain by his cloak and raised right arm, and the warriors by their extravagantly horned helmets. Looking surprisingly modern, the figurines constitute the main source of information about this obscure phase of the island's history. Other nuraghic items have a more primitive look: fragments of pots, axe-heads, jewellery and various domestic implements. For more information on Sardinia's nuraghic culture, see p.349–350.

The other collections housed in the museum complex contrast wildly with each other, and all are worth exploring. The smallest is also the most surprising: the **Mostra di Cere Anatomiche** (Tues–Sun 9am–1pm & 4–7pm; €1.55) displays 23 somewhat gruesome wax models of anatomical sections, early nineteenth-century works by the Florentine Clemente Susini. Items include cutaways of a head and neck, showing the intricate network of nerves and blood vessels linking the brain and facial organs, and one of a pregnant woman displaying the foetus within the womb.

Further up, another building holds the **Museo d'Arte Siamese** (Tues–Sun: mid-June to mid-Sept 9am–1pm & 4–8pm; mid-Sept to mid-June 9am–1pm & 3.30–7.30pm; €2), a splendid assemblage of items from Southeast Asia collected by a local engineer who spent twenty years in what is now Thailand. Chinese bowls and boxes sit alongside Japanese statuettes and a fearsome array of weaponry, but most of the work is from Siam, including vases, silk paintings and ink drawings featuring vivid portrayals of Hindu and Buddhist legends.

Lastly, the Cittadella dei Musei contains an art gallery, or **Pinacoteca** (Tues–Sun 9am–8pm; €2, or €5 with Museo Archeologico; see p.77), holding an excellent collection of primarily Catalan and Italian religious art from the fifteenth and sixteenth centuries. You can pick up a free catalogue with English translation on the way in. The paintings, well displayed on three levels, have mostly been brought here from local churches; they include wooden altar-pieces by the foremost Sard painters of the time, Pietro Cavaro and Antonio Mainas, as well as Flemish work and even a Sienese *Madonna* that ended up in Cágliari on account of a mistaken attribution. Other works to look out for include a *Giudizio Universale* (Last Judgment), showing distinct African elements, by the Sard Mastro di Olzai, and, next to each other on the top level, a trio of large, multi-panelled altar-works: the *Retablo di San Bernardino* by Joan Figuera and Rafael Thomas, an *Annunciazione* by Joan Mates and a *Visitazione* by Joan Barcelo. The lowest floor displays a collection of traditional Sardinian jewellery – amulets, necklaces, earrings and rosaries – worked in silver and gold, mostly dating from the nineteenth century. In addition to the above, two separate ethnographic museums are planned to open in the Cittadella, one housed in the old prison near the entrance.

The Galleria Comunale d'Arte

From Piazza Arsenale, walk though the Porta di San Pancrazio and down Viale Regina Elena to reach the Giardini Púbblici, a brief area of flat greenery below the walls of the Castello. At one end of it, Cágliari's **Galleria Comunale d'Arte** (Mon and Wed–Sun: July–Sept 9am–1pm and 5–9pm, Oct–June 9am–1pm and 3.30–7.30pm; €3.10) offers a more contemporary slant than the town's *pinacoteca* on Sardinia and its people. Exhibitions of Sard artists take place alongside a permanent collection of some of the island's best modern artworks. Among the most notable of these are a collection of paintings by Tarquinio Sini (1891–1943), a skillful caricaturist of the 1920s who specialized in *contrasti* – unlikely encounters between traditionally-garbed Sards and bright young flappers of the day – and, from a decade later, Giuseppe Biasi (1885–1945), who drew upon his travels in Africa to produce work influenced by Gauguin and Matisse. Among the pieces by other artists, the portraits of islanders and the local landscapes illustrate aspects of the Sard experience, often underlining Sardinia's interactions – and simmering tensions – vis-a-vis the outside world. Bronzes from the 1960s recall nuraghic *bronzetti*, while works from the 1970s and 1980s show women artists such as Mirella Mitelli and Rosanna Rossi – represented by some strongly coloured abstracts – beginning to make their mark in Sardinia.

Marina

Like Castello, the lanes of the **Marina** quarter are narrow and dark, but unlike those in the upper town, these streets are always animated, busy with the coming and going from the city's biggest grouping of restaurants and hotels. Marina's proximity to the docks meant that it was heavily bombed during World War II, the damage still starkly visible in places; elsewhere, the bombed-out buildings have been replaced by modern constructions, sometimes startlingly at odds with the quarter's predominantly medieval flavour. One of the victims of the bombardment was the very un-Sardinian **Palazzo Comunale** or *Municipio* (town hall) that presides over Piazza Matteotti. White and pinnacled, with bronze eagles and heraldic devices, this nineteenth-century neo-Gothic concoction with more than a hint of Art Nouveau was rebuilt to match its pre-war appearance. The upstairs rooms (usually Mon–Fri 4–6pm, Sat 4–8pm & Sun 9am–1pm; free) contain some notable tapestries and works by the sixteenth-century painters Antonio Mainas and Pietro Cavaro, among others.

Elsewhere, within the area bounded by Largo Carlo Felice, Viale Regina Margherita, Via Roma and the Castello, Marina preserves a number of sequestered treasures within its many churches. **Sant'Eulalia**, in the piazza of the same name, is currently closed for renovation, but its principal interest, the museum and archeological area beneath the church, remains open. The most remarkable part of the **Museo del Tesoro e Area Archeologica di Sant'Eulalia**, abbreviated to MUTSEU (Tues–Sun 10am–1pm & 5–8pm; €3), is the subterranean complex directly under the altar of the church, in which a fragment of the Roman city dating from the first century AD has been unearthed. A raised walkway provides a good overview of the broad limestone slabs of a wide road. The absence of wheel-ruts suggests that it was probably not a major thoroughfare; it's more likely to have been a pedestrian avenue giving access to a major temple – ongoing excavations may reveal the answer. Another road leads down towards the port, and there are also a couple of wells and even a public urinal. Most of the walls now visible belong to the medieval city built on the ruins of the Roman one, abandoned some time between the sixth and eighth centuries.

Upstairs, the **Treasury** displays priestly mantles and fine silverware, as well as a couple of interesting paintings: one, a fourteenth-century *Madonna and Child*, is Tuscan in style, with additions by a Sard artist of the sixteenth century; the other, a Flemish *Ecce Homo* of the seventeenth century, has been painted on both sides, the rear of the canvas giving a close-up of Christ's gorily flayed back.

Climbing further up Marina's backstreets, drop into the church of **San Sepolcro** (daily 10am–1pm & 4.30–8pm) in the eponymous piazza off Via Dettori. The building was re-opened at the end of 1998 after a 28-year closure, during which the surprisingly spacious interior was painstakingly restored and its treasures cleaned up. The most eye-popping of these is the huge gilded altarpiece covering one entire wall, created in the seventeenth century to hold a Madonna revered by the wife of one of the Spanish viceroys after a supposed miracle. The viceroy had to drastically alter the church's fifteenth-century structure to fit the outsize wooden structure inside, which he did by knocking through two chapels built into the rock, accounting for the church's unorthodox shape. At the same time, the **crypt** (€1) now lying below it was hacked out of a natural hollow in the rock, comprising two bare rooms – again, surprisingly large – devoid of decoration but for some images of Death on the walls and ceilings, one of them bearing the words *Nemini parco* ("I spare nobody") scratched onto his scythe. Back in the nave of the church, the sacristy to the right of the altar gives access to a much older relic of the building's long history: a large-scale paleochristian **baptismal font**, thought to date back to the fourth century. Set into the ground, the wide, circular basin in which converts were completely immersed was unearthed during routine maintenance work in 2000.

△ Torre dell'Elefante

Stampace and the Roman remains

Lying to the west of Largo Carlo Felice, the quarter of **Stampace** has given its name to Cágliari's – and Sardinia's – most influential school of art. Founded by Pietro Cavaro (died 1537), the *scuola di Stampace* affected painting throughout Sardinia in the sixteenth century, where the impact of the Renaissance was slow to arrive. It included artists such as Antioco Mainas and Pietro's son Michele Cavaro, and drew much of its inspiration from Spain, blending the influence of Raphael with late Gothic elements. Major works by members of the school can be seen in Cágliari's Pinacoteca (see p.78) and Oristano's Antiquarium Arborense (see p.166 & 168); few examples remain in Stampace itself, though the district's churches are still redolent of the tight-knit community that gave birth to the school.

At the top of Largo Carlo Felice, **Piazza Yenne** was the site of the old Porta Stampace before the destruction of the quarter's walls. The cobbled square that now forms a pedestrianized enclave to one side of the thick traffic marks the start of the Carlo Felice highway, Sardinia's main north-south artery (now the SS131). A pair of monuments recall the building of this: a bronze statue of its instigator, King Carlo Felice, dressed in Roman garb and for some reason gesturing away from the road, and, across the street, a pointed ball on top of a simple stone column. From here, the highway starts its journey up **Corso Vittorio Emanuele**, today a busy thoroughfare that begins grandly but soon narrows as it cuts through Stampace. Contrasting with the predominantly medieval character of the quarter, Cágliari's most impressive Roman remains are easily accessible to the north of the Corso.

Stampace's churches

Running off the top of Piazza Yenne parallel to Corso Vittorio Emanuele, Via Azuni gives access to four of Stampace's historic churches. On the right, the monumental white neoclassical facade of the **Church of Sant'Anna** (Tues–Sat 8–11am & 3.30–6.30pm), with its two tiers of Corinthian columns, stands atop a grand flight of steps. The present building was begun during the Savoy era in 1785, on the site of an earlier Pisan church, though not completely finished until the 1930s. Faithfully reconstructed after serious damage during the bombing raids of 1943, the late Baroque design is marked by strong Piedmontese features. The airy interior holds a fourteenth-century wooden crucifix from the Stampace church of San Francesco (destroyed by fire in the nineteenth century), a statue of Amedeo di Savoia by Andrea Galassi, the Sássari sculptor responsible for the statue of Carlo Felice in Piazza Yenne, and a painting by the nineteenth-century Sard master Giovanni Marghinotti, depicting *Christ the Saviour*.

To the left of Sant'Anna, the narrow Via Sant'Efisio leads north past the piazzetta and church of **Santa Restituta**, a mainly sixteenth-century structure, to a doorway which gives entry to the **Cripta di Santa Restituta** (Tues–Sun 10am–1pm; free). Originally a place of pagan rites linked to the water collected here, this subterranean cavern was subsequently dedicated to Restituta, a victim of Diocletian's persecution, and provided a home for refugees from Africa during the fifth century, and later for a Greek Orthodox community. Later still it served as a prison, while the scribbled signatures faintly visible on the walls of the crypt belong to locals who sheltered here during air raids in 1943. The interior is mostly bare, but for an altar and a statue of the saint in the main chamber, which has niches and murky corridors running off it.

Popularly represented as a flamboyant knight with a plumed helmet, **Sant'Efisio** was born in Elia, Asia Minor, and served as a soldier in the Roman army during the reign of the emperor Diocletian (AD 283–310). According to tradition, he was sent to Sardinia to combat the tribes of the Barbagia in the interior. Having refused to renounce his Christian faith, he was imprisoned in the hypogeum that is now the crypt of the Stampace church that bears his name, then taken to Nora where he was beheaded in 303. A cult soon grew up around the saint, increasing over the centuries with the attribution of various miracles to him – notably the rescue of the city from a plague in 1652 and the repulsion of the French attack on Cágliari in 1792–3.

Since saving the city from plague, the saint has been commemorated annually at the beginning of May in Sardinia's biggest religious festival, the **Festa di Sant'Efisio**. Setting forth from Sant'Efisio church on the morning of May 1, a solemn procession embarks on the long walk to Nora, 40km south along the coast, bearing the holy statue of the saint which at other times is kept in the church. As the procession makes its way through Cágliari, it is preceded by a long column of costumed participants from every part of the island, sometimes mounted, often accompanied by traditional singing and the playing of drums and instruments such as the *launeddas* (shepherd's pipes). The costumed part of the procession melts away once it reaches Via Pula, south of the train station, but the holy statue continues with a small retinue, joined for part of its way by villagers and bands in the places it passes through, before arriving at Nora on the evening of the following day. After religious services have taken place, the statue departs from the church at Nora on the evening of May 3, entering Cágliari the next evening to a much more muted reception.

The festa is a spectacular affair, and a great chance to view a panoply of traditional costumes from the villages, as well as to hear authentic Sard music. If you can't be present for the whole four-day event, the May 1 festivities are the highlight, for which you might consider a ticket for the stadium-like seats (*tribune*) around Piazza Matteotti and surrounding streets on the route, giving a high, unimpeded view of the proceedings. Tickets, costing €15–18, normally go on sale from January, and are quickly sold out: the AAST tourist office at Via Mameli 97 (℡070.664.195) usually deals directly with ticket sales, alternatively they can give you the number of the organization currently responsible. This is also the main information point for any other queries regarding the festivities. It's worth booking accommodation in advance if you're planning to be in Cágliari between April 30 and May 5.

Further up the street, the **Cripta di Sant'Efisio** (Tues–Sun: summer 9am–1pm & 5–8pm; winter 8.30am–5.30pm; free) may be even older, as it served as one of the many hypogea or cisterns of the Punic-Roman city of Karalis. According to tradition, Efisius, a Roman soldier from Asia Minor, was imprisoned here for his Christian beliefs before being taken to Nora to be decapitated. You can see the column where he was supposedly bound, an object of worship for local believers. There is evidence of a church in existence here as far back as the fifth century; more recently, the crypt served as an air-raid shelter and rubbish dump. If the entrance is closed (which is often), there may be someone to show you around in the present **Chiesa di Sant'Efisio** just up the street (same hours as crypt). The small church was built in the eighteenth century, and is intimately connected with the martyr and with the large-scale festa dedicated to him, which starts here (see box above). The second chapel on the right holds the effigy of the saint that provides the focal point of the procession, and the holy cross carried at Easter is in the third chapel on the right. A wooden altar on the left side of the church has a more dashing image of the saint in the guise of a bearded, armoured figure with a plumed helmet. At the back of the church, look out for the cannonballs embedded in the wall, originally fired by the French fleet during their attack on Cágliari in 1793 – the rout of the fleet was another miracle attributed to Sant'Efisio.

Return back to Via Azuni to reach the triple-arched facade of the church of **San Michele** at the end of this street (Mon–Sat 7.30–11am & 5–8pm, Sun 8–11am & 7–8pm). Consecrated by the Jesuits in 1738, the highly ornamented building is one of Sardinia's most opulent examples of the Baroque. The striking porticoed facade gives a foretaste of the majestic interior, a densely stuccoed and painted octagonal space, sumptuously marbled and topped by a frescoed cupola. On the steps outside, a richly decorated pulpit – said to have been used by Charles V before setting off on his expedition against Tunis in 1535 – stands on four Corinthian columns.

The Anfiteatro Romano and Orto Botánico

With its entrance on Viale Sant'Ignazio da Láconi, the **Anfiteatro Romano** (Tues–Sun: summer 10am–1pm & 3–6pm, winter daily 10am–4pm; €3) is reachable from Castello on Viale Buon Cammino, or from Stampace by walking up from Corso Vittorio Emanuele. Cut out of solid rock in the second century AD, the amphitheatre could hold the entire city's population of about 10,000. Despite its state of decay (much of the site was cannibalized to build churches in the Middle Ages), you can still see the trenches for the animals, the underground passages and several rows of seats. There are open-air concerts here in summer, with details and tickets available from the ticket office.

Turning left out of the amphitheatre, walk down Viale Sant'Ignazio da Láconi to the **Orto Botánico** (daily: April–Oct 8am–1.30pm & 3–7pm; Nov–March 8am–1.30pm; €0.50), one of Italy's most famous botanical gardens, with over five hundred species of Mediterranean and tropical plants, including examples of local carob trees, lentisks and holm oaks, as well as exotic yuccas, palms, papyrus, cacti and some carnivorous species. The collection was initiated in the seventeenth century and transferred to this site in the second half of the nineteenth century; the mother of the writer Italo Calvino later became director of the gardens. Informative guided visits take place (sometimes in English) on the second and fourth Sunday of each month at 11am, but you don't need to be a plant enthusiast to enjoy this quiet and shady retreat, especially on a sizzling afternoon.

The Casa di Tigellio

On the other side of Viale Sant'Ignazio da Láconi, a railed enclosure on Via Tigellio shields another remnant of Cágliari's Roman era. The **Casa di Tigellio** (Tues–Sun 9am–1pm; free) was traditionally held to be the villa of Tigellius, a Sardinian poet whose singing and versifying were appreciated by the Roman Emperor Augustus but loathed by perhaps better judges such as Horace and Cicero. Whether or not this was in fact his abode, excavations have brought to light a later villa of the second and third centuries, quite a substantial complex arranged on either side of a narrow lane. In its present state, however, it's not easy to make much sense of the litter of calcareous blocks that make up the site.

On one side, a set of thermal baths is identifiable by the raised floor of the hypocaust, while three buildings from the imperial era with tetrastyle porticos stand opposite. The first, the atrium, where guests were received, has two Ionic columns and a *tablinum* (room giving onto atrium) with mosaic decorations, and is paved with black and white mosaics; the second – the "stuccoed house" – has remnants of patterned decoration on the walls; few traces remain of the third. Excavations continue, sometimes throwing up oddments like the lapidary monuments from nearby tombs currently displayed here. The overall effect is rather spoiled by the twentieth-century apartment blocks crowding in on all sides, and there is no attempt to explain the site very fully, though there are plans to display finds in an exhibition room at the top end. Note that there's a good chance the site will be closed anyway, due to ongoing funding problems, but you can always get a good view of it from the railings.

Villanova

Much of the quarter of **Villanova** is modern and traffic-thronged, but the streets to the east of Viale Regina Margherita hold two important religious sites of great historical significance. On the slopes of **Monte Irpinu**, east of Piazza Garibaldi and accessible from Viale Europa or Via Pietro Leo, Cágliari's biggest public garden affords the city's best views.

The Basilica di San Saturnino

At one end of the broad Piazza San Cosimo, just off the busy Via Dante, the fifth-century **Basilica di San Saturnino** (Mon–Sat 9am–1pm; free) is one of Sardinia's two oldest churches (for details of the other, San Giovanni di Sinis near Oristano, see p.173). It's one of the most important surviving examples of early Christian architecture in the Mediterranean. The basilica was erected on the spot where the Christian martyr Saturninus met his fate during the reign of Diocletian (283–310). The building sustained severe bombardment in World War II, and today the weathered stone of the tall, domed structure is offset by the modernistic darkened glass which makes up most of three sides. Despite this, the church retains an unmistakable Middle Eastern flavour, with its palm trees and cupola.

The monument is entered through an open atrium, within which a palm is surrounded by various remnants from the past: shattered pillars, fragments of Roman sarcophagi, slabs of stone carved with Latin inscriptions, and seven cannonballs. The church's stark **interior**, of ponderous dimensions, is empty of any decoration or distraction, though the glass walls allow you to see the necropolis which is still being excavated, the tombs clearly visible on either side of the nave.

To reach Piazza Repubblica, where the FdS station is located, turn left up Via Cimitero, behind Piazza San Cósimo. Nearby on Via San Lucífero, **Exma** (Tues–Sun: June–Sept 9am–2pm & 4–10pm; Oct–May 9am–8pm; €3) is Cágliari's former *mattatoio* (slaughterhouse), now converted into a cultural centre, arranged around an open space in which jazz and classical concerts are performed in summer (small-scale concerts are held indoors all year). As well as the one permanent exhibition tracing the restoration and transformation of the old building, there are usually two other shows, mainly featuring the work of Sard artists. There's also a good café and bookshop on either side of the entrance.

The Santuario di Bonaria

Turning right down Via Cimitero from Piazza San Cósimo leads past the **Cimitero Monumentale di Bonaria**, where there are several grandiose tombs and mausoleums, to Viale Bonaria and Piazza Bonaria. Here, rising above Viale Armando Diaz, the hill of **Bonaria** affords commanding views out to sea. Valued for its clean air (*"Buon'aria"*) and for its distance from Cágliari's pestilential conditions, this was an important military base for the Aragonese during their efforts to prise the Pisans out of Cágliari. The fortifications quickly evolved into a significant city and port with a population of 6000, and Bonaria was even for a while the seat of the archbishop and of the administrative organization governing the whole of Sardinia and Corsica. It was only when the Catalans were persuaded to transfer to Cágliari's castle in 1336, ten years after the Pisans were finally expelled from there, that Bonaria's fortifications were abandoned, and a few decades later they were in ruins.

Prosperity returned, however, following the recovery of a legendary image of **Our Lady of Bonaria** from a shipwreck. When a Spanish trading vessel was caught in a storm on the way to Italy in 1370, its crew jettisoned everything on board in their efforts to save themselves, including one chest that refused to sink, and which allegedly had a miraculously becalming effect on the waters. When the chest washed up ashore, at a spot now marked by a column, it was found to contain an image of the Madonna holding a child in one hand, a lit candle in the other. The ship's grateful survivors built the **Santuario di Bonaria** (daily 8am–noon & 5–7pm) in her honour, which soon became a place of pilgrimage, of special significance to all sailors who have traditionally invoked the Madonna di Bonaria as protectress. The sanctuary has always been tended by monks of the Mercedari order, who arrived in Sardinia around 1300 from Barcelona, under the protection of the Aragonese royal house. The order specialized in negotiating the liberation of Christian slaves from pirate kidnappers, usually by means of ransoms. One of their last missions was the rescue of the hundreds of inhabitants of the island of San Pietro captured by North African pirates at the end of the eighteenth century and held as slaves in Tunisia for fifteen years. A handful of Mercedari monks still run the sanctuary, inhabiting the convent to the left.

Viceroys, bishops and popes – including John Paul II – have traditionally paid their respects to the Madonna di Bonaria, and in recent centuries the approach to the church has been aggrandized by a geometric swathe of steps. Inside, the holy image is the centrepiece, conserved on the high altar in the Gothic apse – said to be the first example of the Gothic-Catalan style in Sardinia, built by the Aragonese in 1325. The statue of the Madonna and Child, both crowned, is fashioned from a single piece of locust-tree wood, finely carved and painted. The first chapel on the right has an even more ancient and much venerated statue, the Madonna del Mirácolo, which has stood here since the church's construction in 1325.

In the middle of the apse hangs a small ivory **model ship** dating from 1400, just thirty years after the arrival of the Madonna di Bonaria. It's the oldest of the gifts donated to the sanctuary by shipwrecked sailors as a token of thanksgiving for their survival; many more are on show at the next-door museum (see p.86). The particular model is significant in that it depicts one of the first examples of an Italian ship with a single stern rudder, as opposed to the steerboards (lateral rudders) mainly used at that time. More mysteriously, it is also said to signal the direction of winds in the gulf.

The spot remains a reassuring beacon to sailors approaching the shelter of Cágliari's harbour, but the adjacent **Basilica di Bonaria** (same hours as Santuario) is the most significant landmark here – its imposing Neoclassical front completely overwhelms the plain lines of the sanctuary. Constructed in 1704, the basilica had all of its frescos, stuccos and precious decoration devastated by a bomb in World War II, but its marbled interior has been carefully restored, and today it takes an integral role in the ceremonies next door. Adjoining the Santuario on the other side, the **Museo Marinaro** (same hours as Santuario; free) occupies the floor above the monastery's cloister. The collection consists largely of a diverting hoard of ex-voto model ships, most of them dating from the eighteenth century and later, which together form an important chronicle of evolving nautical styles and maritime art. Amid shelf-fulls of silver galleons, clippers, steamers, warships, Arab dhows and assorted fishing boats – some in bottles – there are several French, US and British ships reproduced, including an *Ark Royal* which burned in 1587 (and here made of matches), a *Bounty* and a couple of *Cutty Sarks*. There are also eighteenth- and nineteenth-century paintings of dramatic shipwreck scenes, many painted with the initials VFGA, standing for *votum feci gratiam abui* ("I made a pledge and received grace"), or PGR, *per grazia ricevuta*, referring to prayers answered.

Other gifts are from liberated slaves and some from nobles and sovereigns, such as the golden crown offered in 1816 by King Vittorio Emanuele I and Queen Maria Teresa, and a silver anchor given by Queen Margherita di Savoia on the safe return of an expedition to the North Pole in 1899, led by her son. Apart from the nautical exhibits, the museum also holds a miscellany of other objects of local interest, including finds from the excavation immediately to the west of the sanctuary: nuraghic odds and ends (obsidian blades and ceramics), a few Punic coins from the sixth to the third centuries BC, clay figurines, fragments of sarcophagi, amphorae and cinerary urns from the third century BC to the first century AD. You'll also see a cistern from the Aragonese castle built here in 1325, used by the monks of the convent until the beginning of the twentieth century, as well as swords and arms donated by soldiers. One unexpectedly gruesome display case contains the mummified bodies of four members of the noble Alagon family, who died of plague in 1604, the three adults and child still fully clothed.

The sanctuary's original Aragonese belltower is visible from the park at the back of the church. There's a good **bar** in the piazza below it for coffees and cakes (see p.89). You can save the walk here or back to the centre by taking any **bus** connecting Poetto with Piazza Matteotti, or the frequent #5, #30 or #31 from Via Roma, which stops right in Piazza Bonaria.

West along Viale Sant'Avendrace

West of Piazza Matteotti, Via Roma turns into Viale Trieste, joining Viale Trento to become Viale Sant'Avendrace. This has always been Cágliari's main route inland, and the traffic flows thick and fast past begrimed palazzi. Unpromising though these untidy suburbs may appear, the district does harbour two **ancient monuments**, which are well worth the short bus ride (#1 from Largo Carlo Felice, Corso Vittorio Emanuele or Via Mameli every 5–10min, or the #9 from Piazza Matteotti approximately every 15min; for the latter you must buy a €1.29 bus ticket, valid 2hr).

Grotta della Vípera

Shortly after the junction with Viale Trieste (the bus stop is opposite the CRAI supermarket), a grand quarried rock marks the **Grotta della Vípera** (Tues–Sun 10am–1pm; free), more properly known as the Sepolcro di Attilia Pomptilla. The popular name derives from the two snakes decorating the classical pediment surmounting the entrance to this shrine, which commemorates the much-loved wife of a Roman official, Cassius Philippus, during the reign of Nero (AD 54–68). She was apparently a woman of exemplary goodness, according to the Greek and Latin inscriptions found at the spot, though you'll need to get someone to point out what's left of the faint carvings. The work of time has erased much of the elaborate tomb that once stood here, its atrium and columns long disappeared, and the site now is little more than a shallow grotto, with collapsed passages leading off into the rock – now filled with water – and a sea of pigeon droppings (keep a wary eye up). Even if the grotto is closed, you can still see quite a lot through the gates.

Tuvixeddu

A far more impressive site lies at the top of this calcareous mass, accessible from a flight of cracked concrete steps 200m further up Via Sant'Avendrace on the right (turn right at the top). The high, boulder-strewn wasteland is honeycombed with tombs chiselled out of the rock. This extensive burial place is the Punic necropolis of **Tuvixeddu** (24hr; free), used between the sixth century BC and the first century AD, first by Carthaginians and then by their Roman successors; much of the wealth of archeological evidence it has yielded up can be seen in Cágliari's Museo Archeologico (see p.77).

The neat square or oblong **chambers** are either hewn out of the vertical rockface on multiple levels or cut sheer into the ground – watch your step among the grass and cactus. A few of the chambers, mostly consisting of single or twin tombs, display much-eroded carvings, in particular of a warrior who might be the Punic divinity Sid, curer of all ills. Dark corridors are tantalizingly visible at the bottom of the deep ground-dug tombs, though you'd need ladders and torches to explore this hidden network.

The whole area – one of the most complete and intricate Punic remains on the island – is shockingly neglected, with all work to maintain, protect and open up the site having been stalled for years while a property dispute is unresolved. In the meantime, despite the litter of plastic bags and broken glass and the complete absence of explanatory signs, the site is still a fascinating place to wander about, and the high ground offers good views over the gulf. You'll need more than flip-flops to explore the higher tombs.

Poetto and Calamosca

When you need a break from the city centre and a swim, head for the suburb of **Poetto**, a fifteen-minute bus ride (bus "PF" or "PQ") from Piazza Matteotti past Cágliari's Sant'Elia football stadium. Poetto has 6km of fine sandy beach (the Spiaggia di Quartu), with small bars and showers conveniently located nearby. Behind the beaches are the choppy waters of the **Stagno di Quartu** lagoons, north of which stands the town of Quartu Sant'Elena itself, now little more than an industrial suburb of Cágliari.

The liveliest of Poetto's beaches is at the southernmost end, where there's the tidy **Marina Píccola** – an anchorage for boats and an area for concerts and outdoor cinema in July and August (films usually nightly at 9.30pm; €4). Other spots along this beach strip can get equally raucous throughout the summer. "PF" or "PQ" buses run along the whole length of it, allowing you to take your pick of the various stretches of sand, though there's little to distinguish between them, and all have similar facilities. Some, clearly marked, are reserved for the police or air force.

If you don't have your own parasol with you, it would make sense to bathe from one of the lidos lining the beach, where you pay the standard daily rate of a few euros for entry and use of showers and toilets. Parasols and deck-chairs are available for daily hire, and from the same places it's usually possible to rent pedalos, canoes and surf-bikes; some places also offer windsurfing and sailing.

Though **bars** and other refreshment stops are ten a penny in Poetto, there's less choice when it comes to **eating** in the area; the main lido, *D'Aquila*, however, has a mediocre restaurant, *Da Pietrino* (closed Thurs in winter) which overlooks the sea, and there's also the Chinese *Draco d'Oro* close by. The next-door *Stabilimento Il Lido* also has a pizzeria and disco, open summer only.

The Sella del Diávolo

The **Sella del Diávolo** ("Devil's Saddle") rears above the marina at Poetto's southern end, most of the rocky promontory a military zone and therefore off-limits. Its name is connected with a legend relating how the Archangel Gabriel won a battle here against the devil himself (the name of Cágliari's gulf, Golfo degli Ángeli, is also a reference to this celestial tussle). On the western side of this outcrop – for which you need to backtrack along Via Poetto, then turn left into Viale Calamosca – a lighthouse overlooks the **Calamosca** locality, little more than a small sandy cove with one good hotel (see p.72). It can get crowded on this small beach, but if you want a quick dip from Cágliari, this is the nearest patch of sand to the centre. To get here by public transport, take any of the "P" buses from Cágliari, changing at the Amsicora stadium for bus #11, which leaves every quarter-hour.

Eating, drinking and nightlife

Cágliari has the best range of **restaurants** on the island, most clustered around Via Sardegna in the Marina quarter. Many don't start serving until 8.30–9pm and are full within thirty minutes, so pass by earlier or telephone to make a booking if you want to be sure of a table. You'll find a similar choice of food everywhere, almost invariably traditional Sard recipes with a strong emphasis on seafood, though the local places have been joined in recent years by a handful of burger bars, Chinese restaurants and a North African restaurant, providing the only real alternatives – and they're generally cheap. For **takeaway food**, try one of two *salumerie* (delicatessens) on Via Baylle, in the heart of Marina, which rank among Sardinia's oldest: Vaghi, here since 1902, and the slightly younger Pisu.

Restaurants

Antica Hostaria Via Cavour 60 ☎ 070.665.870. Upmarket though not over-formal ristorante, with antique trimmings. Meat and fish are given equal billing, and are usually good. You'll spend around €30 a head, excluding drinks. Closed Sun. Expensive.

Buongustaio Via Concezione 7. Close to the port, this casually smart restaurant is a notch up from the other cheapies in the neighbourhood, and is favoured by locals. Prices are still comparatively low, however, and there are occasional fixed-price menus. Closed Mon eve & Tues. Moderate.

La Damigiana Corso Vittorio Emanuele 115. Unpretentious wood-panelled neighbourhood trattoria for good fixed-price meals in this area. Closed Mon & Tues eves. Inexpensive.

Downtown Piazza Yenne. Grotto-like pizzeria and *távola calda* that makes a useful stop for lunch or fast-food snacks. Closed Sat morning & Sun morning. Inexpensive.

Da Fabio Via Sardegna 90. Easy-going trattoria offering tourist menus and pizzas, with an English-speaking boss. You'll share dining space with the artfully incorporated remains of a Roman wall and cistern. Closed Mon & two weeks in Nov. Moderate.

Il Gatto Viale Trieste 15 ☎070.663.596. Spacious, vaulted restaurant and pizzeria outside the main dining zone, off Piazza del Cármine. It's a little more innovative than most, but has the usual selection of seafood or meat dishes all immaculately prepared, plus a huge range of desserts and imported bottled beer. Closed Sat & Sun lunchtimes. Moderate.

Trattoria Gennargentu Via Sardegna 60c. The plain narrow rooms have a rustic flavour; good Sardinian staples are served at reasonable prices, for example the tasty *Spaghetti alla Gennargentu*, made with ham, bacon, olives and tomatoes. Closed Sun. Moderate.

Ristorante Italia Via Sardegna 30 ☎070.657.987. Well-rated first-floor restaurant that's strong on fish, but has a dull, old-fashioned feel. Closed Sat lunch & Sun all day. Moderate–expensive.

La Kasbah Via Santa Margherita, off Piazza Yenne. North African restaurant serving couscous, kebabs and panini; there's also a takeaway service. Closed Mon. Inexpensive.

Da Lillicu Via Sardegna 78 ☎070.652.970. A large, fashionably bare dining area in the heart of Marina is the place for this straight-talking Sard trattoria, with plain marble tables. The food is basic but meticulously prepared, with a limited menu of local meat and fish specialities and a wider choice of antipasti. It's regularly packed out, so booking is essential. Closed Sun. Moderate.

Pechino Via Santa Margherita 19. Probably Cágliari's best Chinese restaurant, offering an €8 fixed-price dinner and such dishes as *ánatra pechinese* (Peking duck). Open daily. Inexpensive.

Quattro Mori Via Angioy 93 ☎070.650.269. Just off Corso Vittorio Emanuele, this place has built a solid reputation for its endless courses of delectable Sard dishes. Despite the relatively high prices, there's a regular full house and the atmosphere can get quite rowdy, even Bacchanalian. Booking essential. Closed Sun eve & Mon. Expensive.

Queto Via Roma 133. Sleek café-restaurant at the top of the Rinascente department store, with great views of the port. A good choice for a self-service lunch, a fuller evening meal, or just a late-night drink. Closed Sun & Mon. Moderate.

Da Serafino Entrances at both Via Sardegna 109 and Via Lepanto 6. Down-to-earth trattoria with low prices, that's popular with younger locals. Closed Thurs. Inexpensive.

Bars and *birrerias*

Cágliari is well endowed with drink stops, starting with the cafés under the arcades of Via Roma, most of which add 50–80 percent to the bill for table service. For a morning coffee or afternoon tea, Piazza Yenne is a pleasant spot to sit out, at a safe distance from the traffic and getting quite lively at *passeggiata* time. The Castello quarter is worth exploring after dark for new bars and *birrerias* opening up. In summer, **Poetto** offers a gaudier atmosphere, a blitz of bars, pizzerias, fairgrounds and ice-cream kiosks by the sea to provide an evening's entertainment.

Antico Caffè Piazza Costituzione. Old coffee shop with character next to the Bastione San Remy. There are outdoor tables, though the traffic can be oppressive. Good lunches available.

Caffè Libarium Nostrum Via Santa Croce 33. Castello bar with tables outside on the city walls, providing perfect views and a fun atmosphere on late summer nights. Snacks served. Closed Mon.

Caffè Mediterraneo Viale Armando Diaz, opposite the Santuario di Bonaria. Great coffee-and-pastries spot attached to the *Mediterraneo* hotel, where locals congregate; you can sit outside in summer. Ice creams are also available.

De Candia Via Marco de Candia 1–3, Bastione San Remy. Great location for this modern bar, which has tables outside and live music from around 11pm in summer.

Isola del Gelato Piazza Yenne 35. Cágliari's top ice-cream parlour offers a range of lip-smacking concoctions, including yoghurt with fresh fruit, making this a good breakfast stop. Closed Mon Oct–Feb.

Il Merlo Parlante Via Portascalas. Tucked up an alley off Corso Vittorio Emanuele, this boisterous *birreria* offers draught beers, music and *panini* until 2am. Open evenings only.

Old Coffee Via La Mármora 91. Traditional-looking bar in front of the cathedral, with small marble tables and snacks served.

Bar Olympia Via Roma 77. A cinema foyer that doubles as a daytime bar, serving good cappuccinos and with no surcharge for waiter service.

Sotto La Torre Piazza San Giuseppe. This series of elegantly beamed and furnished rooms lies right opposite the Torre dell'Elefante, agreeable surroundings for a long cappuccino by day and cocktails or beers till late at night. Buns and snacks also make this a good breakfast or lunch spot. Closed Sun June–Sept & Wed Oct–May.

Svizzero Largo Carlo Felice 6–8. Antique-style café, with vaulted ceiling and slightly genteel ambience. Tables inside and, sheltered within a glassed-in verandah, out on the busy Largo. Closed Mon.

Festivals and entertainment

Apart from Sant'Efisio (see box on p.82), Cágliari has a few other **festivals** which are worth catching. In February or March, **Carnevale** is always a rowdy affair, kicking off with a carousal through the streets of Castello on the first official day of the season – a long procession with dancing and extravagantly costumed celebrations, all accompanied by *sa ratantina*, a deafening drum tattoo. **Easter** is also taken seriously in Cágliari, with a procession from the Chiesa di Sant'Efisio up to the Cattedrale taking place on the morning of Easter Monday, and cowled columns trailing through town on Easter Friday and Easter Sunday.

In summer, **music**, **dance** and other entertainments are staged at the Anfiteatro Romano, with tickets costing €10–70; ask at the tourist office for details, or call the Teatro Comunale (also called Teatro Cívico or Teatro Lírico) in Via Sant'Alenixedda, north of Castello, which organizes the events (ticket office open Mon–Sat 10am–2pm & 6–8pm; ☎070.408.2230, ⓦteatrolirico .tiscali.it). The brutalist Teatro Comunale is Cágliari's main venue for **classical music** and **ballet** performances, which take place all year, with tickets ranging in price from €5 to €60. The Exma complex on Via San Lucífero hosts chamber music and soloists (☎070.666.399), while open-air **rock concerts** are held regularly in summer at the Fiera Campionaria, Viale Diaz 221.

The smaller-scale Teatro Alfieri stages a full winter programme of **theatre** performances ranging from Shakespeare to the Alice stories at Via della Pineta 213 (☎070.301.378), as does Teatro delle Saline on Viale La Palma (☎070.341.322), both on the eastern side of town; for more experimental theatre performances, check out the Teatro dell'Arco in Via Portoscalas 47 (☎070.663.288). Mainstream films are screened at **cinemas** in Via Roma and Via San Lucífero, while Cineclub Namaste, at Via Ospedale 4, is an arts cinema which periodically shows foreign-language films. Open-air screenings take place at Poetto's Marina Píccola nightly July–September at 9.30pm (tickets €4). For information on all upcoming concerts and other events, pick up the free *Vivi Cágliari*, available from Cágliari's various tourist offices, or visit ⓦwww.zonanet.com/digica/eventi.

Shopping

Via Manno, descending from the Bastione di San Remy to Piazza Yenne, is the place to find **boutiques** and fashion shops. In Castello, Via La Mármora, below the cathedral, has a concentration of galleries and **antiques shops**. In the lower town, Via Sardegna has a couple of army surplus shops with a range of equipment for campers and travellers, cheap T-shirts and other practical items.

On Via Roma, Rinascente is a well-stocked, quality **department store** (Mon–Fri 9am–8.30pm, Sat 9am–9pm, Sun 10am–9pm), while Largo Carlo Felice is a popular spot for Senegalese and Korean traders hawking everything from leather handbags and African masks to lighters and nail-clippers. Via Roma's newspaper kiosks sell foreign **newspapers and magazines**, including same-day English titles.

Sardinian **craftwork** is sold in numerous shops in the Castello and Marina districts; the best selection can be found in the government-sponsored ISOLA shop at Via Bacaredda 176, east of Viale Regina Elena (Mon–Fri 9.30am–1pm & 4.30–8pm, Sat 9.30am–1pm), though prices here are quite steep. For **antique and curio markets**, Piazza del Carmine becomes a scene of low-level haggling on the first Sunday of the month, as does Piazza Carlo Alberto (in front of the cathedral) on the second and fourth Sundays, while there's a **flea-market** on the Bastione di San Remy every Sunday except during August; all close down by lunchtime. On Via Francesco Cocco Ortu, a brief walk north of Castello, the vivacious San Benedetto **covered market** is open every morning from Monday to Friday and all day Saturday for foodstuffs and household goods of every description on two floors. A bigger **outdoor food market** sprawls around the Stadio Sant'Elia, west of the centre, on Sundays. For bookshops and supermarkets, see "Listings" below.

Listings

Airlines Air Dolomiti ☎800.013.366, ⓦwww .airdolomiti.it; Airone ☎800.900.955, ⓦwww.airone.it; Alitalia national flights ☎848.865.641, international flights ☎848.865.642, ⓦwww.alitalia.it; Alpi Eagles ☎041.599.7788, ⓦwww.alpieagles.com; Meridiana ☎199.111.333, ⓦwww.meridiana.it; Minerva ☎0481.772.711.

Banks and exchange Cágliari's centre has a choice of banks, all with ATMs. Most are on or around Largo Carlo Felice, including Banco Nazionale di Lavoro, Banco di Nápoli and Crédito Italiano (Mon–Fri generally 8.25am–1.25pm & 2.50–4pm). Some, like the Banca di Roma, on Piazza Yenne, are also open Saturdays (8.25am–11.55am). Hay Elettronica Service at Via Napoli 8, off Via Roma, can change money and is the local agent for Western Union transfers (Mon–Sat 9am–1pm & 4–8pm).

Bookshops Le Librerie della Costa, Via Roma 63–5, has a good range of books including English-language publications and books on Sardinia. Mon–Sat 9am–8.30pm, Sun 10am–1.30pm & 5.30–9pm.

Bus operators The main company is **ARST** (Piazza Matteotti ☎800.865.042, ⓦwww.arst.sardegna.it); FdS (Piazza Repubblica ☎070.5793.0361, ⓦwww.ferroviesardegna.it); FMS (Bar Mura, Viale Cristóforo Colombo 24 ☎800.044.553,

ⓦwww.ferroviemeridionalisarde.it) – buses also stop near the Spano pharmacy on Via Roma (tickets from the nearby newspaper kiosk), and there are stops on Piazza Cármine and Viale S. Avendrace; **PANI** (Stazione Maríttima ☎070.652.326); **Turmo** (Piazza Matteotti ☎0789.21.487, ⓦwww.gruppoturmotravel.com). For Turmo, buy tickets on board, otherwise tickets should be purchased from the respective ticket offices.

Car rental Easycar, Aeroporto di Elmas ☎070.240.806, or toll-free ☎840.501.655; Eurorent, Aeroporto di Elmas ☎070.240.129, ⓦwww.rent.it; Hertz, Piazza Matteotti 8 ☎070.651.078 and airport ☎070.240.037, ⓦwww.hertz.it; Sardinya, Aeroporto di Elmas ☎070.240.444, ⓦwww.autonoleggiosardinya.it; Pinna, Aeroporto di Elmas ☎070.240.276; Ruvioli, Via dei Mille ☎070.658.955; Sixt, Aeroporto di Elmas ☎070.212.045, ⓦwww.e-sixt.it.

Hospital Via Peretti 21 ☎070.543.266.

Internet access Le Librerie della Costa, Via Roma 63–5; €3 for 30min, €5 for 1hr.

Laundry Coin-operated *lavanderia* at Corso Vittorio Emanuele 232 (daily 9am–9pm). Service wash at Lavanderia Yenne, Via Santa Margherita 2, off Piazza Yenne (Mon–Sat 8.30am–1pm & 5–8pm); they charge around €3 for trousers or skirts, €2.50 for shirts.

The Trenino Verde

Cágliari is a starting point for expeditions into Sardinia's interior on the small-gauge trains of the Ferrovie della Sardegna company (FdS) – also known as Ferrovie Sarde, or Ferrovie Complementari Sarde. Most FdS lines form part of the island's public transport network, while an additional service – the **Trenino Verde** – is strictly for leisure, often driven by antique steam locomotives and usually only running in the summer months. If you're in a hurry, take one of the more efficient train or bus services to reach your destination; otherwise sit back and enjoy the ride through some of Sardinia's most remote and scenic countryside.

From the station in Cágliari's **Piazza Repubblica**, seven trains daily (Mon–Sat; about 1hr 45min) run to Mandas; but the really interesting part is the separate service between Mandas and **Arbatax**, the port on Sardinia's eastern coast (mid-June to mid-Sept twice daily, currently at 8.30am and 3pm). The Mandas–Arbatax stretch takes nearly five hours, a meandering, often tortuous and stomach-churning journey through the beautiful highlands of the Sarcidano and Barbagia Seulo. Reckon on about six and a half hours for the whole one-way journey, for a fare of around €26. It's a good way to see some of Sardinia's remotest tracts and to reach the island's eastern port, though the laborious slog can be daunting and excruciatingly slow. For timetables, ask at the FdS station or call ☎070.580.246 or toll-free ☎800.460.220, or visit ⓦwww.treninoverde.com.

Left luggage Ticket office at train station (daily 7.30am–7.30pm; €2.58 per bag for 12hr). There's also a free service at the Stazione Maríttima for holders of ferry tickets.
Post office Piazza del Cármine. Mon–Fri 8.10am–6.40pm, Sat 8.10am–1.20pm; closes 4pm on last day of month, or noon if this is a Sat.
Supermarket Iperpan, in shopping centre on Viale La Plaia, the road out of town behind the train station. Daily 9am–9pm.
Taxi Ranks at the airport and Piazza Matteotti; Coop Radio Taxi 4 Mori (☎070.400.101) operate 5.30am–2am.

Telephones Unstaffed office at Via Angioy 6. Daily 8am–10pm.
Train information FS in Piazza Matteotti ☎848.888.088, ⓦwww.trenitalia.it; FdS in Piazza Repubblica ☎070.491.304, ⓦwww.ferroviesardegna.it.
Travel agents CTS, Via Balbo 4 (☎070.488.260); Sardamondial, at Via Roma 9 (☎070.668.094) can book bus and train tickets as well as flights and ferries, while Viaggi Orrù, at Via Roma 95 (☎070.659.858) can arrange train tickets but not buses.

Travel details

Trains

(FS unless otherwise indicated).
Cágliari to: Carbonia (Mon–Sat 8 daily, Sun 2, most involving change at Villamassargia; 1hr 10min); Ísili (FdS; Mon–Sat 3 daily, Sun in summer 1 daily; 2hr); Dolianova (FdS Mon–Sat hourly, Sun in summer 1 daily; 40min); Iglésias (Mon–Sat hourly, Sun 8; 55min); Mandas (FdS; Mon–Sat 6 daily, Sun in summer 1 daily; 1 hr 35min–2hr); Olbia (4 daily, may involve change at Oristano or Ozieri-Chilivani; 4hr–4hr 40min); Oristano (hourly; 1hr 10min–2hr); Sanluri (hourly; 50min); Sássari (5 daily, may involve change at Ozieri-Chilivani; 3hr 20min–4hr 15min).

Buses

(ARST unless otherwise indicated).
Cágliari to: Barúmini (Mon–Sat 3 daily, Sun 2; 1hr 20min–1hr 40min); Buggerru (FMS; 1 daily; 2hr 40min); Burcei (Mon–Sat 5–8 daily; 1hr 15min); Calasetta (FMS; 3–4 daily; 2hr 20min–3hr); Capitana (mid-June to mid-Sept 8–11 daily; mid-Sept to mid-June Mon–Sat 5 daily, Sun 2; 40min); Carbonia (FMS; 5–7 daily; 1hr 30min–2hr); Costa Rei (mid-June to mid-Sept 8–10 daily; mid-Sept to mid-June 2–3 daily; 2hr 5min–2hr 35min); Dolianova (FdS; Mon–Sat 10–11 daily, Sun 4; 45min); Iglésias (FMS; 6–7 daily; 1hr 20min); Ísili (FdS; 1–2 daily; 1hr 50min); Mandas

(FdS; 1–2 daily; 1hr 15min); Muravera (Mon–Sat 11 daily, Sun 3; 1hr 35min–3hr 15min); Nuoro (PANI; 4 daily; 3hr 35min); Olbia (Turmo; 1–2 daily; 4hr 15min–4hr 50min); Oristano (4–6 daily; 1hr 35min–2hr); Porto Torres (PANI; 2 daily; 4hr 20min); Portovesme (FMS; 3 daily; 1hr 15min–2hr); Sanluri (ARST & PANI; 1–2 hourly; 50min–1hr 5min); Sant'Antíoco (FMS; 4–5 daily; 2hr–2hr 35min); Santa Teresa di Gallura (Turmo; 1 daily; 6hr 10min); Sássari (PANI; 7 daily; 3hr 15min–3hr 50min); Villasimius (mid-June to mid-Sept 8–11 daily; mid-Sept to mid-June Mon–Sat 5 daily, Sun 2; 1hr 25min).

Ferries

Two ferry companies operate from Cágliari: Linea dei Golfi (℡0565.222.300, ⓦwww .lineadeigolfi.it), for sailings to Livorno; and Tirrenia(℡199.123.199, ⓦwww.tirrenia.it), for sailings to Genoa, Civitavécchia, Naples, Palermo and Trápani. Offices for both companies are at the Stazione Maríttima at the ferry port.

Cágliari to: Civitavecchia (1 daily; 14hr 30min–16hr 30min); Genoa (mid-July to Aug 2 weekly; 20hr); Livorno (1 weekly; 19hr); Naples (1–2 weekly; 16hr); Palermo (1 weekly; 13hr 30min); Trápani (1 weekly; 11hr).

The southwest

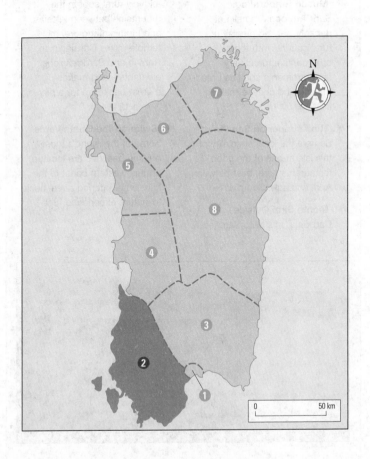

✳ **Drive or bike the Costa del Sud** One of Sardinia's most stunning coastlines, rugged and undeveloped, and offering photo-opportunities at every turn. See p.106

✳ **Museo Etnográfico, Sant'Antíoco** A small but densely-packed display of rural culture, with tools, ornaments and culinary accoutrements such as bread-making and cheese-making kit. See p.112

✳ **Tuna supper on San Pietro** Sample the local speciality of this isle at one of the good restaurants here, best between April and July. See p.114–117

✳ **Monte Sirai** Outside Carbónia, this hilltop archeo-logical site has some fascinating Carthaginian tombs and the remains of streets – but the real draw is the magnificent views. See p.118–119

✳ **Témpio di Antas** Occupying a lovely rural spot in the mountains between Iglésias and Fluminimaggiore, this temple mixes Carthaginian, Roman and Sard religious elements – and makes a great backdrop for a picnic. See p.124

✳ **Swim off the Costa Verde** Some of the island's most pristine beaches are located off this western coast of the Iglesiente, offering a real back-to-nature experience. See p.126

△ Chia Beach

2

The southwest

Predominantly mountainous, Sardinia's **southwest** corner is a complex area of diverse identities, where you'll encounter superb beaches, thick forest, long swathes of undeveloped coast and a scattering of mountain villages, modern resorts and workaday towns. The region's eventful history is reflected in its numerous remains of settlements, temples and fortifications founded by Phoenicians, colonized by Carthaginians and occupied by Rome, most notably **Nora**, once an important centre, its ruins now picturesquely spread out over a promontory in the Golfo di Cágliari. The lively inland resort of **Pula** is the main centre for this area, including **Santa Margherita di Pula**, one of Sardinia's most luxurious holiday enclaves. For swimming, however, you'd do better to continue to **Chia** and beyond, where broad, dune-backed beaches stretch south as far as **Capo Spartivento**. The craggy, undeveloped **Costa del Sud** runs west from here, a highly scenic string of tranquil creeks and coves studded with Pisan and Spanish watchtowers.

The western side of this region is still known as **Sulcis**, a name originally given to it by the Carthaginians, who established their main base on the island of **Sant'Antíoco**. The eponymous town here is packed with interest, not least the Punic remains at the top of the town and the nearby Christian catacombs. Sant'Antíoco and the neighbouring isle of **San Pietro** are among the area's most appealing destinations, bustling in summer, serene at any other time, and supplied with some excellent restaurants.

Historically, the region's importance was due mainly to the mining of ores and minerals, which continues to play a prominent role in Sardinia's economy today. The industry was given a boost by Mussolini, who, in his drive for Italian self-sufficiency, founded the inland mining town of **Carbónia**, just below another ancient Carthaginian settlement on **Monte Sirai**, whose hilltop site enjoys stunning views over sea and mountain.

The **Iglesiente** territory to the north shows more evidence of mineworks, often in a poignant state of abandon, especially around **Iglésias**, the main inland centre of these parts, which retains an attractive old core. A short distance north of here, the Roman **Témpio di Antas**, owes its fine state of preservation to its remote valley location, while some of Sardinia's choicest **beaches** lie to the west, where the **Pan di Zúccero** outcrop sprouts dramatically out of the sea.

Southwestern Sardinia is a compact region, and much of it can be visited on excursions from Cágliari. But with so much to see, it deserves a more prolonged tour, with hotel stops in the towns and villages en route. Although the area includes several well-developed holiday resorts, **accommodation** can be scarce, and you'd do well to plan your itinerary and make reservations,

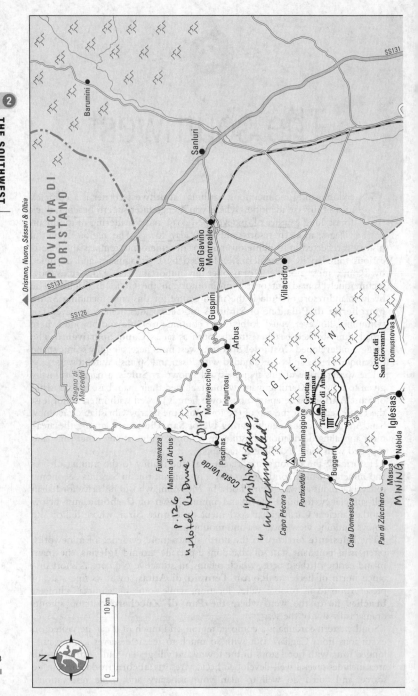

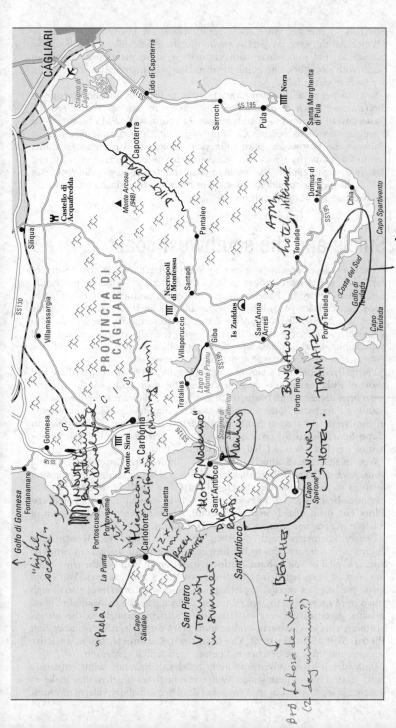

especially in summer when some seaside places are booked up months in advance. All the same, as long as you're mobile and flexible, you will usually manage to find somewhere with vacancies – we've mentioned options in places with not much else going for them, but which are useful last resorts if everywhere else is full.

You can get to all the main attractions in the area by **public transport**, though most beach destinations are only served in summer, if at all. ARST **buses** cover Pula (for Nora) and the southern coast, while FMS buses provide a regular service to Iglésias, Carbónia and Sant'Antíoco, running as far as Calasetta and Portovesme, both embarcation points for San Pietro. FS **trains** run to Carbónia and Iglésias (for Carbónia, change at Villamassárgia). Cycling is a good way to explore the southern coast and its islands: you can rent bikes at Pula, Sant'Antíoco and Carloforte. For more information on bus and train connections, see Travel details on p.127.

Sulcis and the southwest coast

Pockets of development have not seriously detracted from the beauty of Sardinia's **southwest coast**, while its hinterland remains practically untouched. Settled by Phoenicians as early as the ninth century BC, this was once the territory of **Sulcis**, an important link in their network of trade routes which extended to France and the Iberian peninsula. The area was also a valuable source of minerals, extracted with the help of the enslaved local population. Carthaginians and Romans followed in the wake of the Phoenicians, all keen to exploit the lucrative mines.

Thirty-five kilometres south of Cágliari on the SS195, the large village and resort of **Pula** makes an obvious first stop, as the main centre for the area and just a brief distance from **Nora**, the region's most important archeological site. South of Pula, swish hotels and more modest campsites lie amid thick swathes of eucalyptus and pine at **Santa Margherita di Pula**. From here down to **Capo Spartivento**, the coast is an almost unbroken succession of beaches, the best of which lie around **Chia**, 18km south of Pula.

West of the cape, Sardinia's southernmost littoral, the **Costa del Sud** is a visual feast, the jagged shore sheltering a few patches of sand and a profusion of rocks to swim from. On the far side of **Capo Teulada**, you'll find more extensive beaches and a flurry of tourist activity around the resort of **Porto Pino**. The main inland centre is **Santadi**, where there's a small museum of folklore and impressive caves nearby at **Is Zuddas**.

Twenty kilometres north of Porto Pino, a well-preserved Romanesque church at Tratalias testifies to the former importance of this quiet town. The former capital of Sulcis, **Sant'Antíoco**, stands on an island of the same name just west of here, tethered to Sardinia's coast by a road causeway. You could spend the best part of a day exploring the various relics of its long past, though you'd need more time to explore the local coastline, with its handful of good beaches. Alternatively, you could continue straight through to the island's northern port of **Calasetta**, embarcation point for the smaller island of **San Pietro**, 5km across the strait. The main town, **Carloforte**, has an attractive seafront, and there are beaches and beauty spots within easy reach.

Both islands have evolved into lively holiday destinations, while remaining fairly relaxed out of peak season. With some first-class beaches, they make an enticing place to hide out for a couple of days, free of holiday villages or tourist hype. If you're thinking of staying, it's worth venturing outside the islands' main towns for the small selection of **hotels** and **campsites** next to the sea. If you're really stuck, there's usually more availability at **Portoscuso**, an off-putting industrialized town on the Sardinian mainland, though once you're past the chimneys, its fishing harbour and centre are quite agreeable. The large town of **Carbónia**, 10km inland, is equally unprepossessing, but its time-frozen Fascist architecture has curiosity value, and there are a couple of good museums, one of them showing finds from the nearby Carthaginian site on **Monte Sirai**. A visit to the remains of this once impregnable fortress is highly recommended, affording stupendous views out to the islands and inland.

ARST **buses** from Cágliari run every hour or so along the coast to Pula, some continuing on to Chia, then turning inland towards **Teulada**. There's a less frequent service along the Costa del Sud in summer only, and a summer bus connection between Teulada and **Porto di Teulada**, its tiny coastal off-shoot, where there's a beach and a useful campsite and agriturismo. Carbónia is on the **train** line from Cágliari, though the station is a local bus ride from the centre. Carbónia, Sant'Antíoco and Portoscuso are served by regular FMS **buses** from Cágliari; the bus to Sant'Antíoco continues to Calasetta, from which frequent **ferries** cross the short distance to San Pietro. Carloforte is also linked by equally frequent ferries with Portoscuso (or rather its port, Portovesme) on the Sardinian mainland, the most convenient crossing for travellers to or from Cágliari, Carbónia and Iglésias.

The road to Pula

The road south of Cágliari runs past and over the extensive complex of lagoons known as the **Stagno di Cágliari**. Picked over by flamingos and swooping cormorants, the brown, occasionally choppy waters also attract legions of fishermen, often perched in rows over the bridges, spinning their curious hand-made reels. The peaceful scene disappears as the smoking towers of the refinery at **Macchiareddu** hove into view on the banks of the lagoon. Undeterred by its ominous presence, a small beach resort has grown up at **Lido di Capoterra**. The only reason to stop here, however, would be to dine at its renowned fish **restaurant**, *Su Cardiga e Su Schironi*. Close enough to Cágliari to draw in the crowds, it's reckoned to be one of the island's best, though prices remain refreshingly low: a smallish but exquisite *risotto alla pescatora*, for example, costs just €8, and other fish dishes are €3–4 per *etto* (100g). Treat the menu as a guide only: fish are available according to what's in season, and can be prepared in any way (☎070.71.652; closed Mon, also Sun eve in winter, but open daily in Aug).

The village of **Capoterra** itself, 5km inland, is the starting point for the one very minor road running through the range of mountains, some of them rising to over 1000m, that occupies the interior here. It's a laborious drive, mostly on a stony surface, running some 40km to Santadi (see p.107), but it allows you to glimpse the wildest and remotest part of the Iglesiente mountains, forested with oak and thick with coloured and scented maquis – especially evocative in winter or spring.

A few kilometres down a dirt road from Capoterra, a protected wildlife zone has been established around the woody slopes of **Monte Arcosu**, destined to become the core of a nature reserve to provide a sheltered habitat for the *cervo sardo* (deer), now an unusual sight in Sardinia though common before the twentieth century. Other rare wildlife includes martens, wildcats and boars, not to mention kestrels, buzzards, hawks and even golden eagles. Where the granite slopes are not forested with holm oaks, there is a thick mantle of Mediterranean *macchia* which is crossed by waymarked paths. There's a Visitor Centre (sporadically open) with information on walks; if you want a guide, contact *Cooperativa Il Caprifoglio* (Mon–Fri ☎070.968.714, otherwise ☎347.346.3546), or the local WWF branch (☎070.670.308).

Ten kilometres south from Lido di Capoterra, the vast oil- and chemical refinery at **Sarroch** is the biggest industrial complex on the whole island, its malevolent tangle of pipes, container drums and flaming chimneys covering an enormous area that nudges into the village itself, filling the air with acrid odours. The villagers – most of them dependent on the works for their livelihood – don't complain, but it's a zone for anyone else to rush through with windows wound up. All the same, if you're really stuck for somewhere to stay near Pula (not uncommon in summer), there are a pair of comfortable and economical little **hotels** here, the *Lanterna Verde*, on the main road leading towards the sea (☎070.900.396; ❷), and *Villa Rosa*, Via Cágliari 53 (☎070.900.171; ❷; no credit cards); both have restaurants.

Pula

Seven kilometres past the smoking chimneys and foul air of Sarroch, the large inland village of **PULA** has become something of a tourist centre thanks to its proximity to the seaside archeological site at Nora (see p.103–104). Apart from its hotels and restaurants, the village makes an essential stop, either before or after a visit to Nora, on account of its **Museo Archeologico** (daily: 9am–8pm; €5.50, including site at Nora), signposted at Corso Vittorio Emanuele 67. The one large room here is mainly dedicated to the digs at Nora; as you enter, you'll see a model of the site as it would have appeared in the first century AD. Although the display is small – the most significant finds are in the archeological museum at Cágliari – the plans and explanations (in Italian and English) help put the site into context. Most of the items were fished out of the sea, notably the cups, glassware and pottery fragments, variously from Phoenician, Iberian, Greek, Gallic and Punic sources. A room upstairs is given over to temporary exhibitions relating to Nora.

Practicalities

Hourly ARST **buses** connect Cágliari with Pula, of which two a day continue to Nora in summer. If you're not on one of these and want to go straight to the site, get off the bus at Pula's Via Corinaldi, from which there are six departures daily (fewer in winter) on local services #1 or #2 (buy tickets on board) – alternatively walk or hitch the four kilometres. Coming by bus from the south, get off at Pula's Municipio just up from the museum, for the same local bus service.

Pula has a couple of **hotels**, including the very cheap *Quattro Mori*, a one-star *locanda* at Via Cágliari 10 (☎070.920.9124; ❶; no credit cards), whose nine simple rooms include singles with and without private bath, and doubles all with shared facilities. Further along the same street at Via Cágliari 2, the slightly boxy rooms at the *Sandalyon* (☎070.920.9151; ❹) all have private bathrooms and come with TV and telephone; there's an outdoor pizzeria/ristorante, and breakfast is included in the price June–September. Other choices in the neighbourhood lie 3km away at Nora (see p.103).

There's a choice of **restaurants** in town, including the smartish *Eleonora* at Via Nora 35 (closed Wed in winter; no smoking), which has outdoor seating in a narrow courtyard, and, off the central Piazza del Pópolo, the less formal but similarly priced *Sa Macinera* (closed Mon in winter), a ristorante/pizzeria where you can also eat *al fresco* in summer. On Piazza del Pópolo, *Su Nuraghe* is a snack bar, café and pizzeria with tables outside (closed Thurs in winter), just across from *Crazy Art*, which offers wonderful **ice creams**, *frappés* and yoghurt concoctions (closed Oct–Easter). *Su Nuraghe* stays open late in the evenings, as does *Madrigal*, an Irish pub which also serves snacks, on Via XXIV Maggio.

An old villa on Piazza del Pópolo, Casa Frau, houses Pula's Pro Loco **tourist office** (℡070.924.5250, Ⓦwww.prolocopula.it; July–Sept daily 10am–1pm & 7–11pm, Oct–June Mon–Sat 9am–1pm & 4–7.30pm), and there's a summer-only kiosk with tourist information outside the Municipio and near the museum. The all-purpose private tourist office, Le Torri, is also a useful stop, near one of the Cágliari bus stops on the corner of Via Nora and Via Corinaldi (℡070.920.8373, Ⓦwww.agenzialetorri.com; Mon–Sat 9am–1pm & 5–8pm, June–Sept also Sun 9am–1pm). Apart from issuing general information on the locality, they rent out **cars, bicycles** and **motorbikes**, and also **apartments** in or around town, if you were thinking of staying a week or more in the area. Car rental rates are comparatively low (starting at €70 per day, or €180 for three days), and you can rent bikes for €10 a day, though you can rent bikes more cheaply (for about €8 per day, less in winter) at Serra (signed Biciclette Legnano) at Corso Vittorio Emanuele 68. **Change money** at Le Torri, or at the Banca di Sássari, Via delle Palme, which has a bancomat, or at the banks on Via Lamármora.

July and August see plenty of action in Pula's Piazza del Pópolo, with **concerts** and dances almost nightly and free art **exhibitions** in Casa Frau, while there's a programme of nightly **open-air films** at the Cine Arena, on Via Santa Croce (behind the Municipio off Corso Vittorio Emanuele), starting at 9pm. Entertainments are also organized at Nora's Roman theatre (see p.104).

Nora

Founded by the Phoenicians and settled later by Carthaginians and Romans, **Nora**, four kilometres south of Pula on the Capo di Pula promontory, was abandoned after the third century AD. Now partly submerged under the sea, the site requires some imagination to grasp its former scale, but its position on the tip of a peninsula gives it plenty of atmosphere, overlooked by a defensive tower built by the Spanish in the sixteenth century.

The Phoenicians who first settled the site in the ninth and eighth centuries BC were clearly drawn by its strategic location, dominating the Golfo di Cágliari from its southwestern approaches. Controlled by Carthage from the sixth century BC, the city expanded to become the biggest urban centre on the island, a position it retained after it was taken by the Romans in 238 BC, under whom it became the provincial capital for the whole island. However, the gradual incursion of the sea meant that the site became increasingly precarious, and the arrival on the scene of the Vandals in the fifth century AD led to its abandonment.

The archeological site

Today, a good part of the **site** (daily: April–Oct 9am–1hr before sunset; €5.50, including Pula museum) is submerged beneath the sea. As for the rest, crashed arches and walls give some idea of the original size of the buildings, but little has survived above ground level apart from a few solitary Roman columns. Evidence of the long Carthaginian dominion is particularly scanty, despite the intense commercial activity suggested by the foundations of warehouses and the contents of tombs dug up here, a slight elevation holds the ruins of a temple dedicated to Tanit, goddess of fertility. Other pre-Roman remnants, among them a Phoenician inscription featuring the first recorded use of the name Sardinia, can be viewed in Cágliari's archeological museum. Most of the remainder belongs to the Roman period, including, near the Spanish watchtower, a temple, with a single column still standing, and a small theatre – much reconstructed, but splendidly sited, and still used for concerts. Further on, four upright columns mark a patrician's villa, surrounded by one- and two-room dwellings. The villa's well-preserved black, white and ochre-coloured mosaic floors are among Nora's most arresting sights; the opulence of their simple but splendid designs – taken together with the town's four sets of baths and good network of roads with their drainage system still intact – suggests something of the importance of this Roman outpost. Free **tours** of the excavations, in Italian, take place whenever there are enough people to make a group and the guides are available; otherwise you can get a pretty good picture by wandering about under your own steam, aided by diagrams and bilingual explanations.

One memorable way to experience the site is to attend one of the **evening performances** taking place in Nora's Roman theatre in July and August. The annual season, entitled *La Notte dei Poeti* (ⓦ www.lanottedeipoeti.it), features poetry readings, theatre, musical events, and occasionally dance on the theme of the spoken word. Tickets cost around €16–20 and can be bought at the gate, but it's better to book in advance: contact the tourist offices in Cágliari or Pula, or Pula's *Le Torri* agency (see p.103), or call ⓣ070.270.577.

Around Nora

Immediately north of the archeological site, the exquisite sandy bay of **Spiaggia di Nora** is lapped by crystal-clear water, though in season this can rapidly transform into day-tripper hell. Following the bay north for 500 metres or so, you'll come to another beach at **Su Guventeddu**, which may be less congested. Behind Nora's beach stands the rather ordinary-looking **church of Sant'Efísio**, built by Vittorini monks in the eleventh century on the site of the saint's martyrdom. Efisius, a Roman soldier of the third century who converted to Christianity, was credited with stemming an outbreak of plague in 1656, since when the church has been the ultimate destination of Cágliari's Mayday procession (see p.82). A new facade robs the front of the church of much of its character, but the inside is more pleasing: a narrow nave lined with thick pillars and round arches.

South of the archeological site (to the right of the entrance), a placid circle of water, the **Laguna di Nora**, shelters a small nature reserve and, on a rocky causeway, a learning centre with an **aquarium** and exhibition rooms illustrating and explaining the local ecology. School parties and other groups are guided on a ninety-minute tour (currently June–Sept daily at 10am, 11.30am, 5pm & 6.30pm; €4). The Laguna is also a monitoring centre for dolphins, whales and turtles, hence the section dedicated to these creatures in the centre. Supervised snorkelling and canoe trips on the lagoon are also offered, again with the primary aim of exploring the local eco-systems. In winter the place only opens for bookings (ⓣ070.920.9544, ⓦ www.lagunadinora.it).

Practicalities

If you want to **eat** in the area, *L'Approdo* is a pizzeria/ristorante with an outdoor terrace opposite the church of Sant'Efísio – a touristy place, but useful for a snack. For a good-quality, moderately priced meal head for *Su Guventeddu*, a small pensione a kilometre up the road back to Pula. At just a hundred metres from the beach of the same name, this makes a good place **to stay**: the atmosphere is relaxed and friendly, and the rooms are clean and modern, all with TV, telephone and private bath (℡070.920.9092, ✉gio.mon@tiscalinet.it; ❹). Buses #1 and #2, connecting Nora with Pula, stop directly outside. The nearest **campsites** are in Santa Margherita di Pula (see below), on the #2 bus route.

Santa Margherita di Pula

The locality of **SANTA MARGHERITA DI PULA** constitutes a southern Sardinian version of the Costa Smeralda, though marginally more downmarket and decidedly less picturesque. Like its northern counterpart, this exclusive retreat has no history prior to the 1960s, owing its existence primarily to the presence, just outside Pula, of the luxury *Is Molas* golf course and a cluster of equally swanky **hotels**, discreetly concealed among the trees and accessible from the main SS195 coast road. Catering largely to groups, their prices will put off most individual travellers who haven't pre-booked; however, if you fancy a splurge, most offer quite good-value low-season discounts. The biggest and flashiest of them is the *Forte Village* complex, made up of separate four- and five-star hotels spread over a huge area and under a single management, and equipped with pools, sports facilities, shops and restaurants (late-March to Oct; ℡070.92.171, ⊛www.fortevillageresort.com; ❾). If you're in the luxury stakes, however, you might prefer the more select *Flamingo* (April–Oct; ℡070.920.8361, ⊛www.hotelflamingo.it; ❾), where you can stay in rooms in the main building or in detached villas; the half-board requirement bumps up the price. At the other end of the scale are the area's two **campsites**, next to each other on the minor seafront road beyond the pinewoods: the one nearer to Nora is *Flumendosa* (℡070.920.8364), while *Cala d'Ostia* (April–Sept; ℡070.921.470, ✉cop.tur@tin.it) lies closer to the wide sandy beach of the same name. Bus #2 from Pula and Nora stops right outside the sites. You don't need to be rich **to eat** around here: try the *Urru* bar-restaurant, on the road between the SS195 and the seafront.

Chia and around

Like Santa Margherita di Pula, **CHIA** is a dispersed locality without any centre as such. The interesting bit lies at the end of the minor road signposted "Torre di Chia" that branches left off the main SS195, 10km beyond Santa Margherita. You'll soon see the **Pisan watchtower** after which the place is named; it stands above one of the best **beaches** on the southern coast, a perfect sandy arc with a small lagoon behind. Around the tower have been found the remains of the fourth-century-BC Phoenician and Carthaginian town of **Bythia**, mentioned in Ptolemy's *Geography*, but never attaining the same importance as Nora or Tharros. Traces of the settlement were uncovered during a storm in 1933, including some tombs and parts of a temple probably dedicated to the Egyptian deity Bes, but systematic excavation has revealed little of importance. A climb up the tower affords marvellous views south down the coast, taking in a range of inviting beaches. Just behind the Chia beach, there's a handy three-star **campsite**, *Torre Chia* (June–Sept; ℡070.923.0054, ⊛www.campeggiotorrechia.it), equipped with a tennis court and also small villas for up to four people, available for rent for €85–115 in peak season. Immediately south of Chia, the immense beach of **Sa Colonia** makes an irresistible spot for a dip, and there's the *Gabbiano* **pizzeria/ristorante** behind; the same family has six comfortable rooms to rent nearby at *Sa Colonia* (Easter–Sept; ℗070.923.0001), where obligatory half-board comes to €70 per person, less out of peak season.

A series of lagoons and sandy bays unfurls as you head south from Chia, right up to the point at **Capo Spartivento**. There are a couple of **hotels** here – the last for a while – including the relatively cheap *Su Giudeu* (℗070.923.0260, ℉070.923.0002; ❻); comfortable and modern, it requires half- or full-board in summer (and non-residents can eat in the **restaurant** here). The road to the cape ends at the last good beaches on this stretch of coast, backed by unshaded car parks which charge between June and September (€3–4 for the day).

The Costa del Sud MAP p. 98

West of Capo Spartivento, the road runs briefly inland, then climbs and swoops for some 20km along the largely deserted **Costa del Sud**, one of Sardinia's most scenic drives. To the north, groves of olive and eucalyptus give way to a backdrop of bare mountains, while the jagged coast of the **Golfo di Teulada** presents a procession of indented bays punctuated by lonely Spanish watchtowers. It can be a rewarding hike, though walkers will need to follow much of the route by road, making it something of a grind. Much of the time, too, the sea is difficult or impossible to reach, though swimming is possible from rocks or the few strips of sand along the way. **Tuerredda,** a stop on the ARST bus route, is one of the more populated bathing spots, with parking facilities and a bar/pizzeria. Next, the road skirts round **Malfatano**, a deep bay providing shelter for boats and some scraps of beach. A right turn here leads to the jetty and beaches of **Porto Teulada**, an anchorage for fishing boats and pleasure craft, where you can have *panini* and beers at a kiosk in summer, or a seafood meal at *Da Gianni*. In summer you can go diving or rent dinghies, canoes or pedalos from the port, which is also the embarkation point for a tour by yacht of the coast as far as Capo Teulada, Sardinia's southernmost point at the far end of the Golfo di Teulada; call the operators ℗347.943.0139 for details.

Beyond Porto Teulada, there are alluring beaches at and around **Tramatzu**, and a well-situated and popular **campsite**, *Porto Tramatzu* (℗070.928.3027), where you can hire self-catering caravans for the night (€53 for a two-berther in peak season). There's a much smaller inland site at *Agriturismo Fenu*, signposted off the Porto Teulada turn-off about a kilometre up a driveable track, where, apart from the camping facilities, there are six self-catering **rooms** in a peaceful, rustic location (℗349.360.2181; ❹; no credit cards). Prices drop considerably outside peak season, and **riding** is also offered here.

Teulada and around

Back on the main SS195, a right turn leads to the small inland town of **TEULADA**, its drowsy air enlivened by odd pieces of sculpture dotted around its streets and squares. Sculptors come from all over the world to compete in the town's annual exhibition; they're given a block of local marble, granite or trachyte in June, when the theme – usually locally-inspired – is announced. The pieces are finished by September, and then placed around the village. Other than sculpture, Teulada is distinguished for its **handicrafts**, available for sale in various shops in the centre, in particular embroidery, tapestries, carpets, cork objects and terracotta pipes. The only **place to stay** in town is the *Sebera*, on Via San Francesco, which has ten simple rooms and a restaurant (℗070.927.0876, ℉070.927.0020; ❷); in August there's a ten-day minimum stay and a requirement to take half- or full-board (half-board €43 per person in peak season). You can snack at the *Capolinea* bar on Via Cágliari, which offers **Internet access**. If you need cash, the nearby *Banco di Sardegna* has a **bancomat**.

West of Teulada, the SS195 loops inland of the cliffy coast and Sardinia's southernmost tip, **Capo Teulada**, which is occasionally used for military exercises and effectively inaccessible. A right turn at the village of **Sant'Anna Arresi** (the last stop on the bus route from Cágliari) brings you to the pinewoods, lagoons and beaches of **Porto Pino**. It's a favourite spot for day-trippers from the towns and villages nearby – the shady picnic spots and dazzling sand beaches can get a bit claustrophobic, but the place is less busy on weekdays outside August. Right behind the main beach, there's a **campsite,** *Sardegna*, with bungalows available (May–Sept; ☎0781.967.013).

Santadì and around

Some 8km north of Sant'Anna Arresi, the village of **Giba** stands at a crossroads just below the **Lago di Monte Pranu**. Like almost all Sardinia's lakes, this was artificially created, formed by a barrage on the River Palmas. You can see something of it from the track leading north from the main crossroads at Giba, but it's hardly worth the detour, since the route is slow and unsignposted, presenting plenty of opportunity to get lost. The only reason you might want to linger in the village is the *Antica Locanda Rosella* on Via Piemonte (☎0781.964.029; ❸), a family-run **restaurant** (closed Wed in winter) with rustic touches, and twenty well-equipped **rooms** upstairs.

A right turn at the Giba junction leads 10km east to **SANTADÌ**, an agricultural centre on the banks of the Rio Mannu. The otherwise nondescript village is famous for its *matrimonio maureddino*, a re-enactment of a Mauretanian wedding on the first Sunday of August, said to derive from an African colony here during the Roman era; contact the **Pro Loco** on Via Veneto for details (Mon, Wed & Thurs 4–9.30pm; ☎0781.955.178). The village also has a couple of small museums worth a glance: the **Museo Archeologico** on Via Umberto (Tues–Sat 9am–1pm & 4–7pm, 3–6pm in winter; €2.55), a roomful of various finds dug up in the area, and, on nearby Via Mazzini, the **Museo Etnográfico Sa Domu Antiga** (same times, same ticket), a grand name for a small house typical of the peasant dwellings of the Sulcis region, filled with a motley assortment of traditional items relating to rural life, including a loom, bread-making equipment and agricultural tools. Ask at either of these places about excursions into the surrounding area organized by the Cooperative Fillirea, which also runs the museums; the tours focus specifically on local history, wildlife, rural culture and gastronomy.

Is Zuddas and Pantaleo

A more engaging attraction can be found 8km south of Santadi, off the SP70: the **Is Zuddas** grottoes (April–Sept daily 9am–noon & 2.30–6pm; Oct–March Mon–Sat tours at noon & 4pm, Sun 9am–noon & 2.30–5pm; €6.50). Hour-long guided tours through the five main chambers of this cave system reveal how the slow work of millennia has created stalagmites to resemble frozen cascades, organ pipes and Walt Disney characters; the delicate white spiky aragonite, which, in apparent contradiction of the laws of gravity, grows here in every direction, is especially lovely. The relative coolness of the caves (16°C) makes them a welcome respite from a baking sun, and an English-speaking tour guide is usually on hand.

Travelling east out of Santadi, following signs for *Bosco di Pantaleo*, after seven kilometres you'll come to **Pantaleo**, a cluster of buildings in the midst of a small wood. The main attraction here is the *Su Commeo* **restaurant**, housed in an old coal-processing plant, and specializing in local mountain dishes including roast or grilled pork. In July and August, it's open daily, otherwise it's closed Tuesday, but in winter the restaurant opens for lunch only, and even then you should ring first to make sure (℡0781.955.822; no credit cards). You could always drop by on the way through the mountains to or from Capoterra (see p.101): the dirt road begins shortly after Pantaleo.

Montessu

West of Santadi and 3km north of the village of Villaperuccio, off the SP293 Giba–Siliqua road, is the necropolis of **Montessu** (daily 9am–1pm & 4–8pm, 2–5pm in winter; €5), one of Sardinia's most important prenuraghic burial sites. Hewn out of a natural amphitheatre of trachyte rock by people of the Ozieri culture of the fourth and third millennia BC, the forty-odd tombs – popularly called *domus de janas*, or "fairy-houses" – show diverse forms. The square openings either in the top or sides were originally sealed with stone doors (one is still in place); four have wide canopies, behind which circular areas are marked out by stones, probably used for funerary rites. Niches and small annexes in several of the clean-cut chambers are pointed out on the hour-long guided tour: look out for the sacred symbols cut into the walls – graffiti, reliefs and incisions linked to earth cults, mostly representing the mother goddess and bull god. The best are visible in the **Tomba delle Spirali**, showing a cluster of alien-looking spirals, possibly the "eyes" of the goddess, and the **Tomba delle Corna**, with multiple horn shapes.

Linked to the same complex is a group of **menhirs** up to five metres tall situated in the open country about a kilometre south of Villaperuccio, in the **Terrazzu** district. Associated with obscure fertility rites, the stark monoliths are conspicuous landmarks amid the flat cultivated fields.

Tratalias

Heading west, a short diversion from the SS195 Giba-to-Sant'Antíoco road brings you to **Tratalias**, once an important centre in the area, as attested by its Romanesque church of **Santa Maria** (Mon–Tues 9am–2pm, Wed–Sun 9am–2pm & 4–8pm, reduced times in winter), which was consecrated in 1213 as cathedral for the entire Sulcis region. The transfer of this status from Sant'Antíoco was part of a general move inland from exposed coastal sites throughout this period of increasing insecurity, and helps to account for the church's excellent state of preservation. The building lies in the semi-abandoned Vecchio Borgo, the original nucleus of the town before the creation of Lago di Monte Pranu forced its inhabitants to relocate to the newer town a little way north. The church fuses Pisan and French styles, with a small rose window and, curiously, a section of an external staircase at the top of its simple square facade. There's more of the staircase visible inside, where the thick columns and plain bricks are topped by a wooden roof, though all the finery has long since disappeared. Elsewhere in the Vecchio Borgo, a few palazzi near the church preserve their medieval lines, but most of the historic buildings have disappeared.

Sant'Antíoco

The island of **Sant'Antíoco** is joined to the Sardinian mainland by a three-kilometre isthmus that meets the coast 8km west of Tratalias. This causeway has existed since Carthaginian times, though the last section now runs over a modern bridge, which dwarfs the adjacent remains of its Roman predecessor. The waters of the **Stagno di Santa Caterina** on the right are the occasional habitat of flamingos, and you may also spot cormorants and herons. The lagoon is associated with the local legend of two lovers, a monk and a nun, who, attempting to elope to the island, were turned to stone in a visitation of divine disapproval. The petrified figures – rocks or *faraglioni* – are in fact prenuraghic menhirs, thought to have been associated with fertility rites. Popularly named **Su Para** and **Sa Mongia** ("the monk" and "the nun"), the pair are stranded in the middle of an open field: take a side track on the left just after crossing the bridge to view them.

The port area of **Sant'Antíoco town** lies at the end of the new bridge, a low-key harbour for yachts, fishing vessels and freighters. Most of the action, however, is to be found north and west of here towards the historical centre in the upper town, for which you should turn right after the bridge and continue

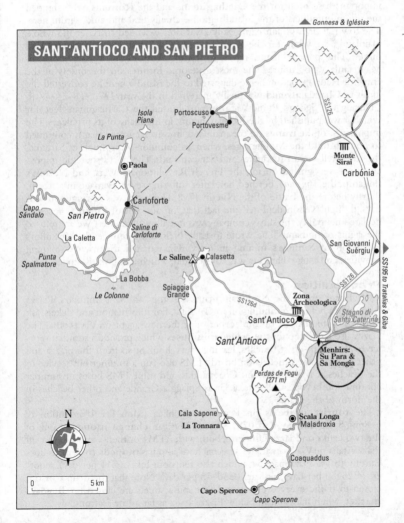

along Via Nazionale, which becomes Via Roma, Corso Vittorio Emanuele and Via Regina Margherita, the long axis interspersed by piazzas Repubblica, Italia and Umberto. All the historical sites lie at the top of the town, at the end of Via Regina Margherita. The SS126 continues northwest from here towards Calasetta; to reach the island's southern zone, turn left soon after the bridge (signposted *spiagge*). The road south follows the coast past bays and beaches before swinging over to the island's rocky western shore; only primitive tracks cross the hilly interior.

Some history

Founded around the eighth century BC, the core of Sant'Antíoco's upper town has been continuously inhabited since **Phoenician** times. As a defensible anchorage commanding the whole of Sardinia's southwest coast, it was an important base both for the **Carthaginians** and the **Romans**, who shipped the mining products of the inland region – chiefly lead and zinc – from here. The town's Carthaginian name, Sulki, was later extended to cover the whole mainland area, while for the Romans, it was Plumbea, after the nearby lead mines. The present name refers to **Saint Antiochus**, a slave born in Mauretania who endured the most gruesome tortures on the orders of the emperor Hadrian, before being deported to the island where he converted the locals to Christianity and was finally martyred in the year 127.

During the Second Punic War, the port hosted the Carthaginian fleet, for which it was punished by the Roman victors, losing many of its privileges. The importance of the **mines** on the mainland, however, ensured that it continued to flourish until the Middle Ages, when, in common with much of Sardinia, the town fell victim to pirates and Saracen raids. The port's strategic importance was recognized during the French Revolutionary Wars, and **Nelson's flagship**, the *Vanguard*, berthed here after suffering severe damage in a storm, shortly before the Battle of the Nile in 1798. The vessel was re-rigged in four days, though Nelson deplored the fact that, on account of Sardinia's recently declared neutrality, the ship's company was not allowed ashore. "We are refused the rights of humanity," he wrote to Lady Nelson. More recently, Mussolini's expansion of Sardinia's mining industry reinvigorated the town's shipping activities, and a new harbour was constructed, which is still in use today.

Practicalities

FMS **buses** from the Sardinian mainland stop on Sant'Antíoco's Piazza Repubblica before continuing on to Calasetta. For information and tickets, ask in the *Sanitari* chemist on the corner or at the newsagent on Via Roma. The piazza also has a stop for the orange **minibuses** which provide a summer service to the south-coast beaches, leaving every hour or so from the piazza and other stops in town (tickets on board). FMS also run a summer bus service to the beaches at Maladroxia and Coaquaddus, and some FMS buses in summer continue on beyond Calasetta as far as Spiaggia Grande and other beaches in the north of the island.

The **tourist office** is on Piazza Repubblica (Mon–Fri 10am–noon & 5–8pm, Sat 10am–noon; ☏0781.82.031). You can **change money** at one of the two banks on Piazza Umberto, both with ATMs, or there's another just off Piazza Italia on Via Roma. The *Moderno* hotel also has **mopeds to rent**, as does Euromoto, Via Nazionale 57, which also rents out bikes (€11 per day), scooters (€26–50 per day) and cars (€50–75 per day). Note that the main Corso is closed to traffic every evening, and that some streets are closed for Tuesday's **market**, when stalls spread below Piazza Italia as far as the seafront.

Accommodation

At Via Nazionale 82, a few steps away from the tourist office, lies the town's only cheapish **hotel**, the small *Moderno* (T0781.83.105, Wweb.tiscali.it /albergomoderno; ❹). Further up the street, at Corso Vittorio Emanuele 32, *Hotel del Corso* (T0781.800.265, Wwww.hoteldelcorso.it; ❺) is fancier and has a panoramic roof-terrace. In the upper town, at the far end of the town's main axis, there's the somewhat dowdy *Eden* (T & F0781.840.768; ❹), right next to the church of Sant'Antíoco on Piazza Parrocchia, and convenient for the museums and archeological site. For more inspiring choices elsewhere on the island, within a shortish drive or bus-ride from town, see p.113.

Eating, drinking and nightlife

The rich choice of restaurants and bars in town makes up for their sparsity elsewhere on the island, and Sant'Antíoco's streets are a-buzz with amblers and scooters on most evenings. Some of the best **restaurants** are on Lungomare Vespucci, a few minutes' walk from Via Nazionale – for example, *Da Ignazio* (closed Sun in winter) and *Del Passeggero* (closed Thurs in winter), both of which offer quality meals – mainly seafood – at moderate-to-expensive prices. Of the numerous **pizzerias** lining Via Nazionale and Via Roma, the bamboo-roofed garden restaurant attached to the *Moderno* hotel at Via Nazionale 82 is one of the most popular, as is the *Pizza House 2*, round the corner in Via Toscana (closed Mon Oct–June), and *Su Giuali*, Via Nazionale 56, both with the regular range of pizzas, plus pastas and other fast food. For a twist on the pizza theme, seek out *Caligola*, on Via Garibaldi (off Piazza Umberto), where the decor is cod-Roman and the pizzas have names such as *Colosseo* and *Messalina*. Despite the gimmickry, the pizzas are good, and you can eat at pavement tables in summer (closed Wed in winter). **Snacks** are available from the bars on Piazza Italia, though for ices, chocolate croissants and good coffee, the *Bar Nuovo Sport* on Corso Vittorio Emanuele is unbeatable. For late **drinks**, *Pierre-Pub* and *Arizona*, both on Corso Vittorio Emanuele, are perennially popular.

Summer sees a full programme of evening entertainments, including **concerts** in July and August on Piazza Umberto and Piazza Italia, and **open-air films** at the *Cinema in Laguna*, just below Piazza Repubblica on Lungomare Vespucci, starting at 9.45pm. Most people, however, content themselves with the slow promenade through the centre of town, eating ice creams and pausing at the many pavement bars along the way. The biggest date on the island's calendar is the **Festa di Sant'Antíoco**, taking place around the second Sunday after Easter; this prolonged four-day affair features traditional songs, poetry recitations and dancing, ending in a procession to the sea and fireworks.

The Town

At the top of Via Regina Margherita, the **church of Sant'Antíoco** makes a good place to begin a tour of the old town. Hidden behind the dilapidated facade of a bishop's palace, the Romanesque construction dates from the twelfth century, and is built over Christian catacombs. Near the entrance to the church, look out for a statue of the saint himself, who was interred in the catacombs – a second burial, after his miraculous resurrection. The entrance to the **catacombs** (Mon–Sat 9am–noon & 3–6pm, also 7–9pm in summer, Sun 10–11am & 3–6pm; €2.50) is in the right transept. Early Christians enlarged these in the sixth century from five existing Carthaginian *hypogea* (underground vaults). Guides are on hand to tour the dark and dingy corridors, pitted with numerous low-ceilinged mini-chambers and graves in which authentic skeletons are displayed – the mortal remains of Christians buried in the eighth century – along with reproductions of ceramic objects unearthed during excavation, some of them of Byzantine origin. You'll also see the remains of a rare Byzantine tomb, and fragments of primitive frescoes.

One hundred metres down Via Regina Margherita, the small **Museo Archeologico** (daily 9am–1pm & 3.30–7pm; €2, or €6, including tophet, ethnographic museum, Forte Su Pisu and necropolis) shows a sample of the finds from the hilltop excavations, a tiny fraction of what is claimed to be one of the largest collections of Carthaginian ware outside Carthage itself. Most of the collection is currently stashed away out of view until a new on-site museum has been completed, but it's worth making a stop here for the few exhibits: mainly inscribed stelae, ceramics and items of jewellery found within the Punic necropolis, along with maps, diagrams and a twenty-minute video about the archeological site. The reproduction of a section of the tophet at one end of the room seems unnecessary, however, when the real thing lies just a few minutes away. To see this, cross the road and follow signs up Via Castello, a side road outside the church. On the way, you'll pass the **Forte Su Pisu** (also called the *Fortino Sabaudo*, or just *Castello*), part of a Piedmontese fortification built in 1812; three years later its garrison was massacred by corsairs. Beyond the tower is the main part of the *zona archeologica*, commanding a lofty view of the sea and Sardinian mainland. At the top of the site stand the meagre remains of the **Punic acropolis**, little more than a few truncated columns and the surviving blocks of what once must have been massive walls.

About 500m further north, another hilltop holds Sant'Antíoco's extensive **Punic tophet** (same hours as museum; €2, or €6 including other sites), or burial site, dedicated to the supreme Phoenician god, Baal-Hammon, and the fertility goddess Tanit. The rocky, panoramic site is centred on the ruined walls of a sanctuary surrounded by a scattering of funerary urns, many of them modern reproductions. The original urns were long held to contain the ashes of the sacrificed first-born children of Phoenician and Punic aristo-crats, but this is now thought to have been Roman propaganda: the ashes, it seems, were the cremated remains of children still-born or dead from natu-ral causes, and of animals. At the summit of the site stand the massive square blocks of a Punic temple. Multilingual audio guides are planned to explain and identify different parts of the area, in the meantime you will either be shown around or supplied with a plan and commentary to be returned on exiting.

There's a quite different tone in the last museum on the circuit, located about 350m back towards the town on Via Necrópoli (signposted). The small but engrossing **Museo Etnográfico** (daily: April–Sept 9am–8pm; Oct to March 9am–1pm & 3–6pm; €1.50, or €6 including other sites) is little more than one capacious room crammed to the rafters with examples of rural cul-ture – tools, agricultural implements, craftwork, bread- and pasta-making equipment, most of them only recently superseded by modern machinery – all enthusiastically explained (in Italian) by a guide. The same guide can accompany you – or point the way to – a well-restored **Punic necropolis**, a little further down the street (same hours as ethnographic museum). The sub-terranean complex consists of numerous narrow chambers of one or two rooms, each accessible via a flight of steps. Well-informed guides explain (in Italian) the structure and use of the tombs, and steer visitors into the more accessible ones. Many of the chambers were taken over and inhabited by townsfolk in later centuries. Near the entrance to the necropolis, look out for the cannons dredged up from the sea and re-located here, belonging to a French man-of-war sunk in local waters in 1793.

The rest of the island

Outside town, the **island of Sant'Antíoco** mainly consists of *macchia*-covered slopes, with a few white houses dotted among the vineyards and scrub. Most of the **beaches** lie on the southern and eastern shores, accessible from the road running south out of town: take a left turn after 5km for some of the best, signposted **Maladroxia**. You'll soon come to an attractive cove fringed by a strip of sand, though there's more space further on at Maladroxia's enclosed bay. It's overlooked by one of the island's best budget **hotel** choices, the *Scala Longa*, with seven simple rooms (each with shower), a panoramic terrace, and a rather uninspired restaurant; you may be asked to take half- or full-board in summer (mid-April to mid-Sept; ☎0781.817.202; ❸).

The road ends at the bay. By continuing on the main road south, you'll curl round towards the island's highest point, **Perdas de Fogu** (271m), from which hikers can enjoy the distant views stretching out over the Sardinian mainland. Another turn-off to the left leads to one of Sant'Antíoco's best beaches at **Coaquaddus**, equipped with deckchairs and parasols to hire, and a couple of bars. Much of the coastline around here is high and rocky, especially at the southern tip of the island at **Capo Sperone**, occupied by a solitary watchtower and a luxury **hotel** – the family-orientated *Capo Sperone*, with bungalows around a central complex, a range of sports facilities including a pool, and fairly reasonable prices (June–mid-Sept; ☎0781.809.000, ☎0781.809.015; ❻). Non-guests can swim at the nearby beach, walking down from the tower.

Bathing spots on the remoter **western side** of the island are harder to find: the best is probably **Cala Sapone**, a sheltered inlet with swimming mainly from rocks. One of Sant'Antíoco's two **campsites** sits alongside, *Tonnara* (April–Sept; ☎0781.809.058, ✉tonnaracamping@tiscalinet.it), with caravans and chalets available. Beyond here the going gets slow as the road loses its asphalt, and access is easiest from the north.

Calasetta

At the island's northern extremity, Sant'Antíoco's second town and port, **CALASETTA,** lies 10km from the main town. The right-angled grid of lanes here holds little of interest, but a brief distance southwest, **La Salina** offers a dune-backed sand beach, or follow the crowds to **Spiaggia Grande**, a couple of kilometres further down, where umbrellas, deck-chairs and boats are available to rent, and a bar serves refreshments. The road becomes a dirt track soon after.

If you want to stay in Calasetta, the *FJBY* is the nearest **hotel** to the port at Via Solferino 83 (☎0781.88.444, ✉htl.fjby@tiscalinet.it; ❹), a modern, functional two-star which, in common with most hotels hereabouts, insists on half- or full-board in late-July and August (€68 and €75 per person respectively). Further out, the three-star *Cala di Seta* offers very reasonable rates at Via Regina Margherita 61 (☎0781.88.304, ⊛www.caladiseta.go.to; ❺), while the smaller *Bellavista* stands above a lovely arc of beach a short walk north of town (☎0781.88.211, ⊛www.calasettabellavista.it; ❸). All three hotels have **restaurants**; if you don't want to eat at one of these, *L'Approdo*, right on the port, specializes in seafood (closed Thurs in winter), or you can just have a drink and snack at the bar in front. The smaller of the island's two **campsites**, *Le Saline*, lies next to La Salina beach (☎0781.88.615, in winter ☎0781.88.489).

Moving on from Calasetta, Saremar **ferries** make the 5km hop to San Pietro roughly every hour (40min; €1.10–2.20 per person, depending on period and day – winter weekends are cheapest). If you're in a car in August, make sure you're here in good time, as you'll need to queue. From mid-July to mid-September, Delcomar ferries also make night-time crossings between Calasetta and Carloforte every 1–2 hours (€2.50 per person, €5 for a small car; buy tickets on board).

San Pietro

The dialect in **San Pietro** is pure Piedmontese, over two and a half centuries after the Savoyan king Carlo Emanuele III invited a colony of Ligurians to settle here in 1738. Originally from the town of Pegli, west of Genoa, the immigrants came from the island of Tabarka, near Tunisia, where they had scraped a precarious living as merchants and coral-gatherers since settling there in 1541. The newcomers were not left in peace for long, however: in 1793, San Pietro was occupied by French forces, and five years later it was the target of one of the last great corsair raids, when nearly a thousand of the Ligurians were abducted back to Tunisia and enslaved. The islanders eventually returned to San Pietro on payment of a hefty ransom by Vittorio Emanuele I in 1803. Ligurian elements remain in the local cuisine and dialect, and some of the buildings hark back to Genoan styles of architecture.

San Pietro today preserves a laid-back air, despite the boatloads of holidaymakers who flood the island every summer. While most visitors confine themselves to the only town, **Carloforte** (named after Carlo Emanuele), the rest of the island is well worth exploring. Although the island's eastern seaboard is not exactly enhanced by the prospect of Portoscuso's smoky industrial works on the Sardinian mainland opposite, the few beaches on the southern coast are pleasantly secluded, while the high western shore vaunts some exquisite panoramas as well as one or two great places for swimming and snorkelling. The cliffy terrain here provides sanctuary for a protected species of falcon, just as it did in former times – the names by which the island was known by the Carthaginians (Enosim) and the Romans (Accipitrum) both refer to the numbers of sparrowhawks that once dwelt here. The present name derives from a legend according to which Saint Peter washed up on the island after being

La Mattanza: San Pietro's tuna bloodbath

Though the annual tuna massacre is also enacted on Sant'Antioco (at Punta Maggiore, southwest of Calasetta), San Pietro's age-old rite of *La Mattanza* is a much bigger, bloodier affair. Nets are laid down as early as March, but the killing mainly takes place in May and June, when the tuna pass through the northern straits on their way to their mating grounds in the eastern Mediterranean. Channelled through a series of nets culminating in the **camera della morte**, or death-chamber, the fish are bludgeoned to death as the net is slowly raised.

The *Mattanza* – the word is from Spanish roots ("the killing") – has mixed **origins**. The methods are identical to those used at other places where the Ligurians settled, such as the Égadi Islands off Sicily's western tip, but there's also a strong Arab influence evident in the use of titles like *Raìs* (Arab for chief), referring to the coordinator of the operation. Although deplored by many for its brutality, the practice attracts crowds of spectators every season, and has even been appropriated as a selling-point by the tourist office. Even so, the gory details are understandably played down in San Pietro's numerous restaurants that serve tuna, the island's top speciality. You can learn about the customs and methods of the *Mattanza* – and see graphic photos – in Carloforte's Museo Cívico (see p.116).

shipwrecked (a claim made by dozens of other Mediterranean islands), subsequently teaching the locals new fishing techniques. The most famous kind of fishing performed on San Pietro now, however, is the annual slaughter of tuna fish, *La Mattanza*, which takes place in May and June (see box on p.114).

Arrival and information

A **bus service** links Carloforte with La Punta, Capo Sándalo and La Caletta, with a stop on Piazza Carlo Emanuele (tickets from Bar Cipollina, off the square on Corso Tagliafico). An ideal way to tour the island is by **bicycle** or **scooter**, for which you'll find a hire shop at Via Roma 18, Di.Be., offering scooters for €10 per hour or €35 for the day, and mountain bikes for €2 per hour, €10 per day; prices are halved outside July and August. To book a bike, and when the shop is closed, call ☏0781.854.392 or 333.461.5956. Alternatively, consider a **boat-tour** of San Pietro's coast: excursions taking about three hours depart from the port at 10.30am and 3pm daily (June–Sept), visiting all the most important grottoes and some secluded beaches. Tickets (€20 per person) can be bought from the white port-side caravan (☏0781.854.244). **Ferries** leave once or twice an hour either back to Calasetta or, for those moving on to the Sardinian mainland Portvesme, the port next to the industrial plant outside Portoscuso. Delcomar also runs a night ferry service to Calasetta (tickets on board). The Saremar ticket office is on Piazza Carlo Emanuele, next to the *Banca Commerciale Italiana*, which has an **ATM**.

Most of the island's facilities are located in Carloforte. Opposite the port, the main Piazza Carlo Emanuele III holds San Pietro's **tourist office** (June–Sept Mon–Sat 10am–noon & 3–9pm, Sun 10am–noon; ☏0781.854.009); there's also a kiosk on the quayside for new arrivals (April–Sept daily 9am–noon & 3–6pm). For general information on the town and island, visit the **websites** ⓦwww.carloforte.net, ⓦwww.carloforte.com and ⓦwww.carloforte.it, all packed with practical tips for walkers, wildlife enthusiasts and divers, as well as overviews of San Pietro's history and culture.

Accommodation

The most stylish of the only two **hotels** in Carloforte is the ornate, Art Nouveau *Hieracon* at Corso Cavour 62 (☏0781.854.028, ⓦwww.hotelhieracon.cjb.net; ❺), a few minutes' walk up from Piazza Carlo Emanuele. Some of the *Hieracon's* rooms have harbour views; at least half-board (at €67 per person per night) is required in peak season. The only alternative is the plain and friendly *California* near the lagoon at Via Cavallera 15, about ten minutes' walk from the port (☏0781.854.470, ⓔcalifornia.hotel@tiscalinet.it; ❻). If both are full and you want to stay in town, the main tourist office can provide a list of **rooms to rent** in and around Carloforte.

Elsewhere on the island, there are just five hotels, all slightly inland and all reachable on a regular bus service. One of them, the three-star *Paola*, signposted off the road to La Punta 3km north of town, offers surprisingly cheap rates, probably due to its relative distance from the sea (about a 10min walk), though it enjoys a great view and has a terrace restaurant (☏0781.850.098, ⓦwww.carloforte.net/hotelpaola; ❻).

Carloforte

The town centres on the broad and animated Piazza Carlo Emanuele. Planted with palms, the square opens onto the port, where water-polo matches take place in cordoned-off sections in summer, and dockside booths offer boat tours round the island. From the port and piazza, Corso Battellieri runs south along the seafront to a placid lagoon where pink flamingoes can sometimes be seen. An observatory sits between the lagoon and the sea, located on the exact line of the thirty-ninth parallel.

A wander around Carloforte's *carruggi*, or alleys, should take in the small **Museo Cívico** on Via Cisterna del Re (mid-June–Sept Tues, Wed & Sat 5–9pm, Fri 9am–1pm; Sept–mid-June Tues & Fri 9am–1pm, Sat 3–7pm; €2), housed in a former guard-house at the entrance to the old citadel (follow signs from Piazza Repubblica). It's a tidy collection of items displayed in five small rooms, each dedicated to a specific aspect of the island's history and culture. The Sala dei Galanzieri evokes local life in the nineteenth century, while the Sala della Tonnara has photos and diagrams illustrating how tuna are caught in the island's annual *Mattanza*, with examples of nets and the hooks used to drag the fish out of the sea. Other rooms highlight fossils, molluscs and historical documents. In front of the museum stands the **Cisterna del Re**, a curious domed archway marking the site of a cistern dating back to the town's construction in the eighteenth century.

Eating, drinking and entertainment

Carloforte has a great range of fish **restaurants**, mostly on the expensive side, and all serving tuna in summer. Other local favourites worth sampling include *zuppa di pesce*, priced at €12–20, and *cuscus* – a variation on the Tunisian dish. One of the best fish restaurants is just up from Piazza Carlo Emanuele, *Da Nicolo*, at Corso Cavour 32 (℡0781.854.048), with pavement seating (under a canopy), where the *Cus Cus Carlofortino* weighs in at €11. You can eat in more elegant surroundings at *Al Tonno di Corsa*, Via Marconi 47 (closed Mon in winter), in an alley most easily reached from the Lungomare via the steps at the top of Via Caprera. A little cramped, but with a pretty veranda for dining *al fresco*, the restaurant is dedicated to tuna dishes, though plenty of other fish are also present on the menu, notably among the excellent *antipasti*; an all-round sampling menu costs €35. More moderate eating choices include *Da Vittorio*, a regular fish restaurant on Corso Battellieri (closed Tues in winter), and the pleasant and relaxed *A Galaia*, Via Segni 36, where fixed-price menus cost €18–33 for land-based dishes, or €25–35 for those from the sea (closed Mon, plus Tues & Wed eves in winter). Otherwise, there's plenty of choice when it comes to pizzas and fast food on and around the main piazza, or try *La Cantina*, a tiny *rosticceria* at Via Gramsci 34, with panini and other local snacks to eat in or take away. For **drinks**, the modish *Barone Rosso* at Via Venti Settembre 26 has a funky charm and stays open till the small hours in summer (closed Mon in winter). *L'Oblò* at Via Garibaldi 23 is another pub which also offers *panini* and other snacks, occasional live music and **Internet access** (closed daytime, also Tues mid-May to mid-Sept).

During the first week of September, Carloforte hosts an **international festival** of film, music, theatre and dance, with nightly performances by big-name companies or stars; contact the tourist office for details. Another highlight of the year is the week-long **Festa di San Pietro**, involving concerts, dances and a picturesque procession of boats, taking place at the end of June.

The rest of the island

Dotted with white villas, most of the island's **interior** is covered with *macchia* that gives way to bare craggy or round peaks, the slopes rising to a height of about 200m. A car is not necessary to explore it: a bus service (3 or 4 daily) covers most of the island, though a bike would give you most independence (see p.115 for a rental shop). The best route from Carloforte is along the twisty road leading across to the western shore at **Capo Sándalo**, a rugged beauty spot on the western tip affording memorable views along the coast, most of which is inaccessible without a boat. However, the road running south out of Carloforte winds round to a popular beach at **La Caletta** (also called Spalmatore), where there's a cluster of houses, while more rough strips of beach lie sheltered in a series of inlets on the island's southeastern edge, for example **La Bobba**, where the twin rock formations known as *Le Colonne* spring abruptly out of the sea. North of Carloforte, a six-kilometre road (bear left at the Agip garage) ends up at **La Punta**, a bracing spot on San Pietro's exposed northern corner, looking towards the offshore **Isola Piana**. This is the venue for the annual tuna slaughter, but you can see the old *tonnare*, or tuna fisheries, at any time.

Portoscuso

On the mainland coast facing San Pietro, the smoking stacks of **PORTOSCUSO** are the biggest blot on the otherwise undeveloped coast of Sulcis. Built as an aluminium extraction plant after coal exports dried up following World War II, Portoscuso looks worse from afar than it does close up, and does not suffer from the chemical-tainted air that permeates Sarroch, near Pula. There's an attractive fishing port where you can see the old tuna fisheries, and even if there's nothing else of particular interest, Portoscuso does have a range of useful facilities: Avis and Hertz **car hire** agencies on the main road into town, a Banco di Sardegna with an ATM, and a couple of slightly tatty but adequate **hotels**. Cheapest of these is the simple *Panorama* (☎0781.508.077, ⓦwww.panoramahotel.ca; ➍), a three-star hotel on the main Via Giúlio Césare with rooms overlooking the fishing port, but without a restaurant. The better-equipped *Hotel Don Pedro*, at Via Vespucci 15 (☎0781.510.219, ⓦweb .tiscalinet/hoteldonpedro.it; ➎) is a slightly more attractive option.

Carbónia

Mussolini's push for self-sufficiency in the 1930s led to a series of initiatives to boost Sardinia's economy, the most ambitious of which was the founding of **CARBÓNIA** in 1938 as a coal-mining centre 15km north of Sant'Antíoco. With the dwindling of mining operations since the 1950s, mainly due to the costs of extraction and the poor quality of "Sulcis coal", the town has lost much of its raison d'être, but it's still worth a visit on account of its historical interest – you can sense the Duce's presence in the orderly streets of regimented workers' houses that give the place such an un-Sardinian air, and its museums of archeology and paleontology are excellent.

Far from being the fulcrum of local industry that Mussolini had intended, Carbónia now has a high level of unemployment, which gives the place a somewhat somnolent pace. At the centre of town, **Piazza Roma** is dominated by the red tower of San Ponziano (a copy of the campanile of the cathedral of Aquileia) and the stout, foursquare Municipio. At time of writing, work is underway to give the broad square a complete facelift, which may inject a bit of life, but currently all the town's activity is concentrated on Viale Gramsci, a modern shopping street leading off from the top of the piazza. Any vitality that this and the neighbouring streets might possess is soon dissipated, however, as they give way to anonymous, right-angled residential quarters.

A drink in a pavement café on Piazza Roma should be enough to absorb the atmosphere before striking out down Via Nápoli to the Giardino Púbblico, site of Carbónia's **Museo Archeologico** (Tues–Sun 9am–1pm & 4–8pm, 3–7pm in winter; €2.10, or €6.50 with Museo Paleontologico and Monte Sirai). Housed in the former residence of the director of the local mining operations, this well-displayed collection consists mainly of finds from Monte Sirai (see below). The most noteworthy exhibits are˙ from the tombs found in the necropolis there: bone, silver and gold ornaments from the sixth century BC; an iron dagger, and a necklace made of bone and shells. In one corner of the museum, a computer gives a good overview of the excavations, allowing you to view the site as it must have once appeared and home in on details, with full explanations (in Italian). There are also objects from further afield, including a smattering of pre-nuraghic items from the so-called Bonnanaro culture – necklaces and domestic implements – and Phoenician and Carthaginian amphorae from Sant'Antíoco.

Across the park, in Via Campania, take time to view the **Museo Paleontologico-Speleologico** (Tues–Sun 9am–1pm & 4–8pm, 3–7pm in winter; €1.60, or €6.50 with Museo Archeologico and Monte Sirai), a couple of rooms packed with rock specimens, fossils and cave-delving bric-a-brac. Even a total ignorance of paleontology, mineralogy and speleology shouldn't prevent the items here eliciting some interest: the Sulcis area holds the oldest fossils anywhere in Italy, and the display is augmented by non-Italian material donated from around the world, such as echinoids (sea-urchins) from Mexico. The paleontological section progresses in chronological order, the oldest exhibits being trilobites from 590–225 million years ago. Ammonites from the mesozoic era (225–65 million years ago) are followed by corals, fish, fossilized wood and even four ants set in amber. From the quaternary period (about one million years ago), a fossilized tree trunk, a skeletal reconstruction of the *Prolagus sardus* rodent unique to Sardinia (a sort of tailless rabbit extinct for the last thousand years), and the jaws and tusk of a dwarf elephant from the Palermo area take us up to the present. The speleological collection is smaller, consisting mainly of photos and diagrams of local cave complexes, and a few glass cases containing bits and pieces of caving equipment.

Practicalities

Carbónia's Piazza Roma is the terminus for **buses** from Cágliari, Iglésias and Sant'Antíoco, and for the regular local buses that connect with the **train station** a couple of kilometres west of the centre. There's no tourist office (but look up the informative website ⓦwww.sardinia.net/carbonia) and no hotels here (the nearest are at Sant'Antíoco, Gonnesa, Portoscuso and Iglésias), and Carbónia's **restaurants** are unexceptional. Centrally, *Ristorante Bovo*, around the corner from Via Gramsci on Via Costituente, offers an extensive but over-priced menu, and a leaden atmosphere (closed Sun); you'd do better heading out of the centre to *Il Caminetto*, Via Roma 59, about one kilometre down from Piazza Roma (and near the southern link with the SS126), an unpretentious trattoria and pizzeria with a good range of standards. You could also sit down for an ice cream or snack at *La Paninoteca* on Viale Gramsci.

Monte Sirai

Four kilometres northwest of Carbónia, off the SS126 Iglésias road, a poorly-marked turning leads up to the high, flat top of **Monte Sirai** – there is currently no bus service, though one is planned to link the site with Carbónia. After ejecting a pre-existent nuraghic settlement, Phoenicians occupied the site around the eighth century BC. They were displaced in turn by Carthaginians at the end of the sixth century BC, who made this their principal military base in the whole of Sardinia. The Romans then occupied the site, but abandoned it at the end of the second century AD for reasons which have never been identified.

The strategic advantages of the location are immediately obvious: from a height of nearly 200m, it dominates the surrounding tracts of sea and land for an immense distance. Today, the view encompasses the stacks and industrial paraphernalia of Portoscuso as well as the islands of Sant'Antíoco and San Pietro, but it's still a thrilling vantage point – the panorama is best at sunset. Guided tours – sometimes in English – show you the most interesting features of the **site** (Tues–Sun: summer 9am–1pm & 4–8pm, winter 9am–5pm; €2.60, or €6.50 with Museo Archeologico and Museo Paleontologico, both in Carbónia), which was first excavated by a Tunisian team in 1966. Three streets of terraced houses were unearthed, of which only the foundations are now visible; everything else, made of mud and straw, has long since disappeared. Since then, the tombs of a substantial necropolis have come to light, many marked with the symbols of Tanit, the Phoenician goddess: a circle, horizontal line and triangle, looking something like a character from *Charlie Brown*. Some of the tombs can be entered, and you can see Tanit's symbol – for some reason upside down – in tomb number five. Apart from the red rubble of the crumbled walls, little else remains of the Phoenician/Carthaginian settlement. The main interest, anyway, lies in the glorious location, with dwarf palms and olive trees bent almost double under the force of the *maestrale* wind.

The Iglesiente

The Iglesiente is the name for the mainly mountainous and sparsely populated region north of Sulcis, centred on the town of **Iglésias**, 25km north of Carbónia and 57km due west of Cágliari. Though it lacks much tourist infrastructure, this inland town is the biggest and liveliest in the area, with a handful of medieval churches worth visiting and the impressive ruins of a huge mine on the outskirts. The Iglesiente coast benefits from the lack of development, though the tourist industry is beginning to wake up to the charms of the highly scenic **Golfo di Gonnesa**, swamping the old mining town of **Buggerru** with holiday villas. Elsewhere, the coast maintains an almost pristine feel, nowhere more than on the **Costa Verde** – acres of untrammelled sand backed by an impressive system of dunes and lapped by uncontaminated waters.

Public transport facilities are rudimentary throughout the region, though Iglésias is connected to Cágliari by **train** and FMS **buses**, and there are infrequent ARST and FMS bus services from Iglésias to the coast. For all practical purposes, however, you need your own transport to do any exploring.

Iglésias

Surrounded by mine-shafts and quarries gouged out of the red rock, the principal city of the Iglesiente region, **IGLÉSIAS**, is an appealing place to stop, with a decidedly Spanish-tinged atmosphere, especially during its flamboyant Easter festivities. The town is also a viable base for exploring the clutch of beach resorts a short drive away, which have little in the way of accommodation. In fact, there's not a great choice in Iglésias either, but since the place is way off the tourist trail, there's a good chance of finding room in one of its three hotels.

Ugolino della Gherardesca

Iglésias enjoyed its greatest prosperity under the rule of the **Gherardesca family**, one of the foremost Tuscan dynasties, whose lands included the counties of Gherardesca, Donoratico, and Montescudaio, near Pisa. At the beginning of the thirteenth century, they led the pro-imperial Ghibelline party of the Pisan republic against the pro-papal Guelf party led by the Visconti family of Milan, but **Ugolino della Gherardesca** (died 1289) became the most reviled member of the family by switching allegiance from the Ghibellines to the Guelfs. Having assumed control as the tyrannical master of Pisa, he soon alienated his allies, and was eventually accused of treason in 1288 by the archbishop Ruggieri degli Ubaldini, who wanted to revive the republican order. Imprisoned in the tower of Gualandi along with two of his sons and two of his grandsons, Ugolino was said to have eaten his own children before himself dying of starvation, an event depicted in numerous works of art, most famously in Dante's *Divina Commedia*, in which the poet encounters the tyrant frozen in the ice of the ninth circle of hell (*Inferno*, canto 33); Archbishop Ruggieri's also there.

Ugolino is remembered with more affection in Iglésias, where, in the course of exploiting the area's mineral resources, he succeeded in introducing Tuscan methods of planning and political organization. The resulting **statutory code** of local rights was enshrined in a *Breve*, or law book, a meticulously drafted volume which is viewable on application in the town's Archivio Stórico, in Via delle Cárceri, near the church of Santa Maria delle Grázie (Mon–Fri 9am–1pm & 4–6.30pm; ☏0781.24.850). Ugolino's son, Guelfo, was imprisoned in the Castello di Acquafredda (see p.124).

Best known for its numerous churches, of which a good number survive, Iglésias was formerly known as Villa di Chiesa. Its livelihood has depended more on its **mining** operations, however. The town owes its foundation to the notorious Pisan Count Ugolino della Gherardesca (see box above), who re-opened the old Roman mines in the thirteenth century. Gold, silver, iron, zinc and lead have all been extracted here at different times, making Iglésias the chief mining centre of Sardinia, despite bearing little resemblance to the stereotyped image of a grimy mining town.

Arrival and information

The main **FS train station** is on Via San Salvatore, while all out-of-town buses stop at the **Giardini Púbblici**, on Via Oristano (tickets and timetables from the bar opposite the stop). Both of these entry points are a five-minute walk from **Piazza Quintino Sella**, the centre of the new town. **Parking** is not always easy to find, but you should find availability fairly centrally in blue-line spaces, for which the parking attendant will charge about €0.60 per hour. The **tourist office** is housed in the public library just off Piazza Sella on Via Gramsci (Mon–Fri 9.30am–1pm & 4–7pm, Sat 9am–12.30pm; ☏0781.41.795, ⓦwww.prolocoiglesias.it). Two **banks** on Piazza Sella have exchange facilities and ATMs. For **Internet access**, CyberTecn@ is just off Via Oristano at Via Diaz 9 (Mon–Fri 9am–1pm & 5–7pm, Sat 9am–1pm; €5 per hour).

Accommodation

Of the **hotels** in Iglésias – all three-star – the most central is the *Artu* (☏0781.22.492, ⓦwww.hotelartuiglesias.it; ⑤) at Piazza Sella 15, recommended both for its premium location and its small garage (parking is

generally problematic in Iglésias). While it lacks character, the rooms are spacious and clean, and there's a bar and restaurant. The business-class *Leon d'Oro*, at Corso Colombo 72 (℡0781.33.555, ℻0781.33.530; ❺), is flashier, pricier and has a pool, but it's located in a dull district on the eastern side of town, and not particularly convenient for the centre (follow Via Crocefisso, running along the south side of the rail tracks, and Corso Colombo for about a kilometre). A third hotel, *Il Sillabario* (℡0781.33.830, ℻0781.33.790; ❹), also geared towards expense-account travellers, is relatively cheap, and also has a pool; however, it lies even further out, 6km east of town on the main SS130, so is only a viable option for drivers. If you're coming this far out, you might as well cut your bills by staying at the much more pleasant *Lo Sperone*, an *agriturismo* clearly signposted just below town on the SS126 south, opposite the Masua turn-off (℡0781.36.247; ❸; no credit cards). It's a relaxed spot, convenient for the Fontanamare beach (see p.125), with eight rooms available (four sharing bathroom facilities, at a small discount), with half- or full-board required in July and August (respectively €42 and €57 per person). The owners also have an **apartment** for weekly rent, and **riding** is available from their stables. Otherwise, there's a *pensione* at Gonnesa, 7km further south (p.125).

The Town

The focus of the action in the modern town is the central **Piazza Sella**, a lively forum by day and the noisy rendezvous of throngs of people every evening. At the top end of the square, what's left of the ruined Aragonese (originally Pisan) **Castello Salvaterra** crowns a knoll, its impact softened by landscaped flowerbeds. The castle is currently closed except for occasional exhibitions.

The old town's labyrinth of lanes and traffic-free squares runs off Piazza Sella's western side. Pedestrianized Corso Matteotti is the main artery, threading through the heart of the *città vecchia* almost as far as the sequestered **Piazza Município**, the only true square in the old town and one of the few really typical Italian piazzas on the whole island. It's an elegant composition, with the town hall taking up one entire side opposite the cathedral and bishop's palace, which are joined by a harmonious enclosed bridge. The **Duomo** itself (currently closed for long-term restoration work) shows a mixture of Pisan and Aragonese styles, reflecting the two dominant (and warring) powers in Iglésias during the Middle Ages, though the building wasn't completed until the seventeenth century. The bell in the squat tower was cast by the great Tuscan sculptor Andrea Pisano in 1337. Once the work on the Duomo is complete, you'll be able to view the low-vaulted, interior, whose main interest is in the spectacular, gilded altar piece in the left transept, carved in the seventeenth century to hold the relics of Saint Antiochus, which had been removed here for safekeeping from the church at Sant'Antíoco during a spate of pirate raids. However, the bones – which were kept behind the curtain in the middle panel – were forcibly reclaimed in the nineteenth century after the clerics of Iglésias refused to return them. An image of the saint adorns the front of the sculpture, his hands blackened, according to legend, from the barrel of pitch in which he had been forced to hide to escape persecution; he appears again in the painting behind the altar in the bottom left corner, opposite Saint Clare.

Across the piazza from the Duomo, take Via Pullo to reach the church of **San Francesco** (daily 8am–noon & 5–8pm), a predominantly Catalan-Gothic structure built between the fourteenth and sixteenth centuries. Behind a minimalist facade of pinkish trachyte stone, perforated by three circular windows, the nave has a wooden ceiling and seven chapels on either side, each framed by an ogival arch. The first chapel on the left shows a recently restored Retablo della Vergine, a lovely tryptich of the Madonna with saints from the sixteenth century by Antioco Mainas. Off Via Zecca, the tiny Piazza Manzoni holds a much humbler church, **Santa Maria delle Grazie** (daily 7.30am–noon & 5.30–8pm), its medieval base incongruously topped by a Baroque upper portion, squeezed between houses on either side.

The other historic churches of Iglésias can be a labour to reach, but it's worth making an effort to track down **Nostra Signora di Valverde**, behind the station near the cemetery. Dating from the end of the thirteenth century, the facade is similar to that of the Duomo, though here the austerity is relieved by lively carvings of animals. Lastly, on an elevation just west of the old quarter stands the simple white **Nostra Signora di Buoncammino**, reconstructed in 1968 according to its original eighteenth-century design. It's worth the drive or hike (up a track off Via Campidano, off the Fluminimaggiore road) for the excellent views of the town and its surrounding mountains.

The more down-to-earth side of Iglésias is represented by its Art Nouveau-style mining institute on Via Roma, which houses the **Museo delle Arti Minerarie** (April–June Sat & Sun 6–8pm; July–Sept Fri–Sun 7–9pm; in winter, call ☎333.447.9980 or 347.833.3257; €4). The museum displays mining machinery, models, photos and recreations of the pit-face, though the real attraction here is the eight thousand or so specimens of the minerals dug out of the local rock. It's worth checking times of opening before heading out to this exhibition, since it keeps erratic hours: contact the tourist office or call ☎0781.22.304 for the latest update. If you're intrigued by the industrial archeology of the area, you should make a point of seeing the evocative site at **Monteponi**, a vast desolate area of mineworkings west of town, visible as you enter Iglésias on the SS126. The place was abandoned surprisingly recently – given the extent of its decay – in 1992, when most of the operation was transferred across to Campo Pisano, visible across the valley. For guided visits around the ruins, contact the Igea cooperative (☎0781.491.300 or 348.154.9556, ⓦwww.igeaminiere.it), which conducts ninety-minute tours of the Galleria Villamarina, a tunnel dug in 1852 (daily at 9am, 10.30am and noon, also 3.30pm, 5pm and 6.30pm June–Sept; €8).

Eating, drinking and entertainment

It is not only hotels that Iglésias lacks: the town's **restaurant** facilities are also limited. The best location – though not necessarily the best food or prices – can be found at the *Villa di Chiesa* on Piazza Municipio, where you can eat in the square in summer (closed Mon Oct–June). For indoor atmosphere, choose *Il Gazebo*, a medieval-style, brick-vaulted hall at Via Musio 27, off Corso Matteotti; there's a regular, moderately priced restaurant menu which offers pasta with fresh vegetables and again, somewhat mediocre food (closed Sun & mid-Oct to mid-Nov). The *Volters & Murion* pub, with outdoor seating on Piazza Collegio, offers good-value, fixed-price meals at €8 and €12, or you might just come here for a late-night drink (closed Tues Oct to mid-June). Finally, for picnic ingredients, there's an indoor **market** open Monday–Saturday mornings just up from the Pro Loco on Via Gramsci.

In summer, outdoor **concerts** take place at various points of the old town, and there's open-air **cinema** in Piazza Collegio. The Pro Loco has a full list of events.

Iglésias festivals

Iglésias comes into its own during its famous **Easter festivities**, when processions weave solemnly between the churches of the old town in a tradition dating back to the seventeenth century. Marching to the rhythm of traditional instruments, the white-robed, sometimes cowled, cortege (the dress is known as *baballotti*) performs this ritual during the whole of Easter week, though the highlight is the second procession, Christ's funeral, on Good Friday evening. Another traditional ceremony, I Candelieri, takes place on or around August 15. As in the better-known festa at Sássari that occurs on the same day (see box on p.230), seven (sometimes eight) huge candles, one for each section of the city, are borne through the streets in the evening, from the Chiesa del Collegio to the cathedral, to be returned eight days later. If you're thinking of visiting Iglésias at any of these times, fix up your accommodation first.

Around Iglésias

The SS130 dual carriageway runs due east of Iglésias over mainly flat terrain, connecting drivers with Cágliari in less than an hour. If you're not in a hurry, it's worth making a detour at Domusnovas, 10km east of Iglésias. Signposted at the back of the village, a small road straggles 4km to the **Grotta di San Giovanni**, a 750m-long natural rock tunnel where the road passed through until recently, when it was diverted for safety and conservation reasons. There's a bar and restaurant at the grotto, and thick woods which provide some nice picnicking spots, though you can't penetrate far into the tangled vegetation. The road soon deteriorates to a dirt track that climbs high into the mountains. In theory, it's feasible to follow this road as far as the Témpio di Antas, but in practice there are no indications and it's easy to get lost: the preferable route is north from Iglésias (see below).

Further east along the Cágliari road, look out for the ruins of the **Castello di Acquafredda**, on a jagged elevation 4km south of Siliqua. Built in the thirteenth century, the castle was the prison for Guelfo, son of Ugolino della Gherardesca (see the box on p.120). If you want to stretch your legs, it's a steep but panoramic climb to the top.

Fifteen kilometres north of Iglésias, a right turn off the twisty mountain road to Fluminimaggiore (the SS126) wanders down a valley to the remote **Témpio di Antas** (April–Oct daily 9.30am–1hr before sunset; Oct–April Sat & Sun 9.30am–4pm; other times call ☎347.181.4733; €2.60), a Roman temple built on the site of a nuraghic and later Carthaginian sanctuary. Its Punic origins are thought to date back to around 500 BC, but it probably assumed its final form in the third century AD. As an inscription records, the Romans dedicated the temple to Sardus Pater Babay, a local deity worshipped as the father of the Sards in the kind of synthesis of imperial and local cults that was practised throughout the Roman Empire. The Ionic-style columns are still standing, topped by a simple pediment, and you can see inside the remains of the sacred chambers, while rooms and houses used by the priests and other members of the ethnically mixed population are faintly visible behind. It's an idyllic spot, the air full of the aromas of the *macchia* and the jangle of distant goat bells, spoiled only by the pylons and cables strung across the valley.

A little way north of the Témpio di Antas, the **Grotta Su Mannau** (Easter–Oct daily 9.30am–6.30pm; €6) is one of the most accessible of the many grottoes scattered throughout this area. A tourist trail penetrates for 350m, enough to see some spectacular rock formations, while cavers can go for about a kilometre inside the mountain. Fifty-minute tours leave every half hour; in winter, call Fluminimaggiore's Società Su Mannau Grotte, Via Vittorio Emanuele 81 (☎0781.580.189 or 347.687.748) for bookings.

You can reach both of these sites on any **bus** running between Iglésias and Fluminimaggiore, though there's a brief walk from the main road in either case.

The Iglesiente coast

West of Iglésias, the remote villages and beaches on the coast have few transport links with the outside world, but are easily accessible under your own steam. The villages and resorts here are hardly the attraction anyway: the real appeal is the refreshing emptiness of the coast, either cliff-hung tracts or wildernesses of bare dunes. Getting to the best places may involve a lengthy haul along dirt roads, so make sure your vehicle is in good working order.

Accommodation, too, is scarce: all options have been listed here, though you should be prepared to make detours to reach a convenient hotel or campsite.

The Golfo di Gonnesa

The coast of the **Golfo di Gonnesa** is mainly high and cliffy, with the exception of one good beach which attracts crowds from Iglésias and from inland **Gonnesa**, 9km southwest of Iglésias. This fairly unremarkable village has a useful **hotel**, the basic *Frau*, next to the *Bar La Piazzetta* on Via della Pace (T0781.45.104; ❶; no credit cards), run by a friendly signora who can also rustle up a meal at short notice; all rooms share bathroom facilities, and there's a bank nearby. On the SS126, outside the village, the *Piedra del Sol* (T0781.36.394, Wwww.piedradelsol.net; ❸) offers a higher standard of comfort and more modern facilities; at least half-board (at €54 per person) is required in August. The good **restaurant** here is open to all.

From the SS126, a road branches west to the long sandy beach at **Fontanamare**, just 4km from Gonnesa. It's a popular bathing spot, with bars and a pizzeria open in summer, but quiet the rest of the time. There are no other facilities until you reach the nearby village of **Nébida**, high above the coast, at the far end of which the *Pan di Zúcchero* hotel offers simple **accommodation**, including some rooms with good views and a restaurant (T0781.47.114; ❷). A small lane next to the hotel dives steeply down to a tiny sandy cove, **Porto Banda**, where two large *faraglioni*, needle-shaped stacks of rock, poke up from the sea. Elsewhere in the village, next to a public garden and sports ground, a path rounding a cliff face gives access to a **belvedere** offering the area's best views of the sheer coast on either side, as far as the Pan di Zúcchero *scoglio* to the north (see below). Below this path, at the bottom of a four-hundred-step descent, the **Laveria La Mármora**, is a ramshackle building, built in 1897 for the filtering and washing of mine products but now abandoned. A **bar** built into a grotto on the cliff path, *Café del Operaio*, serves drinks and snacks until late.

North of Nébida, the mountain road winds three or four kilometres on to **Masua**. Another huge mining site dominates the knot of houses here, dedicated to extracting zinc and lead, the two main products of this region. Below, a lovely but restricted beach backed by shade-giving rocks and ruined walls faces the colossal outcrop known as the **Pan di Zúcchero** (Sugarloaf), whose prodigious white hulk is depicted on countless postcards. Owing its name to its unique shape and colour, it's said to be the oldest such *scoglio*, or rock formation, in Italy. From Masua, where there are bars and a pizzeria, a tortuous road climbs inland; it's mostly unsurfaced, though work is currently underway to upgrade it.

Ten kilometres further north, **Buggerru** is a fishing port and tourist resort superimposed on another old mining centre. Once accessible only by sea, Buggerru was largely self-sufficient during its mining days; it was the first place in Sardinia to have a regular electrical system, and the miners enjoyed health- and recreational facilities long before such practices were introduced by other companies. Today, the ramshackle remains of the mine buildings overlooking a regimented marina packed with small pleasure boats are the most attractive thing about this overdeveloped resort, though there are some superb **beaches** in the vicinity. The most solitary of these is at **Cala Domestica**, little more than a deep, sheltered sandy inlet (bring your own shade) four or five kilometres south of Buggerru; alternatively, you can head north to the much wider **Portixeddu**, a sweeping swathe of sand with little or no construction nearby. Eight hundred metres inland of here, *Ortus de Mari* offers **camping** with minimal facilities (June–Sept; ☎0781.54.964), the only site on this stretch of coast. The road ends a little further north at **Capo Pécora**, a wild, deserted spot with a small stony beach.

The Costa Verde

There is little that's "green" about the **Costa Verde**, stretching north from Capo Pécora, most of it consisting of arid rock, scrub and sand. Access is from the SS126, either from the village of Gúspini, from where a road twists for 25km to the desolate coast, or, 13km further south, via the dirt road threading westwards from the deserted mining town of **Ingurtosu**. If your car can stand it, this is the preferable route; it's shorter, and allows a stop at the ghostly ruins of this once vibrant community. Nine kilometres below, the road emerges on the coast at **Piscinas**, a barren spot, about as remote as it gets in Sardinia, with superb swimming. Apart from a few traces of nineteenth-century mineworks, there's nothing here but immense sand dunes – and the thankfully subdued *Hotel Le Dune* (☎070.977.130, ⓦwww.leduneingurtosu.it; ❽). If you can afford the bill (with prices ranging from €125–153 per person for half-board in summer, lower rates in winter) at this chic luxury retreat, it would be a fabulous place to hole up for a few days. If not, you may be grateful for the bar, which serves *panini*, and expensive restaurant, open to anyone; in summer you'll find fast-food kiosks in the vicinity. If you don't want to pay to stay, camping rough is feasible in this out-of-the-way area.

From Piscinas, another dirt road follows the coast north, passing more dune-backed sands and perfect seas, until it meets civilization among the shops, restaurants and holiday homes of **Marina di Arbus**. There are more good beaches here and a couple of kilometres north at **Funtanazza**, lying below and out of sight of an eyesore of a ruined 1950s holiday complex, and reached along a private road that is barred at night but otherwise open to anyone. From the junction beyond, a winding but scenic road threads inland towards the villages of Gúspini and Arbus, passing through what was once a productive mining area centred on **Montevecchio**. A tour of this complex provides an informative insight into the life of the thriving community here; for details and bookings, call ☎335.531.4198. Ten kilometres east of here, Gúspini has a bank, petrol station and **trattoria** – *Sa Lolla*, on the main road heading south out of town – to meet all immediate requirements. Travelling east from here, the road crests the ridge of mountains, giving long views over the plain of Campidano (see p.134).

Alternatively, heading north up the coast from Funtanazza, you'll reach a superb, broad sand beach backed by high dunes at **Torre dei Corsari** (about 10km north of Funtanazza). The towering cliffs beyond, ending at **Capo Frasca**, are inaccessible by land. Curling eastwards, the road gives access to a causeway/bridge running across the Stagno di Marceddi and into Oristano province (see p.155).

Travel details

Trains

Carbónia to: Cágliari (Mon–Sat 11 daily, Sun 3; 1hr); Iglésias (Mon–Sat 9 daily, Sun 1; 30min–1hr). Most routes from Carbónia involve changing trains at Villamassárgia.

Iglésias to: Cágliari (Mon–Sat hourly, Sun 7; 50min–1hr); Carbónia (with change at Villamassárgia; Mon–Sat 8 daily, Sun 2; 30min–1hr).

Buses

Calasetta to: Cágliari (4–5 daily; 2hr 15min–3hr); Carbónia (hourly; 50min–1hr); Iglésias (5–7 daily; 1hr 40min); Sant'Antíoco (1–2 hourly; 25–30min).

Carbónia to: Cágliari (6–8 daily; 1hr 25min–2hr 10min); Calasetta (4–5 daily; 50min); Iglésias (8–9 daily; 50min); Portopino (2–4 daily; 50min); Portoscuso (7–11 daily; 30–50min); Sant'Antíoco (1–2 hourly; 20–30min).

Giba to: Portopino (5–6 daily; 20min).

Iglésias to: Buggerru (5–7 daily; 1hr 15min); Cágliari (6–10 daily; 1hr); Calasetta (3–5 daily; 1hr 40min); Carbónia (7–8 daily; 45min); Fontanamare (Mon–Sat 10 daily, Sun 4–7; 15–25min); Gonnesa (7–8 daily; 15min); Masua (Mon–Sat 9 daily, Sun 4; 30min); Nébida (Mon–Sat 9 daily, Sun 4; 25min); Portixeddu (Mon–Sat 6–8 daily, Sun 4; 1hr 5min); Portoscuso/Portovesme (Mon–Sat hourly, Sun 8; 40min–1hr); Sant'Antíoco (3–5 daily; 1hr 15min).

Portoscuso/Portovesme to: Cágliari (2–3 daily; 1hr 15min–2hr 10min); Carbónia (Mon–Sat hourly, Sun 8; 30–40min); Iglésias (Mon–Sat 7–11 daily, Sun 5; 25–55min).

Pula to: Cágliari (Mon–Sat 1–2 hourly, Sun 5–7 daily; 50min); Santa Margherita di Pula (Mon–Sat 1–2 hourly, Sun 6–8 daily; 10min); Chia (Mon–Sat hourly, Sun 6–8 daily; 25min); Sarroch (Mon–Sat 1–2 hourly, Sun 5–7 daily; 15min); Teulada (Mon–Sat hourly, Sun 5–7 daily; 1hr).

Sant'Antíoco to: Cágliari (4–5 daily; 2hr–2hr 40min); Calasetta (1–2 hourly; 25–30min); Carbónia (1–2 hourly; 20–30min); Iglésias (4–5 daily; 1hr 20min).

Teulada to: Porto di Teulada (summer only, 4 daily; 15min).

Ferries

Calasetta to: Carloforte (hourly; 40min).

Carloforte to: Calasetta (hourly; 40min); Portovesme (1–2 hourly; 30min).

Portovesme to: Carloforte (1–2 hourly; 30min).

3

Campidano, La Marmilla and Sarrabus

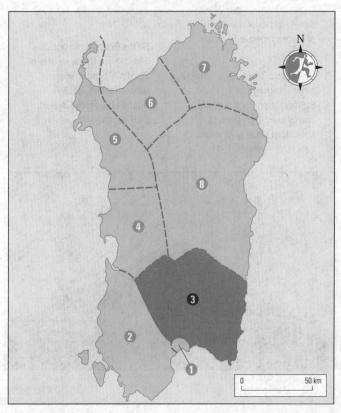

CHAPTER 3

Highlights

* **Chiesa di Santa Maria, Uta** This gem of a church is southern Sardinia's finest example of the Romanesque. See p.135

* **Castello di Eleonora d'Arborea, Sanluri** Delightfully eclectic collection of historical bric-a-brac, taking in everything from Napoleonic curios to flags and arms from World War II, all housed in a well-preserved medieval castle. See p.136

* **Su Nuraxi** The largest and most intriguing of Sardinia's ancient nuragic complexes – an unmissable sight on any itinerary. See p.141–142

* **Giara di Gésturi** A conspicuous landmark rising above La Marmilla, this high basalt plateau teems with wildlife, from rare orchids to miniature wild horses. See p.142–143

* **Costa Rei beaches** Superlative swimming from flawless sandy beaches interspersed with secluded coves. See p.148–149

* **Sette Fratelli mountains** Stretch your legs in one of Sardinia's great scenic wildernesses, easily accessible from Cágliari. See p.149–150

△ Las Plassas Castle

3

Campidano, La Marmilla and Sarrabus

The regions to the north and east of Cágliari are remarkably diverse in tone and physical appearance, and include some essential stops as well as several places well off most tourist itineraries. Much of this disparate territory could be explored on excursions from the island's capital, or on brief detours on your way further afield. The main route north of Cágliari, for example, takes you through **Campidano**, Sardinia's most extensive plain, stretching for a hundred kilometres as far as Oristano. Though scenically dull when compared with most other regions of the island, it includes several places that are well worth a brief stop, for example the Romanesque church in the village of **Uta** and the public sculpture in the village of **San Sperate**. Most compelling of all is the well-preserved but rather diminutive medieval castle in the centre of **Sanluri** that is home to what must be Sardinia's most eccentric museum collection. Further up the SS131, you might pause at **Sárdara** for its diverse historical remnants, and at the nearby **Castello di Monreale**, if only for a photo.

East of the highway, in the northern reaches of the province of Cágliari, the uniformity of Campidano gives way to the hill country of **La Marmilla**, named after the mammary-shaped elevations that characterize the landscape. Some of the island's most important nuraghic remains are located here, notably **Genna Maria**, near Villanovaforru, and the extensive complex of **Su Nuraxi**, the largest and most famous relic of this shadowy culture, located just outside the village of **Barúmini**. North of here, La Marmilla ends at the high plateau of **Giara di Gésturi**, a protected area that is one of the last refuges of Sardinia's miniature wild ponies. You'll need a little luck and a lot of cunning to spot these shy creatures, but in any case it's an excellent spot for walking, and in the spring the plateau is a regular stopover for migrating birds. Among the ring of villages at its base, **Tuili** merits a stop to view a superb painted panel in one of its churches, dating from the middle ages.

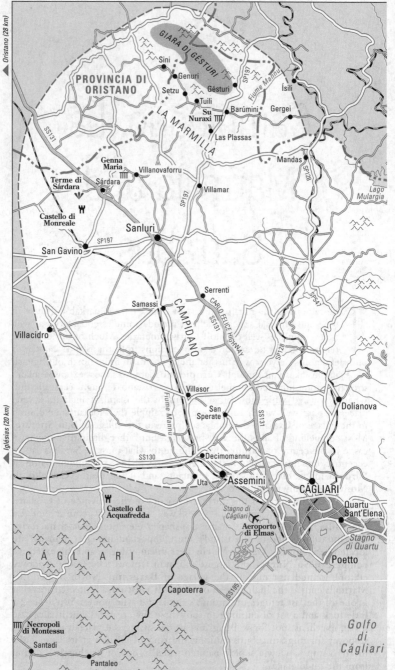

Láconi (10 km) & Aritzo (27 km)

Oristano (28 km)

Iglésias (20 km)

GIARA DI GÉSTURI

PROVINCIA DI ORISTANO

Sini

Genuri

Gésturi

Setzu

Tuili

Su Nuraxi

Barúmini

Ísili

Gergei

La Marmilla

Las Plassas

Mandas

SP128

Lago Mulargia

Genna Maria

Villanovaforru

Terme di Sárdara

Sárdara

Villamar

SP197

Castello di Monreale

Sanluri

SP197

San Gavino

Serrenti

CARLO FELICE HIGHWAY

SS131

Samassi

CAMPIDANO

SP547

Villacidro

Fiume Mannu

Villasor

San Sperate

Dolianova

SP128

SS131

SS130

Decimomannu

Uta

Assemini

CÁGLIARI

Quartu Sant'Elena

Castello di Acquafredda

CÁGLIARI

Stagno di Cágliari

Aeroporto di Elmas

Stagno di Quartu

Poetto

Capoterra

SS195

Golfo di Cágliari

Necropoli di Montessu

Santadi

Pantaleo

Twenty kilometres north of Cágliari, the town of **Dolianova** holds another church that's worth a detour, a good example of the rustic Romanesque. The farming country runs out east of here, for most of **Sarrabus**, the region occupying Sardinia's southeastern corner, is wildly inhospitable. Dominating its interior, the **Sette Fratelli** mountains can be admired from the SS125, the twisty road linking Cágliari to the island's eastern seaboard, but they are best appreciated from close up, preferably on a hike. The emptiness and desolation of these inland tracts are far removed from the holiday ambience of the Sarrabus coast, at least in summer, when the fine sand beaches indenting the rocky coastline attract crowds from Cágliari and further afield. Development is fairly intense all along the south-facing coast of the **Golfo di Cágliari** as far as the main resort hereabouts, **Villasimius**, and it also thickens around the popular **Costa Rei** north of here. In between the pockets of construction lies some of the island's most alluring coastline, however, and though the area gets very busy in July and August, come at any other time and you'll have the beaches pretty much to yourself. Alternatively, you can always escape from the beaten track on inland jaunts to such places as **Castiadas**, site of a former penal colony in the middle of woods, and **Nuraghe Asoru**, one of the rare relics of nuraghic civilization in these parts.

With the exception of the towns of Villasimius and **Muravera**, another inland resort north of the Costa Rei, Sarrabus has few accommodation options. Indeed, **hotels** are thin on the ground throughout the regions covered in this chapter. All the most useful ones are detailed here, and you can always take advantage of the much larger choice to be found in Cágliari and Oristano (a possible base for La Marmilla). On the coasts, **campsites**, at least, are easily found in summer, usually right by the sea and offering bungalows or other options if you don't have your own tent.

Drivers will find the **SS131** dual carriageway, Sardinia's main north-south artery, fast and convenient for Campidano and La Marmilla, while the **SS125** is a slower link to Muravera and the eastern coast. Non-drivers will experience problems in visiting some of the smaller places described here, to which transport services can be sparse. However, there are frequent **buses** running from Cágliari to Sanluri, Villasimius and Muravera, while you can use **trains** to reach Decimomannu (close to Uta and San Sperate), Sanluri, San Gavino (for Sárdara and more frequent trains to Sanluri) and Dolianova. For schedules and connections, see Travel details on p.153.

Campidano

To the northwest of Cágliari, **Campidano** is Sardinia's richest agricultural region, nourished by the numerous rivers flowing into it, and benefiting from past drainage and anti-malaria schemes. Its flatness was exploited by King Carlo Felice in the 1820s when he routed the long highway which still bears his name through the region, also known as the SS131. If Campidano lacks the scenic drama of Sardinia's more mountainous zones, it compensates with its range of cultural and historical sites. If you have a flexible schedule, you might make a brief detour from the Carlo Felice highway to visit the Romanesque church of Santa Maria outside the village of **Uta**, about 20km out of Cágliari off the SS130 Iglésias road. You could combine it with a tour of the "open-air museum" of murals and sculptures at **San Sperate**, 12km northeast. Otherwise, head up the SS131 to **Sanluri**, holding Sardinia's only continuously inhabited medieval castle, once one of the last strongholds of resistance against the Aragonese aggressors, and today the home of the counts of Villa Santa. Inside, there's an absorbing museum that recalls another struggle against foreign oppression, the Risorgimento – Italy's lurch to nationhood in the nineteenth century. Further up the SS131, **Sárdara** is known for its weaving industry and its curative waters, appreciated since nuraghic times. A museum here exhibits items from this era, as well as from the derelict remains of the **Castello di Monreale**, capping a hill just to the southeast of here.

Campidano's few **accommodation** options are scattered; if you want to make an overnight stop, try the small selection of lodgings in Sanluri or Sárdara. All places mentioned here are accessible on frequent ARST **buses** from Cágliari; PANI buses from Cágliari and Oristano are the quickest way to reach Sanluri and Sárdara. By **train**, both towns are close to the station at San Gavino, 9km west of Sanluri and 7km south of Sárdara; Sanluri's own station has less frequent connections and lies 5km southwest of town; buses and taxis can transport you from the stations into town.

Uta and San Sperate

West of Cágliari, the small towns of **Decimomannu** and **Assémini** are renowned for their decorated ceramic output as well as for their eel-filled *panadas* (pasta cakes), though neither place has much else to merit more than a quick passage through. Six kilometres west of those towns, however, on the other side of the River Mannu flowing into the Stagno di Cágliari, the agricultural centre of **UTA** has arguably the loveliest Romanesque church in southern Sardinia, the **Chiesa di Santa Maria** (May–Sept daily 9am–12.30pm & 3–8.30pm). Built by the Vittorini monks from Marseille around 1140. The church stands by itself at the eastern end of the village, its light stonework embellished with arcading running round under the roof, at the base of which human heads, rams, dogs, stags, calves and various abstract devices are chiselled. This florid Provençal style is fused with Pisan elements, apparent in the portals and the bare interior, where two columns of perfect round arches have well-restored capitals. The Benedictine Vittorini house was as instrumental in diffusing Romanesque building styles in the south of Sardinia as the Tuscans and Lombards were in the island's north – its great influence proceeding from the good relations with the papacy and the Sardinian *giudici* that the order enjoyed after 1089, when it was assigned the churches of San Saturnino in Cágliari, Sant'Efisio in Nora and Sant'Antíoco in the town of the same name. Eventually, the Vittorini even took over control of Cágliari's salt pans.

Make a circuit round the church's outside to appreciate the intricate carving of the figures and differently-coloured stones used in Santa Maria's construction. During the last week of August, the **Festa di Santa Lucia** is celebrated with a procession to the church of peasant carts, or *traccas*.

Six kilometres northeast of Decimomannu, the village of **SAN SPERATE** is famous for its murals and sculptures. The startling images daubed over the walls of houses are not as vibrant as those in Orgósolo, near Nuoro (see p.325), but there are still some engaging works to be seen, in a variety of styles, including *trompe l'oeil* domestic scenes, portraying an older, simpler and more parochial society. San Sperate also has several open-air sculptures by Sardinia's best-known contemporary sculptor, **Pinuccio Sciola**, born in San Sperate in 1942. Sciola works almost exclusively in Sardinian trachyte; its mutating, seasoned appearance makes it particularly appropriate for his outdoor pieces, which resemble menhirs or even nuraghic *tombe dei giganti* burial stones.

Sanluri

Occupying a commanding position in the hinterland between the *giudicati* of Arborea and Cágliari, 45km to the southeast, Campidano's biggest town, **SANLURI**, grew around the castle built here in the thirteenth century, a linchpin of the Sard-Aragonese conflict that embroiled the island during the fourteenth and fifteenth centuries. The **Castello di Eleonora d'Arborea** – named after the warrior queen who spent a lifetime in arms against the Aragonese (see p.165) and who briefly resided here – was the venue for a treaty signed by her father Mariano IV and the Aragonese king, Pedro IV. Though this allowed the *giudice* of Arborea a measure of peace, it turned out to be merely a breathing space, and following Eleonora's death, Pedro's son, Martino, won a definitive victory at Sanluri in 1409 against forces commanded by the new *giudice*, Gugliemo, husband of Eleonora's younger sister. This defeat marked the end of Arborea's resistance, and was followed by the swift occupation of almost the whole island by Aragonese forces.

The castle, a high, square keep surrounded by railings and fir trees, lies on the main road slicing through the centre of Sanluri, Via Carlo Felice. Modern artillery pieces have been arranged on the tidy verge, giving some hint of what you can expect to find within. Despite its name, the **Museo Risorgimentale** inside (March to mid-June & Oct–Dec Sun 9.30am–1pm & 3pm–sunset; mid-June to Sept Mon–Thurs 4.30–9pm; €5) has a much wider ambit than the Risorgimento – Italy's struggle for independence in the nineteenth century – though much of it has a strong military flavour.

The core of the motley collection of curios, portraits and trophies was assembled by the local count, Generale Nino Villa Santa, and was augmented by the donations of various enthusiasts in the 1920s. The castle itself, however, is as interesting as the contents of its numerous display cases. Joined by a fine staircase, the two floors present a succession of beamed rooms richly furnished with rugs, tables, dressers and paintings, mainly from the eighteenth and nineteenth centuries. The soldierly theme is strongest in two large halls, one above the other: the ground-floor Salone delle Milizie has photos, flags, maps and armaments from Garibaldi's campaigns against the Austrians and from the Carso and Piave fronts during World War I; above, the Salone della Giustizia, with a Gothic-Aragonese window, focuses chiefly on the little-known Italian-Turkish war of 1911–12 and on Mussolini's Ethiopian campaign of 1936, and includes Fascist mementos and oddments from World War II, such as English postcards.

Other rooms hold an engaging miscellany, such as, in the first-floor study, fragments of writings by the controversial Italian man of letters and swashbuckling patriot, Gabriele d'Annunzio, and, in an adjoining room, a sabre belonging to Joachim Murat, Napoleon's brother-in-law, and drinking glasses used by Josephine, marked "J". The next room along has a collection of around 350 wax figurines, some dating as far back as the sixteenth century, and some by the master in the field Clemente Susini, whose works are also on display in Cágliari (see p.77). The most arresting waxwork, however, is "La Putrefazione" by Gaetano Zumbo (1656–1701), a horrifically graphic study of a plague victim, half-consumed by rats and worms. Other items on this floor to look out for include an iron bed belonging to the Genoan Doria dynasty from the eighteenth century.

The present head of the Villa Santa family is often on hand to point out objects of interest, and lectures regularly to visiting groups in the central courtyard. Ask him or one of the attendants if you can gain access to the castle's roof for a good view of the town and country. Two of the four crenellated turrets here (the northernmost ones) are purely decorative, added to the original structure for the sake of symmetry.

Across the road from the castle, signposted up the tree-lined Via San Rocco, the church of **San Rocco**, a sixteenth-century construction in the Gothic-Aragonese style, stands on an elevation alongside a Franciscan convent. The latter holds another idiosyncratic collection, the **Museo Etnográfico Cappuccino** (daily 9am–noon & 4–6pm; €3), dedicated to the work of the Capuchin friars who established themselves in Sardinia in 1591. On two floors, the museum displays vestments, psalters and items of religious art together with a more practical selection of workaday articles that evoke the highly active part this community played on the island in a variety of occupations. Basketwork, woodworking tools and even a collection of some sixty watches reflect the diversity of crafts with which the Franciscans occupied themselves, in accordance with the precepts eschewing idleness laid down by their order. There are also a few archeological finds from the Campidano area, mainly jewellery and coins, and a statue thought to represent the Roman emperor Tiberius.

Practicalities

There are usually a couple of taxis outside Sanluri's **train station**, 5km southwest of the centre, also a stop on some bus routes heading into town. In fact, by public transport, it's simpler to reach Sanluri on any of the frequent buses that pass this way from just about everywhere. If you want to stay in town, the functional *Mirage* **hotel** (℡070.930.7100; ❷) lies just by the exit onto the Carlo Felice highway (SS131) at Sanluri's northern end. Open all year, the hotel also houses the *Moulin Rouge* nightclub. Outside town, on the Carlo Felice road, the *Motel Ichnusa* has spacious rooms with or without bath and a restaurant (℡070.930.7073; ❸); note that to reach it you must head south on the SS131 (look out for it to the left as you pass), leaving the superstrada at the first exit and heading back north on a parallel side road. Other accommodation possibilities lie further afield, in the village of Serrenti, 10km south down the SS131, where the central *Campidano* hotel offers absurdly cheap, very basic facilities (but with a/c) at Via Gramsci 38 (℡070.915.8551; no credit cards; ❶), and at Samassi, about the same distance due south of Sanluri (also a stop on the rail line), where another *Campidano* (℡070.938.8121; no credit cards; ❷) lies near the station at Viale Stazione 29, with a restaurant.

For lunches or evening **meals**, head for *La Rosy*, a ristorante/pizzeria marked out by its pale green exterior at Via Carlo Felice 510, along from the *Mirage* hotel (℡070.930.7957; closed Fri). It's modern and capacious and does a good range of reasonably-priced meals, including pizzas. In the centre of town, in Piazza San Pietro, *Baffo d'Oro* is a sit-down bar selling snacks, and you can pick up excellent takeaway ingredients just up from here at Il Buongustaio, a deli specializing in local salamis and cheeses at Via Carlo Felice 260. Call in at any baker for a loaf of the local bread – huge and flavoursome, it's renowned throughout the Campidano. Off Piazza San Pietro, the Banco di Sardegna has **exchange** facilities and a bancomat.

Sárdara and the Castello di Monreale

Nine kilometres northwest of Sanluri on the SS131, the otherwise unexceptional village of **SÁRDARA** clusters around a handful of relics from the nuraghic, Roman and medieval periods. At the top of a flight of steps in the centre of the village stands the attractive fourteenth-century church of **San Gregorio**; the tall, narrow facade with its graceful rose window mixes

Romanesque and Gothic styles. Late-Gothic workmanship dominates in the fifteenth-century church of **Sant'Anastasia**, at the village's highest point and close to a much more ancient centre of worship, the **Témpio Nurágico** (Tues–Sun 9am–1pm & 5–8pm, 4–7pm in winter; €2.58, or €4.13 with Museo Cívico, see below). Constructed in basalt and calcareous bricks, this sacred well dates from the eleventh or tenth centuries BC and is known locally as Funtana de Is Dolus, or "Fountain of Pains", on account of the various ailments its waters were supposed to cure. The site has yielded some notable finds, including heavily ornate water jugs, some of them to be seen in the **Museo Cívico** in Sárdara's ex-town hall on Piazza Libertà (same hours as Témpio Nurágico; €2.60, or €4.20 with Témpio Nurágico). The eight rooms here also display items unearthed at various other archeological sites in the locality – mostly pottery fragments – and bits and pieces from the Castello di Monreale (see below).

The waters around Sárdara were not only valued by Sardinia's prehistoric people. The Romans built the now-vanished Aquae Neapolitanae here, close to the spot a couple of kilometres west of the village where a modern spa now stands amid pine and eucalyptus groves, the Complesso Termale di Santa Maria Is Acquas, more simply known as the **Terme di Sárdara**. The sodium-rich waters that issue from the five hot springs are still used to treat liver and digestive complaints. Next to the hotel complex (see below), the late Gothic church of **Santa Maria Is Acquas** is the venue for a festival deriving from a pagan water cult, taking place on the penultimate Monday of September.

Two kilometres to the south, the **Castello di Monreale** was one of Arborea's key strongholds, equidistant from Cágliari and Oristano and controlling the routes between those cities. The squat ruins crown a hillock overlooking the surrounding plain – an evocative backdrop, even if the sparse remains don't really merit closer exploration. Back in the village, which is a stop on several local bus routes, there are a couple of budget **hotels**: the small *Sárdara da Silvano* at Via Cedrino 5 (☎070.938.7811; ❷) and the *Monreale*, north of the centre at Via Oristano 193 (☎070.938.7139; ❸); both have restaurants. The spa hotel at Terme di Sárdara, eponymously named, is much fancier and you get use of all the facilities, sometimes at an extra cost (☎070.938.7200, ⊛www.termedisardara.it; ❹).

Five kilometres south of the Castello di Monreale, and seven or eight kilometres south of Sárdara, **SAN GAVINO MONREALE** is one of Campidano's larger villages, site of a foundry for the lead and zinc ores extracted from the nearby mines. It is also Sardinia's main centre of saffron (*zafferano*) production. Harvested from the violet-coloured *Crocus Sativus* on the same day or soon after it has flowered, the stuff is used as a dye and in cooking. The village recently enjoyed further fame when the otherwise unremarkable fourteenth-century church of **San Gavino** hit the headlines in 1983, after portraits of the four most prominent figures of the *giudicato* of Arborea – Mariano IV, his daughter Eleonora d'Arborea (see p.136), her husband Brancaleone Doria and her brother Ugone III – were discovered in the apse, the only contemporary likenesses known to exist (but unfortunately presently unviewable). In fact, there's little to detain you in the village unless you're looking for a **hotel** for the night: the one-star *Italia* is on Piazza Césare Battisti 25 (☎070.933.7258; no credit cards; ❷), offering all rooms with private bath and air-conditioning, and there's a separate restaurant below. San Gavino is a stop on the Cágliari–Oristano train line, and the station here is for once centrally located.

La Marmilla

On the confines of the provinces of Cágliari, Oristano and Nuoro, the hilly region of **La Marmilla** is a feast of scenic variety after the monotonous plains of Campidano to the south and west. Its very name, thought to derive from *mammella*, or breast, conjures up the shape of the land, the flat expanses interrupted by small, solitary protuberances, round and regular in form. Traditionally a cereal-growing area, it's also rich in nuraghi, including two of Sardinia's most important sites – one, the recently unearthed **Genna Maria**, dating from the middle of the second millennium BC, outside the village of **Villanovaforru**, where a museum exhibits the huge quantity of graceful ceramics and other finds from the site covering a period of eight centuries. Far more striking, however, is the great nuraghic complex of **Su Nuraxi**, outside the village of **Barúmini**, best reached via the local SS197 leading northeast from Sanluri. On the way, you can't miss the distinctive conical hill at **Las Plassas**; clearly visible on the round summit, the fragments of a twelfth-century castle are a landmark for miles around.

Beyond Barúmini, you could spend an invigorating afternoon tramping through the woods and scrubland covering the high plain of the **Giara di Gésturi**. It shelters a variety of birdlife and other fauna and flora, most famously a breed of miniature wild pony. Carless hikers can explore a good part of the plateau on foot from one of the bordering villages of Tuili, Setzu, Sini, Genuri or Gésturi, all accessible on local bus routes, as are Barúmini and Villanovaforru, which offer the best accommodation possibilities.

Villanovaforru and Genna Maria

Roads trail north and east from Sanluri and Sárdara into the hills of **Marmilla**. At its southern fringes, the village of **VILLANOVAFORRU**, founded by the Spanish in the seventeenth century, has a spruce appearance, testimony to its importance as a grain market for the surrounding area. In Villanovaforru's centre, a tastefully restored villa on Piazza Costituzione holds the **Museo Archeológico** (Tues–Sun 9.30am–1pm & 3.30–7pm, 3.30–6pm in winter; €2.50). It's well worth a visit by anyone also going to the nearby archeological site or interested in the prehistory of the whole Marmilla zone, as it exhibits some of the earliest evidence of local settlements in the Iron and Bronze Ages. The well-lit displays mostly consist of the contents of prenuraghic and nuraghic tombs: a procession of ritual vases, oil lamps (some boat-shaped), myriad brooches and necklaces, and assorted ceramics, sometimes painted with complex geometric patterns. Many of the items are distinctively polished, an effect attained using bones specially crafted for the purpose. Finds from Su Nuraxi (see p.140–141) are well represented, and one room is entirely devoted to Carthaginian and Roman objects, including coins, the clay contents of a Punic tomb found at Villamar and part of a Roman millstone. Many of the artifacts were for domestic use, others testify to the intense religious and commercial activity characterizing this region until the Middle Ages. The importance of water to the local communities is reflected in the abundance of containers found, often with elegantly curving designs.

Though stripped of its original furnishings, the villa's interior retains its beamed ceilings, arched walls and a central well on the ground floor. Behind it, the small **Sala Mostre** (same times as Museo Archeológico; €1) hosts occasional exhibitions to do with the town and the region. The slow-moving village has little else to detain you, though a couple of bars and *alimentari* on or within a few steps of the piazza can provide refreshments.

Occupying the summit of the Marmilla's highest hill (408m), the **Nuraghe di Genna Maria** (same times as Museo Archeológico; €2) commands far-reaching views over the surrounding area. A kilometre west of Villanovaforru, a left turn off the Collinas road leads to the car park from which it's a short but fairly steep climb, the path lined on both sides with pungent rosemary and other herbs. The site itself covers an extensive area dominated by a central ruined tower and the surrounding circular structures of a village. The remains are in worse condition than some of Sardinia's other nuraghic monuments, partly a result of the use of local sandstone as building material, but this still ranks among the island's most important sites, not least for the quantity of finds it has yielded. First excavated between 1951 and 1954 by Sardinia's greatest archeologist, Giovanni Lilliu, but only fully revealed in 1977, the site is still the subject of digs. A raised walkway above the walls, in parts 3m high, allows you to look down on the chambers and passages of the main building, and the lower walls encircling the crowd of small rooms pressed up against it.

The difficulties of building on this elevated site are shown in the many successive **stages of construction**. The central keep (*mastio*) was erected during the first phase, possibly as early as the fifteenth century BC, while the quadrilobate bastion and part of the curtain wall (*antemurale*) certainly go back to the thirteenth century BC. A new phase extended over the thirteenth and twelfth centuries BC, while the village dwellings were built between the twelfth and ninth centuries BC, the beginning of Sardinia's Iron Age. Finally, the curtain wall was completed during the ninth and eighth centuries BC. The village, some of whose buildings have a central courtyard, was also inhabited in Carthaginian and Roman periods until the third century AD.

To one side of the site, a new stone-built construction shelters diagrams illustrating how the complex might once have looked, while one map shows how densely the Marmilla is filled with other nuraghic settlements. From this high windy spot, you can sight many of the hills and areas identified on the map, the most significant landmark being the flat and high Giara di Gésturi, to the north (see p.142–143). For more on Sardinia's nuraghic culture, see p.349–350.

A short lane right opposite the turn-off to the site leads to *Le Colline* (☎070.930.0123; ❸), a smart, friendly three-star **hotel** with great views on all sides. The same management runs the next-door *Il Lecco* (☎070.933.1021; ❺), a modern four-star. Back in Villanovaforu, there's the large, convent-like *Funtana Noa* on Via Vittorio Emanuele III (☎070.933.1019, ⓦwww .residencefuntananoa.it; ❸), with tiled floors, beamed ceilings and a cloister-like courtyard. The spacious **restaurant** has pizzas among the menu items, and moderate prices.

Barúmini and Su Nuraxi

East of Villanovaforu stretches a varied landscape of cultivated fields interspersed with some pasturage, all overlooked by a horizon of knobbly brown peaks. The most prominent feature for miles around is the extraordinary conical **hill of Las Plassas** (274m), on whose round pinnacle fragments of the twelfth-century **castello di Marmilla** stick up like broken teeth. The hill is a perfect example of the bosomy bumps characteristic of the Marmilla region. To get closer, take a left turn off the straight SS197, just before the Agip petrol station at the southern entrance to the hamlet of **Las Plassas**; alternatively a brown signpost in the village points you in the same direction. Five hundred metres along, opposite the majolica-tiled dome of the seventeenth-century church of **Santa Maria Maddalena**, a path weaves up the hillside to the scanty ruins: there is little to see of the castle itself, but the view makes it worth the brief spurt of exercise necessary to reach it. Traces of a previous nuraghic settlement have been unearthed below the castle.

Three kilometres to the north of Las Plassas, **BARÚMINI** is a larger, though still fairly run-of-the-mill village, best known for the nuraghic site of **Su Nuraxi** (daily 9am–dusk; €4.20), located just outside it (coming from the south, turn left at the village's central crossroads). As the largest nuraghic complex on the island, as well as one of the oldest (dating from around 1500 BC), it has attracted more funding than any other site, and has been continuously excavated since 1949. Despite all the research, however, its origins remain largely obscure, though it seems likely that this was a palace complex at the very least, possibly even a capital city. The whole area is thought to have been covered with earth by Sards and Carthaginians at the time of the Roman conquest, accounting for its good state of preservation.

There's plenty to take in. The imposing central tower, built of dark-grey basalt blocks, lies at the centre of a tight mesh of walled dwellings separated by a web of lanes. All visits to the site are escorted by guides who can provide a knowledgeable commentary (usually only in Italian), and will warn you to keep off the walls, which would otherwise invite much clambering over. The first traces of human settlement date from the middle Bronze Age (sixteenth–thirteenth centuries BC); the place was destroyed in the seventh century BC, then rebuilt and resettled until the Roman period. In between, the complex was constantly being expanded, with towers added to the central bastion, which were joined by a stone wall. The bulky **central tower** originally reached 21m (now shrunk to about 14.5m), and contained three chambers, one above the other, of which two remain. At the end of a corridor, the *tholos*-type lower chamber has alcoves once lined with cork, and an opening halfway up the walls suggesting the existence of a wooden flight of stairs to reach the next storey. To reach this room now you have to backtrack along the elaborate network of passageways and rugged steps connecting the various inner chambers. Most of the topmost storey is now missing, but you'll still enjoy a good vista over the whole site from here.

Next to the central tower on ground level, a deep crescent-shaped **courtyard** holds a well that still contains water, and gives onto three of the four external towers which form the corners of the quadrilobate outer defences, part of a second phase of construction, probably in the thirteenth or twelfth centuries BC. The height of the walls enclosing this courtyard was raised at a later period, an alteration clearly visible in the contrast between the more regular masonry of the later work and the rougher-hewn stones of the lower parts.

The outer walls were strengthened between the twelfth and tenth centuries BC, and encompassed within a further line of defence: a polygonal **curtain wall** studded with (now roofless) round towers. The same period saw the expansion of the settlement, though most of the **nuraghic village** dates from later, between the tenth and sixth centuries, when the nucleus of the settlement was already in a state of decay. Scattered around the curtain walls, it's a dense, untidy outgrowth of over two hundred circular and horseshoe-shaped buildings, all now roofless, but many reconstructed to a height of about two metres.

The dialect name of the site means simply "the nuraghs". Sardinian x's are pronounced either with a "sh" sound, or like the French "j". "Su Nuraxi" is thus pronounced "Su Nurashi" or "Su Nuraji".

In appearance, these huts must have resembled the small stone-roofed shepherd's *pinneddas* still used today in some parts of Sardinia (see p.181). For more on Sardinia's nuraghic culture, see p.349–350.

In the village, the Renaissance-influenced **Palazzo Zapata** (also called Casa degli Zapata), former residence of a Spanish family granted the fiefdom of La Marmilla in 1541, is destined to hold a museum of finds from Su Nuraxi when restoration work is complete. Until that time, the seventeenth-century church of **Santa Tecla** (July–Sept daily 9am–1pm & 3–7pm; Oct–June Sat & Sun 10am–1pm & 3–6pm; €1.03), right by the crossroads at the centre of the village and distinguished by its swirling rose window and battlements on a square facade, holds various exhibits, including explanatory panels and diagrams, a multilingual audiovisual commentary on a CD-Rom, a model reconstruction of Su Nuraxi, and a few objects dug up from the site, mainly ceramic items. There is currently much more material to be seen at the archeological museum at Villanovaforru (see p.139).

Barúmini has one other attraction which will appeal particularly to children, **Sardegna in Miniatura** (Easter–Sept daily 9am–sunset; Oct Sat & Sun 9am–sunset; €5), located a kilometre west of the village, off the road to Tuili. The centrepiece is a (mainly) 1:25 scale version of Sardinia's most famous monuments and sights arranged on a miniature Sardinia-shaped island, from Cágliari's cathedral in the south, perched above a port where Tirrenia ferries are docked, to Olbia's airport and the nearby beaches of the Costa Smeralda in the north, taking in Pisan churches and various archeological sites – including Su Nuraxi itself – en route. You can tour the model reconstructions by boat and get an overview of it from a wooden tower. The park also holds a near life-size version of huts in a nuraghic village, complete with bearded mannequins and explanatory commentaries in Italian and English. There's a picnic area and restaurant here too.

Practicalities

Barúmini is connected by two or three **buses** daily, calling here en route from Cágliari to Désulo, Láconi and Samugheo. If you want to stay in the area, there are several **accommodation** options in the village. Of these, the swankiest is *Sa Lolla* (℡070.936.8419; ❸), a ranch-style hotel on Via Cavour, with a fantastic restaurant as well as a pool and tennis court. However, with only seven rooms – tastefully minimalist in design – availability may be limited. The alternatives are a string of B&Bs, mostly clustered near the post office on Viale Umberto, all of a similar standard and identically priced (❷): try *Casa Sanna* at Viale Umberto 61 (℡070.936.8157 or 348.058.2175), which has en-suite bathrooms; *Casa del Rio*, Trav. I Principessa Maria (℡070.936.8141 or 328.675.6025), or *Casa Piras*, Trav. II Principessa Maria 15 (℡070.936.8372 or 349.883.7015). They are not marked, so you may have to ask around to find them.

As for **eating**, the best choice is *Sa Lolla* (see above), whose renowned restaurant concentrates on local specialities and is open to non-guests; prices are moderate to expensive, and booking is recommended. Otherwise, there are a couple of plain trattorias catering largely to coach parties across the road from Su Nuraxi, as well as a **bar** where you can buy drinks and *panini*.

La Giara di Gésturi

North of Barúmini, the high tableland of the **Giara di Gésturi**, or *Sa Jara*, is an ever-present feature of the landscape. Roughly 12km long, covering some

42 square kilometres at a maximum height of 560m, it is the largest of a series of basalt plateaux thrown up in ancient eruptions – the most noteworthy others are the Giara di Siddi and that of Serri – and the subject of plans to protect it as a natural reserve. The area is controlled now by rangers, but is uncrossed by any roads; there are, however, surfaced tracks winding up from the villages at its base, leading to places where you can leave your vehicle. The Giara ("plateau") is fairly bare on its lower flanks, but as you climb you'll come across thicker brushwood and groves of twisted cork trees. On the flat summit, the impervious basalt rock has created *paulis*, or depressions, which fill up with rainwater to create swampy ponds; these, together with the thick vegetation, help to provide a perfect terrain for a variety of **wildfowl**, from buzzards to bee-eaters. Spring is the best season to visit, when the area is at its greenest and a magnet for migrating birds.

The plateau has also become home to goats and wild boars, though the most rarely seen beasts are those which appear most frequently on the tourist literature – packs of **wild ponies**, or *cavallini* (in dialect, *is quaddedus*). At the last count there were around five hundred of these diminutive creatures, which measure less than 130cm at shoulder height; a smaller number live in the Arca di Noe protected zone at Porto Conte, near Alghero (see p.208). Their origins are unknown, but they are thought to have links with oriental breeds, possibly introduced by the Phoenicians 3000 years ago. Though free to roam at will, the ponies are generally claimed by local farmers – the branding ceremony is one of the highlights of the year, taking place at the end of August.

You're allowed to wander where you please over the rough terrain (you'll need stout shoes), though you might also consider using an experienced **guide**. Ask in the bars of the low-lying villages, or one of the forest rangers, normally stationed in shacks near the car parks – rates are negotiable, depending on time, numbers and season.

Access to the area is easiest from the villages of Génuri, Setzu, Tuili and Gésturi. One to two ARST **buses** from Cágliari and Barúmini link Tuili and Gésturi daily, while Génuri and Setzu have two daily weekday connections to Sanluri and one to Oristano. None of the villages has much in the way of tourist facilities.

Tuili

The most interesting of the villages circling the Giara di Gésturi is **TUILI**, 3km west of Su Nuraxi's site, whose church of **San Pietro** contains a real treasure. Lying opposite a ramshackle old villa, the church is easily locatable by its neat, round-topped belltower. Within the unprepossessing exterior, the **retablo di San Pietro** occupies the whole of a chapel at the back of the right-hand aisle. Painted by the artist known only as the Maestro di Castelsardo, this vividly coloured polyptych is the only one of his works to bear a date – 1500, according to a legal document specifying his fee. Its style is predominantly Gothic, with few signs of the impact of the Renaissance. Against richly detailed landscapes, the central panels show Christ crucified and the Madonna with saints; on the left, St Michael (slaying the devil) and St Peter are depicted, on the right are St James and St Paul, respectively above and below. Considered by some to be Sardinia's finest work of medieval art, it's a solemn and absorbing study, the facial expressions and garments superbly rendered. To view it properly in the church's dim interior, ask someone to turn on the lights (the switch is behind the painting on the left). The rest of the building is also richly painted – there's another *retablo* on the corresponding chapel on the other side of the nave, dated 1534, painted by another anonymous artist.

The village has a couple of other lavishly endowed churches which point to an impressive concentration of wealthy local patrons. Other than a few bars and a Banco di Sardegna, there's not much else in the village, though it makes a good starting-off point for expeditions to the Giara di Gesturi, rising bare to the north, towards which there are unmissable signs ("Altopiano della Giara"). Plans are afoot to open an **information centre** dealing with the Giara, on Tuili's main road, right by the ARST bus stop.

Gésturi

Five kilometres north of Barúmini, the campanile of **Santa Teresa d'Ávila** dominates the village of **GÉSTURI**. The church is reckoned to be Sardinia's very latest example of the Catalan-Gothic style, dating from 1674. The main road through the village has a handy **bar/pizzeria**, *Fra Nicola* (closed Mon in winter), which also arranges **excursions** on the Giara di Gésturi on foot, bike or horseback (☎070.936.9425). There are the same brown signs to the *Altopiano della Giara* as Tuili, but again, nowhere to find general information. Gésturi is a stop on the ARST bus routes from Cágliari to Désulo, Láconi and Samugheo, the same services which run through Barúmini.

Sarrabus

Sardinia's southeastern corner, **Sarrabus**, is refreshingly wild and sparsely populated, much of it too desolate even for shepherds. At its heart lies the rugged wilderness of the **Sette Fratelli** mountains, noted for their abundant birdlife and excellent hiking possibilities. The only village hereabouts, **Burcei**, provides the main necessities, most usefully a bank and places to stock up on food and drink. You'll find considerably more development squeezed along the Sarrabus coast, where ranks of identical-looking holiday homes have scarred the rocky shore, with the biggest concentration around the resort of **Villasimius**, a fully-fledged holiday town on the eastern tip of the Golfo di Cágliari. Despite the development, there are still unforgettable views over isolated coves and rocky promontories, enhanced by the occasional Spanish watchtower. There are also some superb beaches to swim from, including the perfect golden sands of the **Costa Rei**, the holiday coast north of Villasimius. To escape the colonies of unsightly tourist homes, however, you must follow the coast up to **Capo Ferrato**, 30km north of Villasimius, and to the twelve kilometres of beach extending beyond the cape as far as the port and holiday resort of **Porto Corallo**. The only centre in these parts is **Muravera**, a dull inland town with a traffic problem, though it makes a useful base for beach devotees. On the far western edge of Sarrabus, in the fertile flatlands due north of Cágliari, the agricultural centre of **Dolianova** is worth visiting chiefly for its Romanesque ex-cathedral, the only important religious monument in these parts.

Villasimius holds the area's best choice of hotels and restaurants; elsewhere, **accommodation** may be thin on the ground, though campers will find a good choice of sites scattered along the coast, many with bungalows available. Exploring Sarrabus can be a lengthy business, especially in summer when the few roads linking the region are encumbered by slow-moving traffic, not least the SS125 to Muravera, the main route linking Cágliari with Sardinia's east

△ Nuraghe Su Nuraxi

coast. From Cágliari, Dolianova can be reached on the FdS **trains** on weekdays, and **buses** run daily to Dolianova, Villasimius and Muravera.

Dolianova and around

Fifteen kilometres north of Cágliari, off the SS387, the market town of **DOLIANOVA** is the main centre of a region renowned for its olives and olive oil, and for its wines, which include Nuragus, Moscato and Malvasia. Though mostly a workaday place with a few handsome nineteenth-century palazzi, Dolianova does have one interesting relic: the **Chiesa di San Pantaleo** (daily 10am–noon & 3.30–7pm), reached through an archway signposted off the town's main thoroughfare. Occupying one side of the large courtyard or small piazza and topped by a short belltower, the church – formerly a cathedral – sports blind arcading running right round the walls, sculpted with eroded stone carvings of animals, plants, moons and some human forms. Started between 1150 and 1160 by a team who had previously worked on the church of Santa Giusta, outside Oristano (see p.176), the grey stone exterior was completed by Arab architects a century later, accounting for its *mudéjar* style, which mixes Romanesque, Gothic and Arab elements. Next to the entrance, a Roman sarcophagus protrudes incongruously from the main body of the church, suspended on slender columns.

The **interior** is decorated with an impressive array of murals, one of them depicting Christ crucified on what looks like the tree of life; it is, in fact, an *álbero genealógico*, a favourite theme in medieval art showing Abraham and the prophets (a quarter of it is missing). Next to this, an oriental-looking *ancona*, or six-panelled altarpiece, shows the martyrdom of San Pantaleo, probably the work of an unknown Spanish painter in the sixteenth century. There's a horribly immolated Christ on one wall of the church, and at the back, a stone *baldacchino* (canopy) which, like the wonky columns of the nave, is crudely carved with figures of animals, angels and a man and woman embracing.

Continuing north from Dolianova, you can rejoin the SS387 as far as Sant'Andrea Frius, from where you can choose between branching left onto the SS547 for Mandas and the heart of the Barbágia, or staying with the SS387 as it twists eastwards into the highlands of **Gerrei**, a little-visited mountain area north of Sarrabus. You can also reach the main settlement in Gerrei, **San Nicolò Gerrei**, directly from Dolianova along an even more tortuous mountain road without a building to be seen along its whole thirty-three-kilometre length. Continuing a further 11km north from San Nicolò Gerrei will bring you to Ballao, from where you can continue on into the Barbágia or else follow the SS387 southeast along the path of the River Flumendosa, which descends to Muravera and the coast (see p.151). All of these options offer exhilarating mountain scenery, but they can be fairly strenuous drives. Bus passengers might have a more relaxing experience, though services to San Nicolò Gerrei and Ballao from Cágliari, Dolianova and Muravera are few and far between.

The Golfo di Cágliari

Thankfully, the main roads east out of Cágliari quickly bypass the snarled-up centre of **Quartu Sant'Elena**, separated from the northern curve of the beaches at Poetto by the brown waters of the Stagno di Quartu. The road soon narrows as it traces the littoral eastward along the **Golfo di Cágliari**, and can get congested with traffic, especially in summer. Much of the coming and going is accounted for by the swelling carpet of holiday villas covering a substantial section of the rocky slopes. Despite these hostile factors, it's still a pretty drive, with good views across the gulf back to Cágliari and the western shore. The coast grows progressively emptier and, despite the closeness of the capital, it's still possible to find inlets for a relatively secluded dip. The nearest **campsite** to Cágliari lies in one of its nicer sections in the **Capitana** district, about 6km from Quartu Sant'Elena's beach and not too far from beaches to either side. The *Pini e Mare* (mid-April to Nov; ℡070.803.103, ⦿web .tiscalinet.it /piniemare) also has two-, three- and four-person cabins available for €62–103 per night in high season; other sites lie outside Villasimius (see below) and on the Costa Rei (p.148–149).

East of here, there are excellent sandy beaches tucked away at **Cala Regina**, **Torre delle Stelle** and **Solanas** – the prettiest village on this stretch, next to one of the sentinel towers that dot this entire coast. East of Capo Boi, the **Golfo di Carbonara** – named after the charcoal produced in the nearby forests (a byproduct was the black powder added to gunpowder for its damp-proof qualities, favoured by Nelson among others) – also holds scraps of beach, sometimes visible from the mainly high coast road. However, it's difficult to ignore the intrusions of the holiday industry, for the most part uniform rows of peach-coloured villas and four-star hotels which charge handsomely for their prime locations. If you're looking for somewhere to stay, you'd do better to push on to Villasimius, which has some cheaper choices. Note that all the places mentioned above are accessible from any of the frequent buses between Cágliari and Villasimius.

Villasimius

Not so long ago a quiet village, **VILLASIMIUS** has assumed the typical dual identity of a medium-size resort town. Incredibly lively in summer, when it's a hotbed of bars, boutiques, pizzerias and revving scooters, it slumbers the rest of the time, and visitors between October and May may find most facilities closed. The main road through town is Viale Umberto, leading to Piazza Gramsci and the smaller Piazza Generale Incani, from where Via del Mare leads down to the nearest stretch of beach, just 1.5km away at **Simius**. The arc of sand here faces the offshore isles of **Serpentara**, a long strip of bare rock, and the more southerly **Isola dei Cávoli**, visited by boat tours from the beach in summer. Simius is the most developed of the area's bathing spots, dominated by luxury hotels; you can find wilder sections walking south towards **Capo Carbonara**, where the eastern shore of this thin peninsula is backed by the calm **Stagno di Notteri**, a stopover for flamingos in winter, and the **Fortezza Vecchia**, a square fortification probably dating from the fourteenth century, now used for exhibitions (mid-June to mid-Sept Mon–Wed & Fri–Sun 10am–1pm & 6–9pm; mid-Sept to mid-June Fri–Sun 10am–1pm & 3–5pm; €1). You can drive here by turning right out of Villasimius and following the road for two or three kilometres. This is also the road for the **Marina di Villasimius**, a new yachting port on the Golfo di Carbonara, and for **Spiaggia del Riso**, another magnificent stretch of sand surrounded by turquoise and aquamarine waters, close to a campsite (see p.148).

Practicalities

A small office at the Comune on Piazza Gramsci dispenses **local informa-tion**, including lists of diving centres in the area and rooms to rent (mid-June to mid-Sept Mon–Sat 10am–1pm & 9pm–midnight; mid-Sept to mid-June Mon & Thurs 10am–1pm & 3.30–6.30pm, Fri 4–7pm, Sat 10am–1pm; ℡070.793.0208 or ℡070.793.0232, ⦿www.villasimiusweb.com). The best and cheapest **place to stay** in town is around the corner at Via Vittorio Emanuele 25: the *Stella d'Oro* (℡070.791.255; ❹), where at least half-board, at €82 per person, is required in August. Rooms are regular and clean, and the good fish restaurant has an internal courtyard. Other choices include the much smarter *Blu Marlin*,Via Giotto 7 (℡070.790.357, ⓦwww.hotelblumarlin.it; ❼), a small place offering excellent low-season deals and discounts for last-minute bookings. If you want to stay nearer the sea, hotel prices soar into the luxury bracket, though you'll find more reasonable rates at *Fiore di Maggio* at Località Campulongu, 2km from town and 80m from the beach, separated by pinewoods (April–Sept; ℡070.797.382, ⓦwww.fioredimaggio.it; ❸). Nearer town on Via del Mare, the *Tre Lune* (℡070.790.302, ⓦwww.trelune.it; ❼) is another place with plunging rates out of season, but charges €115 per person for obligatory half-board in August; it lies some 200m from the sea. A well-equipped **campsite**, *Spiaggia del Riso* (May–Oct; ℡070.791.052, ⓦwww .villaggiospiaggiadelriso.it), is located right on the beach of the same name on Capo Carbonara, with four- or five-bed bungalows to rent at €110–132 per night in peak season. Other campsites are north of town at Cala Sinzias (see below).

Villasimius has plenty of scope for food and refreshment, with bars and **restaurants** on every corner. Among the best are the moderately priced *Stella d'Oro* (see above) and the *Carbonara*, a more sober fish restaurant with slightly steeper prices at Via Umberto 60 (closed Wed in winter). On Piazza Incani, *La Página* has an upstairs room for seafood dishes (closed Mon in winter), while the more casual *Tartana* next door has a terrace where you can snack on pastries and rolls, and also has a restaurant/pizzeria upstairs. A food **market** operates on Saturday mornings in Via Donatello, next to the Carabinieri barracks.

The Carboni agency at Via Umberto 99 (℡070.790.376) rents out **cars**, **scooters** and **mountain bikes**: a Fiat Punto costs around €75 a day, scooters are €45, bikes €10. In summer, the office transfers to the Tanka Villaggio holiday village at the Simius beach. The Banco di Sardegna on Piazza Gramsci (Mon–Fri 8.20am–1.20pm & 2.35–3.35pm) has an ATM to **change money**, and the **post office** is at Via del Mare 72 (Mon–Fri 8.10am–1.20pm, Sat 8.10am–12.30pm, last day of month closes at noon). The main **bus stop** is on Piazza Gramsci for ARST buses (buy tickets from the photography shop on Piazza Gramsci or the newspaper kiosks next to the church at Via Marconi and on Via del Mare), and Vacca Viaggi also runs a beach service connecting Villasimius with Capo Boi, Porticciolo and all the neighbouring beaches eight–ten times daily between July and mid-September (buy tickets on board).

The Costa Rei

West of Villasimius, the road dips and swings as it follows the contours of the coast, affording glorious views towards the islands of Serpentara and Isola dei Cávoli. The first good beach lies eighteen circuitous kilometres further north along this road, at **Cala Sinzias**, a broad swathe of sand cupped within the arms of a small bay, virtually free of development. There are two campsites here, however, *Limone Beach* (℡070.995006, ⓦwww.limonebeach.it), and, right in front, *Garden Cala Sinzias* (July–Sept; ℡070.995.037, ⓦwww.calasinzias.com), both with bungalows and caravans available, and the *Limone Beach* also has cheaper tents to rent (€65 in peak season).

A short distance north of here begins the long ribbon of beaches that make up the **Costa Rei**. If your taste is for shimmering expanses of fine white sand but not for the area's full-on holiday mania, make sure you're here outside the months of June–September, when things have quietened down and prices have fallen. Almost all of the available accommodation is in villas rented out by the week, booked through agencies in Villasimius – when they're not block-booked by package companies – though there are some **hotels** which might appeal to families, such as the *Albaruja* on Via Cristóforo Colombo (mid-May to Sept; ☎070.991.557, ⊛www.albaruja.it; ❺), which has villa accommodation near a pool and tennis courts. In common with all other hotels here, it requires at least half-board in high season. At the other end of the scale, the *Capo Ferrato* **campsite** (Easter to mid-Oct; ☎070.991.012, ⊛www.campingcapoferrato.it) is shaded by mimosa and eucalyptus and has bungalows available (around €55 per night); it's right by a broad sweep of sand, though perhaps too close to the dreary ranks of orange and pink holiday villas for comfort. There are wind-surfing and canoeing facilities nearby, and you'll find a few **supermarkets** here.

At the top end of this bay, there are remoter scraps of sandy beach towards **Capo Ferrato**; these may be reached via dirt tracks running off the road parallel to the coast. The only place around here for **eating and drinking** is the *Capo Ferrato* bar/pizzeria, which serves roast chicken alongside the *panini* and pizzas (closed Tues Oct–May). Not too far distant is the upmarket *Porto Pirastu* campsite (April–Sept; ☎070.991.437, ⊛www.portopirastu.net), with caravans and bungalows to rent by the sea (up to €63 for two people per night); ARST buses from Cágliari stop right outside the bar. A short way north of here, the asphalt degenerates into a dusty track that winds behind the pine-clad Capo Ferrato to the next bay, and more premium beaches.

Castiadas

Inland of the Costa Rei, the land is flat and verdant. Signposted 7km west of the main road, **CASTIADAS** is a straggle of buildings around the flaking pink walls of an abandoned penal colony set up in the nineteenth century. There's not much to do here, but there is an inviting **trattoria** – *Le Vecchie Carceri* (closed Oct–April and weekdays May–June), with pizzas, horse and donkey on the menu, and good fixed-price deals – and it makes a good starting point for exploring the **Foresta di Minniminni**, a couple of kilometres to the south. This protected area of holm oak and thick *macchia* is only passable on foot, donkey or, to an extent, in 4WD vehicles. As well as the ubiquitous arbutus, juniper and cyclamen of the *macchia*, the area holds two plantations of pine trees left by the inmates of the penal colony, one from 1875, when they arrived, the second from when the colony was closed down in 1956. Though the summit of Monte Minniminni is only 723m, it affords wonderful views over the surrounding coast. In Castiadas, contact the Cooperativa Monte dei Sette Fratelli (Via Centrale, ☎070.994.7200 or 338.462.9860) for guided excursions in the Foresta and in the Sette Fratelli range. A half-day ride in an off-roader costs €41 per person (negotiable). The group also leads walking expeditions in spring and autumn at around the same price. Some hikes are also described on the website ⊛www.castiadasonline.it, which is packed with general information on the whole district.

Monte dei Sette Fratelli

Linking Cágliari with Muravera, the tortuous and highly scenic SS125 cuts through the heart of Sarrabus, passing through the dramatic **Monte dei Sette Fratelli** ("Seven Brothers") range, which reaches a height of about 1020m. If you want to strike out on foot, there are plenty of opportunities to stop along the way, and we've outlined one of the best walks which can be undertaken without any particular skills (see box below). For more ambitious climbs in these parts, however, you'll need expert guidance, such as the excursion group based in Castiadas (see p.149). The steep, granite slopes are either *macchia*-covered or forested with cork oak and holm oak, and provide a habitat for the rare *cervo sardo*, the short Sardinian stag for which this is a protected zone.

The region is uninhabited apart from a couple of isolated settlements. About 20km northeast of Quartu Sant'Elena, a good road left wanders 7km up to **BURCEI**, a small village at a height of 648m, famed for its cherry trees, which come to full, flamboyant blossom in May. Dominated by the fat dome of the church of Santa Maria di Monserrato, the village holds a Banco di Sardegna in Piazza della Repubblica (with a bancomat), and the friendly *Sa Prana* birreria/ristorante at Via Roma 70 (opposite the Íssimo supermarket), which offers a good selection of antipasti, meat dishes, panini and salads, but no pasta or pizza (no smoking; closed Wed).

A walk in the Monte dei Sette Fratelli

This moderately easy **hike** in the Sette Fratelli takes you into the heart of the range, along paths lined for much of the way with wild clematis and fennel. Climbing skills are not required, but bring stout shoes, at least one litre of water and some sun-protection; also, let other people know where you're bound (there's a Forestry Corps station near the beginning of the walk), and beware of rapidly falling nights. The entire walk should take less than four hours, not counting breaks.

You can reach the **start of the route** on public transport along the SS125 from Cágliari or Muravera. Coming from Cágliari, soon after the junction for Burcei on the left, look out for a bridge over a small river (signposted Rio Campuomo), on the far side of which there is a clearing on the right where drivers can park, immediately before a Corpo Forestale station. The path begins here, signposted "Sentiero Italia, Campuomo, Castiadas". The route is waymarked with the symbol of a white diamond with a red stripe across.

Follow the level track for about ten minutes until you reach a fork, where you should bear left (uphill); there's no symbol here, but you'll see them again soon. It gets a little steeper up the rough path, before it emerges onto a good unasphalted road, where there's a signpost: follow "Conventu" to the left. A few minutes later, there's an unsignposted second fork – take the right-hand path, slightly descending before levelling out and climbing again. About 45 minutes after setting out, you'll reach the ruins of the **Conventu de Sette Fradi** (also called Convento dei Sette Fratelli) that once stood here, in a shady clearing (600m). The name of the range might derive from the erstwhile inhabitants of the monastery, or it may refer to the peaks themselves. Travellers on the route between Burcei and Castiadas would lodge here for the night.

Proceed past the monastery; after five minutes or so, take a right-hand fork onto a rough mule-track, which descends through woods to a river, the **Riu Guventu**. If there's water here, you can cross on stepping stones, before climbing steeply up the far side (following the symbols) along a smaller river-bed. The trail soon diverges to the left, continuing up through dense woods, where the symbols are fairly sparse. The path continues uphill in a similar vein, with occasional clearings affording good views on the way, until, less than an hour after leaving the convent, you'll reach the bare summits of the Sette Fratelli. The path dives in and out of the woods as far as the highest peak, **Punta Sa Ceraxa** (1015m). From here, the trail continues towards Castiadas. From Sa Ceraxa, your return journey should take another ninety minutes or so.

Nuraghe Asoru

Soon after the Burcei junction, the SS125 descends through the desolate gorge of the River Picocca, littered with monolithic boulders. After another 16km the road levels out and passes the **Nuraghe Asoru** (also called **Nuraghe S'Oro**), unmissable on the left-hand side of road. Built between the tenth and eighth centuries BC in a dominating position over the surrounding plain and the inland approaches, it's the only *nuraghe* worthy of note in southeastern Sardinia, which evidently proved too barren even for this hardy folk. There's a small internal courtyard, and a hole in the coarse masonry of the wall reveals a bench running all around its interior. In perfect condition since its 1976 restoration, the *nuraghe*'s lovely tawny colour is in perfect harmony with its surroundings.

Muravera and around

The Riu Sa Picocca flows into a flat, fertile area, with thick groves of citrus and lesser growths of almonds and other fruit and nut trees. Having accompanied the river as far as its outlet on the coast, the SS125 swings north, passing close to the beach of San Giovanni before heading inland again to enter **MURAVERA**. The only town between Villasimius and Tortolì, it's not a particularly endearing place, its main Via Roma a constant stream of traffic alongside which pedestrians are squeezed onto minuscule pavements.

Although heavily dependent on the local tourist industry, for which it serves as a centre, Muravera also thrives as an agricultural town, and is known as the island's citrus capital. With the neighbouring villages of Villaputzu and San Vito, it's renowned for the authenticity of the rural produce, such as honey, wine and *dolci*. All three places are also famed for the preservation of their local traditions, as shown in their much respected local festivals, whose ebullience goes some way to compensating for the essentially drab appearance of the villages.

In Muravera itself, the biggest **festival** is the *Sagra degli Agrumi* (Citrus Fair) on the first or second Sunday before Easter – usually in March or April – to celebrate the end of winter, marked by parades of peasant wagons laden with fruit; the other main dates are around August 28, when the music and costumed festivities last four days, and December 6, for two days of poetry competitions, singing and dancing. **Villaputzu**, 3.5km north of Muravera, has four days of costumed processions and traditional dances around the second Sunday in October, while **San Vito**, 4.5km north of Muravera, is at its best on its saint's day, June 15; on the first Sunday in August, and during the marathon five days of poetry and singing competitions and concerts that take place around the third Sunday in October.

From San Vito, the SS387 curls inland along the course of the River Flumendosa and into the hilly Gerrei region, a panoramic route into the interior (see p.146). East of Villaputzu, the river joins the sea near **Porto Corallo** where, on the approximate site of a long-disappeared Phoenician port, a small harbour has been recreated, this time for pleasure craft. On the left of the road stand the scanty remains of the hilltop **Castello di Gibas**, less a castle than a fortification, erected by the Spanish together with the cylindrical watchtower overlooking Porto Corallo. The latter was the scene of one of the last battles against North African pirates, when the locals succeeded in driving back their attackers in 1812. To the south of the river mouth, a broad beach stretches southwards, backed by eucalyptus woods; it's a popular spot in fine weather, with picnic tables and a bar/pizzeria and gelateria close at hand.

North of Muravera, the road follows the course of the River Quirra, parallel to the coast and separated from it by a wall of mountains. It's a fertile area, much of it cultivated, with scattered nut trees that burst into blossom in early spring. Twenty-two kilometres north of Muravera, the road crosses the Cágliari–Nuoro provincial boundary on its way north to the village of Tertenia and the Ogliastra region around Tortolì (see p.342).

Practicalities

Muravera's helpful **tourist office** is behind Piazza Europa at Via Machiavelli 2 (summer daily 9am–7pm; winter Mon–Sat 8am–1pm, also Tues & Wed 4–7pm; ℡070.993.0760 or toll-free 800/258.142). Despite being the main centre for this holiday region, the town has only two **hotels**, both along the main Via Roma. At no. 31, the most central, the modern *Corallo* (℡070.993.0502, ⓦwww.albergocorallo.it; ❺), is also the smartest, with 45 well-equipped rooms and an outdoor pizzeria. A few doors down, opposite the petrol station at Piazza Libertà 3, *Sa Férula* is dowdy but adequate for a night (℡070.993.0237; ❸; no credit cards). There's a welcome **B&B** nearby, however, at *Casa Speranza*, off Via Roma on Via Speranza (℡070.999024 or 340.004.5487, ⓦwww.discoversardinia.com; ❷). The Irish-German couple who run this also offer B&B accommodation 9km down the coast at Colostrai – where the seaside *Villa Philippine* is named after a Belgian princess who was the previous owner – as well as self-catering apartments. If all else fails, head north to Villaputzu, where the *Seralapis* hotel on Piazza Marconi offers functional accommodation above a bar between June and September (℡070.997.433; ❸; no credit cards).

There are a couple of beach-side **campsites** in the area: the *Quattro Mori*, a couple of kilometres south of Muravera at Località Is Perdigonis (Easter–Sept; ℡070.999.110, ⓦwww.4mori.it), where self-catering four-bed mini-apartments are available for rent for up to €126 per night in high season, less than half that outside July and August, and *Torre Salinas*, a kilometre or two further down (April to mid-Oct; ℡070.999.032, ⓦwww.camping-torre-salinas.de), which has cheaper tents and caravans for rent at €25–35 a night. Both have sports facilities and pizzerias, and both offer riding excursions.

Restaurants are easy to find in the summer season, less so in winter. At Via Roma 257 (the northern end of the drag), *Su Nuraxi* stays open all year and provides a reliable if unexceptional menu of the usual items, with a wood-fired oven for good pizzas (closed Wed Oct–May; moderate). Further north up the road, opposite the Polizia Stradale station, *Sa Foredda* is a more upmarket place offering Sard specialities (closed Tues). For **snacks**, the *Paderi* bar at Via Roma 63 has crepes and ice cream (closed Mon in winter), and there is also good ice cream at *L'Oasi* north of the centre. *Rockburgers* at Via Roma 128 (closed Mon) has pizzas and beers as well as burgers. Off Via Roma, Piazza Europa is the venue for nightly **concerts** and other entertainments in summer. At Porto Corallo, refreshment is provided by the *Top Sound* bar/pizzeria/ristorante, open all year (but closed Wed in winter), which is also the main place in the neighbourhood for tobacco, telephones, bus tickets and newspapers.

Muravera's **post office** is off Piazza Europa at Via Europa (Mon–Fri 7.50am–1pm, Sat 8.10am–12.30pm), and you can **change money** at the Banco di Sardegna, back on the main street opposite *Rockburgers* (Mon–Fri 8.20am–1.20pm & 2.35–4.05pm); there's also a bancomat here. **Car hire** is available from Francesco Musiu at Via Matteotti 23 (℡070.993.0741). If you want to **dive** in the local waters, contact *Casa Speranza* (see p.152), which can also arrange **riding** and other activities. Before leaving the area, take away with you some of Muravera's fresh produce, sold at the fruit market off Via Roma on Monday mornings.

Travel details

Trains

Dolianova to: Cágliari (Mon–Sat 10–14 daily; 40–50min); Ísili (Mon–Sat 3–4 daily; 1 hr 15min); Mandas (Mon–Sat 6–7 daily; 55min).
Sanluri to: Cágliari (every 1 or 2 hours; 50min); Oristano (9 daily; 45min–1hr).
San Gavino to: Cágliari (hourly; 35min–1hr); Oristano (hourly; 40min).

Buses

Barúmini to: Cágliari (2–3 daily; 1hr 20min–1hr 40min); Gésturi (2–4 daily; 7min); Láconi (1–3 daily; 35min); Tuili (2 daily; 5min).
Costa Rei to: Cágliari (mid-June to mid-Sept 6 daily; mid-Sept to mid-June 2–3 daily; 2hr 5min–2hr 25min); Muravera (Mon–Sat 3 daily; 35min–1hr); Villasimius (mid-June to mid-Sept 6 daily; mid-Sept to mid-June 1–3 daily; 35min–1hr 10min).
Dolianova to: Ballao (1–2 daily; 1hr 30min); Cágliari (Mon–Sat 10 daily, Sun 4; 45min); San Nicolò Gerrei (1–2 daily; 1hr).
Gésturi to: Barúmini (2–4 daily; 7min); Cágliari (2–3 daily; 1hr 30min–1hr 50min); Sanluri (Mon–Sat 2–3 daily; 35–50min); Tuili (1 daily; 12min).
Muravera to: Ballao (1–3 daily, not Sun in winter; 1hr); Cágliari (Mon–Sat 11 daily, Sun 3; 1hr 35min–3hr 25min); Castiadas (Mon–Sat 3 daily; 55min–1hr 15min); Costa Rei (Mon–Sat 3–4 daily;

45min–1hr); Villasimius (Mon–Sat 3–4 daily; 1hr 20min–2hr).
Sanluri to: Aritzo (1 daily; 2hr); Barúmini (1–2 daily; 35min); Cágliari (1–2 hourly; 45min–1hr 15min); Gésturi (1–2 daily; 40); Láconi (1–2 daily; 1hr 20min); Oristano (4–6 daily; 50min–1hr 10min); Sárdara (1–2 hourly; 10min); Tuili (Mon–Sat 2–3 daily; 35–50min).
San Sperate to: Cágliari (Mon–Sat hourly, Sun 7; 30min).
Sárdara to: Cágliari (Mon–Sat hourly, Sun 9; 1hr–1hr 20min); San Gavino (Mon–Sat 3–4 daily; 15min); Sanluri (1–2 hourly; 10min).
Tuili to: Barúmini (2 daily; 5min); Cágliari (1–2 daily; 1hr 40min–2hr); Gésturi (1 daily; 12min); Sanluri (Mon–Sat 3 daily; 35–50min); Sárdara (Mon–Sat 1 daily; 40min).
Uta to: Cágliari (Mon–Sat 11–14 daily, Sun 3; 45min).
Villanovaforru to: Cágliari (Mon–Sat 3 daily; 1hr 25min–2hr); San Gavino (Mon–Sat 3–4 daily; 25min); Sanluri (Mon–Sat 2–3 daily; 25min); Sárdara (Mon–Sat 5–8 daily; 15min); Tuili (Mon–Sat 1 daily; 25min).
Villasimius to: Cágliari (mid-June to mid-Sept 6–9 daily, mid-Sept to mid-June 2–4 daily; 1hr 25min); Castiadas (Mon–Sat 2–3 daily; 40min–1hr 20min); Costa Rei (mid-June to mid-Sept 6–8 daily, mid-Sept to mid-June 2–3 daily; 35min–1hr 10min); Muravera (Mon–Sat 4–6 daily, Sun 2; 1hr 20min–1hr 50min).

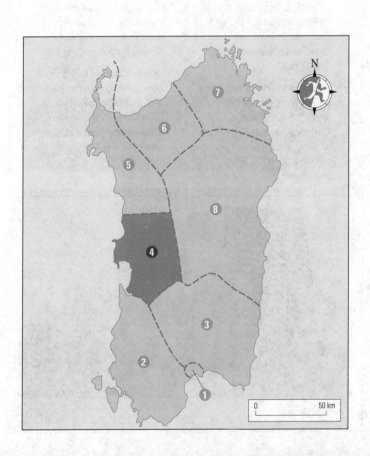

Oristano province

CHAPTER 4

Highlights

✳ **Antiquarium Arborense**
Oristano's premier attraction is
a superb collection of art and
archeology, from Roman
glassware to Renaissance
canvases, with copious material on nearby Tharros. See
p.166–168

✳ **Festa di Sa Sartiglia**
Costumed pageantry and
thrilling equestrian prowess
make this one of Sardinia's
most flamboyant festivals.
See p.167

✳ **Tharros** In one of Sardinia's
pre-eminent archeological
sites, the ruins of a
Carthaginian and Roman city
occupy a magnificent spot on
the very tip of the Sinis
peninsula. See p.173–174

✳ **Cycling around Sinis** The
flat landscape of this compact peninsula west of
Oristano makes it ideal for
touring on two wheels. See
p.170–175

✳ **Casa Gramsci, Ghilarza**
Dedicated to one of the
architects of communism in
Europe, this small museum
staffed by enthusiastic volunteers draws devotees from
across Europe. See p.183

✳ **Santa Cristina** In the midst
of an olive grove, the sacred
well and other monuments
from the nuraghic era exude
a powerfully pagan atmos-
phere. See p.182

△ Nuraghe Losa

Oristano province

S ardinia's smallest province, **Oristano**, was created as recently as 1974 out of bits hacked off the provinces of Cágliari and Nuoro, but it roughly corresponds to the much older entity of Arborea, the medieval *giudicato* which championed the Sardinian cause in the struggle against the Spaniards. Then as now, the city of **Oristano** was the region's main town, and today it retains more than a hint of medieval atmosphere, mixed with equal measures of a burgeoning youth culture and a prim parochialism. For the visitor, the prevailing small-town, pedestrian-friendly tone makes this an undemanding stop whose top attraction is one of Sardinia's best museums, the **Antiquarium Arborense**.

West of Oristano, you could spend a full day roaming the **Sinis Peninsula**, a flat, largely empty wedge of land, with good beaches and some important historical sites. You can still spot the traditional rush-constructed boats, or *fassonis*, on the peninsula's lagoons, used by fishermen and hunters, or just for local races. You'll find a museum dedicated to the lagoons' past inhabitants in **Cabras**, the only town hereabouts, with the best choice of accommodation locally. There's a lot more zip in the nearby summer resort of **Marina di Torre Grande**, however, though this too reverts to a more lethargic pace out of season. Further west, pagan and Christian strands are interwoven in the church of **San Salvatore**, the destination of an annual barefoot race from Cabras. Almost middle-eastern in appearance, the much older church of **San Giovanni di Sinis**, stands on the southern tip of the peninsula, and very close to **Tharros** – one of the best-preserved classical sites on the island. Comparable to Nora (see p.103–104) in scale and location, the extensive remains of this venerable Punic-Roman town lie on a prong of land jutting from the coast. Elsewhere on Sinis, the watery terrain is a magnet for all kinds of birdlife, while the dune systems backing the coast are also a protected zone – thankfully helping to preserve the choice **beaches** around here from excessive development.

On the southern outskirts of Oristano, don't miss the basilica of **Santa Giusta**, one of the earliest of Sardinia's Pisan-Romanesque churches. The fertile land south of here was drained and farmed by settlers from the mainland, who recreated a little corner of their native northern Italy in the town of **Arborea**, which still retains a "foreign" flavour. There are more Roman traces a short way inland at **Fordongianus**, where a system of baths occupies a scenic spot on the banks of the River Tirso. Just off the main route north of Oristano lie a couple of important nuraghic sites: **Santa Cristina**, where a pleasantly ramshackle *nuraghe* and an impressive sacred well are nestled within an ancient olive grove, and the monumental complex of **Losa**. Just east of Losa, **Ghilarza** has a museum devoted to the great political theorist Antonio Gramsci, who

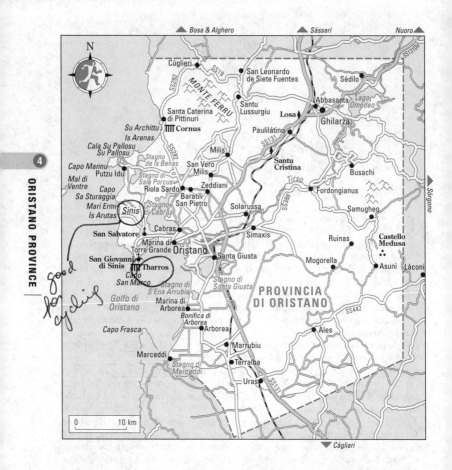

grew up here. Near the coast, **Cornus** was the scene of a historic Roman victory and provides a few archeological remnants in a remote-feeling but easily accessible spot. The prize beaches flanking the resort of **Santa Caterina di Pittinuri** are just a brief hop from here.

Neither of the nuraghic sites is much more than a twenty-minute drive northeast from Oristano on the SS131; Santa Caterina is about the same distance up the SS292, running inland of Sinis, while the Roman baths are slightly longer on the smaller SS338 eastwards. **Public transport** isn't much use to reach some of the remoter historic sites, but you can rely on buses from Oristano (which is on the main north–south rail line) to Sinis in summer, and there are regular year-round services to Cabras, Santa Giusta Fordongianus and Santa Caterina di Pittinuri. For other destinations, non-drivers should be able to negotiate a reasonable taxi fare, especially if there are three or four of you. For more information on bus and train connections, see Travel details on p.187–188.

Accommodation is scattered rather thinly throughout the province, with the best selection in Oristano itself. Apart from hotels and a few campsites (which are all on the coast), you'll find a range of B&Bs both here and in the smaller centres; Oristano's EPT can supply a booklet with full details. The province has some of the island's most compelling **annual festivals**, mostly with a horsey theme: Oristano's medieval **Sa Sartiglia** at Carnival time is the most famous of these, and well worth going out of your way for, but there are smaller, less trumpeted affairs at **Sédilo**, northeast of Abbasanta, and **Santu Lussúrgiu**, in the wooded folds of Monte Ferru.

Some history

In prehistoric times, the area that subsequently became Oristano province was the cradle of an active **nuraghic culture**. The complexes of Nuraghe Losa and Santa Cristina are only the most visible remnants of this civilization; in fact the area around Paulilátino has the highest concentration of *nuraghi* anywhere on the island, and the Sinis peninsula, too, was the scene of much construction. The arrival of the **Phoenicians** in the second half of the eighth century halted the growth of the nuraghic culture; the archeological evidence suggests that while Phoenician ways largely supplanted the local customs, the two peoples lived chiefly in harmony. The Phoenicians' main base was at Tharros, which was to remain the centre of commercial and political activity for the best part of the next two millennia.

Phoenicians and Sards joined forces against **Carthaginian incursions** during the sixth century BC, and both peoples suffered as a result of the Punic triumph. As the island passed under the direct control of Carthage following the treaty with Rome of 509 BC, North African colonies were established at Neapolis, on the southern coast of the Golfo di Oristano, and at Cornus, near present-day Cúglieri. As elsewhere on the island, the partial integration of the indigenous people into the Phoenician/Carthaginian cultural framework took its course, and it was a combined force of Sards and Carthaginians that suffered a decisive defeat by the **Romans** at Cornus in 216 BC, an event which helped to bring about the total occupation of Sardinia by Rome. The Oristano region was thoroughly penetrated by the new rulers, as witnessed by the thermal baths of Forum Traiani, now Fordongianus. Tharros was revitalized by the new conquerors, and remained the local capital until its decline and eventual evacuation in the face of Arab assaults during the second half of the first millennium.

Most of the inhabitants of Tharros resettled inland at Oristano, which became the principal power base during the **Middle Ages**, and the capital of one of Sardinia's four *giudicati* (autonomous territories) in the tenth century. In common with all of these, the **Giudicato of Arborea** was created as a result of a complex of conventions between the noble families and the local judicial structures; its authority, however, depended on the endless power shifts and temporary alliances that characterized the centuries of rivalry between Pisa, Genoa and Aragon throughout the island. Arborea reached its zenith during the thirteenth and fourteenth centuries, first under **Mariano II** (d.1298), and later at the forefront of the island's resistance to the Aragonese. **Eleonora d'Arborea** emerged as the champion of independence in the few areas of the island that remained free of Aragonese domination. Her fortitude and success ensured that she would become one of the greatest figures in Sardinia's history, though her near-legendary fame is also due to the **Carta de Logu**, a body of laws promulgated by her in 1390, which formed the basis of Sardinia's legislative structure until 1817. For more on Eleonora, see the box on p.165.

After Eleonora's death in 1404, anti-Aragonese resistance collapsed, and her realms joined the rest of the island under Aragonese – and subsequently Spanish – colonial rule. Arborea itself disappeared, while Oristano sank into provincial oblivion, languishing in neglect until Sardinia was taken on by the **Piedmontese** in the eighteenth century. The linking of Oristano to the Carlo Felice Highway (now the SS131) in the 1820s gave the town a much-needed boost, and some programmes of social reform were attempted, but other problems – principally the malarial marshland which increasingly encroached on large tracts of this otherwise fertile land – were not addressed until **Mussolini**'s initiatives got under way after 1924. His land reclamation scheme south of Oristano was sustained by colonies of settlers from northern Italy, centred on the new town he originally called "Mussolinia" – later renamed Arborea, as if to reclaim the town itself for the local population. Despite the slow but steady development, however, the area did not achieve **provincial status** until 1974, and Oristano's population still hasn't risen in line with the expansion of Cágliari and Sássari.

Oristano

The city of **ORISTANO**, 100km northwest of Cágliari, is a flat, unprepossessing place whose old walls have been mostly replaced by busy traffic arteries. Its quiet centre has a relaxed yet purposeful ambience, however, with quiet nooks and unexpected pleasures, repaying a leisurely wander. The city has an inland air, though it lies just 4km from the sea and is surrounded by lagoons, irrigation systems and the River Tirso, which empties into the sea just north of town. Together, these factors have contributed to making Oristano the centre of a richly productive agricultural zone, fuelling its growth and prosperity.

At its heart, Oristano's **Duomo** is as old as anything in town, dating from the early thirteenth century, though a seventeenth-century refashioning has given it an opulent Baroque flavour. The medieval stamp is more evident in the central Piazza Roma, where the **Torre di Mariano II** has been a sturdy survivor of the city's chequered fortunes since its erection in the thirteenth century; another, much smaller remnant of the old defences, the **Portixedda**, lies a short walk away. But the old town's most essential attraction is the marvellous repository of prehistoric and classical finds and medieval works of art at the local museum, the **Antiquarium Arborense**, one of Sardinia's top three or four collections.

The best time to be in Oristano is for the colourful medieval **Sa Sartiglia**, a vivid, highly ritualized horseback competition at Carnival (see box on p.167). Advance bookings are essential if you hope to get **accommodation** during that time; indeed, they're a good idea at any period, since hotel space is scarce. Oristano is better provided with **restaurants** and **bars**, and the local cuisine makes good use of the area's agricultural produce and seafood.

Arrival and information

Oristano's **train station** is situated at the eastern end of town, a twenty-minute walk from the centre, to which it is linked by local buses that run every 20–35 minutes. Buy tickets (€0.57) at the bar outside the station in Piazza Ungheria: the bus stop is across the road from here. Buses of the Linea Rossa ("Red Line") and Linea Verde ("Green line") terminate at Piazza Mariano, and Linea Verde buses also stop at Piazza Roma; however, it's always worth telling the driver your intended destination, as there may be a more useful stop. Alternatively, there are **taxis** stationed in Piazza Ungheria; the fare, on the meter, should be less than €5 or less to any destination in town.

Oristano's **bus station** is more central, on Via Cágliari, with access onto Via Episcopio, off Via Vittorio Emanuele. All ARST buses pull in here, also making a stop at the train station, though PANI buses from Cágliari, Nuoro and Sássari stop onVia Lombardia, from which Piazza Roma is a five-minute walk alongViaTirso. For details of moving on from Oristano, see the box on p.170.

Tourist information is handled by three separate offices.The mobile office on Piazza Roma is only open mid-July to mid-September, Carnival and Christmas, usually daily 9am–1pm & 4.30–9pm. The **Pro Loco** is off Via Duomo atVia Ciutadella di Menorca 8 (Mon–Fri 9am–12.30pm & 4–7.30pm, 4.30–8pm in summer, Sat 9am–noon; ℡0783.70.621, ⓦwww.inforistano.it). Both of these offices have information on the city only; for the whole province, go to the **EPT** at Piazza Eleonora 19 (Mon–Fri 8am–2pm & 4–7pm, Sat 8am–2pm; ℡0783.36.831). **Drivers** should observe parking restrictions and obtain a ticket from an attendant for parking between the blue lines between 8.30am and 1pm, and from 4 to 7.30pm (€0.55 for the first hour). For **local bus** information, call ℡0783.357.183.

Accommodation

Oristano has just five **hotels**, none of them particularly inspiring, though adequate for a short stay, which is probably all you'll want to give this town. Alternatively, there are a couple of B&Bs. During the *Sa Sartiglia* festivities in particular, you'll need to book way ahead. The nearest **campsites** are 6km away at Marina di Torre Grande, Oristano's lido (see p.172).

Antonella B&B Via Sardegna 140 ℡0783.73.863 or 349.495.4060. Not exactly central, but little more than five minutes' walk from Piazza Mariano, this friendly B&B in a modern flat has three rooms (one single) that share bathroom facilities. No credit cards. ⑤

Eleonora B&B Piazza Eleonora 12 ℡0783.704.35 or 347.481.7976, ⓦwww.eleonora-bed-and -breakfast.com. Right on the old town's central piazza, this unusual B&B is in a medieval palazzo and has large rooms, some with frescoed ceilings and balconies. The ones at the back are quietest, overlooking the garden where breakfast can be taken in summer. No credit cards. ②

ISA Piazza Mariano 50 ℡ & Ⓕ0783.360.101. This business-travellers' hotel has polish but no great charm; in its favour, it's comfortable, capacious (there are 56 rooms), and it's close to the town centre at the bottom of Via Mazzini. ⑤

Mistral Via Mártiri di Belfiore ℡0783.212.505, Ⓕ0783.210.058. A grey five-storey block in a dull part of town, at least this bland three-star has bright, fully-equipped rooms, and it's not too far to walk to Piazza Roma. ④

Mistral 2 Via XX Settembre ℡0783.210.389, Ⓕ0783.211.000. Pricier, more upmarket version of the *Mistral*, and owned by the same people. This one is even more pointedly business-orientated, though the large pool might entice you. ⑤

Piccolo Hotel Via Martignano 19 ℡0783.71.500. Oristano's cheapest and most central choice is also the most difficult to find, tucked away in an area of unmarked streets behind Piazza Martini, between Via del Cármine and Via Angioy (sign-posted from Via Angioy). It's a quiet place with smallish rooms (some bathrooms are tiny) and dodgy a/c. The front-facing rooms on the second floor have balconies. No credit cards. ③

Villa delle Rose Piazza Italia ℡0783.310.101, Ⓕ 0783.360.101. A good choice on a quiet piazza off Via Lombardia (useful for PANI bus connections), this place is a ten-minute walk from Piazza Roma, and there's a city bus stop right outside on the Linea Verde for connections with Piazza Mariano and the train station. Rooms are solidly furnished, each with a spacious bathroom. Part of the hotel doubles as an old folks' home. ④

The Town

Oristano is initially disorientating, with few straight roads connecting the major landmarks. The principal squares of the town centre are **Piazza Mariano**, terminus of most local bus routes and marked out by a white war memorial; **Piazza Roma**, unmistakeable with its fortified medieval tower, and the pedestrianized **Piazza Eleonora d'Arborea**, site of the *Municipio* in the

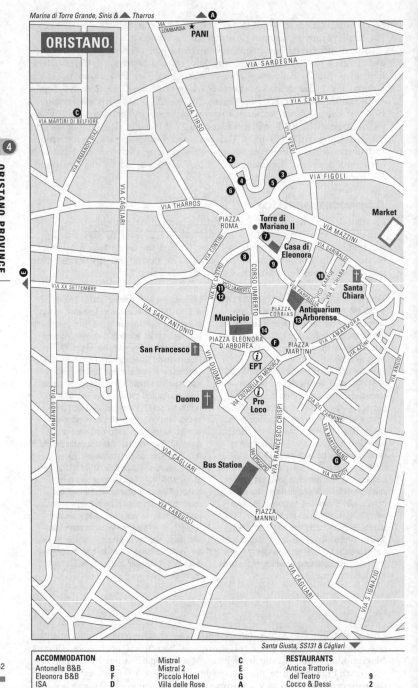

ORISTANO

Marina di Torre Grande, Sinis & ▲ Tharros ▲ Ⓐ

VIA LOMBARDIA
★ PANI

VIA SARDEGNA

VIA CANEPA

VIA TIRSO

Ⓒ
VIA MÁRTIRI DI BELFIORE

VIA ARMANDO DIAZ

VIA CAGLIARI

VIA THARROS

PIAZZA ROMA

VIA FIGOLI

Ⓔ
VIA XX SETTEMBRE

VIA CONTINI

VIA DE CASTRO

CORSO UMBERTO

VICO UMBERTO

Market

VIA MAZZINI

Torre di
Mariano II ●

VIA VERDI

Casa di
Eleonora

VIA GARIBALDI

VIA PARPAGLIA

VIA S. CHIARA
VIA GARAÚ

Santa
Chiara

Antiquarium
Arborense

PIAZZA
CORRIAS

VIA SANT'ANTONIO

Municipio

VIA DUOMO

PIAZZA ELEONORA
D'ARBOREA

San Francesco †

Duomo †

VIA CIUTADELLA DI MENORCA

EPT ⓘ

Ⓕ

PIAZZA
MARTINI

VIA LAMARMORA

VIA AZUNI

VIA ANGIOY

Pro
Loco ⓘ

VIA CAGLIARI

Bus Station

VIA FRANCESCO CRISPI

VIA EPISCOPIO

VIA DEL CARMINE

VIA MARTIGNANO

VIA ANGIOY

Ⓖ

VIA CARDUCCI

PIAZZA
MANNU

VIA CAGLIARI

VIA S. IGNAZIO

Santa Giusta, SS131 & Cágliari ▼

ACCOMMODATION				RESTAURANTS	
Antonella B&B	**B**	Mistral	**C**	Antica Trattoria	
Eleonora B&B	**F**	Mistral 2	**E**	del Teatro	**9**
ISA	**D**	Píccolo Hotel	**G**	Cocco & Dessi	**2**
		Villa delle Rose	**A**		

⓸ ORISTANO PROVINCE

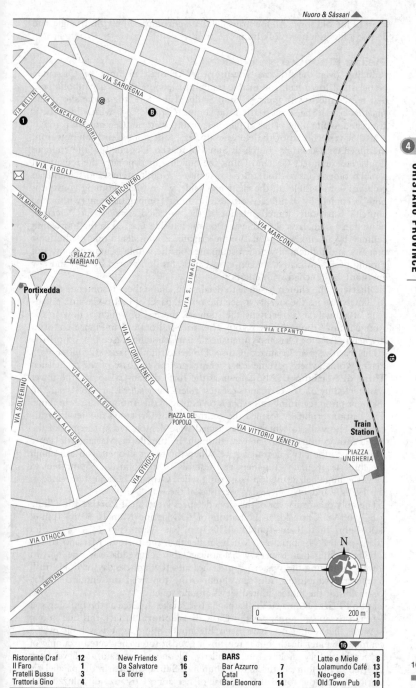

VIA SARDEGNA

@

Ⓑ

VIA BELLINI
VIA BRANCALEONE DORIA

❶

VIA FIGOLI

✉

VIA MARIANO IV

VIA DEL RICOVERO

VIA MARCONI

Ⓓ

PIAZZA MARIANO

VIA S. SIMACO

Portixedda

VIA LEPANTO

VIA VITTORIO VÉNETO

▶ ⑮

VIA SOLFERINO

VIA VINEA REGUM

VIA ALAGON

PIAZZA DEL POPOLO

VIA VITTORIO VÉNETO

Train Station

PIAZZA UNGHERIA

VIA OTHOCA

VIA OTHOCA

VIA ARISTANA

N

0   200 m

⑯ ▼

Ristorante Craf	12	New Friends	6	**BARS**		Latte e Miele	8
Il Faro	1	Da Salvatore	16	Bar Azzurro	7	Lolamundo Café	13
Fratelli Bussu	3	La Torre	5	Çatal	11	Neo-geo	15
Trattoria Gino	4			Bar Eleonora	14	Old Town Pub	10

heart of the old town. All the main sights are encompassed by this triangle, and lie just a few minutes' walk from one another.

Piazza Eleonora and around

Presiding over the **Piazza Eleonora d'Arborea** in front of Oristano's Neoclassical town hall, the marble statue of Eleonora strikes a symbolic pose that recalls the town's greatest hour. Sculpted in 1881, the statue shows the *giudichessa* with the scroll bearing the famous *Carta de Logu* with which she is associated, while inset panels depict her various victories (see box on p.165).

At the western end of the elongated piazza, four stout Ionic columns front the nineteenth-century church of **San Francesco**. Designed by the eminent Cagliaritan architect Gaetano Cima, the building incorporates the remains of a much older construction, traces of which – Gothic arches and Corinthian columns – are visible on the right-hand side, where the adjoining convent is now occupied by a military office. The most compelling item within the church's capacious domed interior is the so-called *Crocifisso di Nicodemo*, housed in a Neoclassical marble altar on the left side. Carved in the fourteenth century by an unknown Catalan, the crucifix is considered one of the most precious and influential wooden sculptures on the whole island; the powerful carving of an emaciated, sunken-eyed Christ, his skin scored by cuts and raw abrasions, is drenched with emotion.

Otherwise, the church has little to detain you, unless there is someone around to allow you into the sacristy to see the central panel of Pietro Cavaro's polyptych of Saint Francis receiving the stigmata, the rest of which is now in the Antiquarium Arborense (see p.166). The space in front of San Francesco forms the main arena for Oristano's annual *Sa Sartiglia* festivities (see box on p.167).

The narrow, pedestrianized Corso Umberto links Piazza Eleonora with Piazza Roma, where pavement bars cluster around the base of the crenellated **Torre di Mariano II**. Also known as the Torre di San Cristóforo, the tower was erected by one of Oristano's greatest rulers, the *giudice* Mariano II in 1290; the inscription recording this event is on display in the Antiquarium Arborense. The bastion originally formed the centrepiece of Oristano's medieval fortifications. The walls to which it was joined were demolished at the end of the nineteenth century; the gateway through it, the Porta Mariano or Porta Manna, was the city's northern gate. When the tower is open, you can climb the three levels (daily Aug–Sept and festivals 10am–noon & 3–5pm; free) to view the huge bell at the top – last rung when Oristano became a province in the 1970s – and, on a clear day, for vistas of the sea.

The only other survivor of the city's defences is the squat **Portixedda** ("little gate"), off Via Garibaldi at the bottom of Via Mazzini (Mon 10.30am–1pm & 4.30–7pm, Tues 10am–1pm & 4.30–7pm, Sat 10am–1pm & 4–6pm, Sun 10am–noon & 4–6pm; free). Much smaller than the Torre di Mariano II, and wholly lacking that tower's visual impact, the Portixedda was one of two towers protecting the western approaches into town; these days it holds small temporary exhibitions. You can climb to the top from the entrance in Via Garibaldi for the rather limited views around town.

Just off Piazza Roma, at Via Parpaglia 6–12, take a glance at the building still referred to on some maps as the **Casa di Eleonora**. In fact, this fine house, now derelict, could not have been Eleonora's home as it was built over a century after her death, but it remains a good if sorely neglected example of sixteenth-century architecture. Similarly, Eleonora was said to have been interred in the fourteenth-century church of **Santa Chiara**, in the parallel Via Garibaldi, but the tomb there is that of her aunt, Costanza di Saluzzo. The

As the last of Sardinia's medieval rulers to enjoy any significant success against the island's aggressors, **Eleonora of Arborea** (c.1340–1404) is venerated throughout the island. Occupying a sort of Joan of Arc role in the popular imagination, she also made a significant contribution to the evolution of **civil rights** in Sardinia with her promulgation of a book of law that eventually became the benchmark of local freedoms for the whole island.

When Eleonora's father, the *giudice* Mariano IV (reigned 1346–76) – himself a Catalan – was required by the Aragonese King Pedro IV to have his two daughters betrothed to Spanish princes, he matched one, Beatrice, with Amerigo VI of Narbonne, but allowed Eleonora to be wedded instead, in 1366 or 1367, to the Genoan **Brancaleone Doria**, scion of Spain's main rivals in Sardinia at that time (though they were nominally Aragon's vassals). Eleonora spent most of the following fifteen years in Castelsardo (then called Castelgenovese) and Genoa itself, where she ingratiated herself with the Doge and laid the foundations of a future anti-Aragonese alliance.

Following the assassination of her brother, she returned to her native city and became **regent of Arborea** in 1383. As the wife of a vassal of Aragon, Eleonora managed to negotiate a delicate balance of power and a degree of independence, allowing her space to concentrate on the concerns of her subjects. In a short time she had acquainted herself with the entire *giudicato*, her tours round the Oristanese territory greeted with enthusiastic acclaim. Her popular appeal was no doubt enhanced by the ten years of **tax exemptions** she granted to the downtrodden population, exhausted by the economic hardship induced by the long period of war.

The struggle against Aragon simmered on, however. Even when her husband Brancaleone was imprisoned (an event interpreted by some as his desertion to the enemy), Eleonora refused to submit. Her intransigence finally paid off in 1388, with the signing of a **treaty** that guaranteed Arborean independence in return for restoring to Aragon the cities occupied by the *giudicato*, and even returned Brancaleone to the fold. From her new position of strength, Eleonora forged a tactical alliance with the Genoans and launched a new offensive against the Spanish, as a result of which, Brancaleone, with Genoan help, even managed to occupy Sássari on her behalf.

Of more lasting benefit was Eleonora's formulation in 1395 of a legal code, or **Carta de Logu**, for Arborea. Although her statue in the centre of Oristano represents this as a brief scroll, in fact the document comprised 198 chapters, addressing rural, civil and penal issues, and attempting to define the legal status and rights of people at every level of society – including children, slaves and (in particular detail) women. First mooted by her father Mariano IV, the code was far ahead of its time in its scope and application, and it remains the most enduring legacy of Eleonora's rule. Adopted by the Aragonese in 1421, it was later extended throughout the island, and remained in force until the enactment of the Carlo Felice code by the Piedmontese in 1817. As the eighteenth-century English lawyer and traveller John Tyndale put it: "The framing of a body of laws so far in advance of those of other countries, where greater civilization existed, must ever be the brightest ornament in the diadem of the Giudichessa."

Eleonora's **military achievements**, however, did not long survive her death from plague in 1404, following which the Aragonese were quickly able to occupy Arborea and its territories. Her rule marked the final glorious chapter of Sardinian independence, and her brief triumph was all the more poignant in light of the obstacles she faced on every side – not just her severely circumscribed role as regent for infant male heirs, but above all her status as a woman in a feudal, male-dominated society.

church is part of a convent, making access difficult, but mass is held daily at 4.30pm in winter, 6pm in summer, and you can arrange a guided tour by contacting the resident Clarisse sisters (☎0783.78.093).

The Duomo

Oristano's **Duomo** (daily: April–Oct 8am–1pm & 4–7pm; Nov–March 7am–1pm & 3–6.30pm) stands in its own square off Via Duomo, behind Piazza Eleonora. With its detached octagonal, onion-roofed belltower, dating from the fourteenth century, and the seminary (built in 1712) next door, it forms an atmospheric ensemble. The present building is mostly the result of a Baroque-era renovation; the only parts to have survived from the original thirteenth-century cathedral are sections of the apses.

The Duomo's spacious if fussy **interior** has three ornate chapels on either side of the nave. The first on the right has a painted wooden statue of the *Annunziata*, or Annunciation of the Madonna, thought to be by Nino Pisano (c.1315–68). Full of expression, the statue is surrounded by a majolica- and gilt altar busy with *putti* (cherubim). The two marble panels in front of it were carved by an anonymous Catalan in the fourteenth or fifteenth century: on the left, figures of prophets, an *Annunciation* and *Christ in Judgment*; on the right, Paul and the Apostles, and saints Antonio Abate and Chiara. Far more interesting, however, are the other sides of the slabs, carved 300 years earlier: here you can see eleventh- and twelfth-century sculptures in the Byzantine tradition, illustrating biblical scenes, including, on the right, a portrayal of Daniel in the lions' den.

The transepts are dominated by large Neoclassical altars at either end, and, on the right, the fourteenth-century Cappella del Rimedio survives from the Duomo's earlier incarnation. Two fierce marble lions salvaged from an ancient pulpit flank the steps leading up to the main altar, behind which the raised presbyterium has large nineteenth-century canvases above wooden Renaissance choirstalls.

Antiquarium Arborense

A handsome sixteenth-century merchant's house on Piazzetta Corrias, just off Via Parpaglia, holds one of Sardinia's most absorbing museums – Oristano's **Antiquarium Arborense** (Tues–Sun 9am–2pm & 3–8pm; €3). As well as featuring rotating exhibitions of its extensive collection of nuraghic, Phoenician, Roman and Greek artefacts, the museum gives permanent space to Tharros and its occupants, and includes a good gallery of medieval art (though this may in the future be relocated in the Galleria Comunale on Via Sant'Antonio).

The **ground floor** contains the museum's earliest exhibits, from the prenuraghic and nuraghic eras, including a quantity of neolithic blades, axeheads and spearheads – many of obsidian or flint – from the Sinis peninsula, and a small collection of jewellery, bone hairpins and other personal items recovered from tombs. More gripping is the wealth of material from Carthaginian Tharros, much of it from burial sites, including masks to ward off the evil eye, elegantly shaped *askoi* (curved vessels), and terracotta figurines, mostly from the fifth century BC and often Ionic Greek in inspiration. There are equally numerous exhibits from the Roman period in Tharros: pins, plates, ceramic objects, bottles and myriad other glass containers including first-century-AD cinerary urns from northern Italy and Gaul. One display case is devoted to items of foreign manufacture found in Tharros tombs, including Cretan, Etruscan and mainland Greek ceramics.

The Antiquarium's **first floor** holds an imaginative reconstruction of Roman Tharros as it might have appeared at its maximum extent (in the fourth

Sa Sartiglia

Oristano's flamboyant **Sa Sartiglia** festival is the biggest date in the town's calendar, prepared months in advance and the subject of intense speculation – some complain it's the only thing that moves this insular, provincial town. The event takes place between the last Sunday of the Carnival period and the following Tuesday (Shrove Tuesday), usually in February.

The **arcane rituals** of the festival perhaps originated with knights on the Second Crusade, who may have brought the trappings of Saracen tournaments to Sardinia in the twelfth century. On the other hand, it could be a Spanish import – a similar annual festival, *La Sortilla*, is held on the island of Menorca in June. Whatever the case, similarly lavish feasts were held for Oristano's ruling knights at regular intervals throughout the year during the Spanish domination; in time, these celebrations took on a more theatrical aspect, finally merging with the annual Carnival revelries. With all participants in the various stages of the ceremonies masked and costumed, the whole three-day affair exudes a theatrical spirit unrivalled by Sardinia's other festivals.

The main events take place on the first and third days, staged by the guilds of San Giovanni (representing the farmers) and San Giuseppe (the carpenters) respectively. Each event is presided over by a white-masked arbiter known as **Su Componidori**, chosen from the "knight" contestants according to his riding prowess. The *Componidori* represents the continuation of the *giudice*'s role, and is decked out in a bizarre pastiche of medieval garb, complete with mask, ribbons and top-hat – the process of dressing him is itself a highly formal ceremony, and follows precise rules. The *Componidori* initiates the proceedings, riding up and down the sanded track on Via Duomo, blessing the track, contenders and audience alike with a bouquet of violets, after which the joust commences, involving a succession of mounted charges with the aim of lancing with a rapier a star-shaped ring – *stella* or *sartiglia* – suspended three metres above the ground. Each charge is heralded by a fanfare of drums and trumpets, and followed by groans of disappointment or wild cheering according to whether the ring is speared or missed; traditionally, more hits represent a better chance of a good harvest and thus good luck for the townspeople. The ring has a diameter of 33mm, but after a record twenty rings were lanced in 1999, there were calls to reduce the diameter. There has also been criticism of the attention given to the number of hits, at the expense of the style and grace of the run-up.

After the *corse alla stella*, the afternoon is given over to **Le Pariglie** – hair-raising horseback stunts (for example several riders balancing on steeds tied together at full gallop), usually taking place on a sanded track along Via Mazzini, with prizes given to the greatest equestrian feats. The whole rigmarole is repeated two days later for the *gremio* (guild) of San Giuseppe, while on the second day a relatively new event takes place – the **Sartigliedda**, dedicated to younger riders mounted on the miniature horses of the Giara di Gésturi (see p.142–143). Other highlights of the festa include the proclamation at the beginning of each day to announce the opening of the proceedings, read out by a mounted herald accompanied by a phalanx of drummers and trumpeters (normally around 10am in Piazza Roma and Piazza Eleonora), and singing and traditional dancing in Piazza Eleonora on the eve of the festivities and at the end of them.

Although the festival draws big **crowds** of both locals and tourists, it's usually possible to get a view of the events. The best vantage, however, is from the **grandstand seats** on Via Duomo and Via Mazzini (tickets cost around €18, or €5 for the Sartigliedda, available from the Pro Loco). If you don't want to attend the whole three-day event, Tuesday is the best day to be here, when the crowds are smaller. It's worth asking to be present at the *vestizione*, or formal dressing of the *componidori*, which generally takes place in Via Aristana for the San Giovanni *sartiglia*, and in the church of Sant'Efisio for San Giuseppe's – though, with limited space, this may not be an option. A similarly elaborate ceremony, the *svestizione*, or disrobing, takes place at the end of each day.

century AD), to a scale of 1:200. Around it, texts in Italian explain the various buildings and monuments: the port, baths, amphitheatre, the tetrastyle Doric temple, the houses, roads, aqueduct and excavated tombs. Display cases on the balcony surrounding the model show funerary items from a Phoenician necropolis excavated at San Giovanni di Sinis (see p.173) from the seventh and sixth centuries BC, plus amphorae, brooches, oil burners and other objects from Tharros and Cabras, including Roman glassware and relics of the Byzantine era (sixth–seventh century AD), such as little jugs with circular fluting and oil lamps that may have originated in Egypt.

Next door to this room, the air-conditioned **pinacoteca** houses a small but interesting collection of medieval and Renaissance art. The chief exhibits come from the studio of the *cagliaritano* Pietro Cavaro, one of Sardinia's best painters from this era. His most outstanding work, the nine-panelled *Retablo del Santo Cristo* (1533), previously in Oristano's church of San Francesco, depicts the most important Franciscan saints, portrayed with great subtlety and sensitivity. The central panel of this polyptych, showing Saint Francis receiving the stigmata, has been left in the sacristy of San Francesco (see p.164).

There are two other famous *retabli* (paintings on wood) here, the *Madonna dei Consiglieri* by Antioco Mainas (also from Cágliari) in 1564–5, depicting five white-bearded town councillors around the Madonna and baby Jesus, with Saint Andrew and John the Baptist, and the much earlier *Retablo di San Martino*, two parts of a triptych (the left panel long disappeared) by an anonymous Catalan in the first half of the fifteenth century. The remaining central panel shows the Madonna surrounded by angels playing medieval instruments; the right panel shows Saint Martin in the act of cutting off part of his cloak to give to a beggar, while a top section shows the saint's consecration as bishop. The gallery also contains various lapidary inscriptions commemorating episodes in the construction of the city, including one recording Mariano II's strengthening of its defences at the end of the thirteenth century.

Eating

Oristano has a good range of **restaurants**, mostly within the central ambit. Prices are generally reasonable, and the best places concentrate on fresh produce from the nearby sea and lagoons, and the fertile hinterland. You might finish your meal with a glass of the area's celebrated *Vernaccia* dessert wine.

Antica Trattoria del Teatro Via Parpaglia 11. Seafood features strongly on the menu of this rather flash place, which offers fixed-price menus at lunchtime – tapas for €10 or a two-course meal for €15 – and sampling menus in the evening (€25–40). Closed Tues. Moderate.

Cocco & Dessì Via Tirso 31 ☎0783.300.720. Slightly reminiscent of a retro cinema foyer, this place has loads of character and excellent food, best experienced on one of their sampling menus costing between €45 and €50 (excluding drinks). There are five eating spaces, including a gazebo, a balcony and a non-smoking room. Closed Sun eve & Mon. Expensive.

Ristorante Craf Via de Castro ☎0783.70.669. Small and intimate, this restaurant specializes in local dishes, especially meat, including horse and donkey. Vegetarian dishes include the delicious

risotto alla bonarcadese, with mushrooms. The atmosphere is chic without being too formal. Closed Sun. Moderate–expensive.

Il Faro Via Bellini 25. Oristano's fanciest restaurant serves local haute cuisine; the changing menu features seasonal items from spit-roasted goat to *zuppa di fave* (bean and pasta soup), but with seafood all year. The atmosphere is elegant-to-posh. Expensive.

Fratelli Bussu Piazza Roma 54. This place combines a fast-food *panini* bar and, at the back, a straightforward trattoria offering unexceptional restaurant fare and pizzas at reasonable prices. Closed Tues in winter. Inexpensive–Moderate.

Trattoria Gino Via Tirso 13. A straightforward, central and reliable restaurant off Piazza Roma offering traditional Sardinian items without frills, for example *ravioli sardi* (made with butter and sage) and, for dessert, *sebadas* (cheese-filled pastry-cases topped with honey). Everything is well-prepared, and service is polite and friendly. No smoking. Closed Sun. Moderate.

New Friends Via Tirso 16. Stand-up fast-food joint for hot dogs, pizzas, chips and sandwiches, open daily until midnight. Inexpensive.

Da Salvatore Via Carbonia 1 ℗0783.357.134. The relatively remote location means that this place is often empty – a shame, considering the great seafood dishes and low prices. It's on the southern outskirts of town, signposted to the right of the main road into town from Santa Giusta; the Linea Rossa bus route passes nearby. Closed Sun eve. Moderate.

La Torre Piazza Roma. Popular place for a cheap and basic pizza; the speciality is *pizza ai funghi porcini*. Gets very lively on weekends. Closed Mon. Inexpensive.

Bars and nightlife

Oristano has plenty of decent **bars** to while away an afternoon or evening, some of which stay open late, but if you're looking for anywhere livelier in summer, or for a late-night bop, head for the bars and clubs in Marina di Torre Grande (see p.172).

Bar Azzurro Piazza Roma. Central people-watching bar with snacks and tables outside, under the Torre di Mariano. Closed Wed.

Çatal Via De Castro 32. Wine bar with a huge range of wines from all round the world and cool music; snacks are also available. Late opening; closed Sun.

Bar Eleonora Piazza Eleonora. A great breakfast bar or coffee stop at any time, with *cornetti*, pastries and *pizzette*, and comfortable seating.

Latte e Miele Via De Castro 14. Busy sit-down café with rolls, *cornetti* and pastries; table service adds 25 percent to the bill. Closed Sun.

Lolamundo Café Piazzetta Corrias. Stylish bar that makes a useful pre- or post-Antiquarium stop. It's also good for snack lunches, with tables in the piazza in summer. Stays open until 1am on Fridays and Saturdays, otherwise 9pm. Closed Sun.

Neo-geo Via Ghilarza 9. Behind the train station (on the far side of the tracks), this is the current in-place for drinking and dancing until late, sharing premises with a gym. Nice atmosphere and funky sounds. Open Thurs–Sat eves only.

Old Town Pub Vico Antonio Garau. Lively Guinness bar with music and videos, open till 1am or 2am. You can sit in booths inside and in a small garden on hot summer evenings. Closed Mon and lunchtime on Sat & Sun.

Listings

Ambulance ℗118 or *Croce Rossa* ℗0783.74.318.

Banks and exchange Central banks with ATMs include the Banca Nazionale di Lavoro (Mon–Fri 8.20am–1.20pm & 3–4.30pm) and Banco di Nápoli (Mon–Fri 8.25am–1.40pm & 3.10–4.25pm, Sat 8.25–11.55am) on Piazza Roma, and Banca Commerciale Italiana on Via Garibaldi (Mon–Fri 8.20am–1.25pm & 2.50–4.30pm, Sat 8.20–11.50am).

Bike rental Mountain bikes can be hired for €8 per day at Marco Moto, Via Cágliari 99 ℗0783.310.320. Scooters and mopeds also available for around €25 per day.

Books La Pergamena, Via Ciutadella di Menorca 24, has a good range of guides and some English-language books.

Car hire Inter Rent are represented by Tharros Viaggi, Via Cágliari (℗0783.73.389); Sardinian Way, Via Carmine 14 (℗0783.75.172, ®www .sardinianway.it) charges from around €80 for 3 days, €170 for a week, plus tax.

Hospital Ospedale San Martino, Via Rockefeller ℗0783.3171.

Internet access Internet Haus, Via Brancaleone Doria 28 charges €2.50 for 30min, open Mon–Sat 9am–1pm & 5.30–8.30pm.

Laundry Centro Igiénico Elensec, Via Figoli 15, charges about €3 for shirts, a little more for trousers and dresses, usually ready after 1–2 days. Open Mon–Fri until 8pm.

Left luggage Facilities at the bus station, open daily 6am–7.30pm; €1.55 per piece per 24 hours is the standard rate.

Markets The main food market is between Via Mazzini and Via Mariano IV (accessible from either), while clothes, household goods, fruit and vegetables are traded on Via Aristana, near the train station; both Mon–Sat mornings only. On the first Sat of the month, an antiques and curiosity market sets up stall in Piazza Eleonora.

Pharmacy See rota posted on pharmacy doors for current late-night opening.

Moving on from Oristano

Frequent **trains** link Oristano to Cágliari and the rail junction of Ozieri-Chilivani, from where there are frequent connections to Sássari and Olbia.

Most local **bus services** are operated by ARST (℡0783.78.001 or toll-free ℡800.865.042, ⓦwww.arst.sardegna.it) from the bus station at Via Cágliari 102, while PANI (℡0783.212.268 or 070.652.326) operates longer-distance services to Cágliari, Mácomer, Nuoro, Porto Torres and Sássari. Departures on PANI buses are from Via Lombardia, just north of the centre, and tickets are sold at *Blu Bar*, Via Lombardia 30; when the bar is closed (Sunday), you can buy tickets on board the bus on payment of a small supplement.

See Travel details on p.187–188 for full schedules.

Post office The main office is on Via Mariano IV (Mon–Fri 8.15am–6.30pm, Sat 8.15am–1pm, closes at 4pm on last day of month, or noon if this is Sat), where you can also change cash and travellers' cheques.
Supermarkets Upim on Via Mazzini (Mon–Sat 9am–1pm & 4–8pm); no food hall, but there's a food supermarket, Vinci, across the road (Mon–Sat 8.15am–8pm).
Taxis Stands at Piazza Roma (℡0783.70.280) and outside the train station on Piazza Ungheria (℡0783.74.328).

Tours Sardinian Way, Via Carmine 14 (℡0783.75.172, ⓦwww.sardinianway.it) organizes excursions in the area as well as riding and sailing activities, accommodation and car hire.
Train information All trains ℡848.888.088; Oristano station 0783.72.270.
Travel agencies Tharros Viaggi, Via Cágliari ℡0783.73.389, and Alerica, Via De Castro 59 ℡0783.300.203, can arrange tickets for air, sea and rail journeys.

The Sinis peninsula

For many visitors, Oristano is just a stop en route to the Punic and Roman city of **Tharros**, one of the island's most important archeological sites. The ruined city is superbly situated by the sea, 20km west of town on the **Sinis peninsula**, the low-lying promontory at the northern end of the Golfo di Oristano. Fringed with beaches and dotted with lagoons where reserves have been established to protect the birds that nest here for part of the year, Sinis is physically unlike anywhere else in Sardinia, and merits an unhurried exploration, ideally by bike.

The marshes and lagoons teem with fish, a continuous source of income for the locals, who have perfected the art of negotiating the watery terrain on reed-built craft, or **fassonis** – the coracle-like, flat-bottomed boats for which Sinis is famous. There is evidence of these in use since prehistoric times, and though they are now mainly taken out for ceremonial occasions, you may still see the flimsy-looking vessels on remote backwaters, usually being punted along from a standing position. Resembling truncated canoes, they can be assembled by experts in a matter of minutes.

A museum in the peninsula's main town of **Cabras** gives a good overview of the history and geography of the area, though there is little other reason to hang about here apart from the useful facilities, which include a couple of hotels. Accommodation is otherwise extremely sparse in Sinis, though the campsites at **Marina di Torre Grande**, the nearest beach area to Oristano, can be fun in summer. Tharros is served by four ARST **buses** daily in summer, and there are good year-round connections to Cabras and Marina di Torre Grande, otherwise public transport is sparse.

Cabras

Spread along the eastern shore of the Stagno di Cabras lagoon, **CABRAS** is a low-key, low-built town, unruffled by much commotion or excitement of any kind. With the lagoon mostly out of view, the bulky domed profile of the seventeenth-century parish church of **Santa Maria** is the only distinctive feature, behind which you might pick out the scanty traces of a castle belonging to the *giudici* of Arborea that once stood here. Lacking a central piazza or other focal point, however, the town has rather an aimless air, and, unless you're here for its accommodation possibilities, doesn't merit much more than a cursory visit. If the occasion arises, take a peek through one of the doorways giving onto courtyards around which the low, flat local dwellings typical of the region are constructed.

In fact, the site of Cabras has been settled since Sardinia's earliest prehistory, as shown by the abundance of archeological finds in the area. Most recently, work around the southern mouth of the lagoon – at **Kukkuru S'Arriu**, also called Cúccuru is Arrius, three or four kilometres south of Cabras – has revealed a huge shrine and necropolis with finds going back to the Bonu Ighinu culture of the fourth millennium BC. Only since the late 1990s have these been documented and displayed in the **Museo Cívico** at Via Tharros 190 (daily 9am–1pm & 4–8pm, 3–7pm in winter; €2), on the banks of the lagoon near the southwest entrance to town. The collection is well worth a look, the exhibits imaginatively displayed on the ground floor of the modern purpose-built block. As well as the nuraghic and prenuraghic items from throughout the Sinis peninsula, there are shelves full of objects from Tharros – including a Roman milestone, stelae, needles, amphoras and vases – and a good part of the museum space is also given over to temporary exhibitions relating to the area, such as local archives, etchings and the lagoon culture. The museum explains plenty about the ecology and flora of the peninsula too, and gives a close-up look at the wonderful *fassonis* – the rush-constructed boats traditionally used on the lagoons. When you've had your fill, take a breather along the eucalyptus-fringed lagoonside behind the museum.

Cabras has a pair of two-star **hotels**, both plain and clean: *Hotel Summertime* (T & F0783.392.089; ❷), up by the museum, offering rooms with or without bath, and *El Sombrero*, on the other side of town at Corso Italia 26 (T & F0783.290.659; ❹). The larger and more modern *Villa Canu*, at Via Firenze 7 (T0783.290.155, F0783.395.242; ❺), offers a generally higher level of comfort. Alternatively, try the **B&B** at Via Toscana 71, *Il Nido* (T0783.290.590 or 339.477.7223, Wweb.tiscali.il/ilnido; ❸), a tidy, traditionally-furnished villa in its own garden. All rooms have private bathrooms, and one has a whirlpool bath. Make sure you book ahead if you're planning to stay for the famous *Corsa degli Scalzi*, a race to the church of San Salvatore during the first weekend of September (see p.172).

The local *stagni* are abundant sources of fish, especially eels and mullet, the main ingredient in one of the oldest-known dishes on the whole island: *sa merca*, salted mullet cooked in herbs (the dialect name suggests a Phoenician ancestry). You can sample the local produce at any of the town's **restaurants** – for example *Il Caminetto*, Via Cesare Battisti 8 (closed Mon), or the more casual *La Lanterna*, a ristorante/pizzeria near the museum at Via Tharros 119 (closed Tues). A **birreria** next door offers cool drinks and stays open late.

Cabras has a couple of **banks** with ATMs on the main drag, Crédito Italiano and Banco di Napoli.

Marina di Torre Grande

The main lido for both Oristano and Cabras, **Marina di Torre Grande** is located 8km west of the provincial capital along the SP1. It's a lively place to visit of an evening if you're spending any time in the area in summer, mainly for its animated bars and pizzerias and the late-night scene along the seafront. The nightlife kicks off with a vivacious *passeggiata* along Lungomare Eleonora d'Arborea, which runs for about a kilometre behind the beach, lined with ranks of holiday homes on the landward side – all of them shut up in winter – and dwarf palms and the view across the gulf to Tharros on the other. The resort is centred on the solid cylindrical Aragonese watchtower for which it is named, usually a-buzz with the bikes and blaring radios of Oristano's youth. The beaches here attract windsurfers: contact *Eolo*, which sets up right on the beach in summer, for courses and equipment hire (℡335.384.440 or 329.613.661, ⓦwww.eolowindsurf.com). They also organize various beach sports, rent out loungers and parasols, and operate a beach bar.

In summer, the resort fairly heaves with bars, gelaterias and pizzerias, though most places close out of season. Among the many **restaurants**, which fill up fast in summer, the *Maestrale* does good seafood and has a terrace on the seafront; pizzas are also served (closed Mon in winter). You'll find a little more character and lower prices by venturing a kilometre or so further west along the shore to *Il Pescatore*, an isolated white building right on the beach specializing in grilled fish (℡0783.22.054; closed Wed in winter). The three-course set-price menu costs €18.

The only **hotel** around here is the expensive *Del Sole*, a modern block at one end of the Lungomare (℡0783.22.000, ℻0783.22.217; ⑤), but there are two well-equipped **campsites**: the *Torre Grande* (May–Sept; ℡0783.22.228), lying about 150m from the sea, and, right on the shore, the better-equipped but pricier *Spinnaker* (mid-April to mid-Oct; ℡0783.22.074, ⓦwww .spinnakervacanze.com), with a private beach and pool. Both have bungalows for rent, and both are reachable on frequent buses from the ARST bus station. The resort is also on Oristano's Linea Azzurra city bus line.

San Salvatore

Six kilometres west of Marina di Torre Grande (signposted off the Tharros road), the sanctuary of **San Salvatore** (daily 9.30am–1pm & 3.30–6pm) is one of Sardinia's *chiese novenari* – churches open for just nine days a year, when devotees live in nearby *cumbessias*, or pilgrims' lodgings. The *novena* of San Salvatore takes place between August and September, culminating in one of Sardinia's most interesting festas, the **Corsa degli Scalzi** – a barefoot race run on the first weekend of September in a re-enactment of a frantic rescue mission undertaken four centuries ago to save the statue of San Salvatore from Moorish attackers. Departing from Cabras, 8km away, the first part of the race is run on the Saturday at dawn by a throng of the town's boys, barefoot and clad only in white shirts and shorts. The following day, the boys return, bearing aloft the holy statue from his sanctuary to safe custody in Cabras. It's a spirited caper, infused with the rowdy enthusiasm of the many participants and spectators.

The rest of the time the place is eerily deserted, the sixteenth-century church surrounded on all sides by the shuttered pilgrims' shacks. Indeed, the scene recalls nothing so much as an adobe-built ghost-town, and if it all looks vaguely familiar, it may be because the place was used as a set for various spaghetti

Westerns in the 1960s and 1970s. Belying its unexceptional appearance, however, San Salvatore reveals a fascinating past, since it was erected on top of an ancient **pagan sanctuary**, connected in nuraghic times with a water cult and later dedicated to Mars and Venus. When the building is open, a guide will accompany you down into the fourth-century subterranean chambers, where you can just make out some faded frescoes of Venus, Cupid and Hercules.

In addition to these, there are black-inked drawings and graffiti from a number of sources, most intriguingly a repeated "RF". This may be a Carthaginian prayer for healing (*Rufu* in their semitic language), but the use of the Latin alphabet suggests that a degree of Punic culture survived later into the Roman era than was previously thought. Greek and Arabic writing adds to the cultural mix, which can be explained by the fact that the holy site lay close to Tharros, then an important port. The pictures of boats – including a Sard *fassonis* and a Spanish galleon – were possibly ex-voto drawings, while an image of a person in a cage could well be a prisoner's doodle from when the chambers were used as a gaol during the Spanish period.

At the entrance to the huddle of *cumbessias*, the *Abraxas* **bar** – appropriately decked out in the style of a western saloon – offers snacks and beers (closed Mon in winter).

San Giovanni di Sinis

Four kilometres south of San Salvatore, the fifth-century church of **San Giovanni di Sinis** (daily 9am–7pm) vies with Cágliari's San Saturnino for the title of Sardinia's oldest church. Standing on the roadside at the base of the limb of land on which Tharros sits, the paleochristian church presents quite an oriental – or at least Byzantine – appearance, with its red dome, irregular stonework and roof slung low over an asymmetrical facade. That it should still be standing at all after its long years of exposure to pirate raids is largely thanks to the French Vittorini monks who took it over in the eleventh century. Thoroughly renovated and purged of later elements added on to the original structure, the interior is pleasingly bare, stripped clean of all decoration.

Near the seashore behind the church, look out for the thatched huts, or *domus di cruccuri*, long used by local fishermen, now converted into happily unobtrusive holiday homes. Opposite the church, a line of **bars**, **pizzerias** and **restaurants** caters to the stream of coach parties visiting Tharros. The comings and goings of these, combined with the bustle of people attracted to the perfect arc of beach a few hundred metres further up the road, makes for a fair amount of confusion around here in high summer.

Tharros

In shape, the spit of land on which **Tharros** was built resembles a clenched fist, with a sturdy Spanish watchtower dominating its highest point. Protruding into the Golfo di Oristano, the peninsula, which ends at Capo San Marco, afforded a perfect vantage point for any military installation based there, and also provided safe anchorage on either side, according to the direction of the wind. Inevitably, given its strategic advantages, Phoenicians settled the site during their period of expansion, as early as 800 BC. Tharros flourished under Carthaginian occupation, and after 238 BC maintained its importance under the Romans, who furnished it with the baths and streets seen today. However, the town had already declined by the Imperial era; with the demise of the *Pax Romana*, it fell prey to Moorish raids, and was finally abandoned in 1070 in favour of the more secure Oristano.

You can tour the **site** (daily 9am–1hr before sunset; €4) on your own, but it makes more sense to use a guide for at least part of the way to get the full picture. There is usually one available who speaks English, though you may have to wait for a sizable group to form (note that guides are usually not available 1–4pm).

For the most part, the site consists of Punic and Roman houses arranged on a grid of streets, of which the broad-slabbed **Decumanus Maximus** and **Cardo Maximus** are the most impressive, the latter with a deep open sewer visible down the centre, now partly covered over. This was probably the main shopping street – a large number of coins have been found along it, along with other clues such as a slab of stone with a groove for a sliding door and holes at either end to support it. At the top of the Cardo Maximus, a basalt Roman wall stands near the remains of a **tophet** (burial ground) from the earlier Punic settlement, and the hill is crowned by the former Carthaginian acropolis, with a wide ditch alongside that was used for defence by the Carthaginians and as a burial site by the Romans, as evident from the tubular-shaped tombs dug up here.

But the site's most prominent remains are the two strikingly white **Corinthian columns**, remnants of a first-century BC Roman temple (the portico would originally have had four). Alongside lies the site's best-preserved Carthaginian structure, a **cistern** walled with large rectangular blocks. Towards the sea, east of here, stand the remains of a bath house from the end of the second century AD, though these are not as large or impressive as the **thermal complex** on the southern edge of the site, which dates from a century later. The sheltered site to the north of the earlier baths, overlooking the sea, was probably used for a theatre by the Romans; seating has been provided for the performances that take place in summer. The Romans also built a minuscule amphitheatre; its remains are still visible on the hill near the Punic tophet.

Although Tharros has much in common with Nora, there are also significant differences. Tharros was a much bigger, more important centre for far longer than Nora, which soon decayed into a summer resort for Romans from Karalis before being abandoned altogether, several centuries before Tharros was evacuated in favour of Oristano. However, like Nora, Tharros has much more waiting to be revealed, submerged underwater as a result of subsidence, and marine archeologists periodically return to fish out more valuable traces.

You can also experience the site at night, by attending one of the **performances** of Greek theatre, classical and light music and poetry that take place here more or less weekly between mid-July and the end of August, on a makeshift stage backed by the sea. Events begin around 9.30 or 10pm; tickets at €10–15 are available directly from the site's ticket office (℗0783.370.019).

Before or after visiting the archeological site, you might be tempted to climb the **Torre Spagnola** (daily 9am–1pm & 4–8pm, 2–6pm in winter; €2), a restored Spanish watchtower overlooking the ancient city, and offering sweeping views over the peninsula and the Sinis area.

The Sinis coast

Outside the holiday season, an air of profound calm lies over the peninsula's western coast, and even in summer there's a stillness and sense of space here. Straight roads branch westwards over the Sinis peninsula to a string of undeveloped **beaches** (there is no coast road), and even if the crowds get oppressive, it's always possible to wander a short distance north or south to find an unoccupied stretch of sand.

One of the best beaches, **Is Arutas**, consists of a long white strand lent interest by rocky outcrops to north and south, beyond which more sand extends in both directions. Rollers attract surf enthusiasts, and can also bring pungent heaps of seaweed ashore. There's a bar open during the season, and pedalos and windsurf-boards are available for rent. The beach can be reached from Oristano, Cabras and San Giovanni di Sinis on a five-times-daily bus in summer, and there's a large unshaded car park (pay in summer, 8am–9pm).

Apart from passing ships, the only feature punctuating the horizon is a small island 10km out, the oddly-named **Mal di Ventre** ("stomach ache"). The origin of the name is uncertain, but, in view of the fast winds that can make for rocky sailing conditions hereabouts, it may either refer to seasickness, or be a corruption of *Malu Entu*, dialect for bad wind. The island is uninhabited and has recently been made a marine reserve, though boats call here daily in summer from Mandriola and Putzu Idu (see below). The remains of a double-towered *nuraghe* testify to the island's occupation in prehistoric times.

Three kilometres further north (drivers have to backtrack inland, then head north and west again), the beach at **Mari Ermi** presents a similar picture to Is Arutas, with bar and beach facilities, but here the sands back onto a small lagoon, and there is a high headland a brief distance north, **Capo Sa Sturaggia**. North again, there is a much larger lagoon, the elongated **Stagno di Sale**, which often hosts a swarm of flamingos in winter, and may dry out completely in summer. The area is managed by LIPU (the Italian bird protection society). There are more signs of civilization – and ugly holiday homes – around the peninsula's only developed resort at **Putzu Idu**. There's a sheltered beach here, but you'll find better swimming on the north side of the peninsula, from **Cala Su Pallosu** and the endless **Is Arenas**, noted for its dunes. You can reach the first of these with your own transport; for the second you need a four-wheel drive, or else walk, from either Putzu Idu or Santa Caterina di Pittinuri (see p.187).

South of Oristano: Santa Giusta and Arborea

The flat lands south of Oristano form the northern reaches of Sardinia's long Campidano plain – a scenically uninspiring landscape, but by no means devoid of interest. The first stop out of Oristano should be the Romanesque church of **Santa Giusta**, a Pisan construction that remains central and relevant to the local community that shares its name. From here the 131 superstrada swerves southeast towards Cágliari, by-passing the extensive reclaimed *bonifica* that remains one of the most enduring legacies of the Fascist era in Sardinia. To see this and its main town **Arborea**, founded only in 1928, take the southbound SS126, the main artery across this prosperous landscape, from which roads shoot off to the mainly sandy coast to the west. Most of this littoral remains undeveloped, though there's a handful of hotels for those who want to spend time on the beach; one of them, set amid the thick belt of pine woods that backs onto the beach, is one of the island's premier bases for **horseriding**. The road ends at the **Stagno di Marceddi**, a natural frontier between Oristano's cultivated plains and the rugged hills of Cágliari province, where the small village of **Marceddi** offers a choice of fish restaurants by the waterside.

Santa Giusta and Arborea are easy enough to reach by **bus** from Oristano, but you'll need your own transport for the smaller places described here.

Santa Giusta

Three kilometres south of Oristano, eucalyptus woods around the **Stagno di Santa Giusta** provide shade for picnics and birdwatchers intent on the itinerant population of aquatic wildfowl that continues to feed here, despite the passing traffic and the industry along the lagoon's western shore. On the first Sunday of August a **regatta** is held on the lagoon, using the *fassonis*, the traditional reed-made boats of the area (see p.170). Both the lagoon and the nearby village of **SANTA GIUSTA** – once the Punic town of Othoca, now little more than a suburb of Oristano – are named after the austere Romanesque **Basilica di Santa Giusta**, one of the earliest of that string of Tuscan-style constructions which went up in the eleventh to fourteenth centuries across central and northern Sardinia. This one, whose severe lines suggest Lombard influence, dates from around 1135 and was elevated to cathedral-status in the sixteenth century. Prominently sited at the top of a flight of steps behind a public garden in the centre of town, the church's façade displays a black basalt cross and a triple-mullioned window, topped by a typically Pisan recessed rhomboid motif in the tympanum. Below the cross, the tall portal is flanked by two truncated columns and a pair of stone lions. Three rusting cannons lie within a railed area to the right, while the main entrance is on the left side of the building.

Inside, a wooden-beamed ceiling covers the **nave**, which is illuminated by slit windows cut into the walls and apses, and lined with a motley array of marble and granite columns. Fluted and plain, some of these were taken from the ruined city of Tharros, while the first two columns on the left and the second on the right show evidence of Arab workmanship. Round arches give access to brick-vaulted aisles and a series of lateral chapels, the first of which on the right has a painted altar and ceiling and a wooden crucifix. Otherwise, there is little concession to ornament in the basilica's interior. Round the back of the church, the square, rather graceless belltower is less than a hundred years old, a poor replacement for the original *campanile*. The Basilica is the venue for four days of celebration around its saint's day of 14 May, featuring a large bonfire in the piazza.

A short distance south of the square on Via Giovanni XXIII, the church of **Santa Severa** (open only for mass on Sun 7.30–8.30am) stands amid the necropolis of Punic Othaca. The unmatched sandstone masonry of the church betrays its different periods of construction, going back to the fourteenth century. The spiral staircase next to it leads down to the subterranean tombs, part of a funerary area discovered in 1861 and excavated in 1910 and again from 1984 to 1989. The tombs are of different types, and include one monumental example immediately south of the church, apparently intended for a high-ranking official, judging by similar ones found in Morocco, Tunisia, Cyprus and southern Spain. Probably originating with the Phoenicians around the seventh century BC, the necropolis remained in use until the Roman period in the first century BC, and has yielded Phoenician, Carthaginian, Greek and Etruscan ceramics, as well as gold and silver jewels, seals, amulets and weapons of bronze and iron, most of these now preserved in Cágliari's archeological museum. The much simpler Roman tombs have also brought to light ceramics, glass and coins. The site is normally locked – visitors should apply for access at the Pro Loco on Via Ampsicora (☎0783.358.160).

Around the corner from the church on Via Garibaldi, *Da Leonardo* **pizzeria/ristorante** offers simple, reasonably-priced meals.

Arborea and around

Another smaller lagoon, the **Stagno di S'Ena Arrubia**, 5km south of the Stagno di Santa Giusta, has a greater variety of birdlife, including sandpipers, herons and the rare whiteheaded ducks. Although this area has been left a protected site, the land south of here, the **Bonifica di Arborea**, was reclaimed and rehabilitated as cultivable fields after 1919.

The quiet, rural centre of **ARBOREA** is a twentieth-century settlement whose name is a conscious throwback to the old *giudicato*. Founded in 1928 during the campaign to maximize Sardinia's domestic production, the town was originally called "Mussolinia", and was intended to house the rural colonies introduced into the area from the Veneto, Friuli and Emilia-Romagna regions of Italy, to which the town owes its incongruous northern Italian appearance. This is most noticeable in the main square, Piazza Maria Ausiliatrice, where a formal garden with neat flowerbeds and palm trees is overlooked by a red-brick parish church and town hall, all surrounded by right-angled, tree-lined streets.

The whole place exudes the cardinal Fascist values of planning and orderliness, and the neo-Gothic church, **Cristo Redentore**, even sports a tidy grotto carved into the left side, with a Madonna presiding. At the opposite end of the square, the grand Liberty-style town hall houses a small but immaculately-kept collection of archeological finds from the locality, the **Collezione Archeológica** (open when the town hall is open, usually Mon & Tues 10am–1pm & 3.30–5.30pm, Wed–Fri 10am–1pm; free). Six display cases show items mainly from the Punic and Roman settlements in the area: bracelets, rings, urns, oil-burners and amphorae, as well as bits of ceramics and glass, and bronze coins from different periods. Many of the exhibits were unearthed during the land-reclamation work of 1932, when a Punic necropolis and numerous Roman sepulchres came to light. Most striking of these is an unusual second- or third-century-BC vase in the shape of a child's head.

Beyond the main square, the neat appearance of the houses ends abruptly, and there's precious little to warrant any further exploration. The town could make a useful alternative to staying in Oristano, however, especially as it possesses a comfortable and cheap **hotel** right on the main square, the endearingly old-fashioned *Gallo Blanco* (T & F 0783.800.241; ❷). The attached **restaurant** (open to non–guests) offers a moderately-priced menu of Sard and Italian dishes. If you want food to take away, Via Sardegna, off the south side of the square, has a baker and an indoor **market** (open 9am–1pm and 4–7.30pm except Wed afternoon and Sun).

Marina di Arborea

Outside Arborea, the fruits of the large-scale land-reclamation scheme that made the town possible are readily apparent: the whole district, formerly a malarial swamp, has been transformed by drainage, canalization and irrigation into a richly productive zone. Fruit and vegetables, vineyards, tobacco and beetroot all thrive here, and the area also supports herds of dairy cows, which account for most of the island's milk production.

Much of the coast is fringed by a dense pine forest, interspersed with the occasional wartime pillbox and some superb sandy beaches, all within sight of Tharros across the Golfo di Oristano and accessible along any of the straight roads leading westward. At the end of one of these, you come upon **MARINA DI ARBOREA** – little more than a handful of houses behind the shore. One of them is a small **restaurant** and **hotel**, *Il Canneto* (T 0783.800.561; ❷), right on the sandy beach – its eight rooms fill quickly in summer.

△ Oristano Cathedral

A much grander affair, the *Ala Birdi* hotel complex (☎0783.8050, ⓦ www.alabirdi.it; ⓢ), lies just up the coast (reachable from the turn-off opposite the unattractive *La Pineta* hotel, on the main road north of Arborea), where there are good facilities for families, with a pool and the beach just a few steps away beyond the curtain of pinewoods. The main attraction here, though, is the hotel's **riding facilities**, among the best in Sardinia. All ages and levels are catered for, and excursions organized along the coast, through the woods, and inland. The hotel also has one- and two-room apartments for rent. Ask about family rates, discounts for longer stays and half-board, which may be compulsory in summer.

Marceddi

South of Arborea, Terralba and its surrounding country is mainly interesting for its wine production; the reclaimed land west of here is also flat and fertile, but is lent more character by the placid lagoon, the **Stagno di Marceddi**, that separates this area from the hilly region on the other side, part of Cágliari province. The banks of the lagoon, which lies 11km south of Arborea off the SP69, have tables and benches under the pines for picnics. Near the mouth of this stretch of water, the sleepy village of **Marceddi** has a low-key port, or *porticciolo*, where fishing boats and pleasure craft are anchored, and a small selection of restaurants, among which *Da Lucio* (closed Thurs except Aug) has good seafood dishes and quantities of the renowned Terralba wine; *panini* and *pizzette* are available from bars nearby. A narrow causeway runs south across the mouth of the lagoon to Sant'Antonio di Santadi and the Costa Verde (see p.126).

East of Oristano: into the mountains

There are two or three places in the hills **east of Oristano** worth seeking out, all in the former territory of medieval Arborea. The SS388 veers inland through nondescript villages and landscape that is initially flat and uninteresting, but soon becomes hillier and more varied. **Fordongianus** is the prime attraction in these parts, the site of some well-preserved Roman baths on the banks of the Tirso river and an interesting 400-year-old Aragonese home. The village's volcanic trachyte stone – brownish-red, pink or grey – is the predominant building material in this area, quarried around the old Roman resort. Further east, the roads become more tortuous and the villages more isolated. Near the textile town of **Samugheo**, a good excursion on foot or by car can be made to the splendidly isolated **Castello Medusa**, right on the confines of Nuoro province.

ARST **buses** to and from Oristano stop at Fordongianus and Samugheo; **hotels** are sparse but, for the most part, cheap.

Fordongianus and around

Twenty-eight kilometres up the River Tirso from Oristano, **FORDONGIANUS** was a Roman spa town founded at the end of the first century AD under the emperor Trajan; the present name is a corruption of Forum Traiani. The town conserves its old Roman bridge over the river, on whose banks and the baths are still in fairly good condition and visitable on the river bank.

The town has several examples of public **sculpture** carved out of the local red trachytic stone. Some are entries for – or past winners of – an international competition held annually in Fordongianus; if you're here in July and August, you'll see the sculptors chiselling away in the streets. A couple of the pieces stand outside the **Casa Aragonese** (Tues–Sun 9.30am–1pm & 3–7.30pm, 2.30–5pm in winter; €3, including Terme Romane), a signposted left turn from near the western entrance to the town. Also constructed from the distinctive red stone, and marked out by its pillared portico, the dwelling is thought to date from the end of the sixteenth or beginning of the seventeenth century, and to have been built for a noble Catalan family. Until 1998, the building housed the local library, and there are moves afoot to install a museum or gallery here, but for the present the rooms are bare, showing few signs of the people who once inhabited them. Even so, and despite some unfortunate cement restoration work from the 1980s, the interior is worth a quick whirl. Guides will point out the Gothic decorated windows and doors, and the window seats where the ladies of the household would sit and sew. There are more of the trachytic stone sculptures in the garden at the back of the house.

At the lower end of town, the **Terme Romane** (signposted) stand on the banks of the River Tirso (daily 9.30am–1pm & 3–7.30pm, 2.30-5pm in winter; €3, including Casa Aragonese). Half the pleasure here is the evocative riverside site, the water steaming as it gushes into the river at a temperature of 54° centigrade. Local women still use the hot spring water to scrub their laundry, as they have done for millennia. A few metres up from the waterside, enclosed by railings, the Roman baths retain much of their original structure, the oldest sections including the main pool, while the frigidarium, tepidarium and calidarium date from a third-century enlargement. Behind the main building, part of a forum still stands, from which a stairway leads to what is thought to be either an ancient hotel or butcher's shop, partly frescoed.

If you feel like a wash-down in the healthy mineral waters, someone at the ticket office can provide you with a key for one of the **Bagni Termali**, the dank nineteenth-century bath-houses tucked away below the road by the river, 200m from the Roman baths (Mon–Sat 8–10am & 2.30–4.30pm; €3.50). Anyone wanting a dash more luxury only has to cross to the other side of the river – there's a pedestrian viaduct – to the **Terme Sardegna**, a modern thermal complex where you can sample a range of treatments from massage to mud-packs (though you should book to make sure of availability: ☎0783.60.037). The centre is open Monday–Saturday 8am–noon & 2–6pm).

A kilometre or so west of Fordongianus, the thirteenth-century **chiesa di San Lussório** stands within its walled enclosure by the side of the SS388. The wonky red trachyte facade looks rough and unadorned at first glance, though closer inspection reveals a very eroded relief around the base of the doorway, and another on one of the columns around the apse, where excavations of a paleochristian necropolis are currently under way.

There's nowhere to stay hereabouts, but there are a few **restaurants** in town – try *La Befana*, a pizzeria on Via Santíssimi Mártiri (closed Tues), or the smarter *Su Montigu* restaurant, nearby at Via Carlo Alberto Dalla Chiesa, which has local dishes (☎0783.60.018; closed Sun and most s except with prior booking; no credit cards).

Samugheo and Castello di Medusa

East of Fordongianus, the SS388 twists into the mountains of the Barbagia, passing close to the dam at the southern end of Lago Omodeo (see p.183–184), and taking in the village of **Busachi** before reaching the mountain town of Sórgono (see p.332). A right turn off this road leads south to Allai (a much shorter route than the zigzagging SP33 going directly there from Fordongianus) and **SAMUGHEO**, a large village famous for its textiles (*tessile*). Throughout August, a craft fair, the Mostra dell'Artigianato del Mandrolisai, takes place here, with huge piles of rugs, blankets, tapestries and furniture for sale in the shops and stalls. At other times, it's not a particularly exciting place to hang about in, though it does have a couple of banks, a hotel/restaurant, and – opposite the *Municipio* in Piazza Sedda – a good-looking church worth a brief wander round. Built in the seventeenth century of pink trachyte blocks, **San Sebastiano** has an unusual Gothic interior with a low-vaulted altar and a lovely old wooden pulpit, carved with faces and resting on a single stone column.

At Via Vittorio Emanuele 37, the town's only **hotel**, the modern *Bittu* (☎0783.64.190; ❶; no credit cards), offers standard rooms with bath, and it has a decent **ristorante/pizzeria** attached.

Three or four kilometres south of Samugheo on the SP38 Asuni road, a dirt track – indicated by a yellow signpost on the left – leads off towards the **Castello di Medusa**, a ruined redoubt which makes a rewarding trip either on foot or with your own transport. On the way you'll pass several *pineddas*, the unusual igloo-type constructions used by the local shepherds; they resemble miniature *nuraghi* at first glance, but are made of much lighter, smaller stones. As you follow the high ridge with steep drops below, look out for glimpses of the distant peaks of the Gennargentu mountains to the east. The castle itself is about 5km along the track: for orientation, aim for the orange church visible on the horizon. The ruins appear suddenly below the track on the left, utterly isolated above a gorge, though the messy evidence of sporadic restoration work detracts from the site's remote flavour.

Little is known of the origins of the castello, though it's thought that it was an outpost of Fordongianus during the Roman occupation, and the fortified site was later used by Arborea's *giudicati*. The straggling ruins give little idea of how the castle might have appeared when intact, but it's a grand spot nonetheless, for solitary contemplation or for heading off on foot into the surrounding hills. By crossing the river to the track on the other side, it would be feasible to reach Asuni, about 3km south, through high pastoral country crossed by dry-stone walls and dotted with herds of goats and sheep, and with sudden rocky outcrops.

North of Oristano

The northern half of Oristano province contains a couple of essential sites – the nuraghic complexes of **Santa Cristina** and **Losa** – and a handful of non-essential but still rewarding spots which you could take in on easy detours from your main route. Unless you're stopping for wine or oranges in the rich farming country immediately north of the provincial capital, the *nuraghi* should be your first halts – they're easily the most important such sites in the province. At Abbasanta, near Losa, the SS131Dir branches east off the Carlo Felice Highway towards Nuoro. Anyone with an interest in **Antonio Gramsci** should head a couple of kilometres up this road to see the small exhibition of documents and letters relating to the Communist theorist in his former home in the village of **Ghilarza**, just west of the dammed **Lago Omodeo**. Still further up this route, the much venerated church of Sant'Antine, outside **Sédilo**, is the venue of the hectic **S'Ardia** horse race, famous throughout the island.

Horses also feature prominently in the village of **Santu Lussurgiu**, west of Abbasanta, where riding skills are put to the test in the local Carnival celebrations. Rounding the northern reaches of the extinct volcano **Monte Ferru** will bring you to **Cúglieri** and within sight of the sea. There are **beaches** below around **Santa Caterina di Pittinuri**, and an atmospheric paleochristian site at **Cornus**.

Any of these places could be visited on day-trips from Oristano, and all but the nuraghic sites are reachable on ARST **buses**. It's feasible to reach both Ghilarza and Nuraghe Losa on foot from the train station at Abbasanta (2km and 3km respectively) – and Paulilátino is also on the main line. **Accommodation** is thin on the ground, however, with more choice around Cúglieri and on the coast.

Santa Cristina and Paulilátino

Travelling up the main SS131, you'll soon pass through the "Vernaccia triangle", an area bounded by the villages of Zeddiani, Barátili San Pietro and Solarussa, which forms the core of the Vernaccia wine-producing region. The villagers of Barátili San Pietro are also famous for their skills in making and navigating the reed-built *fassonis*. Further on, you might stop to buy a kilo or two of what are reputed to be Sardinia's best oranges, grown around **Milis**; the season extends over ten months of the year. About 25km north of Oristano, look out for the signposted exit from the superstrada to the nuraghic complex of **Santa Cristina** (daily 8.30am–1hr before sunset; €3.10), a wide-ranging site scattered among a shady grove of olive trees, comprising a *nuraghe*, a sacred well and other nuraghic buildings, some of them dating back to 1800 BC. The *nuraghe's* main tower, about fifteen metres high, has an egg-shaped "tholos"-type interior, in which niches and alcoves have been hewn. From the top, the views over the green wooded surroundings take in other fragments of this extensive site, including a **capanna lunga** – a long, stone-built, open-topped structure of unknown function, which has yielded Roman finds from the third century BC. But the most impressive part of the complex is the **sacred well** and underground shrine a short walk away. An extraordinary feat of engineering, the shrine is reached down a narrow-walled flight of perfectly smooth steps – so well-preserved you could mistake them for a modern reconstruction. Back on the surface, a round meeting room stands nearby, similar in form to those in other nuraghic sites, and you'll come across other fragments of buildings in varying states of preservation.

It's an impressive grouping, the overall effect enhanced by the mossy green ambience. One of the sprawling olive trees here is said to be 1000 years old. The entry ticket includes a guided tour of the site, and also allows entry into the **Museo Archeologico-Etnográfico** in the centre of **PAULILÁTINO**, 5km further up the road (Tues–Sun 9am–1pm & 4.30–7.30pm, 3–5.30pm in winter). Housed in a handsomely-restored building from the seventeenth century, the disparate and diverting collection includes archeological finds from Santa Cristina on the ground floor, and local photographs, traditional furnishings, tools and other items of folkloric interest upstairs, with temporary exhibitions on the roof and in the courtyard.

Ghilarza

Although born near Oristano, the great political theorist **Antonio Gramsci** spent most of his youth in the village of **GHILARZA**, between Abbasanta and Lago Omodeo. The modest house where he and his family lived at Corso

Antonio Gramsci (1891–1937)

Italy's most influential political theorist of the left, **Antonio Gramsci**, was born in the village of Ales, southeast of Oristano, but grew up in Ghilarza, where his father worked with the land registry. Never physically strong, Antonio suffered from rickets as a child, a condition aggravated by poverty after his father was jailed for "administrative irregularities". Despite such obstacles, the young Gramsci doggedly pursued his education, leaving Ghilarza before he was eighteen to attend the lyceum in Cágliari, where his brother Gennaro was already involved in socialist politics.

By the time he was twenty, Antonio had enrolled to study letters at the university of Turin. Here, he was drawn into working-class politics, and in 1921 became one of the founders of the **Italian Communist Party**. The following year, he took part in an Italian delegation to Moscow, where he met his future wife, Giulia Schucht. Returning to Italy, he was elected to the Chamber of Deputies, where he became one of the most effective and articulate **opponents of Fascism**. Inexorably, the regime closed in. "We must prevent this brain from functioning for twenty years," Mussolini is reported to have ordered. Gramsci was arrested in November 1926; he was 35, and would spend the rest of his life in jail, dying of tuberculosis in 1937.

Paradoxically, Gramsci's imprisonment had allowed him to develop his ideas untainted by Stalinism, and his **Prison Notebooks**, when they were published immediately after the end of World War II, helped to revitalize the discredited Left during the 1950s and 1960s. The alternative theoretical framework that he provided was a decisive factor not just in the reformation of the Italian Communist Party but in the development of the "Eurocommunism" that underlay the electoral successes of his fellow Sard Enrico Berlinguer in the 1970s.

Umberto 57, near the church on the town's narrow main street, has been converted into the **Casa di Antonio Gramsci** (Wed–Sun & Mon 10am–1pm & 5–8pm, 4.30–7.30pm in winter; free, but donations welcome), a study centre and museum dedicated to Gramsci's life and writings. Much of the small building is taken up by a meeting hall and library, where taped reminiscences by people who knew him are stored alongside shelves of books and documents. Items on display are a curious mix of the personal – letters to his mother, boyhood photographs, toys – and writings relating to his academic and political development. Photos of and objects from the prison cell outside Bari, where he spent five years for anti-Fascist activities, can be seen upstairs. You could spend an absorbing hour or so here (though a knowledge of Italian would help) – but note that the museum, run by volunteers, does not always adhere to its official opening hours, and you'd do well to telephone first (☎0785.54.164).

Ghilarza might not be the most exciting place to spend a night, but if you need it, the village has a comfortable **hotel**, *Su Cantaru*, at Via Monsignor Zucca 2 (☎0783.54.523; ❸). If you need a meal, there's a **restaurant** through the arch opposite Corso Umberto 132, *Al Marchi*, an impressive space overlooked by a trio of unicorns; pastas, pizzas and local meat dishes are on the menu (closed Mon). Alternatively, stock up on *panini* and other takeaway items at the store across from Gramsci's house. You can **change money** at the Banco di Napoli (with an ATM) at Corso Umberto 71.

Lago Omodeo and Sédilo

East of Ghilarza, **Lago Omodeo** is Italy's largest artifical lake, covering an area of 22 square kilometres. Created by damming the River Tirso, it's named after the engineer who planned it in 1923, and supplies electricity as well as drinking water and irrigation to the area. It's extremely scenic, but difficult to get close to the water; if you felt like a paddle, there are places where access is possible, especially on the eastern shores around the village of Bidoni.

Just north of the lake, the town of **SÉDILO** hosts the annual **S'Ardia** horse race, held in honour of the Roman emperor Constantine in his saintly guise of San Costantino. The race takes place at dawn on July 6 and 7 at breakneck speed and over a danger-strewn course, around the church of **Sant'Antine di Sédilo**. It's an attractive, woody spot outside the village and within sight of Lago Omodeo, though tranquillity is notably absent during the S'Ardia itself. The risks to participants and spectators alike are increased by people whose sole job is to harass the horses and their riders, to the extent of shooting dud bullets at them. It's a thrilling spectacle, full of hot tempers, commotion and displays of virility. The church of Sant'Antine – a *novena* church, open for nine days a year – deserves a look for the copious ex-voto graffiti scribbled on its walls.

ARST **buses** (8 daily, Sun 3; 15–30min) run to Sédilo from Ghilarza and the station at Abbasanta, but there are no direct connections from Oristano.

Nuraghe Losa

Standing alone in bare flat country just west of the SS131, the **Nuraghe Losa** (daily 8am–1hr before sunset; €3.50) makes an easy stop for anyone following Sardinia's main north–south highway in either direction (look out for the exit signs). It's also possible to reach the site by public transport, if you don't mind the three-kilometre walk from the train station at Abbasanta. If you're coming this way, turn left out of the station, cross the lines at the level crossing, and follow the road straight, turning right at the signpost.

Dating from the Middle Bronze Age (the second millennium BC), the flat, grassy site is encompassed within a prodigious perimeter wall, giving a better idea of the extent of a nuraghic settlement than other similar structures in Sardinia. Either before or after visiting the *nuraghe* itself, take a bit of time to follow this wall round for new perspectives on the central structure, and to explore the three shattered **external towers**, which provided secondary entrances to the complex. The perimeter wall encloses the scanty remains of a prehistoric village and, just inside the site's main entrance, exposed cinerary urns from the settlement's post-nuraghic phase, the remains of a first- to second-century-AD cemetery.

What commands most of your attention, however, is the massive sheer-walled trilobate (three-cornered) *nuraghe* – the compact, fortified structure grows in impact as you approach. Composed of regular basalt stones half-covered with striking orange lichen, the tapering walls of the truncated **central tower** are smoother than those of most other *nuraghi*, today reaching a height of nearly thirteen metres. The design and arrangement of the various parts of the complex are, as ever, baffling. Directly in front of the *nuraghe's* main entrance, a circular meeting chamber leaves little room for coming and going, and there are equally cramped spaces on the *nuraghe's* western side, where an inner rampart forms an additional protective belt, enclosing a small courtyard accessible through a lintelled door. Two minor **defensive towers** – now topless – are incorporated into the rampart, furnished with narrow slits for viewing the surrounding area and for archers to fire through. Cradled within the rampart at the northern end are more remains of stone buildings, and an entrance – again tiny – for access to the northern tower of the trilobate.

On the other side of the bastion, the **main tower** is entered through a narrow corridor with a large recess hacked out of the right-hand wall (possibly for a sentry). To the left, a flight of stone steps curls up to a second-floor chamber, continuing on to the open terrace from which, on a clear day, you can see the peaks of the Gennargentu mountains to the east. Back on ground level, the main corridor also has lateral passages leading to the bare windowless chambers within the bastion's two southern towers. The main central tower, the oldest part of the structure, has a tall conical interior, dimly lit by electric lighting, with alcoves and niches gouged out of the walls. With little evidence of the use to which this monument was put or of the society that created it, one has to resort to imagination to fill in the gaps, but there is no single explanation: the overall complex shows continuous occupation from the middle Bronze Age (around 1500 BC) to the seventh century AD, while most of the village to the northeast and southwest of the bastion has yet to be uncovered.

The site also holds a small **museum** of very fragmentary finds from the vicinity. Needles and vases from the nuraghic period fill one display case, pottery with zigzag designs from the fifth and sixth centuries AD are in another, and there are photos and notes from other *nuraghi* in the area from which some of these finds originate. There is nothing particularly arresting, however, since the best stuff is on view or in store in Cágliari's museum (see p.77). For more on Sardinia's nuraghic culture, see p.349–350.

Santu Lussurgiu and around

The village of **SANTU LUSSURGIU** sits in the crater of an extinct volcano some 35km north of Oristano and 15km west of the Carlo Felice highway on SP15, amid bare craggy hills and woods of olives and chestnut. This was once a highly volatile seismic zone, though nowadays there's little suggestion of anything erupting in this intensely peaceful corner of the island.

Though many of the local dwellings are modern in appearance, the nucleus of the village is a web of steep cobbled lanes, among which the heavily buttressed church of **Santa Maria degli Ángeli** stands out on an elevation. Above the public gardens on the left of the main street, the grey stone and unusual shape of this late fifteenth-century building is enough to lure you inside, where there's a good wooden altar.

Immediately below the gardens, the **Museo della Tecnologia Contadina** (also known as the Centro di Cultura Popolare) on Via Deodato Meloni is an admirably comprehensive and scrupulously-catalogued collection of everyday items from different eras and different parts of Sardinia. The eleven rooms are dedicated to different aspects of rural culture, starting with agricultural tools and taking in weaving, bread-making, wine-making, children's toys, craftwork and archeology. The museum has no fixed opening hours, however – either just turn up and hope to find someone there, or telephone the non-English-speaking curator to make an appointment (☎0783.550.617 or 0783.550.706). Expect to pay around €2.60 for entry.

The museum gives little space to the main passion in Santu Lussurgiu, however – **horses**. Rearing and riding them is in the blood here, and at no time is this more apparent than in the village's annual party, a horse race spread over three days during **Carnival** (usually Sunday, Monday and Shrove Tuesday). As in Oristano's Carnival binge, riders gallop hard through the narrow streets of the old town, though there are few or no costumed theatrics here – this is serious bareback riding, and highly exciting to watch. The village's saint's day, around **21 August**, is also an excuse to saddle up for horseback competitions during four days of festivities. Santu Lussurgiu takes a break from the horses at **Easter**, however, which is celebrated with choral singing, but the local craft-work for sale in the shops includes anything to do with horses, from saddles to pen-knives.

For **eating**, the village has a pleasant trattoria/pizzeria, *Bellavista*, Viale Azuni 70, on the road going out of town towards San Leonardo (closed Tues), where you'll pay around €5.50 for a good lasagne. Santu Lussurgiu is served by regular buses from Abbasanta (about 25min), and also has direct bus links to Oristano.

San Leonardo de Siete Fuentes

North of Santu Lussurgiu, weekend picnickers head up the minor road towards Macomer (see p.217–218) for the wooded area around the hamlet of **SAN LEONARDO DE SIETE FUENTES**. The village's Spanish name is a reference to its highly-prized mineral waters, which attract droves of connoisseurs. The crumbly old Romanesque church is the burial place of Guelfo, son of Count Ugolino della Gherardesca, who died in 1292 (see p.120). San Leonardo is also the scene of a **horse fair**; held every June 2, it's one of Sardinia's most important markets of this kind. The small **pensione** in the village makes an excellent place to stay at any time of year: *Malica*, at Via Macomer 5 (☎ & ℱ0783.550.756; ❷; no credit cards), but as they only have twelve rooms, you'd better book in advance if you're coming during the fair. There's also a trattoria here.

Cúglieri and around

West of Santu Lussurgiu the mainly forested **Monte Ferru** – the name a reminder of the iron once mined here – which reaches a height of over 1000m. This former volcanic zone is now endowed with an abundance of rivers and springs which nourish its thick forests of oak, elm and chestnut. Mouflons and deer inhabit parts of it, such as the Sa Pabarile area. If you're tempted to get a closer look, the twisty and highly scenic SP19 heading north and west of Santu Lussurgiu offers opportunities to explore on foot – Sa Pabarile can be reached from the lane on the left leading up to the RAI TV transmitter, 8km from the village. Seventeen kilometres along the SP19, the silver dome of the basilica at the top of the village of **CÚGLIERI** makes a prominent landmark for miles around. The superb panoramic views from here repay the short detour, though the basilica itself is a disappointment, its broad brown exterior only feebly enlivened by two marble carvings on either side of the portal. The ruined castle on a promontory southeast of town is the **Castello di Monte Ferru** (in Sard: "Casteddu Etzu"), a twelfth-century redoubt subjected to over-zealous restoration. A side-road off the SP19 provides easy access.

If you were thinking of **staying** off the beaten track, Cúglieri has a very reasonable choice, *Hotel Desogos* on Vico Cugia (☎ & ℱ0785.39.660; ❶; no credit cards), off the one-way Via Cugia, the main road descending through the old town from the basilica. Plain rooms are available with or without private bathroom, and there is a restaurant. Other **trattorias** in town include *Meridiana* and *La Villa*, both close by. Cúglieri is a stop on the ARST **bus** route between Oristano and Bosa (see p.188).

Santa Caterina and Cornus

From Cúglieri, the SS292 heads rapidly downhill and south along the western flank of Monte Feru to the main resort on this stretch of coast, **SANTA CATERINA DI PITTINURI**, a busy holiday centre in summer, but pretty dead at any other time. In winter, the local economy relies on olive production – the surrounding country is famed for its olive groves, and is one of the island's major sources of olives and olive oil. The **beaches** around here are also renowned, a mixture of sand and rocks sheltered within pretty inlets. The most photogenic are at **Su Archittu**, a couple of kilometres south of town, where a ruined watchtower stands on a point. The place is named after a natural rock arch which you can swim through and climb above. South of here, the long, dune-backed strand Is Arenas extends for 6km.

Santa Caterina itself, however, almost overwhelmed by holiday homes, has little of interest. Neither does the town have much in the way of **accommodation**: Corso Alagon has the pleasant and reasonably priced *La Scogliera* (T & F0785.38.231; ❷), near the beach and with a fish restaurant and pizzeria, but with only seven rooms, it's often full. A second, larger hotel, *La Baja* (T0785.389.149, F0785.389.003; ❹), signposted off the main road, is currently closed for renovation. Near Su Archittu, try *S'Istella* (T0785.38.484; ❸), a plain pensione with shared bathrooms and a restaurant. There are several **campsites** in the area, however, all of which have bungalows or caravans for rent: *Europa* (May–Sept; T0785.38.058), in the Torre del Pozzo neighbourhood, *Nurapolis* (T0783.52.283, Wwww.nurapolis.it) and the smaller *Is Arenas* (April–Oct; T0783.52.284), the last two close to the beach at Is Arenas. All have sports facilities, shops and pizzerias.

A kilometre or so south and inland of Su Archittu, a dirt road leads off to the left, signposted **CORNUS**: veer right just before the cemented section of the track to reach the site, which is always open (free). The settlement here was the focus for the gathering opposition of the allied Carthaginian and Sard forces – under the local chieftain Ampsicora – to the growing power of Rome. The rebellion was swiftly crushed by Roman forces in 216 BC, Ampsicora took his own life, and with the Carthaginian threat banished for ever, the way was clear for Rome's undisputed domination of the island.

The battlefield itself is a little further inland on a hill, though there's nothing to mark out the exact spot of the epic conflict. The main site, however, reveals the interesting remains of an early Christian centre of worship. The outlines of a double-apsed basilica are clearly visible, with tombs jammed into every available space, even the apses. Further along, you'll come across the baptistery, marked out by a well-preserved cruciform font. It's a serene, deserted spot, within sight of the sea, and ideal for a quiet picnic.

Travel details

Abbasanta to: Cágliari (8–10 daily; 1hr 30min–2hr 15min); Macomer (8–11 daily; 20–30min); Olbia (2 daily; 2hr 35min); Oristano (8–10 daily; 30min); Ozieri-Chilivani (5–6 daily; 1hr 15min); Paulilátino (3–6 daily; 10min); Sássari (3 daily; 2hr 10min).
Oristano to: Abbasanta (8–11 daily; 25–45min);

Cágliari (hourly; 1hr–1hr 40min); Macomer (8–11 daily; 45min–1hr 10min); Olbia (2 daily; 2hr 40min–3hr); Ozieri-Chilivani (5–6 daily; 1hr 30min–2hr); Paulilátino (4–7 daily; 30min); Sássari (2 daily; 2hr 25min–2hr 40min).
Paulilátino to Abbasanta (4–7 daily; 10min); Cágliari (3–5 daily; 1hr 30min–2hr); Macomer (4–7 daily; 35min); Olbia (1 daily; 2hr 35min); Oristano (3–5 daily; 25min); Ozieri-Chilivani (2 daily; 1hr 30min).

Buses

Cabras to: Is Arutas (July–Aug 5 daily; 35min); Oristano (Mon–Sat 1–2 hourly, Sun 5–10; 15min); San Giovanni di Sinis (July–Aug 5 daily; 20min).

Oristano to: Abbasanta (Mon–Sat 11 daily; 1–2hr); Arborea (Mon–Sat 1–2 hourly; 25min); Bosa (Mon–Sat 5–6 daily; 2hr); Cabras (Mon–Sat 1–2 hourly, Sun 5–10; 15min) Cágliari (4–6 daily; 1hr 25min–2hr); Cúglieri (Mon–Sat 6–7 daily, plus July–Aug Sun 2; 1hr–1hr 10min); Fordongianus (Mon–Sat 9–10 daily; 40min); Ghilarza (Mon–Sat 2 daily; 2hr); Is Arutas (July–Aug 5 daily; 50min); Láconi (Mon–Sat 6–7 daily; 1hr 30min–2hr); Marina di Torre Grande (Mon–Sat 12 daily, Sun 5; 25min); Nuoro (4 daily; 2hr); Putzu Idu (Mon–Sat 2 daily, July–Aug also Sun 1; 35–50min); Samugheo (Mon–Sat 5–6 daily; 1hr 10min); Santa Caterina di Pittinuri (Mon–Sat 6–8 daily, July–Aug also Sun 2; 40–50min); Santa Giusta (Mon–Sat 1–2 hourly; 10min); San Giovanni di Sinis (July–Aug 5 daily; 35min); Sássari (4 daily; 2hr 15min); Sórgono (Mon–Sat 5–6 daily; 1hr 30min–1hr 45min); Tharros (July–Aug 5 daily; 35min).

The northwest coast

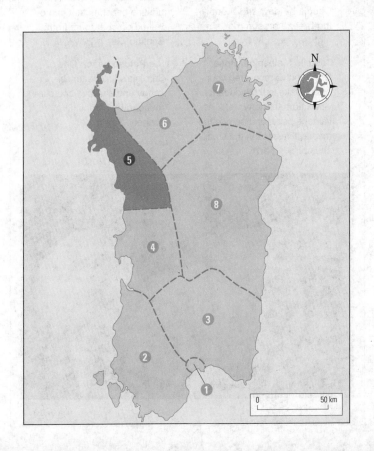

CHAPTER 5

Highlights

* **Seafood in Alghero** Push the boat out with a banquet in one of the town's renowned fish restaurants – lobster is the local speciality. See p.202–203

* **Walk along Alghero's sea walls** The formidable old walls of the port are usually almost deserted, but offer great views across to Capo Caccia by day, and a cooling breeze on summer nights. See p.201

* **Castello Malaspina, Bosa** Once you've recovered your breath, take in the wonderful views from this lofty vantage point, and admire the medieval frescos in the small church. See p.215

* **Cycle along the Alghero–Bosa coast** This wild stretch of coast warrants a leisurely ride, with stops at secluded beaches along the way. See p.210–211

* **Boat excursion to Asinara** Off-limits for centuries, the island shelters wildlife and pristine beaches that can be visited on boat tours from Stintino. See p.222–223

* **Le Pelosa beach** One of Sardinia's top beaches, sandy and shallow, and surrounded by magnificent scenery. See p.222

△ Miniature donkeys

5

The northwest coast

S ardinia's **northwest coast** shelters a trio of the most attractive seaside resorts on the island, interspersed with some really spectacular coastline. The principal resort on this stretch, **Alghero**, has become a major package destination, yet it has retained its distinctive Catalan character – the result of intense colonization in the fourteenth century. Paradoxically, given this faintly exotic tinge, it is simultaneously the most "Italian" of Sardinia's holiday towns, its old centre a tight web of narrow lanes packed with boutiques, bars and restaurants. Alghero is often compared to mainland towns like Sorrento or San Remo, and if it lacks their glamorous edge, it's also refreshingly free of their cynical hard sell. Even a short stay should be enough to get acquainted with the abundance of enticing beaches in the vicinity and to investigate the area's most important archeological sites, not to mention the famous **Grotta di Nettuno** (Neptune's Grotto) on the point at Capo Caccia.

The area around Alghero also has plenty of interest. To the north, the ghost town of **Argentiera** and Sardinia's only natural lake, **Lago di Baratz**, make intriguing half-day trips, while the unspoiled rocky coast south of town is one of the last habitats in Sardinia of the griffon vulture. At the end of this stretch, the riverside port of **Bosa** is still waiting to be discovered by the big package companies. With its compact warren of streets topped by a ruined castle, the town is not exactly tourist-free, but has a quiet, undemanding atmosphere perfectly in tune with the slow rhythms of the local fishing community. At the outlet of the River Temo, **Bosa Marina** keeps the beach aficionados happy, though connoisseurs may prefer the more secluded scraps of sand on the coast north. Inland of Bosa, **Macomer** has some diverting nuraghic sites within close range, but should otherwise detain you only as a transport junction.

The resort of **Stintino**, at Sardinia's northwestern tip, is much smaller than Bosa and Alghero, and more subject to the whims of the tourist industry. The real attraction here is the largely undeveloped coastline on either side – especially the once-seen, never-forgotten sands around the point at **La Pelosa**, where calm, turquoise waters extend to rocky offshore isles. Boat excursions from Stintino call at the biggest of these islands, **Asinara**, a nature reserve with some exquisite beaches.

Outside the resorts, the northwest coast presents a wild and rocky aspect, sparsely populated and ideal for roaming. Although **public transport** services are adequate for travelling between the main towns and villages, your own car gives you more freedom, while renting a bike is a fun way to cover the shorter distances. **Walkers** will find the terrain rewarding, with few overly strenuous

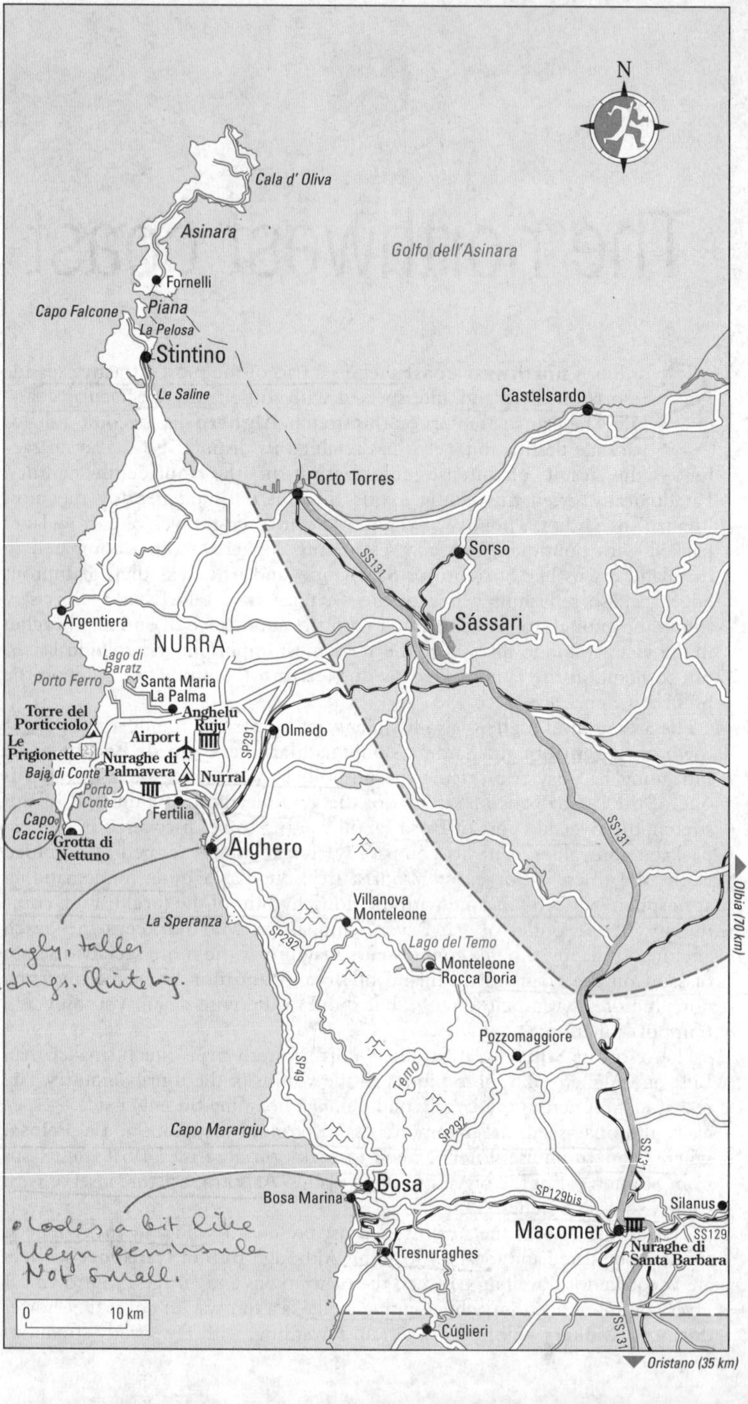

looks great.

o Some ugly, taller buildings. Quite big.

o Looks a bit like Lleyn peninsula Not small.

tracts, though they should be aware that the rough and rugged nature of the coast means that much of the alluring Alghero–Bosa stretch, for example, must be tackled on the road – fortunately, it's free of much traffic most of the time.

Accommodation options are rather limited in Stintino and Bosa, but plentiful in Alghero, which also has most of the **campsites**. Two of Sardinia's five **HI hostels** are at Bosa and Fertilia (near Alghero). Bear in mind that availability can be very scarce throughout the region in summer, with many places closed altogether between October and April.

Alghero and around

ALGHERO is a very rare Italian phenomenon: a tourist town that is also a flourishing fishing port, giving it an economic base entirely independent of the summer hordes. The predominant flavour here is Catalan, owing to the wholesale Hispanicization that followed the overthrow of the Doria family by Pedro IV of Aragon in 1353 – a process so thorough that the town became known as "Barcelonetta".

According to some, Alghero's name is derived from the Arabic, *al-ghar*, meaning cave or cavern, possibly a reference to the celebrated **Grotta di Nettuno** nearby. Others suggest that its original name was *S'Alighera* (*L'Alguer* in Catalan), meaning "seaweedy" or "place of algae", though there's little evidence of this today in the clear blue seas here. In fact, it is the purity of the water together with the spectacular coast – not to mention Neptune's Grotto – which have helped to put the town on the map in recent times. Tour operators homed in on Alghero in the post-war holiday boom, which gave birth to the welter of hotels and restaurants that exist today, catering to a constant influx of mostly British and German tourists.

Thankfully, the resort has escaped the fate of many another Mediterranean holiday niche and resisted the lure of quaintness and fakery. Instead, it remains a fairly easy-going place, with a sharp but good-humoured population, who themselves like nothing better than a good night out in a trattoria. All the same, you'll find fewer signs of foreigner fatigue outside the main tourist season – another reason not to visit in high summer, when facilities are stretched and prices are higher. As you might expect, the choice of **accommodation** is extensive, but booking is essential at any time. As for **restaurants**, the quality of the food is generally impressive – the presence of the fishing port ensures a regular supply of the freshest seafood, and the varied local cuisine also makes good use of the Catalan culinary tradition. The town is additionally blessed by its proximity to some of Sardinia's most famous vineyards, producing eminently quaffable wines.

However, the real attraction of Alghero is its atmospheric **old town centre**, a puzzle of mainly car-free lanes, at the heart of which Via Carlo Alberto, Via Principe Umberto and Via Roma have most of the bars and shops. The old town's finest architecture dates from the sixteenth century, built in a congenial Catalan-Gothic style; a walkabout should also take in the series of seven towers which dominate Alghero's centre. The Spanish connection is never far away: the street names are all in the Catalan dialect – *carrer* for "via", *plaça* for "piazza", *iglesia* for "chiesa" and *palau* for "palazzo". Beyond the stout girdle of walls enclosing this historic core, the new town's grid of parallel streets has little of interest beyond its restaurants and hotels.

Most visitors to Alghero make the boat trip to the **Grotta di Nettuno**, justifiably famous and worth the ride, though by no means the only essential stop. If you visit the grotto by boat, you'll pass the glorious deep bay of **Porto Conte**, one of Sardinia's most celebrated beauty spots, favoured by sailors and windsurfers, part of which is set aside as a wildlife reserve. The land journey will take you through the low-key resort of **Fertilia**, an alternative place to stay if Alghero is full, and close to the area's most important nuraghic complex, **nuraghe di Palmavera**, not to mention some fine beaches. Inland, you could drop into another archeological site belonging to an earlier era, the necropolis at **Anghelu Ruju**, set amidst the endless vineyards that produce some of the best of Sardinia's wine.

Further afield, the undeveloped coast **south of Alghero** is a jagged and dramatic interplay of rock and sea, with a few select beaches tucked out of sight. There are no habitations here, not until you climb to the village of **Villanova Monteleone**, situated inland amidst a bare mountainous terrain. In the opposite direction, the country **north of Alghero** is much flatter, but there are a couple of places worth exploring: **Lago di Baratz**, harbouring protected wildlife, and the abandoned mining centre of **Argentiera**, dominated by the eighteenth-century workings of a once flourishing industry.

Local **buses** from Alghero (service AF) run every forty minutes to Fertilia, less frequently to Porto Conte and Capo Caccia (for Grotta di Nettuno). Other places must be reached by **taxi** or your own transport, though there's a regular bus service to Villanova Monteleone. For more information on bus and train connections, see Travel details on p.223.

Some history

While archeological finds in the area around Alghero suggest a degree of social organization as early as 6000 BC, the history of the modern town really begins in the first half of the twelfth century with the fortification of what had been an obscure fishing port by the Doria family of **Genoa**. The town successfully defended itself from assaults by the Pisans and Aragonese until 1353, when, after the conquest of Cágliari and Sássari, a large **Spanish fleet**, supported by the Venetians, routed the Genoans at the nearby bay of Porto Conte and took possession of Alghero. Following an uprising in which the Spanish garrison was massacred, the town was subjected to a thorough "ethnic cleansing", in which waves of **Catalan settlers** displaced the locals, forcing them to settle at Villanova, a mountain village 25km to the south. Laws were passed limiting the number of native Sards who could enter, and compelling them to leave town at the sound of a trumpet signal.

Because of its geographic and strategic importance on Sardinia's northwestern coast, Alghero quickly became the foremost **port** for traffic between Sardinia and Catalonia. Between the fourteenth and sixteenth centuries, its defences were massively strengthened; most of the ramparts and towers still standing today date from this period, when they sheltered a substantial garrison and fleet, providing a powerful bulwark against seaborne incursions against Sássari and the whole western interior.

The town suffered a downturn in its economic fortunes following the expulsion in 1492 of its substantial **Jewish community**, or *Aljama*. This forced the Aragonese to reopen Alghero to foreign and Sard traders – though the core of the town remained stoutly Catalan in character and culture. The historic links with Spain were bolstered in 1541, when the emperor **Charles V** made a historic visit to the town, accompanied by his admiral Andrea Doria – the most eminent member of the Genoan dynasty, formerly in the vanguard of the emperor's enemies before becoming his staunch ally. The two were en route to flush out the corsair **Hassan Aga** from his lair in Algiers, for which they had assembled one of the biggest fleets ever seen. (The pirate chief was himself a Sard: born of shepherds, he was abducted as a slave, forcibly converted and castrated for harem service, and swiftly rose to become right-hand man to the feared Khair al-Din, or Barbarossa).

After Sardinia was taken over by the **House of Savoy** in 1720, Alghero became an increasingly marginalized enclave. The destruction of its landward-facing walls in the nineteenth century was unable to arrest its steady decline, a process that was only halted in the 1960s, with the flow of new money into the town in the wake of its discovery and development as a package **tourist resort**. The last fifty years have seen the establishment of Sardinia's greatest concentration of hotels and restaurants in Alghero, with a string of new development erected along the coast north of the centre. However, the town's remoteness from the mainland has enabled it to escape total mass-market annihilation, while its well-established port has ensured the continuation of the key role of fishing in the local economy. At the same time, the most obvious index of Alghero's distinctive culture, the *catalano* or *algherese* **dialect**, has largely lost the battle against uniformity. While old people – many of whom still regard themselves primarily as Catalans – are attached to it, few of the post-1960s generations are at all adept, and the existence of evening classes for locals to learn or perfect their knowledge of *catalano* is a significant gauge of its present precarious state. Today, the best way to hear the *algherese/catalano* dialect is to drop in on one of the church services conducted in the local vernacular at the church of San Francesco (see p.200).

Arrival, information and getting around

Alghero's **airport** lies 10km inland, outside the town of Fertilia. The building has a **tourist office** (usually daily 8.30am–7.30pm; ☏079.935.124) and a **bank** with an ATM; the post office here can also change cash. Local FdS **buses into town** leave about eight times a day in summer, four or five times daily in winter, timed to coincide with Airone arrivals from the mainland; buy tickets (€0.57) from the shop at one end of the terminal. There are less frequent departures from the airport to Sássari, Stintino, Nuoro, Oristano, Cágliari, Castelsardo, Santa Teresa di Gallura and Olbia operated by different companies (buy tickets on board); some of these services are summer-only. **Taxis** into Alghero cost around €20.

FdS **trains** arrive some way north of the centre, and the small station is connected to the port by frequent **local buses**; you can buy tickets from the bar inside the station, and the bus stop is across the road. Buses AP (every 20min) and AF (hourly) run into town; in the opposite direction, the AF runs to Fertilia, for people heading straight to the hostel or campsite there. Local and regional buses arrive in Via Catalogna, on the Giardini Púbblici. If you're **driving** into town, you'd do well to park before reaching the old centre as spaces here are extremely limited; try on the portside off Via Garibaldi, just north of the centre.

For **getting around town**, your feet should be enough for most journeys, though you may use local buses for journeys to the train station, the campsites and Fertilia; tickets from *tabacchi* and bars cost €0.57. A good alternative for short trips around the town and its environs is by bike (see p.204). For information on tours in and around Alghero, see the box on p.201.

Alghero's **main tourist office** (April–Sept Mon–Sat 8am–8pm, Sun 9am–1pm; Nov–March Mon–Sat 8am–2pm; ☏079.979.054, ⓦwww .infoalghero.it), at the top end of the Giardini Púbblici, is easily the most efficient on the island; its multilingual staff are equipped with reams of maps, accommodation lists and tour details.

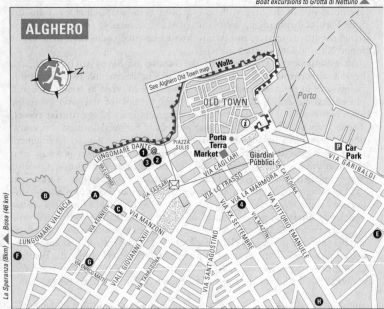

SS292, Scala Piccada (10 km) ▼ & Villanova Monteleone (25 km)   ▼ Santuario di Valverde (6 km)

Accommodation

Of the twenty-eight **hotels** listed in Alghero, only seven or eight remain open in winter, of which five are four-stars, greatly reducing choice during this time. However, there's a good chance of finding a room in one of the less expensive options that remain open all year, such as the resort's numerous **B&Bs**. During July and August, however, when prices rise by up to 25 percent, advance booking is essential. The **campsite** listed here is an easy bus ride north from the centre. There are two other sites located 6km along the coast at Fertilia (see p.206–207), one of them open all year, and there's a fourth, more secluded one at Torre del Porticciolo (p.208). Alghero's youth hostel is also at Fertilia.

There's also a good choice of **private apartments** to let, available through *Immobiliare* agencies, a full list of which can be obtained from the local tourist office. Off-season rates are particularly favourable, but don't expect to find many bargains or any availability at all (unless you've booked far ahead) in August. For example, four- to five-bed apartments range from €600 to €900 per week during high season, normally with a week's minimum stay. Try the Mario Cau agency at Via Don Minzoni 159 (☏079.952.478, ⓦwww.mariocau.cjb.net), or Mamajuana, Vicolo Adami 12 ☏339.136.9791, ⓦwww.mamajuana.it.

Hotels & B&Bs

El Balear Lungomare Dante 32 ☏079.975.229, ⓕ079.974.847. A white, boxy building a few minutes south of Piazza Sulis, mainly catering to groups. It's bright and modern, overlooking the sea and has attractive rates; there's no price difference between sea- and non-sea-facing rooms, although

breakfast is extra. Open March–Oct. ⑤

Carlos V (Carlos Quinto) Lungomare Valencia 24 ☏079.979.501, ⓦwww.hotelcarlosv.it. Once one of the plushest hotels in town, this place is badly in need of an uplift – the air of luxury fostered by palm trees around the good-sized pool is undermined by unreliable plumbing and peeling paint.

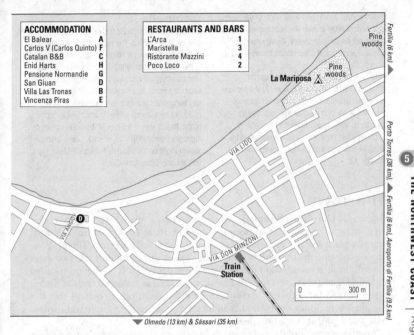

ACCOMMODATION

El Balear	A
Carlos V (Carlos Quinto)	F
Catalan B&B	C
Enid Harts	H
Pensione Normandie	G
San Giuan	D
Villa Las Tronas	B
Vincenza Piras	E

RESTAURANTS AND BARS

L'Arca	1
Maristella	3
Ristorante Mazzini	4
Poco Loco	2

Olmedo (13 km) & Sássari (35 km)

All the same, it offers very reasonable low-season rates, with a supplement for sea-facing rooms. ⑥
Catalan B&B Via Manzoni 41 ☎079.981.909 or 347.833.5230, ⓦwww.algherocasavacanze.it. Modern apartment in the new town, a 10min walk from the old centre. Three rooms are available with shared bathroom. No credit cards. ③
Enid Harts Via Mazzini 156a ☎079.950.283 or 347.408.1378, ⓔenidbb@tiscali.it. A 20min walk from the centre, this friendly B&B in a modern, third-floor apartment has two plain double rooms and a shared bathroom. English, French, German and Dutch are spoken, and rates only just creep into its price category. ②
Mamajuana Vicolo Adami 12 ☎339.136.9791, ⓦwww.mamajuana.it. Very central B&B in the old town. The three doubles and one single are squeezed into an old building, all tastefully renovated and with tiny en-suite bathrooms. Breakfast is served in a nearby café. The managers also offer houses and apartments to rent in the vicinity (see Listings on p.204). No credit cards. ④
La Margherita Via Sássari 70 ☎079.979.006, ⓔhotel.margherita@tiscalinet.it. Close to Piazza Sulis and the old town, this old-fashioned three-star is clean and reliable. All rooms have TVs, a/c and private bathrooms, some with tubs; the front-facing ones have a small balcony, with the best

views from the fourth floor (there's a lift). ⑤
Pensione Normandie Via Enrico Mattei 6 ☎079.975.302, ⓔhotelnormandie@excite.it. In the newer part of town, between Via Kennedy and Via Giovanni XXIII, this very cheap but basic place has spacious double rooms, some with private bathrooms. One (bathless) single is also available, while a third bed adds 45 percent to the bill. ③
Vincenza Piras Via Asfodelo 69 ☎079.953.294 or 340.407.8041. A couple of streets back from the seafront, this modern B&B lies a 10min walk from the centre, with three decent-sized rooms, one with its own bathroom. Breakfast is self-service, with unlimited coffee. No credit cards. ③
San Francesco Via Machin 2 ☎079.980.330, ⓔhotsfran@tin.it. Alghero's best-value hotel and the only one in the old town, so it's often full. Formerly a convent attached to San Francesco church and lying just behind it, the hotel retains a cloistered air; the 21 rooms are clean and quiet, with telephones, a/c and private bathrooms. The bill includes breakfast. Parking is a problem, but a garage is available nearby at an extra cost of €5 per night. It may close for a few weeks in November. ⑤
San Giuan Via Angioy 2 ☎079.951.222,

℗ 079.951.073. A 15min walk north of the centre, this modern hotel is near the beaches, and all the rooms are en suite. In theory, it stays open in winter; in practice, it often closes for weeks at a stretch. ❹

Villa Las Tronas Lungomare Valencia 24 ℗ 079.981.818, ⓦ www.hvlt.com. At the top end of the market, this castellated former baronial mansion is full of character, still retaining an aristocratic air with its old-fashioned furnishings. Superbly sited on a promontory surrounded by small beaches east of town, it makes a terrific splurge. ❾

Campsite

La Mariposa Via Lido 22 ℗ 079.950.360, ⓦ www.lamariposa.it. The nearest site to Alghero, 2km north of town, *La Mariposa* has direct access to the beach, part of which is sectioned off for site users. Eucalyptus and pine provide welcome shade and soft ground; there are shops and a restaurant, and bungalows and caravans available for rent (€27–58 for a double). The Phoenix Diving Center is also based here. Take bus AP from the station or Alghero's Giardini Púbblici, or walk 10min from the station (right on Via Minzoni, left on Via Malta, right on Via Lido). Open April–Oct.

The Town

Alghero's **Giardini Púbblici**, which effectively divide the right-angled regularity of the new town from the intricate maze of the old, are the usual starting place for any exploration of the *centro stórico*. The **Porta Terra**, at the top of the gardens past the tourist office, was originally one of the two gates into the walled town. Also known as the Torre del Portal, it has been identified by some scholars as the *Torre dels Ebreus*, mentioned in medieval texts as having been erected by Alghero's Jewish community, though others believe that this lay elsewhere. Today, the tower has an incongruous Art-Deco-style war memorial, and a tourist bookshop has been installed inside.

Another remnant of the old town's defensive structure lies at the bottom of the gardens, towards the port, where the huge hollow shell of the **Bastione La Maddalena** has one of the town's seven towers, embedded within the crumbling ruins. The bastion is sometimes the venue for open-air cinema in summer, and also provides access to the centre of the old town, **Piazza Cívica**, a traffic-free but bustling arena of locals and tourists, lined with expensive bars and boutiques. The elongated square gives onto the port through the **Porta a Mare**, the second of the main gates to the old city. The opposite side of the square holds the Gothic **Palazzo d'Albis** (*Palau Albis*), the former governor's palace from which the emperor Charles V addressed the crowds in 1541 before embarking for Algiers to fight his African campaign against the Turks. He is said to have uttered the words, long-remembered in local lore as granting instant nobility to the assembled throng: *Estade todos caballeros* ("You are all knights"), and to have described Alghero as *bonita y bien asentada* ("pretty and well-situated"). Mullioned Gothic and Renaissance windows adorn the facade; next door, a comfortable-looking sailors' club occupies the ground floor of the former town hall.

The Cattedrale and around

At the western end of the square, Via Manno leads into Piazza Duomo, where four tall, fluted columns dominate the white Neoclassical facade of Alghero's **Cattedrale** (daily 6.30am–noon & 5–8pm), a grandiose entry somewhat out of keeping with the sixteenth-century edifice. Founded in 1510, just seven years after Alghero was promoted to city status, the cathedral was not fully completed or consecrated until 1730, though it had long since been established as the customary place for Spanish viceroys to take a preliminary oath before assuming office in Cágliari.

The **interior** is a bit of a hodgepodge: the alternating pillars and columns on either side of the lofty nave survive from the original construction, while the

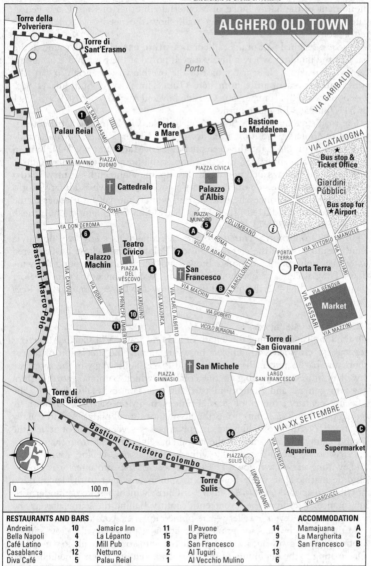

Excursions to Grotta di Nettuno

ALGHERO OLD TOWN

Torre della Polveriera
Torre di Sant'Erasmo
Porto
VIA GARIBALDI

1 Palau Reial
VIA SANT'ERASMO
Porta a Mare
2 Bastione La Maddalena
VIA CATALOGNA
★ Bus stop & Ticket Office

VIA MANNO PIAZZA DUOMO
PIAZZA CÍVICA
Giardini Púbblici
Bus stop for ★ Airport

✝ Cattedrale
Palazzo d'Albis **4**

VIA ROMA
PIAZZA MUNICIPIO
VIA COLUMBANO
VIA VITTORIO EMANUELE
VIA CAGLIARI

VIA DON DEROMA
6
A5
VIA ROMA
PORTA TERRA
Porta Terra

Palazzo Machin
Teatro Cívico
7 VICOLO ADAMI
VIA GENOVA

VIA CAVOUR
PIAZZA DEL VÉSCOVO
8
✝ San Francesco
B
VIA BARCELLONETTA
VIA SASSARI
Market

VIA DORIA
VIA PRINCIPE UMBERTO
VIA ARDUINO
VIA MAIORCA
VIA MACHIN
9
VIA MAZZINI

10
VIA CARLO ALBERTO
VIA GIOBERTI
VICOLO BURAGNA

11
12
Torre di San Giovanni

✝ San Michele
LARGO SAN FRANCESCO

Torre di San Giácomo
PIAZZA GINNASIO
13

Bastioni Cristóforo Colombo
15
14
VIA XX SETTEMBRE
C

VIA KENNEDY
Aquarium
Supermarket

N

PIAZZA SULIS
LUNGOMARE DANTE

Bastioni Marco Polo

0   100 m

Torre Sulis
VIA CARDUCCI

RESTAURANTS AND BARS						ACCOMMODATION	
Andreini	10	Jamaica Inn	11	Il Pavone	14	Mamajuana	A
Bella Napoli	4	La Lépanto	15	Da Pietro	9	La Margherita	C
Café Latino	3	Mill Pub	8	San Francesco	7	San Francesco	B
Casablanca	12	Nettuno	2	Al Tuguri	13		
Diva Café	5	Palau Reial	1	Al Vecchio Mulino	6		

impressive dome and creamy marble central altar date from the eighteenth century, and the lateral chapels are predominantly Neoclassical or Baroque. Behind the altar, an ambulatory said to derive architecturally from the Islamic mosque of the old Moorish city (and recalling similar designs in cathedrals at Salamanca and Segovia) gives onto five radiating chapels, also part of the original building. The left transept holds the well-executed marble funerary monument of the Savoy Duke of Monferrato, brother of King Carlo Felice, dated 1799. Elsewhere, the flaking walls show the need of a long overdue restoration.

To see an original part of the cathedral's **Gothic exterior**, walk round to the back of the building, where a lovely carved portal at the base of the octagonal campanile makes a pleasant contrast to the overblown entrance. You can take **tours of the campanile** from here (Tues, Thurs, Sat & Sun: July & Sept 7–9.30pm; Aug 6–11pm; €1.50). Outside July and August, call ☎079.973.3041 or 347.785.8562 for guided visits.

The road stretching south from the campanile, **Via Príncipe Umberto**, is one of the quietest and most attractive of Old Alghero's lanes. Notable buildings include, on the right, the decrepit **Palazzo Machin** at no. 9–11; built in the seventeenth century for a local bishop, it still preserves its Catalan-Gothic windows and Renaissance portal. Further up, the eighteenth-century **Teatro Cívico** occupies one side of Piazza del Véscovo (also known as Piazza Vittorio Emanuele). Performances are held here in winter, but half-hour **tours** of the theatre are also conducted (Tues, Thurs, Sat & Sun 7–9.30pm; €1.50); check first by calling ☎079.973.4045.

From the front (north) entrance of the cathedral, walk a few steps down Via Sant'Erasmo to view the elegantly austere **Palau Reial**, whose well-restored exterior is enlivened by elaborate brown-and-white patterns around the windows. The palace was probably owned by the Jewish Carcassona family before their eviction in 1492; the ground floor is now a stylish restaurant, *Palau Reial* (see p.202).

Via Carlo Alberto

Of the long lanes running the length of the Old Town, **Via Carlo Alberto** is the busiest, crowded with amblers browsing among the succession of tourist shops and bars between Piazza Cívica and Piazza Sulis. Many of the shops are jewellery stores, specializing in the coral for which Sardinia's northwestern coast in general and Alghero in particular are famous. Halfway along, the fifteenth-century church of **San Francesco** (Mon–Sat 9.30am–noon & 5–6.20pm, Sun 5–7.30pm) fronts the eponymous small piazza. Architecturally the finest of Alghero's churches, it encompasses several different styles; the Gothic campanile and some of the lateral chapels – survivals from the original construction – blend successfully with the Renaissance ceiling, round arches and swirling carved windows. The centrepiece of the dim interior is a polychrome marble altar, while bound to a column on a pier to the left stands a horribly emaciated (*grattugiato*) figure of Christ which, despite its modernistic appearance, dates from the seventeenth century. Behind the statue, prayers and personal items – even jewellery – are pinned up as ex-voto offerings.

To the left of the altar, the presbytery, with its happily irregular cross-vaulted Gothic ceiling, gives onto a simple **cloister** with round, rough-hewn arches. Originating at the beginning of the fourteenth century, it was modified at the end of the following century and again in the eighteenth. In summer, the cloister is the occasional venue for al fresco classical concerts (currently at 8pm). **Services** in Catalan are held in the church of San Francesco at 7pm on Sundays, 6pm in winter.

Further up Via Carlo Alberto, the majolica-tiled cupola of **San Michele** (open daily from twenty minutes before masses, currently Mon–Fri 7am and 10am, Sat 7.30pm and Sun at 7am, 9am and 7.30pm) is a sparkling feature of Alghero's skyline, though from close up the flaky facade does not invite further exploration. In fact, the haughty interior remains true to its seventeenth-century Jesuit origins, with a high, rough-looking ceiling above round arches and swirling columns. One of the elaborately stuccoed and decorated chapels contains a sculpture of St Michael slaying the dragon; look out also for the gilt wooden choir box over the main entrance.

Via Carlo Alberto ends a few metres further south at Piazza Sulis, site of the sturdy **Torre Sulis**, also called Torre dello Sperone (*Torre dell'Esperò Real* in Catalan), which dominates the seashore here. The tower once served as a place of detention, and is named after its most celebrated prisoner, Vincenzo Sulis, incarcerated here for thirty years for his part in the Cágliari uprising of 1794–5. Today, the area around the tower is a meeting point for many of the town's youth (and their bikes); it's an airy, pleasant space, marking the end of the old town and the start of the traffic.

On the far side of the piazza, next to the Oviesse department store, Alghero's **Aquarium** (daily: April–Oct 10am–1pm & 3–7pm in April & May, 4–9pm in June & Oct, 5–11pm in July & Sept, 5pm–12.30am in Aug; Nov–March weekends and public holidays only 3–8pm; €6) makes a diverting place to while away an hour or two. The underground complex is not particularly big, but there are over a hundred species of marine life here, including piranha and beautiful spotted leopard sharks. Via Kennedy runs north from here, past Largo San Francesco, site of another of Alghero's towers, as far as Porta Terra and the Giardini Púbblici.

The waterfront

An alternative route from Piazza Sulis is along the perimeter of the sea-facing walls, or **bastioni**, girding the old town, reached by turning right out of Via Carlo Alberto. You'll pass three more of the town's defensive towers this way, Torre di San Giácomo, Torre della Polveriera and Torre di Sant'Erasmo, and the views out to Capo Caccia are superb. It makes a good place to escape Alghero's bustle, though evenings and night-time in summer see a fair amount of coming and going between the bars here.

North of the old quarter, most of the tourist activity revolves around the **port** abutting the lofty walls, its wide quay nudged by rows of colourful fishing boats and bordered by more bars. This is the embarkation point for excursions to Neptune's Grotto and along the coast. Further up begin the hotels and beaches, most of them an easy walk from town. Some of the more opulent,

---

Tours in and around Alghero

If you've got kids, or you're just tired, you might want to tour the old town on the **Trenino Catalano** (April to mid-Oct), a miniature train which does a circuit of the old centre every thirty minutes or so, leaving from the port. Buy tickets on board (€5, or €3 for 2–8-year-olds).

Cooperativa SILT, Via Petrarca 14 (☎079.980.750) organizes one- or two-day **guided tours** of Alghero, taking in the archeology and wildlife of the surrounding district. Dune Viaggi, Via XX Settembre 118 (☎079.952.600), conducts half-day tours of the Alghero area, including Capo Caccia, Palmavera, Anghelu Ruju and the Sella and Mosca wine cellars, and also go further afield.

For **boat tours**, the main company, Navisarda, has a booth at the port and an office at Via Diaz 3a (☎079.950.603); they arrange a variety of boat tours in the immediate vicinity of Alghero, sailing up and down the coast and including spaghetti lunches and suppers under the stars. These "mini-cruises" last from two hours to the entire day. Sun Sails (☎347.669.0784) arranges **sailing excursions** from the port to the beaches of Le Bombarde and Lazzaretto.

older-looking villas were formerly owned by a resident expatriate community, mainly central European refugees who fled here after World War I. The **beaches** themselves aren't particularly alluring: it's worth carrying on a while to where the pinewoods begin, though even here you'll have to share the water with a couple of campsites located within a few steps of the sea, and you can find much better beaches a short drive out of town (see p.208).

Eating and drinking

Alghero's **restaurants** are famous for their fish and seafood, which is always fresh, inventively prepared and tastefully presented; spring and winter are the best seasons. You might find *paella* on the menu, following the Catalan tradition, while lobster (*aragosta*) is the local speciality. This is pricey, however; the best way to order it is on a set-price menu, usually €30–40 per person (though one portion is often enough to share). Fixed-price menus are common and offer good value, though as a rule don't expect a wide choice or huge portions. Most places close for a few weeks in winter.

For **snacks**, the fast-food joints by the port aren't bad, though you're better off dropping in at the daily market (8am–1pm) off Via Sássari between Via Génova and Via Mazzini for the freshest fruit and vegetables. Good foodstuffs and *panini* can also be had at the nearby Antica Formaggeria, which does a good line in Sard specialities, on the corner of Via Génova and Via Cágliari.

Restaurants

Andreini Via Arduino 45 ☏079.982.098. This elegant and upmarket restaurant specializes in land-based dishes such as kid and boar, not to mention the Sard classic *maialetto* (young pig roasted on the spit). The antipasti is excellent, and a few tasty fish dishes are also available. Fixed-price menus are €20 and €39. Closed Mon except Aug. Moderate–expensive.

Bella Napoli Piazza Cívica 29 ☏079.983.014. Popular Neapolitan-run ristorante/pizzeria just off Piazza Cívica, with generous portions, good salads and a lively atmosphere; traces of an ancient *frantoio*, or olive-mill, are visible inside. Closed Wed in winter. Inexpensive–moderate.

Casablanca Via Príncipe Umberto 76 and Via Arduino 45. A buzzing pizzeria in a long vaulted room; as well as superb pizzas, you can also have a *fritto misto* (battered fish fry-up), and the lemon sorbets are wonderful. Non-smoking section. Closed Wed in winter. Inexpensive–moderate.

La Lépanto Via Carlo Alberto 135 ☏079.979.116. Just off Piazza Sulis, with large windows looking out to sea, this top-class restaurant is renowned for its fish – take your pick from the enticing choice laid out. As a rough guide to prices, a good sized *spígola* (sea bass) should cost around €15. Meat dishes are excellent too, and there's a delectable range of Sardinian sweets also on view. Closed Mon in winter. Moderate–expensive.

Maristella Via Kennedy 9 ☏079.978.172.

Reasonable prices, tasty fare and terrific desserts at this place near Piazza Sulis. Popular with locals, so it's worth booking; there's also some pavement seating. Moderate.

Ristorante Mazzini Via Mazzini 59. A modern-town restaurant with less pretension and lower prices – if less atmosphere – than the places in the *centro stórico*. The food's fine if you stick to basics, and the service is friendly; there's a wood-fired oven for pizzas, and minstrels strum their stuff. Moderate.

Nettuno Vía Maddalanetta 4 ☏079.979.774. This pizzeria/ristorante overlooking the port is touristy, but worth a try, if only for the rooftop terrace open in summer, for which there is a fifteen-percent supplement, and balcony seating, for which booking is essential. Closed Nov–Dec. Moderate.

Palau Reial Via Sant'Erasmo 14 ☏079.980.688. Occupying the ground floor of a medieval Jewish palazzo, this is a classy joint where you can feast on sea-urchin mousse and other delicacies of *la cucina algherese*. There's a €25 fixed-price menu, or à la carte. Closed Thurs in winter. Expensive.

Il Pavone Piazza Sulis 3 ☏079.979.584. A few outside tables provide an exclusive enclave to sample some of the best of Alghero's cuisine, including meat and vegetarian dishes. First courses weigh in at around €10–12, main courses at €14–16. Inside, the two small mirrored rooms can get stuffy and over-formal. Closed Sun in winter, Sun eve in summer. Expensive.

Da Pietro Via Machin 20 ☏079.979.645. Popular with tourists, this fish restaurant is highly variable – dishes range from very good to very mediocre, and the place often comes across as downright seedy. Closed Wed Oct–June. Moderate.

San Francesco Piazza San Francesco. *Paninoteca*, pizzeria and general fast-food place outside San Francesco church; pastas and salads are also available. Closed Mon in winter. Inexpensive.

Al Tuguri Via Maiorca 57 ☏079.976.772. Minuscule restaurant – two rooms on two floors – specializing in Catalan cuisine. The name is dialect meaning "old abandoned house", helping to explain the faintly rustic ambience. If you can afford it, opt for one of the sampling menus at around €28 for a five-course feast. First courses must be accompanied by a main course. Closed Sun. Expensive.

Al Vecchio Mulino Via Don Deroma 3 ☏079.977.254. Atmospheric low-vaulted cellars in the heart of the old town, with friendly staff and a good selection of white wines. For a change from seafood, try the *spaghetti al Vecchio Mulino*, made with mushrooms, ham and cream; pizzas are also available. Closed Mon–Fri lunchtime, all day Tues in winter, but open all day in July & Aug. Moderate.

Cafés, bars and birrerias

Surprisingly, Alghero doesn't have a great selection of bars and cafés, and the ones there are can look pretty dismal out of season. Things liven up in summer, of course, when many stay open until the small hours; you can find the current flavour of the month along the Lungomare south of the centre. The following are some of the best places staying open all year:

L'Arca Lungomare Dante 6. Laid-back seafront bar with table football and live music on Fri and Sat eves.

Café Latino Piazza Duomo 6. An elegant venue for whiling away an afternoon, with outside tables beneath white parasols on the walls overlooking the port. *Panini*, salads and ice creams are also available. Closed Tues in winter.

Diva Café Piazza Municipio 1. Fashionable central bar with a terrace for sitting outside, tucked up a side street off Piazza Cívica. No smoking in main room. Closed Sun.

Jamaica Inn Via Príncipe Umberto 57. A pub with snacks and cocktails, more wines than beers. Open late. Closed Mon.

Mill Pub Via Maiorca 37. For the homesick, an Italian-style "pub", with regular live music in summer. Closed Tues in winter.

Poco Loco Via Gramsci 8. Beers, pizzas, live music (usually Fri & Sat) and general carousing in this spacious hall off Piazza Sulis, with bowling upstairs (not Mon). Open till late; closed daytime.

Clubs

Clubs and discos proliferate in Alghero and the surrounding area in summer, but tend to disappear altogether in winter. Ask at the tourist office for the latest spots, which come and go; many are attached to hotels. The two below are permanent fixtures, and both require a car to reach, their out-of-town location pulling in the punters from Sássari and other nearby centres. Count on about €10–20 entry, usually including the first drink; subsequent drinks are €5–10. *Ruscello* (☏079.953.168; summer only, from about 11.30pm) lies about 2km from Alghero on the Olmedo road, opposite a large supermarket; it has open-air dance floors and occasional live bands. *Siesta*, Scala Piccada, 10km southeast of town on the SS292 ☏079.980.137; Fri and Sat nights from about midnight, nightly in Aug, usually closed in winter) sometimes has live bands, but the best feature of this outdoor club are the magnificent views over the deserted coast.

Festivals and entertainment

Alghero's Spanish inheritance is particularly manifest during its **Easter** festivities, when the rituals of the Incontru (the symbolic meeting of the Virgin with Christ) and Misteri (representing the Passion of Christ) are enacted, with statues carried through town amid solemn processions. In contrast, **Carnival** is a pretty feisty affair, involving plenty of masked antics and the burning of the *pupazzo* (a "guy" representing a French soldier), ceremonially put on trial and burnt on the bonfire on Shrove Tuesday. May sees a steady procession of pilgrims to the sanctuary of Valverde, 6km east of town, in thanksgiving for the Madonna's intervention at times of disaster. The other major milestone in the year is **Ferragosto** (August 15), in which the Feast of the Assumption is celebrated with a range of musical and folkloric events, boating competitions and fireworks.

Religion and secular games are mixed on Sant'Agostino's day on August 28, and there are waterborne events and feasting organized as part of the **Sagra dei Pescatori**, or Fisherman's Fair, on a Saturday or Sunday in September, the precise date varying from year to year.

Apart from these yearly fixtures, summer sees a range of **events** (usually free) taking place in various parts of the town, including concerts, cabaret and folk dances – consult the tourist office for details. Theatre and cinema are poorly catered for in Alghero, though there are **open-air film screenings** at the Bastione della Maddalena in July and August, in Italian or, occasionally, Catalan.

Listings

Airport Aeroporto di Fertilia lies 10km north of Alghero. For information on Airone flights, call ℡079.935.034 or 848.848.880, ⓦwww.flyairone.it; Ryanair ℡079.935.282 or 199.114.114, ⓦwww.ryanair.com; Volare ℡800.454.000, ⓦwww.volare-airlines.com.

Banks and exchange Banks in Alghero are generally open Mon–Fri 8.20am–1.20pm and 3–4.30pm. Most have ATMs, including all the central branches, such as the Banco di Sardegna in Largo San Francesco, and Banca Nazionale di Lavoro at Via Vittorio Emanuele 5, on the Giardini Púbblici. There's also a small exchange office with longer opening hours at Banca 121, Via Vittorio Emanuele 11 (Mon–Fri 9am–1pm & 3–6pm), and the post office (see p.205) also changes cash. The best banks for speedy money transfers are Crédito Italiano, Via Sássari 43, and Banco di Sássari on Via La Mármora.

Bike rental Cicloexpress, off Via Garibaldi at the port (℡079.986.950 or 336.327.048), Silvio Noleggio, Via Garibaldi 113 (℡079.987.243 or 347.596.7924), and MTB, near the public gardens at Via Catalogna 28 (℡079.952.992 or 329.460.6608). All charge €8–10 per day for a pedal bike and €15 for a tandem. Cicloexpress and Silvio also rent out scooters: €25 per day for a 50cc scooter, or €30–40 for a bigger scooter, for which a driving licence is required. All vehicles can be hired on an hourly basis, and 600cc motorbikes are also available.

Bookshops You'll find English books, guides and maps at Ex-Libris, Via Carlo Alberto 2, and on sale in the Porta Terra tower.

Buses For information on local routes and times, call FdS ℡079.950.458.

Car rental Most of the rental agencies have offices out at Fertilia airport, such as Avis (℡079.935.064), Pinna (℡079.935.130) and Maggiore (℡079.935.045). In town, try Autoexpress, Via Satta 48 (℡079.951.505), and Avis and Maggiore also have offices, respectively at Piazza Sulis 9 (℡079.979.577) and Via Sássari 87 (℡079.979.375). At the port, Cicloexpress (see Bike rental above) also rents out cars. Expect to pay around €75 for one day or €180 for three days for a Punto with unlimited mileage; some agencies offer lower daily rates, but charge a supplement per kilometre.

Diving Blue Services Diving Center, Via Lido 18 (℡079.987.197 or 338.185.2663, ⓦwww.blueservices.it) and Centro Immersioni Alghero Nautisub, Via Garibaldi 45 (℡079.952.433 or 330.935.350, ⓦwww.nautisub.com) both offer courses and equipment rental; there are other dive centres at La Mariposa campsite (see. p.198) and Porto Conte (see p.208).

Internet access Two places on Via Gramsci have Internet points: the *Poco Loco* (only open lunchtime and eves) at no. 8, and the Bar *Miramar* at no. 2, both charging around €3 for 30min or €5.20 for 1hr.

Laundry Central laundries include La Suprema, Via Catalogna 60 and Tintoria Flórida, Via Mazzini 20. You have to leave your clothes to be washed and pressed, ready within one or two working days.

Left luggage At the train station (open while the station is open, until around 9pm); €0.77 per piece for 24hr.

Moving on from Alghero

From Alghero's station, FdS **trains** provide a frequent rail link to Sássari (approximately every hour), from where FS trains run to Cágliari, Oristano, Porto Torres and Olbia.

Several companies operate **bus services** out of town:

ARST buses run to Sássari, Porto Torres and local villages. The ticket office is on Via Catalogna, next to the bus stop at the Giardini Púbblici ☎079.950.179, ⓦwww.arst.sardegna.it.

Deplanu/Redentours buses run from Fertilia Airport to Nuoro, twice daily (10am and 10pm). For information and bookings, call ☎0784.30.325.

FdS buses run to Sássari, Bosa, Porto Conte, Porto Ferro and Villanova Monteleone, stopping on Via Catalogna and at the port. Buy tickets from the office on Via Catalogna ☎079.950.179 or 079.950.458, ⓦwww.ferroviesardegna.it.

Turmo Travel buses run to Olbia and Olbia airport (1 daily, currently at 8pm); buy tickets on board. For information, call ☎0789.26.101.

Note that from Sássari there is a fast and frequent **PANI** service to Cágliari (see p.223).

For full schedules, see Travel details on p.223.

Markets A daily food market occupies the block between Via Cágliari and Via Sássari, and Via Genova and Via Mazzini (currently being enlarged). Wednesday mornings see a lively fish market on Via de Gásperi, on the southern outskirts.

Pharmacy Farmacia Cabras, at Piazza Sulis 20, is the most central pharmacy (Mon–Sat 9am–1pm & 4–8pm, or 5–9pm in summer). The night-time rota is posted on this and other pharmacy doors.

Post office The only central office is at Via Carducci, off Via Sássari (Mon–Fri 8.15am–6.15pm, Sat 8.15am–1pm; last day of the month closes at noon). You can also change cash here.

Supermarket Sisa on the corner of Via Sássari and Via XX Settembre (Mon–Sat 8am–8.30pm, Sun 8.30–1.30pm & 5–8.30pm) has a good food hall.

Taxis There's a taxi rank on Via Vittorio Emanuele, at Giardini Púbblici (☎079.975.396); otherwise, call ☎079.974.409 or 338.702.1446.

Telephones Cabins at Piazza Sulis, the Giardini Púbblici and by the port.

Train information For information on FdS trains to Sássari, call ☎079.950.785 or visit ⓦwww.ferroviesardegna.it; for FS services, call ☎848.888.088 or visit ⓦwww.trenitalia.it.

Travel agency Agenzie Marittime Sarde, Via Vittorio Emanuele 27 ☎079.979.005.

Around Alghero

It's almost de rigueur for visitors to Alghero to make the trip out to the **Grotta di Nettuno**, one of Italy's most awesome cave complexes, on Capo Caccia, 15km due west of town. Most people visit on one of the frequent boats that leave from the port throughout the year. It's a thrilling ride along the coast, though it's cheaper and in some ways more rewarding to go the slow way by bus. There are also good public transport services for a pair of important sites from the nuraghic and prenuraghic eras in the area, the necropolis of **Anghelu Ruju** and the **Nuraghe di Palmavera**, which make a stimulating contrast to the sun-and-sea attractions of the rest of the region.

Fertilia, 7km west of Alghero, was one of Mussolini's projects linked to the local land reclamation programme. There's not much going on here today – indeed, it appears remarkably quiet after the vivacity of Alghero, but there are enough beaches, trattorias and hotels to make this a worthwhile outing. Some of the region's best **beaches** lie beyond Fertilia, around the deep bay of **Porto Conte**, a centre for diving and sailing. The area could easily be biked, and there's even a protected bicycle lane running part of the way to Porto Conte.

Grotta di Nettuno

The most touted of the excursions you can take from Alghero's port is west along the coast to the **Grotta di Nettuno**, or Neptune's Grotto (daily: April–Sept 9am–8pm; Oct 10am–5pm; Nov–March 9am–2pm; last tour 1hr before closing; €8). Boats operated by Navisarda depart hourly in summer, at 9 and 10am, 3 and 4pm in April, May and October: return tickets cost €10, not counting the entry charge to the grotto, the return trip taking about two and a half hours. The thirty-minute **boat ride** along the cliffy coast takes you past the lovely long bay of Porto Conte as far as the point of Capo Caccia, where the spectacular sheer cliffs are riddled by deep marine caves. They include the Grotta Verde and Grotta dei Ricami – visited on some tours – but the most impressive is the Grotta di Nettuno itself, just west of the point.

From the grotto's entrance, **tours** lasting 45 minutes depart on the hour every hour, led single-file by guides who provide commentaries in Italian, and sometimes also in German, French or English. The long, snaking passage delves far into the rock, past fantastical, dramatically-lit **stalagmites** and **stalactites** and along walls shimmering with phosphorescence. The guides relate the discovery by fishermen of this masterwork of nature, pointing out imagined resemblances to helmeted warriors, toothy witches and popes. Less fanciful are the likenesses of organ pipes and columned cathedral interiors, after which two of the chambers are named. Signs point out that touching the rock and photography are both forbidden, though no one takes much notice. The green colouring visible on some of the rock is mould, mostly caused by the lighting system. Navisarda also operates occasional boat departures from Cala Dragonara, an inlet on the western arm of Porto Conte (see p.208).

A cheaper alternative to the boat trip from Alghero is to drive or take a **bus** to Capo Caccia from Via Catalogna, a fifty-minute ride (June–Sept 3 daily; Oct–May 1 daily; €1.76 one-way, €3.25 return). Once you're deposited at the end of the line, there's a spectacular 654-step descent down the **Escala del Cabirol** (the Catalan name means "goat's steps", presumably a reference to the only animal that could negotiate the perilous path before the construction of the stairway in 1954). The sheer cliff-face and dark-blue water below is almost as impressive as the grotto interior itself. Make sure you time your arrival at the cave so that you don't have to wait up to an hour for the next tour: the descent takes ten to fifteen minutes. On the way back, leave some time before the bus goes for a well-earned ice cream or thirst-quencher at the bar opposite the top of the steps.

Fertilia

From Alghero, you can walk or cycle the eight flat kilometres along the seafront and past pine-fringed beaches to **FERTILIA**, if you don't want to take local bus AF from the Giardini Púbblici, seafront or the train station. Once out of town, you'll pass a long lagoon on the right, the Stagno di Cálich, which collects the outflow of two rivers. Its mouth is crossed by a medieval bridge sinking picturesquely into the water, known locally as the **Ponte Romano**, or "Roman" bridge; it has been superseded by a modern road bridge, and the old structure is now mainly used as a perch for fishermen.

Fertilia itself is nothing special, a creation of Mussolini in the 1930s, named to evoke the agricultural abundance that local land drainage would bring about (indeed, the rich agricultural land has produced some excellent wines, notably Torbato, a fairly sweet white). The arcaded **Via Pola** is the main avenue through town, connecting Piazza Venezia Giulia with the broad Piazzale San Marco next to the sea, marked by a memorial to the migrants who settled the area from the Friuli-Venezia region of northeast Italy. There's little else in the town, and little movement more frenetic than the slow padding of stray dogs.

If hotel space in Alghero is scant, Fertilia makes a reasonable place to sleep. The best **hotels** are *Bellavista*, near the seafront on Lungomare Rovigno (℡079.930.124, ⓕ079.930.190; ❻; may close in winter), offering fairly standard rooms, some with balconies, and much favoured by groups, and the even less charming *Hotel Fertilia*, on the airport road (℡079.930.098, ⓕ079.930.522; ❹), both with restaurants. Fertilia's **youth hostel** (open all year; ℡079.930.478, ⓔhostalalguer@tiscali.it), lies at the western end of town, on the secluded Via Zara. It's modern and clean, if slightly institutional in tone, with rooms with four or six beds for €14 each, and family rooms with private bathroom for €18 per head. There are no cooking facilities, but evening meals are prepared (€9), and there's a laundry and Internet access. Non-IYHF members can buy temporary membership for €2.58. Call first to check availability, as it's popular with groups even in low season.

Fertilia has two **campsites**, one on the coast towards Alghero, *Calik*, just across the road from the beach (June–Sept; ℡079.930.111), the other, the much smaller *Nurral* (℡079.930.485), 100m along the SS291 running north to Santa Maria La Palma. The latter is open all year; though it's not that close to the sea, it has good facilities and four-bed self-catering bungalows to rent at €105 for two people.

The town has a few **bars and restaurants** – nothing too inspiring, though the *Acquario*, close to Piazzale San Marco at Via Pola 34, has a straight-up menu with reasonable prices (closed Mon in winter) and the restaurant in the nearby *Bellavista* has a good-value fixed-price lunch menu at €8.50. Best of all is the *Paguro* (closed Wed in winter), quite near the hostel at Via Zara 13, which has a garden.

Nuraghe di Palmavera and around

On the Fertilia–Porto Conte road, 10km west of Alghero, you'll pass the **nuraghe di Palmavera** (daily: April–Oct 9am–7pm; Nov–March 9.30am–4pm; €3.60 with guide, €2.10 without, or €3.60 and €6.20 with/without guide including Anghelu Ruju – see p.209), located just by the side of the road. One of the largest in this region, the site comprises a ruined palace dating from the fourteenth and thirteenth centuries BC, surrounded by fifty or so circular huts.

The corridor in the entrance to the central tower has two niches on either side, probably for sentries, and a trap door in the roof for extra security. The interior is of the rounded "tholos" type, with more shallow niches. An elliptical bastion and a minor tower were added to the main building in the second phase of construction, around the ninth century BC, when some of the round huts scattered outside the ramparts were also erected. Most of these were probably dwellings, but one, the **Capanna delle Riunioni**, distinguished by a low stone bench running round the circular walls, is believed to have been used for meetings and religious gatherings. The stool at the centre is a plaster copy of the original, now on display in Sássari's Museo Sanna (see p.233), along with numerous other finds from the site. A third building phase took place a hundred or so years later, when more buildings were added, this time in limestone, as opposed to the softer sandstone of previous stages. The complex is thought to have been abandoned in the eighth or seventh century BC, possibly on account of fire. For more on Sardinia's nuraghic culture, see p.349–350.

Nearby, on the opposite side of the road, side-roads lead to two of the area's best **beaches**, set in beautiful sandy coves facing Alghero across the bay. A signpost points to the beach of **Le Bombarde**, nearly a kilometre further on at the end of a straight and narrow track, a lovely sandy crescent where **windsurfing** courses are held, and you can rent equipment, as well as parasols, deck-chairs, pedalos and canoes from J & B Sailing, based here in summer (T336.594.404). The beach of **Lazzaretto**, guarded by a Spanish watchtower, lies only about 700m further west, at the end of another signposted turn-off, and also has beach equipment for hire in July and August. Both of these swimming spots can get quite busy in summer, though Lazzaretto has a string of smaller, less popular beaches beyond, and you can count on having these pretty much to yourself on weekdays out of season.

Porto Conte

The lovely inlet of **Porto Conte** lies a couple of kilometres beyond Lazzaretto, about 10km west of Alghero. Romantically named Portus Nimpharum ("Lake of the Nymphs") by the Romans, the intensely blue bay is a favourite anchorage for luxury yachts, which can be admired from the terraces of the clutch of top-notch hotels nestled among the trees. The road tracing the bay's eastern shore ends at a lighthouse; if you're looking for good bathing spots, follow the main road to Capo Caccia, turning left for the beach of **Baja di Conte** near the hotel of the same name. There are some **Roman ruins** here – unfortunately little more than a scattering of broken walls – and facilities for **windsurfing** and **diving** on the beach. Divers should head to the Base Nautica, where Adventure and Diving (T079.942.205 or 333.184.7750, Wwww.portoconte.it) and Diving Center Porto Conte (T079.942.122 or 338.325.3695, Wwww.divingportoconte.it) provide equipment and tuition at various levels. Not for nothing is this coast known as the Costa del Corallo – the two promontories at the southern end of Porto Conte are walled with coral colonies, mainly in underwater grottos, ideal for diving. On the far side of the bay, **boat excursions** to the Grotta di Nettuno (see p.206) leave hourly between June and September, taking about ninety minutes for the round trip; return tickets cost €8, excluding entry to the grotto. There are also sporadic departures in April, May and October.

To the west of Porto Conte, the peak of Monte Timidone (361m) holds **Le Prigionette** (Mon–Sat 8am–4pm, Sun 9am–5pm; free), a protected wildlife zone where the flora includes a rich abundance of Mediterranean *macchia*, and among the fauna are miniature horses, asses from Asinara (see p.222–223), mouflons and even Tibetan goats, as well as assorted wild boar, deer, griffon vultures and peregrine falcons. You can also tour the area on horseback: ask at Alghero's tourist office for details.

The biggest and swishest of the **hotels** in the area, *Baia di Conte* (mid-May to Sept; T079.949.000, F079.949.021; ❽), has the full gamut of sports facilities including boating and windsurfing on the bay; the cheapest choice is *Corte Rosada* (T079.942.038, F079.942.158; ❺), a little further along the road to Capo Caccia, boasting almost as full a range of facilities. For something a lot less grand, there's a good **campsite** about 5km north on the road to Santa Maria La Palma (signposted): lying on the western coast, *Torre del Porticciolo* (May–Sept; T079.919.007, Wwww.torredelporticciolo.com) is the largest campsite in the region. It has tennis courts, a pool and bungalows, and there's a good beach in the marvellous round bay below. The German admiral Von Tirpitz owned an extensive estate here before World War I, and it is said that the nearby bays and inlets were much used by submarines for nocturnal rendezvous.

Anghelu Ruju

The necropolis of **Anghelu Ruju** (daily: April–Oct 9am–7pm; Nov–March 9.30am–4pm; €3.60 with guide, €2.10 without, or €3.60/6.20 with/without guide including Nuraghe di Palmavera – see p.207), a pre-nuraghic cave complex of some forty hypogea, lies 10km out of Alghero on the road to Porto Torres. The site was discovered by chance in 1903, shortly after the land was purchased by the Sella e Mosca winery, now one of Sardinia's most celebrated wine producers. The necropolis – which now stands in the midst of the vineyards of *cannonau* grapes beneath the planes roaring to and from Fertilia airport – is a creation of the late Neolithic Ozieri culture dating back to about 2900 BC, though it was reused throughout the Copper Age (2900–1500 BC). The tombs, gouged out of the ground and accessed by low-lintelled doorways, constitute Sardinia's best examples of the so-called *domus de janas* (fairies' or witches' houses), of which there are scores on the island, for the most part murky chambers, or groups of them, some connected by sloping passages. The dead were embalmed within, occasionally in mass burials, sometimes half-cremated and in some cases skinned before burial.

Visitors are free to scramble around the tombs, though there is little specific to see: the rich contents have been removed to the archeological museums of Cágliari and Sássari. In some cases, however, you can just make out, carved on the lintels or in the depths of the darkness, symbolic shapes including bulls' horns in tombs A, XXb, XXVIII and XXX, the last of these – carved on the left wall of the "atrium" – a simple line which could also be a boat. Bring a torch, and be prepared for some serious stooping.

Copies of some of the finds from Anghelu Ruju, together with diagrams of the site, are contained in Sella e Mosca's **Museo e Tenuta Vitivinícola**, less than a kilometre north on the Porto Torres road. The main focus of the museum, however, is **winemaking**, whose various stages are explained on guided tours taking place Monday–Saturday at 5.30pm between June and mid-October, other times by appointment (⊕079.997.700). Vittorio Sella's black-and-white photographs add life to the history of the vineyard. You can buy the end product from the on-site wine shop (daily: mid-June to Sept 8.30am–8pm; Oct to mid-June 8.30am–1pm & 3–6.30pm).

North of Alghero

Travelling north from Alghero, Fertilia or Porto Conte, good roads lead across the territory of Nurra to **Lago di Baratz**, Sardinia's only natural lake. A path curves round the reeds and marshes of the perimeter, allowing a close-up of some of the protected plants and – if you're lucky – animals gathered here. Among these is a species of turtle (*Emys orbicularis*), while wildfowl include the little- and great-crested grebes as well as a multitude of mallards and coots. The *macchia* which partially encroaches on the shores is a pungent mêlée of rosemary, myrtle, wild lavender and numerous species of wild orchid.

Just over a kilometre west from the lake, easily walkable (there's also a road for drivers), the bay of **Porto Ferro** is guarded by three watchtowers and framed by a luscious long beach. North of the lake, an unasphalted track crosses a desolate tract of mountain to the hamlet of Palmádula, which can also be reached on the more reliable main roads. However, it's a long detour: back towards Sássari, turning left for Porto Torres, then left again.

Palmádula is not a place to linger, so continue another 5km west to reach the old abandoned mining town of **Argentiera**. As its name implies, this was a silver-mining centre, once the greatest producer of silver on the island. Worked since Roman times, the seams were exhausted and extraction halted in 1963, and now the little town sits by itself at the end of a road on one of the most deserted expanses of the western coast. Its forlorn, haunted air is full of the echoes of its former industry: shafts lie abandoned, miners' quarters stare blindly out, and there is little movement at all outside July and August. There are some good shingles and sand beaches around here, though, one of which you will have passed on the way into town. The wonder is that the whole place has not been bought up and converted into a holiday village, a tribute to the planning laws in force in Sardinia. Still, Argentiera is unlikely to stay the same for very much longer. If you feel like stretching your legs, head out to **Capo dell'Argentiera**, a headland with good coastal views about 3km southwest of the old mining centre.

Summer sees a little more action, with bathers attracted to the beaches in the vicinity, and there's a bar attached to a **trattoria**, *Il Veliero*, serving mixed salads and meat and fish dishes, as well as a range of milkshakes and "beer-shakes" (closed mid-Oct to mid-June; no credit cards). *Il Patio*, on the remains of the piazza, also has pizzas and other meals in summer.

Argentiera is linked to Sássari by ARST **buses** (Mon–Sat several daily).

South of Alghero

There are two routes running south of Alghero, both strongly recommended, but very different from each other. As one route runs inland and the other along the coast, and each ends at Bosa (see p.211), you could cover both on a round-trip excursion to that town from Alghero. The **inland route** follows the SP292 from the crossroads at the south end of town, signposted Villanova. The road soon climbs above the coast, affording magnificent views back towards Alghero. After 25km of increasingly twisting road, you reach **VILLANOVA MONTELEONE**, the place to which the original *algherese* population was banished in 1354 after their town had been taken over by the Spanish. There's precious little to see or do here, though the village would make a lively destination at the end of August, when the local **Festival of St John the Baptist** involves processions and horseback races. The local craft speciality is linen embroidered with angular animals and other geometric designs.

A right-turn out of Villanova takes you along a minor, little-used road which eventually winds up in Bosa, an arduous forty-kilometre trawl through an empty but often inspiring wilderness of *macchia* and mountain. Alternatively, continue east another 9km on the SS292 to the dammed **Lago del Temo**, from which the eponymous river flows down to Bosa on the coast. It's a good place to mosey around, with some grassy banks ideal for picnics. Rising on a hill just beyond the lake, the village of **MONTELEONE ROCCA DORIA** was a Dorian foundation which endured a three-year siege by the combined forces of Aragon, Sássari, Bosa and Alghero, ending with its complete destruction in 1436. Monteleone's refugees joined Alghero's deportees in Villanova (hence that village's composite name), though the ruined Monteleone was later resettled and rebuilt.

The **coast road** south of Alghero travels through an equally rugged landscape, though now the vistas encompass an ever-changing succession of coves and inlets. Some of these shelter first-class **beaches** where, in the summer months, you are charged a few euros to park and there are umbrellas and drinks available. **La Speranza**, for example, lies 8km south of town, and Alghero–Bosa coastal buses stop here; ideally, however, the tract should be walked or biked through at a leisurely pace. The mercifully undeveloped rocky terrain holds Sardinia's only significant colony of **griffon vultures**, though only about sixty were thought to exist here in 2003 (a few others nest around Capo Caccia, west of Alghero). Many of these predators are being wiped out by the poisons left out by local farmers for foxes and stray dogs, though strictly enforced measures have helped to stabilize their numbers in recent years. Visitors to the area should take special care not to approach nesting sites in July and August.

The best chances of spotting a griffon vulture is around **Capo Marargiu**, 12km north of Bosa, one of the remotest sections of the coast. The area achieved a brief notoriety in the 1980s when it was revealed that a secret right-wing commando group, Gladio, used the headland as a training ground. There are good swimming spots from the rocks around here.

If you want to see the coast by **public transport**, make sure you get on one of the Bosa–Alghero buses that take the coastal route, as some services take the inland alternative via Villanova Monteleone. For schedules, see Travel details on p.223.

Bosa and around

As the only town on the brief western seaboard of Nuoro province, **Bosa** has little in common with most of that inland sheep-rearing country. Not only does it exude a much stronger historical atmosphere, but it's far more closely related to the sea, despite its location 5km inland. It has a self-contained air, and from whichever direction you arrive, the town appears curiously suspended, stranded in the middle of one of Sardinia's last remaining stretches of undeveloped coast and cocooned from the main currents of Sardinian life. For all of these reasons, and for the placid river flowing through on its way to the coast, it makes a soothing place to hole up for a few days, refreshingly uncommercial and yet within reach of some good beaches. The town, however, is becoming increasingly aware of its tourist potential – it's already a stop on coach-tour itineraries, and development is beginning to make a significant impact on its western outskirts.

Most of the tourist activity is concentrated at **Bosa Marina**, Bosa's coastal offshoot 3km west, where a sandy arc of beach is backed by hotels, bars and restaurants. On summer weekends, the resort is connected by the **Trenino Verde** (see the box on p.92) to **Macomer**, 30km inland, where you could drop in to see a couple of notable nuraghic remains. Apart from these, this is a fairly dull town, which you may well be passing through en route to somewhere else, as Macomer is one of the island's major transport hubs. More practical than the Trenino Verde are the frequent **bus** connections to Bosa itself. Between them, the two Bosas have a small selection of **accommodation**, including a youth hostel and a good agriturismo, and Macomer also has a few lodgings.

Bosa

Though built on the banks of the Temo, Sardinia's only navigable river of any length, **BOSA** has no easy links to any of the island's major towns. Encircled by mountains, it huddles around the base of a hill capped by a ruined castle, its very isolation having largely preserved it from the incursions of ill-considered construction. The lingering, unkempt look of much of the place shows that Bosa has escaped the makeover to fully-fledged resort, though this also means that not everything works at maximum efficiency. The castle, river and a couple of churches are the main sights, all easily reached on foot, making this an ideal place to mooch around at leisure. The lower town, **Sa Piana**, is traversed by Corso Vittorio Emanuele, running parallel to the river; north of here, the medieval quarter, **Sa Costa**, is a succession of tight lanes winding round the Serravalle hill. Bosa Marina is a bit of a toil to reach on foot; buses leave from Via Nazionale, on the south side of the river.

Some history

Phoenicians and Romans are known to have settled the banks of the River Temo, the Roman town was located near the site of the church of San Pietro, a couple of kilometres upstream from the present town. After the Romans left, Bosa fared badly, and was repeatedly battered by barbarian and Moorish raids. In the twelfth century, the settlement was refounded by the Ligurian **Malaspina family** around their fortress on the Serravalle hill. Many who had been living on the coast, near present-day Bosa Marina, willingly migrated to this more defensible spot, establishing the Sa Costa quarter on the slopes of Serravalle.

Bosa changed hands several times during the ensuing vicissitudes of war, at one time allying itself with the anti-Aragonese coalition headed by Eleonora d'Arborea, but eventually forging a happy working relationship with the **Spanish**, under whom it prospered. After an interlude of decay, the town achieved wealth and security in the eighteenth and nineteenth centuries, when it was briefly a provincial capital renowned for the working of precious metals, coral-gathering and leather-tanning. Much of Sa Piana, the lower town, dates from this era.

Arrival and information

Buses to Bosa pull up at various points of the town: on Viale Alghero, Piazza Zanetti and Via Nazionale, and some also make stops at Bosa Marina and Turas, south of town. Bosa's main bus terminal is in Piazza Zanetti, where there's an FdS office. ARST tickets can be bought from the *Bar Mouse* in the piazza (it also sells FdS tickets when the office is closed), and from the *tabacchino* next to the *Perry Clan* hotel on Viale Alghero. There's another ARST bus stop here, and inland services also pick up passengers at Via Nazionale

If you're arriving **by car** from the south or inland, park before entering the old town, preferably near the old town bridge; alternatively, find a slot on Lungotemo Álcide de Gásperi, a left turn immediately after the bridge. Driving or biking from Alghero, turn left at the first roundabout onto Viale Alghero, which becomes Viale Giovanni XXIII and then Corso Vittorio Emanuele, the pedestrianized main street of the old town; again, parking by the river is probably the easiest option, to avoid narrow lanes and one-way systems. Another newer bridge crosses the river further downstream, nearer Bosa Marina (for which, turn right after crossing). Here, the small FdS station is the terminus for the **trenino verde** in summer, a steam train service from Macomer, usually running on summer weekends or for group bookings.

Bosa's **Pro Loco** is off Piazza Gioberti at Via Azuni 5 (Mon–Sat 10am–1pm & 5.30–8.30pm; ☎0785.376.107, ⓦwww.bosa.it), though winter opening may be erratic, and there's another seasonal office in Bosa Marina, near the station on the main Via C. Colombo (mid-June to mid-Sept daily 10am–1pm &

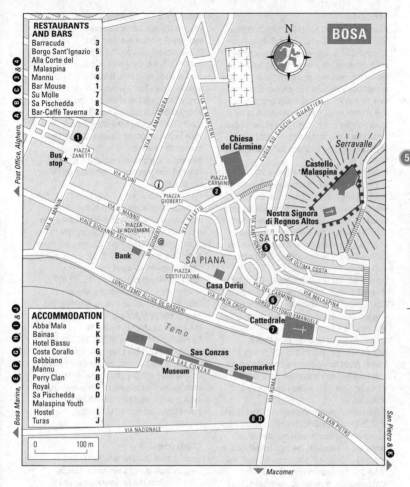

RESTAURANTS AND BARS

Barracuda	3
Borgo Sant'Ignazio	5
Alla Corte del Malaspina	6
Mannu	4
Bar Mouse	1
Su Molle	7
Sa Pischedda	8
Bar-Caffè Taverna	2

ACCOMMODATION

Abba Mala	E
Bainas	K
Hotel Bassu	F
Costa Corallo	G
Gabbiano	H
Mannu	A
Perry Clan	B
Royal	C
Sa Pischedda	D
Malaspina Youth Hostel	I
Turas	J

6–9pm; ☎0785.377.108) – again, the timetable may change, or the office may not open at all.

Accommodation

Most of Bosa's **hotels** stay open all year, and most require half- or full-board in high summer. There are none within the town's central core, though a couple lie within walking distance. The lion's share of the accommodation, however, is in Bosa Marina; all of these hotels are close to the sea, though none has much character. The modern resort also has one of Sardinia's rare **youth hostels**; the nearest **campsite** is a couple of kilometres south down the coast, connected by bus in summer.

If you're stuck with nowhere else to go, find out about **rented apartments** from the tourist office or the *Perry Clan* hotel (see p.214). Most properties are modern and small, located in Bosa's newer districts or at Bosa Marina.

Hotels

Abba Mala Località Abba Mala, 3km from Bosa ☏0785.375.565, ⊛www.abbamala.com. This fully-equipped holiday village offers two-, four- and five-person bungalows, charging up to €650 per week in peak season, though you may be able to negotiate a discount, and you can sometimes book for less than a week. Prices drop considerably at other times. The main drawback is the distance from the beach – it's 1.5km inland – requiring at least a bike to make this a practical option. To compensate, there's a pool and other sports facilities. ❻

Bainas On the road to San Pietro ☏0785.373.793 or 339.209.0967. An attractive agriturismo in the middle of fields, about a 10min walk from town, with clean rooms giving onto a veranda. It's worth taking half-board here (€52 per person in high season) to sample the excellent food, much of which is homegrown and all is organic (and you can buy a bag to take away). Use of the kitchen is €10 per day. No credit cards. ❸

Hotel Bassu Via Grazia Deledda 15, Bosa Marina ☏ and ⊕0785.373.456. A modest one-star in a bland modern block, 50m from the beach. Rooms with and without bath are functional and clean, and there's a restaurant. ❸

Costa Corallo Via Colombo, Bosa Marina ☏0785.375.162, ⊕0785.375.529. Run by a friendly young family, this smart two-star on the riverside offers very reasonable rates. Rooms, all with a bath, are fairly ordinary and there's a restaurant. ❺

Gabbiano Lungomare Mediterraneo, Bosa Marina ☏0785.374.123, ⊕0785.374.109. This unexceptional three-star tourist lodge has standard a/c rooms and a restaurant. The main advantage is the proximity of the beach, just across the road. Half- or full-board is required in season. ❹

Malaspina Youth Hostel Via Sardegna 1, Bosa Marina ☏ and ⊕0785.375.009. This scrupulously clean hostel has 48 beds in dormitories for €9.50 each, and a bar and restaurant where you can get meals for €8. The hostel should remain open all year, but check in winter. It's closed 1–3.30pm each day. The beach is a 5min walk.

Mannu Viale Alghero ☏0785.375.306, ⊕0785.375.308. You'll need your own transport to use this place, as close to Bosa Marina as to the main town (less than a kilometre in either direction), on the north side of the river. The main attraction is its plaudit-winning restaurant (see p.217). The three-star hotel offers fairly good value for its comfortable facilities, though the location on a main road is hardly inspiring. Bike and boat rentals and excursions can be arranged from here. Half- or full-board only in summer. ❸

Perry Clan Viale Alghero 3 ☏0785.373.074. Just off Piazza Dante at the far end of Corso Vittorio Emanuele, a 10min walk from Bosa's centre, this is primarily a noisy bar and restaurant with rooms above – rather characterless, but clean and cheap. A minimum of half-board (€55 per person per night) is required in August. ❷

Royal Viale Alghero ☏ and ⊕0785.377.037. Brash modern hotel opposite the *Mannu*, with better all-round facilities than its neighbour and correspondingly higher prices. Guests have access to a private beach and a sauna. ❺

Sa Pischedda Via Roma ☏0785.373.065. The best choice in Bosa itself, just across the bridge from the old town, this fine old palazzo is the only hotel with any atmosphere. A grand staircase leads up to quiet, comfortable rooms, some of which are quite cramped. There's also a good restaurant (see p.217). Booking essential. ❸

Campsite

Turas ☏0785.359.270, ⊕0785.377.310. Lying a couple of kilometres south down the coast from Bosa Marina (connected by bus in summer), this is a shady site just up from the beach. A shop and nearby pizzeria provide food. Open June–Sept.

The Town

Bosa's colourfully-domed **Cattedrale** (daily 10am–noon & 4–7pm) lies on the northern side of the bridge, its fifteenth-century origins largely obscured under an overlay of Baroque. The Rococo facade gives access to a lavish interior, a riot of polychrome marble among which there are some individual items to pick out: carved lions subduing dragons on the altar steps; frescos in the apse painted by Emilio Scherer at the end of the nineteenth century, and, behind the seventeenth-century altar, another fresco from the same period showing a town plan of Bosa – the town's appearance is scarcely different today.

From the cathedral, the main **Corso Vittorio Emanuele** heads west, its tone set by well-preserved palazzi on either side. Halfway along on the right, at no. 159, the nineteenth-century **Casa Deriu** occasionally hosts cultural exhibitions. At the Corso's western end, the grand Palazzo Don Carlos, dating from the eighteenth century, overlooks the outdoor bars on **Piazza Costituzione**, beyond which lie the newer outskirts of town. Take any of the lanes to the right of the Corso to penetrate the web of alleys that make up Bosa's Old Quarter, **Sa Costa**. Full of medieval gloom, the corridor-like streets follow up the steep contours of Serravalle, involving a healthy amount of huffing before you reach the brow of the hill and the castle. If this is the direction you are headed, you can't go wrong by taking any way that goes up; it's about a twenty-minute climb. On the way up or down, drop in on the **Chiesa del Cármine**, on Via del Cármine, a richly decorated Baroque edifice with an elegant facade from 1779.

The Castello Malaspina

Only the shell of Bosa's **Castello Malaspina** (daily 10am–12.30pm & 3.30–5.30pm, but erratic hours in winter; €2.50) survives, but that and the commanding position are enough to give the flavour of this medieval fortress. Erected by the powerful Malaspina family in 1112, the walls incorporate a series of towers, notably the **torre nord**, open-sided in the fashion of other towers in Oristano and Cágliari, and the **torre maggiore**, taller and more refined than the others, and thought to have been the work of Cágliari's celebrated military architect Giovanni Capula, who designed the Torre di San Pancrazio and Torre dell'Elefante in his home city; the pentagonal **torre ovest** is Aragonese.

Within the walls, the only building standing is the church of **Nostra Signora di Regnos Altos**, which contains a rare cycle of vibrant, Catalan-style frescos from about 1300, and a couple of statues of the Madonna. The bird's-eye views from the castle's red trachyte ramparts are worth savouring, allowing the chance to get to grips with the area's geography. If you're driving, you can reach the entrance by following signs along the road skirting the back of town, leading round to the castle gate. From the castle, walkers can proceed east along this road and on tracks into the mountainous hinterland on a circular walk taking around three hours. It's difficult to get lost, but you'll need a good supply of water.

Along the river

From the castle's ramparts, the landscape's clearest feature, the broad Temo **river**, invites closer investigation. Near the bridge, you can wander the quayside among **Sas Conzas**, the former leather tanneries – relics of an industry that was central to the local economy from the eighteenth century to World War II. One of the buildings houses a small **museum** devoted to the tanning industry (daily 10am–1pm & 6–11.30pm, or 4–6pm in winter; €2.50), displaying old photos and equipment. A rank of palms lines the opposite bank of the river, where most of the fishing boats are moored, their nets draped over the quay.

San Pietro

The best walk, however, runs 2km east along the south bank, where a rural road running parallel to the river leads to the former cathedral of **San Pietro** (daily 10am–noon & 4–7pm, or 3–5pm in winter). Built over an early Christian necropolis (see the upside-down Latin inscription on one of the stones at the base of the apse, at the back of the church), the original construction dates from 1073, although the Gothic facade was added by Cistercian monks at the end of the thirteenth century. Beneath a trio of small rose windows, the architrave of the west door is embellished with naively-carved vignettes of the Madonna and Child with saints Paul, Peter, and Constantinus de Castra, the church's founder (or it may represent San Costantino), taken from a tomb. The square belltower and the apse date from the twelfth century.

The main body of the church, however, is pure Lombard Romanesque in inspiration, though it was modified at later stages. The sombre interior has two rows of solid, broad-stoned, rectangular columns; on one of them, the first on the right, you might just be able to make out an inscribed dedication by Bishop Constantinus de Castra. With little other kind of decoration, it's a silent, moody place. Opening hours can be erratic, especially in winter, so walkers who want to avoid a fruitless journey should confirm it's open before setting out (call ☎333.544.5675).

Bosa Marina

At various times in its history, Bosa has transferred its site to different points along the banks of the River Temo, one of them being what is now **BOSA MARINA**, at the mouth of the river. Today, it's a conventional minor resort with a small choice of hotels and trattorias, a terminal for the tourist steam train connecting the town with Macomer in summer, and a broad beach. Guarded by a stark Spanish watchtower, yachts and fishing boats lie at anchor in the lee of the islet of Isola Rossa, now linked to the mainland by a bridge. In July and August the tower is opened for occasional exhibitions of local arts and crafts. The sheltered beach is a favourite place for windsurfers, with equipment usually available to rent in summer, but can get pretty thronged. Remoter patches of sand lie 2km south in the **Turas** neighbourhood, though if you're looking for true isolation, you're best off visiting the rugged littoral north of Bosa, where you'll find rocks to swim off, interspersed with some fine sandy beaches (see p.211).

Eating, drinking and entertainment

Bosa doesn't have a huge choice of **restaurants**, but you'll eat well and fairly cheaply in the few there are. If you're self-catering, try the Discount Mio supermarket (see Listings on p.217). At some point, make sure you sample the local **Malvasia** dessert wine, for which the Bosa area is renowned; it's served at most bars and restaurants. The two main **clubs** in the area open in summer only: *Sas Covas*, at the end of Viale Alghero on the north side of the river, and *Al Paradise* in the Turas neighbourhood, a couple of kilometres south of Bosa Marina. You may find one or two other places in Bosa Marina, also open just in summer, while the only winter choice is *Zia Maria*, on Viale Alghero. None of the above deviates too far from mainstream dance beats and Latin salsas.

Restaurants and bars

All of the places listed below are in the main town; Bosa Marina has a few more choices, mainly attached to hotels, but the fare is pretty standard. The bars in Piazza Costituzione are good for a long drink, but the service charge is high.

Barracuda Viale Repubblica 17. Honest local cuisine at sensible prices, though the modern setting lacks much charm. It's a 5min walk west of Piazza IV Novembre. Closed Wed in winter.

Borgo Sant'Ignazio Via Sant'Ignazio 33. Hidden in an alley above the Corso, but well-signposted from just about everywhere in the old town, this cosy bistro offers local land and sea dishes in tasteful, traditional surroundings. Closed Tues.

Alla Corte del Malaspina Corso Vittorio Emanuele 39. Friendly birreria that stays open late, with a good selection of draught and bottled beers. *Panini* and chips are also served, and rock videos screened. Closed Sun.

Mannu Viale Alghero ℡ 0785.375.306. Attached to a hotel (see p.214), a kilometre or so from the centre, you'll need your own transport to reach this place. Though lacking much ambience, it has won awards for its culinary excellence, and such local dishes as spaghetti with lobster and fried mussels won't disappoint. Booking advisable. Expensive.

Su Molle Lungomare De Gásperi. Neighbourhood bar opposite the old bridge, with outdoor tables and late closing.

Bar Mouse Piazza Zanetti. Cool wine bar and café with terrace seating. Meals also available. Closed Sun. Moderate.

Sa Pischedda Attached to the eponymous hotel (see p.214), this informal place has generous portions, fine Sard wines and a busy atmosphere. Worth booking ahead. Moderate.

Bar-Caffè Taverna Piazza Carmine. Drinks, *panini* and other snacks served here, inside or on the terrace. Closed Tues Oct–April.

Festivals

The best **festivals** are centred on the river: the Festa dei Santi Pietro e Paolo on June 29 involves a regatta as far as the church of San Pietro, with local food-stuffs available to be sampled, while in the Sagra di Santa Maria del Mare, on the first Sunday of August, an image of the Madonna is transported by boat from Bosa Marina to the cathedral, returning in the afternoon when an open-air mass is held and fireworks are set off. The Sagra di Nostra Signora di Regnos Altos on the second Sunday of September is a great chance to attend an open-air mass at the castle, watch local groups perform traditional songs and dances, and to enjoy local food and drink. In addition, Carnival and Easter are both enthusiastically celebrated in Bosa, and there's a country festival, the Festa dei Santi Cosma e Damiano, on September 26, accompanied by traditional singing and dancing.

Listings

Banks and exchange The Banco di Sardegna in Piazza IV Novembre (Mon–Sat 9am–1pm & 4.30–7pm) has an ATM. The post office also changes cash.

Bike rental Iguana, Piazza Costituzione ℡ 347.466.2002, charges €7 per 24 hours for a mountain bike, €25 for a scooter, or try the *Sa Pischedda* hotel (see p.214).

Diving Excursions, supervision, instruction and equipment rental are offered at Bosa Diving Center, Via Colombo 2, Bosa Marina ℡ 0785.375.649.

Internet access Web Copy Internet Point, Via Gioberti 12 (Mon–Sat 8.30am–1pm & 4.30–8pm); €3 for 30min. Fax service and photocopies also available here.

Pharmacy Farmacia Solinas, Piazza IV Novembre; Farmacia Sardu, Corso Vittorio Emanuele. The night-time rota is posted on pharmacy doors.

Post office Via Pischedda, off Viale Giovanni XXIII (Mon–Fri 8.15am–6.30pm, Sat 8.15am–12.45pm, last day of month closes 4.30pm or noon on Sat). You can change cash here.

Supermarket Discount Mio, just by old bridge on southern bank of the river. Mon–Sat 8am–1.15pm & 5–7.45pm.

Taxis Call ℡ 0785.37.410, 335.659.0568 or 335.760.8451.

Telephones Kiosks on Piazza IV Novembre.

Train information FdS trains to Macomer and Nuoro ℡ 0785.376.107, ⓦ www.ferroviesardegna.it; FS services from Macomer ℡ 848.888.088, ⓦ www.trenitalia.it.

Travel agency Sardinian Welcome Service, Corso Vittorio Emanuele 41 ℡ 0785.374.391.

Macomer and around

Thirty kilometres inland of Bosa on the SS129, **MACOMER** has little to recommend anything more than a brief glance. Called Macopissa in Roman times, when it was a major military base, the town was the site of the last serious revolt against the Aragonese by the Sards in 1478. More recently, it has become a centre of livestock, dairy farming and wool.

Although Macomer has no intrinsic interest, a few sights in the surrounding area repay the small detour required. Chief among these are a couple of *nuraghi*, the most noteworthy of an intense concentration of nuraghic sites in the area. A kilometre or two north of the centre, the **nuraghe di Santa Barbara**, signposted between the Bosa road and the Carlo Felice highway, has a mossy central tower that reaches 15m, with primitive cupolas, minor towers and bastions tacked on to the main structure. Little more is known about the building's origins than that it was abandoned in the ninth century BC, but used again in the Carthaginian and Roman era as a centre of worship. Nearby, on the other side of the highway, the ruined state of **nuraghe Ruju** (or Ruggiu) reveals a cross-section of how a nuraghic cupola was constructed. *Domus de janas* tombs are scattered about below it, their contents on view at Sássari's Museo Sanna (see p.233).

Twelve kilometres east of town on the Nuoro road (SS129), just outside the village of **Silanus**, the charming little Byzantine chapel of **Santa Sabina** is harmoniously juxtaposed with a small *nuraghe* close by.

Practicalities

Right on the SS131 highway, Macomer is a stop on most long-distance bus routes between Oristano, Sássari and Nuoro, lies on the main FS north–south train line, and is the terminal for FdS trains for Nuoro. The **bus and train stations** lie near each other at the western end of town. The rattly old small-gauge trains for Nuoro leave from here approximately every hour. The town has three **hotels**, all fairly central and very reasonably priced: *Su Talleri* on Via Cavour (☎0785.71.422; ➋), a three-star with all rooms en suite with telephone and TV; the much larger and similarly well-equipped *Motel Macomer* (☎0785.748.119; ➌), and the two-star *Marghine* (☎ and ☎0785.70.737; ➋) on Via Vittorio Emanuele, with rooms with or without bathroom; all have **restaurants**.

On Sant'Antonio Abate's day, January 17, a mighty bonfire is lit outside Macomer's church of Santa Chiara for the **Festa di Su Tuva**.

Stintino and around

The thin peninsula that forms the western arm of the **Golfo di Asinara** is an inhospitable, sparsely populated landscape of rock and *macchia*. The only town here is **Stintino**, until recently nothing more than a remote jumble of fishermen's cottages jammed between two narrow harbours. Fortunately, its discovery by the tourist industry has not drastically altered it, and it remains a small, laid-back, if slightly bland place with a few bars, banks, restaurants and lodgings. The big hotels have established themselves further up the coast, where most of the sunning and swimming take place around the ravishing beach of **La Pelosa**. At the end of the peninsula, **Capo Falcone** overlooks the isles of **Piana** and **Asinara**, one a tiny blip, the other the only known habitat of a miniature white ass from which the gulf and island both take their name. It's one of Sardinia's more spectacular corners, though increasingly threatened by encroaching tourist developments.

Stintino has a small selection of **hotels**, though if you want to stay nearer the bathing, head up the coast towards the cape. You'll need a bit of forward planning to find anything available in the summer season, however, with many rooms booked by the week. There is greater scope for finding self-catering apartments, and though most of these are set aside for block bookings by tour companies, you can find some real bargains in low season. There are no campsites in the area, though discreet space for a tent could be found among the remoter tracts.

△ River Temo at Bosa

Try to be in Stintino at the end of August for the **Regata della Vela Latina**, when the waters are filled with yachts, some of them restored vintage vessels. The other major **festival** is on September 8, when a procession re-enacts the exodus of Asinara's inhabitants to their new home in Stintino.

Stintino is connected by regular **buses** from Porto Torres and Sássari (see Travel details on p.223).

Arrival and information

Between three and six ARST **buses** a day go to Stintino from Sássari, and there are also organized trips from Alghero in the summer months. Buses stop outside the town hall at the start of the main Via Sássari. Call in at the small **tourist office** at Via Sássari 77 for general information (Mon–Sat: summer 9.30am–1pm & 5–8pm; winter 9.30am–1pm; ☎079.523.788), or see Stintours below.

The Stintours agency (see below) is the place for information on almost everything, and you can also **rent cars**, **mopeds** and **bikes** from them: for a car, expect to pay around €35 per day plus €0.30 per kilometre, or €70 per day with unlimited kilometres; for a moped it's about €35 a day, and for a push-bike around €10 a day. Prices drop in low season, and motorboats and dinghies are also available.

Accommodation

There are just three **hotels** in town, cheapest of which is the *Lina*, overlooking Porto Vecchio at Via Lepanto 30 (☎079.523.071; ❺), where there's no restaurant and therefore no half-board requirement. Half the plain rooms here (no telephone or TV, but all with private bathroom) have balconies facing the boats, the others have no view but go for the same rates. All of the other places demand half- or full-board in summer. In Stintino's centre, the much smarter *Silvestrino* at Via Sássari 12 (☎079.523.007, ⓦwww.silvestrino.it; ❻), has full modern facilities (private bath, TV, telephone), and demands a three-day minimum stay and half- or full-board in July and August. The latter requirement shouldn't be too great a sacrifice since its restaurant is one of the region's best (see p.221). At Via XXI Aprile 4, *Geranio Rosso* (☎079.523.292; ❺) is a little bland and impersonal in style, but the rooms are airy and comfortable, and there's a good pizzeria at street-level (half-board, at €70–80 per person, is the rule from mid-June to mid-Aug).

The Stintours agency on Lungomare Colombo (☎079.523.160, ⒻO79.523.777, ⓦwww.stintours.com) deals with **apartment rentals** in and around Stintino, available even for two or three days, according to demand. Prices depend on distance to sea and season, rising to €1000 per week for four people (obligatory extras such as laundry and cleaning might be added on).

The Town

Some 50km north of Alghero and 30km west of Porto Torres, **STINTINO** was founded little more than a century ago, when the Italian state appropriated the island of Asinara for use as a penal colony. The 45 families of the resident fishing community were transferred to this sheltered spot between two natural inlets. The town today holds a population of about one thousand, to which must be added the thousands more who flock here every year, replacing fishing as the main source of income for many of the locals. While escaping the mass development undergone by other more accessible resorts, Stintino is undeniably a tourist town, even if tourists are extremely scarce for most of the year. The place lives for the summer, and the contrast between the vitality that prevails then and the inertia of the other nine months is striking.

The compact town is simple enough to grasp, a right-angled grid of mainly residential streets spreading out from the main Via Sássari. Two harbours lie on either side of the promontory: to the north, **Porto Nuovo**, also known as Portu Mannu, caters mainly to pleasure craft, while the southern **Porto Vecchio**, or Portu Minori, is crowded with fishing vessels. There is no central piazza, the two ports providing the only reference points.

Next to Porto Nuovo, the **Museo della Tonnara** (June–Sept daily 7pm–midnight; free) outwardly appears like an ordinary quayside warehouse, but is arranged within to reflect the various stages in the process of trapping and killing tuna, once a major activity in these parts, introduced by Ligurians on Asinara. The six rooms from the *Cámera Grande* to the *Cámera della Morte* ("death chamber") trace the role of tuna in the ecology of the Mediterranean and the intricacies of the centuries-old methods used each year to snare them. Maps, filmed interviews and videos of the final bloody scenes fill out the picture, and will probably tell you all you want to know and more of this practice.

The one-way street running round the seaward side of the promontory, **Lungomare Colombo**, provides a route for an easy stroll around town, which, after a couple of bar-stops, exhausts the things to do here aside from Stintino's good restaurants.

Eating and drinking

All of Stintino's **restaurants** specialize in seafood, and the larger ones have fresh lobster on offer. The best place to eat is at *Silvestrino*, the hotel on Via Sássari, where a limited menu includes decent lobster soup, seafood risotto and scrumptious prawns – it's worth booking, and there's outdoor seating in summer (moderate–expensive; closed Thurs in winter, plus Jan). Round the corner on Via Marco Polo, *Da Antonio* aspires to the same high standards, but fails on every count: it's over-priced, pretentious and slow. At Porto Vecchio, the *Porto Vecchio* has outdoor seating and reasonable prices for its variable food, while on Lungomare Colombo, *Lu Fanali* is a popular snack bar, pizzeria and gelateria with an open-air terrace. Check out the **birreria** *L'Ormeggio* just up from Porto Nuovo at Via Asinara 41 for snacks, billiards and late drinks (closed Wed in winter).

Around Stintino

With most of the shore around Stintino rough and rocky, you'll have to go north or south of town to find decent beaches. About a kilometre to the south, near an old watchtower, a narrow road leads to the *macchia*-backed beach of **Le Saline**, once site of a salt works owned by the monks of Santa Maria di Tergu (see p.251). There's a Spanish bastion here, and often a flock of flamingos attracted to the salt-pan/lagoon here.

North of Stintino, tourist villages clutter the hills backing the coast almost as far as the northern tip of **Capo Falcone**, site of Torre Falcone, a Spanish

---

Diving around Stintino

The exceptionally clear waters of La Pelosa and the islands offer superb opportunities for **diving**. For equipment rental and courses, contact Asinara Diving Center (☏079.523.223 or 338.968.5721) at the *Ancora* hotel, 2km north of Stintino (☏079.527.085).

watchtower. Leading up to the cape, the otherwise idyllic beach of **La Pelosa** is one of Sardinia's premier swimming spots, lapped by a shallow, turquoise sea of crystalline clarity. You probably won't be alone here, and the tiers of holiday homes spreading over the slopes are an annoying blot on the landscape, but the perfect views over the outlying islands of Piana and the much larger Asinara are enchanting, and the swimming is good too.

Between mid-June and mid-September, hourly **buses** connect Stintino with La Pelosa; buy tickets on board. At other times, you can reach the beach by taxi (☎079.523.382 or 333.266.4463) or hired bike from Stintino.

A range of flashy three- and four-star **hotels** in the vicinity offer surprisingly favourable rates, especially out of season, and are just steps away from the sea. The biggest – and most obtrusive – of these is the *Roccaruja* (May–Sept; ☎079.529.200, ☏www.gestitur.it; ➐), where there's an Olympic-size pool; an extra €31 a week allows guests paying half- or full-board to participate in a number of activities including tennis, windsurfing, canoeing and sailing. With self-contained apartments also available, the hotel is popular with families, many of them attached to groups coming from northern Italy. Among the other choices, *La Pelosetta* (April–Oct; ☎079.527.188, ☏www.lapelosetta.it) is extensive, right behind the beach of La Pelosa, and boasts a renowned **restaurant** with stupendous sea views. Obligatory half-board here is €98 per person, half that in low season. The hotel also has a snack bar right on the beach (April–Sept) – both places are open to non-hotel guests.

Piana and Asinara

In summer, regular boat tours depart from Stintino (and occasionally from La Pelosa) to sail round the islands' coasts and make a landing. On **Piana**, what

---

Tours of Piana and Asinara

Access to the islands of Piana and Asinara is only possible on authorized **boat excursions** from Stintino or – less frequently – Porto Torres (see p.242), normally departing between Easter and September. Once on Asinara (most boats sail past Piana without stopping), you can only travel in groups and in designated areas. The tours take in the various features of the coast and some of the prison buildings, with the rest of the time devoted to lazing on the pristine sandy beaches of Fornelli, Cala d'Oliva and others in the north of the island. You can choose between transport by bus (€2.75), tourist "train" (€17) or four-wheel drive (€24). You're allowed a certain degree of freedom, however, by renting bikes on the island, which can only be ridden on the surfaced roads. In addition, walking and biking expeditions can be arranged with the agencies listed below. Bring your own food and drink, because there's nothing available on the island.

From Stintino, excursions on the *Ogliastra* motor launch currently leave at 9.30am, returning at about 1.50pm and 5.30pm, later in summer; return tickets cost €22. When there's sufficient demand, there may be additional departures and returns during the day. **From Porto Torres**, the *Zaffiro* leaves at 9am and returns at 6pm, though again, this will depend on demand and may be cancelled altogether; return tickets cost €29).

You can get further information and purchase tickets at the toll-free ☎800.561.166 or from Asinara's website, ☏www.parcoasinara.it. In Stintino, La Nassa agency at Via Sássari (☎079.520.060) deals with ticket sales; at Porto Torres, contact Cooperativa Sardegna Nord-Ovest, based near the Capitaneria at the port (☎079.510.659). Stintours (see p.220) and Scopri Sardegna (☎079.512.209) also organize walking, biking and nature-watching expeditions.

you see is what you get: a tiny flat patch of land with a solitary watchtower standing guard. There is more on **Asinara**, 16km long, though visitors are only permitted within certain areas on organized boat tours. Access to the island has been severely restricted since the establishment of a prison colony there in 1885, and, after its closure in the late 1990s, of a national park to preserve the natural environment. The wildlife that you probably won't see – it's out of bounds – includes breeding turtles.

Called Sinuaria by the Romans on account of its indented form – making it appear from a distance like a whole archipelago of separate islands – Asinara has been sporadically inhabited in the last two millennia, and was even occupied in 1638 by French pirates as a base for their raiding missions against shipping bound to or sailing from Porto Torres. The Savoyan king sold it to the Duke of Vallombrosa in 1775, but it never yielded a significant income, and was used both as a quarantine hospital for victims of cholera and a place of incarceration. At its northern end, the island's highest point (408m) is poignantly named **Punta della Scomúnica** ("Excommunication Point").

Asinara's off-limits status has allowed a range of **wildlife** to thrive, including the white wild donkeys for which the island is named, falcons, mouflons, pigs and goats. Both islands are still used to pasture cattle, which are walked across the shallow straits between Capo Falcone and Piana twice a year, in November and May.

Travel details

Trains

Alghero to: Sássari (Mon–Sat 11 daily, Sun 6; 35min).
Bosa Marina to: Macomer (July–Aug Sat & Sun 1 daily; 1hr 45min).

Buses

Alghero to: Bosa (Mon–Sat 4 daily, Sun 2; 1hr 5min–1hr 40min); Capo Caccia (1–2 daily; 50min); Olbia (1 daily; 2hr); Porto Conte (7–8 daily; 30min); Porto Ferro (3–4 daily; 1hr); Porto Torres (5–8 daily; 50min); San Marco for Anghelu Ruju (Mon–Sat 3 daily; 30min); Sássari (hourly; 1hr); Villanova Monteleone (Mon–Sat 8–9 daily, Sun 6; 45min–1hr 25min).
Argentiera to: Sássari (Mon–Sat 5–6 daily; 1hr 10min).
Bosa to: Alghero (Mon–Sat 4 daily, Sun 2; 1hr 15min–1hr 40min); Cúglieri (Mon–Sat 7–8 daily; 1hr); Macomer (10 daily; 25min); Olbia (1 daily; 3hr); Oristano (Mon–Sat 6–7 daily; 2hr); Sássari (3–6 daily; 2hr 10min–2hr 30min); Villanova Monteleone (Mon–Sat 2 daily; 1hr).
Stintino to: Porto Torres (Mon–Sat 5–6 daily, Sun 2–3; 1hr 40min); Sássari (Mon–Sat 5–8 daily, Sun 3–6; 1hr 15min).

Sássari and around

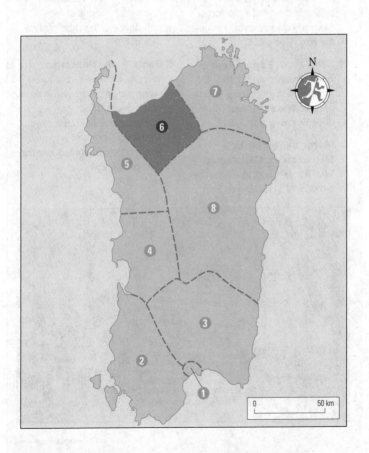

CHAPTER 6

Highlights

✳ **Sassari's old quarter** The maze-like old town preserves its medieval air, with the glorious Baroque Cathedral at its heart. See p.233–238

✳ **Nuraghe Santu Antine** A fascinating relic of Sardinia's culture, this venerable prehistoric palace is the most imposing of the many *nuraghi* strewn about the area. See p.256

✳ **San Gavino, Porto Torres** Beautifully preserved, this atmospheric monument is one of the island's grandest Pisan churches. See p.243–244

✳ **Museo dell'Intreccio Mediterraneo, Castelsardo** With its far-reaching views, the old citadel's castle is an extraordinary location for a collection of the town's highly distinctive basket-ware. See p.249

✳ **La Cavalcata, Sássari** One of the island's most flamboyant festivals, with feats of horsemanship, traditional costumes and performances of music and dance in the main piazza. See p.230

✳ **Santa Trinità Saccargia** With its rocket-like belltower rising abruptly above the bare countryside, this Romanesque church makes a striking landmark and also has a finely preserved interior. See p.253–254

△ San Pietro delle Immágini, Bulzi

6

Sássari and around

Encompassing the ancient territories of Logudoro and Anglona, the western half of Sássari province ranges from high tableland riven by unexpected gullies around the provincial capital to craggy peaks and valleys further east, and a long sandy arc edging the Golfo dell'Asinara on the northern coast.

Sardinia's second city, **Sássari**, is for many the island's most interesting town, with its crowded medieval centre and Spanish associations. It's a less cosmopolitan place than Cágliari, its inland location accentuating its inward-looking mentality, though there's also a high level of culture here, and enough interest in the city's churches and excellent archeological museum to fill at least a couple of days.

A short ride northwest of Sássari will bring you to an ancient monument that is unique not just in Sardinia but in the whole Mediterranean basin – the "ziggurat" of **Monte d'Accoddi**, a sanctuary dating from around the third millennium BC. Some excellent beaches line the coast north of here, where the only blot is the extensive refinery outside **Porto Torres**, the original capital of the *giudicato* of Torres. Unless you're passing through on one of the ferries to or from the mainland, the principal reason to visit this industrial port is the **Basilica di San Gavino**, considered by many to be the island's finest example of Pisan-Romanesque architecture. The local lido of **Platamona** lies east of town, one of a string of small summer resorts dotted along the sandy coast of the Golfo dell'Asinara, in between which you'll find less crowded spots for a swim.

To the south and east of Sássari, the old territory of **Logudoro** is richly endowed with **medieval churches**, most of them splendidly positioned in improbably remote corners of the countryside, saved from despoilation by their very inaccessibility. The most famous of them, **Santissima Trinità di Saccargia**, lies just off the Sássari–Olbia road, though others require a little more perseverance to reach. The medieval refinement of these buildings forms a sharp contrast to the ramshackle grandeur of the *nuraghi* that are an equally striking feature of the region. The densest concentration of them is at **Torralba**, where there is an outstanding museum of nuraghic culture and, a short distance outside the village (and very near to the SS131), the grand **Nuraghe Santu Ántine**, one of the island's most important nuraghic complexes.

Nuraghi and prenuraghic structures are also scattered across the mountainous **Anglona** region, northeast of Sássari. Its principal town, **Castelsardo**, occupies a fortified site on the coast; this scenic location, and the local skill with handicrafts, have made it a magnet for tourists, but don't be put off exploring the old citadel to enjoy the far-reaching views. There are some good scenic drives inland from here, while the best beaches lie to the east of town, around

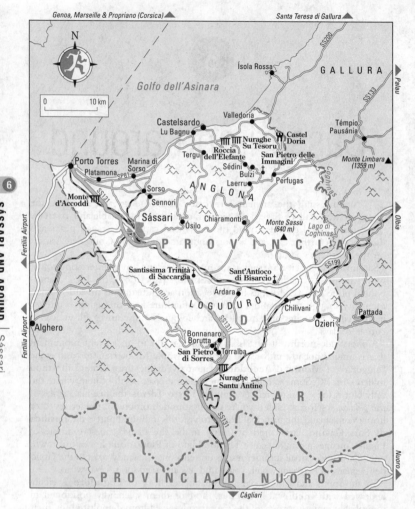

the mouth of the **River Coghinas**, which marks Anglona's eastern boundary. Sássari is the area's major transport hub. Apart from the fifteen-minute **train** connection between Sássari and Porto Torres, and the occasionally useful line to Ozieri-Chilivani, non-drivers will have to rely on **bus services** to reach most places. The north coast is well-served by frequent buses bound for Santa Teresa di Gallura, but most inland places have extremely limited connections, sometimes with just one or two ARST or FdS buses passing through on weekdays. For more information on bus and train connections, see Travel details on p.257.

Sássari

First impressions of Sardinia's second city, **SÁSSARI**, do little to encourage anything more than a cursory visit; its inland location and sparse tourist facilities might seem a poor substitute for the holiday diversions of the nearby coast. But it is this very lack of tourist glamour that gives Sássari its special interest as an unpretentious – and not unattractive – working town, steeped in tradition, albeit without the rustic and folkloric elements of Sardinia's villages. To the outsider, it presents a proud, self-sufficient, even self-absorbed aspect, an impression that becomes overwhelming once you penetrate the **old quarter**'s dense network of medieval streets, old churches and *palazzi*, among them some rare examples of Renaissance buildings in Sardinia. This atmospheric labyrinth is connected to the modern city by a sequence of squares, culminating in the impressive Piazza Italia, whose imperial tone sits oddly next to the old town. Close by, the **Museo Sanna** houses one of the island's top archeological collections, second only to Cágliari's.

Sássari has a good range of **bars and restaurants**, though not so much choice when it comes to accommodation. Nonetheless, with its network of transport connections, the town makes a handy base for the many coastal or inland attractions in the vicinity, or else a stimulating diversion from a more permanent base by the sea. Note that if you're coming to Sássari by **train** from the south or east, you'll probably have to change at the nondescript town of Chilivani (its station is usually referred to as Ozieri-Chilivani).

Some history

Built on an ancient site known as **Tatari**, or Tathari, the modern city of Sássari has roots going back to settlers from the Roman colony, Turris Libyssonis, the modern Porto Torres. As the port declined, so the inland town expanded; by the fourteenth century it possessed its own statute of laws and a ring of walls. Sássari was inevitably sucked into the conflict between Pisa and Genoa, making strategic alliances with both sides as the situation demanded. Then, in 1323, **James II of Aragon** established a power base here and, after a brief interlude under the control of the *giudicato* of Arborea, the city spent the next four centuries as an integral part of the Catalan-Aragonese hegemony, though that did not prevent it from being plundered several times by Moorish pirates. Ten years under Austrian rule preceded the coming of the House of Savoy in 1720, whose cautious programme of reforms and investment was briefly interrupted when an anti-feudal revolt led by a coalition of urban democrats and rural peasants provoked a fierce campaign of repression between 1793 and 1802. In the course of the nineteenth century, the Aragonese castle and walls were demolished, allowing the city to expand gradually.

The Spanish stamp is still evident in Sássari, not least in its churches. The city also has a strong tradition of intellectual independence; in the sixteenth century the Jesuits founded Sardinia's first **university** here, which continues to excel in the spheres of law, medicine and politics. In recent years, Sássari has produced two national presidents, Antonio Segni and Francesco Cossiga, as well as the long-time head of the Italian Communist Party, Enrico Berlinguer (1922–84) – a cousin, incidentally, of the Christian Democrat Cossiga.

Today, with its 120,000 inhabitants (about half Cágliari's population), Sássari is grappling with rapidly changing **economic conditions**. Belying the well-to-do urbanity of Via Roma's café society, the city's youth especially has been caught between the seemingly intractable problems of unemployment and heroin addiction, which have generated a degree of petty crime, though matters on all counts have improved in recent years. Outsiders have little to fear, anyway, and most *sassaresi* are rarely less than courteous and hospitable, albeit imbued with a deep cynical streak.

One of Sardinia's showiest festivals – **La Cavalcata** – takes place in Sássari on **Ascension Day** (the fortieth day after Easter), the highlight of a month of cultural activities. Northern Sardinia's equivalent to Cágliari's Sant'Efisio festival (see p.82), it attracts hundreds of richly costumed participants from villages throughout the province and beyond. Originally staged for the benefit of visiting Spanish kings and other dignitaries, it lapsed in the eighteenth century until it was revived, first in 1899, and then more recently by the local branch of the Rotary Club.

The festival is divided into three stages, the morning featuring a **horseback parade** and a slow **procession**, in which the embroidered and decorated costumes unique to each village are displayed. In the afternoon, the scene shifts to the **Ippodromo** (race track) on the southern outskirts of town, where hectic **horse races** and ever more daring equestrian feats are performed before a large crowd. Saturday night and Sunday evening are devoted to traditional songs and dances in Piazza Italia, showcasing groups from all over the island – the close-harmony singing is especially impressive. A large fair takes over the centre of town during the week leading up to the Cavalcata, so expect lengthy traffic hold-ups.

A much more local affair held on the afternoon of August 14 is **I Candelieri** (or *Li Candareri*), linked to the Pisan devotion to the Madonna of the Assumption. It became a regular event when an outbreak of plague in Sássari mysteriously abated – though there is some dispute as to which particular plague it was, those of 1528, 1580 and 1652 being the main contenders – since when the ritual has been repeated annually on the eve of the feast of the Assumption as a token of thanks. For all its religious intent, I Candelieri is a crowded, rumbustious occasion, involving bands of **gremi**, or medieval guilds of merchants, artisans and labourers, decked out in Spanish-style costumes, staggering through the old town under the weight of nine gigantic wooden "candlesticks", eight metres tall, weighing 200–300kg, and laden with colourful ribbons and other symbols of the guilds they represent. **La Faradda** (the descent through the town) usually begins at Piazza Castello, ending at the church of Santa Maria di Bethlem, with a stop en route at the Teatro Cívico, where the representative of the farmers hails Sássari's mayor with a hearty *A zent'anni!* ("May you live a hundred years!"), a traditional salute to all the *sassaresi*. The *Faradda* starts at 6pm; if you're in town on the previous afternoon, you should drop in on the **palio**, or bareback horse race, that takes place in the Ippodromo.

Arrival and information

The **train station** is at the bottom of the old town, from which it's a ten-minute walk uphill to the modern city. Most long-distance bus services arrive at and depart from the **bus station** on Corso Vico, a right turn out of the train station. ARST buses run the thirty-kilometre, thirty-minute journey between the bus station and Alghero's **Fertilia airport** (see p.195) eleven times daily. Note that you can buy most bus tickets at bars and tobacconists indicated by stickers or posters.

Everything of interest in Sássari is easily reached on foot, and you're unlikely to need to use **local buses**; however, if you want to get to or from the train station quickly, #8 is the most useful service, plying a circular route every twelve minutes between the station, Corso Trinità, Piazza Italia and Via Roma. Buy tickets before boarding at *tabacchi* (€0.57) or the kiosk on Via Tavolara, in the Giardini Púbblici, the main terminus for local services. If you're **driving**, make sure you stay on the right side of the parking attendants; seek them out and buy a ticket (€0.60 per hour) to avoid a fine during the times when

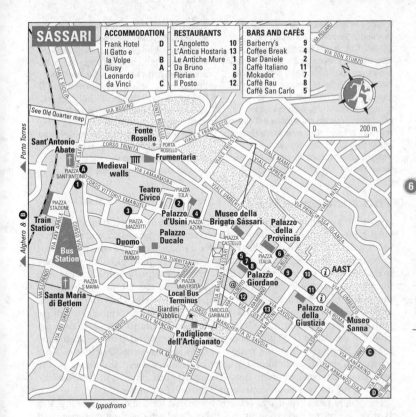

SÁSSARI

ACCOMMODATION		RESTAURANTS		BARS AND CAFÉS	
Frank Hotel	D	L'Angoletto	10	Barberry's	9
Il Gatto e		L'Antica Hostaria	13	Coffee Break	4
la Volpe	B	Le Antiche Mure	1	Bar Daniele	2
Giusy	A	Da Bruno	3	Caffè Italiano	11
Leonardo		Florian	6	Mokador	7
da Vinci	C	Il Posto	12	Caffè Rau	8
				Caffè San Carlo	5

▼ Ippodromo

restrictions are in force (Mon–Fri 8.30am–1pm and 4–8pm, Sat 8.30am–1pm). Free spaces can be hard to find: try around the station area, Emiciclo Garibaldi or Viale Umberto, or if you're desperate use a garage (see p.240).

Sássari's **tourist office** is right next to the Museo Sanna at Via Roma 62 (Mon–Thurs 9am–1.30pm & 4–6pm, Fri 9am–1.30pm; ☏079.231.777, ⓦ www.comune.sassari.it); alternatively, the staff at the AAST office at Viale Umberto 72 (Mon–Wed 8am–1.30pm & 4–7pm, Thurs & Fri 8am–2pm; ☏079.231.331), though primarily concerned with administration, are generally helpful and also have maps, brochures and accommodation lists to give away.

Accommodation

Staying in Sássari can be a real problem, as there are few reasonably priced **hotels** – you'd do well to phone ahead. There are **youth hostels** at Fertilia (p.207) and Castelsardo (p.251), both about forty minutes away, and **campsites** in Alghero or on the north coast east of Porto Torres, on a bus route from Sássari.

Frank Hotel Via Armando Diaz 20 ☏079.276.456, ⓦ www.frankhotel.com. Smart three-star geared towards groups and conferences, but useful for staying in the modern city. Rooms are spacious, and there's a moderate pizzeria/restaurant in the basement, and garage parking. ❹

Il Gatto e la Volpe Monti di Jesgia 23, Caniga, 6km west of Sássari ☎079.318.0012 or 333.695.7118, ⓦwww.ilgattoelavolpebandb. A rustic B&B that makes a great alternative to staying in town, only about 10min by car or bus from the centre (hourly buses call here from Via Tavolara). It's a large country house with friendly young owners (both drummers), a spacious garden and lots of rooms, including one separate, self-catering apartment for longer stays; other bathrooms are shared. Bikes can be hired and excursions arranged, including sailing trips. It's hard to find, but you can call to be met. No credit cards. **❷**

Giusy Piazza Sant'Antonio ☎079.233.327, ⓕ079.239.490. Conveniently near the station on Piazza Sant'Antonio, and the only choice in the old town. It's seen better days, and suffers from traffic noise, but all rooms have TV and telephone, and triple rooms are available; there's no restaurant. **❷**
Leonardo da Vinci Via Roma 79 ☎079.280.744, ⓦwww.leonardodavincihotel.it. Like the *Frank* but glitzier, with similar accoutrements – garage parking, rooms with TVs, telephones and minibars. Just up from the museum, it's marginally closer to the centre and has higher prices. There's a bar and breakfast room, but no restaurant. **❺**

The modern city

It's hard to say where the true centre of Sássari lies; the city is split into different, largely self-contained quarters. However, the largest piazza, and the venue of most of the city's festas, is **Piazza Italia**, a magnificent area which can claim to be the grandest piazza in Sardinia, and one of the most monumental public spaces anywhere in Italy. Virtually traffic-free, its generous expanse is a sure cure for any claustrophobic feelings induced by the old town. One whole side of the square is occupied by the imposing **Palazzo della Provincia**, built in 1880, looking more like a presidential palace than a mere provincial office; perhaps surprisingly, the neo-Gothic **Palazzo Giordano** facing it (now the offices of the Banco di Napoli) dates from the same period. Between them, surrounded by palm trees in the middle of the square, a pompous statue of King Victor Emanuel II lends almost a colonial flavour, somewhat deflated by the pigeons usually perched on his head. The statue's inauguration in 1899 was the occasion for the revival of Sássari's main festival, *La Cavalcata*.

The stately mood of Piazza Italia is continued for a short distance up **Via Roma**, where the succession of smart shops and cafés is abruptly terminated by a stern relic of the Fascist era, the hulking **Palazzo della Giustizia**. Its ponderous dimensions are slyly undermined by the semi-restored Rococo villa opposite at no. 46, sporting a cream-coloured facade adorned with whimsical *putti*.

South of Piazza Italia, Via Carlo Alberto leads down to the Emiciclo Garibaldi, a wide semicircle of shops and cars, and the **Giardini Púbblici**, a shady oasis of calm amid the traffic rushing past on all sides. The gardens are home to a permanent exhibition of island art, the **Padiglione dell'Artigianato** (Mon–Sat 9am–1pm & 4.30–7.30pm), Sardinia's best showcase for current arts and crafts, with all items for sale. Carpets, ceramics, jewellery and leatherwork jostle for space here; prices are on the high side and, unlike in some other shops, non-negotiable, though quality is guaranteed. Even if you don't intend to buy, it's a good opportunity to see what's available and note items that you might find cheaper elsewhere.

At the bottom of Piazza Italia, off its northwestern side, the short arcaded Portici Bargone e Crispo shelters cafés filled with gossiping regulars watching the coming and going between the square and the long sloping Piazza Castello. The site of an Aragonese castle until the nineteenth century, this piazza is still lined on one side by a barracks. This now houses the **Museo della Brigata Sássari** (Mon–Fri 9am–12.30pm & 2.30–4.30pm, Sat 9am–noon; free), dedicated to the renowned Sardinian regiment whose bravery and heavy losses during World War I are taught in every Italian school. Fighting mainly against Austrians in the Alps, the troops were involved in a horrific campaign of trench warfare which cost them nearly 4000 missing or dead and more than 9000 wounded. You don't need to be a military buff to enjoy the old photos, posters and mementos collected in the half-dozen rooms here, though anyone interested in the period will also appreciate the uniforms, maps and documents.

The Museo Sanna

The modern city's principal attraction, the **Museo Sanna** (Tues–Sun 9am–8pm; €2) lies on via Roma within its own garden. Sardinia's second most important archeological museum is housed in a modern, well-planned block, and organized chronologically from prehistoric through nuraghic to Phoenician, Carthaginian and Roman items. Most of the **prehistoric** items date from around 2700 BC, including pottery fragments and necklaces belonging to Sardinia's Ozieri culture, and numerous slivers of the smooth obsidian, used to make arrow heads and cutting tools, which was the island's major export in neolithic times. One room holds a laser image of the unique Copper Age *ziqqurat* temple at Monte d'Accoddi (see p.241–242), while objects from the Bonnanaro culture include sacred skulls, trepanned for reasons that remain obscure.

It is the finds from the **nuraghic** culture, however, that constitute the museum's prime attraction. Collected on the upper floor, the fragments of pottery, jewellery and household implements are interspersed with plans and cross-sections of *nuraghi*, and explanations (in English and Italian) of their structure. Most engrossing is the display of **bronze statuettes**, smaller than the collection in Cágliari but a good taster if you can't make it to see that one; it includes warriors with boldly stylized ox-head helmets, a motif repeated on the boat-prows modelled here, and one figurine of a shepherd holds either a dog or goat on the end of a lead. The material was unearthed at various sites throughout the province, especially the concentration in the Valle dei Nuraghi (see p.256). Some of the finds – a bronze statuette of a bearded man from the Levant, Phoenician ceramics, a necklace of Baltic amber – demonstrate the nuraghic people's strikingly far-flung trading contacts. One of the oldest of these items, a Mycenaean vase from around 1600BC, was recently excavated at Nuraghe Arrubiu. For more information on Sardinia's nuraghic culture, see p.349–350.

Back downstairs, the Carthaginian, Roman and classical sections hold a miscellany of coins, ceramics, busts and mosaic floors. From the **Phoenician and Carthaginian period** (sixth–fourth centuries BC), there are beautifully preserved articles of jewellery, terracotta masks, Greek-inspired amphorae painted with battles and sex scenes, and inscribed *stelae*. **Roman** remains include material from Nora and Tharros: statuettes, gold rings, pendants, knives, and a decree carved in stone from AD 69 commanding a group of mountain-dwellers to leave the low-lying region of the Campidano. Elsewhere on the ground floor, space has been set aside for temporary art exhibitions. You can join an informative guided tour of the museum (weekdays 9am–1pm & 4–7.30pm, weekends 9am–2pm; €3.10).

The old quarter

The compact **old quarter** is a quirky corrective to the straight lines of Sássari's modern streets. Bounded by Corso Margherita di Savoia and Viale Umberto to the south and north, Via Brigata Sássari and Piazza Castello to the east, and Piazza Sant'Antonio and the station area to the west, the area is surrounded by

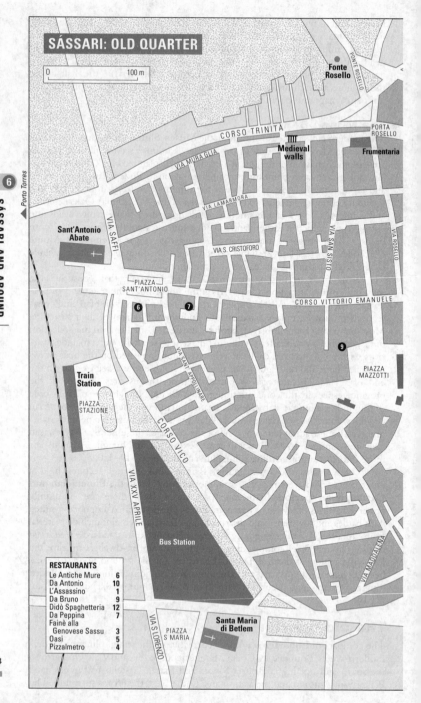

SÁSSARI: OLD QUARTER

0   100 m

Porto Torres

Fonte Rosello

CORSO TRINITÀ

Medieval walls

PORTA ROSELLO

Frumentaria

VIA MURA GLIA

VIA LAMARMORA

Sant'Antonio Abate

VIA SAFFI

VIA S. CRISTOFORO

VIA SAN SISTO

VIA ROSELLO

PIAZZA SANT'ANTONIO

CORSO VITTORIO EMANUELE

6

7

9

Train Station

PIAZZA STAZIONE

VIA SANT'APOLLINARE

PIAZZA MAZZOTTI

CORSO VICO

VIA XXV APRILE

Bus Station

VIA MADDALENA

RESTAURANTS

Le Antiche Mure	6
Da Antonio	10
L'Assassino	1
Da Bruno	9
Didó Spaghetteria	12
Da Peppina	7
Fainè alla Genovese Sassu	3
Oasi	5
Pizzalmetro	4

VIA S LORENZO

PIAZZA S MARIA

Santa Maria di Betlem

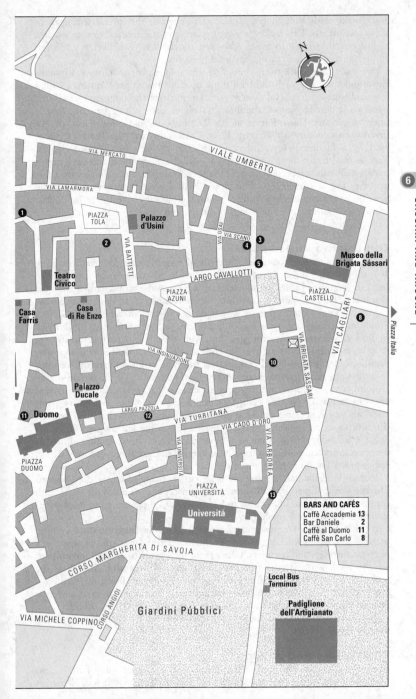

VIA MERCATO

VIALE UMBERTO

VIA LAMARMORA

1

PIAZZA
TOLA

**Palazzo
d'Usini**

VIA USAI

VIA SCANO

3

4

VIA BATTISTI

2

5

**Museo della
Brigata Sássari**

Piazza Italia

LARGO CAVALLOTTI

**Teatro
Cívico**

PIAZZA
AZUNI

PIAZZA
CASTELLO

**Casa
Farris**

**Casa
di Re Enzo**

8

VIA CAGLIARI

VIA INSINUAZIONE

10

VIA BRIGATA SÁSSARI

**Palazzo
Ducale**

LARGO PAZZOLA

12

VIA TURRITANA

VIA CADO D'ORO

11 Duomo

PIAZZA
DUOMO

VIA UNIVERSITA

VIA ARBOREA

PIAZZA
UNIVERSITÀ

13

Università

BARS AND CAFÉS	
Caffè Accademia	**13**
Bar Daniele	**2**
Caffè al Duomo	**11**
Caffè San Carlo	**8**

CORSO MARGHERITA DI SAVOIA

CORSO ANGIOI

**Local Bus
Terminus**

VIA MICHELE COPPINO

Giardini Púbblici

**Padiglione
dell'Artigianato**

noisy main roads, though little traffic can penetrate the interior network of alleys and piazzas. This makes it a great place to stroll around, easy to get lost in but equally simple to leave. Although much of it is derelict, it's still got enough in and around it to justify a foray or two.

The main axis, effectively bisecting the old town, is **Corso Vittorio Emanuele**: a long, partly cobbled slope up from Piazza Sant'Antonio, with a few easily-missed medieval doorways, flaking palazzi and fragments of Gothic windows jammed in among the shops and alleys. Look out in particular for the fifteenth-century **Casa Farris** at no. 23, the Catalan-Gothic **Casa di Re Enzo** from a century earlier at no. 42, and, across the road, the **Teatro Cívico**, built by a Piedmontese architect in 1830 as the seat of the municipality. Transformed into a theatre after 1880, it's still the place where the city's mayor traditionally meets representatives of the local guilds during the Candelieri festival (see the box on p.230). The facade has been elegantly restored, but the interior, which you might get to see while at a play or concert here, holds little of architectural interest. For details of drama and classical music at the Teatro Cívico, call ☎079.232.182. Tickets start at €10–12.

The Duomo and around

At the core of the old town, the **Duomo di San Nicola** (daily 9am–noon & 4–7pm; not Sun during masses) is an unexpected eruption of flamboyance amid the cramped jumble of streets. Rearing above the semicircular Piazza del Duomo, its florid seventeenth-century facade is Sardinia's most dazzling example of Baroque architecture, in which statues of the *turritani* saints, Gavino, Proto and Gianuario (see the box on p.244) are set, surmounted by San Nicola. Behind this extravagant frontage, however, the basic structure is simpler Aragonese-Gothic work of the fifteenth and sixteenth centuries. The **campanile** alongside is even earlier, a survival from the original thirteenth-century construction, with gargoyles and other Gothic details. The **interior** of the Duomo has escaped the full Baroque treatment that the facade suggests, and you can still make out the plain Gothic lines. The eighteenth-century choir stalls are worth seeking out, and there's some interest in the small **museo diocesano** of ecclesiastical treasures reached from the left transept (Tues, Fri & Sat & feast-days 10am–noon & 4–6pm; €2). Part of this collection of medallions, ceramics and devotional objects is housed in the church of San Michele, opposite the Duomo's main entrance.

Behind the cathedral, fighting for space on Via Santa Caterina, the **Palazzo Ducale** was designed by a Piedmontese architect at the end of the eighteenth century for the Duke of Asinara, and today houses the *comune* and hosts occasional exhibitions and concerts.

At the back of the Duomo and palazzo, the long **Via Turritana** was a centre of gold- and silver-working, a tradition maintained today by the presence of a few watchmakers and jewellers. Take a right turn off here up Via Università to see the nucleus of Sássari's university in **Piazza Università**. As well as the main library and administration offices, the building still holds the faculty of law, which, with medicine, has been the university's principal field of academic excellence since its foundation by the Jesuits in 1562. Its original late-Renaissance appearance is best appreciated round the back, on the side facing the Giardini Púbblici.

Piazza Tola and around

Sássari's old commercial centre was located on the other side of the Corso Vittorio Emanuele, at the now sequestered **Piazza Tola**, where a daily market is a faint reminder of its former role. The piazza, known until the last century as *Carra Manna* (Sard for public weighing machine), takes its present name from the judge and historian whose statue stands at its centre, Pasquale Tola (1800–74). Various building styles face the square, most notably the **Palazzo d'Usini**, a Renaissance building dating from 1577.

A much more exquisite relic of the Renaissance stands a short distance away at the end of nearby Via Rosello, another jewellers' lane that leads to the north-eastern edge of the old city. The pretty **Fonte Rosello** (May–Sept Tues–Sat 9am–1pm & 5.30–8.30pm, Sun 9.30am–8.30pm; Oct–April Tues–Sat 9am–1pm & 4–7pm, Sun 9am–1pm; €1) lies hidden away at the bottom of a grassy flight of cobbled steps accessible from Corso Trinità. The small, square monument, sculpted by Genoese stonemasons in 1606, and with a Latin dedication to the Spanish King Philip III, is delicately carved with four statues representing the seasons, one on each corner, with dolphins curled around their feet. The original statues were damaged in riots in 1795, and replaced by these in 1828 (the statue of San Gavino surmounting it is a copy of the original).

Fed by a spring that was once one of Sássari's principal sources of drinking water, the fountain was traditionally one of the busiest hubs of local life, where throngs of women would converge to scrub clothes and exchange gossip. The reconstructed wash-house alongside helps to recall its former importance, though, as there's usually no one here apart from the occasional tourist, its former bustle has given way to a more intimate charm, the tranquillity only shattered by the flyover arching overhead. Nonetheless, the *sassaresi* continue to regard this as their greatest treasure.

Across Corso Trinità, through the Porta Rosello, an old grain-store has been converted into a gallery, the **Frumentaria** (Tues–Sat 9am–1pm & 5–7pm, Sun 9am–1pm; €1.50). Dating from around 1600, the building holds exhibitions on various local themes. Further down Corso Trinità, there are several surviving remnants of the **medieval walls** which girdled Sássari until they were pulled down in the nineteenth century. On one section, just by the petrol station, you can make out three heraldic devices bearing symbols of the alliance on which the old city depended: a tower represents Sássari; a cross for the church, and a lily for Pisa. Further down this busy road, turn left onto Via Saffi where, at the bottom of Corso Vittorio Emanuele, the church of **Sant'Antonio Abate** stands above the piazza of the same name. It's a noble Baroque structure of clean lines and elegantly-proportioned arches within, where the star attraction is a gigantic gilded wooden altarpiece, executed by local craftsmen on a design by Bartolomeo Augusto, a Genoan master of the seventeenth century.

Santa Maria di Betlem

Piazza Sant'Antonio once held the busy northern gate of the old town; Sássari's northwestern gate, on the other side of the train station, is still used by a stream of traffic to and from Alghero and Fertilia airport. The most striking landmark here is the silver dome of **Santa Maria di Betlem**, one of the city's oldest churches and the one dearest to the local people. The building has accumulated a range of different styles during its long lifetime, with much of its simple Gothic structure overlaid with a heavy Baroque touch. Its best and oldest feature is the Romanesque facade, with its sprinkling of Gothic and even Arab styles in the zigzag cornice, rose window and French Gothic columns. The lowest part dates back to the thirteenth century, to which the upper part containing the rose window was added in 1465. The inside, however, while conserving its fifteenth-century Gothic vaults, is overwhelmingly Baroque, the result of a going-over in the last century, when the elliptical cupola was added. The lateral chapels are still there, though, each one dedicated to one of the local guilds which became attached to the church and convent in the thirteenth century, when this was the city's chief Franciscan centre. Least retouched of the chapels is the first on the left, the Catalan-style stonemasons' chapel; others belong to wallmakers, carpenters, tailors and so on. You can see the *candelieri*, or massive wooden candles associated with the guilds, stored here in between their annual outings at the festival of I Candelieri (see the box on p.230), each one heavily festooned with ribbons and decoration. If they're not displayed in the church, they're usually kept in the adjoining cloisters.

Eating

Sássari has a good range of **restaurants** scattered in different parts, sometimes difficult to track down. In the old town, you'll come across several places serving *fainè*, a popular local dish originating in Genoa, a legacy of that city's former close association with Sássari. This winter speciality (most *fainè* places are closed in summer) is made of *ceci* (chickpea) flour fried into a sort of thick pancake, served either plain (*normale*), or cooked up with onions (*cipolle*), sausage (*salsicce*), anchovy (*acciughe*), or some combination of these. They're generally dispatched more quickly than pizza, with second and third helpings as the occasion demands; beer is the usual accompaniment. You might find them heavy-going, but they make a good fast-food snack and are cheap at around €4 per helping. Horsemeat (*cavallo*) is especially prized in these parts, and you'll often find donkey (*asinello*) and snails (*lumache* or *monzette*) on the menu too. Fish is not a particular *sassarese* favourite, though it's usually available; in autumn, it's worth sampling the local mushrooms (*porcini* or *antunna*). If you're self-catering, see "Markets" and "Supermarkets" in Listings on p.240–241.

The old quarter

Le Antiche Mure Piazza Sant'Antonio. At the bottom of the Corso and close to the train station, this restaurant has occasionally offhand service but the food is fine: the *gnocchetti alla furba* is the name here for the ubiquitous *mallorreddus alle sarde*, with tomato, fresh sausage and mild *peperoncino*. Pizzas are available, but there is no carafe wine. Best of all, you can eat on the "verandah" – effectively, out in the piazza. Closed daytime & Sun. Moderate.

Da Antonio Via Arborea 2 ☏079.234.297. Bright and modern in appearance, this place serves only traditional *sassarese* specialities, such as *trippa alla parmigiaba* (tripe with parmesan) and roasted snails. Wines are all from Sardinia. Closed Sun. Moderate.

L'Assassino Vicolo Ospizio Cappuccini 1, off Via Rosello ☏079.235.041. Casual trattoria in the heart of the old town with photos and paintings of Sássari. Dishes are from Sássari or Gallura, and can be sampled on fixed-price menus (currently €18 and €20, minimum of two people). Closed Sun eve. Moderate.

Da Bruno Piazza Mazzotti 11. A basic ristorante/pizzeria, with some tables outside – if you can bear sitting in what must be the ugliest piazza in Sardinia. Try the Sassarese pizza, with *antunna* (local mushrooms) and *melanzane*. At lunch, €6- and €9-menus are available, for a meal, drink and coffee.

Didò Spaghetteria Largo Pazzola 8. A good range of pastas at very reasonable prices; *Spaghetti Didò*, with sausage, olives and cheese, will leave you reeking of garlic. Non-pasta dishes are also served, and good-value fixed-price menus are available. Closed Sun. Moderate.

Fainè alla Genovese Sassu Via Usai 17. An unpretentious central place for *fainè* fans. There's nothing else to eat here, and you can't get wine – only beer, soft drinks or water. Service is brisk. No credit cards. Closed Sun and June–Sept. Inexpensive.

Oasi Via Usai 7. The first of three restaurant options on this short street linking Piazza Castello and Piazza Tola. This one is a regular trattoria offering the usual regional and national items, with pasta dishes at €5–8, including *alle vóngole* (with clams) at €6.20. You can try *fainè* here, or local crepes. Closed Sun. Moderate.

Da Peppina Vícolo Pigozzi, an alley off Corso Vittorio Emanuele. A good place to sample the local specialities of horsemeat, donkey, pork or snails. No Credit cards. Closed Sun. Inexpensive.

Pizzalmetro Via Usai 10. Pizzas are ordered here by the metre: just point out how much you want. The *Antunna*, made with local mushrooms, is luscious. Open eves only. Closed Tues. Inexpensive.

New town

L'Angoletto Via Mazzini 2. Self-service *távola calda* charging €8.50 for first and second courses, *contorno* and a drink. No credit cards. Lunchtime only; closed Sun. Inexpensive.

L'Antica Hostaria Via Cavour 57 ☎079.200.066.

Small, upmarket place whose creative versions of traditional Sard dishes have earned it a gourmet reputation. Closed Sun & Aug. Expensive.

Florian Via Bellieni 27 ☎079.236.251. A well-established, top-class restaurant, with excellently prepared Sard and Italian dishes. The atmosphere is formal, though prices are surprisingly reasonable. Closed Sun. Moderate–Expensive.

Il Posto Via E. Costa 16 ☎079.233.528. A casually smart trattoria in the new town, its pale pink, vaulted interior hung with tasteful artworks. Pizzas are available alongside a good range of pastas, including *tagliatelle ai quattro formaggi* (with four cheeses) for €6. Closed Sun.

Drinking and entertainment

There's no lack of good **bars** in Sássari, most of them packed out and open late during summer. The ones in Piazza Castello and along Via Roma are liveliest, sometimes with live music. There are also a few **clubs** in town for a late bop: the most central is *Sergeant Pepper* on Via Asproni, where smart dress is the rule, while you'll need a car to reach the larger *Meccano* (Wed, Fri & Sat) and *Atrium* (winter only, Fri–Sun), located on Sássari's eastern periphery at Via Carlo Felice 33 and Via Milano 40 respectively. Music tends to be mainstream dance, entrance charges are €10–20, and they close around 6am. Check in the daily *La Nuova Sardegna* for more details on discos, concerts, **theatre** performances (see Listings on p.240–241 for theatre details) and **cinema** programmes – including open-air screenings in summer at Monte Rosello (July–Aug 9.30pm; €5). Otherwise, there's little to appeal to nightbirds from out of town, since, as in Cágliari, social life tends to be concentrated in members-only *círcoli*, or clubs.

Sássari's biggest **events** are of course the annual festivals, especially the Holy Week processions, the costumed and equestrian celebrations of the Cavalcata, forty days after Easter, and the mid-August Candelieri celebrations – all good times to be here, if you don't mind crowds. For more information on Sássari's festivals, see the box on p.230.

Bars and cafés

The old quarter

Caffè Accademia Via Torre Tonda 11. Pleasant place with an enclosed verandah for sitting with an ice cream, snack or *Marocchino* (espresso mixed with chocolate). Closed Sun.

Coffee Break Piazza Azuni 19. Cosy bar for a daytime bite or a late drink; there's a huge range of *frappés*, also *panini*, *pizzette* and pastas. Closed Sun.

Bar Daniele Piazza Tola. A comparatively quiet nook for a late drink or snack.

Caffè al Duomo Piazza del Duomo. Convenient place for a sit-down in the heart of the old town, with good coffees and pastries. Closed Mon.

Mokador Piazza Castello. A favourite local hangout by day or night, serving snacks and ice creams.

Caffè San Carlo Portici Bargone e Crispo. A traditional people-watching bar selling good ice creams.

New town

Barberry's Via Roma 18. A late-night crowd-puller, selling the usual beers and ices. Closed Sun.

Caffè Italiano Via Roma 42. Chic bar with tables outside and stylish decor within. Live music most Friday evenings, either on the pavement or in an internal room. Closed Sun.

Caffè Rau Piazza Italia. Ices, yoghurts and other snacks at this smart place, which has tables under the arcades and, in summer, on the square.

Moving on from Sássari

Sássari is on the main FS **train** network, with frequent departures to Ozieri-Chilivani, the main junction for Cágliari, Olbia and Oristano. There are frequent FdS services to Alghero.

All **bus** departures are from Sássari's bus station, though PANI is currently the only company with a ticket booth there; buy ARST and FdS tickets from bars or *tabacchi* showing the companies' stickers, such as La Piccola Tabaccheria at Corso Vico 33 (opposite the passenger entrance to the bus station), or from the newsagent inside the nearby train station.

ARST (☎079.263.9206, ⓦ www.arst.sardegna.it) run services to Alghero; Ardara; Bosa; Castelsardo; Fertilia; Fertilia airport; Monte d'Accoddi; Nuoro; Olbia; Porto Torres; Santa Teresa di Gallura; Santa Trinità di Saccargia and Stintino. Buy tickets from bars and *tabacchi*.

FdS (☎079.241.301, ⓦ www.ferroviesardegna.it) run services to Alghero; Arzachena; Bosa; Castelsardo; Fertilia; Palau and Tempio Pausánia.

Nurágica (☎079.510.494, ⓦ www.nicosgroup.it) operates daily services to Olbia and, in summer, to Stintino and the northern coast as far as Porto Cervo, taking in Porto Torres, Castelsardo and Santa Teresa di Gallura. Buy tickets on board.

PANI (☎079.236.983) operates long-distance services to Cágliari; Macomer; Nuoro; Oristano and Porto Torres. The ticket kiosk is at the bus station.

Listings

Airport bus For Fertilia airport: at least ten daily departures on ARST buses; for Olbia airport: three or four departures daily with Nurágica Tour. Both services operate from Sássari's bus station – call for departure times, or ask at a travel agency. See above for contact information and tickets.

Airport enquiries For flights from Fertilia airport, near Alghero, contact: Airone ☎079.935.034 or 848.848.880, ⓦ www.flyairone.it; Ryanair ☎079.935.282 or 199.114.114, ⓦ www.ryanair.com; Volare ☎800.454.000, ⓦ www.volare-airlines.com. For flights from Olbia, call ☎0789.52.634.

Ambulance Call ☎118 (24hr).

Banks and exchange It's not hard to find banks in Sássari, nearly all with exchange facilities. Among the central ones with ATMs are: Banca Commerciale Italiana and Banco di Nápoli, Piazza Italia; Banco di Sardegna, train station, Via Pais (corner of Corso Vittorio Emanuele) and Piazza Castello, and Unicredit Italiano, Via C. Battisti 2 (corner of Corso Vittorio Emanuele and Piazza Azuni). Most open 8.20am–1.20pm & 3–4.30pm; Unicredit also opens Sat 8.20am–12.45pm. In addition, you can change cash at the main post office (see p.241).

Bookshops Gulliver, at Portici Bargone e Crispo (on the corner of Piazza Italia) has a good choice of books on Sardinia and English-language novels. Daily 9am–9pm (closed Sun 1–5pm).

Car hire Avis, Via Mazzini 2 ☎079.235.547; Eurorent, Via Roma 56 ☎079.232.335; Hertz, Corso Vico ☎079.232.184; Maggiore, Viale Italia 3a ☎079.235.507; Saccargia, Corso Margherita di Savoia 115 ☎079.231.363; Sardinya, Viale Caprera 8/A ☎079.291.113.

Garage Autorimessa Bonfigli, Corso Margherita di Savoia 8.

Hospital Ospedale Civile Santa Annunziata, Via de Nicola ☎079.206.1000; Ospedale Civile Santa Annunziata, Via de Nicola ☎079.206.1000.

Internet access Dream Bar, Via Cavour 15–17. Mon–Sat 9am–9pm; €2.60 for 30min.

Laundry Cid at Via Duomo 24 can provide a service wash. 9am–1.15pm & 4–8.15pm.

Left luggage Train station. Mon–Sat 8am–8.30pm; €2.58 per piece for 12hr.

Markets Every morning (not Sun) in Piazza Tola, mainly household items and clothes, but also some fruit and veg. The main food market is behind, on Via Mercato, also mornings only, while Monday morning sees a much bigger open-air market of clothes, toys and tools on Piazza Segni, near the stadium (up Via Adua from Piazza Conte di Mariano at the end of Viale Umberto). An antiques fair is held in Piazza Santa Caterina on the last Sunday of each month (Sept–June 8am–1pm).

Pharmacy V. Simon on Piazza Castello, open 24hr apart from 1–4.30pm.

Post office Central Ufficio Postale is on Via Brigata Sássari. Exchange facility for cash; stamps are available from a separate room on the right, and Poste Restante (*Fermo Posta*) from yet another room entered from round the corner. Mon–Fri 8.15am–6.15pm, Sat 8.15am–1pm.

Supermarkets Íssimo on Piazza Bruno (Mon–Sat 8am–1.30pm & 4.30–8pm); Multimarkets, on the corner of Via Cavour and Via Manno (Mon–Sat 8am–8.30pm). Super Discount supermarket, 2 or 3km out of town on the Porto Torres road, is also open Sunday.

Taxis Ranks on Emiciclo Garibaldi, Piazza Castello and the train station, or call ☎079.253.939 or 079.260.060 (24hr).

Theatres The old Teatro Cívico on Corso Vittorio Emanuele (☎079.232.182) is the best place for drama or classical music in Sássari, with tickets starting at about €12; otherwise check out the programmes at the Teatro Il Ferroviário (☎079.263.3049), next to the train station, where more modern productions are staged, and the Teatro Verdi (☎079.239.479), on Via Politeama (off Piazza Castello), which also has plays, dances and concerts.

Train information FS for Cágliari; Olbia; Oristano; Ozieri; Porto Torres: ☎848.888.088, ⊛www .trenitalia.it; FdS for Alghero; Nulvi; Sorso: ☎079.241.301, ⊛www.ferroviesardegna.it.

Travel agencies Agitour (Piazza Italia 13, ☎079.231.767) and Ajo Viaggi (Piazza Fiume 1, ☎079.200.222) for internal and international tickets.

Porto Torres and the Sássari Riviera

Northwest of Sássari, the Carlo Felice highway ends its long run from Cágliari at **Porto Torres**, once the main Roman base on this coast. Although surprisingly little of historical interest has survived, what remains easily justifies a sortie: a gem of Pisan church-building, some Roman excavations and an antiquarium. A smoky industrial zone dominates the western side of town, but to the east the coast offers a choice of fine sand **beaches** along the so-called Sássari Riviera. Around Sássari's main resort of **Platamona**, these tend to get very crowded, but further east they soon empty out, sheltered from the SP81 coast road by a curtain of pines, eucalyptus and juniper trees. Inland of Porto Torres, you could make an easy stop at the pre-nuraghic sanctuary of **Monte d'Accoddi**, off the SS131. There are a few **hotels and campsites** on the coast; the alternative is to lodge in Sássari or Porto Torres.

Apart from the fifteen-minute **train** connection between Sássari and Porto Torres, non-drivers will have to rely on **bus services** for all places mentioned in this section. For the Sássari Riviera, there is a good service (marked "Buddi Buddi") leaving from Via Tavolara every forty minutes, stopping at Platamona and the less visited spots along this stretch, and there are onward links as far as Marina di Sorso. Porto Torres is equally well served by frequent buses from the provincial capital, any of which will also do for the site of Monte d'Accoddi, approximately halfway between the two towns.

Monte d'Accoddi

The stretch of the Carlo Felice highway (SS131) that links Sássari with its parent city, Porto Torres, is mainly dual-carriageway, running northwest through cultivated rolling country. Near the junction for Platamona, 12km out of Sássari, a right turn brings you round to **Monte d'Accoddi** (daily: summer 9am–6pm; winter 9am–5pm; last entry 30min before closing; €2.07) where, surrounded by cereal fields, a sanctuary dating back to the Copper Age (2450–1850 BC) has been unearthed. In fact, there's little visible construction remaining, but the long earthen ramp and the platform at its top are clearly defined. This alone sets the site apart from anything else found in Sardinia, or in the entire Mediterranean for that matter. The flat-topped pyramid would appear to have more in common with Mesopotamian or Aztec temples, hence its popular name, *ziggurat* or *ziqqurat*.

The mound, measuring 30m by 38m, tapers inward, with a long ramp ascending on one side to a flat top. The outlines of various structures – including stonewalled dwellings and even a menhir – can be seen on either side of the ramp, and there's evidence that there may have been some kind of sacred spot here from as early as 5000 BC. It's believed that this first altar was destroyed by fire and rebuilt on what is now the top of the ramp. The sanctuary was probably used for sacrifices and other ceremonial functions, though you need to make an imaginative leap to picture it as it might have once appeared – it helps to have seen the laser images in Sássari's Museo Sanna (see p.233). It's an impressive site, nonetheless, with views back to Sássari and seaward to the Golfo dell'Asinara, over the industrial chimneys of Porto Torres. **Guided visits** in Italian lasting about thirty minutes are available while the site is open (€3.10).

Porto Torres

The unprepossessing town of **PORTO TORRES**, 6km northwest of Monte d'Accoddi, is one of the main gateways into Sardinia. There have always been settlements on this site, drawn to its natural harbour and position at the mouth of the Riu Mannu, one of the island's longest rivers. Any trace of its pre-Roman past, however, has long been effaced, though there is considerable evidence of the Roman colony, Turris Libyssonis, which developed as an important shipping stop between the Italian mainland and the Iberian peninsula.

The town subsequently assumed a religious significance as the centre of a cult devoted to the *mártiri turritani* (see the box on p.244), and by the tenth century it had become the capital of one of Sardinia's four *giudicati*. Now called Torres, the town continued to wield commercial influence under the Pisans, though Saracen raids and Genoan assaults eventually led to its decline and a transfer of power inland to Sássari. The building of the Carlo Felice highway linking Porto Torres to the rest of the island contributed to its revival in the nineteenth century, and today the town is thriving once more, its economic role buoyed by the petrochemical works to the west of town as well as constant shipping traffic. Opposite the port, covered stalls provide a lively focus for the busy townsfolk by day, while the town's central axis, Corso Vittorio Emanuele, is humming with promenaders most evenings

It is not necessary to venture into the centre, however, to visit its prime attractions: the magnificent Romanesque **Basilica di San Gavino** and various **Roman remains** lie on the outskirts. Perhaps this is just as well – Porto Torres is a gritty working port that does not invite much idle rambling, although it does have a couple of good restaurants and a sensational *gelateria* off its main artery, Corso Vittorio Emanuele.

There are some good-looking **beaches** to the west of town, but their emptiness is explained by the proximity of the oil refinery, and you'll have to go almost as far as Stintino (see p.218) to find safe swimming spots in this direction. To the east, however, there are some enticing sheltered places immediately outside town where you can bathe off the rocks, and a full-scale beach resort at Platamona, 7km out from the centre (see p.245).

Arrival and information

Most **ferries** use the industrial port 2km west of town, where there's a fleet of taxis awaiting every arrival and an irregular local bus service. **Buses** arrive at

Piazza Colombo, by the old town port. The **train station** is ten minutes' walk west of here, near the museum.

Information on sights, events and transport connections can be obtained from the **Pro Loco** at Via Roma 3 (Mon–Sat 8am–noon & 3–5pm, 4–8pm in summer; ℡079.515.000), a left turn off the Corso if you're walking up from the old port. Ask here about scheduled tours to the island of Asinara (see the box on p.222); if there's no regular service, they can put you in touch with a tour company, though most excursions start from Stintino (p.218).

Accommodation

Nearby, Corso Vittorio Emanuele, holds a couple of banks with cash machines, several travel agents and most of the town's bars and restaurants. If you've been deposited by ferry in Porto Torres, you may be looking for somewhere to spend the night, though **accommodation** isn't so thick on the ground. There are three hotels in the central area, all about the same price: the *Royal* (℡079.502.278; ❹; no credit cards) at Via Sebastiano Satta 8, a side-street reached by taking Via Príncipe di Belmonte up from the Lungomare, or Via Petronia from the Corso, with eight large, if uninspiring, rooms, all with TV; the *Eiisa*, a three-star with standard rooms and low on atmosphere, right on the port at Via Mare 2 (℡079.513.260; ❹), and, further up in the town, on Via Sássari 75 (a left turn off the Corso), the much fancier *Torres* (℡079.501.604, ⓦwww.albergotorres.com; ❹), with access to a pool. Other hotels and campsites lie along the beaches and resorts east of town (see p.246).

The Basilica di San Gavino

Coming from Sássari, you can find the **Basilica di San Gavino** (8am–1pm & 3.30–8pm, Sun opens at 10.30am; €1) signposted to the left on your way into Porto Torres (from the port, continue straight up Corso Vittorio Emanuele). Originally in the open country, its present back-street location diminishes the monument's grandeur, especially in the context of the work presently being undertaken on either side of the building to display an excavated necropolis (which may be complete by the time you read this). Nonetheless, as Sardinia's largest and – according to some – finest Romanesque structure, it still makes quite an impact, worth taking a minute to absorb. The slits of windows and blind arcading around the fine yellowy stonework contribute to its austere, fortified appearance, a reminder that it survived innumerable Saracen attacks during the Middle Ages.

The basilica was started by Pisans in around 1050 and finished by 1111, over eight hundred years after the martyrdom of the *mártiri turritani* (see the box below), and on the site of a Roman necropolis. Unusually, the church was given a second apse when it was enlarged in the twelfth century, lending it a slightly confused, directionless look. Of the three lateral doors, the one on the north side is oldest, decorated with human and animal figures; the other two are later additions, one of them, the main entrance, Catalan-Gothic from 1492.

Gloomily lit by the narrow windows and barely decorated, the three naves of **the interior** are separated by 28 marble columns, dug up from the old Roman town. The main nave has a harmonious wooden roof and, at the back, a prominent catafalque carries wooden images of the three saints to whom the church is dedicated, near a dashing seventeenth-century statue of San Gavino on a horse. Across the nave, stairs lead down to the first of the basilica's two **crypts**, a long room lined with statues of saints and several Roman sarcophagi, one of them elaborately carved with figures of a seated man and woman – whose tomb this was – surrounded by Apollo and the Nine Muses.

At the far end, a door gives access to the foundations of the original paleochristian church that stood here in the sixth century. From the ante-crypt, more steps lead down to a lower crypt, where the bones of the martyrs – placed here in the nineteenth century – are displayed in arched niches together with more sarcophagi. **Guided tours** of the church and crypt are offered (May–Oct Mon–Sat 8.30am–1pm & 3.30–7pm, Sun from 10.30am; €1.50); in winter, these can be booked by calling ☎079.514.433 or 333.806.1382. A free **festival** of polyphonic music takes place in the Basilica in the first week of September – contact the tourist office for details.

The Mártiri Turritani

The Basilica di San Gavino commemorates the three martyrs, known as the **mártiri turritani**, upon whom the town's religious fame is based. **San Gavino** was a Roman commander based in the city of Turris Libyssonis, as it was then known, at the time of the emperor Diocletian's last-ditch attempt to stamp out Christianity. He was converted by two condemned Christians, Proto and Gianuario, and all three were beheaded in 304 – Gavino on a small headland to the east of town, where the little church of San Gavino a Mare now overlooks the sea.

After Diocletian's abdication the following year, the persecutions came to an end, and within two decades his successor Constantine – commemorated by an inscription in the crypt – had recognized the new religion. The town soon became a **place of pilgrimage**, and by the sixth century a paleochristian church existed on the site. The construction of the present building – the largest and most impressive basilica on the island – both reflected and further enhanced the prestige that the cult devoted to the martyrs had attained by the eleventh century. When the bones of the saints were exhumed in 1614, "frequent perfumes" and various miracles were reported. The three are commemorated every May 3, when the wooden figures displayed in the nave are carried in **procession** from the Basilica to San Gavino a Mare.

The Antiquarium and the Roman remains

The other main focus of interest in Porto Torres lies by the train station on the western edge of town (take Via Ponte Romano from the Corso). Keep your eyes open to locate the poorly-marked **Antiquarium Turritano** (Tues–Sun 9am–8pm, closes 11pm on certain days July–Sept; €2), which displays finds from various digs in the area of Turris Libyssonis, including some of the most interesting items unearthed from the remains of the Roman city that extend alongside and behind the museum. The ground floor is devoted to ceramics, votive ornaments, mosaics and frescos from the central baths, and there's a model of the archeological site. First-floor exhibits are mainly from the site and from the necropolis on Monte Agellu, where the church of San Gavino now stands, and include a Roman lead sarcophagus.

The archeological site, or **Palazzo di Re Bárbaro**, is entered from the museum. The so-called Palace of King Barbarus gets its popular name from the semi-mythical Roman governor who presided over the martyrdom of the town's saints. The site principally consists of the shattered main baths complexes, or *terme*, of the Roman town, dating from the third or fourth century BC, some well-preserved mosaic floors and a network of flagstoned roads bordered by stumps of columns. A lot of it won't mean much to most visitors, but you can get a much better picture by joining an hour-long **guided tour** of both museum and archeological area, available all day (€2.50). The ruins are used in summer for occasional late-evening **exhibitions and concerts**.

Another 200m further out of town, taking the left fork, you can glimpse the seven arches of the **Roman bridge** crossing the Riu Mannu near the turn-off for the Stintino–Alghero road. This well-preserved monument was used by traffic until the 1980s, but now looks sadly redundant on the outskirts of town, almost hidden between newer bridges and thick growths of bamboo. You can visit the bridge on the same guided tours that go round the museum and archeological site (€3.50 for all); ask at the museum.

Eating

Porto Torres has a plethora of **eating** places, most of them geared towards fast food. The *Elisa* hotel, for example, has a handy and inexpensive self-service canteen on the ground floor. Better fare is available at *Tana* on Via Cavour, a side street off Corso Vittorio Emanuele; it's a pizzeria/ristorante with swift service, friendly staff, and a wood-burning oven for the cheap and tasty pizzas (closed Tues Oct–June). On the other side of the Corso, *Gli Ulivi* offers a tourist menu for €10 with plenty of choice and pavement seating in summer (closed Sun in winter). For a do-it-yourself lunch or food for the ferry, drop in at the *La Bottega* at the bottom of the Corso; they sell *panini* and a range of local cheeses, salamis, wines, yoghurt and bread. Any of the **bars** along the Corso, such as *Gli Ulivi*, would do for a sit-down with a drink. Finally, before or after a visit to San Gavino, take time to sample one of the fifty-odd flavours of **ice cream** from *Gelateria Capriccio* at Corso Vittorio Emanuele 114 (open until late in summer): utterly irresistible, they come in cones, cups and frappés, up to five flavours at a time.

Platamona

A small, summer and weekend beach resort for exhausted city-dwellers, **PLATAMONA** is just a twenty-minute drive from Sássari, linked by regular local buses (every 40min from Via Tavolara). A right turn off the Porto Torres road brings you through a eucalyptus wood to a brief parade of bars, restaurants and lidos. The few sections of pavement are strewn with the wares of Senegalese and Korean traders, while children's play areas, bars, pizzerias, even a pool, stand a stone's throw from the sea. If you want the facilities and don't mind the crowds, you might as well stop here for a swim. At the lidos you'll pay a few euros a day for an umbrella and deck chair, and the use of showers and car park (elsewhere car parks charge around €0.60 per hour).

There are all kinds of fast-food places around, none of them particularly exciting, and you can stay about 500m east from the centre at the *Toluca* **hotel** (T079.310.234; ⑤), with half- or full-board only available in August (half-board is €101 per person), and good reductions are available outside peak season. Some rooms have balconies with sea views, all have bathrooms and TVs, and there's a pool. You can **camp** right next to the sea at the *Golfo dell'Asinara* (June–Sept; T079.310.230, Wwww.campingasinara.it), which also has a pool and tennis court, and caravans and chalets are available for rent (€50–90 a day for two people). **Buses** from Sássari stop right outside.

East along the coast

Heading eastwards, the beaches get wilder and more secluded, offering numerous hideaways for a private swim or even camping rough in the endless pinewoods backing the sands (being extra careful not to start fires). Small lanes disappear north off the SP81 coast road, leading to relatively isolated spots with just enough space for a few vehicles and a bar in summer, and surrounded by sandy wilderness. The buses from Sássari (marked "Buddi Buddi") conveniently stop all along this road, so you can choose your spot and take your chances. If you want the comforts of a three-star **campsite**, however, head for *Li Nibari*, signposted off the road after a few kilometres (T079.310.303, Wwww .campinglinibari.com). Bar, restaurants and a supermarket cater to a crowd of campers, and there are also sports facilities but no pool – the private beach is just metres away. Two- and four-bed caravans and bungalows are available for €47–78 for two in high season, half that at other times.

There's another concentration of beachside activity at **Marina di Sorso**, albeit on a much smaller scale than at Platamona. The beaches here are nothing special: again, you've only got to shift a few hundred metres to find perfect isolation. Five kilometres inland, the village of **Sorso** lies above a fertile valley, whose fruit and vegetable produce liberally fills the pavements. The local *Cannonau* wine is one of Sardinia's best, and the place is also famed for its baskets woven with dwarf-palm leaves. There's not a lot to look at in the village, but there is a **pensione**, the small *Romangia*, on Via Porto Torres (T079.352.868; ②), which has its own restaurant.

Above Sorso, and almost joined to it, the sister village of **Sénnori** has a winding road back to Sássari (10km).

Anglona

Northeast of Sássari, the compact region of **Anglona** is a mountainous landscape scattered with the remains of a "petrified forest". Bound by Logudoro and Gallura to the south and east, the area's rocky northern littoral is the perfect setting for Anglona's main town, **Castelsardo**, picturesquely draped over a promontory at one end of the Golfo dell'Asinara. The robust fortified citadel here was the Doria power-base in Sardinia for nearly 250 years, and the historic centre preserves a pungent medieval flavour, though the modern lower town is mostly dedicated to milking the coach tours that regularly call in here. Castelsardo makes the area's best **place to stay**, a short drive from some good beaches and the ruined castle of **Castel Doria**, an inland outpost of the Dorias. A scenic but tortuous drive further south brings you to another connection with the powerful Genoan dynasty, the village of **Chiaramonti**, a fast 35-kilometre ride from Sássari.

Non-drivers travelling in Anglona will have to rely on ARST **bus services** for most places mentioned in this section. Castelsardo is well served by frequent buses from Sássari, though the other inland destinations covered here have only infrequent connections.

Castelsardo

Travelling east along the coastal SS200, the first view of **CASTELSARDO** is an impressive one, the reddish-grey houses huddled below the stout castle, with the cathedral's tall campanile visible to one side and a belt of scrub-covered hills to landward. The powerful Genoan Doria dynasty established a stronghold at Castelsardo at the start of the twelfth century, giving it the name of "Castelgenovese". Embroiled in the power clashes between Genoa, Pisa and Spain throughout its ensuing history, the strategically crucial town was one of the last Genoan centres in the Torres *giudicato* to hold out against the Spaniards. When he finally took possession of the town in 1448, Alfonso V immediately changed its name to Castel Aragonese, though the locals were mollified when, in 1511, Charles V accorded the port the same rights and privileges as the rival Spanish sea-base at Alghero. Supported by 4000 French troops, the Dorias made a last, futile effort to recapture their home-base in 1527, then virtually disappeared from the Sardinian scene altogether. The town's present, safely neutral name was given by the Savoyard kings in 1769.

Today, its small port still active, Castelsardo is one of the few fishing centres on the north Sardinian coast, while its well-preserved citadel and photogenic setting above a small beach have assisted its transformation into a fully-fledged **holiday resort**. Tourists are also lured by the town's pre-eminence as a centre of Sard handicrafts, which are prominently displayed in stores in the lower town and dotted around the narrow lanes of the old quarter (see the box on p.248).

It's possible to visit Castelsardo on a day trip from Sássari, just an hour away on frequent buses (last one back at 8.50pm). However, despite its somewhat tacky side, it's a pleasant spot to spend a little more time, especially outside August, and an excellent place to break your journey travelling up the coast. The **Easter festivities** are known for the dramatic torchlit procession, *Lunissanti*, a tradition pre-dating the Spanish conquest of the town, in which a cortege of cowled figures threads through the old town on Easter Monday to the accompaniment of medieval choral chants in Latin and Sard. The town's other major festival is August 2, when the Madonna degli Ángeli is celebrated with games and traditional dancing.

Arrival and information

All ARST **buses** stop at the central Piazza Pianedda, at the bottom of the old town, and there's another bus stop by the beach in the lower town. If you're driving, leave your vehicle in the piazza, or in the car park reached from the piazza's top-right corner. You *could* drive up the main Via Nazionale and take your chances parking on the road leading to the citadel, but don't get tangled up in the tight web of alleys that make up the old centre unless you want to get involved in frantic reversing and scraped bodywork.

Artigianato in Castelsardo

Many people come to Castelsardo purely to shop, and the lower town has plenty of outlets to meet this demand, mostly geared towards parties on coach stops. All come in search of the famed Castelsardo **artigianato**, or handicrafts, which has grown in the last twenty years from a small cottage industry to a major year-round money-spinner. Cork, coral and ceramic goods are here in abundance, as well as shelves full of the African-looking Sard wooden masks, but the main craft for which Castelsardo is known is *l'intreccio*, or **basketwork**. Straw, wicker, reeds, raffia and asphodel leaves are all used to create an incredible variety of containers, trays and furniture, though the material most associated with Castelsardo is dwarf-palm leaves, locally picked. You can see plenty of examples in Castelsardo's countless small shops and stores, but you'll have to wade through a large proportion of junk to find the ideal gift or souvenir, and much of it may have been made elsewhere, using synthetic materials.

A good place to visit before shopping is the **museum of basket-weaving** in Castelsardo's castle (see p.249), to get an idea of what the best examples of the genre should look like. As for the emporia, don't spend too much time shopping around – you'll see the same products everywhere, with very similar price tags. You should, however, at least view the merchandise at **ISOLA** on the main road at Via Nazionale 104, a branch of the network of officially-recognized outlets for Sardinian craftwork (Mon–Sat 8.30am–1pm & 5–8.30pm). Alongside the raffia vases and wicker products on display are carpets, ceramics, wall hangings, metalwork items, masks, handbags and carved wooden ornaments; prices, however, tend to be on the high side. If you've honed your bargaining technique, there's no reason why you shouldn't deal directly with the producers up in the old town, where you can see the locals working the stuff on their doorsteps. This is the place to find cheaper prices, if sometimes cruder products. You can also find some good work in nearby villages such as Tergu (see p.251), where the quality is at least as good as that in town.

A small **tourist office** operates out of a temporary kiosk in Piazza Pianedda during the summer (June–Aug daily 9am–1pm & 5–9pm – times may vary), or consult Ⓦ www.castelsardo.net. For **banks**, there's a Banco di Sardinia with an ATM just up from the piazza, another on the road down to the Lungomare (Mon–Fri 8.20am–1.20pm & 2.35–3.35pm).

Accommodation

The seafront, Lungomare Anglona, is where Castelsardo's meagre choice of **accommodation** can be found; it's about a one-kilometre walk from the citadel. Many of the hotels will demand a minimum stay of three nights or even a week in mid-August. If everywhere else is full, try the beach resort of Lu Bagnu (see p.251), where there's also a good hostel; the nearest campsites lie a few kilometres east of town (see p.252).

Castello Lungomare Anglona 15 ℡079.470.062, Ⓦwww.gattei.it/castello. This 1970s-style three-star has rooms with balconies and a spacious roof terrace, but it's all rather run-down and the back-facing rooms are grim. Closed Nov. ④

Marina Via Roma 108 ℡079.470.137. Overlooking the town beach, this is a simple holiday hotel with fairly basic rooms, only a few of which have sea views, but all have showers.

Breakfast is extra. Open March–Sept. ③

Nadir Via Colle di Frigiano 1 ℡079.470.297, Ⓦwww.hotelnadir.com. The unfortunately named *Nadir* is actually one of the two smartest hotels on the Lungomare, a considerable step up in price from the other choices (though rates are up to fifty percent lower outside the peak months). There's also a good restaurant. ⑥

Pinna Lungomare Anglona 7 ☎079.470.168. Castelsardo's cosiest option is not as small as it appears, above a popular trattoria; half-board (€60 per person) or more is required during August. ❷

Riviera Lungomare Anglona 1 ☎079.470.143, ⓦwww.hotelriviera.net. Like the *Nadir*, this has plush, fully-equipped rooms and a good seafront restaurant, but is slightly nearer the centre. Prices plummet in low season. Open April–Sept. ❸

The Town

It's a steep but rewarding ascent up the streets and steps of Castelsardo's old quarter. Home-made baskets and other artifacts are displayed in doorways, brightly-coloured plants are draped over walls, and time-weathered arches and crumbling doorways adorn the minute lanes. Glimpses of the rocky shore and sea below bring relief from the closed, insular air of the place, though the best views, of course, are from the top, crowned by the battlements of the heavily restored **castello** (April–May daily 9.30am–1pm & 3–7.30pm; June daily 9.30am–1pm & 3–8.30pm; July–Aug daily 9am–midnight; Sept daily 9.30am–1pm & 2.30–9.30pm; Oct & March Tues–Sun 9.30am–1pm & 3–6.30pm; Nov–Feb Tues–Sun 9.30am–1pm & 3–5.30pm; €2). From here, it's an uninterrupted prospect across the gulf to the isle of Asinara, off Sardinia's northwestern point; to the northeast, it's sometimes possible to sight the coast of Corsica – though for this the conditions need to be particularly good. The sunsets here are especially memorable.

The abode of the powerful Doria dynasty for two centuries, and for ten years home to Eleonora d'Arborea and Brancaleone Doria after their marriage in 1376 (see p.165), the castle now houses the **Museo dell'Intreccio Mediterraneo** (same hours as castle), a basketwork and weaving museum artfully incorporated into the small chambers. There's much to admire in this assortment of bowls, plates, bottles and lobster traps, often skilfully patterned, some of the most prized items woven from the leaves of the local dwarf-palm. For the most part, these are the traditional tools of everyday life, utilized by bakers, farmers and fishermen; there's even a grass-woven boat here – the truncated-looking *fassoni* used around Oristano (see p.170). But without any labelling of the displays or much explanation of any kind, the exhibition becomes somewhat monotonous to all but a dedicated enthusiast, and it's diverting to find amid this collection a quotation from *Ulysses*, translated into the Sard dialect, daubed onto a door; a remnant of a former art installation, it speaks of local people's attachment to the land.

From the castle, it's a short walk round to the **church of Santa Maria** (daily: summer 7am–8pm; winter 7am–5.30pm), a misshapen building squeezed into the available space. The richly decorated church holds a special role among the townspeople, as the repository of the sacred *Critu Nieddu*, or Black Christ, a fourteenth-century crucifix, as well as being the focus of the Easter Monday processions.

After Santa Maria's cramped site, it's a surprise to find, lower down, the relatively large terrace that accommodates Castelsardo's cathedral, **Sant'Antonio Ábate** (daily: summer 7am–8pm; winter 7am–5.30pm), but the gradient is not so steep here, and there is even room for a public garden laid out on the ramparts and the rocky slope below. Overlooking reddish boulders washed by the sea, it's a lovely spot, the octagonal campanile with its majolica-tiled cupola adding a splash of colour. The church itself retains some evidence of the original Gothic structure, and its sixteenth-century rebuilding and Baroque accretions are not unsympathetic. In front of the painted wooden pulpit hanging off one of the piers, at the centre of the fussy marble altarpiece, the main treasure here is the **Madonna with Angels**, a fragment of a work by a local fifteenth-century painter known simply as Maestro di Castelsardo, whose synthesis of Italian and Flemish Gothic elements were hugely influential in Sardinia. Other items worth looking out for are the sculpted figures of musicians and animals on the capitals of the pillars on either side of the altar, and, behind this, some good carved choir-stalls. To the left of the altar, a flight of steps leads down to the **cripta** (daily: summer 7am–1pm & 3.30–8pm; winter 7am–1pm & 3.30–5.30pm; €2), where there is much more of interest, notably more sections of the *retablo* on the altarpiece, one depicting four apostles, another – with liberal use of Byzantinesque gold – showing the holy trinity. Connected by narrow stairs, the four sombre stone chambers display various other items of religious art, and there's a glorious rendition of the archangel Michael slaying a dragon.

There's little else of specific interest to see in the old centre – and, beyond the shops and trattorias, neither does the newer town at sea-level have much to offer. The disordered agglomeration of modern constructions, many of them boxy holiday homes, scars the shoreline, though the rocky cove immediately below and west of the citadel, sheltering an attractive sand beach, is undeniably pretty. On the coast to the west, you'll pass the **Porto di Frigianu** fishing anchorage, watched over by an old defensive tower, and the new marina, where posher boats are moored. There are a couple of bars if you want to sit and watch the low-key activity here. Eastward, there's another small beach squeezed up among the rocks on the far side of town.

Eating

Castelsardo has a good selection of places to eat and drink, some (in the old town) quite expensive. There are plenty more bars and trattorias lower down, some with good-value tourist menus; it's worth remembering that the *Pensione Pinna* here has a cheerful trattoria with a terrace facing the sea, and the *Marina* hotel also has a fairly regular pizzeria/ristorante with sea views (see p.248 for both).

Aragona Via Manganella. Just along from the cathedral, a bar which also serves pasta dishes and other light meals until late at night, a good choice if you're looking for snacks with views. Closed Mon in winter. Inexpensive.

Bounty Via Lamarmora 12. Each of the two floors here has its own character, the brick-vaulted lower floor connected by spiral staircase to the more modern part upstairs. Tourist menus are €13 (meat) and €15.50 (fish). Closed Wed in winter. Moderate.

Il Cormorano Via Colombo 5. Smartish place round the corner from Piazza Pianedda, with good local dishes and a verandah. Closed Tues in winter. Moderate–expensive.

La Guardiola ✆079.470.428. Just below Castelsardo's castle, this restaurant serves quality dishes and has a terrace with romantic views over the sea, but it's pricey. Closed Mon in winter. Moderate–expensive.

La Trattoria Via Nazionale 20. An excellent mid-range choice on the main road up from Piazza Pianedda, informal and friendly. The menu includes creamy *pasta mazzafrissa*, made with sheep's cheese (minimum two people). May close Mon in winter. Moderate.

Around Castelsardo

Castelsardo makes an ideal base for exploring the rest of the Anglona region, whose contoured terrain is a thinly-inhabited area of stirring vistas. West of town, the appeal of **Lu Bagnu** is mainly in its seaside location, but most of the interest hereabouts lies inland, where scattered historical relics make good targets for rural excursions. Of these, the pair of medieval churches at or near the villages of **Tergu** and **Bulzi** are good examples of Sardinia's

Pisan-Romanesque style. Much older remains can be seen at the remarkable **Roccia dell'Elefante**, a huge trachyte rock in the shape of an elephant, and in the village of **Sédini**, where there are prehistoric *domus de janas*, while the island's later nuraghic culture is represented by the nearby **Nuraghe Su Tesoru**. For scenery, however, head deeper inland, to where the Doria strongholds of **Castel Doria** and **Chiaramonti** watch over Anglona's mountainous borders. Back on the coast, **Valledoria** is a thriving holiday locality at the mouth of the River Coghinas, with good swimming from its beaches.

Lu Bagnu and Tergu

Five kilometres west of Castelsardo, **LU BAGNU** has good swimming in limpid waters off the rocks at the bottom of cliffs, but the modern holiday surroundings may put you off spending much time here. You might, however, get a taste of the resort's bar-life on a night out from Castelsardo, and you could find yourself **staying** here if that town is full: the cheapest option is *Ampurias*, off the main road on Via Imperia (℡079.474.008, Ⓦwww.ampurias.net; ❹), and in front of the Sacro Cuore beach, with a restaurant attached. On the edge of the resort, signposted at Via Sardegna 1, the modern *Golfo dell'Asinara* **youth hostel** lies amid greenery and with great views from its wide terrace (Easter & May–Sept; ℡079.474.031, Ⓔostello.asinara@tiscalinet.it). Beds in dorms are €11, or you can sleep in a two- or three-bed room with en-suite facilities (€15). Prices include breakfast, and you can eat dinner here for €10.

From Lu Bagnu, a road winds 7km inland to **TERGU**, a small village whose square-faced Pisan-Romanesque church of **Nostra Signora di Tergu** (also called Santa Maria) dates from the early thirteenth century. The facade is the most interesting feature, with blind arcading and red trachyte stone alternating with paler limestone, and there are the ruins of a once-powerful Benedictine monastery alongside. A visit to the village would be a good opportunity to search out examples of local craftwork, often similar to the items on sale in Castelsardo, but cheaper.

The Roccia dell'Elefante and Sédini

Exiting eastwards from Castelsardo, the road soon leaves the sea behind. Right by the junction for Sédini, you can't miss the famous **Roccia dell'Elefante**, a wind-eroded rock structure whose elephant-shaped profile is featured on hundreds of postcards. It's difficult to miss the trachytic monolith on the roadside, its drooping trunk practically swishing the passing vehicles. Clearly the rock has long held an emblematic power, for there are some pre-nuraghic *domus de janas* tombs hewn from beneath it; look carefully on the wall of the right-hand chamber to make out a carving of the curling bull-horns which are such a pronounced motif on nuraghic figurines.

At **SÉDINI** itself, another 11km southeast on the SP134, there are some more of these ancient tombs gouged out of a massive calcareous rock known as **La Rocca**, situated right on the main road in the centre of the village. The chambers were utilized as a prison in the Middle Ages, incorporated into a dwelling in the nineteenth century, and currently hold a small exhibition of agricultural tools and other ethnographic items. In summer, a local group of volunteers is on hand to provide guided tours of the tombs, at other times you may have to book at the *Municipio* 200m away (℡079.588.581). Many of Sédini's houses are Aragonese-Gothic in style, including the church of **Sant'Andrea**, dating from 1517, with a fine square portal and a handsome pointed campanile alongside.

Bulzi, Chiaramonti and around

Arguably the prettiest of the churches scattered around Sássari's hinterland is **San Pietro delle Immágini** (also called San Pietro di Simbranos). Marooned in a flowery meadow in a valley below **BULZI**, a village 7km east of Sédini on the SP134, it makes a picturesque sight. The church was founded by monks from Monte Cassino in 1112, became an important Benedictine centre during the twelfth and thirteenth centuries, and owes its excellent state of preservation today to its safe distance from the ravagings of coastal raiders in the past.

The **facade**, added together with the apse and transept in the thirteenth century, shows a singular blend of Romanesque and Gothic styles, with a brown-and-white striped pattern similar to that of Tergu's church, and possibly worked on by the same builders. The Gothic elements are stronger here, however, with pointed blind arches on the second level surmounted by a pediment, and there is no belltower. Above the door, a lunette holds a crude relief of an abbot with arms raised and two monks – the "images" from which the church takes its name. Worth looking at in the interior is the stoup formed from trunks of petrified – or, more accurately, silicified – trees, of which the surrounding area holds a considerable quantity. You'll be lucky to find the church open, though: weekends are the best bet, or be here for the Festa di San Pietro, forty days after Easter.

If you're taking the slow but scenic route back towards Sássari, you'll pass through the village of **Laerru**, 4km further south, which boasts an international reputation for the carving of briar, olivewood and juniper pipes. Shortly before the good SS127 Sássari–Tempio road, **Chiaramonti** has an intricate network of narrow streets grouped around the base of a Doria fortification from the twelfth century. Though not particularly high (440m), the ruins offer a fantastic vantage point over the mountains on all sides, most strikingly Monte Limbara (1359m) to the east and Monte Sassu (640m) – a famed haunt of bandits and kidnappers – to the southeast.

Nuraghe Su Tesoru and Valledoria

Alternatively, head east from the Roccia dell'Elefante on the Valledoria road, making a stop almost immediately to see the well-preserved **Nuraghe Su Tesoru** (more properly known as Nuraghe Paddaggiu), erected during the last phase of nuragh-building. The niched central room and stairs up to the second storey still survive.

By the time you reach **VALLEDORIA**, you're back by the sea and in holiday country, with beaches as far as the eye can see, finally giving way to the pink rocks around Isola Rossa (see p.297), some 10km away. Of the three **campsites** in the area, the best is *La Foce* (mid-May to Sept; ☏079.582.109, ⓦwww.foce.it), with excellent facilities including a pool, and a lagoon across which a small craft ferries campers to the good sand beach on the other side. Bungalows and caravans are available (from €60 for two in high season). From the campsite, New Kayak Sardinia rents out **kayaks and canoes** in summer (from €7 per hour), and lead tours (from €16 for 3hr) up the River Coghinas. ARST and Nurágica buses to Santa Teresa di Gallura stop several times daily at Valledoria, from where you have to walk or hitch. Among the **hotels** in the area, there are two on Valledoria's Corso Europa, including the modern, fully-equipped *Park Hotel* (☏079.582.800, ⓦwww.parkhotelweb.it; ④), with a garden; others lie closer to the sea in the La Ciaccia and San Pietro neighbourhoods.

Castel Doria

Inland of Valledoria, follow the course of the River Coghinas for 8km up the

Perfugas road to reach the poetic ruins of **Castel Doria**. Poised over the Lago di Castel Doria, the castle (now inaccessible) was built here in the twelfth century to guard Anglona's eastern approaches. It's a deserted, craggy spot, full of atmosphere, and repays a brief wander. Marking the boundary with Gallura, the river feeds the artificially created lake, which has allowed the drainage of Anglona's only plain of any size, around Valledoria. The lake holds one of Sardinia's four main hydrothermal spring sites, whose therapeutic mud baths draw spa devotees from all over Italy.

South of Sássari: Logudoro

The country south of Sássari is sparsely populated, consisting of swathes of sloping fields interspersed by small villages. The historical name, **Logudoro**, derives from the former *giudicato* of Torres, whose heartland this was. Its former wealth and importance is attested today by the presence of numerous noble churches throughout the region, many of them established by Pisan merchants. The present-day inhabitants of the territory retain the distinction of having the purest form of Sard, softer and more rolling than the island's other dialects.

Although few places justify a lengthy stay around here, several are well worth a stop en route to somewhere else, notably the Pisan churches of **Santissima Trinità di Saccargia**, **Sant'Antíoco di Bisarcio** and **San Pietro di Sorres**, each stranded in open countryside, though within easy reach of the main roads. Close to the last of these stands one of Sardinia's most important nuraghic complexes, the **Nuraghe Santu Antine**, whose construction and background is lucidly explained in the nuraghic museum at the nearby village of **Torralba**. The area's only town of any size, **Ozieri**, holds remnants of the neolithic culture to which it has lent its name, and also has some of the only **accommodation** to be found hereabouts.

Ozieri-Chilivani is a major rail junction for **trains** to Sássari, Olbia and Cágliari, and Logudoro's former capital of **Árdara** is also on the Sássari line; other places covered here really need a car to reach, though most villages have a sketchy service of one or two **buses** daily from Sássari. Note that the village of Torralba is a stop on the Sássari–Oristano PANI bus route, though visitors to the nuraghic site will have to walk or hitch the last 4km.

Santissima Trinità di Saccargia

Some fifteen kilometres southeast of Sássari (and glimpsable from the Sássari–Chilivani train), the church of **Santissima Trinità di Saccargia** (April–Oct daily 9am–sunset; €1, or €2.50 with guided tour) makes a stunning apparition to anyone travelling on the main Sássari–Olbia SS597. Standing tall and solitary amid the surrounding flat country, its zebra-striped facade and belltower conspicuously mark its Pisan origins.

The church was built in 1116, and supposedly owes its remote location to a divine visitation that took place while the *giudice* of Torres and his wife stopped here on the way to Porto Torres, where they intended to pray for a child at San Gavino's shrine. During the night, a celestial messenger informed the *giudice*'s wife that the pilgrimage was unnecessary since she was already pregnant, whereupon the grateful *giudice* built an abbey on this spot. The basalt and limestone facade was added some sixty years later, and, like the rest of the structure, has survived remarkably well, although the abbey's outhouses are either ruined or converted into barns, and much of what you see of the church has been subject to a thorough restoration. Some of the carved dogs, cows and other beasts on the lovely Gothic **capitals** at the top of the entrance porch, for example, are reconstructions. Nonetheless, the place has an authentic medieval air, best appreciated in the absence of one of the coach parties that regularly descends.

Showing elements of Lombard architecture, the stark, tall-naved **interior** is mostly unadorned, but for a gilded wooden pulpit embedded in one wall and some vivid eleventh- or twelfth-century **frescos** covering the central apse. These, illustrating scenes from the life of Christ, are attributed to a Pisan artist and are a rare example in Italy of this type of Romanesque mural. Look out, too, for the stone image at the front of the nave on the left, possibly representing Costantino I, the *giudice* supposed to have founded the church and thought to be buried here. Masses are held in Santa Trinità di Saccargia during the weeks leading up to Easter, and at some other religious festivals.

Árdara

The nondescript village of **ÁRDARA**, 15km further east along the SS597, shows few traces of its one-time role as capital of the Logudoro region, though the restored basilica of **Santa Maria del Regno** (daily 9am–1pm & 3–7pm), visible immediately on entering the village, hints at its former glory. Built by Pisans in around 1100, using black and brown basalt, the Romanesque church provided the model for a series of lesser churches in the region. The interior, which has frescoed columns, is dominated by an ornate tableau of thirty gilded panels behind the altar, the work of various artists in the sixteenth century (look for the date 1515 painted below the hand of Jesus at the bottom of the central panel). There's plenty to take in here: scenes from the lives of the Virgin Mary, Jesus and various prophets, saints and martyrs. Some of the scenes are reproduced on the frescoed columns. The church was the venue for the marriage in 1239 of Enzo, son of Frederick II of Hohenstaufen, by which he came into possession of the *giudicati* of Torres and Gallura, enabling him to claim the title of king of Sardinia. Though Enzo abandoned wife and island soon afterwards, he clung on to the title, even during the last 23 years of his life spent in prison in Bologna. The church is the focus of a costumed **carnival** with horses every July 29. If it's closed when you visit, call ☎079.400.069 or 338.569.0009 to request entry. Masses are held Monday–Saturday at 6pm, Sunday at 10.30am.

There's yet another isolated Pisan relic visible about 10km further along this road on the left, the church of **Sant'Antíoco di Bisarcio** (daily 9am–1pm & 3–7pm). Built in 1090 and reconstructed in 1170, it was later given cathedral status and was the venue for the coronations of many of Logudoro's *giudici*. Subsequent centuries saw the gradual abandonment and dilapidation of the church, though a long-overdue restoration should retrieve something of its original splendour. In the meantime, it may be closed, though it's worth checking out anyway, and even if you can't enter, a walk round the building is enough to appreciate the French-style portico, apse, blind arcading and *campanile*, and the views over the hills.

Ozieri and around

A signposted right turn from the main SS597 brings you to **OZIERI**, the main centre for this area. Arrayed along a slope that creates a natural amphitheatre, it's a wealthy-looking place, with stuccoed, sometimes faded, Neoclassical houses, though you'll also come across vividly-coloured contemporary murals depicting scenes of rural life and the horrors of war. The town's prominence stems from the surrounding fertile country, mainly used for cattle-rearing and dairy-producing; the best-known local products, however, are the little almond biscuits known as *suspirus* (also called *sospiri*, or *guelfos*), for sale in any of the town's bakeries and most bars.

The town has given its name to a whole era of Sard prehistory, the **Ozieri culture**, which prevailed mainly in the northwest of Sardinia in the fourth and third millennia BC. This is also known as the San Michele culture, after the grotto where most of the finds identified with it were discovered, many of which can be seen in the town's **Museo Archeologico** (Tues–Fri 9am–1pm & 4–7pm, Sat & Sun 9.30am–12.30pm, extended opening in summer; €2, or €3.50 with grotto), annexed to the Convento Clarisse, signposted at the top of the town, a few minutes' walk from the main Piazza Garibaldi. The displays include the bone jewellery and ceramics painted with a spiral pattern that are characteristic of this people, and other objects retrieved from the local area, notably nuraghic ornaments, Punic and Roman coins, and domestic items from the Middle Ages.

You can visit the **Grotta di San Michele** (guided tours daily 9am–1pm & 3–7pm; €2.60) where many of these finds were unearthed, a walk or brief drive from here along the panoramic Viale Vittorio Veneto, on the northern edge of town (next to the sports ground, signposted). The complex of caves consists of little more than a deep hole in the limestone, with connecting tunnels and passages, where the key items relating to the Ozieri culture were discovered in 1914.

Back in the lower part of town, make a stop at Ozieri's **Cattedrale dell'Immacolata**, whose Neoclassical facade fronts an Aragonese-Gothic structure overladen with Neoclassical and Baroque additions. Among several sculptures and paintings here, there's a noteworthy polyptych, the *Madonna di Loreto*, its seven panels painted by the so-called Maestro di Ozieri, the foremost Sard painter of the sixteenth century.

The last Sunday of September sees Ozieri's biggest **festa**, La Sagra della Madonna del Rimédio, during which groups from all over the island participate in medieval chanting and costumed processions.

Ozieri wouldn't be a bad place to bed down if you're travelling in these parts: there's only one **hotel** in town, however, the *Mastino*, a large, modern, rather characterless place with a restaurant at Via Vittorio Veneto 13 (℡079.787.041, ℻079.787.059; ❸), on the road to Pattada, 15km west, where there is an alternative choice (see p.320). Regular buses connect Ozieri with the train station 10km west towards **Chilivani**, a main junction for passengers between Sássari, Olbia and Cágliari, and close to the island's most important racecourse and horse-breeding stables (visible from the train).

Torralba and around

Thirty kilometres south of Sássari, an easy detour from the SS131 takes you to the village of **TORRALBA**, whose only interest is a remarkable nuraghic museum, a short distance from one of Sardinia's greatest prehistoric monuments, the Nuraghe Santu Ántine. It doesn't matter which you visit first – the same ticket will let you into both. Easy to find in the centre of the village, the **Museo di Torralba** (daily: April–Oct 9am–8pm; Nov–March 9am–5pm; €3, including Nuraghe Santu Ántine) focuses on the nearby nuraghic complex. You can see a model of this on the ground floor, though most of the material relating to this is displayed upstairs in the **Sala Santu Ántine**, including some of the 17,000 shards of pottery found on the site, which testify to the continuous use of the monument and surrounding area from the twelfth century BC until the Roman era. Other items include ceramic combs, smith's tools and projectiles, while bits and pieces of Phoenician and Greek ware illustrate the extensive trading links that this settlement enjoyed. Also on the first floor, the **Sala Romana** has examples of columns and capitals dug up in the area, with displays of coins and pottery fragments, and there are more Roman finds in the garden, reached by steps from the Sala Santu Antine, including a collection of inscribed milestones found alongside the Cágliari–Olbia road, the first one built by the Romans on the island.

The Nuraghe Santu Ántine

The **Nuraghe Santu Ántine** (daily: April–Oct 9am–sunset; Nov–March 9am–5pm; €3, including Museo di Torralba) lies just over 4km south of the village, in the heart of the so-called Valle dei Nuraghi, an area copiously dotted with the ancient structures. This royal palace is the biggest and most impressive of them – hence its common name *Nuraghe Majore* – and is considered to be technically the finest nuraghic structure on the island. The oldest sections date back to the fifteenth century BC, though the site was continuously worked on and added to during its long history, not least by the Romans. Built of square basalt blocks, the central complex consists of three external bastions, mostly crumbled, connected by a defensive wall and grouped around the original massive three-storey circular tower, with walls up to 5m thick and 17.5m high. The tower is thought to have once reached 21m, before the uppermost of its three circular rooms was demolished in the nineteenth century. Corridors and staircases link the different parts of the tower, and the grounds include a well in an internal courtyard. It's a fascinating place to scramble around, an intricate network of steps, ramps, chambers and curving passages.

From the railed area on top, other *nuraghi* are visible among the cultivated fields – though the closest and most perfect specimen is a recent reconstruction. A scattering of circular huts lies around the walls of the main complex, the ruins of the nuraghic village on which Carthaginian and Roman structures were added. Note that guided tours are available (€2), though not always in English. A bar at the entrance to the site serves rolls and other snacks, and there's a shop with guides to the site in English. The site lies about a kilometre north of an exit from the SS131.

San Pietro di Sorres

The hilly area north of Torralba holds one of the best-preserved of Sardinia's Romanesque churches, the twelfth-century basilica of **San Pietro di Sorres** (Mon & Fri 8.30–11.45am & 3.30–5.45pm, Tues–Thurs & Sat 8.30–11.45am & 3.30–7.15pm, Sun 8.30am–12.30pm & 3.30–7.15pm). Surmounting a bluff with sweeping views over the villages of Bonnanaro and Borutta, the former cathedral is still attached to a Benedictine convent (accounting for its immaculate condition), whose monks have become specialized in book restoration among other fields. The church displays more Tuscan precision than Sardinia's other Pisan churches, while its grand dimensions and ornate style also suggest French influence. The partly striped facade of white and dark grey stone has three levels of blind arcading, each embellished with coloured geometrical motifs and intricate stonework.

The slightly forbidding **interior** restates the two-tone scheme and contains a few items of interest, in particular a decorated Gothic pulpit supported by four arches and an open sarcophagus from the twelfth century, belonging to a local bishop. Back outside, if the gates are open, take time to wander round to the rear of the building, past the monks' plantations in pinewoods, to enjoy the extensive views over the high cultivated country on every side.

Travel details

Trains

Ozieri-Chilivani to: Cágliari (6 daily; 2hr 45min–3hr); Macomer (6 daily; 50min); Olbia (8–10 daily; 1hr–1hr 10min); Sássari (7–8 daily; 45min).

Porto Torres to: Cágliari (2–3 daily; 4hr–4hr 20min); Sássari (Mon–Sat 9–10 daily, Sun 3–4; 15–20min).

Sássari to: Alghero (Mon–Sat 10–11 daily, Sun 6–7; 35min); Árdara (7–8 daily; 30–40min); Cágliari (4 daily; 3hr 45min–4hr); Macomer (4 daily; 1hr 30min–1hr 45min); Olbia (Mon–Sat 7 daily, Sun 4; may need to change at Ozieri-Chilivani; 2hr); Oristano (4 daily; 2hr 20min–2hr 35min); Ozieri-Chilivani (7–8 daily; 50min); Porto Torres (2–5 daily; Mon–Sat 9–10 daily, Sun 3–4; 20min); Sorso (Mon–Sat 14 daily, Sun 8; 15min).

Buses

Castelsardo to: Santa Teresa di Gallura (ARST & Nurágica; Mon–Sat 4–6 daily, Sun 2–4; 1hr 25min–2hr); Sássari (ARST & FdS; Mon–Sat 12–16 daily, Sun 9; 1hr–1hr 10min); Sédini (ARST; Mon–Sat 5–6 daily, Sun 2; 35min); Sorso (ARST; Mon–Sat 8–11 daily, Sun 5–6; 30min); Tempio Pausánia (Nurágica; 3 daily; 1hr 30min); Valledoria (ARST & Nurágica; 4–6 daily; 20–25min).

Porto Torres to: Alghero (ARST; Mon–Sat 5–6 daily, Sun 3; 50min); Fertilia airport (ARST; Mon–Sat 1–3 daily, Sun 1–2; 40min); Monte d'Accoddi (ARST; 1–2 hourly; 10min); Olbia airport (Nurágica; 3–4 daily; 1hr 50min); Sássari (PANI, Nurágica & ARST; 1–2 hourly; 35min);

Stintino (ARST; Mon–Sat 5–7 daily, Sun 2–4; 40min); Torralba (PANI; 3 daily; 1hr 15min–1hr 45min).

Sássari to: Alghero (ARST & FdS; hourly; 50min); Argentiera (ARST; Mon–Sat 5–6 daily, Sun July–Aug 1; 1hr 10min); Bosa (ARST & FdS; Mon–Sat 5–7 daily, Sun 1; 2hr 10min–2hr 30min); Cágliari (PANI; 7 daily; 3hr 15min–3hr 45min); Castelsardo (ARST & FdS; Mon–Sat 11–13 daily, Sun 6; 1hr–1hr 10min); Chiaramonti (Mon–Sat 8 daily, Sun 2; 45min–2hr); Fertilia airport (ARST; 11 daily; 40min); Marina di Sorso (ARST & FdS; Mon–Sat 11–13 daily, Sun 6; 50min); Monte d'Accoddi (ARST; 1–2 hourly; 20min); Nuoro (PANI & ARST; 6–8 daily; 1hr 50min–2hr 35min); Olbia (ARST & FdS; 1–2 daily; 1hr 30min); Olbia airport (Nurágica; 3–4 daily; 1hr 30min); Oristano (PANI; 4 daily; 2hr 20min); Ozieri (ARST; Mon–Sat 7 daily, Sun 2; 1hr–1hr 25min); Platamona (city buses; 1–2 hourly; 30min); Porto Torres (PANI, ARST & Nurágica; 1–2 hourly; 35min); Santa Teresa di Gallura (ARST & Nurágica; Mon–Sat 4–6 daily, Sun 2–4; 3hr); Sédini (ARST; Mon–Sat 5 daily, Sun 2; 1hr 35min); Sorso (ARST; Mon–Sat 10–12 daily, Sun 4–5; 30min); Stintino (ARST; Mon–Sat 5–8 daily, Sun 3–5; 1hr 15min); Torralba (ARST & PANI; Mon–Sat 12 daily, Sun 5; 35min–1hr 30min); Valledoria (ARST & Nurágica; Mon–Sat 5–6, Sun 2–3; 20min–1hr).

Ferries

Porto Torres to: Genoa (Tirrenia & Grandi Navi Veloci 1–3 daily; 10–11hr); Marseille, France (SNCM; 1–4 weekly, 11–18hr).

Gallura

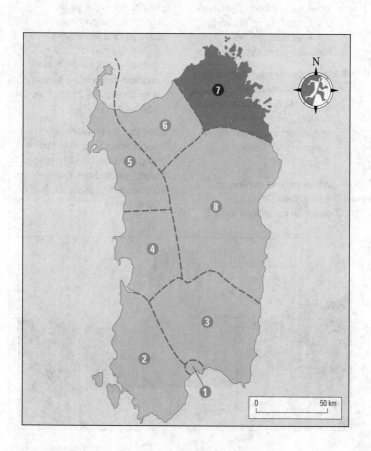

CHAPTER 7

Highlights

✳ **Capo Testa's beaches** The dramatic granite rockscape west of Santa Teresa di Gallura makes a fantastic backdrop for memorable swims. See p.296

✳ **Il Purgatorio restauraunt, Tempio Pausania** Tuck in to top-notch, authentic gallurese dishes such as grilled lamb, hare and boar, served in traditional surroundings. See p.300

✳ **Mountains around Aggius** This rugged, inland area includes some of Gallura's most spectacular highland scenery, strewn with imposing granite outcrops and boulders. See p.301–302

✳ **Wind- or kite-surfing at Porto Pollo** Enjoy the excellent conditions around this resort, which attracts windsurfers and other water-sports fans of all levels. See p.285

✳ **Arzachena's prehistoric remains** Scattered in fields and woods and way off the tourist track, the various nuraghic and prenuraghic sites around Arzachena – including a pair of "giants' tombs" – make a refreshing contrast to the more sensory pleasures of the coast. See p.280–281

✳ **Boat tour to Tavolara** Spend a day cruising around and swimming from this beautiful craggy island, whose stark profile dominates the coast south of Olbia. See p.273

△ Giants' tomb near Arzachena

Gallura

Sardinia's northernmost region, **Gallura**, is a land of raw granite mountains and startling wind-sculpted rocks, which combine with its extraordinary coastline to imbue the area with a unique edge-of-the-wilderness appeal.

The largest town in this wedge, **Olbia**, owes its recent phenomenal growth in the last half-century or so to the huge annual influx of tourists bound for the numerous holiday spots on this coast. Although not many visitors linger, the town acts as a base for the whole region, and has a good selection of hotels and restaurants. If you're stuck here for an afternoon, you might as well visit its main item of interest, the Pisan-Romanesque church of San Símplicio that is the focus for the town's biggest festa. The lurking presences of **Tavolara** and **Molara** form a constant feature on the coast **south of Olbia**, and may be visited by boat from the modern resort of **Porto San Paolo**. This and **San Teodoro**, further south, typify the insipid holiday developments that have defaced much of this coast – deserted for most of the year, they can get over-whelmed in summer, when the combination of alluring bathing spots and lively bars and restaurants creates quite a vibrant atmosphere.

North of Olbia, the port of **Golfo Aranci** has more beaches within a short radius, but glamour-seekers should follow the tide to one of the Mediterranean's loveliest stretches of coast and premier holiday zones, the **Costa Smeralda**. The five-star development of the "Emerald Coast" has not only transformed the economy of the region but also kick-started the tourist industry in the entire island, setting new standards of planned, environment-friendly tourism. On the whole, the devotion to luxury has not compromised the extraordinary natural beauty of the indented rocky coast, but you'll need a full wallet to get the most out of it.

Fortunately, the Costa Smeralda is only a tiny part of Sardinia's northeastern littoral; elsewhere on the coast, it's still possible to have fun without spending stacks of money. Near the inland centre of **Arzachena** – itself worth a visit for the prehistoric sites lying within a short distance – there are miles of shoreline still undeveloped and a profusion of minor islands, over sixty in all, which you can explore on boat tours from points along the coast. From the resort of **Palau**, a daily ferry service runs to **La Maddalena**, the biggest island of this archipelago of sun-baked rocks, and the only one that's inhabited (apart from the NATO base on a neighbouring isle). Linked to La Maddalena by a road causeway, **Caprera** has an absorbing museum devoted to Giuseppe Garibaldi, the hero of Italy's independence movement, located in his former home.

West of Palau, the SS125 passes a succession of lovely bays before reaching **Santa Teresa di Gallura**, Sardinia's northernmost point. This port for ferries

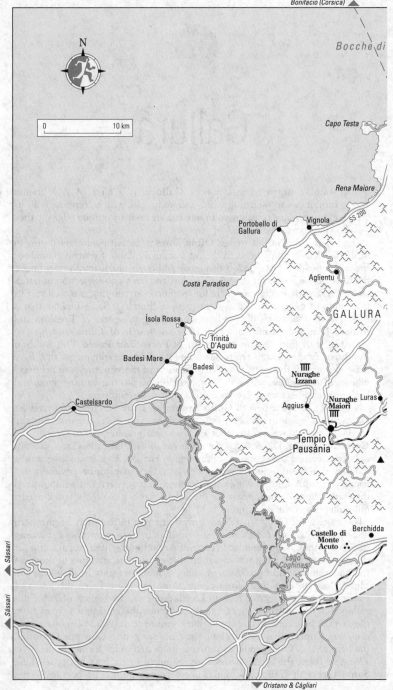

Bonifacio

Razzoli
Santa Maria
Arcipélago della
Maddalena
Budelli
Punta Falcone
La Marmorata
Santa Teresa
di Gallura
La Maddalena
Spargi
La Maddalena
Porto Pozzo
SS133 bis
Santo
Stéfano
Caprera
Palau
Capo
d'Orso
Golfo delle
Saline
Baia Sardinia
SS125
Cannigione
Tempietto
Malchittu
Porto
Cervo
Li Muri
Li Lolghi
Arzachená
Cala di
Volpe
Coddu Vecchio
Nuraghe
Albucciu
Costa
Smeralda
Nuraghe
Capichera
Porto Rotondo
Lago di
Líscia
Golfo di
Cugnana
SS125
Sant'Antonio
di Gallura
Golfo
Aranci
Capo Figari
Figarolo
Calangianus
Pittulongu
PROVINCIA
DI
SÁSSARI
Olbia
Monte
Mandriolo
(126 m)
Capo Ceraso
Monte Limbara
Punta Balistreri
(1359 m)
Porto
Istana
Piana
Tavolara
Molara
Nuraghe
Maiori
Capo
Coda Cavallo
Monti
La Cinta
SS125
San Teodoro
263
Agrustos
Budoni
PROVINCIA DI
NUORO

to Corsica is also one of the island's liveliest holiday centres, within easy reach of some of the most splendid **beaches** anywhere in Italy, cradled in coves and inlets on either side. Sailors and windsurfers have long appreciated the brisk wind conditions in the Straits of Bonifacio, and there are numerous outfits around to cater to watersports enthusiasts.

The ever-present backdrop to this indented shore is the jagged line of granite **mountains** which are the dominant motif in Gallura. Hidden within them is the secret heart of the region, a world that most tourists never discover, thickly forested with the **cork oaks** which, after tourism, provide most of Gallura's revenue. Now somewhat isolated from the main currents of life in the region, the grey granite town of **Tempio Pausánia** lies within sight of the pine-clad slopes of the region's highest mountain, **Monte Limbara**, and within easy reach of some of the interior's best walking routes. Excursions can also be made in the bizarre landscape of granite rubble around **Aggius**, northwest of Tempio, and in the cork forests surrounding **Calangianus** to the east.

Accommodation is available throughout the coastal area in summer, but harder to find inland and in winter. Prices on the coast soar during July and August, when vacancies can be hard to find. The cheapest option is to camp, and there are plenty of sites dotted along the shore, though all get uncomfortably crowded in peak season.

Public transport is adequate for all the towns mentioned here, and there's a fuller service in summer. Olbia is linked to Golfo Aranci by **train**, while a summer-only train service runs twice daily through the mountainous heart of Gallura from Tempio Pausánia to Palau – an appealing if somewhat slow and laborious way to see parts of the region you might otherwise miss. As well as the frequent ARST **bus** connections, some local buses from Olbia are useful for destinations within a short distance of town; #5, for example, plies between Porto Rotondo (across the Golfo di Cugnana from the Costa Smeralda), via Olbia to Porto Istana, a bathing locality east of town. For more information on bus and train connections, see Travel details on p.304. Bus passengers and drivers alike may find traffic unbearably slow on Gallura's coastal roads, especially in summer when motor-homes add to the congestion already created by trucks bearing massive loads of quarried granite.

Olbia

When the English barrister John Tyndale visited **OLBIA** in the 1840s, he compared its Greek name, meaning "happy", with the state he found it in: "A more perfect misnomer, in the present condition of the town, could not be found… The whole district suffers severely from *intemperie*. The wretched approach across these marshes is worthy of the town itself. The houses, none of which have an elegant or neat appearance, are built mostly of granite, and are whitewashed, as if to give a greater contrast to the filth and dirt within and around them."

The "intemperie" of which Tyndale complained was malaria, which, together with the marshes and the filth, has long vanished as a result of the land-drainage schemes and DDT-saturation of the 1950s and the tourist invasions of the 1960s. Olbia today is once more a happy place, enjoying its new-found income both as the nearest Sardinian port to the mainland and the main gateway to the Costa Smeralda.

Nonetheless, few of the tourists pouring through the docks and airport stay long in town, for Olbia – the least Sardinian of all the island's centres – holds

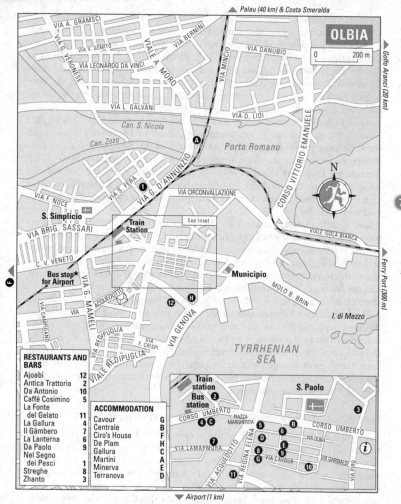

OLBIA

Palau (40 km) & Costa Smeralda

Golfo Aranci (20 km)

Ferry Port (300 m)

0   200 m

VIA A. GRAMSCI
VIA V. GEMITO
VIA G. VERONÉSE
VIA LEONARDO DA VINCI
VIALE A. MORO
VIA BERNINI
VIA DANUBIO
VIA MINCIO
VIA L. GALVANI
VIA D. LIDI
Can. S. Nicola
Can. Zozo
Porto Romano
CORSO VITTORIO EMANUELE
N
VIA F. NOCE
VIA S. FERA
VIA G. D'ANNUNZIO
VIA CIRCONVALLAZIONE
S. Símplicio
VIA BRIG. SASSARI
Train Station
See Inset
VIALE ISOLA BIANCA
C. V. VENETO
Bus stop★ for Airport
VIA G. MAMELI
ACQUEDOTTO
Municipio
MOLO B. BRIN
I. di Mezzo
VIA CAMPIDANO
VIA
VIA REDIPUGLIA
VIALE REDIPUGLIA
VIA F. CRISPI
VIA GENOVA
TYRRHENIAN SEA

RESTAURANTS AND BARS

Ajoabi	12
Antica Trattoria	2
Da Antonio	10
Caffé Cosimino	5
La Fonte del Gelato	11
La Gallura	4
Il Gámbero	7
La Lanterna	6
Da Paolo	9
Nel Segno dei Pesci	1
Streghe	8
Zhanto	3

ACCOMMODATION

Cavour	G
Centrale	B
Ciro's House	F
De Plam	H
Gallura	C
Martini	A
Minerva	E
Terranova	D

Train station
Bus station
CORSO UMBERTO
S. Paolo
PIAZZA MARGHERITA
CORSO UMBERTO
VIA OLBIA
VIA LAMARMORA
VIA REGINA ELENA
VIA CAVOUR
VIA ACQUEDOTTO
VIA GARIBALDI
VIA PIRO

Airport (1 km)

no more character than most transit towns. The best **view** of it is from the surrounding hills, a wide panorama embracing the flat hinterland and the wide Golfo di Olbia, where a small group of islands clusters out to sea, most prominently the immense mass of Tavolara. From close up the town is less inviting, awash with traffic and ugly apartment blocks that spoil what might once have been an attractive seafront. Its appeal is scarcely enhanced by dull back-streets, crossed by canals, railway lines and flyovers. There is a little more charm in the old centre, where the narrow lanes are lined with bars and restaurants that are generally crammed with tourists, sailors and service personnel from the NATO base further up the coast. Apart from the Pisan-Romanesque church of **San Símplicio**, there's little in the way of sights, but it is at least a manageable place, the bus and train stations conveniently located in the centre of town and the airport and ferry port just short bus rides away.

265

Some history

Olbia was the first Sardinian town to be taken by the **Romans**, who captured it in 259 BC, expelling the Carthaginians who had been established here since the fourth century BC. The great Carthaginian general Hanno was killed in the fighting, and was buried with full military honours by the victorious Lucius Cornelius Scipio. Under Rome, the city expanded and flourished as the only natural port on Sardinia's eastern seaboard, though malaria was almost always prevalent due to the surrounding marshy lagoons.

Having survived numerous Vandal and Saracen raids in the Dark Ages, Olbia – or Civita, as it became – was completely rebuilt by Pisa after 1198. It went on to become one of the principal strongholds of the *giudicato* of Gallura, preserving its independence from Spain until the fifteenth century. Now called **Terranova Pausánia** (a name which it retained until 1939), the city suffered complete destruction in 1553 at the hands of the Turkish admiral Dragut, in alliance with France against Charles V of Spain, and half its population was carried away as slaves.

Spain's shift of focus towards its Atlantic empire deprived the port of its prominent role, and Olbia languished in neglect. In 1711 the English Admiral Norris briefly occupied the city, and six years later an **Austrian army** landed and took possession of the town, intending to march on Alghero. But, according to the story, the priest they commandeered as a guide led them into a trap, and the Austrians were captured and led back to Olbia by a Sardinian force – a triumph of cunning that is still the subject of mirth among the local population.

The last century has seen the arrival of the railway, a good road connecting the port with the SS131, and the eradication of malaria, all of which have helped to restore the fortunes of the city. Sophisticated, wily, but still friendly, the people of Olbia – today numbering over 40,000 – are well-used to having large numbers of foreigners in their midst – not just tourists but sailors from the port and large numbers of US service personnel from the nearby NATO base on Palau and the Maddalena archipelago.

Arrival, transport and information

Ferries from Civitavecchia, Piombino, Genoa and Livorno (see the box on p.270–271 for details of services) dock at the island of Isola Bianca, connected to the mainland by a two-kilometre causeway along which you can walk or take an hourly #3 bus (tickets €0.57 from the information office); alternatively, take a train to Olbia's main station, though these are infrequent. The **Stazione Maríttima** at the port holds the main ferry offices, as well as a bank with an ATM, a left-luggage office, car and scooter rentals, a bar and restaurant, and an **information office** (daily 6.20am–1pm & 2.30–9.10pm, later closing in summer; ☎0789.24.696). There are bus departures from here to Arzachena, Nuoro, Palau, Santa Teresa di Gallura and Sássari (see Travel details, p.304). In town, there are shipping agencies at the bottom of the main Corso Umberto.

Of Sardinia's three airports, Olbia's **Aeroporto di Costa Smeralda** is the most convenient, connected with the town by half-hourly bus #2 (hourly on Sun), which takes just ten minutes to reach the central Piazza Regina Margherita (tickets €0.57, or €1.30 on board) from the bar in the terminal; last departure around 8pm). A summer-only **bus service** (5 daily) departs from the airport for the resorts of Arzachena, Palau and Santa Teresa di Gallura (see p.280, 283 & 292), obviating the need to go to Olbia at all if you're bound for the beach-chequered coast northward. **Taxis** into town charge about €15; if you want to reach other destinations directly by taxi from the airport, expect to pay around €50 to Arzachena, €60 to Palau.

Trains from Sássari and Cágliari arrive several times daily at the station just off Corso Umberto; some trains continue to the Stazione Maríttima. The ARST **bus station** is round the corner from the main train station, also reachable from platform 1. Buy tickets here or from the FS ticket booth at the train station.

Olbia's **tourist office** is on Via Piro, a sidestreet running off Corso Umberto (Mon–Sat 8.30am–1pm & 4–7pm, reduced hours in winter; ☎0789.21.453, Ⓦwww.olbia.it).

Accommodation

There's no shortage of **hotels** in Olbia, though most are on the expensive side. The nearest campsites are north of town near the Golfo di Cugnana (see p.276) or south at Porto San Paolo (p.272), both about twenty minutes' drive or bus-ride away.

(see p.276) ... at Porto San Paolo (p.272)

Cavour Via Cavour 22 ☎0789.204.033, Ⓦwww.cavourhotel.it. Just off Piazza Margherita, this hotel successfully combines modern décor and fittings with the traditional style of the building, to produce a cool, white ambience. Triples and quadruples also available. ⑤

Centrale Corso Umberto 85 ☎0789.23.017, Ⓦwww.hotelcentraleolbia.it. A tidy little three-star on the main street, with elegant, smallish rooms; soundproofing keeps the noise level down. There's a bar serving breakfast, but no restaurant. ⑤

Ciro's House Via Aspromonte 7 ☎0789.24.075 or 338.504.7598, Ⓔcirocan@email.it. In a quiet residential neighbourhood a couple of kilometres from the centre (a right turn after the Agip garage), this modern villa offers friendly B&B in simple rooms with a separate shared bathroom. Buses #1 and #3 stop close by. No credit cards. ⑤

De Plam Via de Filippi ☎0789.25.777, Ⓦwww.hoteldeplam.it. Standard business-class hotel on the seafront, with boxy rooms, some of them enjoying the best views in Olbia. You can bring the price down by skipping breakfast, and there's a separate ristorante/pizzeria next door. ⑥

Gallura Corso Umberto 145 ☎0789.24.648, Ⓕ0789.24.629. On the main drag opposite the bus station, this smart, family-run three-star is an excellent central choice. The rooms are clean and fully-equipped, with nice bathrooms, and there's a renowned ground-floor restaurant. Breakfast included. ⑤

Martini Via D'Annunzio ☎0789.26.066, Ⓦwww.hotelmartiniolbia.com. Posh hotel with sumptuous rooms and wonderful views over the bay, though some distance from the town centre. There's no restaurant, but the classy *Adriano* is almost next door. ⑦

Minerva Via Mazzini 7 ☎ & Ⓕ0789.21.190. What was Olbia's best budget choice is undergoing an overhaul at time of writing, but is likely to be upgraded, and to offer much the same quality and rates as the *Terranova* next door (see below). It's well situated, off Via Garibaldi and near Piazza Margherita.

Terranova Via Garibaldi 3 ☎0789.22.395, Ⓦwww.hotelterranova.it. Comfortable, fully-equipped but otherwise unremarkable rooms in this central choice near Piazza Margherita, which has its own restaurant. ⑤

The Town

The centre of town is reached from the seafront by the pedestrianized Corso Umberto, at the bottom of which the Art Nouveau **Municipio** (town hall) ranks as one of Olbia's more interesting architectural features, dating from 1932. Other than this, the main if not the only sightseeing item in town is the little **Basilica di San Símplicio** (daily 6.30am–1pm & 3.30–8pm), on the street of the same name lying over the level-crossing from Corso Umberto. Set in a piazza apart from Olbia's bustle, the simple granite structure is considered the most important medieval monument in the whole of Gallura.

The church formed part of the great Pisan reconstruction programme of the eleventh and twelfth centuries, though also displays distinct Lombard influences.

The lower part of the exterior as far as the blind arcading, which shows traces of stone carvings, dates from the first period of construction at the end of the eleventh century. The building's best feature, the facade, was added in the twelfth century, capped by a mullioned window. The nave's narrow windows hardly lighten the murky **interior**, whose three aisles are separated by columns recycled from Roman constructions; even the stoup for the holy water was formerly an urn that held cremated ashes. The only adornment is the two thirteenth-century frescos in the apse, showing San Simplicio on the left and, on the right, a figure possibly representing Vittore Vescovo, a bishop ordained by Pope Gregory the Great in the sixth century. Two carved capitals, also Lombard in inspiration, are also worth looking at, one carved with a human head, the other with that of a ram. Outside, the piazza makes a quiet spot for a sit-down, and there's a bar.

The only other church of note in Olbia is **San Paolo** just off Corso Umberto, easily recognisable by its multi-coloured cupola. The church, built in 1747 on the site of a Punic temple, is a good example of Gallura's typical building style of that time. Within the unadorned granite-faced exterior, a lovely wooden pulpit of the eighteenth-century Venetian school has inlaid panels and a canopy from which a wooden hand grasping a crucifix is thrust out. The date 1421, engraved on one of the arches of the nave, suggests San Paolo was raised on a site where there was already a church, or else that its builders utilized material from another church. Other buildings in town display dates from the seventeenth and eighteenth centuries carved into their granite lintels (look on Via Garibaldi), though the prevailing tone of the centre's right-angled lanes is modern and rather faceless.

Sa Testa and Pittulongu

If you need to kill some time before a ferry departure, there's an easy excursion you can make just **west of town** on the SP82 Golfo Aranci road, that would make a viable bike ride (or else take any bus bound for Golfo Aranci). About 5km out of the centre, look on your right for the entrance to **Sa Testa**, a sacred well from the late nuraghic era (eighth–sixth century BC), set in a dry, grassy site. The well is approached through a spacious circular area bounded by upright stones – probably a sort of waiting room for devotees who had come to perform their rites. The vestiges of a bench run round the circumference, and there's also rudimentary seating in the small paved recess at the far end, from where seventeen steps lead down to a tholos-shaped chamber holding the spring. The site's state of preservation is due to the fact that it remained buried until 1938 – however, it's one of Sardinia's cruder examples of sacred well, and you can see much more sophisticated ones at Santa Cristina, near Oristano (see p.182) and Su Tempiesu, near Nuoro (see p.319).

A kilometre or two further along this road, you can cool down with a swim at Olbia's favourite bathing spot, **Pittulongu**, where, in summer, the wide arc of sand is lined with bars, and deck-chairs and parasols can be rented.

Restaurants

The centre of Olbia is well-furnished with fast-food places and more sedate **restaurants**. You'll find good-value tourist menus in most places in summer, when everywhere gets pretty crowded.

Antica Trattoria Via Pala 6 ☎0789.25.725. Popular place off the Corso, with a buzzing atmosphere and tasty food: good-value tourist menus are available. Worth queuing for. Moderate.
Da Antonio Via Garibaldi 48. A little cheaper than most of the local trattorias, this has a chi-chi feel, but the food is good. Moderate.
La Gallura Corso Umberto 145. Attached to the eponymous hotel (see p.267), this is one of the best places in town, with delicious, authentic

gallurese dishes featuring strongly on the vast menu, which lists some fifty varieties of soup. Booking is advisable. Moderate.

Il Gámbero Via Lamármora 6. Locals and tourists alike appreciate the rustic trimmings, including a broad fireplace, a mantelpiece piled with pots and ceramics, and hangings. The fare is mainly seafood, and there are fixed-price menus; good antipasti include *pesce spada affumicata* (smoked swordfish). Closed Sun. Moderate.

La Lanterna Via Olbia 13. This subterranean dive off the Corso is good for pizzas, also offering vegetarian choices, and there's a tourist menu for €23. Closed Wed in winter. Moderate.

Da Paolo Via Garibaldi 18 (entrance also at Via Cavour 17). Run in conjunction with the *Cavour* hotel, this old building (1723 on the lintel) has three rooms, one of them granite-walled with a polished wooden ceiling. Over-zealous service but good food, including excellent *zuppa gallurese*. Closed Sun eve. Moderate.

Nel Segno dei Pesci Via D'Annunzio 68. Outside the main restaurant area, on the other side of the rail tracks, this place is spacious and relaxed and offers a good choice of dishes including pizzas (eves only). Meat dishes include *salsiccia alla griglia* (grilled sausages). Closed Sun. Moderate.

Streghe Via Cavour 3. Near the central Piazza Margherita, this *osteria* offers good-value dishes of the day, although it's a bit touristy and gimmicky; you can also eat at benches outside. Moderate.

Zhanto Via delle Terme 1b. Just off the Corso, this small and elegant place with a garden is always busy with locals; fresh pasta dishes feature on the menu, there's a wide range of antipasti, with pizzas served at lunchtime. Closed Sun. Moderate.

Bars, nightlife and entertainment

On Piazza Margherita, *Caffè Cosimino* is good for coffees and fresh **cornetti**; sit outside or inside, where the walls have faded photos of old Olbia (closed Sun). You can also pick up an **ice cream** or iced yoghurt at *La Fonte del Gelato* at Via Regina Elena 12 (closed Sun).

Live **music** and DJs can be heard at *Ajoabi*, Via de Filippi 34 (usually open Fri–Sun only). It's a spacious cellar dive, where *panini* and steaks are served alongside the draught beer, staying open until late; entry is normally free. A posher clientele can be found at *Capricorno Club*, a semi-exclusive **nightclub** on the corner of Via Piro and the Corso, open at weekends for mainstream dance.

The Basilica di San Símplicio is the venue for Olbia's biggest **festa**, three days of processions, costumed dancing, poetry recitals, traditional games and fireworks around May 15, commemorating San Símplicio's martyrdom in the fourth century. The other big local festivals are on Sant'Agostino's day on June 24 and Santa Lucia's day on the first Sunday of September, both lasting three days. Olbia also hosts a cultural festival, **L'Estate Olbiense**, with concerts and other events throughout the summer from the end of July, including almost nightly performances on Piazza Margherita.

Listings

Airport Aeroporto di Costa Smeralda lies 3km east of Olbia. For flight information, call ☏0789.52.634 or consult a travel agent.

Banks Banco di Sardegna at Corso Umberto 142 (Mon–Fri 8.20am–1.20pm & 2.35–4.05pm) has an ATM; there's also a Crédito Italiano at Corso Umberto 165 (Mon–Fri 8.20am–1.20pm & 2.50–4.20pm, Sat 8.20–11.50am).

Bike hire On the Road, Via Sássari 8 (☏0789.206.042) rents out bikes (€12 per day) and scooters (€35 for a 50cc); Gallura (see Car hire) rents out 50cc scooters from about €25 a day, or €150 per week.

Bookshop Gulliver, Corso Umberto 154, has guidebooks and a few English-language books. Tues–Sat 9am–1pm & 4–8pm, Sun 10.30am–1pm & 5–8pm.

Buses For information on Olbia's city buses, call ASPO at ☏0789.553.856.

Car breakdowns Call ☏116 for roadside assistance.

Car hire All the major companies have agencies at the airport, for example Ellepi ☏0789.69.055. Agencies in town include Gallura, Viale Aldo Moro 359 (☏0789.51.518) and Holiday Car, Via Genova 71

(☏0789.28.496). Rates vary according to whether or not you have a kilometre rate; Ellepi and Holiday Car charge €40–50 for a Panda for one day, €90 for a three-day weekend, with a supplement of €0.10 per kilometre driven over 100km or 150km per day. Gallura, offering unlimited mileage, charges just €50 per day for a Panda, €135 for a long weekend. Prices may rise about fifteen percent in July and Aug.

First aid ☏118.
Hospital Viale Aldo Moro ☏0789.552.201.
Luggage deposit At Stazione Maríttima. Daily 6am–12.40pm & 3.20–10pm; €2 per bag for 24hr.
Market Covered fruit and veg market in Via Bari, Mon–Sat 8am–1pm & 4.30–8.30pm.
Pharmacy Most pharmacies are open 9am–1pm & 4.15–7.35pm, closed on Sat afternoon & Sun, though Lupacciolu at Corso Umberto 134 stays

Moving on from Olbia

By air

Olbia's Costa Smeralda Airport lies 5km south of town, connected by Bus #2 (every 30min, hourly on Sun; last daily departure at 7.30pm). The bus stop is outside the Ragazze Italiane boutique, just past the level crossing on Via Mameli; from the same stop, the bus marked "Circolare Impis" (Mon–Sat every 30min) also runs to the airport. Buy tickets for both from the Small Coffee bar on Piazza Margherita, or from the bar just beyond the bus stop.

By train

Frequent **trains** leave from the main station for Cágliari, Golfo Aranci, Oristano and Ozieri-Chilivani (see Travel details on p.304 for schedules). There are also infrequent departures to the same destinations from the Ísola Bianca station at the port.

By bus

ARST (☏0789.21.197 or toll-free 800.865.042, ⊕www.arst.sardegna.it) run services to Nuoro, Sássari and along the coast as far as Santa Teresa di Gallura; **Nurágica** (☏079.510.494, ⊕www.nicosgroup.it) run services to Sássari and Alghero's airport. See Travel details on p.304 for schedules.

By ferry

Olbia is Sardinia's main ferry port, with daily connections to the Italian mainland. All **tickets** can be bought from the offices at the Stazione Maríttima (ferry terminal) or at the agencies (see "Listings" for opening hours). Ask about discounts: for example, return tickets for car plus passengers and midweek daytime departures in low season. Book as early as possible for the lowest fares and to guarantee availability, which in August can be limited. Note that Sardinia Ferries to Livorno and Civitavecchia leave from Golfo Aranci, 15km up the coast (from Olbia, 4–7 trains daily; see the box on p.276).

All the companies operating out of Olbia have ticket offices at the Stazione Maríttima: Tirrenia (☏199.123.199, ⊕www.tirrenia.it; Mon–Fri 8.30am–12.45pm & 4.45–10.50pm, Sat & Sun 5.15–10.50pm); Grimaldi/Grandi Navi Veloci (☏010.209.4591, ⊕www.gnv.it; Mon–Fri 8.30am–12.45pm & 2.30–8.30pm, Sat 8.30am–12.15pm); Moby Lines (☏0565.9361, ⊕www.moby.it; Mon–Fri 8.30am–12.30pm & 4–10pm, Sat 7.30am–12.30pm & 6–10pm, Sun 7.30 am–9pm & 6–10pm). You can also pick up tickets (including for Sardinia Ferries from Golfo Aranci) at travel agencies; there's a trio clustered at the bottom of Olbia's Corso Umberto, for example Unimare, Corso Umberto 1 (☏0789.25.560; Mon–Fri 8.30am–12.30pm & 3.30–7.30pm). Book early for all departures.

To Civitavecchia

Tirrenia (☏199.123.199, ⊕www.tirrenia.it) operates a year-round service of ferries (traghetti) **to Civitavecchia** (north of Rome), departing every night at 11pm,

open weekdays until 10pm. Night rotas are posted on pharmacy doors or in the local newspaper.

Post office Main office at Via Acquedotto. Mon–Fri 8.15am–6.15pm, Sat 8.15am–1pm (last day of month closes at 1.45pm).

Supermarket Superpan, Via Genova, on the seafront (Mon–Sat 8.30am–9pm); Auchan super-store on the SS125 east of town, just past the air-port (daily 9am–9pm in winter; 9am–10pm in summer). North of Olbia, the Terranova shopping centre on the road to Arzachena has similar hours.

Taxis Ranks at train station ℡0789.22.718, Stazione Maríttima ℡0789.26.852 and airport ℡0789.69.150.

Train information FS for Sássari, Oristano and Cágliari ℡848.888.088, ⓦwww.trenitalia.it.

Travel agent Unimare, Corso Umberto 1 ℡0789.25.560.

arriving at 7am, apart from June to mid-August, when ferries depart at 11am and arrive at 7pm. Between June and early September, Tirrenia also runs daily **fast fer-ries** (*mezzi veloci*), with departures at midnight, arriving at 6am, and additional day-time departures from July to early September at 8.30am (arriving at 12.30pm), 2pm (arriving at 6pm) and, during the last two weeks of August, 7pm, arriving at 11pm (there may be more sailings according to demand). Between April and September, Moby (℡0565.9361, ⓦwww.moby.it) also operates a daily fast-ferry service, with departures at 9am, arriving at 1.45pm. On the regular ferries, tickets are around €20–25 for a semi-reclinable seat, €35–40 for a berth, €90 for a medium-size car; for the fastest vessels, tickets are €40–55 (night-crossings are cheaper), and medium-size cars cost €90–100. These are peak-season prices; you'll pay less at other times of the year, and special deals and last-minute discounts are usually available.

To Genoa

Ferries operated by Tirrenia, Moby and Grimaldi/Grandi Navi Veloci (℡010.209.4591, ⓦwww.gnv.it) connect Olbia **to Genoa**. Tirrenia ships leave three times weekly (Tues, Thurs and Sat) at 8.30pm between early September and late June, arriving at 10am the following day, daily or twice-daily in summer, with departures at 9am, 6pm, 8.30pm or midnight. High-season fares are €40–52 for deck class, around €47 for a reclinable seat, €60–80 for a berth. Ferries run by Moby Lines and Grimaldi/Grandi Navi Veloci operate June–September. Moby ferries leave at 10pm and arrive at 7.30am; Grimaldi ferries leave at 9pm until mid-August, then at 9.30am (journey time 8–10hr). Both companies charge €40–80 for a reclinable seat, according to day of departure, €55–90 for a berth in a four-person cabin (more for a cabin with a porthole), and €80–130 for a medium-sized car.

To Livorno

Moby Lines boats leave **for Livorno** once or twice daily in winter, up to three times daily June to mid-September, with departures currently at 8pm, 9pm and/or 10pm, plus 10am in summer (8–12hr). Tickets are around €50; reclinable seats cost an extra €10, and berths €70 or so; a small-to-medium size car costs about €115, motor-bikes €55, and bikes go free. Linea dei Golfi (℡0565.222.300, ⓦwww.lineadeigolfi.it) also links Olbia with Livorno, daily except Sunday all year. Crossings are by night (11–13hr), slightly longer than Moby's but costing less, at about €40 for deck, €55 for a berth, €86 for a smallish car.

To Piombino

Linea dei Golfi ferries also leave **for Piombino** in Tuscany, once or twice daily in winter, two or three times daily in summer. Departures are at 7.30am, 12.30pm and/or 8pm (8–9hr). High-season fares are around €35, or at least €50 for a cabin, with cars from €80.

South of Olbia

The coastal stretch **south of Olbia** has rapidly grown from a wilderness of rock and scrub to become a favourite with Olbians and other holiday-makers, who throng the area's beaches every summer. The cubic pink and coral-coloured constructions that have sprouted haphazardly in the last couple of decades have blighted much of the landscape, though the seaward view remains thankfully unaltered, dominated by the dramatically looming shapes of the islands of **Tavolara** and **Molara**. You can visit them from points along the coast, most easily from **Porto San Paolo**, a recently developed resort village 14km south of Olbia, catering like other holiday centres along this coast mainly to families. Further south, **San Teodoro** is more of the same, a bland colony of bungalows interspersed with hotels and campsites around a reasonable beach.

Porto San Paolo

From Olbia, the southbound SS125 runs past the airport and the first suitable bathing beach at **Lido del Sole** after another four or five kilometres. The road twists just inland of the coast, but always within sight of the monolithic flat-topped islands of Tavolara and Molara. The #5 bus route (6 daily) from Olbia terminates at **Porto Istana**, a sandy bay sheltered by the hulking forms of the islands. A nice excursion around here is to **Capo Ceraso**, the southern tip of the Golfo di Olbia; you can drive most of the way, or walk along a mainly tarmacked road that cuts north about 200m off the SS125 on the Porto Istana road. There are some good beaches among the thick growth of *macchia* and pink rocks, and a stairway once used to reach a World War II gun emplacement leads to the top of **Monte Mandriolo** (126m); the views from here across to Capo Figari north, and the island of Tavolara to the east, are fabulous.

In summer, **boat tours** depart from Porto Istana to visit Tavolara and Molara (see the box on p.273), though the main embarkation point is a few kilometres further south at **PORTO SAN PAOLO**, a lively summer resort that gets very dull out of season. Beyond the battery of bars and pizzerias, boats leave for the islands every half hour or hour from the Pontile della Marina; buy tickets from the kiosks here. The small quay is also used by fishing boats.

Most of the vacationing on this stretch of coast takes place in holiday apartments, accounting for the sparseness of other types of accommodation. The one **hotel** in Porto San Paolo is the extremely swish *San Paolo* (☎0789.40.001, ✆0789.40.622; ◑; April–Oct), with a tennis court and private beach among the facilities; prices fall sharply outside July and August. Three kilometres south of here, the beachside *Tavolara* **campsite** has a tennis court, bike and boat rental and a diving centre; caravans can also be rented (☎0789.40.166, ⊕www.camping-tavolara.it). For a **meal**, seek out *Lu Striglioni*, an agriturismo signposted at Bivio Diriddò a short way inland (☎0789.40.524 or 333.600.6126), where good fixed-price dinners are offered in the evenings for about €23. Information on any of these places and on boat tours is on hand at Porto San Paolo's **Pro Loco** (☎0789.40.172; summer only).

San Teodoro

Just south of the Sássari-Nuoro provincial boundary, the cape known as **Capo Coda Cavallo**, or "horse's tail", curls round to within 3km of the island of

Rising sheer above the flat coast south of Olbia, the islands of **Tavolara** and **Molara** make an excellent day-trip from the Sardinian mainland. Boat excursions combine close-up views of these tall eruptions of rock with opportunities to swim in crystal-clear waters from one of the sheltered beaches around their sides.

Tavolara is the more impressive of the two islands: a giant wedge 4km long and just 1km wide, its precipitous walls towering to a height of 564m. Peregrine falcons and storm petrels are among the rare birds to look out for here. Its eastern flank is a military zone and therefore off-limits, but the western side, which is inhabited and even has a cemetery, is freely accessible, and there's a good beach at Spalmatore di Terra on the southern tip. In summer, refreshment and victuals are supplied by bars and a couple of restaurants, *La Corona* and *Da Tonino*.

In recent years, the island has hosted an occasional open-air **film festival** of non-mainstream Italian movies, screened on the beach during four or five nights in mid-July. Special boat excursions ferry ticket-holders to and from the al fresco arena. For dates and times, contact the tourist office at Olbia or Porto San Paolo, or visit Ⓦhttp://web.tin.it/cinematavolara.

In contrast to calcareous Tavolara, the smaller, circular isle of **Molara** is composed of granite, and it's greener too, with a covering of wild olives trees. On its eastern shore, at Cala di Chiesa, are the remains of a medieval village, **Gurguray**, with the shell of a church, San Ponziano.

At Easter and between June and September, **boats to the islands** leave at regular intervals from Porto Istana and Porto San Paolo, with further sailings outside these periods according to demand. The most regular service is from Porto San Paolo to Tavolara, leaving every half-hour or hour from 9.30am until 1pm, with returns from 3.30pm to 6.30pm (you can choose to come back at any time throughout the afternoon); return tickets are around €10. There's a less frequent service to Molara, and some operators also make a stop at **Piana**, a tiny rock just big enough to hold a lovely sandy beach. There are also **longer cruises** around all the isles, with optional swims, costing around €20. These currently depart daily from Porto San Paolo (Easter and June–Sept) at 9.30am, arriving at Tavolara at noon, with returns at 12.30pm, then 3.30–6.30pm, as you choose.

For more information on all excursions, call one of the boat companies (try ☎0789.40.210 or 0789.53.065), or contact Porto San Paolo's tourist office at ☎0789.40.172.

Molara. There's another good **campsite**, *Cala Cavallo* (☎0784.834.156; June–Sept), on the cape; it's well equipped, with its own pool and tennis court. The views over the islands from this little peninsula are awesome. Eight kilometres further south, past the long Stagno di San Teodoro lagoon, used by wading flamingos and cranes, **SAN TEODORO** is another popular beach resort, its modern villas, bars and restaurants thickly planted behind the **Cala d'Ambra** beach. There's another great beach north of town on **La Cinta**, a long bar of sand separating the lagoon from the sea, but Cala d'Ambra is the preferable area to stay in if you're looking for accommodation in San Teodoro. *L'Eságono*, a three-star **hotel** (☎0784.865.783, Ⓕ0784.866.040; ❹; mid-April to Oct), has relatively cheap rates and provides a range of facilities and activities for children and adults, including horse-riding, a tennis court, pool and disco, and there are organized children's games and baby-sitting. Away from the sea, Via del Tirreno has most of the hotels, including the reasonably priced *Al Faro* (May to mid-Oct; ☎0784.865.665, Ⓕ0784.865.565; ❺), and one of San Teodoro's two **campsites**, the *San Teodoro* (☎0784.865.777; mid-May to mid-Oct), which offers bungalows from around €80 per night. The other site, however, *Cala d'Ambra* (☎0784.865.650; June–Sept), has lower prices and is situated right by the sea.

San Teodoro sports an abundance of **places to eat** in summer: *L'Eságono* hotel has a terrace right on the beach, and other choices include, near the resort's centre, *La Lámpara* ristorante/pizzeria, with a verandah, a wood-fired oven for pizzas, and meat and fish served on the spit (good-value tourist menus are available). Other popular hang-outs include the *Gallo Blu* ristorante/pizzeria and the *Zanzibar* café, both nearby. For afters, treat yourself to good **ice cream** and pastries from either of the two branches of *Anna gelateria/pasticceria*, at Via Sardegna and Via Rinaggiu. San Teodoro also boasts a good choice of **clubs**, including, near the beach, open-air dance floors at *L'Eságono* hotel and *Cala d'Ambra* campsite; nearer the centre, the *Idolhouse* disco-bar has billiards and serves *panini*.

⑦ Budoni

The minor road south from San Teodoro takes you past more beaches and campsites, eventually rejoining the main SS125. If you're looking for accommodation in the area, **BUDONI**, 10km south of San Teodoro, has a couple of hotels on its main drag, *Isabella* (☎0784.844.048, ☎0784.844.409; ❹), which has a restaurant, and *Solemar* (☎0784.844.081; ❹); they're both pretty characterless, though they do stay open all year. To the north of Budoni, the beach neighbourhood of **Agrustos** has the impressively equipped *Eurovillage* (☎0784.846.020, ☎0784.846.043; ❺; April to mid-Oct) among several much pricier options, and three of the numerous campsites in these parts. Apart from the beach, however, there's not a great deal to recommend a stay in this area, and you might as well press on south to the mouth of the River Posada and the Nuorese village of the same name (see p.336).

Golfo Aranci and the Costa Smeralda

The Golfo di Olbia reaches its northern extent at **Golfo Aranci**, a major port which has taken an increasing portion of Olbia's shipping traffic. Its picturesque name – "Gulf of Oranges" – fails to convey the more down-to-earth reality, and apart from some decent beaches and a nature reserve in the vicinity, there's no pressing reason to come here unless you need to cross on the daily ferries to the mainland. Much of this long peninsula has been invaded by the uniform holiday villas that become increasingly dominant along this stretch of coast, not least around the modern holiday town of **Porto Rotondo**. However bland the architecture, the vegetation is always exuberant, with bougainvillea, tiger lily and hibiscus injecting a tropical brilliance to the granite rock.

This clash of nature and artifice is even more pronounced on the **Costa Smeralda**, the "millionaire's playground" which occupies the western shore of the Golfo di Cugnana. At least here, however, the development has been subject to stringent controls which have limited the damage. Accordingly, large areas of *macchia* and mountain have been left undisturbed, though the pockets of development that exist are not always as unobtrusive as they are claimed, and they are gradually expanding.

It is not just the natural beauty of the granite littoral which is striking, but the cleanliness and transparency of the sea – another beneficiary of the planning regulations in force here. If you don't mind bathing off rocks, then you can swim virtually anywhere; **beaches** are much less obvious, but many are indicated with brown signs.

Although Golfo Aranci has a couple of good **accommodation** choices, and there's a campsite just south of the Golfo di Cugnana, don't even think of staying on the Costa Smeralda itself unless you have an invitation. Even three-star hotels have five-star prices, and in any case most of the accommodation here is in the form of rentals by the week. If that's your preferred option, consult the agencies in Porto Cervo, Baja Sardinia or Porto Rotondo, who will probably try to persuade you to spend a little more on a patch of real estate; otherwise, stay around Arzachena (see p.279) or camp. There are regular **public transport** connections to Golfo Aranci and Porto Cervo, but you really need your own wheels to reach other spots along this coast.

Golfo Aranci

If you have come from Livorno, La Spezia or Civitavecchia, **GOLFO ARANCI** may well be your first landing in Sardinia. It's not a bad place to touch down if you want to avoid the noise and bustle of Olbia. Golfo Aranci is not a particularly inspiring town, nor a great foretaste of what else Sardinia has in store, but it has good connections to other places in Gallura, with a couple of nice beaches nearby and even a nature reserve, overlooked by most visitors, in the hills behind.

The town developed in the first decades of the twentieth century, when the construction of its port facilities and the railway line to Olbia helped it to take over a portion of the shipping coming to that town. The arrival of the FS ferries in 1961 gave a further boost, as did the establishment of a passenger service in the 1970s; the holiday homes followed soon after.

If Golfo Aranci has any centre, it's the port and train station at the far end of town, where there's also a tourist office open daily in summer. Just a few metres up from the station is Golfo Aranci's only item of historical interest, the **Pozzo Sacro Milis**, a rough-hewn sacred well dating from the nuraghic era.

Behind the town rears the immense mass of rock occupying **Capo Figari**, a protected area where the thick *macchia* is interlaced with holm oaks and a juniper wood. A number of Sardinia's long-horned **mouflons** (wild sheep) have been successfully reintroduced here and on the offshore islet of Figarolo, whose steep slopes are visible from here, similarly clad in *macchia* and twisted old olives. The best **beaches**, however, lie south of town, round the curve of the **Golfo degli Aranci**, where Cala Sássari includes several small sandy coves, one of which, **Sos Aranzos**, lent its name to both the gulf and the major port. The aptly named **Cala Banana** (also called *Pellicano*) is another arc of beach worth seeking out.

Practicalities

Frequent **trains** and (in summer) **buses** connect Golfo Aranci with Olbia. Some trains run right up to the port, though most stop at the central station in town. If you need to stay at Golfo Aranci, there is a handful of **hotels** to choose from, most on or off the long main road connecting the port area with the centre of town. Two are on Via Libertà: *Castello* (☎0789.46.073, ℉0789.46.450; ❼) and the much smaller and cheaper *King's* (☎0789.46.075, ℉0789.46.400; ❺), both open Easter–September. A third option lies nearby: *La Lámpara* on Via Magellano (☎0789.615.140; ❺).

Ferries from Golfo Aranci

Tirrenia (☏199.123.199, ⓦwww.tirrenia.it) operates a fast-ferry (*mezzo veloce*) service **to Fiumicino**, site of Rome's main airport, with frequent connections to the capital (late June to early September 1 daily at 1.30pm; 3hr 30min). Tickets cost around €50 for passengers, €73–86 for a car.

Sardinia Ferries (☏019.215.511, ⓦwww.corsicaferries.com) operate "express" ferries **to Civitavecchia**, north of Rome (Easter to early October 1–3 daily at 12.20pm and 8.40pm; 3hr 45min). Tickets cost €35–50 for passengers, €50–120 for a medium-size car. Sardinia Ferries also runs a slower service to Civitavecchia (mid-June to mid-September 1–2 daily at 8.15am or noon; 6hr 45min); there are also occasional extra crossings at 4pm during peak season, and night-ferries at 9pm and 11.30pm (7hr 30min or 10hr). Passengers pay €17–44, berths start from €22, arm-chairs are €10–15, and medium-small cars are €45–90.

Sardinia Ferries also run slow and express crossings **to Livorno**. The slower service (April–Oct at around 9am, 9pm or 11pm; 8–10hr), costs €24–50 for passengers, €22 for berths, €10–15 for armchairs and €41–117 for a small car. Fast ferries to Livorno (June–Sept 5 weekly at 8.15am or 3.30pm; 6hr) cost €30–60 for passengers, €41–117 for a small car).

It's worth asking about any possible reductions on return crossings, such as stand-bys or advance bookings; in season, you should book early.

The best **place to eat** is near the port, off the main road at Via de' Caduti, where the plain-looking *Manzoni* (closed Nov) offers first-class fish meals for very reasonable prices, and there are pizzas too. The local *sagra di pesce*, or **fish festival**, takes place on August 14, when seafood and wine are doled out to all and sundry.

Porto Rotondo and around

Built in 1963 following the development of Costa Smeralda, **PORTO ROTONDO** does not deviate very far from the main theme. Rows of orange villas snake remorselessly over the *macchia* hills, grouped more thickly around the inevitable round yachting port. Chic boutiques and fashion shops set the tone in the central Piazzetta San Marco, from which a wide stairway leads up to the church of **San Lorenzo**, a modern granite construction holding twenty wooden statuettes on a religious theme. A few metres away, there's an open-air theatre, also granite, built in 1995, where entertainments are staged in summer. There are beaches around the thin headland north of here, **Punta della Volpe**, though these get overwhelmed in summer.

There's nowhere remotely affordable to stay in the area, except for an inland **campsite**. To reach it, backtrack some 10km from Porto Rotondo towards the SS125; turn right before reaching the highway, onto the Porto Cervo road. Having rounded the base of the Golfo di Cugnana, you'll pass almost immediately *La Cugnana*, a three-star campsite (May–Sept; ☏0789.33.184, ⓦwww.campingcugnana.it) that's also the nearest to Olbia and the Costa Smeralda, and the cheapest option for staying anywhere near that exclusive zone – so you can expect a crowd. However, the site has excellent facilities, including a beautiful large pool. Self-contained bungalows are also available here for €70–85 per night for two. The site lies 2km from the beach at Marina di Cugnana, and a minibus shuttles campers to some of the Costa Smeralda's best beaches; ARST **buses** between Olbia and Porto Cervo stop right outside. To **rent bikes**, **scooters** and **cars**, contact Rubix Motorbikes at Località

Castello (☎0789.34.111 or 335.305.900); in high season, bikes cost €13 per day, 50cc scooters €39, with cars from €75m.

The Costa Smeralda

The **Costa Smeralda** is a strictly defined ten-kilometre strip between the gulfs of Cugnana and Arzachena, beginning some 12km north of Olbia. Legend has it that in 1958 the Aga Khan Prince Karim IV, Imam and spiritual leader of the Ismaili Muslims, stumbled upon the charms of this idyllic coast when his yacht took shelter from a storm in one of its narrow creeks. Four years later, the fabulously wealthy tycoon headed a consortium of businessmen with the aim of exploiting this wild coastal strip, and was easily able to persuade the local farmers to part with their largely uncultivable land – though stories have circulated ever since of the stratagems used to dupe the locals into selling their property for a fraction of its value.

The consortium's plans were on a massive scale, limited only by the conditions imposed by the regional government. These included proper sewage treatment and disposal, restrictions on building, and the insistence that the appearance of the landscape should not be unduly changed. On this last point the developers were only partially successful. Although only local building materials may be used along the Costa Smeralda (multi-storey hotels, advertising hoardings, fast-food restaurants and even garish filling stations have been banned), and only indigenous vegetation planted – so that pines, eucalyptus and poplars, for example, are banished in favour of oleander, mimosa, arbutus and myrtle – the coastline can hardly be described as pristine, nor will you find a genuine fishing community surviving hereabouts, nor anything like the kind of local markets you'll see in other parts of the island. Even the supermarkets are self-consciously discreet, and the red-tiled holiday villages, for all their trappings of luxury, have a bland, almost suburban feel about them.

Shorn of the disorderly and spontaneous, what's lacking is that vital human element or local touch that invigorates most other Italian resorts. If you can afford to stay here, you'll probably appreciate the virtues of this insulated holiday oasis, though you may soon tire of the stifling air of opulence.

The keynote in the best hotels is sophisticated, understated class mingled with a kind of peasant chic, most in evidence in the enclave of sumptuous hotels around **Cala di Volpe**. If you really want to mingle with the in-crowd, however, you could start by sipping aperitifs in the Piazzetta in **Porto Cervo**, the only "town" on this coast, with all the shops and facilities. Needless to say, when the summer's gone, so is the jet set, and the whole area sinks into a kind of dispirited torpor – though this might be the best time to appreciate the truly spectacular coast, undistracted by the wannabe high-flyers. June, July and September are the best months to enjoy the glorious **beaches** dotted along the indented coast south of Porto Cervo, which sometimes require a little enterprise and a good sense of direction to reach.

Porto Cervo is linked to Olbia by at least three **buses** daily (not Sun), more in summer – although the most enjoyable way to visit the coast is on a scooter or bike. Note that the nearest **information** office is at Arzachena (see p.282), but the website covering the area may be useful: ⓦwww.portocervo.net.

Cala di Volpe and around

The quiet creeks and inlets north of the Golfo di Cugnana provide numerous anchorages for yachts and often reveal hidden patches of sand from which to bathe. Of the area's broader **beaches**, the most popular include **Rena Bianca**,

Petra Ruia and **Liscia Ruia**, the latter giving onto the bay of **Cala di Volpe**, a locality holding a concentration of some of Europe's most select **hotels**. The most exclusive of these, formerly managed by the Aga Khan's Consorzio Costa Smeralda, are now part of the Starwood hotel group.

Perhaps the most stylish of all is the *Cala di Volpe* (mid-April to late Oct; ☎0789.976.111, Ⓦwww.starwood.com/caladivolpe; ❾) designed by celebrated architect Jacques Couelle and looking something like a mix between an adobe Moorish fortress and a peasant's farmstead, painted in umbers and ochres. Exceptional cuisine, a private harbour, two salt-water pools (one on the hotel's roof) plus a fine sand beach combine to make this a sybaritic delight, if you're loaded: palatial rooms ring in at about €875 a night in high season (half-board per person); the low season rate dips to around €475. The eighteen-hole 72-par Pevero golf course on a rolling expanse of green above the hotel is one of Europe's most prestigious; it's also a masterwork of design, the creation of architect Robert Trent Jones. It's linked to the *Cervo, Romazzino, Cala di Volpe* and *Pitrizza* hotels by a free shuttle service.

Head west of Cala di Volpe for the pick of the area's **beaches**: just follow any dirt track – the rougher it is, the more promising – down to the sea. The more popular ones are signposted, for example **Capriccioli** and **Romazzino**, facing the offshore islands of Soffi and Mortorio.

Porto Cervo

In the "capital" of Costa Smeralda, **PORTO CERVO**, the tidy pastel-coloured architecture characteristic of the region becomes almost surreal. Fascinating to wander round, crime- and litter-free, Porto Cervo has the quality of a film set, more of a virtual version of a "Mediterranean village" than an authentic resort. The huge yachting marina is a curiosity in itself, awash with the ostentatious baubles of the ultra-rich. The marine facilities here are the best in Sardinia, with berths for 650 vessels, each with electricity and fresh water supplies. In uneven years, antique sailing boats gather at the port during the first days of September, usually followed by a race in the Straits of Bonifacio.

The gleaming ranks are overlooked to the west of the centre by the **Stella Maris** church, a rough-textured, whitewashed building which surprisingly houses a couple of good works of art, including a *Mater Dolorosa* by El Greco, the bequest of a Dutch aristocrat. The church was designed in 1968 by the Roman architect Michele Busiri Vici, who was also responsible for the grotto-like shopping arcade in Porto Cervo's centre. At the heart of this warren of paths and passages, the **Piazzetta** is the place to lounge in style, ideally with cocktail in hand and an expensive pair of shades. A small beer at one of the bars here won't leave you much change from €10, though the price includes a front-seat view of the kind of people who frequent this VIP resort. Steps lead down from here to the **Sottopiazza**, an area of posh boutiques and also site of an ISOLA outlet, selling government-sponsored craftwork.

There are also banks, phones, pharmacies, travel agents, estate agents, even a supermarket here, not to mention the top-quality tennis facilities, used for tournaments in the summer and at other times open daily to the public. Unless you opt for this, however, there's not much else to do in Porto Cervo once you've had your eyeful of the Fendis and Vespaces, and admired the incredibly grand yachts at the marina. If you're hungry, head for the supermarket behind the Piazzetta or else buy an expensive *panino* from a bar. For anything more substantial, there are some slightly cheaper **restaurants** than the swanky affairs tucked away in Porto Cervo's alleys, including *Il Pomodoro*, behind the Piazzetta.

The dominant presence in the centre of the resort is the five-star *Cervo Hotel* (℡0789.931.111, Ⓦwww.sheraton.com/cervo; Ⓞ), projecting an air of privileged quiet behind its entrance on the central piazza. If you're tempted to stay here, rooms rise from a low-season price of about €180 to €800 per night in high season, for which you get use of squash and tennis courts, a pool and a boat-service that whisks guests off to a select beach twenty minutes away.

Beyond the obligatory aperitif in the Piazzetta and a couple of late-closing portside bars, Porto Cervo has little or no nightlife as such, though there are venues within a short drive. A couple of kilometres outside town, on the road south, the *Sopravento* has one of the biggest **discos** in the area, also featuring occasional live bands. Across the road from it, *Sottovento* is a less intense piano bar. For **taxis**, call ℡0789.92.250.

Baia Sardinia and around

You'll need your own transport to get to the sequestered **beaches** around Porto Cervo, only a few of which are clearly marked. North of the resort, one of the best is at **Liscia di Vacca**, an exquisite bay at the end of a long bumpy dirt road. Thankfully, the villas of the nearby *Pitrizza* hotel (May–Oct; ℡0789.930.111, Ⓦwww.luxurycollection.com/hotelpitrizza; Ⓞ), which numbers moguls and minor royals among its guests, are safely fenced off, and do not intrude too much on the beach.

West of here, just outside the controlled zone of the Costa Smeralda though sharing its élite ethos, the **Baia Sardinia** locality is dominated by the extensive *Forte Capellini* holiday village, whose lawns and thatched bungalows lie scattered around the granite boulders of the headland here. There are a number of other high-class hotels in and around this modern resort, and also a good **restaurant** that's not excessively expensive, the *Grazia Deledda*, on the Cannigione road (open summer only). Also on this road, the *Aquadream* amusement park is a hit with kids (June–Sept), though for young and old the main attraction around here is the beach below the headland.

The Golfo di Arzachena and Palau

Outside the luxury belt but enjoying many of the Costa Smeralda's natural advantages, the **Golfo di Arzachena** is a deep narrow bay whose western shore holds most of the tourist facilities. **Arzachena** itself is inland and not particularly inspiring, though it has its share of excitement in high season. Apart from its hotels, banks and shops, the town also has a couple of curiosities worth exploring, including, a short distance outside, two of Sardinia's "giants' tombs" – the biggest and best-preserved of this type of nuraghic monument in the whole island. These and other sites lying in the middle of the countryside make easy targets for walking or biking expeditions.

Most of the tourists gravitate towards the nearby coasts, with a concentration of facilities around **Cannigione** – a small fishing port and yachting resort on the gulf. There are campsites here, while a minor road leads round the coast to the **Golfo delle Saline**, one of the area's best swimming spots, before reaching the port of **Palau**. The embarkation point for the Maddalena archipelago, Palau is a lively tourist town, well supplied with hotels, though lacking much intrinsic interest. West of here, **Porto Pollo** has a magnificent beach that encompasses the coast's – if not Sardinia's – best windsurfing location.

Driving, you can reach Arzachena from Olbia in about thirty minutes on the SS125. Three **buses** daily leave Olbia on a route that takes in Arzachena and Palau, and several buses daily link Cannigione with Arzachena. Palau is also the terminus for the small **train service** that currently operates in summer only, and then with a very limited service.

Arzachena and its prehistoric sites

Although **ARZACHENA** lacks the glamour of the nearby upscale resorts, it makes a useful base for the area, with a selection of reasonable hotels and restaurants. At the centre of town, Piazza Risorgimento is the venue for nightly entertainments in summer – cabaret, concerts and the like – and the centre of a good **market** for both food and household goods on Wednesday mornings. If you're in town, take a look at the **Roccia Il Fungo**, or "mushroom rock" (also called *Monti Incappidatu*), one of Gallura's weathered natural sculptures, conspicuous on a rise at the end of Via Limbara, a short walk from the piazza. Fragments found here have convinced archeologists that the formation provided shelter to Neolithic and nuraghic peoples; there's no doubting its choice location, commanding extensive views up and down the coast.

Nuraghe Albucciu and the Tempietto Malchittu

Of the other prehistoric sights around Arzachena, the easiest to visit lies 2km southeast of town, right by the side of the SS125, signposted near the Cannigione junction. Surrounded by olives, **Nuraghe Albucciu** (daily: 9am–1pm & 3–7pm, or 4–8pm in July & Aug, reduced hours in winter; €2, or €2.50 with guide) is one of Gallura's best-preserved nuraghic monuments, with one chamber, on the right of the main corridor, still roofed and intact. Near the entrance to the *nuraghe*, you can just make out a groove that was probably made by a device for sealing the door. Linked by sight to other *nuraghi* in the area, the structure is built on an almost rectangular plan, and still displays the jutting supports for the vanished wooden roof. For more information on Sardinia's nuraghic culture, see p.349–350.

Opposite the site, the car park contains a small tourist office (see "Practicalities" on p.283), which can provide information on the archeological sites scattered around this area. You can buy tickets for these here, if you don't want to buy them on the spot, including a combined ticket which allows you to visit two of the sites for €4.50, or three for €6.50, in each case accompanied by a guide.

Behind the office, a track leads north to another archeological ruin, the **Tempietto Malchittu** (daily: 9am–1pm & 3–7pm, or 4–8pm in July & Aug; reduced hours in winter; €2). Having left your vehicle in the car park by the tourist office (the track is a private road), it's an easy stroll, the track winding through fields for less than 2km, curving round a spur in the lee of which lies the roofless ruin, now overgrown with trees and scrub. Little can be said for certain about this rugged oval structure dating from the first nuraghic phase (between 1500 and 1200 BC), except that it's thought to have been a place of worship; finds suggest that sacrifices were made here. The granite walls enclose two rooms connected by a low doorway; very few examples of this kind of construction are known today. While there isn't a great deal to see, it makes a pleasant expedition, and could be a point of departure for longer walks in the *macchia*.

Coddu Vecchiu

Four and a half kilometres south of Arzachena, on the road to Sant'Antonio di Gallura, branch right onto the Luogosanto road and turn left after another 2km to reach the site of **Coddu Vecchiu** (daily: 9am–1pm & 3–7pm, or 4–8pm in July & Aug, reduced hours in winter; €2, or €2.50 with guide), one of the most complete of Sardinia's so-called *tombe dei giganti* ("giants' tombs"). Like other examples of this type of construction, it consists of carved granite slabs laid end-up in a semicircular, or bull-horn-shaped, formation. Their name was given to them by local people who were clearly mystified as to the purpose of these enigmatic objects. They are now known to be works of the nuraghic culture, for which they were simultaneously collective burial chambers and places of worship.

The central stele, over 4m tall, resembles an immense doorway, probably symbolizing the entry into another world. The low opening at the base, which would presumably have been sealed after burial, leads into two long chambers, suggesting two distinct periods of construction during the second millennium BC. Excavations here have thrown up evidence that members of the older Bonnanaro culture also used this site, and that it was later adapted by the nuraghic people.

Nuraghe Capichera and Li Lolghi

A kilometre further up this minor road brings you to a *nuraghe* that was possibly associated with the Coddu Vecchiu site, **Nuraghe Capichera**, also known as *La Prisciona* (daily: 10am–1pm & 3–7pm, or 4–8pm in July & Aug, reduced hours in winter; €2, or €2.50 with guide). Built at any time between 2000 and 1000 BC on a height overlooking the whole Arzachena plain, this trilobate (three-sided) construction stands 6.5m tall. The central tower is surrounded by three smaller towers and the very sparse remains of an external wall. Three niches survive in the main chamber (which is not central in respect of the tower itself). There's a well in the space between the rampart and the wall, and huts have been excavated in the vicinity.

You can visit another giants' tomb by continuing west along the Luogosanto road for nearly 3km, making a right turn and keeping right for another couple of kilometres. Just off this track on the left, **Li Lolghi** (same hours/prices as Nuraghe Capichera) has a lower central stele than Coddu Vecchiu, but its inner chamber is nearly twice as long, and considered to be the finest example of its type in Gallura. Again, the small arched doorway leads into a passage containing the two chambers where bodies were laid. In most respects the site is very similar to Coddu Vecchiu, and no less striking.

Li Muri

From Li Lolghi it's a short distance to the last and oldest of Arzachena's major prehistoric sites, **Li Muri** (daily: 10am–1pm & 3–7pm, or 4–8pm in July & Aug, reduced hours in winter; €2, or €2.50 with guide), reached by backtracking for a couple of hundred metres to take the left-hand (west) fork off the track leading from the Luogosanto road. The track gets pretty rough, so drivers should leave their vehicles at the first suitable place and proceed on foot, unless they have a 4WD.

The **stone circles** that make up the site constituted a necropolis of the third millennium BC, once thought to belong to a so-called "Arzachena culture", though it now looks as though this was a variation of the Ozieri culture (3400–2700 BC). Each of the five central circles (5–8m in diameter) contained a body interred in a crouching position together with votive offerings, while smaller circles dating from a subsequent period are distinguished by a double row of stones with better worked sides. These were probably used in funerary rites but not as tombs; it has even been suggested they were used for the skinning of the corpse prior to burial. It's a complex site, the rugged setting lending it an appealing wild grandeur.

Practicalities

You can pick up maps and details on accommodation and excursions in the Arzachena area from the **tourist office** (Mon–Fri 8am–1.30pm & 3–7pm; Sat 8am–1.30pm; ☎0789.82.624) opposite Nuraghe Albucciu on the SS125 southeast of Arzachena (signposted near the Cannigione junction). Until a new local office is set up, this presently serves the whole Costa Smeralda region, though is best for general advice rather than practical information. The town has four **hotels**, cheapest of which is the capacious *Citti* (☎0789.82.662, ⓦwww.wel.it/hotelcitti; ❺), boasting a small pool but with characterless rooms and no restaurant, on the outskirts of Arzachena on the Palau road (Viale Costa Smeralda 197). At the other end of town, off the road to Olbia at Via Torricelli 3, *Casa Mia* (☎0789.82.790, ⓦwww.hotelcasamia.it; ❻) has small functional rooms and a restaurant, while the glitzy *Albatros* at Viale Costa Smeralda 28 (☎0789.83.333, ⓦwww.albatrosclubhotel.com; ❽) has low-season rooms in the ❹ category, and the small *Delfino*, nearby at Viale Costa Smeralda 51 (☎0789.83.420, ⓦwww.delfinohotel.it; ❼), has gaudily modern rooms, most with a balcony, and there's a roof bar.

There is a dearth of decent **eating places** in town. Apart from the *Casa Mia* hotel, try the *Pizzeria Calipso*, behind the Banco di Sardegna on Viale Costa Smeralda, or the *Quattro Mori* ristorante/pizzeria, with a veranda, at the eastern end on the same road. There are a couple of other trattorias on this road and the main Via Ruzzittu.

You can **rent a car** from Am Service, in the Delfino shopping centre on Viale Costa Smeralda (☎0789.840.094), with prices from around €220 for seven days. For **bike hire**, ask at *Raimondo Casula* at Via Dettori 37 (☎0789.81.288). Leaving town on the Palau road, Arzachena's **post office** is on the left at Viale Costa Smeralda 159 (Mon–Fri 8.10am–6.15pm, Sat 8.10am–1.15pm); it also changes cash, or you can **change money** at the nearby Banco di Sardegna, also on Viale Costa Smeralda (Mon–Fri 8.20am–1.20pm & 2.35–4.05pm), which has an ATM.

Buses pull up on Via San Pietro, off Viale Dettori – the road signposted for Luogosanto. At the *Bar Castello*, Viale Dettori 43 (closed Fri), you can buy tickets for Olbia, Palau, Cannigione and Laconia. When this is closed, buy tickets round the corner at the *Bar Smeraldo*, on Via San Pietro (closed Sun). Arzachena's **train station** is about a kilometre west out of town, with trains stopping twice daily in summer on the Tempio Pausánia–Palau line. **Taxis** can be found on the central Piazza Risorgimento.

Cannigione and around

On the western shore of the Golfo di Arzachena lies the resort village of **CANNIGIONE**, a small fishing port and yacht-stop with some decent beaches to the north. Outside a few weeks in August, Cannigione has a serene, even dull, air; it's the place to find supermarkets, restaurants and an exchange office, but once you've dispatched a *gelato* on a stroll by the portside, you've exhausted its attractions.

The beaches are further up the coast, though most of the **hotels** are in Cannigione itself; none of them is especially cheap (virtually all are over ❼, and most are open only from Easter to October: the cheapest is the *Hotel del Porto*, which enjoys an attractive seafront location on Lungomare Andrea Doria (☎0789.88.011, Ⓕ0789.88.064; ❺), stays open all year, and has a restaurant (other dining spots in Cannigione are pricey).

Cannigione also has a couple of **campsites** which are teeming in high summer. The *Golfo di Arzachena* (March–Oct; ☎0789.88.101,

@www.campingarzachena.com) is inland just south of Cannigione, with a big pool and caravans and mini-apartments for rent (③–⑤), while the preferable *Villaggio Isuledda* (mid-April to mid-Oct; ☎0789.86.003, @www.isuledda.it) lies right on the shore north of the resort, in the Laconia district. It has excellent bathing spots, and a range of non-tent accommodation.

Beyond Laconia, the tiny coast road winds round to the **Golfo di Saline**, a bay sheltering an exquisite **beach** and the *Club Hotel Li Capanni* (May–Sept ☎0789.86.041, ℗0789.86.200; ⑥), which does not impinge too heavily on the undeveloped sandy shores. At the tip of the bay sit the even more lavish four-star *Capo d'Orso* hotel (☎0789.702.000, @www.delphina.it; ⑧), and the far humbler but still fairly grand eponymous **campsite** (☎0789.702.007, @www.capodorso.it), both open from May to September. Equipped with a diving centre, boat hire, windsurf facilities and bungalows and caravans (③–⑤), the campsite would make a great holiday base, but gets extremely congested in high summer. Hotel and campsite are named after the nearby headland, **Capo d'Orso**, which in turn takes its name from a huge outcrop nearby, a strange bear-shaped rock (*orso* = bear), known since ancient times and even claimed to be the dwelling-place of the Laestrigonians, the mythical cannibal tribe which destroyed the fleet of Ulysses when it was docked here. To reach it, you have to pass a gate and climb the slopes of the headland. At 122m high, it makes a lofty platform to view the sensational panorama, embracing the Maddalena islands, Santa Teresa di Gallura and Corsica.

Palau

Until recently, most visitors to **PALAU** – with the exception of the US navy personnel billeted here as part of the NATO presence – were only interested in the ferry out. However, the growth of the local holiday industry has raised the profile of this minor port in the last few years, and it has become quite a lively local centre, with enough bars, restaurants and summer entertainments to keep you amused for an evening or so. There are hotels, too, making useful bases to explore the excellent beaches in the vicinity. The only sight of any interest lies outside town, the **Fortezza di Monte Altura** (daily: April–May 9am–noon & 3–6pm; June–Aug 9am–noon & 5–8pm; Sept to mid-Oct 9am–noon & 3–5pm; €3), a defensive bastion built in the nineteenth century on the rocky slope above Palau. To get here, take the signposted turn-off on the right as you leave town towards the SS125. The winding road leads a couple of kilometres up to a set of impregnable-looking granite walls, and the tall gates from which guided tours leave. Immediately in front of the gates, a surreal-looking flight of stone steps gives access to towers and the empty emplacements for guns installed during World War II, from where you can enjoy panoramic views seaward. Ask at Palau's tourist office about concerts and other performances staged in the fortress in summer.

Practicalities

In summer, Palau is connected by a twice-daily FdS train service to Arzachena and Tempio Pausania (see Travel details on p.304). The **train station** is by the port at the end of the main Via Nazionale, right next to the **Stazione Maríttima**, for ferry departures and boat tours. The town's **tourist office** is further back on this road at Via Nazionale 94 (May–Sept daily 8am–1pm & 4–8pm; Oct–April Mon–Fri 8am–1pm & 3–6pm, Sat 8am–1pm; ☎0789.709.570). As well as holding all the ticket desks for the ferries, the Stazione Maríttima is also the place for **tours** of the Maddalena islands and

As well as connecting Palau with La Maddalena (see the box on p.287), Enermar (℡899.200.001, ⓦwww.enermar.it) operates a ferry service between Palau and **Genoa** (April–Sept 1–5 weekly; 12hr), leaving from Palau at 8pm or 8.30pm, with additional sailings at 9am and 10pm or 10.30pm in summer. Crossings cost €40–65 for passengers, plus €6–10 for a semi-reclinable seat, at least €30–40 for a berth, €66–141 for a car and €38–57 for a motorbike.

Linee Lauro (℡081.551.3352, ⓦwww.medmagroup.it) runs a ferry service to **Naples** (mid-June to mid-Sept; 13.5hr), leaving on Saturdays at 7pm. Crossings cost €40–75, or €45–80 for a reclinable seat, €50–90 for a berth, €85–165 for a car. They also operate a service to **La Spezia** (July–early Sept; 13hr) leaving on Saturdays at 5pm, and costing €25–50 per passenger, plus €5 for a reclinable seat and at least €10 for a berth, plus €60–100 for a car.

For more information and tickets for all these routes, contact Agenzia Bulciolu, Via Fonte Vecchio (℡0789.709.505).

around the coasts, for which you'll pay around €25 for a full-day excursion; ask here for details or call ℡0789.735.419, 338.563.9366 or 0789.735.088.

If you want to **rent a car**, contact Trecentosessantagradi, at Via Brigate Sássari 22 (℡0789.708.565), or Naus Rental, Via Nazionale 97 (℡0789.709.083); a Smart or Fiat Panda costs around €65 a day. Naus also rents out **scooters** for €30 per day (for a 50cc model) and **mountain bikes** for €12.50 per day; Captain Morgan, at Via Fonte Vecchio 10 (℡0789.708.187), charges €40 for a 125cc scooter. You'll find an **ATM** signposted off Via Nazionale, and one at the Stazione Maríttima, and **Internet access** at *Webtime Internet Point* on Via Fonte Vecchia, above the *Grillo birreria*/snack bar.

As for **accommodation**, most places in Palau close in winter, but the following selection stays open all year. Near the port, try the *Serra* at Via Nazionale 17 (℡0789.709.519, ℗0789.709.713; ❷), with adequate but cramped rooms with private bathrooms, or the smaller and swankier *Del Molo*, on Via dei Ciclopi (℡0789.708.042, ℗0789.708.043; ❺). The hotels further back from the seafront enjoy good views: the *Piccada*, about ten minutes' walk from the port at Via degli Asfodeli, off Via Capo d'Orso (℡0789.709.344, ⓦwww.hotelpiccada.com; ❻), which has modern, spacious rooms, those with seaward views and a separate entrance costing a little more (they also rent out apartments by the week), and *La Roccia*, Via dei Mille 15 (℡0789.709.528, ⓦwww.hotellaroccia.com; ❻), which has smallish rooms and is named after the granite boulder that intrudes into the garden and lobby. If you prefer to be near the beach, book into a cabin or caravan (around €18 per person, but half-board required July–Aug) or pitch your tent at the nearest **campsite**, *Baia Saraceno* (March–Oct; ℡0789.709.403, ⓦwww.baiasaraceno.com), on the other side of a pinewood close to Punta Nera, less than a kilometre east of town – it has access to rocky inlets, sandy coves and a naturists' zone.

Palau's **restaurants** include *San Giorgio*, Vicolo La Maddalena 2 (a left turn off the main street going towards the port), where there's a good range of pizzas (eves only) as well as pastas and seafood. For a drink and an ice cream, head for *Bassa Prua* behind the *Serra* hotel on Via Fonte Vecchia, or *Guido's Bar*, a favourite meeting spot opposite the Stazione Maríttima, with a verandah. Nightlife focuses on *Il Big* **disco** at Via Capo d'Orso 30, a haunt of the U.S. service personnel stationed around here.

West of Palau

Between Palau and the port of Santa Teresa di Gallura, the dramatic rocky coastline is indented by a succession of lovely creeks and bays. The few small resorts here get very busy in summer, but are generally deserted the rest of the time, when most of the local hotels and campsites are closed.

Two or three kilometres out of Palau, a right turn brings you 3km along a minor road to **Porto Pollo** (also called Porto Puddu), a scattered locality which has become established as one of Sardinia's busiest watersports centres. A slender isthmus of beach ending in a thick knob of rock divides the two bays of Porto Pollo and Porto Liscia, creating a breakwater and thus ideal conditions for **windsurfing**: downwind of the sand bank, the sea is flat; upwind, it's choppy, fast and more suited to experts. There's a whole network of surf schools and rental operations on hand to cater to the masses of enthusiasts, but even if you're not a surfer, the dune-backed beaches on the two bays are worth going out of your way for, and you can also rent dinghies.

Among the windsurf and kitesurf operations, Sporting Club Sardinia (☎0789.704.016) or Paolo Silvestri Surf and Sail Center (☎0789.704.053), both with stalls on the beach near Isola dei Gabbiani headland should see you right. You can **rent mountain bikes** from Il Borgo (€13 per day).

At the end of the sandy limb, the *Isola dei Gabbiani* **campsite** takes its name from the bulbous promontory which it completely occupies (April–Oct; ☎0789.704.019, Ⓦwww.isoladeigabbiani.it). Caravans and bungalows are also available for rent here at €48–68 per night for two people (officially for a fortnight's minimum stay, but this requirement may be waived), and there are more splendid beaches along the shores of the "island". The only **hotel** hereabouts is *Le Dune* (April–Oct; ☎0789.704.013, Ⓦwww.hotelledune.it; ❺), a castellated three-star on an elevation less than 100m from the sea, with views to the Maddalena islands of Spargi and Budelli; at least half-board is required (€85 per person per day in peak season). The hotel also rents out mountain bikes and organizes riding excursions. There are plenty of **bars** and **pizzerias** around, such as *Il Maestrale*, a bar/pizzeria/*gelateria* complex, and the nearby and groovier *La Papaya*, a surfies' meeting place which also does breakfasts. *Le Dune* (see above) is another focus for socializing, with a bar, *birreria* and restaurant. Look out for posters advertising **local discos** in summer.

The Maddalena Islands

From Palau, the ferry crossing takes just twenty minutes to reach the **Maddalena archipelago**, a cluster of seven larger islands and a sprinkling of smaller ones. The archipelago is a favourite sailing area for yachters, and sees a number of regattas throughout the year. Boats dock at the largest of the group, **La Maddalena**, where almost all the hotels and restaurants are located; there's also a small museum of naval archeology here. From the main island, you can drive, bike or hike across to neighbouring **Caprera**, where Garibaldi spent the last third of his life. The hero of the struggle for Italian unification is remembered in a museum – his former home, which gives a fascinating insight into his long career on the world stage and his reclusive existence on the island.

La Maddalena is also the departure point for a range of boat tours to the other isles, though there is only limited access to **Santo Stéfano**, which is

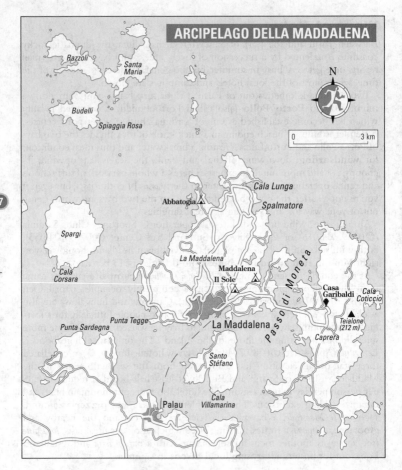

ARCIPELAGO DELLA MADDALENA

N

0   3 km

Razzoli
Santa Maria
Budelli
Spiaggia Rosa

Cala Lunga
Abbatogia ▲
Spalmatore

Spargi

Cala Corsara

La Maddalena
Maddalena
Il Sole

Punta Tegge
Punta Sardegna

La Maddalena

Passo di Moneta

Casa Garibaldi
Cala Coticcio

Teialone (212 m)
Caprera

Santo Stéfano

Palau

Cala Villamarina

almost wholly occupied by a US naval base. The boats also call at the remote, smaller islands of **Spargi**, **Budelli**, **Razzoli** and **Santa Maria**. Set amidst myriad jutting rocks, they have some perfect scraps of beach to swim from, but little else besides rock and scrub.

In 1997, the islands were granted **national park** status (extending as far south as the islands of Martorio and Soffi in the Golfo di Cugnana, and as far north as Lavezzi and Cavallo in Corsican waters). The most conspicuous wildlife in evidence on the islands are gulls, cormorants and herons, which perch on the innumerable granite rocks poking out of the sea. Even before the area was placed under protection, the archipelago harboured a rich range of wildlife, which was left relatively undisturbed as a result of the restrictions imposed by the military base. The national park status limits sailing activities, fishing (on the surface and underwater) and building; prohibitions are tightest on the northern tip of La Maddalena, around Caprera's eastern shore, and cover some of the smaller islands entirely.

Unless you're on a boat tour from Santa Teresa di Gallura (see p.292), **Palau** is the normal port of embarkation for the Maddalena archipelago. **Ferries** for the main island of La Maddalena (every 15–30min) are run by one of the main operators: Enermar (℡899.200.001, ⓦwww.enermar.it), Saremar (℡0789.709.270, ⓦwww .saremar.it) and Tremar (℡0789.730.032). The regular service ends at around 8.45pm in winter, or 11.50pm in summer, when an hourly **night service** takes over (run by Tremar; tickets on board). **Tickets** for daytime crossings are sold at Palau's Stazione Maríttima and cost around €5.50 return per person, €22 return for two people in a medium-sized car. Be warned that it can be a hectic bustle for tickets in high season, and queues are common, so it's worth arriving half an hour early to bag a place. Don't bother arguing with queue-jumpers: the chances are they are island residents who get priority rights (as well as fare discounts). It's much faster for pedestrians, of course; if you don't want to ferry your vehicle, leave it in the **car park** behind the ticket office at Palau (€2.80 for the first two hours, then €0.80 per hour); cars parked in front get fined. However, you can usually find a space in a street not too far away where you can park for free.

La Maddalena

Bearing the same name as the island, the port and sole town of **LA MADDALENA** is an upbeat place, its population of about 12,000 swollen by a large number of Italian and US sailors who lend parts of the town a garrison feel. Their headquarters are on the eastern side, a drab area of monotonous barracks guarded by armed sentries, which the recruits appear eager to leave every evening in favour of the distractions of the centre.

Most of the action takes place in the narrow lanes between the main square, Piazza Umberto I, and **Cala Gavetta**, a natural harbour five minutes' walk west of the ferry port. Now a marina for small boats, this was the original nucleus of the town. The main *passeggiata* takes place here, along Via Garibaldi. Once you've given these areas the once-over, there's little else of specific interest to see in La Maddalena's centre, though Via Améndola, which runs along the seafront between the port and Cala Gavetta, holds a few palazzi from the period of the port's main growth in the eighteenth century, and, not far from here, the modern-looking church of **Santa Maria Maddalena** contains a couple of silver candlesticks and a crucifix donated by Nelson during his sojourn in the archipelago (see the box on p.288).

West of the port in Localitá Mongiardino, however, the **Museo Archeologico Navale** on the Via Panorámica has more interest, though it has very sporadic hours, and may be open only in August. The collection gathers finds recovered from ancient wrecks in the area, notably a Roman cargo ship dragged up from the sea near Spargi in the 1950s. The vessel foundered around 120 BC, and the museum's prize exhibit is a reconstructed cross-section of the hull, showing how some two hundred of the hundreds more amphorae recovered – mostly containing wine from Campania – would have been stored for the sea passage. A second room has lead anchors and various other finds from the sea, as well as photos showing the excavation operations.

Practicalities

Ferries from Palau dock close to the central Piazza Umberto I. La Maddalena's **tourist office** is at Cala Gavetta on Piazza Baron des Geneys (summer Mon–Sat 8.30am–1pm & 4.30–7.30pm, Sun in July–Aug 9am–noon &

Between 1803 and 1805, the fleet of Admiral Nelson was a constant presence in what he called "Agincourt Sound", or the Straits of Bonifacio. It lurked in the waters around the Maddalena archipelago for fifteen months while Nelson stalked the French fleet during the run-up to the Battle of Trafalgar. Throughout this long wait, during which Nelson never once set foot on shore, he sent a stream of letters to the Admiralty in London urging that steps be taken to secure Sardinia for England – it was then the only neutral shore in this part of the Mediterranean: "And I venture to predict, that if we do not – from delicacy, or commiseration of the lot of the unfortunate King of Sardinia – the French will." The French, docked at Toulon (nicknamed "Too-Long" by Nelson's impatient sailors), eventually fled to the West Indies before returning to meet Nelson at Trafalgar.

4.30–7.30pm; winter Mon–Thurs 8.30am–1pm, Fri–Sat 8.30am–1pm & 3–5pm; ☏0789.736.321, Ⓦwww.lamaddalena.it). You can **change money** across the piazza at the Banco di Sardegna, which has an ATM. The town is not particularly well off for **hotels**, considering the volume of tourists; cheapest are the *Arcipélago* at Via Indipendenza Traversa 2 (☏0789.727.328, Ⓕ0789.728.100; ❹) – hard to find (but signposted), a fifteen-minute walk from the ferry port, with small but clean and comfortable rooms – and, in the opposite direction, the *Gabbiano* beyond Cala Gavetta at Via Giulio Césare 20 (☏0789.722.507, Ⓕ0789.722.455; ❹), excellently sited on a point overlooking Santo Stéfano and Palau. Back in the centre, right on the seafront at Via Améndola 7, the *Excelsior* (☏ & Ⓕ0789.737.020; ❺) enjoys views over the port, but has a rather down-at-heel air. All rates drop significantly out of season.

Rooms to rent (*cámere in affito*) are marked in some windows, otherwise pick up a list of addresses from the tourist office, or ask around in bars. There are also three campsites, all outside town (see p.289).

There's an abundance of **eating places**, among them *La Terrazza*, just off Piazza Umberto at Via Villa Glori 6 (closed Tues in winter), where you can eat good food at reasonable prices, either inside or on a terrace. Slightly more expensive, *Sottovento* at Via Indipendenza 1 (☏0789.727.792; closed Mon in winter) has a wide array of *antipasti* and a good choice of fresh pasta. Booking is advised in summer.

Buses run to various parts of the island (every 30min–1hr in summer, every 2hr in winter) from near the Banco di Sardegna at the end of Via XX Settembre. The best way of getting around the island is on a **bike** or **moped**, which can be rented from any of the outlets on the seafront walking towards Cala Gavetta, for €20 a day for a mountain bike, or €50 for a scooter (though prices are halved outside the peak season). Fratelli Cuccu at Via Améndola 30 (☏0789.738.528) and Nicol Sport at Via Améndola 18 (☏0789.735.400) also rent out cars as well as bikes and mopeds; you may be asked for ID or a deposit.

Around the island

The island of La Maddalena invites aimless wandering and offers a variety of sandy and rocky beaches in mostly undeveloped coves. The **beaches** on the northern and western coasts are most attractive, particularly those around the tiny port of **Madonnetta**, 5km west of La Maddalena, and at **Cala Lunga**, 5km north of town. At **Spalmatore**, there's a small sand beach with a jetty, bar and disco. One of the nearest swimming places to town is just 2km southwest at **Punta Tegge**, where the low, flat rocks make access to the sea easy.

There are three **campsites** on the island, all closed in winter. The two nearest to the port lie beyond the barracks east of town: *Il Sole* (mid-June to Oct; ☏0789.727.727), and the better-situated *Maddalena*, in the Moneta district facing Caprera island (April–Oct; ☏0789.728.051). The best location, however, is in the north of the island, in Località Abbatoggia, where *Abbatoggia* (June–Sept; ☏0789.739.173, ⓦwww.campingabbatoggia.it) sits close to some superb beaches; it also has caravans to rent (though these are often fully booked), there's a ristorante/pizzeria on-site, and you can rent bikes, canoes and windsurf equipment.

Caprera

A simple bridge built in 1891 stretches for 600m across the **Passo di Moneta** that separates La Maddalena from **Caprera**. Between October and May, half of Caprera is closed off for military purposes, but there's always plenty of space left to roam this protected woody parkland, which is undeveloped apart from Garibaldi's house in the centre and a couple of self-contained tourist complexes, one of them a *Club Med*.

Giuseppe Garibaldi (see the box on p.290) came to live on Caprera in 1855, after a glorious and highly eventful career in arms, much of it spent in exile from Italy. It was from here that he embarked on his spectacular conquest of Sicily and Naples in 1861, accompanied by his thousand Redshirts, and it was here that he returned at the end of his campaigns, to resume a simple farming life. Having first seen the island on his flight from Rome in 1849, he subsequently bought the northern part of it for £360, no doubt attracted by its proximity to the Piedmontese naval base. While he lived on Caprera, he devoted his time to writing his memoirs and a handful of bad novels, as well as farming. His neighbour was an Englishman named Collins, with whom he had some celebrated disagreements concerning wandering herds of goats, as a result of which Garibaldi built a wall dividing their properties, which can still be seen. After Collins's death in 1864, a group of English admirers provided the money for Garibaldi to buy the rest of Caprera from his ex-neighbour's family.

At the end of a tamarisk-lined road, the **museum** (June–Sept Tues–Sat 9am–6.30pm, Sun 9am–1.30pm; Oct–May Tues–Sun 9am–1.30pm; €2) is in Garibaldi's old house, the elegant South American-style **Casa Bianca**, which has been preserved pretty much as he left it. Visitors are escorted past a collection of memorabilia which include the famous *camicia rossa* (red shirt) with which he was iconized, the bed where he slept, a smaller one where he died, various scrolls, manifestos and pronouncements, a pair of ivory-and-gold binoculars given to him by the future King Edward VII, and a letter from London, dated 1867, conferring on him honorary presidency of the National Reform League. A stopped clock and a wall calendar indicate the precise time and date of his death. The tour ends with Garibaldi's grave in the garden, its rough granite contrasting with the more pompous tombs of his last wife and five of his children. Garibaldi had requested to be cremated, but following the wishes of his son Menotti, his corpse was stuffed. In 1932, fifty years after his death, his tomb was opened to reveal the body perfectly intact.

Elsewhere on the island, you can strike out in any direction to reach tranquil spots that are a welcome relief after the bustle of coach parties around Garibaldi's museum. Caprera's flora and fauna are among the most interesting of the islands, especially during spring when the heather, hawthorn and juniper present a multi-coloured mosaic amid the pines, holm oaks and myrtles, and the birdlife includes royal seagulls, shearwaters, sparrow hawks and buzzards.

Giuseppe Garibaldi (1807–82)

The most famous Italian patriot of all, **Giuseppe Garibaldi** was born in Nice of a family of fishermen and coastal traders, and for more than ten years was himself a sailor. By the age of 26 he had served in the navy of the Kingdom of Piedmont-Sardinia, and had absorbed the influence of both Giuseppe Mazzini, the great prophet of Italian nationalism, and the French Socialist thinker, the Comte de Saint-Simon. In 1834, having taken part in a failed mutiny, he was condemned to death by a court in Genoa, but managed to escape, first to France then to South America, where he lived until 1848.

These years in exile formed his education as a guerrilla warrior and wily strategist. Enlisted as a naval captain by a small republic, Rio Grande do Sul, attempting to break free from the Brazilian Empire, Garibaldi later tried his hand as a cowboy, commercial traveller and teacher, but was sucked back into the swashbuckling life when he was put in charge of the Uruguayan navy in another liberation war in 1842. The following year, he took command of a newly formed **Italian Legion** at Montevideo, the first of the famous "Redshirts" with whom his name was to be permanently linked, and in April 1848 led 60 of them back to Italy to fight for the **Risorgimento** – Italy's war of independence against the Austrians, French and Spanish. After his services were rejected by both Pope Pius IX and the Piedmontese king Carlo Alberto, Garibaldi went to Milan, where Mazzini had already established himself, and quickly won two engagements against the Austrians before withdrawing across the Swiss frontier. Garibaldi next led a group of volunteers to Rome, from which the pope had recently been expelled, and was elected deputy in the Roman Assembly in February 1849. Taking charge of the defence of the city, he managed to repulse an attack by a French army attempting to restore papal government, and defeat a Neapolitan army soon after. His spirited defence of Rome against an ensuing and ultimately unsuccessful French siege was to become one of the most glorious episodes of the Risorgimento.

Although now renowned internationally as the hero *dei due mondi* ("of the two worlds"), Garibaldi was both envied and feared by the leaders of the Risorgimento in Italy, who saw him as something of a loose cannon, and he once more found himself in exile. After time spent in Tangier, New York and Peru, where he returned to his original trade as a ship's captain, he was allowed to return to Italy in 1854, and the following year he bought part of the Sardinian island of **Caprera**, which remained his home for the rest of his life.

There are several small beaches around the shore, the most popular being **Cala Coticcio**, on the island's east coast (about a forty-minute walk from the bridge, less from the museum). A handful of fortifications lie dotted around, some built by the Savoy régime in the eighteenth century, and some from around the time of World War I. You can also climb a long stairway leading to the lookout tower on **Teialone**, at 212m the highest point of the Maddalena archipelago.

Santo Stéfano, Spargi and Budelli

Halfway between La Maddalena and the coast, the island of **Santo Stéfano** was briefly captured by French forces in 1793 in an abortive attempt to take possession of Sardinia. From here, the young **Napoleon Bonaparte**, then a Lieutenant-Colonel in the Corsican National Guard, commanded a bombardment of La Maddalena. The island today is mainly occupied by US and Italian military installations, including a nuclear submarine base. The archipelago has always had a strong naval tradition, harbouring a fleet of the Royal

His career was by no means over, however, and he took up arms again in 1859, when he helped to bring about Piedmont's liberation of Lombardy, and in May 1860, when he set out with his Redshirts on the greatest venture of his life, which was to result in the **conquest of Sicily and Naples**. For this brilliant escapade, he lacked all government support, and, in his eyes, all recognition of his achievement by the Piedmontese conservatives, who still distrusted him. Garibaldi was already deeply offended by Piedmont's having handed his home town of Nice over to France earlier in 1860 (it had become Piedmontese in 1814). Consequently, when the new kingdom of Italy finally came into being in 1861, the popular hero was in virtually permanent opposition. At least he had his now legendary fame to fall back on, which led to his being offered a command in the American Civil War by Lincoln, and to his rapturous reception when he visited England in 1864.

Anxious to keep Garibaldi on his side, Vittore Emanuele, the new king of Italy, recruited him on campaigns against the Austrians and French in Italy in 1862, 1866, 1867 and 1870–71. However, as these irregular expeditions usually went further than the king had authorized, and were anyway only intermittently successful, relations continued to be frosty, and Garibaldi eventually became something of a recluse on Caprera – while still keeping abreast of affairs, receiving numerous deputations and making regular pronouncements on issues of the day. Towards the end he called himself a Socialist (though Karl Marx disowned him) and even a pacifist, and also proved to be a champion of **labour rights** and **women's emancipation**. He showed himself ahead of his time in espousing such unpopular causes as racial equality and the abolition of capital punishment, though he also believed in dictatorship, distrusting parliaments which he saw as nests of corruption.

Opinion in Italy is still sharply divided between those who dismiss Garibaldi as an amateur and meddling charlatan, and others who adore him. Indisputably, he deserves his place in history if only as a pioneer of unorthodox guerrilla tactics and for his ability to inspire reckless loyalty. He certainly succeeded better than any of his contemporaries in rousing the Italian people, by whom he is remembered as a professional rebel and indomitable individualist who refused to retire gracefully, continuing to wear his gaucho costume until he died.

House of Savoy long before NATO arrived, and from a boat tour you can spot traces of the fortifications erected here at the end of the eighteenth century. Trippers can disembark on the eastern side of the island, around the **Spiaggia del Pesce** beach, where there are a couple of holiday enclaves. At the southern end, traces of Neolithic life have been found at **Cala Villamarina**.

The best beach on **Spargi** is on the southern littoral at **Cala Corsara**, with transparent water – though as it's a regular stop for boat tours, it's not exactly untrammelled. Nearby was found the wreck of a Roman vessel from the second century BC, now preserved in La Maddalena's marine museum (see p.287).

On **Budelli** the famous **Spiaggia Rosa** ("pink beach"), immortalized by the director Michelangelo Antonioni in his film *Il Deserto Rosso* (*Red Desert*, 1965), is also a boat-stop, while the limpid waters around the island attract **scuba-divers**. If you're interested, the tourist offices at Palau and La Maddalena can supply lists of local dive operators who come here.

Santa Teresa di Gallura and around

On Sardinia's northern tip, the small town of **Santa Teresa di Gallura** is the main port for ships to Corsica, whose cliffs are clearly visible just 11km away. Not all the people who come here are passing through, however. If **beaches** are your thing, Santa Teresa must rank as one of the island's most attractive holiday destinations, surrounded by scintillating stretches of sand, with exhilarating views across the Straits of Bonifacio. To cope with the demand, the town has Gallura's widest selection of hotels, restaurants and bars, and has recently spawned the region's liveliest bar-culture – though life grinds to a much slower and calmer pace outside the summer months.

From Santa Teresa, a local minibus service transports tourists to the beaches on either side of town: to the east, beyond Punta Falcone to **La Marmorata**, extensive but quite heavily developed, and westwards to **Capo Testa**, a panoramic headland where huge granite boulders make a striking backdrop to the fine sand beaches. Buses bound for Castelsardo make stops at the more distant beaches of **Rena Maiore**, **Vignola** and **Ísola Rossa**, on Sardinia's long northwestern littoral, well worth making the effort to reach. Catch any bus going towards Palau to reach **Porto Pozzo**, presently a small-scale resort, though clearly destined for greater things.

Santa Teresa di Gallura

Like most of Gallura's coastal towns, **SANTA TERESA DI GALLURA**, Sardinia's most northerly town and the main embarkation point for Corsica, has a prosaic, modern look. Though there was a Roman settlement in the region, and garrisons were stationed here at different times by the Genoans and Aragonese, the town was only founded in 1808 by order of the Savoyard king Vittorio Emanuele I, who named it after his wife Maria Teresa of Austria. Apart from a Spanish watchtower, however, few buildings of the town date even as far back as the nineteenth century, and it owes its prevailing tone to its development in the late 1950s as a holiday base. In recent years, the growth of Santa Teresa's marina and the swelling pockets of holiday homes on the eastern side of the Longone creek have helped to make this one of Sardinia's most full-on holiday resorts, while permanently transforming the local landscape.

Santa Teresa is arranged on a regular grid of modern streets, centring on the main Piazza Vittorio Emanuele, site of the tourist office (see p.293) and a bunch of bars and coral shops. Beyond the square, the Via del Mare ends after a couple of hundred metres at a high bluff dominated by the **Torre Aragonese**, a well-preserved Spanish watchtower from the sixteenth century, officially known as the Torre di Longosardo (open in summer; €2). With the help of the telescope installed in the tower, you can take in the sweeping views

---

Boat tours from Santa Teresa

Between Easter and September, tours around the coasts and to the islands can be booked at Consorzio delle Bocche, at Piazza Vittorio Emanuele 16 (☎0789.755.112, ⓦwww.consorziobocche.com), and Marco Polo, Via XX Settembre 16 (☎0789.754.942), or directly at booths at the port. The 9.30am departure takes in the western isles of the Maddalena archipelago, including stops at the beaches of Santa Maria, Budelli and Spargi, a stroll around the town of La Maddalena and a lunch on board, with a return at 5pm, all for around €35 per person, less outside the peak season.

over the Straits of Bonifacio, and, nearer at hand, the minuscule isle of Monica (or Municca). To the east can be seen the burgeoning belt of new developments on the far side of the deep inlet of Longone (or Longosardo). A panoramic path leads beyond the tower and down to the waterside, and there are also steps leading west of the tower to the town's main beach, **Spiaggia Rena Bianca**, the focus of most of the fun in the tourist season.

The **marina** and port area lie out of sight further down the Longone creek, and are best reached from Via del Porto. Kiosks selling tickets for Corsica and the various boat tours (see p.292) are located here, while the capacious marina – also the subject of a continuing programme of expansion – is jammed with yachts and blue and white fishing vessels.

Practicalities

ARST and FdS **buses** arrive and depart from Via Eleonora d'Arborea off Via Nazionale, the main road into town. This is also the terminus for the blue Sardabus **shuttle buses** for beaches in the vicinity (June–Sept; buy tickets on board). For longer routes, tickets and timetables are available from *Baby Bar* on Via Lu Pultali, just round the corner from the bus stop and from Via Nazionale (closed Tues, when you can buy tickets on board or from the *tabacchino* nearby on Via Nazionale). **Ferries to Corsica** are operated by Moby Lines (℡0789.751.449, ⓦwww.moby.it) and Saremar (℡0789.754.788, ⓦwww.saremar.it). A single ticket for foot-passengers is €12–15 and medium-sized cars cost €22–30.

Pick up a map of the town and surrounding area, and accommodation listings, from the **tourist office** on the main Piazza Vittorio Emanuele 24 (June–Sept daily 8.30am–1pm & 3.30–8pm; Oct–May Mon–Fri 9am–1pm & 3.30–6.30pm, Sat 9am–1pm; ℡0789.754.127, ⓦwww.regione.sardegna.it/aaststg).

Accommodation

Santa Teresa di Gallura has a plentiful supply of central **hotels**, and several more outside town where they are best-placed to take advantage of some of Sardinia's most alluring beaches. Many close over the winter months, while vacancies can be difficult to come by in summer, particularly in August when groups from the mainland descend on Santa Teresa. Most places insist on half- or full-board in peak season. The nearest campsite lies 6km west of town beyond Capo Testa (see p.297). See Listings, or ask at the tourist office about **weekly rents** in apartments in and around town.

Bellavista Via Sonnino 8 ℡ & ℗0789.754.162. Considering this hotel's prime position above Rena Bianca beach, you'll find excellent rates for the fourteen comfortable doubles, though these are often booked up months in advance – rooms with balconies and views go first, of course. Half-board (€52–59 a head) is obligatory in July & Aug. Open May–Oct. ❸

Canne al Vento Via Nazionale 23 ℡0789.754.219, ℗0789.754.948. Smart, family-run hotel on the main road into town; the rooms at the back are quiet enough. The hotel has attracted such luminaries as Antonioni in the past, mostly drawn by its renowned restaurant (see p.294). Half-board here is a positive bonus, at €72 each in peak season, much less at other times. Open April–Sept. ❸

Da Cecco Via Po 3 ℡0789.754.220, ⓦwww.hotel-dacecco.com. Great value in this modern palazzo above the port, with a roof terrace and a pink-and-green colour scheme. Open late March to Nov. ❺

Corallaro Rena Bianca ℡0789.755.475, ⓦwww.hotelcorallaro.it. Santa Teresa's classiest hotel, just back from the beach and enjoying superb views over to the Corsican coast from its rooms and terraces. There's a minimum stay of three days, or a week in peak season, and there's a half- or full-board requirement in Aug (half-board in Aug costs €102–120 per person). Prices drop significantly in April–June and Sept. Open April to mid-Oct. ❼

Marinaro Via Angioy 48 ℡0789.754.112, ⓦwww.hotelmarinaro.it. In a quiet spot in the centre of town, this solid, old-fashioned building contains a modern, well-designed hotel, smartly painted in cheerful stripes. Rooms on two floors are a good size, and fully-equipped. In August, guests must take at least half-board, which comes to €75 each. ④

Miramare Piazza della Libertà ☎0789.754.103, ℱ0789.754.675. This unprepossessing hotel occupies one of Santa Teresa's prime scenic locations, for which it commands premium rates. No half-board requirement. Open late May to late Oct. ⑥

Moderno Via Umberto 39 ☎0789.754.233, ℱ0789.759.205. Enthusiastically-run hotel halfway between the bus stop and the main Piazza Vittorio Emanuele, with pleasantly furnished rooms but no restaurant. Open April to mid-Oct. ⑤

Sa Domo Via Genova 18 ☎0789.755.564, ℱ0789.754.124. Family-run and family-based hotel in the centre of town, with huge terraces on the second floor. There's a pool, and music,

cabaret and children's events are staged nightly in summer, with excursions available by day. ④

Sandalion Via Valle d'Aosta 12 ☎0789.754.541, ☒www.hotelsandalion.it. One of Santa Teresa's cheaper options, plain and clean, with English spoken; some rooms have a balcony. At least half-board is required in July and Aug (€47–70). Open late March to mid-Oct. ③

Scano Via Lazio 4 ☎ & ℱ0789.754.447. A good, cheap two-star on the west side of town (off the road to Capo Testa), with relaxed family management and a reasonable restaurant. Rooms are functional, and often booked up. The requisite half-board in July and Aug comes to €40–60 per head. ②

Smeraldo Via XX Settembre 23 ☎0789.754.175, ℱ0789.755.795. Small hotel with only twelve rooms, but centrally located just up from Piazza Vittorio Emanuele, close to the main beach. Street noise can be a problem. ⑤

Eating

Many of the town's abundant choice of **restaurants** offer reasonable fixed-price menus, and most are boarded up after October. For provisions for the beach, call in at the *Bottega* **alimentari** at Via Vittorio Emanuele 4, selling a range of local goodies.

Barbagia Via Valle d'Aosta 2. Rather garish trattoria, with tables outdoors and a good range of set menus (€10–25), which include Sard specialities. Open April–Oct. Inexpensive–moderate.

Canne al Vento Via Nazionale 23 ☎0789.754.219. Elegant restaurant with a bamboo-covered terrace, attached to a pensione (see p.293). The menu includes seafood cooked in all kinds of ways as well as such authentic elements of local cuisine as *suppa cuata* (bread, cheese, and tomato soup) and *porcheddu* (roast suckling pig). Open eves only. Moderate–expensive.

Due Palmi Via Capo Testa. Unpretentious pizzeria/trattoria meal west of the centre, with a small verandah. The staple local dishes can be sampled on set-price menus. Closed Thurs in winter. Moderate.

Pape Satan Via Lamármora 20. Basic back-street pizzeria with small courtyard. No credit cards. Open evenings only. Inexpensive–moderate.

Poldo's Via Garibaldi 4 ☎0789.755.860. Cool and cosmopolitan restaurant and wine bar that's often jammed, despite having plenty of capacity in four rooms (two non-smoking). Service can be slow, but the food is usually worth the wait. Closed Mon in winter. Moderate.

La Torre Via del Mare 36. Busy restaurant (no pizzas) below the Miramare hotel and above the main beach, offering a reliable range of Sard dishes. Moderate. Closed Wed in winter.

Tropican Spiaggia Rena Bianca. Ristorante/pizzeria right on the beach in front of the Corallaro hotel. Inexpensive–moderate.

Bars and entertainment

Santa Teresa's intense **bar life** is loud and fun in summer, but melts away almost without trace in the winter months. Recommended stops on or off the main Piazza Vittorio Emanuele include *Bar Conti* at Via Regina Margherita 2 (closed Wed), *Central Bar 80*, on the corner of the square, both serving *panini* and ice creams, and two places with attached *paninotecas* and upper floors with music: the *Groove Café* on Via XX Settembre (closed Sun in winter), and the glitzier *Caffè Mediterraneo*, Via Amsicora 7 (closed Mon in winter).

If you feel like a dance, the biggest local **club** is *Éstasi* (☎0789.755.570), a turn-off on the right two or three kilometres out of town near the church of Buoncammino. It's open-air and removed from other buildings, so your best bet is to follow your ears. More sedate entertainment is provided by the **open-air cinema** on Via Capo Testa, nightly from mid-June to August. Other diversions are never far away in summer, for example a **sagra del pesce**, or fish festival, with samplings, during the second week of July; a **sailing regatta** between Corsica and Sardinia at the end of July, and a religious procession for the Assumption on August 15. Windsurfing championships are also held in the Straits most years.

Listings

Ambulance ☎118.

Apartments GULP, Via Nazionale 58 (☎0789.755.689, ⓦwww.gulpimmobiliare.it), and Holiday Immobiliare, Via Nazionale 51 (☎0789.741.079, ⓦwww.holidayimmobiliare.it), have apartments in town, or at Capo Testa, Porto Quadro, Marmorata and Rena Maiore. The weekly tariff for a two-bed apartment in town ranges from €200 in May and June to €750 in Aug, up to fifty percent more at one of the bathing localities. A minimum stay of one or two weeks is normally required.

Bank Banco di Sássari in Piazza Vittorio Emanuele (Mon–Fri 8.20am–1.20pm & 2.30–3.30pm, Sat 8.20–11.20am) has an ATM. Banco di Sardegna on Via Nazionale has similar hours. Global Information (see Bike rental) also changes money, open daily in summer 8.30am–1pm & 4–8pm.

Bike rental Global Information on Via Maria Teresa (☎0789.755.080) has mountain bikes (€10 per day), mopeds (€40) and scooters (up to €52) for rent. GULP (see Apartments) also does bike rentals.

Boat hire Contact Lo Squalo Bianco at Spiaggia Rena Bianca (☎0789.750.113) for motorboats, canoes and pedalos.

Car rental Sardinia Car, Via Maria Teresa (☎0789.754.247). The agent for Maggiore is the

Viaggi Sardorama travel agent (see below); for Hertz, the agent is GULP (see Apartments).

Diving Local diving operators include No Limits, Via del Porto 16 (☎0789.759.026, ⓦwww.divingmediterraneo.it), and Centro Sub, Via Tibula 11 (☎0789.741.059, ⓦwww .marinadilongone.it). Dives cost around €35–50 per hour, plus equipment rental. Night dives are also offered.

Internet access Infocell, Via Nazionale 2 (€6 per hour). Open Mon–Sat 9am–1pm & 4–8pm, Sun 9am–1pm.

Laundry Lavanderia Jefferson, Via Genova 31. Leave your dirty washing here for picking up (ironed) after 1–2 days; shirts are €3.70, trousers €4.70.

Post office Via Eleonora d'Arborea, on the corner of the square where the buses come in, open Mon–Fri 8.10am–1.15pm, Sat 8.05am–12.45pm. Cash can be changed here.

Taxis Office on Via Cavour (☎0789.754.286), or try the rank on Piazza Vittorio Emanuele or at the port, or call ☎0789.754.741. The run to Olbia air-port is priced at around €65.

Travel agent Viaggi Sardorama at Via Tibula 11 (☎0789.754.464) can arrange air and sea tickets, as well as excursions in the area and beyond. Also rents cars.

East out of Santa Teresa

Some of Sardinia's most alluring **beaches** lie only a short ride out of Santa Teresa, all with superb views over to Corsica. To reach them from town, turn off at the signposts on the main Via Nazionale, or turn off the SS133bis Palau road; in summer, a local bus service connects the nearest beaches. Swimmers, sailors and windsurfers should all beware of the **strong currents** coursing through the Straits of Bonifacio, particularly around the northernmost cape of Punta Falcone.

There's safe swimming three kilometres or so east along the coast, in the deep inlet of **Porto Quadro**. Another couple of kilometres further east **Punta Falcone** is the Sardinian mainland's most northerly point, sheltering to east-wards the biggest sandy beach along here at **La Marmorata**, an exquisite spot marred by the proximity of vast villa complexes. The swimming, though, is superb, with the serrated profile of the Ísola di Marmorata out to sea. The next beach down, **Marazzino**, is reached from the same turn-off from the SS133bis (and there are capacious parking areas here and at La Marmorata). **La Licciola** also has a scattering of holiday houses, though not enough to overwhelm this small beach.

Porto Pozzo is a small beach and fishing locality about 15km east of Santa Teresa, at the edge of the deepest of the inlets hereabouts, also called Porto Pozzo. At present, this is little more than a bar and a few houses, though things liven up considerably in the season, when you can eat at the beach-side trattoria, and consult the information office on the main Via Nazionale (open summer only).

If you want to spend any time in Porto Pozzo, there's a handful of **hotels** on Via Aldo Moro, including the *Frassetto* (T0789.752.007; ❸), which has a restaurant, and the smaller and more basic *Locanda Porto Pozzo* (T0789.752.124; no credit cards; ❷), opposite the road to the beach, which also leads to the *Arcobaleno* **campsite** (May–Sept; T0789.752.040, Wwww.campingarcobaleno.it), right next to the sea, where caravans are available for €50–60 per night. **Boat trips** to the islands of Spargi, Budelli and Santa Maria leave from the quay here.

West out of Santa Teresa

Three kilometres west of Santa Teresa, **Capo Testa** is one of Sardinia's finest bathing localities, a rocky promontory at the end of a narrow isthmus, surrounded by turquoise sea. Though it gets extremely popular in summer, it makes an excellent destination outside the peak months, and has a handful of hotels worth considering as alternatives to staying in town, all open in summer only. The headland has some scraps of sandy beach and even some meagre remains of a Roman settlement called Tibula – truncated granite columns and some fragments of stone by the waterside. Material from the nearby quarries was used both for the columns of the Pantheon in Rome and for Pisa's cathedral. Beyond, standing amid a clutter of surreal, wind-chiselled rock formations, a lighthouse casts its beam from the point.

Among Capo Testa's **beaches**, take your pick between those facing Corsica on one side, and those with views towards the northern Sardinian coast sloping away westward on the other. The most popular ones are the **Spiaggia dei Due Mari** – situated on either side of the isthmus, facing north and south – and those actually on Capo Testa, such as **Spiaggia Rosa**. The **Spiaggia Levante** (also called Baia Santa Reparata) on the north side, and **Spiaggia Ponente** (or Cala La Colba) on the south, are the places to rent surfboards and other craft, or enrol in a diving or sailing course.

If you want to go farther afield, there are more beaches and plenty of privacy behind the thick pinewoods flanking the SS200 coastal road south and west. First and best of these is the extensive **Rena Maiore** near the tourist village of the same name 8km due south of Santa Teresa of Capo Testa, with snack bars and rental facilities in summer. Smaller beaches follow in quick succession further west, all worth investigating, including a cluster around **Vignola**, about 10km west of Rena Maiore, signposted off the SS200. The locality is named after the vineyards which produce the region's best wine, Vermentino di Gallura.

South of here, the road tracks inland, away from the sea, where a sequence of holiday villa developments lies tucked out of sight at the end of private roads. In fact the coast in these parts is in the process of being privatized, and, following the example of the Costa Smeralda, has been dubbed **Costa Paradiso**. There are indeed some heavenly spots here, but be prepared to backtrack when you reach a barrier across the road with lavish villas on the other side.

Access is easier to the evolving holiday resort of **Ísola Rossa**, reached along a five-kilometre road off the SS200. It's an impressive site, on a promontory opposite the reddish island after which the resort is named, with a small port and a clutch of hotels and trattorias. Overlooked by a stout sixteenth-century watchtower, the indented, craggy coast to the west shelters some small patches of beach among the coves, while sand-seekers will be spoiled by the 10km stretch of virtually undeveloped beach extending to the south of Ísola Rossa at **Badesi Mare**, with hazy views over to Castelsardo, 25km southwest (see p.247).

Practicalities

The best **hotel** in the Capo Testa area is *Bocche di Bonifacio* (April to mid-Oct; ☏0789.754.202; ❸), where you can stay comfortably and cheaply in clean rooms just a few metres above the sands. **Apartments** are also available (to rent by the month only in Aug), and there's a wonderful **restaurant** with cheap Sard specialities. Other hotels here include the much grander *Capo Testa e dei Due Mari* (May to mid-Oct; ☏0789.754.333, Ⓕ0789.754.482; ❺), and the appropriately named *Large Hotel Mirage* (June–Sept; ☏0789.754.207, Ⓕ0789.755.518; ❻). In Ísola Rossa, the swish *Corallo*, 100m from the beach on Via Lungomare and run by a young French-Italian couple (April–Oct; ☏079.694.055, Ⓦwww.hotelcorallo.20m.com; ❸), has excellent facilities and very reasonable rates (though these may increase in future), while across the road, the much more modest *Vitti* (☏079.694.005, Ⓔvittyhotel@tiscali.it; ❸) is a traditional family-run pensione. Half-board is obligatory at all of these places in summer.

The nearest **campsite** to Santa Teresa lies 6km west of town, signposted off the Castelsardo road: *La Liccia* (mid-April to Sept; ☏0789.755.190, Ⓦwww.campinglaliccia.com), spreading out on a shady elevation about 400m from the beach. Caravans and bungalows are available, costing €48–55 for two people per night. There are plenty of other, smaller sites around that are closer to the sea: try *Marina delle Rose* at Vignola (☏079.602.290, Ⓦwww.marinadellerose.com), an "ecological" campsite under shady pines, with bungalows for rent (€70–110 nightly for two).

Buses run to Capo Testa four times daily mid-June to mid-September (30min; about €2 return); buy tickets on board. The last bus back leaves at 5.30pm. Other buses towards Castelsardo can drop you at or near the beaches at Rena Maiore, Vignola and Ísola Rossa.

Inland Gallura

Although most people are content to admire from afar the dramatic mountain-scape backing onto Gallura's coast, you can't fail to be intrigued by the spiky pinnacles lying just a short way inland, where the small towns and villages retain far more of Gallura's essential character than any of the region's coastal resorts. The chief town in these parts, **Tempio Pausánia**, has a calm dignity lacking on the coast, and makes a good base for refreshing excursions into the hills, with most of the region's hotels and a good choice of restaurants. The obvious destination for local outings is nearby **Monte Limbara**, Gallura's highest peak, with glorious views extending in all directions. Southwest of Limbara, one of Sardinia's many artificial lakes, **Lago Coghinas**, also makes a great area to hike around, and the nearby village of **Berchidda** provides handy accommodation.

Where the country is not bare and arid, it's covered with a thick mantle of holm oak and **cork oak** forest, the latter providing the area's main industry. In September and October you are sure to notice lorry-loads of the silver and red bark being transported to processing plants in Olbia and Arbatax, and you can see at all times the lower trunks stripped to their rust-red stems. The main centre for cork-processing is **Calangianus**, a good place to purchase cork products to take home, and close to the village of **Luras**, site of some intriguing prehistoric dolmens. North of here, another lake, **Lago di Liscia**, stands close to a magnificent forest of centuries-old wild olive trees. West of Tempio, **Aggius** is famous for its carpets, and lies close to an extraordinary area of knobbly, rock-strewn slopes.

Come in winter and you'll find the peaks snow-clad, while spring is the best time to appreciate the *macchia*-covered lower slopes, woven with cistus, gorse, juniper, heather, myrtle and a hundred other wild species, pungent with diverse herbal scents. Before leaving, take away with you a jar of the famous bitter **honey** produced in these parts and for sale in the local shops: you'll probably already have sampled it poured over *sebadas*.

This is one of the few areas in Sardinia where you'll see isolated farmsteads, or *stazzi*, originally founded by settlers from Corsica fleeing the strife on that island in the eighteenth century – and the inhabitants of Gallura still have a reputation for the touchy sense of honour and vengeance for which Corsicans are famous.

The area is best reached either from the SS199 running between Olbia and Sássari, or the roads climbing inland from Arzachena, Palau, Vignola and Ísola Rossa. Those without their own transport could make use of the narrow-gauge **railway** that stoically burrows through the region, stopping at Tempio Pausánia, Calangianus and Arzachena on its long, tortuous route from Palau. Beware, though – some of the stations are located in quite remote areas. Far more useful are the regular **bus** services that connect Tempio, Aggius and Calangianus with the main coastal towns.

Tempio Pausánia and around

"Capital" of Gallura since the Romans established camps here to control the region's inland tracts, **TEMPIO PAUSÁNIA** has all the slow-moving solidity of a typical mountain town, conserving an appearance of calm well-being. The town had a greater profile in the eighteenth and nineteenth centuries, when it was the administrative centre of the Gallura region, benefitting also from the presence of therapeutic mineral waters. Though the springs remain, most of the commercial and bureaucratic activity has shifted to the coast in general, and to Olbia in particular. This at least has saved Tempio from the unplanned construction that has blighted much of Olbia since the 1960s, and the present-day town has a homogeneous appearance, its uniform granite-grey centre a pleasant place for a wander, if oddly lacking much of specific architectural interest.

Lowlanders from Olbia and around frequent the resort in the summer, relishing the superb climate which has always kept the area malaria-free. As you might expect at a height of 566m, the air here is crisp and fresh, and long views stretch out on every side, most dramatically towards the region's highest mountain, Monte Limbara (see p.300).

At the centre of town, Tempio's **Municipio** dominates Piazza Gallura, behind which Via Roma leads to the **Cattedrale** in Piazza San Pietro (daily 7am–noon & 3.30–6.30pm). This was originally a fifteenth-century

Tempio's Carnival

Tempio's week-long **Carnevale** celebrations have grown hugely in recent years to become one of Sardinia's principal festivities. The pagan element is strong, featuring parades of outlandish allegorical floats, and the high points include the symbolic marriage of two puppets, Re Giorgo (King George, a sort of Carnival King) and the peasant girl Mennena, on Carnival Sunday, followed by a distribution of corn fritters (*fritelle*); on Shrove Tuesday, King George is burned in a ceremonial bonfire.

Romanesque construction, though its present appearance owes so much to a drastic nineteenth-century restoration that only the belltower is original, and even this was modified in 1822. The interior is now mostly Baroque in appearance, devoid of much interest, though the third and fourth chapels on the left have good wooden altars from the eighteenth century. Opposite the cathedral, the **Oratorio del Rosario** from the same period has an austere but elegant front, mixing Baroque and late-Romanesque motifs. Inside there is another wooden altarpiece, this time decorated with pure gold. The granite ensemble is completed by the **Oratorio di Santa Croce**, located right behind the cathedral and joined to it at its restoration in the nineteenth century. It has a wooden altar from the early eighteenth century, originally from a Franciscan monastery in Alghero, and wood bas-reliefs on the right from the seventeenth century.

Out of town, there are some worthwhile excursions, best made with your own transport. You could walk, though, to the nearest, the **Fonti Rinaggiu**, a wooded spot a couple of kilometres away (follow signs, *Alle Terme*, up Via San Lorenzo from Largo de Gásperi). The waters are prized for their diuretic qualities, and the spring is usually crowded with locals filling up flagons of the stuff. A more compelling sight could also be visited on foot from the centre, 2km north on the Palau road (SS133), where **Nuraghe Maiori** lies signposted off to the right along a dirt road. Surrounded by cork woods, the *nuraghe* has one round room on the right as you enter, another on the left, with a corridor giving access to the main chamber. From here, steps wind up to a parapet, from which there's a wonderful view of Gallura's jagged peaks, also embracing Tempio and Aggius as well as miles of fields and vineyards.

Practicalities

Tempio's **train station** for the summer service to Arzachena and Palau is just west of the centre. ARST **buses** stop here and at two other stops in town. The **tourist office**, on Piazza Gallura (Mon–Fri 10am–1pm & 4.30–7pm, Sat 10am–1pm; ☎079.631.273), sells bus tickets, and can also point you towards the town's three **hotels**: most central is the *Petit*, at Piazza De Gásperi 9 (☎079.631.134, ⓦwww.petit-hotel.it; ⑤), a slick, modern business-folks' lodge, with some rooms enjoying fine views; a kilometre's walk uphill from here, right by the Fonti Rinaggiu, the *Delle Sorgenti* at Via delle Fonti 6 (☎079.630.033, ⓕ079.671.516; ④) has a certain run-down charm and another riveting vista, this time from the edge of town; remotest is the *Pausania Inn* in Località Battino, a kilometre east of town on the Palau road (☎079.634.037, ⓦwww.hotelpausaniainn.com; ⑤–⑥), which has a tennis court and pool and can organize expeditions into the mountains. All three places have restaurants.

In Piazza Gallura, the Banco di Napoli (8.25am–1.20pm & 2.40–3.45pm) can **change money** and has an ATM. The **post office** is on Piazza De Gásperi (Mon–Fri 8.15am–6.15pm, Sat 8.15am–1pm).

Piazza Gallura has a supermarket where you can stock up with provisions, or you can eat at a good range of **restaurants**. At Via Garibaldi 9, next to the church in Piazza Purgatorio, the semi-formal *Il Purgatorio* (closed Tues) is solidly old-fashioned and features such local specialities as hare (*lepre*), boar (*cinghiale*) and snails (*lumache*) for €10–12. *Il Giardino* (closed Wed) is a pizzeria/ristorante dating from 1926 at Via Cavour 1 (off Piazza Gallura), with grilled lamb among the items on the menu, and an open-air verandah. Off Corso Matteotti at Via Novara 2, the *Trattoria Gallurese* serves typical local items such as soup (*zuppa gallurese*), lamb (*scottadito di agnello*) and boar, and has a set-price menu for €20. *Il Fagotto* on Piazza Italia has good take-away **pizzas**. Make sure you sample a glass of the local Vermentino with your meal, a light, dry white wine drunk as an aperitif or with desserts.

In the evenings, you can repair to a cosy Irish **pub**, the *Sporting*, on Piazza Don Minzoni 12, which serves *panini* and *piadine* (unleavened bread with mozzarella and tomato, or fish) and has occasional live music at weekends. *Millennium*, about 3km outside town on Via Panorámica, has a *birreria* below and a dance floor upstairs, with live music on Friday and Saturday; entry is usually around €10. It's an unusual, octagonal building, with outstanding 360-degree views across to the encircling mountains.

Monte Limbara and around

Though not huge by Italian standards, the **Monte Limbara** massif towers above the rest of Gallura. You can drive to this thickly wooded peak by taking a left turn off the main road south to Óschiri after about 8km (signposted); you could park your vehicle here and walk, or else drive up along a narrow road that twists up the pine-clad flanks of the mountain. The road climbs for a long way, affording fantastic views all around, then follows a ridge before reaching a forest of TV antennas and satellite dishes. Near here is a *punto panorámico* where a statue of the Madonna and Child stands festooned with charms and bracelets, an odd miscellany of personal mementos, lighters, hair-grips, even strips of gum, donated by the faithful. Nearby, the plain **Chiesa di Santa Madonna della Neve** stands at the site of a spring.

The road passes within a few hundred metres of the highest summit, **Punta Balestrieri** (1359m). There are bracing views, of course, even as far as Tavolara island, and several of the curious contorted rocks that are such a feature of the area. The peaks of this massif have become the haunt of hiking enthusiasts in recent years, and are also popular with free climbers. There's an endless choice of paths and tracks to explore; the tourist office in Tempio Pausánia can supply you with a very rough map of routes, and with a list of local operators for **guided excursions.**

Lago di Coghinas

The Óschiri road continues south, descending from **Passo della Limbara** (640m); it's a scenic ride through cork forests and *macchia*, the road usually empty but for flocks of sheep. At the bottom of the valley, **Lago di Coghinas** swings into view. Dammed in 1926 to provide a reservoir and hydro-electric power, the artificial lake has a lovely shore, alternately rocky and sandy, that makes a good picnic spot.

The FdS **bus** between Tempio and Ozieri makes a stop at the lake, and FS **trains** between Olbia and Ozieri-Chilivani also stop at the village of Óschiri, just three or four kilometres east of the lake. Between the lake and Óschiri, the scanty ruins of a medieval castle and church, a Roman fort and a *nuraghe* all lie close to each other.

Berchidda

East of the lake, just off the main SS199, **BERCHIDDA** is an important producer of Vermentino wine – one of Sardinia's most renowned whites – as well as of pecorino cheese and an intriguing goat's-milk liqueur. It's not a particularly attractive village, though it's the starting point for expeditions to Limbara and around. An easy ramble from the village follows a track leading 4km west to the **Castello di Monte Acuto**, a desolate ruin once the home of Ubaldo Visconti and later an outpost of the Doria and Malaspina families. The walls are mostly rubble now, but it makes an exhilarating ascent, and you can continue for another four or five kilometres along the path to the shores of Lago Coghinas.

There are two reasonably-priced **hotels** in Berchidda: *Sos Chelvos*, Via Umberto 52 (℡079.704.935, Ⓕ079.704.921; ❷), and the slightly more expensive *Nuovo Limbara*, Via Coghinas (℡079.704.165, Ⓕ079.705.030; ❸), both with en-suite bathrooms and restaurants.

Aggius

Ten kilometres west of Tempio, **AGGIUS** is another popular highland retreat, enlivened by its colour-washed granite houses with wrought-iron balconies. The village, which occupies a superb panoramic position in the midst of massive boulders and corkwoods, boasts a strong choral tradition, its choir having taken part in the Welsh Eisteddfod. The village is also known for its woven carpets, produced using traditional methods, which you can view between July and September, usually in the Pro Loco on Via Andrea Vasa (℡079.620.803). Cork and granite constitute the foundations of the local economy, helping to account for the well-to-do appearance of the solid-looking houses.

On the first Sunday of October, the **Festa di li 'Agghiani** ("Bachelors' Feast") takes over the village. Traditionally an opportunity for the young folk to meet and make merry, it's now mainly an excuse for the locals to consume a lot of *suppa cuata*, the favourite *gallurese* soup dish.

Leaving Aggius northward, a left turn towards Trinità d'Agoltu and Ísola Rossa (see p.297) soon brings you to a wilderness of rocky debris, dubbed **La Valle della Luna**. In this "lunar valley", boulders are strewn across an arena-like hillside, looking – in the words of the travel writer Virginia Waite – "as though a giant has pettishly emptied his playbox of rocks and thrown them carelessly about". Many have been carted away by illegal quarriers, though plenty remain, including some said to resemble human figures – one on the left of the road is said to recall Plato's head. Where the road curves to the left, take a rough track on the right for a few metres to reach the **Nuraghe Izzana**. The road leading northwest of here as far as the coast at Ísola Rossa (see p.297) makes a highly scenic drive or cycle, with numerous possibilities for walks and roadside picnics. You can also take the parallel Strada Panoramica

A Sardinian Vendetta

In the annals of Aggius's past, the area was the hiding place of a sinister character known as **Il Muto di Gallura** – the mute of Gallura, the last scion of a family locked in a long and deadly vendetta in the nineteenth century that claimed 72 lives and left only six survivors. *Il Muto* carried on the feud from this lonely eyrie, from which he descended only to dispatch his enemies. He ended his terror with the murder of the 12-year-old son of his principal antagonist, the head of the opposing family. The boy was of an unsurpassed beauty, so the story goes, and was cut down while walking through the cork forests lost in song.

di Aggius signposted to the left, even more striking and a slightly shorter route to the coast.

There's no listed **accommodation** in Aggius, but there is an excellent *agriturismo* in the neighbourhood: *Il Muto di Gallura* in Località Fraiga (☎079.620.559; ❹), signposted on the left as you approach Aggius from Tempio. You can eat here, and there are discounts for stays of more than a day or two. In the village, you can also eat well at *Calimero*, a rustic **ristorante/pizzeria** signposted to the right off the main Via Roma at Via Li Criasgi 1, open evenings only (no smoking; closed Wed).

Calangianus and around

Seven kilometres east of Tempio, the road skirts Limbara to **CALANGIANUS**, a small town surrounded by a jagged ring of mountains and, closer to hand, cork factories. This is the centre of Sardinia's biggest cork-producing area, and it's no surprise to see the local shops overflowing with the stuff, fashioned into an endless variety of unusual forms. In September, the village stages an **exhibition of cork** and its various uses.

There's a station on the Tempio–Palau rail line in Calangianus, and a **hotel** with a restaurant – *Briantino*, Via Aldo Moro 40 (☎079.678.1005; ❺) – but, once you've sifted through the shelves of cork, there's precious little to do. Three kilometres out of town to the north, however, the village of **Luras** – notable for its *logudorese* dialect, as opposed to the *gallurese* spoken elsewhere – has some prenuraghic dolmens, or funerary stones, which date back to the second or third millennium BC. To reach the most impressive of these, **Dolmen Ladas**, follow the road north through the village, turn right into the

Gallura's cork oaks

No one travelling through Gallura can fail to notice the groves of short, spiky **cork oak** (*Quercus suber*), usually stripped at the waist by foresters to reveal the reddish inner bark. This evergreen grows abundantly in the Mediterranean region – particularly in the Iberian and Italian peninsulas, parts of France and North Africa – usually to a height of about 18m, with a broad, round-topped head and glossy green, holly-like leaves. It is the new outer sheath of bark that's useful, harvested in Gallura since earliest times for a variety of purposes. Ladles and other kitchen utensils, trays, containers and insulation material are all produced from this versatile substance, and its lightness, flexibility and impermeability make it ideal for a number of other industrial and practical uses – ninety percent of Italy's bottle corks come from Gallura's trees. In recent years it has also been fashioned into a variety of unlikely **souvenir objects**, such as postcards, notebooks, masks, ornaments and purses.

The cork oak lives about 150 years, and the first cork is not peeled off the trunk until the tree is 25–30 years old. The product of this initial **de-barking**, or *demaschiatura*, is too porous and plastic to be useful, however; the second stripping, about ten years later, yields a better quality, and thereafter the outer sheath is removed every decade or so. In a healthy tree, 2.5–5cm of new cork forms in three to ten years, and it may continue to be productive for the rest of its life. The stripping itself is still done by hand, by cutting slits in the outer bark, which is then pried loose and peeled away with the help of levers and wedges, taking care not to injure the regenerative layers of the inner bark. Before it can be used, the peel of cork is boiled or steamed to remove soluble tannic acids and increase its flexibility, and its rough woody surface is scraped clean by hand. Among the many by-products, the fibrous tissues that come away with the bark are used to dye sheep's wool and goat hair.

303

△ Yacht

last asphalted street, and follow a dirt track for about 350m, then take the right fork – a couple of kilometres in all. Standing on a low hill, the tall rectangular dolmen measures 6m in height and over 2m in width.

The tiny village of **Sant'Antonio di Gallura** lies 18km northeast of Calangianus on the SP427 (and the same distance south of Arzachena along the same road), close to the **Lago di Liscia**, the artificial lake which supplies irrigation to much of the coastal region and drinking water to Olbia, Arzachena and the Costa Smeralda. The neighbourhood also holds an ancient forest of wild olive trees, some reaching 14m high and 11m broad, among which is thought to be the oldest wild olive tree in Sardinia, estimated to be 2000 years old. You'll need local advice to find it, however: it's out of sight in a secluded little valley near the banks of the lake. The area is also renowned for its Nebbiolo wines.

Travel details

Trains

Arzachena to: Calangianus (mid-June to mid-Sept 2 daily; 1hr); Palau (mid-June to mid-Sept 2 daily; 25min); Tempio Pausánia (mid-June to mid-Sept 2 daily; 1hr 10min–1hr 25min).
Golfo Aranci to: Olbia (4–7 daily; 25min).
Olbia to: Cágliari (4 daily, some with change at Ozieri-Chilivani; 4hr–5hr); Golfo Aranci (Mon–Sat 6–7 daily, Sun 4–5; 25min); Oristano (4 daily, some with change at Ozieri-Chilivani; 3hr–3hr 40min); Ozieri-Chilivani (6–7 daily; 1hr–1hr 20min).
Palau to: Arzachena (mid-June to mid-Sept 2 daily; 25min); Calangianus (mid-June to mid-Sept 2 daily; 1hr 15min–1hr 30min); Tempio Pausánia (mid-June to mid-Sept 2 daily; 1hr 30min–1hr 45min).
Tempio Pausánia to: Arzachena (mid-June to mid-Sept 2 daily; 55min); Calangianus (mid-June to mid-Sept 2 daily; 20min); Palau (mid-June to mid-Sept 2 daily; 1hr 30min).

Buses

Arzachena to: Cannigione (Mon–Sat 5–8 daily; 10–55min); Olbia (8–12 daily; 40min); Palau (8–11; 20min); Santa Teresa di Gallura (5–6 daily; 35min–1hr).
Golfo Aranci to: Olbia (mid-June to mid-Sept 8 daily; 25min).
Olbia to: Arzachena (8–13 daily; 40min); Golfo Aranci (mid-June to mid-Sept 8 daily; 25min); Nuoro (6–7 daily; 1hr 45min); Palau (9–12 daily; 1hr–1hr 10min); Porto Cervo (Mon–Sat 3–5 daily; 1hr 10min); Porto San Paolo (6 daily; 30min); Posada (4–6 daily; 1hr 10min); San Teodoro (6–9 daily; 40min); Santa Teresa di Gallura (5–7 daily; 1hr 35min–2hr); Sássari (1–3 daily; 1hr 30min); Tempio Pausánia (Mon–Sat 6–7 daily, Sun 3; 1hr 25min).
Olbia (Ísola Bianca) to: Arzachena (6 daily;

45min); Nuoro (1 daily; 2hr 35min); Palau (6 daily; 1hr 10min–2hr 15min); Santa Teresa di Gallura (4 daily; 2hr); Sássari (2 daily; 1hr 25min).
Palau to: Arzachena (9–12 daily; 20min); Olbia (9–12 daily; 1hr–1hr 15min); Santa Teresa di Gallura (5–6 daily; 35–45min); Sássari (3 daily; 3hr 30min).
Santa Teresa di Gallura to: Arzachena (5–6 daily; 1hr); Cágliari (1 daily; 5hr 10min); Castelsardo (Mon–Sat 5 daily, Sun 3; 2hr); Olbia (5–6 daily; 1hr 45min–2hr); Sássari (Mon–Sat 4–5 daily, Sun 2–3; 2hr 20min–3hr).
Tempio Pausánia to: Aggius (8–10 daily; 15min); Arzachena (2 daily; 1hr 15min); Cágliari (1 daily; 4hr); Calangianus (Mon–Sat 8 daily, Sun 3; 25min); Ísola Rossa (3–4 daily; 1hr); Palau (2 daily; 1hr 40min); (1hr 30min); Sássari (4–5 daily; 1hr 15min–2hr 15min).

Ferries

Golfo Aranci to: Civitavecchia (mid-June to mid-Sept 1–2 daily; 6hr 45min–10hr), or by fast ferry (Easter to early Oct 1–3 daily; 3hr 45min); Fiumicino (fast ferry service late June to early Sept 1 daily; 3hr 30min); Livorno (April–Oct 1–2 daily; 8–10hr), or by fast ferry (June–Sept 5 weekly; 6hr).
Olbia to: Civitavecchia (Tirrenia; 1 daily; 8hr), or by fast ferry (Tirrenia, Moby; April–Sept 1–5 daily; 4–6hr); Genoa (Tirrenia, Moby, Grimaldi; 3–24 weekly; 8hr–13hr 30min); Livorno (Moby, Linea dei Golfi; 1–3 daily; 8–13hr); Piombino (Linea dei Golfi; 1–3 daily; 8–9hr).
Palau to: Genoa (Enermar; April–Sept 1–5 weekly; 12hr); La Maddalena (Enermar, Saremar; 2–4 hourly, 1 hourly at night; 20min); La Spezia (Linee Lauro; July to early Sept 1 weekly; 13hr); Naples (Linee Lauro; mid-June to mid-Sept 1 weekly; 13hr 30min).
Santa Teresa di Gallura to: Bonifacio, Corsica (Moby, Saremar; 2–14 daily; 50min–1hr).

8

Nuoro province

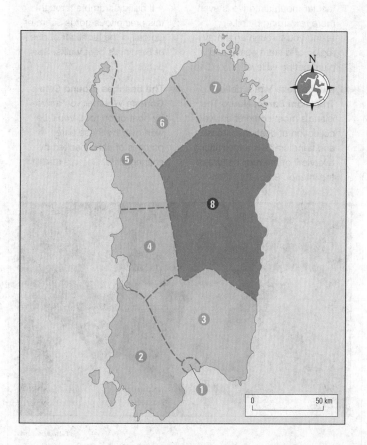

CHAPTER 8

Highlights

* **Nuraghe Arrubiu, Orroli** Set in remote country on the southern edge of Nuoro province, this sequestered nuraghic complex has a poignantly bleak atmosphere. See p.335

* **Cycling the SS125 Dorgali–Baunei** Sardinia's most spectacular mountain drive is even more rewarding by bike, taking you through an empty region of distant peaks and plummeting valleys. See p.342

* **Museo della Vita e delle Tradizioni Sarde, Nuoro** The island's most comprehensive collection of costumes, masks and handicrafts is a fascinating overview of the rural culture of the interior. See p.314–316

* **Easter at Oliena** Grief, joy, drama and exuberant local costumes all feature in the Easter rituals of this mountain village – the accompanying gunfire makes ear-plugs essential. See p.323

* **Hiking in the Gorropu gorge** A thrilling scramble through this precipitous gorge south of Dorgali is the highlight of one of Sardinia's best walks. See p.338

* **The beaches around Cala Gonone** Whether you arrive by boat or on foot, you'll be won over by these bare patches of sand backed by soaring cliffs. See p.340–341

△ Festival costumes

Nuoro province

The huge central **province of Nuoro** has little in common with Sardinia's modern sun-and-sand image. However, for many people it's the most interesting part of the island, dotted with isolated villages which have never known the heel of foreign conquerors. Their inhabitants have retained a fierce sense of independence and loyalty to centuries-old practices, that continued unabated in the inaccessible interior long after most of the coastal towns had shed their traditional culture. The province is consequently the last repository of some of Sardinia's oldest customs, where you won't be surprised to find a few elderly folk still unselfconsciously wearing their local costumes.

All the same, the most practical place to view the region's huge range of costumes – not to mention masks, musical instruments, jewellery and domestic items – is the ethnographic museum in the provincial capital, **Nuoro**. Although unprepossessing, this high inland town has plenty more to discover, often connected to the remarkable roster of artists and writers who lived and worked around here before achieving national fame.

For many, Nuoro is the starting point for trips into the surrounding mountains. North of town, the first obvious stop would be **Su Tempiesu**, a sacred well of the nuraghic era, splendidly sited on the side of a valley east of the village of **Orune**. North of **Bitti**, where there's a small ethnographic museum, the granite landscape of Gallura begins to impinge around **Buddusò**. There's a chance to explore the mountains on foot from outside **Alà dei Sardi**, where an annual fair takes place in a peaceful rural setting. West of Buddusò, **Pattada** is famed for its shepherd's knives, while the castle of **Burgos**, south of here, occupies a lofty perch that offers stunning views over the Tirso valley.

South of Nuoro stretches Sardinia's **Barbagia** region, called *Barbaria* by the Romans who, like Sardinia's other conquerors, never managed to subdue it completely, foiled by the guerrilla warfare for which the mountains here proved ideal. Amid forested slopes, Barbagia's population is concentrated in small, self-contained villages, interconnected by twisting mountain roads. These settlements have changed little since the novelist Salvatore Satta described them as "minuscule settlements as remote from one another as are the stars". Although material conditions have improved in recent years, the region seems a world apart from the whitewashed luxury of the Costa Smeralda just a couple of hours' drive away, and it's still common to see black-shawled old ladies trudging up and down the steep streets of the villages, or shepherds in brown corduroy suits, wrapped up against the cold grey air which envelopes these parts for much of the year.

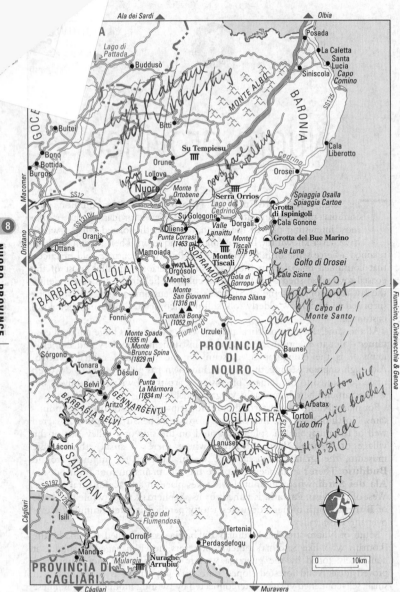

The region is divided into different districts, of which the **Barbagia Ollolai** is the nearest to Nuoro. En route to this area, **Oliena** is the best departure-point for expeditions to **Sopramonte**, the dramatic massif visible from Nuoro, and, with its wide range of accommodation, is a useful base for the whole region. South of here, the village of **Orgósolo** once had one of the island's worst reputations for banditry and violence, though it is now best known for its striking murals. Westwards, **Mamoiada** and **Ottana** present two of

Sardinia's most spectacular Carnival displays, and **Orani** has a diverting museum featuring the work of the artist Costantino Nivola.

Further south, the small town of **Fonni** is one the main gateways to the once impenetrable **Gennargentu** massif, the island's highest range, from which all of Sardinia's major rivers flow – most of them dammed to create sequestered mountain lakes. The loftiest peak, **Punta La Mármora**, can be reached on foot without too much difficulty, one of the scores of treks that can be made in the area. The forested slopes of the **Barbagia Belvì**, which borders this range, shelter more tight communities, of which **Belvì** and **Aritzo** are most attractive. South of here in the **Sarcidano** region, the gradients are milder, though the village of **Láconi**, surrounded by woods, still retains a fresh, mountainous feel. **Ísili**, a local centre, has a superb single-towered nuraghe worth a photo-stop, while **Nuraghe Arrubiu**, below Orroli, is one of the island's grandest nuraghic sites.

The **eastern coast** preserves the rugged character of the interior, though the sheer walls rearing above the sea also leave space for some fantastic beaches. These are more popular in the northern parts, where the town of **Posada** provides a lofty vantage point from its ruined castle. South of the attractive inland centre of **Orosei**, the swimming spots are much more inaccessible apart from those at the holiday enclave of **Cala Gonone** and around **Arbatax**, one of the few ports along this littoral, connected to the mainland by ferry.

The province of Nuoro hosts some of Sardinia's most intriguing **festivals**, much smaller and less lavish than those organized in the cities, but possessed of a fiery exuberance and occasionally imbued with a distinctly dark mood. Each village has at least one *festa*, for which preparations are made months in advance, though the Carnival period, Easter and the festival of the Assumption in mid-August are usually the most spectacular. All provide a good opportunity to see traditional costumes – the tourist office at Nuoro can supply you with an illustrated booklet with full details.

Because of the winter sports and trekking possibilities which draw growing numbers of enthusiasts, there are plenty of **accommodation** choices along the way, though it's always wise to phone first. The province is best explored using your own vehicle, though it's also possible to get around by **public transport**: ARST buses from Nuoro or Cágliari pass through the remotest villages in the area at least once a day (but usually no services on Sun), while PANI buses link Nuoro to Cágliari, Sássari and Oristano. Private FdS trains connect Nuoro with Macomer, and Sórgono, Ísili and Arbatax with Cágliari, though the Cágliari line is a slow one, best treated as a travelling experience rather than as a means of crossing the island. For more information on bus and train connections, see Travel details on p.344–345.

Nuoro

"There is nothing to see in Nuoro: which to tell the truth, is always a relief. Sights are an irritating bore," wrote D.H. Lawrence, after touching down here during his Sardinian excursion of 1921. The town appeared to him "as if at the end of the world, mountains rising sombre behind". Despite the overlay of unsightly apartment blocks, administrative buildings and banks which have overrun **NUORO** in the last half-century, little seems to have changed since then. With faded Fascist graffiti from the 1930s still visible on its walls, an old-fashioned air hangs over the place, its sober dignity and slow pace in stark contrast to the cosmopolitan energy infusing such towns as Olbia and Oristano.

However, while the town shares many of the insular and parochial qualities of many of the villages of Sardinia's interior, Nuoro occupies a unique place in the island's **cultural life**, both for its extraordinary literary fame and the artists who lived and worked here. The town's specific sights afford fascinating glimpses into Sardinia's inner life, while its unpretentious, uncommercialized milieu provides a welcome escape from the gaudy trappings of more touristy areas. Not the least of Nuoro's inducements is its superb position beneath the soaring peak of Monte Ortobene and opposite the sheer and stark heights of Sopramonte, a rather more inspiring panorama than Lawrence's brusque assessment might suggest.

Each of Nuoro's main attractions focuses, in different ways, on aspects of Sardinia's core identity. Contrasting and complementing each other are two museums, the **Museo della Vita e delle Tradizioni Sarde**, an engrossing overview of the island's rural culture including a colourful exhibition of local costumes, and the **Museo d'Arte Nuoro**, which showcases a varied cross-section of modern art, chiefly by local artists. Nuoro's other attractions are rooted firmly in the past: the **Casa di Grazia Deledda**, the restored birthplace of one of the city's literary stars, offering an insight into the city's domestic life of a hundred years ago, and the **Sagra del Redentore**, Nuoro's annual festival, when the traditional costumes on display in the ethnographic museum are brought vividly to life.

Nuoro's *sagra* reaffirms a strong bond that links the city with nearby **Monte Ortobene**, whose summit marks the end-point of the costumed parade. You can visit the mountain at any time of course, to take in the dramatic panorama, and there are some excellent B&Bs here that make up for the shortage of accommodation in town.

As the chief town of Sardinia's interior, Nuoro is known for its **handicrafts** and other rustic artefacts – knives, carpets, musical instruments, masks and the like. It's worth checking out the two floors of folk arts and crafts at the government-sponsored ISOLA shop at Via Monsignor Bua, near the Duomo. The quality is generally good, though prices are often steep; if you're travelling through Barbagia, you might as well do any shopping closer to source, probably for lower prices.

Arrival and information

Nuoro's FdS **train station** is a fifteen-minute walk from the centre of town along Via Lamármora, along which pass frequent city buses #3, #4 and #5 (tickets €1 from the shop inside the station); cross the road for buses to the centre. ARST buses stop at the **bus station** on Viale Sardegna, a few minutes' walk south of the station (take bus #3 from here for the centre), while PANI buses stop at Via Brigata Sássari 15 (parallel to Via Lamármora). At the end of this road is **Piazza Italia**, the centre of modern Nuoro, where the town's – and province's – main **tourist office** (mid-July to Sept Mon–Sat 8.30am–1.30pm & 3.30–8pm, Sun 9.30am–1.30pm; Oct to mid-July Mon–Fri 9am–1pm & 3.30–6.30pm; ℡0784.30.083, ⓦwww.provincia.nuoro.it) is located at no. 19; it may be closed on a Tuesday, in which case go up to the EPT administration office on the fourth floor of the same building (same times). There's also a handier independent office at Corso Garibaldi 155 (℡0784.38.777, ⓦwww.viazzos.it), though it has a more limited range of material to give out and keeps irregular hours. Apart from the brief ride between the stations and the centre, **local buses**, operated by ATP (℡0784.202.447), are mainly useful for reaching Monte Ortobene (see p.316);

buy tickets (€0.57, or €0.80 for 90min, and €1 for Ortobene) before boarding from newsagents or *tabacchini*.

Drivers should avoid the old centre as much as possible; park your vehicle in between the blue lines, for which tickets are available from a parking attendant for €0.52 per hour.

Accommodation

Nuoro is seriously ill-equipped for the few tourists planning to stay here, though the town does have a few business-travellers' **hotels**, which are worth booking ahead. The best options are on Monte Ortobene (see p.316), a short drive or bus-ride away, where there's also a basic, semi-official **campsite** at the *Roccas agriturismo* (☎0784.36.565 or 339.799.7377, ⓦwww.roccas.it). If all else fails, try some of the neighbouring villages, for example Oliena, 12km to the southeast (see p.322).

Casa Solotti Monte Ortobene ☎0784.33.954 or 328.602.8975, ⓦwww.casasolotti.it. One of Ortobene's two B&Bs; at 5km from the Grazia Deledda church, it's the nearer to town, with a bus stop right outside. Like Ortobene's other accommodation options, this has fantastic views from most of its rooms, which are comfortable and quiet, one with private bathroom. There's a kitchen, a large, peaceful garden, and assorted pets; breakfast is a grand affair, which may include homemade yoghurt. Call to be picked up. ❸

Euro Hotel Via Trieste 44 ☎0784.34.071, ⓕ0784.33.643. With 1930s-style furnishings and an unfortunate colour scheme, the *Euro* doesn't invite a lengthy stay, though it has a kind of quirky charm that might appeal to retro-fans. ❹

Fratelli Sacchi Monte Ortobene ☎0784.31.200, ⓕ0784.34.030. Modern, but with stylish rustic trimmings, this offers good value if you want to stay right near the top of Monte Ortobene. Not all the rooms have views, and some have shared bathrooms, but all are clean and comfortable, and there's a popular restaurant and pizzeria. ❸

Grazia Deledda Via Lamármora 177 ☎0784.31.257, ⓕ0784.31.258. Nuoro's classiest hotel is currently undergoing a thorough overhaul, so no prices are currently available, though it's likely that it will maintain its high standards of comfort. It's conveniently located almost opposite the train station, but not so handy for the old centre.

Grillo Via Monsignor Melas 14 ☎0784.38.678, ⓕ0784.32.005. Modern and characterless, this prominent three-star is nonetheless a comfortable and fairly central choice, with all mod cons. ❺

Paradiso Via Aosta ☎0784.35.585, ⓕ0784.232.782. A useful last resort, this hotel is comfortable enough and reasonably priced, but distant from the centre and lacking the personal touch. ❹

Su Redentore Monte Ortobene ☎328.022.5518 or 329.076.1697, ⓦwww.suredentore.it. Well-tended B&B on Monte Ortobene, offering good-value accommodation, a garden and panoramic views. There's also a six-bed apartment available for weekly rents. ❸

The old centre

Nuoro's **old quarter** is the most compelling part of town, spread around the pedestrianized hub of **Corso Garibaldi**, at its best during the buzzing *passeggiata*. Nuoro's newest attraction lies just off here, on the corner of Via Satta and Via Manara. The **Museo d'Arte Nuoro** (Tues–Sun 10am–1pm & 4.30–8.30pm; €2.60) occupies four floors of a renovated nineteenth-century *palazzo*, and is filled with the works of Sardinia's best-known modern artists. The ground and top floors are devoted to temporary exhibitions, while the middle two floors have a permanent display of artists from the nineteenth, twentieth and twenty-first centuries, including moody abstracts by Mauro Manca (1913–69), and sculptures by two outstanding locals, Costantino Nivola (1911–88, see p.327) and the Nuorese Francesco Ciusa (1883–1949). The gallery also hosts occasional poetry readings and classical and jazz concerts.

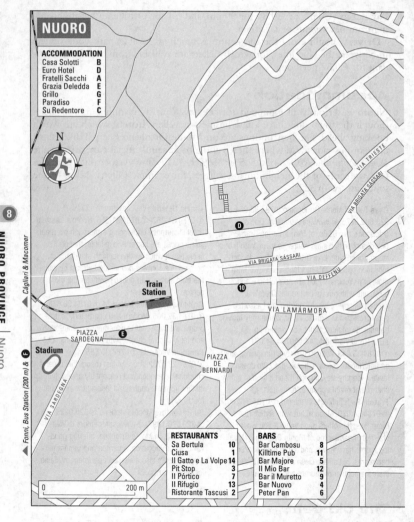

NUORO

ACCOMMODATION

Casa Solotti	B
Euro Hotel	D
Fratelli Sacchi	A
Grazia Deledda	E
Grillo	G
Paradiso	F
Su Redentore	C

N

VIA TRIESTE

VIA BRIGATA SÁSSARI

D

VIA BRIGATA SÁSSARI

VIA DEFFENU

Train Station

VIA LAMÁRMORA

10

PIAZZA SARDEGNA

E

Stadium

PIAZZA DE BERNARDI

VIA SARDEGNA

◀ Cagliari & Macomer

◀ Fonni, Bus Station (200 m) & F

RESTAURANTS

Sa Bertula	10
Ciusa	1
Il Gatto e La Volpe	14
Pit Stop	3
Il Pórtico	7
Il Rifugio	13
Ristorante Tascusi	2

BARS

Bar Cambosu	8
Killtime Pub	11
Bar Majore	5
Il Mio Bar	12
Bar il Muretto	9
Bar Nuovo	4
Peter Pan	6

0   200 m

More works by Nivola and Ciusa can be seen a few steps away at the top of, Via Satta. In the usually deserted **Piazza Satta**, the poet Sebastiano Satta, who was born nearby (see the box on p.314), has been honoured with a cluster of menhir-like granite blocks in which small bronze figures evoking nuraghic *bronzetti* have been placed – the work of Nivola in the 1960s. Just beyond, on the corner of Via Sássari and Via San Carlo Borromeo, a ramshackle house now awaiting renovation was the birthplace of Francesco Ciusa. His tomb lies opposite in the pink, rustic-looking church of **San Carlo** (daily 8am–1pm & 4–7pm), which also contains a copy of Ciusa's most powerful work, *Madre dell'Ucciso* ("Mother of the killed man"), a bronze statue of a barefooted crone swathed in shawl and headscarf, whose bony face is a poignant display of grief.

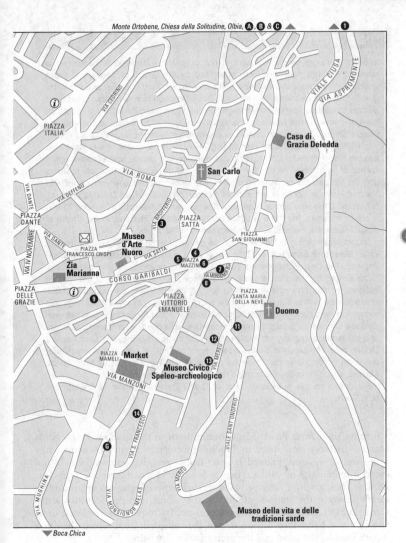

▼ Boca Chica

The original was presented at the Biennale at Venice in 1907, and is now exhibited in Rome's Galleria dell'Arte Moderna.

Corso Garibaldi ends at Piazza San Giovanni, from where a left turn up Via Deledda will bring you to the **Casa di Grazia Deledda** (daily: mid-June to mid-Sept 9am–8pm; mid-Sept to mid-June 9am–1pm & 3–7pm; free), once the home of the Nobel Prize-winning author (see the box on p.314), now restored and partly furnished to present an authentic example of a typical Nuorese house. At present, however, much of the three-storey building is bare (and there will probably be an admission charge once all the furnishings and fittings are in place), and the most interesting items on display consist of manuscripts, first editions, photos, clippings and various other mementoes relating to the author.

In Sardinia, Nuoro seems to have the monopoly where **literature** is concerned, a standing that has been discreetly advertised by the scraps of poetry and prose inscribed on the walls of the old town. The best-known Sard poet, **Sebastiano Satta** (1867–1914), was Nuorese, and his name has been given to innumerable streets and piazzas throughout the island – though he's hardly known outside Italy. In his home town, the street where he lived is named after him, as is the square at one end of it (Piazza Satta), where bronze statuettes depict him at different stages of his life.

In 1926, the author **Grazia Deledda** (1871–1936) became one of four Italians to win the Nobel Prize for Literature. It was a tribute to a steady writing career and a corpus of work based on the day-to-day trials and passions of simple folk in Nuoro and the villages around. Praised by D.H. Lawrence, she has been compared with Thomas Hardy in her style and subject matter. The house where Deledda grew up, described in her autobiographical work *Cosima*, can be seen at Via Deledda 28 and is now a museum; her tomb is at the bottom of Monte Ortobene, in the church of Santa Maria della Solitúdine, which also recurs in her works.

"Nuoro was nothing but a perch for the crows," for the town's greatest modern writer, **Salvatore Satta** (1902–1975), as he wrote in his semi-autobiographical masterpiece, *The Day of Judgement*. No relation to his poetic namesake Sebastiano, Satta earned his living as a jurist, which placed him at the heart of the tangled intrigues of this provincial town, and though his posthumously published book chronicles life in Nuoro at the turn of the twentieth century, much of it still rings true today. The meandering descriptions of the townsfolk and the antagonisms between the local shepherds, peasants and aristocrats tread a fine line between soap opera and existential angst, dry yet easily readable, in some ways recalling Lampedusa's Sicilian epic, *The Leopard*. Satta's achievement has not yet earned him any memorial in his home town apart from the plaque at Via Angioi 1, just up from Piazza Mazzini, which indicates the house where he wrote parts of his novel.

For details of this publication, and of Grazia Deledda's works in English, see p.363–364.

Turning right from Piazza San Giovanni leads to the spacious Piazza Santa Maria della Neve, dominated by Nuoro's nineteenth-century **Duomo** (daily 8am–1pm & 4–7pm). Framed by two bell-towers, its orangey Neoclassical exterior often crops up on local postcards but lacks much presence from close up. The cool, spacious interior holds various items of religious art, including panels showing the stations of the cross by local twentieth-century artists Carmelo Floris and Giovanni Ciusa Romagna. Try to persuade someone to let you into the **belvedere** to one side of the cathedral, from which there is a superb view of the town and the precipitous valley below.

Elsewhere in Nuoro's old town, off Piazza Vittorio Emanuele, the **Museo Cívico Speleo-archeologico** displays a range of rocks, ropes and other equipment relating to the caving that this province is particularly suitable for. It's been closed a long time, however, with no information on its reopening.

Museo della Vita e delle Tradizioni Sarde

Nuoro's most famous attraction lies up on Via Antonio Mereu, a ten-minute walk past the Duomo from the Corso: the **Museo della Vita e delle Tradizioni Sarde** (daily: mid-June to mid-Sept 9am–8pm; mid-Sept to mid-June 9am–1pm & 3–7pm; €5) – more simply known as the Museo del Costume or Museo Etnográfico. Past the crude carts and wine presses that greet you on your way in, the museum has Sardinia's most comprehensive range of local costumes, jewellery, masks, carpets and other handicrafts, arranged in a modern purpose-built complex whose sequence of rooms, steps and courtyards is intended to evoke a Sardinian village.

The most striking exhibits are the **costumes**, showing an incredible diversity of pattern, design and colour, according to both their place of origin and the circumstances in which they were worn: scarves, skirts and bodices for unmarried women or widows; blouses and shawls for mourning or feasting, and shirts, tunics and pantaloons for the menfolk. One of the first rooms, however, deviates immediately from the main theme in its presentation, behind glass, of a well-preserved seventeenth-century **fresco** from a local church. Of unknown authorship, the work shows six of the apostles (presumably there was another fresco portraying the other six) all holding their traditional symbols – Simon the Zealot holds a saw.

Next door, **room 4** is devoted to costumes from the Barbagia villages of Bitti, Fonni, Gavoi, Ollolai and Désulo – black hats and boots for the men, lace shawls for the women – while **room 5** has rugs, carpets and a horizontal-type oak loom from Bono from the second half of the nineteenth century. **Funerary carpets** on which the deceased were placed during wakes are draped on the walls.

Room 6 focuses on Sardinia's **musical instruments**, including various drums (*tamburi*), flutes made from canes from Barbagia and La Marmilla, and rudimentary clarinets (*benas*) made from oat stems. Some of these were tied together to make *launeddas*, or shepherd's pipes, said to be the island's oldest and most original instrument, made of three tubes of cane of differing lengths and diameters, and individually spaced finger holes. Other noise-making gadgets include a simple string bass used at Bosa, Sássari and Gavoi during Carnival time, similar to that used in jug bands but resonating in an inflated pig's bladder instead of a box; whistles, triangles and rattles used at Easter, and cork-popping guns fired by children at Christmas. Another display shows sheep- and goat-bells, the various sizes used to identify different flocks – one of the characteristic accoutrements in Barbagia's masked processions.

The next room has examples of the various *dolci* and **breads** you may have encountered in restaurants and pastry shops throughout Sardinia, but particularly common in the Nuoro region. *Paneddas*, cakes and sweets with bird designs, elaborately designed hearts and bows made of pastry, filled with figs and nuts, are displayed below photos showing how they are prepared. The island's famous *pane carasau* – discs of bread – are also here. Traditionally made once a month, they were at first the preserve of the better-off classes, but are now in general use.

Guns and **swords** share space in the next room with **lacework** and **basketwork**, while **room 10** – downstairs and across a yard – has solemn photos from the end of the nineteenth century, costumes from Atzara and Samugheo, and more carpets on the walls. **Rooms 11–13** display costumes from Oristano and Cabras, lace from Cágliari, and an impressive collection of **jewellery** used by men and women, crafted out of silver plate, polychrome glass, precious stones, and silver filigree work. Among the buttons, pins and earrings studded with pearls and coral, wedding and engagement rings of silver and gold, and necklaces made of coral, gold plate and silver, there are pendants and amulets encrusted with turquoise, marble and obsidian, some of them incorporating fragments of shell, sharks' teeth, boar's tusks and crystals to ward off evil.

Rooms 14 and **15** have sober dark brown and black garments from Macomer and Íttiri, more flamboyant women's dresses from Ósilo decorated with roses and other flowers, and brocaded wedding and feast gowns from

Sénnori, Ploaghe and Bono. The costumes in the last rooms are much more dramatic, including the very sinister-looking black gowns tied with ropes and bells belonging to **Sos Thurpos** of Orotelli – a chain of twenty or thirty hooded and stick-wielding men swathed in thick black cloth with only their soot-blackened faces exposed, who leap upon their victims during the village's Carnival procession and truss them up, as seen in the photos displayed here. You can also see the hairy goatskin costumes of Mamoiada's Carnival, the masks at once menacing and tragic (see the box on p.325), and those of *Sos Merdules* of Ottana (see p.328).

Monte Ortobene

On Nuoro's eastern flank, 8km outside town, the summit of **Monte Ortobene** affords awe-inspiring views over the deep valley separating Nuoro from Monte Corrasi (1463m) and the Sopramonte massif. The heavily wooded slopes are a favourite destination for the townsfolk at weekends, and the **Farcana** locality (signposted off the only road leading up the mountain) has a sports complex that includes a sizeable open-air pool, tennis courts and stables for riding. However, there are still plenty of areas which feel remote enough to get lost in, and the woods are perfect for walks and picnics.

Near the top of the mountain (955m), a huge bronze **statue** of the Redeemer (*Redentore*) stands poised in an attitude of swirling motion over the immense void. The figure attracts pilgrims at all times – as shown by the trinkets and other devotional gifts left here, and by Christ's polished right toe (the only part of the statue within reach of the worshippers) – and is the destination for the procession that weaves up from the town during Nuoro's annual Sagra del Redentore (see the box below). Others come for the stupendous panorama, with its dizzying views down to the valley floor.

Near the statue, stalls sell souvenirs and cold drinks, and you can have a full meal at *Fratelli Sacchi*, which offers hunks of meat roasted on an outdoor spit, and has superb views from its indoor bar and restaurant. *Fratelli Sacchi* also offers hotel **accommodation**, or you can stay in one of the area's B&Bs (for accommodation options, see p.311). Frequent local **buses** (#8) connect Monte Ortobene from outside Nuoro's train station, Corso Garibaldi and Piazza Vittorio Emanuele; the last bus down is at around 8.15pm. In winter there are only two buses daily and none on Sunday.

At the base of Monte Ortobene, where the road up the mountain meets the main road to Siníscola and Olbia, you might pause at the **Chiesa della**

The Sagra del Redentore

Many costumes similar to those displayed in Nuoro's ethnographic museum are aired in the town's biggest annual festival, the **Sagra del Redentore**. Held at the end of August, it involves participants from all over the island, but especially the villages of the Barbagia. The festival combines solemn religious rites with a flamboyant celebration of Sardinia's cultural heritage: the penultimate Sunday of August is dedicated to traditional dancing and singing, enthusiastically performed in the old town's squares, while on August 29, a long, costumed procession trails through Nuoro as far as the statue of the Redeemer on Monte Ortobene and the nearby church of Nostra Signora di Montenero. Together, these events constitute one of the most vibrant events on the island's calendar, and accommodation at this time is at a premium.

Solitúdine (known locally as the *Chiesa di Grazia Deledda*), an austere granite structure at the top of a flight of shallow steps. The church was designed in the 1950s by local artist Giovanni Ciusa Romagna on the site of an earlier church that was often mentioned in the books of Grazia Deledda (see the box on p.314), and contains the author's simple granite tomb.

Eating, drinking and entertainment

Nuoro is not particularly well off for **restaurants**, though prices are generally very reasonable. On some menus, or in bars, you might find traditional **pastries**, such as *Aranciadda nuorese*, a sticky local sweet made with honey and fresh oranges. This and other local specialities are also available from places on the Corso, for example Zia Marianna at no. 174. For fruit, veg and other takeaway items, the covered **market** is open mornings and evenings at Via Santa Barbara, and there's a supermarket opposite the train station.

Sa Bertula Via Deffenu 119. Near the train station, this quiet, rather characterless restaurant specializes in Nuorese cuisine and seafood. Closed Sun. Moderate.

Ciusa Viale Ciusa 55 ℡ 0784.257.052. On the western end of town, this elegant place pulls in regular crowds for tasty dishes such as *risotto* with wine and melted sheep's cheese, meat grills and even prawn curry. Closed Tues. Moderate.

Il Gatto e La Volpe Via San Francesco 8. Modern and a bit flashy, on two levels, this offers good local fare as well as pizzas (eves only). The *fettuccine profumo di bosco* (pasta with mushrooms) is recommended. You'll need to book between 9 and 10pm. Closed Mon. Moderate.

Pit Stop Via Brofferio 19. Quirky place to stop at lunchtime, when there's a fixed-price menu for €10, or in the eves, when pizzas are also available. The place is done up with old racing-car

memorabilia, and there's a convincing copy of a racing pit – thankfully glass-covered – to take you unawares as you enter. Closed Sun. Inexpensive–moderate.

Il Pórtico Via Monsignor Bua 13. With an old-fashioned style, this is one of Nuoro's smarter choices, though not intimidatingly so, and the food is delicious. Closed Tues. Moderate.

Il Rifugio Via Mereu 28. Popular ristorante/pizzeria with a traditional feel and appetizing dishes. It fills up quickly, but the service is brisk. Closed Wed. Moderate.

Ristorante Tascusi Via Aspromonte 11. Local dishes are served in simple white rooms decorated with Sard art. The menu might include *Malloreddus al sugo di cinghiale* (pasta with boar's meat sauce) and *porcettu arrosto* (roast pork), and pizzas are also available. Closed Tues. Moderate.

Bars

As you might expect, Nuoro's **bars** are fairly staid affairs, stronger on atmosphere than energy – the only place that provides much evening excitement is the *Killtime*. If you're looking for a snack for breakfast or lunch, however, or just a place to rest up, try one of the following:

Bar Camboso Via Monsignor Bua 4. On the corner of Piazza Vittorio Emanuele, this is a lively but old-fashioned place with comfy chairs and lots of chat. A good breakfast stop.

Killtime Pub Via Mereu 45 (corner of Viale Sant'Onofrio). The conspicuous modern green and orange building below the museum combines a bar, cafeteria and nightspot. Serves snacks and Guinness too. Closed Mon.

Bar Majore Corso Garibaldi 69. The old fittings, beautifully painted ceilings and mirrors give this small bar plenty of atmosphere.

Il Mio Bar Via Mereu. A handy sit-down place for a lunchtime snack, between the museum and the duomo. Closed Sun.

Bar il Muretto Via Solferino 18. *Panini caldi*, burgers and chips, plus lots of beers, bottled or draught. Closed Sun afternoon.

Bar Nuovo Piazza Mazzini. Good old bar offering *pizzette*, *panini*, ice creams and tables outside. Closed Wed.

Peter Pan Piazza Vittorio Emanuele. The best central place for ice creams.

Moving on from Nuoro

FdS (℡0784.30.115, ⊛www.ferroviesardegna.it) run **train** services from Nuoro to Macomer, a stop on the main north–south FS line (for information on FS services, call ℡848.888.088, ⊛www.trenitalia.it).

Most **bus** routes within Nuoro province are operated by ARST, from the bus station on Viale Sardegna (℡0784.32.201, ⊛www.arst.sardegna.it). The other main companies are PANI, Via Brigata Sássari 15 (℡0784.36.856), for fast buses to Sássari, Oristano and Cágliari; DePlano for Olbia airport (℡0784.295.030) and Redentours/Deplanu for Fertilia airport and Alghero (℡0784.30.325) – the latter two services leave from the bus station (tickets on board).

Entertainment

When the theatre currently under construction in Via Brofferio is finally completed, it will be the main venue for the city's cultural life. In the meantime, check out the local edition of *La Nuova Sardegna* any day except Monday (when sport predominates) for listings of current events. The Mexican-inspired *Boca Chica*, Via Mughina 94, is the only full-time **club** in town, playing upbeat Latino and house music until dawn, with pizzas until 11pm and rooftop dancing in summer. For **live music**, the small *Killtime Pub* on Via Mereu has regular jazz and blues concerts from about 9.30pm, and, outside town, *Farcana* and *Nuovo Parco*, both bars on Monte Ortobene, also stage gigs in summer.

Listings

Ambulance ℡118.

Banks and exchange Banco di Sardegna, Corso Garibaldi 90 (Mon–Fri 8.20am–1.20pm & 3.05–4.30pm); Banca CIS, Piazza Italia (Mon–Fri 8.20am–1.20pm & 3–4pm, Sat 8.20–11.20am). Both have ATMs, and the post office also changes money.

Bookshop Libreria 2R, Corso Garibaldi 93, stocks guides, hiking routes and some English-language novels. Closed Sat.

Buses ATP (℡0784.202.447) operate Nuoro's local network. Buy tickets (€1) from newsagents or *tabacchini* before boarding.

Car rental Maggiore-Budget, Via Convento 32 ℡0784.30.461.

Hospital Piazza Sardegna, west of the train station ℡0784.240.237.

Market Open mornings and eves at Via Santa Barbara, mainly fruit and veg, but there are also other stalls selling clothes and various goods.

Pharmacy Gali, Corso Garibaldi 65 ℡0782.30.143 (8am–1pm & 4–9.30pm). Late-night pharmacies operate on a rota – check on any pharmacy door to see the address of the current one.

Police ℡112 or ℡113.

Post office Piazza Francesco Crispi. Mon–Fri 8.15am–6.30pm, Sat 8.15am–12.45pm; last day of month closes at 4.30pm, or 10.45am on Sat.

Supermarket Upim on Via Lamármora, opposite the train station. Mon–Sat 9am–1pm & 4–8pm.

Taxi Taxi e Basta ℡0784.31.411; Nuoro Taxi ℡0784.203.376.

Travel agent La Nuova Barbagia, Via Dante 28 ℡0784.37.777.

North and west of Nuoro

The country **north and west of Nuoro** has a less dramatic appeal than that of the more famous Barbagia, but its scattered hamlets and high plains merit a slow exploration, preferably with your own transport. Bus connections are sporadic, and accommodation possibilities are virtually non-existent, but much of the region can be conveniently visited on trips out of Nuoro.

Orune and Su Tempiesu

The nondescript hill settlement of **Orune**, 13km north of the provincial capital, has little intrinsic interest, but you'll need to pass this way to visit the remote site of **Su Tempiesu** (daily 8.30am–sunset; €2), a sacred well and temple dating from nuraghic times. At the entrance to the village, take the signposted (and mostly unsurfaced) road that dips 5km east to the entrance to the site, where there's a bar selling drinks and snacks. The temple itself is hidden in the valley below the road, reached along a steeply descending path. Knowledgeable guides will explain (usually in Italian) the significance of the site, which, discovered by a farmer in 1953, constitutes Sardinia's best-preserved example of a **sacred well** from this period, and remains a good illustration of the importance of water at a time when it was often (surprisingly) in chronically short supply. Health-giving and prophetic properties were attributed to springs by the numerous cults growing around them, and temples were built over the outlets. In design, many of these conformed to the general structure of Su Tempiesu, which has sturdy, slab-built walls with a triangular entrance, and topped by a steeply pitched roof. Benches run along the tapering walls of the "atrium", from where shallow, cleanly-hewn steps descend to the spring, and a conduit channels any excess water for when the level rose. The surrounding walls have niches built into them to hold the bronze statuettes and other votive objects that were found during the excavations, some of them dating from between the twelfth and ninth centuries BC.

The visible remains don't take very long to absorb, but the peaceful, bucolic setting and the enthusiasm of the guides, who will point out the various plants and sculptures they have installed along the path, justify the effort. Similar examples of sacred wells, albeit in very different settings, can be seen at Santa Cristina, near Oristano (see p.182), and Sa Testa, outside Olbia (see p.268).

From Bitti to the Monti di Alà

Twelve kilometres of mountain road north of Orune, the village of **BITTI** is famed for its singing tradition; the local male group, Tenores di Bitti, has established an international reputation for its four-part harmonies. There are a couple of bars here, and, signposted up Via Mameli, an alley off the main road (park below), the small **Museo della Civiltà Contadina e Pastorale** (Sat & Sun only: summer 10am–12.30pm & 3.30–6pm; winter 10am–12.30pm & 3–5.30pm; €3.10), devoted to the local farming and peasant culture. It's a diverting collection of tools, costumes and artefacts, but no great loss if you can't come during its limited visiting hours, with little of note that you won't have seen in other museums of the ilk in Sardinia.

Crossing into Sássari province at the Tirso river, the SP389 curls 25km northwest of Bitti to **BUDDUSÒ**, where there's a Banco di Sardegna (with an ATM) and a few shops on the main Corso Vittorio Emanuele. You can have a snack at the **bar** at Corso Vittorio Emanuele 95 (closed Tues), or a fuller meal at *La Madonnina* (☎079.715.500; ❸), one of the region's rare **hotels**, located opposite a sculpture park a kilometre south of the centre; rooms here are quiet and clean but lack much character.

The landscape around Buddusò is pitted with quarries, which have blasted huge craters out of the rock. Continuing north, the SP389 passes through flat country dotted with cork groves before reaching the tidy granite village of **ALÀ DEI SARDI**, 12km northeast of Buddusò. This somewhat isolated local centre has a couple of bars and the *San Lorenzo* **ristorante/pizzeria**, opposite the *Municipio* off the main street. If you prefer the idea of a picnic, follow signs left (heading north) from the main road running through the village for the **Santuario di San Francesco**, two or three kilometres north. Amid woods and fields, the church is the focus of a country festival, the **Festa di San Francesco**, on October 4, when a costumed procession including mounted *cavalieri* ends with a general carousal involving much food, drink and traditional dancing. You can follow paths from here into the **Monti di Alà**, a bare, rocky terrain that culminates in the Senalonga ridge (1076m), affording far-reaching views on all sides.

Pattada and around

Following the SP389dir west from Buddusò brings you alongside the **Lago di Pattada**, an artificial lake that makes another good spot for picnics. Five kilometres west of the lake, the village of **PATTADA** is famed for its shepherds' knives, known as *pattadesa*, for sale in shops all over the island. You can see numerous examples in the shops here at surprisingly steep prices: all have tough, hand-worked steel blades and the best have horn handles from ram or mouflon. The village has an excellent hotel, *La Pineta*, on Via La Pineta (☎079.755.140; ❹), making this a good, out-of-the-way place to halt. At 778m, the village is the highest in the province of Sássari, and there are plenty of good views and walks in tall pine forests within a short distance.

Burgos

From Pattada, the road descends some 15km west to Ozieri (see p.254). To the south lies the high, hilly region of **Goceano**, whose green pastures are dotted with grazing herds of sheep. Beyond the villages of Bultei and Bono, **BURGOS** is visible from miles around, mainly on account of its castle, **La Reggia**, dramatically poised on a granite pinnacle high above the village (daily: 9am–sunset; €3). Completed in 1133, the formidably walled redoubt was strategically vital for its commanding position over the Tirso valley, at a point where the three territories (*giudicati*) of Torres, Arborea and Gallura met. It was briefly occupied by Eleonora d'Arborea (see p.165), and was used as a prison for various unwanted family members – the guides will point out the remains of cells as well as of stables and barracks, and of an extensive space that may have been a church or central dining-hall. At one end, the square tower looming over the ruins was rather incongruously renovated in the 1950s, and may be open for visits in future.

At the base of the castle, the village of Burgos was founded in the fourteenth century by Mariano IV of Arborea, though has a predominantly modern aspect. There's not much here apart from a couple of bars, but the scenic road running 35km northwest towards Torralba (see p.255) passes through the **Foresta di Burgos**, a wooded area that's home to miniature horses, and across high, empty plains, before descending to the SS131.

Sopramonte and the Barbagia Ollolai

Facing Nuoro to the south, the great wall of mountain that is **Sopramonte** makes an irresistible destination for further exploration. Crouched at the base of Monte Corrasi, the long ridge visible from the provincial capital, **Oliena** is the best base for excursions in the area, with abundant accommodation

△ Valle Lanaittu near Tiscali

possibilities. East of the village, the springs at **Su Gologone** are the starting point for hiking expeditions, notably to the nuraghic village of **Tíscali**. To the south and east of Oliena, the villages of the **Barbagia Ollolai** region offer contrasting glimpses into local culture and folklore: **Orgósolo** is famous for its ancient banditry and its vivid, politicized murals; the otherwise unremarkable village of **Mamoiada**, 11km west and 16km south of Nuoro, is the venue of a highly pagan Carnival; further west, **Orani** has an absorbing museum dedicated to Costantino Nivola, one of Sardinia's most respected twentieth-century artists, while **Ottana**, on the southern fringes of the region, is also renowned for its festivities during the Carnival period and possesses a good Pisan church. Lacking the dramatic landscape of other parts of the Barbagia, the area is less suitable for walking, though the **Montes** region south of Orgósolo has an appealing empty grandeur worth experiencing.

If you're looking for **accommodation** for the night, choose places either in or around Oliena or Orgósolo – there's practically nothing elsewhere. All villages are accessible by frequent ARST **buses** from Nuoro.

Oliena and around

The nearest village of any size to Nuoro, **OLIENA** is easily visible from the provincial capital, sprawled along the side of Monte Corrasi to the south. Rising to 1463m, this rugged limestone elevation forms part of the

A walk to Valle Lanaittu and Monte Tíscali

One of the most rewarding expeditions you can make on Sopramonte is to **Valle Lanaittu**, a grand secluded valley overlooked by **Monte Tíscali** (518m), which holds the remains of a nuraghic village within. The official advice is to take a guide, which the tourist office in Oliena (see p.324) can arrange; expect to pay around €30, or €45 including lunch. However, it's a relatively short and straightforward hike, and though there are some tricky sections where there's a risk of straying off the route, it's always possible to retrace your steps to return to your starting point. The following directions should enable you to visit the site unaccompanied. The whole hike to and from Tíscali should not take longer than three or four hours, depending on your setting-off point. Before leaving, make sure you let someone know where you're headed, and that you have adequate equipment: robust walking shoes or boots, protection against the sun, and at least a litre of water per person.

The track into the Valle Lanaittu is signposted from the **Sorgente Su Gologone**, a natural spring just by the *Su Gologone* hotel complex (℡0784.287.512) on the Oliena–Dorgali road. Non-drivers can reach this point on any bus between the two villages, and can avoid trudging along the first easy but uninteresting section (about 10km) by asking at the hotel for a taxi-ride to a point from which to begin the climb, and you can arrange a pick-up time for the return. From the spring, walk or drive along the mainly unasphalted track, sticking to the most travelled route. After about 6km, a signposted turn-off to the right leads to **Grotta Sa Oche**, a cave with a car park alongside. You could leave your vehicle here, but as there are plenty of parking possibilities further along the route, you might as well continue on the main track past the Grotta Sa Oche junction, keeping left. Ignore the next major turn-off to the right after another kilometre or so (signposted "Grotta Helies Arias"). As the track soon afterwards becomes too rough for any but off-road vehicles, look for a place to leave your car around here and continue on foot.

The track curves round to the left before passing through a wide clearing. Keep left until you see a broad path that diverges from the main track to the right, marked by red painted symbols and a cairn of stones. After about thirty minutes of climb-

Sopramonte massif, famed as the haunt of **bandits** until relatively recent times. Oliena itself prefers its reputation as the producer of one of the island's finest **wines** – a dry, almost black concoction that turns lighter and stronger over the years – and as the best base for hiking excursions in the mountainous terrain surrounding it. You can gain access to Monte Corrasi from Località Maccione, a wooded area 3km south of town off the very squiggly old road to Orgósolo, where there's a good hotel and restaurant (see p.325).

Although it's one of the liveliest villages of the region, Oliena lacks much intrinsic interest unless you're here during one of its **feast days**. The most striking are around Easter: on Good Friday, when a mournful procession shuffles through the streets, at the end of which the whole village pours into a pitch-black church to watch an intensely dramatic re-enactment of Christ's Deposition, and on Easter Sunday, a much more boisterous affair, when hundreds gather to witness the *Incontru*, or meeting, between the figures of the Virgin Mary and the resurrected Jesus. On this latter occasion, there's much gunfire, villagers don the local traditional dress (an elegant black-and-white or red-and-white costume, complete with jewellery), and there's dancing, music and free tastings in the main square. The costumes and dancing can also be viewed during the four days of revelry around San Lussorio's day on August 21.

Off the Dorgali road, 7km from Oliena, **Su Gologone** makes a good starting point for mountain expeditions (see the box on p.322); the area is named

ing the stony, zig-zagging path (marked both red-and-white symbols and red arrows), you'll reach a broad **rocky ledge** which provides a convenient platform to enjoy the grand panorama over the valley. Look out for a dead tree painted with a red marker, from where the trail ascends steeply to the left up the mountainside, involving a bit of a scramble, with slippery scree underfoot. After about twenty minutes, the red-and-white markers continue to the right, but you should bear left to the steepest part of the mountain, where a well-hidden narrow cleft leads through the formidable rock wall to a wide ledge, affording stupendous views over the **Valle Lanaittu** to the right. Note the crinkly, grooved surface of the rock here, formed by rainwater, and there are also fossils to be found. The red markers are not always clear, so look out after a few minutes for a rudimentary path over the rocks to the right, which descends to the entrance to the Tíscali cavern, again partly concealed behind trees.

It's a bit of a shock to find, in such an isolated spot, a custodian and ticket desk for the remains of the **nuraghic village of Tíscali** (daily: May–Sept 9am–7pm; Oct–April 9am–5pm; €5), dramatically sited within a vast hollow space inside the mountain itself. Once providing a last refuge from foreign incursions during the first millennium BC, the site was inhabited well into Roman and medieval times, but was only rediscovered about a century ago, and is still under excavation. Few of the buildings have survived in a recognizable form, but it's a fascinating place nonetheless, the yellow limestone walls and stalagmites giving it a weird, ghostly atmosphere. A huge hole punched through the rock where part of the roof collapsed creates a soft twilight within, and once enabled the villagers to keep an eye on any comings and goings in the valley below. There's vegetation and even trees growing inside, but the lack of ready water must have been a constant problem, probably preventing the community from ever growing very large.

From here, unless you have an experienced guide with you, you'll have to retrace your steps back down. With a guide, however, you might continue along the path past Tíscali, descending into the Flumineddu valley to the east.

for a fast-flowing therapeutic spring which emerges from underground close to the church of **San Giovanni**, and there are usually a few locals here with jerry cans. It's a good spot to picnic under the eucalyptus trees, and you can follow the course of the stream or a choice of tracks leading into the mountains. There's a hotel with a renowned restaurant here too, *Su Gologone* (see p.325). ARST buses stop at the turn-off for Su Gologone.

Practicalities

Oliena is connected by regular **buses** from Nuoro, the last one returning at around 8pm (earlier on Sun). The village's **tourist office** lies on the main Via Deledda that weaves up through town, opposite the church on Piazza Santa Maria (Mon–Sat 9am–1pm & 4–7pm; ☏0784.286.078). The office has material on the whole of the Barbagia, with helpful, English-speaking staff, who can put you in touch with guides for excursions in the region as well as local *agriturismi* and B&Bs.

If you're not staying in one of the local hotels, you can consult one of Oliena's tailor-made agencies for all the various **guided expeditions** possible around Sopramonte's caves and crags. The main operators are Barbagia Insólita, Corso Vittorio Emanuele 48 (☏0784.286.005); Levamus, Corso Vittorio Emanuele 33 (☏0784.286.088), and Corrasi, Piazza Santa Maria (☏0784.287.144, ⓦwww.corrasi.com).

Accommodation

There is only one **hotel** in town, the *Cikappa* at Via Martin Luther King 2 (☏0784.288.733, ⓕ0784.288.721; ❸), much favoured by outdoors enthusiasts, with fairly standard but efficient modern rooms; the people here can also arrange expeditions of various sorts. There are several alternatives however, including a useful **agriturismo**, for once right in the centre of the village at Via Bixio 9 (☏0784.287.066; ❷), offering clean and comfortable rooms and home cooking; *Su Marimundu* (☏0784.287.360 or 388.338.4892; 2), a friendly (currently unsigned) country B&B about 1km north of the village (call to be met), and in Località Maccione, a wooded area 3km south of town, the *Monte Maccione*, also known as *Cooperativa Enis* (☏0784.288.363, ⓦwww.coopenis.it; ❸), an excellent stop for mountain walkers, offering clean rooms as well as pitches for **camping** in the woods (€6 per person). It's on a steep, rough-surfaced road that corkscrews up the mountain, signposted off the old road for Orgósolo. The terrace restaurant enjoys phenomenal views. Oliena's third hotel, *Su Gologone* (☏0784.287.512, ⓦwww.sugologone.it; ❸), actually lies 7km east of the village on the Dorgali road, in a rustic setting next to the spring of the same name. It's one of the best-known hotels in inland Sardinia, equipped with a swimming pool, tennis court and fitness centre; though expensive, it's a popular destination for both day-trippers and food pilgrims drawn to its good restaurant (see p.325). It has a full programme of walking, horse-riding and jeep expeditions onto Sopramonte and beyond, and also arranges "lunch with the shepherds" – a hike or jeep-ride which culminates in an open-air feast where punters are pampered with a succulent succession of local dishes cooked over an open fire (vegetarians will have a limited choice).

Eating

You can eat well in Oliena – all the above-mentioned hotels have excellent **restaurants**, specializing, of course, in land-based dishes. The *Cikappa* is fairly cheap and cheerful, and is popular for its pizzas; the harder-to-reach *Monte Maccione* is also reasonably priced, has a more adventurous menu, and benefits from its fabulous views over the valley, while *Su Gologone* has superb, gourmet fare, with high prices. Apart from these, you will also do well at the semi-formal *Masiloghi*, Via Galiani 68 (☏0784.285.696); it's the most "rustic" of Oliena's choices, and offers delicious meat and seafood platters at moderate-to-expensive prices.

Orgósolo and Mamoiada

Deeper into the mountains, at the end of a straggly eighteen-kilometre road from Oliena, **ORGÓSOLO** is stuck with its label of bandit capital of the island. The clans of Orgósolo, whose menfolk used to spend the greater part of the year away from home with their flocks, have always nursed an animosity towards the settled crop-farmers on the Barbagia's fringes, a tension that occasionally broke out into open warfare. On top of this, there was conflict between rival clans, which found expression in large-scale sheep-rustling and bloody **vendettas**, such as the *disamistade* (enmity) that engulfed Orgósolo at the beginning of the twentieth century. The feud arose from a dispute over the inheritance of the village's richest chieftain, Diego Moro, who died in 1903, and lasted for fourteen years, virtually exterminating the two families involved. Between 1901 and 1954, Orgósolo – population 4000 – clocked up an average of one murder every two months. In 1953 the first of the post-war kidnappings,

Mamoiada's Mamuthones

The **Mamuthones of Mamoiada** are among the best-known of Sardinia's traditional costumed figures, associated with the festivities around Carnival time, but with obscure roots going back several centuries. Despite their spooky, rather disturbing appearance – decked out in dark, shaggy sheepskins on which rows of jangling goat bells are strung, and with heavy, black, oversized masks – the *Mamuthones* are symbols of abundance and good times, as manifested by the food and drink liberally dispensed during the proceedings.

The **main events** take place on Shrove Tuesday and the preceding Sunday, usually kicking off at 3pm and 3.30pm respectively. Two columns of masked *Mamuthones* stalk the main street, Corso Vittorio Emanuele, accompanied by red-jacketed **Issohadores** – or *Issokadores* – wielding lassos (*sa soca*). As the *Mamuthones* advance solemnly, they perform curious synchronized leaps, causing the hundreds of goat bells tied across their backs to clang simultaneously, while the *Issohadores* twirl their lassos and ensnare victims, often from metres away, sometimes targeting spectators watching from balconies along the route. At the end of Shrove Tuesday's procession, a masked puppet known as **Juvanne Martis** is hauled on a cart through the village by participants supposedly weeping to lament the end of Carnival, though the evening sees a general carousal in Piazza Santa Croce anyway, with plates of pork and beans, traditional sweets and glasses of the local wine handed around, and dancing. There's also plenty of similarly rustic fare to eat and drink throughout the ceremonies, offered at stalls and shops around the village.

There's an alternative opportunity to view these celebrations at the **Festa di Sant'Antonio Abate**, the traditional beginning of the Carnival period, usually mid-January 16 and 17. Then, bonfires are lit around the village and kept burning through the night, attracting groups of half-drunk revellers shuttling between them. Locals contend this is the best time to view the Mamuthones, when there are fewer distractions from the other costumed Carnival celebrations on the island, and fewer tourists.

At other times, you can view the *Mamuthones* and other local costumes at Mamoiada's Museo delle Máschere Mediterranee (see p.326).

which would soon become endemic to this region of Sardinia, took place near Orgósolo, and the connection was crystallized with the screening of Vittorio de Seta's film *Banditi di Orgósolo* in 1961.

The village's most notorious son is **Graziano Mesina**, the so-called "Scarlet Rose", who won local hearts in the 1960s by robbing only from the rich to give to the poor and only killing for revenge against those who had betrayed him. Roaming at will through the mountains, even granting interviews to reporters and television journalists, he was eventually captured and incarcerated in Sássari prison. Escaping in 1968, he was recaptured near Nuoro and flown by helicopter the same day to appear on television in Cágliari. Mesina last surfaced in July 1992, when he was dispatched to Sardinia from a mainland prison to help negotiate the release of Farouk Kassam, an eight-year-old boy held hostage for seven months in the Barbagia (see the box on p.328).

Saddled with this semi-legendary background, Orgósolo plays host to a constant trickle of visitors hoping to find traces of its violent past amid the shabby collection of grey breeze-block houses, and the locals have obliged by peppering various of the the village's name-plates and signs with bullet holes, and by painting a sinister scarlet and white face on a rock by the side of the main road into town. But this is just a harbinger of things to come, for Orgósolo's narrow alleys have been daubed with a vivid array of **murals**, more strident and better executed than those found in other Sard villages such as San Sperate. Covering whole houses and shop fronts, most have a political element, graphically illustrating themes of exploitation – of the landless and women, for example – or demanding Sardinian independence. Some date back to the 1960s, protesting against the US bombing of Vietnam, while others are more recent, such as recalling the 1993 famine in Somalia; yet others are comic or simply depict village culture. All share a common theme of traditional culture in collision with the modern world. One of the most heavily painted buildings is the *Municipio*, whose garish collection of cartoon figures and slogans are poignantly shot through with more bullet holes – the work of local hotheads.

You could happily spend an hour or two wandering through this open-air gallery, but there's precious little else to do in Orgósolo, unless you're here at Ferragosto (August 14–15), when one of the region's most colourful **festivals** takes place around the little church of the **Assunta**, a nondescript, creamfronted building enclosed behind a wall (but visible below Piazza Caduti). Within easy reach of the village, the high country above Orgósolo is well worth exploring. Following the road through the village, a left turn takes you south out of town and steeply uphill, leading after about 5km to the high plateau of **Montes**, an empty, desolate expanse, green but rugged, suitable for hiking or riding, and site of a good hotel and restaurant (see p.327). A small road continues as far as **Funtana Bona**, at a height of 1052m, only a kilometre or two's walk from the peak of **Monte San Giovanni** (1316m), near the source of the Cedrino river.

Taking the right fork above the village leads instead to **MAMOIADA**, a village every bit as straitened as Orgósolo, judging by its drab appearance, but whose highly theatrical **Carnival rituals** have made it one of the best-known of Barbagia's villages (see p.48). Unless you're here for the twice-yearly masked festivities, there's little to see or do, though you might wander up to the **Fonte Romana** (signposted from Piazza Europa, at the bottom of the Corso), a couple of simple spouts over granite basins; only the lower part is authentically Roman, but the water is drinkable and fresh. The **Museo delle Máschere Mediterranee** (Tues–Sun 9am–1pm & 3–7pm; €4), housed in the *biblioteca* (library) in Piazza Europa, exhibits local masks and costumes and mainly consists of mannequins and photos – not a patch on Nuoro's costume collection, but the video and guided commentaries are informative (though usually in Italian only).

Practicalities

About ten **buses** a day (two on Sun) ply the route to Orgósolo from Nuoro, so it's not necessary to stay over. Should you want to, however, there are a couple of reasonable **hotels** in town. One, *Sa 'e Jana* (℡0784.402.437, ℱ0784.401.247; no credit cards; ❷), on Via Lussu, has a restaurant, discotheque and stupendous vistas; it's at one end of the village on the Mamoiada road, signposted past the graffiti-daubed school. The even cheaper *Petit* (℡ & ℱ0784.402.009; ❷) is right in the heart of things on Via Mannu, with fewer views, and offers rooms with or without private bath. Apart from these places, Orgósolo itself has little in the way of restaurants, though drivers can go a few kilometres in the Montes direction to **Località Settiles**, where there's a wonderful restaurant, the *Monti del Gennargentu*, serving healthy mountain fare (℡ & ℱ0784.402.374). You can also stay here, if you wanted to do any walking or riding around here (stables are nearby): half-board comes to €55 per person, less outside the peak season. It's about 3km from the SS389 Nuoro–Arbatax road, from the junction at Pratobello.

Mamoiada is equally well connected to Nuoro, though the village has no hotels or pensions. You can contact the Pro Loco on Via Sardegna (irregular hours; no telephone), or the *Comune* (town hall) on the Corso (Mon–Fri 10am–1pm, also Mon & Wed 3.30–6pm; ℡0784.56.023). Mamoiada also has more scope for **eating**, including a good trattoria, *La Campagnola*, on Via Satta, which you may have passed on the way into the village from Nuoro. Pizzas are served in the evenings, and are also available more centrally from *Da Mommo*, a simple pizzeria at Corso Vittorio Emanuele 82 (closed Wed). About a hundred metres further up from the latter, at Corso Vittorio Emanuele 92, the *Bar Sarvuleddu* has snacks and tables outside. If you're here during Carnival, pick up a steaming pork sandwich freshly grilled in places along the Corso, which also sell chilled wine.

Note that if you're **driving** here direct from Nuoro, you might prefer to take the fast, straight but poorly signposted route via the Circonvallazione Sud rather than the twisty (but gratifyingly empty) alternative.

Orani and Ottana

The unassuming village of **ORANI** is worth a stop for the museum dedicated to its most famous son, the sculptor **Costantino Nivola** (1911–88). In fact, Nivola only spent a short part of his life here, working with his stonemason father until the age of fifteen before studying in Sássari and then fleeing Fascist persecution in 1938. After spending some time in Paris, he emigrated to the United States, where he forged a long association with Le Corbusier and taught at Berkeley and Harvard. Most of the pieces in the **Museo Nivola** (Mon 4–9pm, Tues–Sun 9am–1pm & 4–9pm, closes 8pm Oct–May; €1.60), a low yellow villa located above the Agip petrol station at Via Gonare 2, are from the last period of Nivola's life, and reflect the artist's attitudes towards his homeland upon revisiting it after his long American exile. Small-scale, the very opposite of monumental, the bronze sculptures are arranged in a white, well-lit room on marble plinths, and in a small courtyard outside. Many of the items are clearly inspired by ancient menhirs and nuraghic *bronzetti*, other works use cement and marble, and the technique of sandcasting (which Nivola pioneered). There are also paintings, sketches and models on display in three further rooms, and also a good bookshop where you can pick up material on Nivola.

OTTANA, on the northern and western fringes of the Barbagia Ollolai, is reckoned to be the dead centre of Sardinia. The twin chimneys of the chemical plant outside town create an unattractive landmark in the predominantly flat countryside – a rare instance of industry in this province. Although its masked and horned Carnival horrors, *Sos Merdules*, vie with those of Mamoiada, Ottana is a dull place. It does, however, possess a good Romanesque church, **San Nicola**, for once centrally positioned on an elevation above the main square. Completed in 1160, the structure's sombre black stone is not immediately appealing, though its bare interior, minimally illuminated by slit windows, has an impressive altarpiece from the mid-fourteenth century. The main **Carnival** procession starts off from here at around 2.30pm on Shrove Tuesday, and features costumed representatives from the villages of Mamoiada, Fonni, Gavoi and Tonara as well as Ottana. The previous afternoon sees folk dances in the piazza below.

The Gennargentu massif and Barbagia Belvì

The **Gennargentu** chain of mountains – the name means "silver gate", referring to the snow that covers them every winter – holds the island's highest peaks, **Punta La Mármora** (1834m) and **Monte Bruncu Spina** (1829m), and the only skiing facilities. Unlike the granite crags of Gallura, these mountains are round and, above a certain altitude, completely bare. The villages scattered about were traditionally shepherds' communities, but nowadays the shepherds send their children to university, or they go to seek work in mainland Italy and don't come back, leaving behind them slowly atrophying communities whose salvation is deemed to lie in a greater awareness of their tourism potential.

Many villages have in fact succeeded in adapting to the new economic reality, serving the expanding leisure industry, even if the season is short and has only a partial impact on the local economy. Though the villages themselves are

Banditry and kidnapping in the Barbagia

Until a short time ago, the villages of the Barbagia were primarily communities of shepherds, whose isolated circumstances and economic difficulties in the postwar years led to widescale emigration and, among those who stayed behind, a crime wave. Sheep-rustling and internecine feuding came to be replaced by the infinitely more lucrative practice of **kidnapping** and ransoming of wealthy industrialists or their families. This phenomenon reached epidemic proportions during 1966–68, when scores of *carabinieri* were drafted into the area to comb the mountains for the hideouts, rarely with any success. The most high-profile case in recent years was that of Farouk Kassam, an eight-year-old abducted from the Costa Smeralda in 1992 and held for seven months on Monte Albo, near Siníscola, who had part of his ear severed by his kidnappers to accelerate the ransom payment. Since then, however, there has been a lull in the kidnappings, partly due to improvements in police intelligence.

often unprepossessing and uniform in appearance – **Fonni**, for example, one of the main centres on the northern outskirts of the Gennargentu range, or **Sórgono**, loathed by D.H. Lawrence during his visit to Sardinia – some, such as **Aritzo** and **Belvì**, Sardinia's cherry capital, are beautifully sited and even have good museums. But the real pleasures here are the bits between the villages: the distant views over thickly-wooded slopes, where you may come across wild pigs and deer and, in the air, goshawks, sparrow-hawks, peregrine falcons, griffon vultures and eagles.

The villages certainly make good bases for **walking**, best undertaken in spring and summer, and there are good, reasonably-priced hotels in the best areas, such as **Désulo** and **Tonara**. For fuller details on walks, you can obtain a handy booklet from Nuoro's tourist office (see p.310). As for **getting around**, roads are convoluted and slow, and public transport is usually infrequent, but every village is connected by at least one route to large centres. The FdS train service is not as bad as in Lawrence's day, but it's still a cumbersome way to travel, only to be used if you have lots of time and patience.

Fonni and around

Sixteen kilometres due south of Mamoiada, in a hilly area thick with vineyards, corks and oak forests, **FONNI** is, at 1000m, Sardinia's highest village. As a popular destination for skiers and walkers in the Gennargentu mountains – whose loftiest peaks, Bruncu Spina and La Mármora, are visible from the village – Fonni is also one of the Barbagia's biggest centres, a role it has occupied since the seventeenth century, when a community of Franciscans helped to make this the focus of the whole region.

The church of **Madonna dei Mártiri** annexed to their convent is still the most significant of the Barbagia's churches, both for its wealth and for its image of the Madonna, said to have been made from the crushed bones of martyrs. You can see the domed church at the highest point of the village, in the centre of a large open space off Piazza Europa, surrounded by *cumbessias* or pilgrims' houses. Outside, the trees have been skilfully carved to depict religious themes. Originally dating from the seventeenth century, but remodelled a hundred years later, the church is a substantial, salmon-coloured building with a tall, grey granite spire. The interior is richly painted; an elaborate shrine on the right as you enter holds the artless but much venerated Madonna. The image is escorted through the streets during Fonni's two principal **festivals**, both in June – on the Monday following the first Sunday in June and again for San Giovanni's day on June 24. Both occasions are costumed extravaganzas, with columns of immaculately turned-out women and men on horseback, also in traditional dress, filing through the village.

The village has two three-star **hotels**: the modern, fully-equipped *Cualbu* on Viale del Lavoro (☎0784.57.054, ⓕ0784.58.403; ❹), signposted on the left as you enter town, and the much smaller *Cinghialetto* on Via Grazia Deledda (☎ & ⓕ0784.57.660; ❸). Both have **restaurants**, or you could seek out the modest *Barbagia* ristorante/pizzeria on Via Umberto, at the southern end of town.

You can also eat and sleep on the slopes of **Monte Spada** at the *Sporting Club* (☎0784.57.285, ⓕ0784.57.220; ❹), a large complex 8km south of Fonni, on a signposted left turn off the Désulo road; catering mainly to groups of skiers, it has a full range of facilities, but is often closed for weeks at a time. Paths from here wind up to the peak of the mountain (1595m). Alternatively, take the right fork before reaching the hotel to reach **Bruncu Spina**, to which you can approach quite close by a tarmacked road. It's a magnificent landscape, with bracken and other hardy shrubs taking over above the tree-line, covered in snow for a good part of the year. The views from the top extend as far as Gallura and even Corsica to the north. **Skiers** can experience Sardinia's only piste from the ski-station here, while properly-equipped hikers can reach the top of the island's highest peak, **Punta La Mármora**, a little way to the south, in less than three hours. You don't need to be an experienced climber to tackle either of these summits, though a guide is essential; excursions can be organized from the various villages on the flanks of the mountains between May and September.

Désulo

DÉSULO lies huddled along the steep slope of a deep forested valley 27km south of Fonni, to which it is connected by bus (less frequent services run from Cágliari and Nuoro). As one of the closest villages to the Gennargentu mountains, it makes a useful hiking base, and as such has a choice of **hotels**, including a small, good-value three-star, the *Gennargentu* (☎ & ℱ0784.619.270; ❷), up Via Kennedy on the left as you enter the village from the north; the *Lamármora* (Dec–March & June–Sept; ☎0784.619.411, ℱ0784.619.126; ❸), on the main Via Lamármora on the right, and *La Nuova* (☎0784.619.251; ❶), further up the same road, which has seven basic rooms with a shared bathroom above a restaurant. At the end of Via Lamármora, another small hotel, *Maria Carolina* on Via Cágliari (☎0784.619.310, ℱ0784.617.156; ❷) has splendid views from its bar, restaurant and pizzeria. None of the hotels currently accepts credit cards.

Belví and Aritzo

West of Désulo, the road descends along a valley to meet the SS295 after about 6km. Turn left (south) to reach **BELVÍ** after another 4 or 5km. This compact cluster of dwellings is, like Désulo, crowded along the side of a valley, and is famed for its cherries. Its former importance is attested to by the fact that the village gave its name to the whole of this sector of the Barbagia, but it's a very low-key place now, with little reason to linger apart from its **Museo Scienze Naturali** (daily: summer 8am–noon & 2–7pm; winter 9am–noon & 3–5pm; free), a collection of minerals, fossils and stuffed mammals, lizards and nearly four hundred birds, all crammed into a private house on Via Sebastiano (corner of Via Roma). It's a diverting assortment, but the numerous stuffed animals look a little tatty in places; if you're very keen, call first to make sure it's open (☎0784.629.806). Close by on Via Roma, the village has a decent **hotel and restaurant**, *L'Edera* (☎0784.629.898; ❷).

Almost immediately after Belví, **ARITZO** is another grey huddle, though it's larger, and has a livelier aspect than many of the other villages round here. The main road, Corso Umberto, holds everything of interest, including the parish church of **San Michele Archángelo**, a handsome edifice with some traces of its late Gothic construction and a good eighteenth-century *Pietà* on the second chapel on the right, and a seventeenth-century *San Cristóforo* in the last. Outside the church, the solitary and oddly square profile of Monte Téxile (975m) is visible on the horizon.

Aritzo also has an excellent **Museo Etnográfico** (daily 10.30am–1pm & 4.30–7pm, 3.30–6pm in winter; €1.60), housed in the *Comune* (town hall). It's a fascinating jumble, mainly connected with rural culture in the Gennargentu, including agricultural implements, articles for cheese- and wax-making, artisans' tools, a few local costumes and some old photos, all in excellent condition. Aritzo once earned a healthy living selling snow, and you can see here the straw-lined chests in which it was transported.

Beyond the church, the imposing crenellated building on the left as you ascend the main road is the neo-Gothic **Castello Arangino**, its tower and loggia lending it a Tuscan character, though it was only built at the beginning of the twentieth century. The Corso also holds the eighteenth-century **prigione d'Aritzo**, used as a gaol until the 1940s.

There are several **hotels** in Aritzo, making this a feasible place to stay. Cheapest is the *Hotel Castello* at the southern end of the village, a modern two-star with plain and clean rooms, some with views (✆0784.629.266; no credit cards; ❷), while the larger *Capannina* on Via Maxia (✆ & ⓕ0784.629.121; ❷), with rooms with or without bath, and, further up, the *Moderno*, with its own little garden and a pleasant restaurant (✆0784.629.229, ⓕ0784.629.675; ❸), have a little more character. There are also a few craft shops and a **bank** on Corso Umberto.

Tonara and Sórgono

Fifteen kilometres north of Aritzo, **TONARA** shares the same forested environment. Chestnuts are one of the foundations of the local economy, and the village is also famed for the manufacture of cattle bells and for its *torrone* nougat – a rich sticky feast of honey, nuts and eggs, usually for sale wherever there's a village festa. Tonara has a handful of small hotels, including the *Belvedere* on the street of the same name (open July–Aug; ✆ & ⓕ0784.63.756; ❷), its more modern sister-hotel *Belvedere 2*, 50m away on Via Monsignor Tore (✆0784.610.054, ⓕ0784.63.756; ❸), and *Su Toni* on Via Italia (✆0784.63.420; no credit cards; ❷). All three have **restaurants**, or you can eat informally at *Aquarium*, a cosy pizzeria/*paninoteca* on the main drag.

D. H. Lawrence in Sardinia

"Comes over one an absolute necessity to move," begins *Sea and Sardinia*, the travelogue by **D.H. Lawrence**, written in response to a restless desire to take a break from Sicily, where he was then living with his wife Frieda. Disembarking in Sardinia in January 1921, the couple made the briefest tour of the island, just six days, for most of which they were in trains and buses, having decided to travel the hardest route – straight up through the interior from Cágliari on the painfully slow narrow-gauge railway. At Sórgono, the Lawrences changed onto a bus to Nuoro and proceeded to Olbia, whence they returned by ferry to the mainland.

It was Sardinia's inland villages that left the deepest impression, however. Sórgono – which at first appeared like "some little town in the English West Country" – possessed just one hotel, the *Risveglio*, where the only bedroom available contained "a large bed, thin and flat with a grey-white counterpane, like a large, poor, marble-slabbed tomb in the room's sordid emptiness; one dilapidated chair on which stood the miserablest weed of a candle I have ever seen: a broken wash-saucer in a wire ring: and for the rest, an expanse of wooden floor as dirty-grey-black as it could be, and an expanse of wall charted with the bloody deaths of mosquitoes." A stroll through the village did not improve his mood: "A dreary hole! A cold, hopeless, lifeless, Saturday-afternoon-weary village, rather sordid, with nothing to say for itself."

Despite the ill humour that characterizes much of the book, it's a good read: a close-up description of travelling on the cheap, crammed with the details of conversations and the minutiae of buying bread or making tea on the "kitchenette", all interspersed with observations on the state of the world in the wake of World War I. For details of publication, see p.362.

West of Tonara, the road careers through forests of chestnut and oak for 10km before reaching the small town of **SÓRGONO**, the northernmost point of the FdS narrow-gauge railway from Cágliari. D.H. Lawrence and his wife Frieda stopped here in 1921, en route to Nuoro, and hated it. As the centre of the Mandrolisai wine region, the town enjoys a certain fame, but it's a long, dull sprawl, devoid of any great interest and useful only as a transport junction and hotel stop. The FdS station is at the eastern end of the village, off the main street, where the Banco di Sardegna has an ATM. There is little to distinguish between the two **hotels**: one, *Da Nino*, is on Via IV Novembre (☎ & ⓕ0784.60.127; ❸), the other is *Villa Fiorita* on Viale Europa (☎0784.60.129; ❸); both have **restaurants**.

The Sarcidano: Láconi, Ísili and the Nuraghe Arrubiu

On the southern edges of the Barbagia, the **Sarcidano** region is a quickly changing landscape of verdant hills and desolate basalt plains. There's ample evidence here of Sardinia's prehistory, starting with a fascinating collection of menhirs in the museum at **Láconi**, a village cradled in a fold of the hills at the top of this area. Further south, **Ísili** – the economic, cultural and administrative centre of Sarcidano – has the imposing **Is Parras** nuraghe on its outskirts, while outside the town of Orroli, between the Flumendosa and Mulargia lakes, the **Nuraghe Arrubiu** is one of the island's grandest monuments from this era.

Either Láconi or Ísili would be good places to break your journey, the latter having the area's best choice of **hotels**, though the former is the more attractive village. Ísili is a stop on the FdS line, and Láconi and Orroli are linked by ARST buses, though you'll need your own transport to view Nuraghe Arrubiu.

Láconi

On the fringes of the mountains, the village of **LÁCONI** retains a fresh, wooded feel; it's a pleasurable place to explore, with a surprising number of attractions. Not the least of these is its elegant Neoclassical **Municipio** on the main Corso Garibaldi, designed in 1846 by Sardinia's most eminent architect, Gaetano Cima (1805–78). Below and behind it is housed Láconi's excellently presented **Museo delle Statue Menhir** (daily: April–Sept 9.30am–1pm & 4–7.30pm; Oct–March 9am–1pm & 4–6pm; closed first Mon of month;

Sant'Ignazio da Láconi

Born Vincenzo Peis, though apparently called "Il Santerello" even in his youth because of his extreme piety, Sardinia's most popular "modern" saint, **Sant'Ignazio da Láconi**, became a lay Capuchin monk in 1721. He spent the next sixty years practising penitence, humility and charity; as an inscription in his birthplace relates, *"Conobbe le cose occulte, penetrò il segreto dei cuori, ed ebbe il dono dei miracoli"* ("he knew occult things, he penetrated the secrets of the heart, and he had the gift of miracles"). Born in Láconi, he lived for most of his life in Cágliari, where he performed various miracles, dying there in 1781 and spawning an enthusiastic cult. Beatified in 1940, he was canonized in 1951.

€3.50), signposted simply "Museo Archeologico", but mainly dedicated to Sardinia's extraordinary prehistoric menhirs, which are particularly concentrated in this area. Although most of the bigger ones, reaching up to seven metres in height (as seen in photographs here), have been left in their original sites, the museum has a fine selection of smaller pieces, imaginatively displayed and grouped according to the genre they represent.

The majority of the menhirs, which are mainly of trachyte stone, date back to the **Neolithic cultures** of Ozieri and Arzachena of the second half of the fourth millennium BC, and are a principal source of information for this obscure era, particularly regarding its divinities. The earliest have few if any characteristic marks, though later ones bear primitive facial characteristics, mainly nose and eyes. These more interesting "anthropomorphic" menhirs may be male or female in form, and are especially common around Láconi; the "males" are distinguished by the horn-shaped tridents embossed on one side, perhaps indicating membership of a warrior class, while "feminine" menhirs have a more inchoate form, though one, in Sala 2, shows a grooved circle below the "neck", perhaps representing a hair arrangement. Others are "asexual", though still retaining the facial features. The museum also displays Neolithic ceramics and obsidian arrowheads.

Opposite the Municipio, the cobbled Via Sant'Ignazio leads to the **Casa Natale di Sant'Ignazio**, family home of one of Sardinia's most revered saints (see the box on p.332). Even non-believers can find something interesting in the house, though you need to go round to the back to appreciate how it must have originally appeared – the rough stonework here is quite unlike the spruced-up exterior of the front. The house itself is little more than a bare room with a typical wood-beamed and bamboo-covered ceiling, and there's a shrine and benches for prayer and meditation. The place is usually left open; if not, call ☎0782.869.027.

Further down Via Sant'Ignazio, turn left at Piazza XXIX Agosto and walk up Via Don Minzoni to reach the church dedicated to **Sant'Ignazio**, conspicuous by its metal dome and square, pointy campanile. The bronze sculpted doors, carved in the 1980s, depict miracles and scenes from the saint's life, and you can see the chapel where he received his baptism.

Below the church, the terraced **Parco Aymerich di Láconi** (8am–sunset) makes an ideal place to take a breather or have a picnic. Once over a bridge that crosses a pretty stream, you'll find a marvellous shady retreat full of surprises: springs, grottoes, waterfalls, a lake with goldfish and much bigger, darker fish lurking, great overhanging rocks and beautifully crafted rustic benches. Best of all, buried within the thick groves, is the **Castello Aymerich**, a ruined redoubt, parts of which go back to 1051. The building has pleasing details, such as the small carving of a castle on the gate and windows resembling an ace of spades. In front of the roofless hall there's a grassy terrace with fine views over the valleys and countless paths curving round the hill. Everything is verdant, damp and mossy. All around are trees from Europe, Asia and the Americas (they are labelled, and a list at the entrance gives their scientific nomenclature, their names in Italian, and in the Láconi dialect).

Practicalities

Láconi has a good, friendly and cheap hotel, the *Sardegna* (☎0782.869.033, ℱ0782.867.005; ❶), above a restaurant at the top of the main street. ARST buses stop right outside here as well as in front of the Municipio (tickets from the kiosk to its left), and the village is a stop on the FdS line, the station a ten-minute walk to the west of town. The Banco di Sardegna on Via Santa

Maria–signposted left off the main street heading north – has a *cambio* but no ATM (open Mon–Fri 8.20–1.20pm).

Ísili

A right turn off the SS128 southward takes you along the SS197 to the Giara di Gésturi, La Marmilla and Barúmini (see p.139–144). Staying on the SS128 leads another 8km across a calcareous landscape studded with outcrops to **ÍSILI**. Like so many of Sardinia's inland villages, it makes little visual impact, though it has a couple of attractions and some good country worth exploring in the vicinity. In recent years it has been a popular base for free climbers, attracted to the sheer rock faces of the surroundings, though the village has a longer-established fame as a centre of *artigianato*, particularly copperware, which is readily available in the shops in and around the central Corso Vittorio Emanuele III. There are also several **domus de janas** in the vicinity – the so-called "fairy-houses" which were actually prenuraghic tombs. A couple of them are easily visitable on foot from the western end of the Corso: a sign points the way along a cul-de-sac on the edge of the village, from where a path leads to square-cut openings giving onto low-roofed chambers.

Far more compelling is the **Is Parras** nuraghe (daily 9am–noon & 2–5pm; free), splendidly sited on Ísili's northern outskirts (unmissable from the SS128 from Láconi or from the FdS train). Exposed on a bare hillock, with wild olive growing out of its walls, this constitutes one of Sardinia's most impressive single-towered nuraghic monuments, and its smooth-walled tholos interior is also, at 12m, the highest on the island. Its other main features are the small chamber in front of the main entrance, and a niche for a sentry on its right-hand side.

Free climbers and passing visitors alike can enjoy some of the desolate sites lying within a short distance of Ísili. The **Lago di San Sebastiano**, visible from the village's western side, is a dammed lake overlooked by the ruins of a church. Also west of town, the canyon of **Is Borroccus**, carved out by the Mannu river, is one of the rare nesting sites in Sardinia of Bonelli's eagle.

Practicalities

Ísili's main FdS station is on the southern end of town, though there's another station to the north. Its fame as a centre of crafts and climbing means that the village can boast four **hotels**, making it a useful overnight stop. Of these, the small *Giardino* lies nearest to the main FdS station, just across from the Agip petrol station on Corso Vittorio Emanuele (℡0782.802.014; no credit cards; ❷), though it's also the dingiest; two mini-apartments have private bathrooms, the other eight rooms share facilities. Of the other choices, the smartest and most modern is the two-star *Del Sole* (℡0782.802.371, ℱ0782.802.024; ❷), at the western end of Corso Vittorio Emanuele. However, *Il Pioppo* (℡0782.802.117, ℱ0782.803.091; ❷), on the corner of Via Dante Alighieri and the Corso – some of whose comfortably-sized rooms have TVs – and the *Cardellino*, a modern, three-storey yellow block next to a public garden on Via Dante (℡0782.802.004, ℱ0782.802.438; ❷), are fine too. All hotels have their own restaurants and charge very similar rates, and all, apart from the *Giardino*, have en-suite rooms.

Nuraghe Arrubiu and Perdasdefogu

From the SS128, the SS198 branches eastward about 8km south of Ísili, from which the towns of Nurri and Orroli are reachable along the SP10. From

Orroli, continue south for another kilometre along the SP10 for the turn-off leading to one of Sardinia's most important nuraghic sites, **Nuraghe Arrubiu** (daily: March–Oct 9am–8.30pm; Nov–Feb 9.30am–5.30pm; €5), occupying an exposed, wind-blown plain another couple of kilometres down this road. Dating from around the seventh century BC, this formidable ruin is the only five-towered nuraghic complex in existence, and is thought to have originally had a much older thirty-metre central tower, of which nothing now remains. The complex takes its name ("red") from the basalt trachyte stone and the lichen that lend it its distinctive hue. The site has only been open since 1996 after a long period of excavation. Curiously, no nuraghic finds have so far been unearthed, only Punic and Roman artefacts, though continuing excavations are expected to throw up more valuable material. The Roman finds, which include mills, basins and stone tools used for pressing olives and grapes, are displayed in a separate walled area to the left as you enter the site.

Visitors are guided round the complex on hour-long tours (no tours in summer 1–3pm). If you're in the area on a summer night, you can sign up for one of the illuminated **night tours** led by the local *cooperativa*, an atmospheric way to view the remains (☎0782.847.269; €6); a minimum of twenty-five people is required, unless you're willing to pay a higher price. You can pick up refreshments from a snack bar at the site. For more information on Sardinia's nuraghic culture, see p.349–350.

The country south and east of here is rugged and empty, though growing greener and gentler once past the Flumendosa river. Continue south to reach the mountainous Gerrei district (see p.146), or head west at Escalaplano for the highly scenic and gloriously deserted minor road that runs through Perdasdefogu before climbing north again towards the Ogliastra region (see p.343). **PERDASDEFOGU** is an undistinguished village whose name ("Fire stones") is thought to derive from either the bituminous coal and anthracite mined here in the nineteenth century, or the local silica, used by primitive tribes to light fires. These days, with its ugly military base, the town has little to recommend a stay, though there are some wonderful walks to be enjoyed in the area, for example in the **Santa Barbara** wood, less than a kilometre from town, and to a lovely set of seventy-metre waterfalls, the **Cascate di Luesu**, to the south (on the right of the new road to Tertenia). The main Corso Vittorio Emanuele has a Banco di Sardegna and post office, and a useful **hotel and restaurant** at no. 55, the *Mura* (☎0782.94.603; no credit cards; ❷).

The eastern coast

Nuoro province's long **eastern seaboard** is highly developed around the resorts of **Posada** and **Orosei**, but further south it preserves its desolate beauty, virtually untouched apart from a couple of isolated spots at **Cala Golone** and, further down, around the small port of **Arbatax**. The SS125 follows the coast down from Siniscola. Frequent daily buses connect Cágliari and Nuoro with Tortolì, which is close to Arbatax. Tortolì and Arbatax are also on the FdS narrow-gauge railway that follows an inland route from Mandas, which has connections with Cágliari; the full journey from the coast to Cágliari takes seven hours.

The **beaches** along this coast are some of Sardinia's wildest. Near Orosei, **Cala Liberotto** has some extremely swim-worthy stretches of sand, as does Orosei's Marina, from where another small road leads a little further south to some more secluded bathing spots. The coast around Cala Gonone is also studded with isolated sandy coves, most of them inaccessible by road. **Hotels** are easy to come by, and the coast also has a good choice of **campsites**.

Posada

Northeast of Nuoro, the SS131dir highway follows the course of two river valleys, passing close to the inland town of Siniscola, the main centre of the rich agricultural land around here. The main road reaches the coast at **POSADA**, sited on a rise a little way inland, near the mouth of the river of the same name. Once a power-base for the surrounding districts, the town was prey to repeated attacks by seaborne raiders during the Middle Ages, and now only the ruins of its once impregnable castle – still commanding impressive views for miles around – attest to its former importance,

To get to the castle, climb up into the old centre; drivers should leave their vehicles in Piazza Eleonora d'Arborea or lower. The **Castello della Fava** (9am–sunset; €3.50) is a five-minute climb up steps above the square, now little more than a single oblong upright tower ringed by broken-down walls. Visitors must climb up five levels of wooden steps and iron rungs to reach the trapdoor at the top, but are rewarded by a sweeping panorama that takes in the citrus groves clustered around the coast and on the banks of the Posada river, the lagoons stretching south to the resort of La Caletta, and Barbagia's inland peaks. The castle owes its strange name – "Bean Castle" – to a medieval legend according to which, when besieged here by Moors, the *giudice* of Gallura took a homing pigeon, forced a broad bean down its gullet, and attached a message addressed to a fictitious army of rescuers. As planned, the Moors intercepted the bird. When they read the message and found the broad bean in its stomach, they concluded that not only was there an army on the way, but that the besieged Sards had plenty of provisions (enough to waste on pigeons, anyway), and promptly withdrew.

Most of Posada's **hotels** are located on the road to the sea, though there is the small three-star *Sa Rocca* in the village (℡0784.854.139, ℻0784.854.166; ❸), an attractive hotel/restaurant below the castle in Piazza Eleonora d'Arborea; half- or full board may be required in summer (€50 per head *mezza-pensione*). On Via Gramsci, between Posada and La Caletta, the *Donatella* has more capacity (℡0784.854.521, ℻0784.854.433; ❸). The **restaurants** in either place can supply good pastas, pizzas and seafood dishes. Posada hosts a **jazz festival** over three or four days around August 20, when bands from Sardinia and the mainland play for free in Piazza Belvedere.

The coast to Orosei

South of Posada, **La Caletta** is a small resort close to a watchtower and some good beaches, with a choice of hotels and snack bars. The fine white sands lie to the south of the small port. For refreshments, *Skipper*, a *birreria* with *panini* and music, is just around the corner from the beach, on Via Lungomare, while the nearby *Cappriccio* has snacks and ice creams. You can get a full meal at *L'Ostrica*, Via Nazario Sauro, where pizzas and inexpensive meat and fish dishes are served; **rooms** are also available here (℡0784.810.286; ❸). Fantasy, on Piazza Berlinguer, rents out bikes, tandems and cars (summer only). **Santa Lucia**, 5km further south, is another holiday resort with a Spanish watchtower. Close to the beach, under pinewoods, are two adjacent **campsites**, *Selema* (May to mid-Oct; ℡0784.819.068) and *La Mandragola* (May–Sept; ℡0784.819.119, ℗www.mandragola-villaggio.com), both fully-equipped. The bigger *Selema* has better sports facilities, while *La Mandragola* has cabins (❹). A little further south in the La Mandras neighbourhood there's a more remote site, *Cala Pineta* (June to mid-Sept; ☎0784.819.184, ⓦwww.calapineta.it), which also has rudimentary caravans (❸) and a tennis court.

Six or seven kilometres south, a turn-off left leads another couple of kilometres on to **Capo Comino**, Sardinia's easternmost point, a wild and desolate spot of jagged rocks and abundant *macchia*. An enticing arc of sand just to the north of the point is backed by more holiday homes and a couple of bars. A further 12km to the south, **Cala Liberotto** is yet another small-scale holiday centre, lacking much in the way of shops, but the pinewoods are scattered with villas and a clutch of **campsites**, including *Cala Ginepro*, right on the sea (May–Oct; ☎0784.91.017); it has bungalows at up to €115 for four people, much cheaper in low season, but usually available only by the week. For a **meal**, head for *Mariposa*, just inland from the sites, which serves good pizzas; like almost everywhere else around here, it's closed in winter.

From Cala Liberotto, the SS125 tracks away from the sea for 12km before crossing the Cedrino river, thick with reeds, to the town of **OROSEI**, the main centre of the Baronia region. Though it now stands 3km from the sea in a flat and fertile zone planted with vines and citrus groves, medieval accounts of Turkish raids suggest that Orosei was a significant harbour before the silting up of the river pushed back the shore. The town certainly shows signs of a prosperous past, in the many fine Spanish palazzi scattered around its interesting old quarter, and in its splendid ecclesiastical architecture, not least the church and towers of **Sant'Antonio**, fifteenth-century but much restored and remodelled. Entered through an ogival arch from Piazza Sant'Antonio, the church precincts consist of a cobbled space surrounded by *muristenes*, temporary pilgrims' dwellings (known as *cumbessias* in Sardinia's other provinces), in the centre of which stands a Pisan tower, converted into a private residence.

Orosei's central Piazza del Pópolo has another group of medieval buildings worth seeking out, foremost among which is **San Giácomo**, a cluster of tiled cupolas and a campanile fronted by a plain white Neoclassical facade at the top of a flight of steps. More steps on the other side of the road lead to Piazza Sas Ánimas, holding the dreadfully neglected remains of a fourteenth-century castle that was later used as a gaol, for which it's called **Castello Prigione Vecchia**. Next to it stands the pretty eighteenth-century **Chiesa delle Ánime**, made of rough brick and stonework with a tiled cupola and good portal. A brief walk away (and well signposted) lie two more churches worth a glance – San Gavino and the ruin of San Sebastiano, which you could take in on a brief stroll through the old town's streets.

Practicalities

Situated below the church of San Giácomo, Orosei's **Pro Loco** can put you in touch with knowledgeable guides for tours of the old quarter. The town has three **hotels**, none of them particularly cheap. The best is *Su Barchile* on Via Mannu (☎0784.98.879, ⓕ0784.998.113; ❺), a modern and friendly three-star with a great restaurant attached, though the *S'Ortale* on Via S'Ortale has more space and is cheaper (July–Sept; ☎0784.998.055, ⓕ0784.998.056; ❹), and also has a restaurant. When it comes to **eating**, however, the first choice must be *Su Barchile*, with delicious local dishes such as *makkarrones de busa* and *porcetto* cooked in myrtle. There's a Banco di Sardegna (Mon–Fri 8.20am–1.20pm & 2.35–4.05pm) across from *Su Barchile* on Via Nazionale, with an **ATM**.

Dorgali and around

Centre of the renowned **Cannonau** wine-growing region, the small inland town of **DORGALI** has also established a reputation for its craftwork. Apart from a couple of significant attractions in the neighbourhood, the handicrafts shops are the main reason to stop here, though you could also visit the town's small **Museo Archeologico** on Via Vittorio Emanuele (daily: March–April 9am–1pm & 3.30–6pm; May 9am–1pm & 3.30–6pm; June–Aug 9am–1pm & 4–7pm; Sept–Oct 9.30am–1pm & 3.30–6pm; Nov–Feb 9.30am–1pm &

A hike into the Gola di Gorropu

The **Gola di Gorropu** (Gorropu canyon), one of the deepest and most spectacular in southern Europe, with walls reaching over 200m high, can be walked for much of its length between April and October. If you're considering it, however, you should ask advice as to the state of the Flumineddu river which bores through it; large sections of the gorge may be flooded, requiring specialist skills and even dinghies to negotiate. When conditions are good, there's little possibility of losing the way, and the walk can be undertaken unaccompanied by a guide. The entire excursion will take a minimum of three hours, its length depending on how far up the gorge you want to – or can – reach.

You'll need your own transport to get to the **start of the trail**, which is best approached from **Dorgali**, about 10km to the north. From the Circonvallazione that by-passes the town to the west, take the side-road signposted for the *Sant'Elene* hotel (southwards). Past the hotel, take the left-hand turn, slightly descending, then the middle road at the subsequent three-way fork. About 5km from Dorgali, you'll pass the Chiesa di Buoncammino on your right, after which you'll see signs for Tiscali. After a further 4km, the unsurfaced road becomes increasingly bumpy before crossing the Flumineddu river. Take the left turn signposted Gorropu, and you'll soon come to a car park, beyond which you must proceed on foot.

The **track** lies behind the car park: follow this southwards, parallel to the river, and after a few minutes take the left-hand fork, which dips before beginning a gentle ascent. Passing in and out of woods, and alongside copious growths of lentisk, myrtle, wild cyclamen and other plants of the *macchia*, the path – occasionally indicated by green arrows – follows the course of the river on its left. About ninety minutes after setting out, you'll finally descend to the **river**. This idyllic spot, with glades of oleander shading the rocky pools on all sides and the sheer walls of the gorge rising dramatically above, makes a good place for a pause. There's usually water here, even in high summer, and in winter it can get torrential.

To enter the *gola*, remain on the right side of the river, keeping as high as possible. The path will eventually become clear and once you're in the canyon, there's no straying from the route, with high rock walls on either side. Much of the time it's simply a matter of negotiating the boulders, usually not unduly difficult, though some parts are challenging and demand concentration. Where **rockfalls** have blocked the way, look out for lengths of rope secured to the rock, which you can use to haul yourself up; these are occasionally marked with green paint.

How far you go, of course, depends on your perseverance and stamina. The total walkable length is about 8km, though you'd need **equipment** and a **guide** to go so far, and with expert help you could even reach the village of Urzulei and beyond. For such an ambitious trek, however, you'll need professional equipment and a stock of provisions; even for shorter distances, some form of head protection is advisable. Apart from banging your head, the biggest danger is of slipping on the smooth surfaces of the rocks – particularly when these are wet – so don't attempt the walk in shoes lacking a secure grip and ankle-support.

2–4.30pm; €3) containing a few relics found in the neighbourhood, from Neolithic to medieval and more recent times, plus a collection of minerals.

Dorgali's hotels and restaurants are not significantly cheaper than those at nearby Cala Gonone (see p.340), nor can they compare in terms of atmosphere or style. **Accommodation** is provided at the modern three-star *Querceto* (April–Oct; ☎0784.96.509, ℉0784.95.254; ❹), on Via La Mármora at the northern entrance to town, and the *S'Adde* (☎0784.94.412, ℉0784.94.315; ❺), on Via Concordia. Both places have **restaurants**, but you'll dine better by heading three or four kilometres south of town to *Sant'Elene* (closed Mon in winter), signposted off the SS125. Set on a hillside (and visible long before you reach it), it offers decent Sardinian specialities and grand panoramic views, and you can also stay here (☎0784.94.572; ❸). Ask at Dorgali's **Pro Loco** at Via La Mármora 108 (July to late Oct Mon–Fri 9am–1pm & 4–8pm; late Oct to Dec Mon–Fri 9am–1pm; Jan–June Mon–Fri 9am–1pm & 3.30–7pm; ☎0784.96.243) about **excursions** to the nearby archeological sites and trekking expeditions, or call the Ghivine excursions group directly, the best of the local outfits run by friendly young guides and specializing in walking, caving and diving trips (☎0784.94.897 or 338.663.850, Ⓦwww .ghivine.com).

The Ispinigoli Grotto

Between Orosei and Dorgali, the **Grotta di Ispinigoli** is signposted a little way off the main road. This deep cave contains one of nature's masterpieces, a mind-bending collection of stalagmites and stalactites dominated by one 38-metre column that appears to hold the whole lot up. Inside have been found traces of some distant human presence – jewels, amphorae and bones, probably dating from Phoenician times. The local name for the cave, Abisso delle Vérgini, probably owes more to popular imagination than to fact, but it is likely that such an impressive natural phenomenon would have attracted some kind of religious ritual.

Tours inside the grotto leave daily on the hour with a gap for lunch, from 9am onwards (last tour at 7pm in Aug; 6pm June–July & Sept; 5pm March–May & Oct–Nov; closed Dec–Feb). The 45-minute tour costs €7 per person. There's a good **restaurant** close to the entrance.

Serra Orrios

Eleven kilometres northwest of Dorgali, near the SS129 running between Nuoro and Orosei, **Serra Orrios** (daily: Oct–March 9am–1pm & 2–5pm; April–June & Sept 9am–1pm & 3–6pm; July–Aug 9am–1pm & 4–7pm; last entry 1hr before closing; €5) makes a fascinating stop. Though it lacks a *nuraghe* as such, it's still one of the region's most engrossing nuraghic sites, illustrating how a typical community was organized. Located in a small plain surrounded by olive trees and overlooked by the peaks of Monte Albo to the north, the remains of the village lie within a long walled enclosure at the end of a 500-metre path through an olive grove.

Entered through a lintelled doorway, the extensive **site** consists chiefly of the closely packed circular walls of the seventy-odd village buildings, about two metres high and separated by paths. Among them are two rectangular temples labelled "Tempietto A" and "Tempietto B", the first of which lies within a round walled area, and is thought to have been used by visiting pilgrims. Tempietto B was probably the villagers' centre of worship – a long building surrounded by a wall, with a doorway at one end topped by a curved slab and a low bench running along the inside. All in all, it's an attractive site to wander around; guides provide a commentary in Italian, but are mainly there to keep you off the walls. Before setting off, it's worth examining the diagram near the entrance showing how the village must once have appeared. There's also a bar and *paninoteca* on the site.

Cala Gonone and around

A couple of kilometres south out of Dorgali, a left turn from the SS125 brings you into a tunnel through the mountain wall, and corkscrewing down through groves of cork to an azure bay. Beautifully sited at the base of the 900-metre mountains, **CALA GONONE** was once a tiny settlement huddled around a harbour, until recently accessible only by boat. Now hotels and villas dominate the scene, though these have not entirely spoilt the sense of isolation, even in summer, when the place positively hums. Abundant activities are offered, most popular of which are the numerous boat excursions to the various secluded coves up and down the coast.

Boat tours (see the box below) as well as dinghy-hire can be booked at the small **port** at the bottom of town, where a line of kiosks vies for business, and the sheltered harbour is crowded with pleasure craft. A curve of sand extends south from here, culminating in a full-size **beach** at the end of the Lungomare. This will do for a dip, but it's a poor substitute for the beaches further afield, all accessible by boat, and some also from the land. North of town, a car or bike would do for the pair of idyllic swimming places at **Spiaggia Cartoe** and **Spiaggia Osalla**, reachable from the narrow road dug out of the mountains that eventually connects up with the SS125. South of Cala Gonone, you can reach one of the best beaches on foot from Cala Fuili, the rocky cove at the

Boat trips and rental from Cala Gonone

From Cala Gonone's port, numerous operators offer a range of trips to and longer tours of the truly spectacular swimming spots dotted along the cliffy coast hereabouts. Between April and September, the most popular **boat trips** ply between the town and the remote inlets of **Cala Luna** and **Cala Sisine**, respectively 6 and 11km to the south. One-way tickets for these cost around €15, and departures are frequent. There are plenty of even more secluded beaches to visit, while other cruises explore some of the area's deep grottoes. The most famous of these is the **Grotta del Bue Marino** (around €15, plus a separate entrance charge of €7) – touted as the last refuge of the Mediterranean monk seal, or "sea ox", in Italian waters. In fact the last of these creatures disappeared some time ago, but it's a good expedition anyway, since this is among Sardinia's most spectacular caves, a luminescent gallery filled with remarkable natural sculptures resembling organ pipes, wedding cakes and even human heads – one of them is known as "Dante", after a fondly imagined resemblance to the poet.

A **minicruise** of the coast – typically heading south for around two hours as far as Arco di Goloritzè or Spiaggia Aguglia for diving, swimming and a *grigliata* lunch (may be included in the price), then returning with stops at Cala Mariolu, Cala Biriola, Cala Sisine, Cala Luna, and Grotta del Bue Marino – can also be booked from the quayside agencies, for around €25–35. Boats depart at about 9.30am, returning at around 6pm. General information of all of these can be obtained from the Nuovo Consorzio Transporti Maríttimi at the port (☎0784.93.305). For longer trips, try to book the day before, and take a sun hat.

Kiosks at the port, such as Noleggio Malù (☎348.765.3503), also offer **boat rental**: a simple motor-driven dinghy costs around €60 for a day, excluding fuel.

southern end of Viale del Bue Marino. From here, a rough track leads parallel to the sea for nearly 4km to **Cala Luna**. It's fairly level, but very stony, so you need more than sandals (and there's no water along the way, so carry at least a litre). The path is signposted with painted green arrows and white arrows chiselled into the rock. If you don't feel like walking back, jump on one of the boats to the port (frequent in summer).

On a very different note, a brief inland expedition from Cala Gonone evokes the area's ancient history. Signposted left off the road leading up to the tunnel back to the SS125, **Nuraghe Mannu** (daily: March 9am–noon & 3–5pm; April–May & Sept 9am–noon & 4–6pm; June–Aug 9am–noon & 5–8pm; €5) lies at the end of a 3km rocky track (not recommended for laden cars). On a ledge over the bay, with a ravine to one side, it's an impressive site, one of Sardinia's few nuraghic structures to be built right by the sea, and affording magnificent views. The topless main tower has steps off to one side, and niches in the central chamber. All around lie the traces of dwellings, some paved, and mostly dating from much later times – there's evidence that the site was occupied as recently as the middle ages.

Practicalities

There's a summer-only **tourist office** in the pine woods above the centre, on Viale Bue Marino (daily: April–June & Sept 9.30am–1pm & 3–6.30pm; July & Aug 9am–11pm; ☎0784.93.696). ARST **buses** pull up in opposite – for those with hotels here or camping – and again by the port on Via Marco Polo. You'll find a **bancomat** at the port, and **Internet access** just up from here at New Age, Via Colombo 5 (Mon–Sat 10am–1pm & 4–8pm, also Sun in summer; €5 for 30min). **Bikes** (from €20 a day) and **scooters** (from €35 a day) can be rented from Prima Sardegna, Lungomare Palmasera 32 (☎0784.93.367), and Dolmen, Via Vasco da Gama 18 (☎0784.93.260, ⓦwww.sardegnascoprire.it), both open roughly April–October. Dolmen also organizes **excursions** inland, while the *Argonauta Diving Club* (☎0784.93.046, ⓦwww.argonauta.it) arranges **dives** and snorkelling tours for all abilities.

Accommodation

Most of Cala Gonone's numerous **accommodation** choices are closed out of season, but a handful of establishments keep things ticking over. If you're interested, the tourist office can supply you with a list of apartments for weekly rentals.

Cala Luna Lungomare Palmasera ☎0784.93.133, ⓕ0784.93.162. At the south end of the seaside strip, a bougainvillea-covered holiday hotel with standard, comfortable rooms with balconies overlooking the sea and direct access to the beach. Open April–Oct. ❹
Camping Village Calagonone Via Collodi ☎0784.93.165, ⓦwww.campingcalagonone.it. In the pine woods above the resort, just along from the tourist office, this well-equipped, popular site rents out caravans, bungalows and chalets from €46 a night in high season. Open April–Oct.
La Conchiglia Lungomare Palmasera ☎ & ⓕ0784.93.448. Small and select, this is smarter than most of the hotels along this seafront, with good views. At least half-board is required in

summer, at €90 per person; rates plummet outside peak season. Open June–Sept. ❻
Miramare Piazza Giardini 12 ☎0784.93.140, ⓦwww.htlmiramare.it. Central, modern hotel, offering standard rooms with sea-facing balconies; there's also a fine restaurant (see p.342). Open April to mid-Sept. ❻
L'Oasi Via Lorca ☎0784.93.111, ⓕ0784.93.444. This quiet *pensione* occupies a scenic site above the town, with lofty views and an air of pampered seclusion; the port is just five minutes away along a steep short cut. Open late April to early Oct. ❻
Piccolo Viale Colombo ☎0784.93.232, ⓕ0784.93.235. One of the resort's few hotels to stay open all year, and one of the cheapest in town. It lies at the bottom of the long, winding

street cutting through town, about 50m up from the port. Rooms are fairly basic, all with small en-suite bathrooms, and some have views through pine trees to the sea. If you find it closed, call ☎0784.93.035. ❸

Pop Via Marco Polo ☎0784.93.185, ⓦwww.hotelpop.com. Right above the port, this modern, fairly functional hotel has friendly staff, and a lively atmosphere in summer, when there's a three-day minimum stay. ❺

Eating and drinking

Cala Gonone is well supplied with **places to eat**, ranging from fast food to gourmet parlours. The **bars** swing into action in the summer, with most places staying open until late.

Aquarius Via delle Ginestre. On the seafront, with a few outdoor tables, *Aquarius* has possibly the best fish in town, and it's also good for pizzas and ice cream. Open all year, but closed Tues in winter. Moderate.

Il Cormorano Via Vespucci. Pleasant trattoria just north of the port with outdoor seating. The good fixed-price menus may include *tagliolini della casa* – fresh pasta with artichokes, tomatoes and *cala-mari*. Open April–Sept. Moderate.

Miramare Piazza Giardini 12. At the hotel of the same name (see p.341), *Miramare* has a reputation for good food, best enjoyed on the terrace; the torpid air of the interior is uninviting. Open April to mid-Sept. Moderate.

Il Pescatore Via Marco Polo. By the port, this does

a brisk trade in seafood dishes. Open Easter–October. Moderate.

Pop Via Marco Polo. The restaurant attached to this central hotel offers good set-price menus, and gets packed out in summer. Moderate.

Roadhouse Blues Lungomare Palmasera. Great *birreria* that also serves snacks until late, right on the seafront. The *panini* have names like Miles Davis and B.B. King. Closed Mon in winter.

San Francisco Via Magellano 4. Mamma's won-derful *ravioli* and *gnocchi* pull in the punters, and the pizzas and seafood are also excellent. Moderate.

La Terrazza Lungomare Palmasera. Pizzeria/ris-torante next door to the *Cala Luna* hotel, with alfresco eating in summer. Inexpensive–moderate.

Arbatax and around

South of Dorgali and Cala Gonone lies one of Sardinia's last truly untouched tracts. Skirting the top of the Gorropu canyon (see the box on p.338) high above the Flumineddu River, walled on the far side by the Sopramonte massif, the SS125 brings you into a majestic mountain landscape, largely devoid of human life. The road climbs into the neighbouring Codula di Luna valley at the **Genna Silana** pass (1017m), the departure point for walking expeditions in the area. From Baunei, the road steeply descends to **Tortolì**, an unremark-able inland town that is the centre of the local region, with banks, shops and tourist facilities.

Five kilometres east, the port of **ARBATAX** is more attractive, though it amounts to little more than a paper factory, a few bars and restaurants, and a port from which ferries ply to Genoa and Civitavecchia four times weekly. The area around here is famous for its red rocks, and there are **beaches** in every direction. One lovely cove, predominantly rocky, lies within easy walking dis-tance of the port, reached from the road behind the Tirrenia office on Via Venezia (turn left after the school). Other spots lie south of town at Porto Frailis, San Gemiliano and Lido Orri. In summer at least, the **Porto Frailis** locality, connected by #2 buses from Viale Arbatax (buy tickets on board), has a bit more life than Arbatax itself, and is the site of most of the local hotels and restaurants. You'll need to drive to reach the series of sand and rock beaches at **Lido Orri** 4km down the coast and accessible from the SS125 south of Tortolì (signposted), but it's worth the effort to enjoy the broad sands here. In summer, all the usual facilities are available on all the major beaches hereabouts.

From the tourist marina at Arbatax, **boat tours** leave for beaches in the Golfo di Orosei to the north, including the sublime sandy cove of Cala Mariolu, and as far as the Grotta del Bue Marino (see the box on p.340).

The mountainous **Ogliastra** region of which this is the edge, offers diversions of a very different order, with forests, rivers and lakes offering a cool respite from the coastal heat. The heart of the region is **LANUSEI**, an attractive mountain village (590m) with a lively old centre, 20km inland from Tortolì on the squiggly SS198. Its accommodation options (see below) would make this a convenient base if you don't want to stray too far from the sea. Six kilometres west on the SS198, the **Parco Archeologico Selene** holds the remains of a nuraghic village and burial site amid a thick forest of holm-oaks and chestnuts, at an altitude of 960m.

Practicalities

There is a seasonal **tourist office** at Arbatax station (June–Sept daily 7.30–10am, noon–1.30pm & 5–9pm, open until 10 or 10.30pm in July and Aug; ☎0782.667.690) with information on **sea excursions**. In winter, Tortolì's Pro Loco on Via Mazzini is open 9am–noon (☎0782.622.824). ARST **buses** stop almost opposite the Tirrenia office on the road to the station (tickets from the nearby bar).

There are several small **hotels** in the Arbatax area, most of them difficult to reach on foot. The only reasonably priced one, the *Gabbiano* (☎0782.667.622; no credit cards; ❹), lies a couple of kilometres south of the port in the Porto Frailis district, near a good beach; it only has four rooms, however, and may be closed in winter. Otherwise, head towards Tortolì, where there is a small selection, including the pleasant *Splendor* on Viale Arbatax (☎ & ⓕ0782.623.037; ❸) – opposite the Esso station on the other side of the rail tracks – and, further up on the left (on the corner with Via Sarcidano), *Dolce Casa* (mid-June to mid-Sept; ☎0782.623.484; no credit cards; ❸), a clean and comfortable place run by an expatriate Englishwoman and her husband. There's a **campsite** in Porto Frailis, *Telis* (mid-April to mid-Oct; ☎0782.667.140), with bungalows and caravans to rent by the week; another one at San Gemiliano, *Sos Flores* (June–Sept; ☎0782.667.485), and a third further south at Lido Orrì, *Orrì* (May to mid-Sept; ☎0782.624.695). Frequent buses connect Tortolì, Arbatax and Porto Frailis.

Ferries from Arbatax

Tirrenia runs a regular **ferry service** to the mainland from Arbatax, sometimes via Cágliari or Olbia. Departures are twice weekly to Civitavecchia (north of Rome) and to Genoa. The crossing to Genoa, leaving in the afternoon, takes up to twenty hours, as it usually makes a stop for a couple of hours at Olbia. A typical fare between Arbatax and Civitavecchia (10hr 30min) in high season would be around €45 in a second-class cabin, €36 in a semi-reclinable seat, €72 for a small or medium-size car, or respectively €36, €28 and €57 in low season. Between mid-July and early September, an additional fast ferry service (*mezzo veloce*) plies between Arbatax and Fiumicino, Rome's main airport (with frequent connections to the city), in 5hr 30min, with fares at €35–48 per person, €65–73 for a small-to-medium-sized car. For full schedules, see Travel details on p.345.

Tickets should be booked as early as possible, especially in summer. The Tirrenia office is on the right near the port, at Via Venezia 10 (Mon–Fri 8.30am–1pm & 3.30–7.30pm, or 4–8pm in summer, Sat 8.30am–1pm, plus Sun & Wed 10pm–midnight; ☎0782.667.067). A general travel agent operates out of the same office.

As for **restaurants**, there are a few seafront joints in Arbatax itself; in the Porto Frailis district, look out for *Il Faro*, overlooking the beach, and with a good choice of fish (closed Mon in winter). There's also *La Baia* pizzeria/ristorante near the *Telis* campsite (closed Tues in winter). A good place for pizzas and full meals as well as late drinks, the *Caffè del Mare* on the Spiaggia di San Gemiliano also has live music.

In **Lanusei**, the main Via Umberto I has the *Belvedere* (℡0782.42.184, ℻0782.482.050; ❹), a handsome three-star hotel with splendid views from its broad terrace, and across the street on the narrow Via Indipendenza, *La Nuova Luna* (℡0782.41.051, ✉lanuovaluna@tiscali.net), an independent **hostel** with beds for €13–16 in modern clean dorms. There's a bar (but no kitchen), washing machines and organized excursions. For a **meal**, head for the excellent *Voltavela* just above the main piazza on Via Zanardelli (closed Sun), for good country cooking (and pizzas). The village is a stop on the FdS Arbatax–Mandas line, the station only minutes away from the centre.

Travel details

Trains

(All FdS)

Arbatax to: Mandas (mid-June to mid-Sept 2 daily; 4hr 50min).

Ísili to: Láconi (July–Aug Sun only 1 daily; 40min); Mandas (Mon–Sat 6 daily; 20min); Sórgono (July–Aug Sun only 1 daily; 2hr 20min).

Láconi to: Ísili (July–Aug Sun only 1 daily; 40min); Mandas (July–Aug Sun only 1 daily; 1hr); Sórgono (July–Aug Sun only 1 daily; 1hr 40min).

Nuoro to: Macomer (Mon–Sat 6–8 daily; 1hr 15min).

Sórgono to: Ísili (July–Aug Sun only 1 daily; 2hr 20min); Láconi (July–Aug Sun only 1 daily; 1hr 45min); Mandas (July–Aug Sun only 1 daily; 2hr 40min).

Buses

(All ARST unless otherwise stated)

Arbatax to: Dorgali (Mon–Sat 1 daily; 2hr); Nuoro (Mon–Sat 1 daily; 3hr); Tortolì (Mon–Sat 5 daily; 10min).

Aritzo to: Barúmini (1 daily; 1hr 25min); Belvì (2 daily; 5min); Cágliari (2 daily; 2hr 45min–3hr); Désulo (1 daily; 30min); Fonni (1 daily; 1hr 15min); Ísili (1 daily; 1hr 20min); Láconi (2 daily; 45min); Nuoro (Mon–Sat 2 daily, Sun 1; 2hr); Sanluri (1 daily; 2hr); Tonara (1 daily; 25min).

Belvì to: Aritzo (2 daily; 5min); Barúmini (1 daily; 1hr 30min); Cágliari (2 daily; 2hr 50min); Désulo (Mon–Sat 2 daily, Sun 1; 25min); Fonni (Mon–Sat 2 daily, Sun 1; 1hr 10min); Ísili (1 daily; 1hr 25min); Láconi (2 daily; 50min); Mamoiada (Mon–Sat 2

daily, Sun 1; 1hr 30min); Nuoro (Mon–Sat 2 daily, Sun 1; 1hr 50min); Sanluri (1 daily; 2hr); Tonara (1 daily; 20min).

Bitti to: Nuoro (Mon–Sat 8–9 daily, Sun 2; 1hr 5min).

Buddusò to: Nuoro (Mon–Sat 2 daily; 1hr 50min).

Cala Gonone to: Dorgali (Mon–Sat 7 daily, Sun 3; 20min); Nuoro (Mon–Sat 5 daily, Sun 1; 1hr 10min).

Désulo to: Aritzo (1 daily; 50min); Barúmini (1 daily; 2hr 15min); Belvì (Mon–Sat 2 daily, Sun 1; 25–45min); Cágliari (1 daily; 3hr 35min); Fonni (Mon–Sat 3–5 daily, Sun 1; 40min); Láconi (1 daily; 1hr 35min); Mamoiada (Mon–Sat 1 daily; 1hr); Nuoro (Mon–Sat 2 daily, Sun 1; 1hr 20min); Sanluri (1 daily; 2hr 45min).

Dorgali to: Arbatax (Mon–Sat 1 daily; 2hr); Cala Gonone (Mon–Sat 7 daily, Sun 4; 25min); Nuoro (Mon–Sat 7–9 daily, Sun 3–5; 50min); Olbia (Mon–Sat 2 daily, Sun 1; 1hr 10min–2hr); Oliena (Mon–Sat 6–8 daily, Sun 3–5; 25min); Orosei (Mon–Sat 3–4 daily, Sun 1; 25min).

Fonni to: Abbasanta (Mon–Sat 1 daily; 2hr 50min); Aritzo (1 daily; 1hr 15min); Belvì (Mon–Sat 2 daily, Sun 1; 1hr 10min); Cágliari (1 daily; 4hr 15min); Désulo (Mon–Sat 2 daily; 40min); Ísili (1 daily; 2hr 35min); Mamoiada (Mon–Sat 3 daily, Sun 1; 20–55min); Nuoro (Mon–Sat 7 daily, Sun 4; 40min); Orani (Mon–Sat 7–8 daily, Sun 4; 1hr–1hr 30min); Oristano (Mon–Sat 2 daily; 3hr); Ottana (3–4 daily; 1hr 15min); Sórgono (Mon–Sat 3 daily; 1hr–1hr 25min); Tonara (Mon–Sat 3 daily, Sun 1; 50min–1hr 5min).

Ísili to: Cágliari (1 daily; 1hr 40min); Láconi (1 daily; 25min); Mandas (1 daily; 25min).

Láconi to: Aritzo (2–3 daily; 50min); Barúmini (Mon–Sat 2 daily, Sun 1; 35min); Belvì (2–3 daily; 50min–1hr 15min); Cágliari (Mon–Sat 4 daily, Sun 3; 2hr–2hr 15min); Désulo (1 daily; 1hr 20min); Fonni (1 daily; 2hr); Ísili (1 daily; 25min); Mamoiada (1 daily; 2hr 20min); Mandas (1 daily; 50min); Nuoro (Mon–Sat 2 daily, Sun 1; 2hr 40min–3hr 10min); Oristano (Mon–Sat 7–9 daily; 1hr 30min–3hr 10min); Sanluri (1 daily; 1hr 10min; Tonara (1 daily; 1hr 11min).

Lanusei to: Nuoro (Mon–Sat 3 daily, Sun 2; 1hr 15min).

Mamoiada to: Aritzo (1 daily; 1hr 35min); Belvì (Mon–Sat 2 daily, Sun 1; 1hr 30min); Cágliari (1 daily; 4hr 35min); Fonni (Mon–Sat 2 daily, Sun 1; 20min); Ísili (1 daily; 3hr); Láconi (1 daily; 2hr 20min); Mandas (1 daily; 3hr 20min); Nuoro (Mon–Sat 10 daily, Sun 5; 20min); Tonara (1 daily; 1hr 10min).

Nuoro to: Alghero and Fertilia airport (Redentours/Deplanu; 2 daily; 2hr 30min–3hr); Arbatax (Mon–Sat 1 daily; 3hr); Aritzo (Mon–Sat 2 daily, Sun 1; 2hr 10min); Belvì (Mon–Sat 2 daily, Sun 1; 2hr); Bitti (Mon–Sat 7 daily, Sun 3; 1hr 5min); Cágliari (PANI & ARST; 6 daily; 2hr 30min–5hr); Cala Gonone (Mon–Sat 6 daily, Sun 3; 1hr 10min); Désulo (Mon–Sat 1 daily; 1hr 20min); Dorgali (Mon–Sat 6 daily, Sun 3; 45min); Fonni (Mon–Sat 8 daily, Sun 4; 50min–2hr); Ísili (1 daily; 3hr 30min); Láconi (Mon–Sat 2 daily, Sun 1; 3hr); Macomer (DePlano & PANI; 6 daily; 1hr 10min); Mamoiada (Mon–Sat 12 daily, Sun 5; 30min); Mandas (1 daily; 3hr 40min); Monte Ortobene (ATP; summer 15 daily, winter Mon–Sat 2 daily; 20min); Olbia and Olbia airport (DePlano & ARST; Mon–Sat 8 daily, Sun 5; 1hr 45min–3hr 25min); Oliena (Mon–Sat 12–13 daily, Sun 6; 20min); Orani (Mon–Sat 8 daily, Sun 1; 30min); Orgósolo (Mon–Sat 8 daily, Sun 4; 35min); Oristano (PANI; 4 daily; 2hr); Orosei (Mon–Sat 9 daily, Sun 3; 1hr 5min); Ottana (DePlano & ARST; Mon–Sat 8–10 daily, Sun 4; 30min); Posada (Mon–Sat 7 daily, Sun 5; 1hr 20min); Sássari (PANI & ARST; Mon–Sat 8 daily, Sun 6; 2hr 30min); Sórgono (Mon–Sat 6

daily, Sun 3; 1hr 35min); Tonara (Mon–Sat 2 daily, Sun 1; 1hr 40min).

Oliena to: Dorgali (Mon–Sat 6–8 daily, Sun 3–5; 25min); Nuoro (Mon–Sat 11–12 daily, Sun 5; 20min).

Orani to: Fonni (Mon–Sat 6–7 daily, Sun 4; 1hr); Nuoro (Mon–Sat 4 daily, Sun 2; 30min); Ottana (3–4 daily; 15min).

Orgósolo to: Nuoro (Mon–Sat 8 daily, Sun 4; 35min).

Orosei to: Dorgali (Mon–Sat 3–4 daily, Sun 1; 25min); Nuoro (Mon–Sat 7–8 daily, Sun 1; 1hr 10min); Olbia (3 daily; 50min–2hr 25min); Posada (2 daily; 1hr 20min).

Ottana to: Fonni (3–4 daily; 1hr 15); Nuoro (Mon–Sat 9–10 daily, Sun 3; 30min); Orani (3–4 daily; 20min); Sórgono (Mon–Sat 4–5 daily, Sun 3; 1hr 5min).

Posada to: Nuoro (Mon–Sat 8 daily, Sun 6; 1hr 25min); Olbia (2 daily; 1hr 5min); Orosei (1 daily; 1hr 20min).

Sórgono to: Abbasanta (Mon–Sat 2 daily; 1hr 25min); Désulo (Mon–Sat 2–4 daily, Sun 1; 45min); Fonni (Mon–Sat 2–4 daily, Sun 1; 1hr 25min); Nuoro (Mon–Sat 6 daily, Sun 4; 2hr–2hr 35min); Oristano (Mon–Sat 6–7 daily; 1hr 30min–1hr 50min); Ottana (3–4 daily; 1hr 5min); Tonara (Mon–Sat 4–6 daily, Sun 1; 20min).

Tonara to: Aritzo (1 daily; 25min); Belvì (1 daily; 20min); Cágliari (1 daily; 3hr 25min); Désulo (Mon–Sat 2–4 daily, Sun 1; 25min); Fonni (Mon–Sat 3–5 daily, Sun 2; 50min–1hr 5min); Ísili (1 daily; 1hr 45min); Láconi (1 daily; 1hr 10min); Mamoiada (1 daily; 1hr 10min); Mandas (1 daily; 2hr 10min); Nuoro (Mon–Sat 4 daily, Sun 2; 2hr 25min); Sórgono (Mon–Sat 3 daily; 20min).

Ferries

Arbatax to: Cágliari (2 weekly; 5hr 15min); Civitavecchia (2 weekly; 10hr 30min); Fiumicino (mid-July to early Sept 2 weekly; 5hr 30min); Genoa, via Olbia (2 weekly; 16–20hr); Olbia (2 weekly; 5hr).

Contexts

Contexts

History

S ardinia's position at the centre of the Mediterranean has ensured that the island has rarely been left to its own devices. For most of its history, it has been subject not only to the great power struggles which convulsed this inland sea, but also to the opportunist depredations of pirates for whom the island's exposed shores were an irresistible target. Only in remote prehistory did the island enjoy relative freedom from external interference, and this period is inevitably the one we know least about.

Prehistoric times

No one can say where the first Sards came from, though various theories suggest they were the followers of Sardus, son of Heracles, or else the descendants of the Libyan Shardana people; the island's name could have derived from either of these sources, or neither – we don't know. The earliest phase of the island's development is also arguably the most intriguing, with mysterious remnants of that distant era still dotting the landscape of modern Sardinia.

Though recent discoveries indicate the presence of communities in the Paleolithic era, the first traces of human settlement go back to before 6000 BC, when a hunting and pastoral society lived in grottoes, creating tools and weapons of flint and obsidian, and crudely decorated ceramic bowls. In the fourth millennium BC, a more advanced culture appeared, called **Bonu Ighinu** after the grotto near Mara where their most significant remains have been found. The people of this society seem to have inhabited villages of huts and practised more advanced systems of agriculture. Finds show that they had trading links with Corsica, southern Italy and the south of France, while statuettes suggest a cult based on a mother-goddess; their dead were interred in caves.

Between around 3400 and 2700 BC, the **Ozieri culture** achieved dominance in the island (also called the San Michele culture, after the grotto of San Michele at Ozieri, its first important settlement). This was a significantly advanced society of hunters, shepherds and farmers, who worked copper as well as flint, obsidian and ceramics, all in a greater variety of forms than seen until then. Their cult of the dead was also much developed; bodies were interred in caves cut into rock that were often decorated and later came to be called *domus de janas* (fairy-houses) by later generations ignorant of their function. The sanctuary of Monte d'Accoddi, near Porto Torres, is one of the most important religious relics from this era.

The fragments surviving of Sardinia's **Bonnanaro culture**, which held sway during the first centuries of the second millennium, show a lower level of artistic achievement than those of its predecessors. This society was soon overshadowed by the new emerging **nuraghic culture**, which has yielded the most ubiquitous and imposing remains of any of Sardinia's historical phases, and which survived until the third century BC or later. The first nuraghic phase, between about 1800 and 1500 BC, overlapped in many respects with the preceding cultures, including the use of *domus de janas* and menhirs. The second, lasting until around 1200 BC, saw the development of the nuraghic towers and the *tombe dei giganti* – "giants' tombs", or collective burial chambers. During the third phase (1200–900 BC), the nuraghic towers became elaborate complexes sheltering sizeable villages, such as those at Su Nuraxi and Santu Antine, while sacred wells indicate the existence of a water cult.

The nuraghic culture reached its apogee between the tenth and eighth centuries BC, trading abroad and cultivating at home. Its fate was sealed, however, when Sardinia became embroiled in the commercial and military rivalries of other Mediterranean powers. The last nuraghic phase is characterized by the increasing engagement of the indigenous people with these more powerful forces, even as they were producing items of growing sophistication such as the **bronzetti**. These bronze statuettes have provided invaluable insights into nuraghic society, suggesting a tribal and highly stratified social organization comprising an aristocracy, priests, warriors, artisans, shepherds and farmers.

The Phoenicians, Carthaginians and Romans

The *bronzetti* and other artefacts reveal the extent of the mercantile network of which Sardinia formed a part, encompassing Italy, North Africa and Spain. From the eastern Mediterranean, **Phoenicians** first began trading in Sardinia around 900 BC, and soon established peaceful commercial bases at Bythia and Nora, both southwest of Cágliari; Monte Sirai and Sant'Antíoco (Sulki, or Sulcis), further west; Tharros, near Oristano, and Cágliari itself (Karalis). The Phoenicians were also attracted by the island's mineral resources – as was every subsequent group of invaders and settlers.

From the sixth century BC, the main protagonists on the scene were the much more warlike **Carthaginians**, whose capital, Carthage, was less than 200km away across the Mediterranean near present-day Tunis, and for whom the island was of crucial strategic importance in their rivalry with the Greek cities of Italy. Intent on drawing Sardinia into their sphere of influence, the Carthaginians took over and expanded the main Phoenician settlements, to the extent that almost all traces of the Phoenician presence were eradicated, and proceeded either to wipe out or assimilate as much as they could of the nuraghic culture.

The Carthaginian expansion in Sardinia was only stopped by their need to concentrate on the growing power of **Rome**, which eventually, in 259 BC, was turned against Sardinia itself. The Sards – now in league with Carthage – fervently struggled against the new aggressors, at first with some success, but their inevitable defeat occurred in 232 BC, followed five years later by the institution of the *provincia* of Sardinia and Corsica.

Resistance continued, however, and towards the end of the **Second Punic War** between Rome and Carthage (201–217 BC), a concerted attempt to shake off the Roman yoke was organized under **Ampsicora**, a Sard of Carthaginian culture who rallied the opposition but suffered a crushing defeat at Cornus, north of Oristano, in 216 BC. Other revolts followed, including one in 177 BC, when 12,000 of the islanders were slaughtered and many more sent away as slaves to the mainland. The survivors of these rebellions, and others who refused to bow to the Romans, fled into the impenetrable central and eastern mountains of the island, where they retained their independence, in an area called Barbaria by the Romans, and known today as Barbagia.

Under the **Roman occupation**, Sardinia was bled of its resources – minerals and agricultural produce mainly, especially grain – and its taxes, without any great benefit accruing to its people. Although the island was rewarded for supporting Julius Caesar in Rome's civil war of 49–45 BC, little was done over seven centuries to instil Roman values or develop the island, which was often entrusted to corrupt officials.

The attitude of the Romans towards the island was summed up in the use they found for it as a **place of exile** for "undesirable elements," including 4000 Jews sent by the emperor Tiberius, and early Christian subversives, who helped to spread the Gospel in Sardinia. Apart from some impressive remains at Nora and Tharros, traces of **Roman building** on the island are few compared to, say, Sicily. The most notable are at Porto Torres, seat of an important colony (Turris Libyssonis); the baths at Fordongianus (Forum Traiani), east of Oristano; the Tempio di Antas in the Iglesiente, which showed the integration of Roman and Sardinian cults, and the amphitheatre at Cágliari. Rome's most lasting contribution was perhaps the strong Latin element that can still be heard in the Sard dialect today.

The Giudicati, Pisa and Genoa

With the eclipse of the Roman empire in the 5th century AD, Sardinia shared the fate of other former territories in becoming vulnerable to barbarian raids and plundering that reached far inland. For a short period the island was held by the Vandals, then, after 534 AD, the **Byzantines**. It was too remote an outpost of Byzantium to benefit greatly from this new rule, though the island was given some protection in fighting off incursions of Goths and Lombards from the European mainland.

One survival of Byzantine rule was the division of the island into **giudicati** for administrative purposes, a system which was to endure right through the Middle Ages. There were four main *giudicati*: Cágliari, Arborea (around Oristano), Torres in the northwest and Gallura, each a small kingdom with an elected king – originally a judge, or *giudice*. In practice, however, these were the preserve of local oligarchies, and the island was left to its own devices, increasingly prey to raids from the new **Muslim** empires of North Africa and Spain, which were to continue sporadically from the eighth century for over 1000 years. In southern Sardinia in particular, travellers today can hardly fail to notice the numerous watchtowers along the coasts, built to warn against these attacks. Though most date from a later era, fear of death or slavery at the hands of the corsairs was a fact of life in Sardinia throughout this period, and had the long-term effect of depopulating the island's coasts. Another reason for the move inland was the increasing prevalence of **malaria** on the coasts and lowlands, the result of neglected irrigation works, deforestation and the silting-up of rivers. This combination of marauders and malaria led to the gradual abandonment of much of the crop cultivation in the lowlands in favour of sheep and livestock farming in the safe highland pastures of the interior.

The Arab threat was not confined to localized attacks: larger forces occupied Cágliari in 720 and further inroads were made in 752. In 1015, a substantial force from the Arab emirate in Spain landed and threatened to take over the entire island; the pope encouraged the Italian mercantile republics of **Pisa** and **Genoa** (which were then expanding their commercial operations) to intervene, and the combined Sard and mainland forces succeeded in ousting the invading army. The Pisans and Genoans themselves, however, proved harder to dislodge, and from this time on Sardinia was increasingly open to trading and political links with mainland Italy. The influence of **monastic orders** from Provence also grew during this period; granted special privileges on the island, they played an important part in restoring the decayed irrigation works and industries such as salt extraction.

By lending their support in the various conflicts between the *giudicati*, the rival cities of Pisa and Genoa were able to take an increasingly active role in their internal affairs. The driving forces were **individual families**, not specifically linked to either of these cities – for example, the Visconti family in Logudoro, the della Gherardescas in Iglesias, and the Malaspinas in Bosa – though the Doria dynasty was closely connected with the city of Genoa. At the end of the eleventh century, the principal **Pisan merchants** had been granted privileges in the northern *giudicato* of Torres, where their influence was evident in the string of remote churches such as San Gavino in Porto Torres, and Santa Trinità di Saccárgia and San Pietro di Sorres, both southeast of Sássari – all apparently transplanted ready-built from Tuscany. In Arborea, there was Santa Giusta, outside Oristano, while further south, Pisan power was centred on Cágliari, where the defences built around that city's citadel still stand. By the end of the thirteenth century, the balance had swung entirely in the favour of Genoa, whose power-bases were in Torres, specifically Castelsardo, on the northern coast, and Alghero.

Around this time a new player appeared on the scene: **Aragon**, whose king, Pedro III, had recently taken possession of Sicily. Keen to resolve the dynastic crisis there, Pope Boniface VIII managed to persuade Pedro's successor James II of Aragon to give up the Aragonese claim to Sicily in return for being granted rights over the newly created kingdom of Sardinia and Corsica in 1297. The title was a mere formality, however, since Aragon was very far from asserting any control over the island, and the ensuing struggle lasted more than a century. The campaign proved easier in the south of the island, with Cágliari taken from the Pisans in 1326; in the north, the biggest obstacle was the Doria family – of whom the king of Aragon was nominally feudal overlord – and there was continual fighting between Aragonese forces and the alliance between Sards, Genoans and the mixed-blood aristocracy.

The islanders' cause was led by the *giudicato* of Arborea, and championed in particular by **Eleonora d'Arborea** (see the box on p.165), a warrior queen who granted Sardinia its first written Code of Laws, the *Carta di Logu*, which – after the Spanish had extended its use throughout the island – remained in force for the next four centuries. Eleonora succeeded in stemming the Aragonese advance, but after her death in 1404, Sardinian resistance crumbled. Following a decisive victory at Sanluri in 1409, the Aragonese finally triumphed.

The Spanish in power

With the unification of the kingdoms of Aragon and Castile in 1479, Sardinia became a colony of a united Spain. Although, when compared with the turmoil that had prevailed in previous centuries, this was an unusually peaceful period in the island's history, the three centuries of **Spanish rule** in Sardinia were not accompanied by any significant improvement in the lot of most

Sards, and there were few attempts to develop or even maintain the infrastructure. Like Sicily, the island was ruled by viceroys who were uninterested in the island's welfare and in any case unable to effect lasting reforms in their short three-year terms. The island's trading links with the Italian mainland were cut while the shift of focus towards Spain's Atlantic empire left Sardinia marginalized and neglected.

The Spanish introduced a **feudal system**, under which the land was parcelled up and distributed among Catalan-Aragonese nobles who enjoyed absolute powers within their domains. The great landlords rarely lived on the island, however, leaving their affairs in the hands of local officials, though the smaller potentates such as the Castelvì, Zatrillas and Alagon families resided on their estates and had a more direct input into the well-being of their territories.

Spanish influence was strongest in the cities, which absorbed elements of Catalan Gothic architecture and were later subjected to a heavy injection of the Baroque in churches and palazzi – notably in Sássari, Iglesias and Alghero. On the coasts, the most visible contribution was the series of defensive towers that still line Sardinia's shores, which provided only a partial defence against the attacks from North African corsairs, who remained a constant threat. The Spanish king (and Holy Roman Emperor) **Charles V** attempted to end these destructive assaults by assembling huge fleets in 1535 and 1541, with which he hoped to extirpate the raiders from their lairs in Tunis and Algiers. But these armadas had only short-term success, and Charles and his successor Philip II were too preoccupied with their far-flung empire and the threat posed by the Protestant Reformation to devote much time to the island's welfare.

Throughout this period, Sardinia was particularly hard hit by the malaria rife in all but the highest points of the island. A devastating toll was also extracted by two other calamities which swept across the island during the **seventeenth century**: plague, which is thought to have dispatched 25 percent of the population during the 1650s, and famine, which might have accounted for around 80,000 deaths in 1680–81. On the positive side, universities were founded in Cágliari in 1626 and Sássari in 1634, encouraging the growth of a professional class which no longer had to leave the island in order to pursue a career.

Overall, however, Spain had only a superficial impact on Sardinia, and the period is in many respects a barren one in the island's history. Relegated to an exploited and deprived backwater, Sardinia shared in the lethargy and decay which infused Spain itself, whose power was ebbing and institutions were moribund. Nonetheless, its hold on the island was never seriously questioned, and the mere hint of a rebellion in Cágliari in 1688 resulted in a harsh repression.

The Kingdom of Sardinia

As Spain declined, events in Europe began to impinge on Sardinia's destiny. During the War of the Spanish Succession in 1701–13, Cágliari was bombarded by an English fleet in 1708 and briefly occupied. In the ensuing negotiations the island was ceded first to Austria, then, according to the Treaty of London of 1718, to the Piedmontese House of Savoy, a duchy on the French-Italian border. The united possessions of Vittorio Amedeo II of Savoy became the new **Kingdom of Sardinia**.

Although Sardinia's Savoy period is associated with the beginnings of reconstruction, reforms did not take place quickly enough to stem the simmering discent engendered by high expectations. The frustration manifested itself in a variety of forms during the **eighteenth century**. *Banditismo* – the phenomenon of factional fighting, clan warfare, robbery and kidnapping that had always existed in the interior – assumed chronic proportions, while the enforced adoption of Italian as the language of government alienated an aristocracy for whom Spanish was the mother tongue.

For the majority of Sardinia's population, the chief problems included the low level of **education**, with schools dominated by the church and illiteracy almost universal; the island's continued vulnerability to seaborne attacks, and Sardinia's very sparse population. The government attempted to solve the last of these by a poorly organized and ultimately unsuccessful attempt to introduce **foreign colonies** to the island. The most deep-rooted cause of Sard hostility to the new ruling elite, however, was the continuing existence of the feudal system.

Matters came to a head after the **French Revolution**; the ensuing turmoil in Europe exposed not only the intransigence of the Piedmont regime vis-à-vis Sardinia's plight, but also the drawbacks inherent in the island's links to the House of Savoy, as the latter's quarrels became Sardinia's. In 1793, French troops attempting to invade the island succeeded in occupying the island of San Pietro, but another force which included the young **Napoleon Bonaparte** was repulsed at La Maddalena, as was a fleet which bombarded Cágliari. Though the Savoyard king rewarded his Piedmontese officials for their part in the rout, the role of the islanders was unacknowledged. What rankled even more was the refusal of the royal court to respond to a delegation from Sardinia bearing the *Cinque Domande*, or "Five Demands", which called for a full constitutional reform, including the restoration of ancient privileges and the regular convocation of an island parliament.

Between 1794 and 1796, an **insurrection** in Cágliari forced the viceroy and his entourage to take flight, and full-scale revolts subsequently broke out all over Sardinia, which ended with Sássari being taken by the rebels. At their head was **Giovanni Maria Angioy**, an aristocrat whose anti-feudal stance made him popular among the peasants, but whose increasingly radical demands for a Sardinian republic alienated the more moderate elements and eventually led to his downfall. In 1796, Angioy was driven out of Sardinia and died in exile in Paris – leaving behind a name which has been given to streets and squares throughout the island – and his followers were savagely persecuted by the Piedmontese.

The French were not the only ones to cast a hungry eye over Sardinia. Even **Admiral Horatio Nelson** expressed an interest in the island as a potential base, during the fifteen months he spent hovering around its coasts in his pursuit of the French fleet that ended at Trafalgar in 1805. "God knows," he wrote in his dispatches home, "if we could possess one island, Sardinia, we should want neither Malta, nor any other: this which is the finest island in the Mediterranean, possesses harbours fit for arsenals, and of a capacity to hold our navy, within 24 hours' sail of Toulon..."

The most noteworthy Savoyard kings in the **nineteenth century** were Carlo Felice (1821–31), who did much to modernize the island's infrastructure, not least by building the Carlo Felice highway – today the SS131 – that runs the length of the island from Cágliari to Porto Torres, and Carlo Alberto (1831–49), responsible for the final **abolition of the feudal system** in 1836–43. Although this led to a bitter conflict over the introduction of enclosures to demarcate private land in the mountains, which limited the ancient liberty of shepherds to wander freely in search of fresh pasturage, it was an essential prelude to rural reform.

Unified Italy

The Kingdom of Sardinia came to an end with the **unification of Italy** in 1861, when Vittorio Emanuele II, son of Carlo Alberto, became the new nation's first king (1861–78). Sardinia played a crucial role in the Risorgimento (the struggle for nationhood), providing both a genuine king to stand as the figurehead of a united Italy, and the base from which Giuseppe Garibaldi, who led the military campaign, embarked on both his major expeditions.

Sardinia's problems entered a new phase with unification. Adjusting to its role as a part of a modern nation-state has been the main theme of recent times, and attempts to force the island to integrate into the new centralized, bureaucratic Italy gave rise to a host of resentments whenever old, traditional ways came up against the new. Colonial attitudes towards the island persisted, its natural resources were ruthlessly plundered, accounting for much of the deforestation still evident today, and wages remained low. Agriculture also suffered, leading to soaring unemployment, which in turn fuelled the banditry that was still widespread and was brutally suppressed. There was little money available to improve the root causes of the problem and less interest in doing so. Although there was a degree of political reform, by the end of the nineteenth century voting rights were still only available to less than five percent of the island's population, leaving the vast majority without a voice or representation.

Nonetheless, Sardinia contributed notably to both world wars, with the Sássari Brigade in particular achieving lasting distinction during **World War I**, albeit at a heavy cost. The experience of war radicalized many Sards, and elections now based on universal suffrage in 1920 and 1921 saw the creation of the **Partito Sardo d'Azione**, or Sardinian Action Party, whose manifesto demanded autonomy; four of its members were elected as deputies, thus making it the island's second biggest party.

Mussolini and World War II

Ironically, Sardinia had to wait for a ruthless centralizing dictatorship before real changes began to make themselves felt. **Benito Mussolini**, the Italian Fascist leader who came to power in 1922, saw the backward island as fertile ground for his social and economic experiments, particularly in the context of his drive for Italian self-sufficiency in the wake of sanctions imposed following his invasion of Ethiopia. In the 1920s and 1930s, the Fascist government initiated a series of schemes which led to genuine improvements: the island's many rivers were harnessed and dammed to provide irrigation as well as power, land was drained and made fertile, agricultural colonies were set up to exploit the new resources, and the new towns of Carbonia, Arborea and Fertilia were founded – though the industrial projects were mostly failures.

The island also suffered in **World War II**, as Cágliari endured some of the heaviest bombing of all Italian cities in 1943, with 75 percent of its houses destroyed. Traumatized, the island awoke to a post-war era in which nothing seemed to have changed – once more, it felt itself to be a second-class member of the Italian state, subject to a remote bureaucracy and irrelevant legislation.

A genuine attempt to offset this was made in 1948, when the *regione* of Sardinia was granted **autonomy** on the same lines as that also given to Sicily and two other areas on the Austrian and Yugoslav borders, allowing the regional government direct control over such areas as transport, tourism, police, industry and agriculture. Two years later, the central government's fund to speed up the development of the South of Italy, the Cassa per il Mezzogiorno, was extended to Sardinia, and the island began to receive hefty injections of capital investment. Perhaps more significantly, through the intervention of the US Rockefeller Foundation, Sardinia was saturated with enough **DDT** in the years immediately following World War II to rid it once and for all of malaria, the centuries-old scourge that had sabotaged all local initiatives.

Sardinia today

The success of this combined effort to haul Sardinia up from a peripheral, third-world status is everywhere apparent, and some areas of Sardinian life are as streamlined and sophisticated as anywhere on the mainland. Visitors to the island today will recognize a piece of Italy – the same shops, cars and language – to the extent that it is growing ever harder to distinguish "the real Sardinia" underneath the Italian gloss.

Much of the island's present-day landscape is a direct result of two crucial decisions made in the same year, 1962. This was when the Italian parliament finally authorized a **programme of industrialization**, which led to the introduction of heavy-duty petrochemical plants completely at odds with the island's traditional activities. At the same time, the Aga Khan's development of the **Costa Smeralda** as an elite jet-setters' enclave and the subsequent opening-up of the tourist industry has given Sardinia a new role which has by and large been embraced by the islanders, and has brought genuine wealth to a substantial section of the population.

These developments have gone hand-in-hand with a new appreciation of the **traditional culture** of the island, a re-evaluation of its dialect and folklore, and a corresponding pride in the Sard identity that had always previously been repressed. The other side of the coin is the often unrestrained and irreversible development of some of the island's most beautiful spots, unregulated construction and the degradation of its natural environment in pursuit of short-term profit – the usual pitfalls connected with tourist economies.

Still, with its relatively prosperous population of 1.6 million, Sardinia today seems comfortable enough with its modern role. Despite certain stains on the surface which most people would prefer to overlook – the pockets of **pollution**, the high rates of **unemployment**, a worrying level of drug addiction in the cities, and the occasional kidnapping in the Barbagia which continues to baffle the police – there is a general satisfaction with the island's place within Italy and the European Union. Italian bureaucracy still infuriates, and there is still a good deal of rancour directed at the Italian state which has imposed on the island, among other things, the largest NATO concentration in the Mediterranean. Campaigning against this presence, and in the longer term for complete independence, the Partito Sardo d'Azione is too marginal to exert much influence, and the general tenor of the island is quiet contentment.

Sardinian wildlife

Sardinia shares with all islands that spark of uniqueness that arises from isolation, in which plants and animals evolve differently from those on the mainland. Many species are found only here, or are shared with neighbouring Corsica (with which Sardinia has much in common), while the proximity of Africa gives the local fauna and flora a distinct, almost tropical character. In addition, Sardinia's location on a key bird migration route between Africa and Europe accounts for the seasonal visitations of a number of bird species.

Sardinia's island ecology also means that a number of species present on the mainland are absent here – notably poisonous snakes, but also wolves, otters and moles. Those species which are present display a brilliant diversity, linked to the range of different terrains – mountain, forest, plain and coast – that exist within a relatively limited area, and to the typically Mediterranean climate, which keeps rainfall between 600mm (24 inches) on the plains to 990mm (39 inches) in the mountains.

Anyone planning a visit to Sardinia with its natural history in mind should consider carefully the timing. A visit in spring or autumn combines the advantages of bird migration with the flowering of many species of plants and shrubs, many of which bloom first in spring and again in autumn, after the summer drought. In winter, there's less to see in higher terrain but the lowlands, particularly around lagoons, still shelter a range of waders and other aquatic bird-life.

Habitats

Sardinia boasts a significant proportion of Italy's **lagoons** and **wetlands**, as well as extensive areas of **maquis** (Mediterranean scrub), remnant **forests**, hot **plains** and high **mountains**. The overwhelming presence of mountains accounts for the island's numerous rivers, of which the Tirso and Flumendosa are the most important.

Lagoons

In ornithological terms, the **lagoons** (*stagni*) and wetlands are perhaps the most important feature of the island. While wetlands around the world have been extensively drained for agriculture and have become one of the most endangered habitats, Sardinia still has 130 square kilometres of protected lagoons, constituting 25 percent of all the lagoons located within Italy. Those in Sardinia are internationally designated both for their importance during migration time and for the presence of rare breeding birds.

The richest *stagni* are to be found in the vicinity of Oristano and Cágliari, where it is common to spot flocks of pink **flamingos**; they have long used both of these areas as a stop-off on their migrations between Africa and the Carmargue region of France, though recently they have also started nesting and breeding on the island. Along with the flamingoe, the lagoons of Sardinia shelter a remarkable range of wetlands species, most notably **black-winged stilt** (in Italian the "cavalier of Italy", named for its extraordinary leggy appearance), spoonbill, crane, avocet, cattle egret, tern, cormorant, glossy ibis, white-headed duck, osprey, pratincole, purple gallinule, ferruginous duck, marsh harrier and Andouin's gull.

In winter, there are large numbers of **duck** and **cormorant**, their V-shaped skeins a prominent feature in the skies, not to mention plenty of waders and great wheeling flocks of **lapwing**. The spring and autumn migrations see significant numbers of passage birds, and this is a good time to see the **curlew sandpiper**, **Caspian tern**, **short-toed eagle** and **red-footed falcon**.

The area around Oristano has the island's best-protected lagoons, not least those on the Sinis peninsula, where the flatlands around the lakeside town of Cabras has the Pauli e Sali reserve, sheltering reeds and a wide range of water-fowl. The nearby Stagno di Sale Porcus is the place to see the extremely rare European crane. Another general feature of these wetlands are the reed beds, home to **great reed**, **fan-tailed** and **Cetti's warblers** and hunted over by the fast, acrobatic **hobby**.

The coastal zones

In coastal areas, **Aleppo** and **maritime palms** lend a tropical feel, while the long **sand dunes** on the west coast of the provinces of Cágliari and Oristano create a more arid environment, notably around Piscinas and Is Arenas. **Turtles** use these and other remote beaches to lay eggs.

On the other side of the island, Sardinia's eastern coast is mainly cliffy and undeveloped. The Gennargentu mountains end in a sheer rocky wall of lime-stone where, at Capo di Monte Santu at the southern end of the Gulf of Orosei, there is a significant colony of the highly unusual **Eleonora's falcon**, a "semi-colonial" nesting falcon. One of a small number of colonies on Sardinia, these are only found in the Mediterranean, named after Queen Eleonora, the medieval warrior queen who decreed that only she was permit-ted to hunt with it. This large bird is one of Europe's rarest and most enigmatic raptors, with long, thin, speedily-vibrating wings. As a migratory falcon, it's most often seen in autumn, since the species breeds late to feed its young on autumn-passage birds, catching its prey on the wing.

The Gulf of Orosei is also important as the last home of the monk or **Mediterranean seal** (in Italian *bue marino*, or "sea-ox"), sadly facing extinc-tion with at best only a handful of individuals remaining scattered in the coves and grottoes of this rocky coast.

Off the Stintino peninsula in the northwest, the island of Asinara, now a National Park, is most famous for its unique and diminutive **albino asses**. Some of these tiny creatures are also to be found south of the peninsula on the massive cliffs of Capo Caccia, where the Priscionera reserve also contains **mouflons** (long-horned wild sheep), **wild boars** and immense **griffon vultures**. The latter have been successfully reintroduced a few kilometres fur-ther south, on the desolate Alghero–Bosa coast, and this now constitutes the largest Italian colony. Also near Alghero, Lago di Baratz, Sardinia's only natural lake, has a species of **freshwater tortoise** and a system of pine-covered dunes and maritime *macchia*.

Plains and plateaux

Sardinia's **plains** constitute another highly important habitat, largely bare and cultivated, with scattered vines and wheatfields. Flatlands such as these are being agriculturally "improved" across much of Europe, but here in Sardinia they still shelter a range of flora and fauna. The Marmilla region between

Cágliari and Oristano is characterized by odd-looking bare hummocks and a series of high tablelands virtually empty of homes or developments. Here, red, white, blue and yellow flowers make a carpet of colour with **asphodel**, euphorbia, poppies, lavender, buttercups and daisies all in abundance.

The largest of these high plateaux is the Giara di Gésturi, where the boundaries of the provinces of Cágliari, Oristano and Nuoro meet. This high basalt plateau is an excellent place to find a concentration of the island's most interesting plants, including a number of rare species of **orchid**; it is also Sardinia's principal habitat of the famous *cavallini* – miniature **wild horses** whose origins are shrouded in mystery and which are notoriously difficult to track down – and shelters a range of other wildlife including hares, boars and foxes.

The most important bird of these plains is the little **bustard**, a turkey-like creature that was once much hunted by aristocratic falcons, providing spectacular sport. The whole bustard family is imperilled in much of Europe, but Sardinia is one of the few places where this particular member of the bustard family is expanding and flourishing in the mosaics of pasture particularly favoured by this species. The plains are also a rich habitat for **partridge**, **buntings**, **woodchat** and **shrike**, while the vividly colourful exotics – **roller**, **hoopoe** and **bee-eater** – are all found here. It is best to visit these areas in springtime when the *macchia* and grasslands are a riot of colour.

The macchia

Sardinia's rocky slopes are everywhere covered with a thick layer of Mediterranean **maquis**, known on the island as *macchia*. This invasive scrub flourishes after fire or the felling of forests and also colonizes abandoned cultivated land. Tangled, heavily scented and richly colourful, *macchia* includes **juniper**, **lentisk**, **myrtle** and **arbutus** (strawberry trees); **heather** and the yellow-flowering **broom** and **gorse** are also common, as are the pink and white petals of the **cistus** family. Leaves here are often thick and gummy to help prevent water loss, and the shrubs are intermingled with herbs and flowers and orchids in more open patches.

Near the coast, the *macchia* has a more typically maritime selection of plants, while in the drier areas it is interspersed with **prickly pear** cactus (introduced from Mexico by the Spanish), the fruit of which ("Indian fig") is considered a delicacy by Italians. The typical **warblers** here – **Sardinian**, **Marmora's**, **subalpine**, **spectacled** and **Dartford** – are all of interest to those more familiar with northern European species. At night one can hear the calls of **Scops owl** and the echoing warm, low churring of the **nightjar** intermingling with the cicadas.

Mountain and woodland areas

As the altitude increases, the shrub layer gives way to taller **woodland** where trees such as cork and holm oak start to appear. Here, the richly lyrical **blackcap** and the **Orphean warbler** become more predominant as the thickening canopy shades out the *macchia*. Traditional olive groves and fruit orchards are very important for a number of species, the most important of which is the rare **wryneck**. Alder and the pink blossom of oleander may mark the line of water courses, often totally dried out in summer, while on the more established streams the semi-aquatic **dipper** can sometimes be seen. Woodland is also one of the favoured habitats of the **Barbary partridge** – apart from Gibraltar, Sardinia is the only place in Europe where this species can be found. You'll be lucky to glimpse one, however, just as you'll need luck and patience to spot the rare **Sardinian salamander**.

Sardinia has the highest level of forest cover of all the Italian regions, and the interior is criss-crossed by ancient trackway ideal for the adventurous hiker or naturalist. **Cork oak** forest stretches from Gallura to the northern Barbagia (the central zone of mountains), providing one of Europe's main sources of cork – the plantations are particularly thick in the area around Tempio Pausánia. The **holm oak** is another ubiquitous tree in Sardinia: the Gennargentu mountains and the Abbasanta plateau near Oristano hold the remnants of a holm oak forest that once covered much of the island. At Sas Badas and Su Lidone on the Sopramonte massif are remains of ancient forest which has never been felled, its gnarled specimens numbering among the last remaining examples in Europe. Sardinia even has a **petrified forest** near Soddi on the shore of Lake Omodeo, the trees submerged by a primeval volcanic eruption.

Higher up in these mountains, where the gentle chiming of sheep and goat bells are a constant accompaniment, the species in the tree line change and one finds **bay oaks** and **maples** whose red leaves give a blaze of colour in autumn. Scattered smaller clumps of **holly** and **yew** are residual vegetation from a cooler era. It is here that other rare wildlife is to be found: **golden eagle** and the rare **Bonelli's eagle** soar in these skies above deep and rugged valleys that cut into the mountains, while **goshawk** and **peregrine falcon** prey on the flocks of **wood pigeon** which multiply in years when there are rich falls of

A checklist of Sardinian wildlife sites

Alghero–Bosa coast Home to Italy's largest colony of griffon vultures. See p.211.

Le Prigionette This reserve has some of the rare mouflon as well as wild boar and griffon vultures, though these are more common further south, on the Alghero–Bosa coast. See p.208.

Capo Figari Mouflon have been reintroduced on this cape and on the offshore islet of Figarolo. See p.275.

Caprera Dense *macchia* and woods, where sea and land birds nest. See p.275.

Foresta di Minniminni and Monte dei Sette Fratelli Rugged terrain sheltering deer, boar, wildcat, and various birds of prey. See p.149–150.

Gennargentu This thickly forested central mountain range has boars and – more visibly – wild pigs. See p.328–329.

Giara di Gésturi A high basalt plateau famous as the island's main habitat of the miniature wild horses (*cavallini*); it's also a good place to see rare species of orchid. See p.142–143.

Monte Arcosu The Sardinian stag (*cervo sardo*) and other forest fauna, as well as a range of predatory birds, can be spotted here. See p.101–102.

Piscinas High dune system where esparto grasses and even wild lilies take root in the sands. See p.126.

San Pietro The island's western cliffs are the habitat for rare sea birds and falcons. See p.114.

Sinis The dunes, marshes and lagoons shelter reeds and a huge range of aquatic birdlife, including the European crane. See p.170–175.

Sopramonte Eagles and other raptors can be seen circling above the mountains here. See p.320–325.

Tavolara The sheer cliffs of this island shelter peregrine falcons and storm petrels among other rare birds. See p.273.

acorn. The **jay** is also common. Towards the summits of the mountains the forests largely disappear, and are replaced by grassland, scattered **junipers** and **dwarf palm trees** bent by the Mistral wind.

Many species of rare and unique mountain plants are to be found in the Gennargentu, but pride of place goes to the **peony**, or "mountain rose" as it is known locally, whose blooming announces the arrival of spring. A notable mammal to be found in this terrain is the **Sardinian stag**, a few hundred of which have survived here and in the forests around Cágliari, for example Monte Arcosu, in the mountains of Sulcis – also the place to see **martens**, **wildcats** and **boar**.

Mouflon, or long-horned wild sheep, which have been hunted to the edge of extinction across much of Italy, are now found only in the mountains of Sardinia, and on Corsica and Cyprus. Numbers here have recovered quite well, and if one keeps a good eye open, herds of this extraordinary animal, with its enormous, regal curved horns, can be glimpsed perched high on inaccessible cliffs. Lower down, the groves of hazel, almond, walnut and chestnut carpeting the slopes of the interior are grazed by both wild *cinghiali* (boar) and the more domesticated pig – which in many cases has interbred with its wild cousin. Although Sardinia's wild boar are hunted assiduously both for the sport and their meat, their numbers have not declined significantly in recent years.

Sardinians are unreconstructed **hunters**, and will shoot at anything that moves. This can be nearly as disturbing as it is destructive, when you come across heavily armed hunting parties of men trailing through the *macchia*, though European public opinion is having an impact on reducing the damaging effects of this "sport", and the provision of protected areas is increasing.

By Peter Hack

Books

Compared with other areas of the Mediterranean, surprisingly little has been written about Sardinia, though the island has provided the inspiration for a small number of outstanding works. Most of the books listed here are in print; out-of-print books are marked "o/p". Titles marked ⊡ are particularly recommended.

Travel and general

Russell King *Sardinia* (David & Charles; o/p). One of the *Islands* series, this is an informed and comprehensive read, with chapters on archeology, industry and bandits. If you can't track down a copy for sale, you'll usually find it in public libraries.

⊡ **D.H. Lawrence** *Sea and Sardinia* (Penguin). Lawrence's hurried six-day journey through Sardinia in 1921 did not give the island much of a chance, and his account is imbued with impatience and irritation. Travelling up from Cágliari to Nuoro and Olbia in the company of the "Queen Bee" (Frieda Lawrence), his highly personal travelogue alternates between disgust and rapture, though his descriptions sparkle with closely-observed cameos and the book repays rereading.

Bernard Lortat-Jacob and Teresa Lavender Fagan *Sardinian Chronicles* (University of Chicago Press). Part of the Chicago Studies in Ethnomusicology series, this work examines the music of the island

through twelve vignettes of locals who continue to practise the tradition of choral singing.

Amelie Posse-Brázdová *Sardinian Sideshow* (Routledge; o/p). Translated from the Swedish in 1932, this light-hearted memoir relates the experiences of the Swedish protagonist and her Middle-European companions in exile during World War I in Alghero. Illuminating mainly for its descriptions of the people of the resort and elsewhere in the island in the days before package tourism.

⊡ **Alan Ross** *The Bandit on the Billiard Table* (Collins Harvill, o/p). A well-written account of a journey through Sardinia in the 1950s, full of sympathetic descriptions of people and places; informative and readable, if a little old-fashioned.

Virginia Waite *Sardinia* (Batsford, o/p). A rambling but well-researched trek through the island, with lots of historical background and first-hand descriptions of the festivals.

Specific guides

Stefano Ardito *Backpacking and Walking in Italy* (Bradt/Hunter; o/p). This guide has a very short chapter on Sardinia featuring two walks on the mountainous east coast, along the Flumineddu river and the Gorropu canyon,

and between Cala Gonone and Cala Sisine.

Giuliano Bugialli *The Foods of Sicily and Sardinia* (Rizzoli). Recipes and background on some familiar – and less well-known – Sard dishes.

Mithra Omidvar *Sardinia*
(Rother Walking Guides). The
best hiking guide to the island, with
fifty walks described, each with a
colour map (1:20,000, 1:50,000 or
1:75,000) and photographs. It's a
good, compact size, printed on hard-
wearing paper. In the UK, the book
is available from Cordee, 3a De
Montfort St, Leicester
(Ⓦ www.cordee.co.uk).

Egidio Trainito *Sardinia Diving
Guide* (Swan Hill Press). Lavishly
illustrated guide outlining Sardinia's
principal underwater ecosystems
and describing 31 dives, with
details of the marine life and also
wrecks to explore. Maps and diagrams show the sites, while colour
photos help to identify fish and
other sea life. However, poor
translation, some serious
omissions regarding dive centres
and background, and unhelpful
artwork may leave the diving
enthusiast disappointed.

History and archeology

**Robert H. Tyke and Tames K.
Andrews** *Sardinia in the
Mediterranean: A Footprint in the Sea*
(Sheffield Academic Press).
Comprehensive (and highly expensive) study of Sardinian archeology
that may be available in some
libraries; it covers Paleolithic and
Neolithic cultures, including
nuraghic, Phoenician, Punic, Greek
and Roman settlements on the island.

Gary S. Webster *A Prehistory of
Sardinia, 2300–500 BC* (Sheffield
Academic Press in UK, Almond
Press in US). Another heavyweight
academic tome bringing together all
the research on Sardinian prehistory,
with particular attention given to
nuraghic society.

Sardinian literature

Grazia Deledda *After the
Divorce* (Quartet Encounters),
Cosima (Quartet Encounters), *Elias
Portolu* (Quartet Encounters), *La
Madre* (Dedalus Modern Classics),
Canne al Vento (Reeds in the Wind,
Italica Press). Grazia Deledda's
Sardinia is a raw place of passion and
instinct, which she evokes in her
simple, unsentimental tales set
around her hometown of Nuoro. In
After the Divorce, first published in
1902, she writes of the grim sense of
exclusion from the tribal mores prevailing in the village of Orlei, where
the main protagonist, Giovanna Era,
is driven to betray her husband who
has been convicted of murder.
Cosima is an autobiographical novel
published posthumously, vividly
evoking the experiences of a
Nuorese girlhood. *Elias Portolu*
(1900) relates the moral and social
dilemmas of a convict returned to
his rigid shepherd's society. *La
Madre*, published in 1920, deals with
the frustrated love of a village priest
and the efforts of his mother to dis-
suade him from giving up his voca-
tion in order to follow his passion.
Canne al Vento (1913), translated as
Reeds in the Wind, tells of the decline
of three noble spinster sisters, the
guilt-ridden, unpaid servant who
looks after them, and the numerous
local characters who inhabit this
densely superstitious society.
Deledda's writing is full of what
D.H. Lawrence called "uncontaminated human instinct" and "the

Sardinian films

Sardinia has no distinctive **film-making** tradition, although a few directors have taken advantage of its landscape to set their films here. The following small selection lists the most notable films associated with the island.

Banditi a Orgosolo (*Bandits of Orgosolo*, directed by Vittorio de Seta, 1961). This film capitalized on the publicity given to the kidnapping and violence as practised by the outlaws living in the hills around the village of Orgósolo, outside Nuoro. The first feature film of this Sicilian-born director, made with minimal technical and financial facilities, it was enthusiastically received at the 1961 Venice Film Festival, but has disappeared almost without trace now.

Il Deserto Rosso (*Red Desert*, directed by Michelangelo Antonioni, 1965). Filmed on Budelli – one of the Maddalena islands – and responsible for propelling its *spiaggia rosa* or "pink beach" to instant fame, the movie has since sunk into obscurity.

Padre Padrone (directed by Paolo and Vittorio Taviani, 1977). This is the most famous film to come out of Sardinia, and the island's rugged mountain backdrops are used to full effect. All the same, it was hated by Sard audiences for giving a negative portrayal of the island, even if its main theme is chiefly an exploration of a boy's relationship with his tyrannical, sadistic father. Based on the autobiography of the writer Gavino Ledda, it relates how he was dragged out of school to tend sheep until army service gave him the opportunity to educate himself and finally rebel against his father. The cruelty and bleak poverty of the shepherd society is perhaps overplayed, but it's a strongly atmospheric piece, the first film to win both the Palme d'Or and International Critics' Prize at Cannes, and for years de rigueur viewing at Communist Party gatherings. Roberto Rossellini, head of the Cannes jury, declared that the film: "embodies everything which is most impressive, vigorous and coherent, and most daring, socially and artistically, in the Italian cinema."

indescribable tang of the people of the island, not yet absorbed into the world." She won the Nobel Prize for Literature in 1926.

Giuseppe Dessi *Il Desertore* (Feltrinelli; o/p). Published in 1961, "The Deserter" is one of the most prestigious works by Dessi (1909–77), who spent most of his life on the Italian mainland. The novel narrates the tale of a young Sardinian shepherd sent to fight in World War I, who flees from the front after killing his captain in a fit of rage. The protagonist returns to Sardinia, where he makes a deathbed confession of his crime. Other works by Dessi include *Paese d'Ombre* ("Land of Shadows"), published in 1972 and winner of the Strega Prize that year.

Emilio Lussu *Marcia su Roma e dintorni* (Edwin Mellen Press). First published in 1933, "March on Rome" is an autobiographical account by a leading Sardinian republican politician of resistance to fascism in Sardinia from 1918 to 1930. It remains a compelling chronicle of how Fascism took hold in Sardinia, and of one man's opposition to it; narrated with humour and evocative descriptions of the island, this is worth seeking out. Other important works by Lussu include *Sardinian Brigade* (1938), an autobiographical novel (published by Prion Books) recounting the largely forgotten Alpine war between Italian troops and the Austro-Hungarian army, and *Un Anno sull'Altiplano* (o/p), a factual account on the same subject (1938). Lussu (1890–1975), a highly decorated officer in the famous Sássari brigade, helped found the separatist Partito Sardo d'Azione, was imprisoned by the Fascists, and later became a senator in Italy's Partito Socialista.

★ **Salvatore Satta** *The Day of Judgment* (Collins Harvill). A respected jurist, Salvatore Satta wrote this classic work of fiction over several years, though it was not published until after his death in 1975. Like Deledda's work, it is set in Nuoro, peopled by a procession of theatrical characters who seem to inhabit a bleak dreamscape of a long-dead past. Lacking any storyline, the book is a powerful evocation of a lost world, set in the remotest recesses of Sardinia's impoverished interior.

Language

Language

Language

The ability to speak European languages other than Italian is increasingly widespread in Sardinia. You'll often find the staff in museums, tourist offices and hotels, as well as guides, able to communicate in English, and students in particular are frequently willing to show off their knowledge. Outside the tourist areas, however, few people actually know more than some simple words and phrases – those more often than not culled from pop songs or computer programs.

Anyone interested in Sardinia and the Sards will find their experience greatly enriched by learning a few basic phrases of **Italian**. Even if only a very superficial knowledge from a phrasebook is gained, just the ability to ask for a glass of water will make you feel less helpless. In any case, it's one of the easiest European languages to learn, especially if you already have a smattering of French or Spanish, which are both very similar grammatically.

To avoid making unnecessary gaffes, it's worth noting some elementary guidelines. When **speaking to strangers**, the third person is the polite form (ie *Lei* instead of *Tu* for "you"); using the second person is a mark of disrespect or stupidity. It's also worth remembering that Italians use "please" and "thank you" far less frequently than we do: it's all implied in the tone, though if you're in doubt, err on the polite side.

All Italian words are **stressed** on the penultimate syllable unless an **accent** denotes otherwise, although in practice accents are often left out. Thus, Cágliari and Sássari are pronounced with the accent on the first syllable. Note that the ending **-ia** or **-ie** counts as two syllables, hence *trattoria* is stressed on the i. We've put accents in, throughout the text and below, wherever it isn't immediately obvious how a word should be pronounced: for example, in *Maríttima*, the accent is on the first **i**; conversely *Olbia* should theoretically have an accent on the **o**. Other words where we've omitted accents are common ones (like *Isola*, stressed on the I), some names (*Domenico*, *Vittorio*), and words that are stressed similarly in English, such as *archeologico* and *Repubblica*.

Lastly, it's pleasantly surprising how much can be communicated by the use of body language alone – gestures, gesticulations, facial expressions and miming – an art at which Italians are supremely adept.

Pronunciation

The rules of **pronunciation** are easy, since every word is spoken exactly as it's written: you articulate each syllable of every word – the louder and clearer the

---

Phrasebooks and dictionaries

The best **phrasebook** is the Rough guides' own *Italian Dictionary Phrasebook* (Penguin; £2.99/$5.00), which has a large but accessible vocabulary, a detailed menu reader and useful dialogues. Collins also publish a comprehensive series: their *Gem* or *Pocket* dictionaries are fine for travelling purposes, while their *Concise* dictionary is adequate for most language needs.

better. The only difficulties you're likely to encounter are the few **consonants** that are different from English:

c before **a**, **o** or **u** is hard, as in **c**at; before **e** or **i** it is pronounced as in **ch**urch, while **ch** before the same vowels is hard.

sci or **sce** are pronounced as in **sh**eet and **sh**elter respectively. The same goes with **g** – soft before **e** and **i**, as in **g**entle; hard when followed by **a**, **o** or **u**, or by an **h**, as in **g**arlic.

gn has the ni sound of o**ni**on.

gl in Italian is softened to something like li in English, as in vermi**li**on.

h is not aspirated, as in **h**our.

The Sard dialect

Italy has been a separate state for only a little over 140 years, and what is now known as **standard Italian** was originally simply the usage of an educated elite deriving from a literary Tuscan dialect. In fact, each of the regions of Italy speaks its own **local dialect** which has only very recently taken second place to "standard" Italian. But in informal family or social circles, it's often still the dialect that is instinctively spoken.

Sardinia, isolated in the middle of the Mediterranean, has a dialect so dense that it almost constitutes a separate language. Every area of the island, almost every village, has its own **variation**, as you might expect in a place that is both mountainous and, from ancient times, poorly integrated. These local strains will incorporate a concoction of ingredients according to each area's particular historical circumstances. Thus on the isle of San Pietro off the southwest coast of Sardinia, a strong **Piedmontese** dialect is spoken, owing to its settlement by a colony of Ligurians, invited by King Carlo Emanuele III in 1737. At around the same time there was a wave of immigration from Corsica into the northern region of Gallura, which still retains a dialect close to that spoken in the southern parts of Sardinia's sister island. And the people of Alghero still speak a variety of **Spanish Catalan** – over 600 years after the Aragonese king made the town his main base in northern Sardinia and flooded it with Catalonians. Visitors there will find Catalan street names in the old quarter, even if they are unable to distinguish the differences in speech.

The influence of **Spanish** permeates all the island's various dialects – hardly surprising in a place that was a Spanish colony for three centuries. The evidence is also on maps, where you will see examples like *riu* used for a river, where the Italian would be *fiume*. The Sard dialects also have large infusions of **Latin**, a residue of the much older Roman occupation. "House," for example, in Italian *casa*, is called *domus* in areas of Sardinia, the same as Latin. The words for "the" in northern Sardinia – *su* and *sa* in the singular, *sos* and *sas* in the plural – are derived from the Latin noun-endings. In the south of the island, "the" is *is*, from the Latin *ipse*. Again, you'll find copious examples on the maps. The region which has the greatest preponderance of Latin in its dialect is Logudoro, in the island's northwestern quarter; its inhabitants boast of speaking the purest form of dialect, which in effect means the form least corrupted by later influences.

Added to the innate **insularity** of islanders, Sards have a particular reputation for being *isolani*, meaning that they are not only insular but a closed and introspective people, with little interest in anything beyond immediate concerns. Whether or not this is still true today, the trait has influenced – and been influenced by – the local variations in speech. Within the artificially imposed provincial boundaries of Cágliari, Sássari, Nuoro and Oristano, Sardinia is a conglomerate of diverse regions – Campidano, Arborea, Logudoro, Gallura, the Iglesiente and Barbagia, to name but the principal ones – each with distinct traditions and a fierce awareness of their differences from one another. The use of dialect became not just a colloquial mode of speech, but also a symbol of **local solidarity**, enabling Sards to identify each other according to the particular area of the island they inhabit, just by listening.

The result of this linguistic confusion is that Italian has become the only means for people of different areas of the island to communicate effectively, and it has been learned, as a foreign language is learned, to perfection. Indeed, it is claimed that Sards speak the most correct form of Italian anywhere. Television, of course, has also played its part, and it's extemely unlikely that you could ever find today a non-Italian speaking Sard.

Basic Italian terms and phrases

Numbers

One	uno	Twenty-one	ventuno
Two	due	Twenty-two	ventidue
Three	tre	Thirty	trenta
Four	quattro	Thirty-one	trentuno
Five	cinque	Thirty-two	trentadue
Six	sei	Forty	quaranta
Seven	sette	Forty-one	quarantuno
Eight	otto	Fifty	cinquanta
Nine	nove	Sixty	sessanta
Ten	diece	Seventy	settanta
Eleven	undici	Eighty	ottanta
Twelve	dodici	Ninety	novanta
Thirteen	tredici	One hundred	cento
Fourteen	quattordici	One hundred and one	centouno
Fifteen	quindici	Two hundred	duecento
Sixteen	sedici	One thousand	mille
Seventeen	diciasette	Two thousand	duemila
Eighteen	diciotto	Three thousand	tremila
Nineteen	dicianove	One million	un milione
Twenty	venti		

Days and months

Monday	lunedì	March	marzo
Tuesday	martedì	April	aprile
Wednesday	mercoledì	May	maggio
Thursday	giovedì	June	giugno
Friday	venerdì	July	luglio
Saturday	sábato	August	agosto
Sunday	domenica	September	settembre
		October	ottobre
January	gennaio	November	novembre
February	febbraio	December	dicembre

Useful phrases

Good morning	Buongiorno	tomorrow	domani
Good afternoon/ evening	Buona sera	day after tomorrow	dopodomani
		yesterday	ieri
Good night	Buona notte	now	adesso
Hello/Goodbye	Ciao (informal; when speaking to strangers use the phrases above)	later	più tardi
		Wait a minute!	Aspetta!
		in the morning	di mattina
		in the afternoon	nel pomeriggio
Goodbye	Arrivederci (formal)	in the evening	di sera
Yes	Sì	here/there	qui/lì
No	No	good/bad	buono/cattivo
Please	Per favore	big/small	grande/píccolo
Thank you (very much)	Grázie (Molte/mille grazie)	cheap/expensive	económico/caro
		early/late	presto/ritardo
You're welcome	Prego	hot/cold	caldo/freddo
Alright/That's OK	Va bene	near/far	vicino/lontano
How are you? (informal/formal)	Come stai/sta?	vacant/occupied	líbero/occupato
		quickly/slowly	velocemente/ lentamente
I'm fine	Bene		
Do you speak English?	Parla inglese?	slowly/quietly	piano
I don't understand	Non capisco	with/without	con/senza
I haven't understood	Non ho capito	more/less	più/meno
I don't know	Non lo so	enough, no more	basta
Excuse me/Sorry	Scusa (informal)	Mr...	Signor...
Excuse me/Sorry (formal)	Mi scusi/prego	Mrs...	Signora...
		Miss...	Signorina... (il signore, la signora, la signorina
Excuse me (in a crowd)	Permesso		
I'm sorry	Mi dispiace		when speaking about someone else)
I'm here on holiday	Sono qui in vacanza		
I live in...	Abito a...	first name	primo nome
today	oggi	surname	cognome

Accommodation

hotel	albergo	Is breakfast included?	È compresa la prima colazione?
Is there a hotel nearby?	C'è un albergo qui vicino?	Do you have anything cheaper	Ha niente che costa di meno?
Do you have a room...?	Ha una cámera...?	full/half board	pensione completa/ mezza pensione
for one/two/ three people	per una persona, due/tre persone	Can I see the room?	Posso vedere la cámera?
for one/two/three nights	per una notte, due/tre notti	I'll take it	La prendo
for one/two weeks	per una settimana/ due settimane	I'd like to book a room	Vorrei prenotare una cámera
with a double bed	con un letto matrimoniale	I have a booking	Ho una prenotazione
with a shower/bath	con una doccia/ un bagno	Can we camp here?	Possiamo fare il campeggio qui?
with a balcony	con una terrazza	Is there a campsite nearby?	C'è un camping qui vicino?
hot/cold water	acqua calda/ fredda	tent	tenda
		cabin	cabina
How much is it?	Quanto costa?	youth hostel	ostello per la gioventù
It's expensive	È caro		

Questions and directions

Where? (Where is/are...?)	Dove? (Dov'è/Dove sono?)	Can you tell me when to get off?	Può dirmi quando devo scendere?
When?	Quando?	What time does it open?	A che ora apre?
What? (Qhat is it?)	Cosa? (Cos'è?)		
How much/many?	Quanto/Quanti?	What time does it close?	A che ora chiude?
Why?	Perché?		
It is/There is (Is it?/Is there...?)	È/c'è (è/c'è...?)	How much does it cost (...do they cost?)	Quanto costa? (Quanto costano?)
What time is it?	Che ora è/Che ore sono?	What is it called in Italian?	Come si chiama in italiano?
How do I get to...?	Come arrivo a...?	left/right	sinistra/destra
How far is it to...?	Quant'è lontano a...?	Go straight ahead	Sempre diritto
Can you give me a lift to...?	Mi può dare un passaggio a...?	Turn to the right/left	Gira a destra/ sinistra

Transport

aeroplane	aeroplano	bicycle	bicicletta
bus	autobus/pullman	ferry	traghetto
train	treno	ship	nave
car	mácchina	hydrofoil	aliscafo
taxi	taxi	hitch-hiking	autostop

on foot	a piedi	Where does it leave from?	Da dove parte?
bus station	autostazione	Which platform does it leave from?	Da quale binario parte?
railway station	stazione ferroviaria	Do I have to change?	Devo cambiare?
ferry terminal	stazione maríttima	How many kilometres is it?	Quanti chilómetri sono?
port	porto		
a ticket to…	un biglietto a…	How long does it take?	Quanto ci vuole?
one-way/return	solo andata/andata e ritorno	What number bus is it to…?	Que número di autobus per…?
Can I book a seat?	Posso prenotare un posto?	Where's the road to…?	Dov'è la strada a…?
What time does it leave?	A che ora parte?	Next stop please	La próssima fermata, per favore
When is the next bus/train/ ferry to…?	Quando parte il próssimo pullman/ treno/traghetto per…?		

Driving

parking	parcheggio	no through road	vietato il tránsito
no parking	divieto di sosta/ sostavietata	no overtaking	vietato il sorpasso
		crossroads	incrocio
one way street	senso único	speed limit	límite di velocità
no entry	senso vietato	traffic light	semáforo
slow down	rallentare		
road closed/up	strada chiusa/ guasta		

Some signs

entrance/exit	entrata/uscita	to let	affítasi
free entrance	ingresso líbero	platform	binario
gentlemen/ladies	signori/signore	cash desk	cassa
wc	gabinetto, bagno	go/walk	avanti
vacant/engaged	líbero/occupato	stop/halt	alt
open/closed	aperto/chiuso	customs	dogana
arrivals/departures	arrivi/partenze	do not touch	non toccare
closed for restoration	chiuso per restauro	danger	perícolo
		beware	attenzione
closed for holidays	chiuso per ferie	first aid	pronto soccorso
pull/push	tirare/spíngere	ring the bell	suonare il campanello
out of order	guasto		
drinking water	acqua potábile	no smoking	vietato fumare

Italian food terms

Basics and snacks

aceto	vinegar	pane	bread
aglio	garlic	pane integrale	wholemeal bread
biscotti	biscuits	panino	bread roll/ sandwich
burro	butter		
caramelle	sweets	patatine	crisps/potato chips
cioccolato	chocolate	patatine fritte	chips
focaccia	oven-baked snack	pepe	pepper
formaggio	cheese	pizzetta	slice of pizza to take away
frittata	omelette		
gelato	ice cream	riso	rice
grissini	bread sticks	sale	salt
maionese	mayonnaise	uova	eggs
marmellata	jam	yogurt	yoghurt
olio	oil	zúcchro	sugar
olive	olives	zuppa	soup

Antipasti and starters

antipasto misto	mixed cold meats, seafood and cheese (plus a mix of other things in this list)	mortadella	salami-type cured meat with white nuggets of fat; in Sardinia, often with pistachios
caponata	mixed aubergine, olives, tomatoes	pancetta	bacon
caprese	tomato and mozzarella cheese salad	peperonata	grilled green, red or yellow peppers stewed in olive oil
insalata di mare	seafood salad (usually squid, octopus and prawn)	pomodori ripieni	stuffed tomatoes
		prosciutto	ham
insalata russa	"Russian salad"; diced vegetables in mayonnaise	salame	salami
		salmone/tonno/ pesce spada affumicato	smoked salmon/tuna/ swordfish
insalata di riso	rice salad		
melanzane alla parmigiana	fried aubergine in tomato sauce with parmesan cheese		

Pizzas

biancaneve	"black and white"; mozzarella and oregano
calzone	folded pizza with cheese, ham and tomato
capricciosa	literally "capricious"; topped with whatever they've got in the kitchen, usually including baby artichoke, ham and egg
cardinale	ham and olives
diávolo	spicy, with hot salami or Italian sausage
funghi	mushroom; tinned, sliced button mushrooms unless it specifies fresh mushrooms, either *funghi freschi* or *porcini*
frutti di mare	seafood; usually mussels, prawns, squid and clams
margherita	cheese and tomato
marinara	tomato and garlic
Napoli/ Napoletana	tomato, anchovy and olive oil (often mozzarella, too)
quattro formaggi	"four cheeses", usually mozzarella, fontina, gorgonzola and gruyère
quattro stagioni	"four seasons"; the toppings split into four separate sections, usually including ham, peppers, onion, mushrooms, artichokes, olives, egg, etc.
romana	anchovy and olives

The first course (*il primo*)

Soups

brodo	clear broth
minestrina	any light soup
minestrone	thick vegetable soup
pasta e fagioli	pasta soup with beans
pastina in brodo	pasta pieces in clear broth
stracciatella	broth with egg

Pasta

cannelloni	large tubes of pasta, stuffed
farfalle	literally "bow"-shaped pasta; the word also means "butterflies"
fettuccine	narrow pasta ribbons
gnocchi	small potato and dough dumplings
lasagne	lasagne
maccheroni	macaroni (tubular pasta)
pappardelle	pasta ribbons
pasta al forno	pasta baked with minced meat, eggs, tomato and cheese
penne	smaller version of *rigatoni*
ravioli	ravioli
rigatoni	large, grooved tubular pasta
risotto	cooked rice dish, with sauce
spaghetti	spaghetti
spaghettini	thin spaghetti
tagliatelle	pasta ribbons, another word for *fettuccine*
tortellini	small rings of pasta, stuffed with meat or cheese
vermicelli	very thin spaghetti (literally "little worms")

The sauce (*salsa*)

aglio e olio (e peperoncino)	tossed in garlic and olive oil (and hot chillies)
amatriciana	cubed pork and tomato sauce (originally from Rome)
arrabbiata	spicy tomato sauce, with chillies
bolognese	meat sauce
burro e salvia	butter and sage
carbonara	cream, ham and beaten egg
frutta di mare	seafood
funghi	mushroom
panna	cream
parmigiano	parmesan cheese
pesto	ground basil, pine nut, garlic and pecorino sauce
pomodoro	tomato sauce
puttanesca	"whorish"; tomato, anchovy, olive oil and oregano
ragù	meat sauce
vóngole (veraci)	clam and tomato sauce (fresh clams in shells, usually served with oil and herbs)

The second course (*il secondo*): meat (*carne*)

agnello	lamb	maiale	pork
ásino	ass, donkey	manzo	beef
bistecca	steak	montone	mutton
capretto	young goat	monzette	snails
cavallo	horse	ossobuco	shin of veal
cervello	brain	pollo	chicken
cinghiale	wild boar	polpette	meatballs
coniglio	rabbit	rognoni	kidneys
costolette/cotolette	cutlets/chops	salsiccia	sausage
fegatini	chicken livers	saltimbocca	veal with ham
fégato	liver	scaloppina	escalope (of veal)
involtini	steak slices, rolled and stuffed	spezzatino	stew
		tacchino	turkey
lepre	hare	trippa	tripe
lingua	tongue	vitello	veal
lumache	snails		

Fish (*pesce*) and shellfish (*crostacei*)

Note that *surgelati* or *congelati* written on the menu next to a dish means "frozen" – it often applies to squid and prawns.

acciughe	anchovies	baccalà	dried salted cod
anguilla	eel	calamari	squid
aragosta	lobster	céfalo	grey mullet
arselle	clams	cozze	mussels
bottarga	salted and dried eggs of mullet and tuna	dattile	razor clams
		déntice	dentex (like sea bass)

gamberetti	shrimps	sampiero	John Dory
gámberi	prawns	sárago	bream
granchio	crab	sarde	sardines
merluzzo	cod	seppie	cuttlefish
múggine	mullet	sgombro	mackerel
orata	gilthead	sógliola	sole
óstriche	oysters	sp'gola	sea-bass
pesce spada	swordfish	tonno	tuna
polpo/pólipo	octopus	triglie	red mullet
ricci di mare	sea urchins	trota	trout
rospo	monkfish	vóngole	clams

Vegetables (*contorni*) and salad (*insalata*)

aspáragi	asparagus	finocchio	fennel
basílico	basil	funghi	mushrooms
bróccoli	broccoli	insalata verde/mista	green salad/mixed salad
cápperi	capers		
carciofi	artichokes	melanzane	aubergine/eggplant
carciofini	artichoke hearts	orígano	oregano
carotte	carrots	patate	potatoes
cavolfiori	cauliflower	peperoni	peppers
cávolo	cabbage	piselli	peas
ceci	chickpeas	pomodori	tomatoes
cetriolo	cucumber	radicchio	red chicory
cipolla	onion	spinaci	spinach
fagioli	beans	zucca	pumpkin
fagiolini	green beans	zucchini	courgettes

Desserts (*dolci*)

amaretti	macaroons	zabaglione	dessert made with eggs, sugar and Marsala wine
gelato	ice cream		
macedonia	fruit salad		
torta	cake, tart	zuppa inglese	trifle

Cheese

| caciocavallo | a type of dried, mature mozzarella cheese | fontina | mild northern Italian cheese used in cooking and in rolls |
| dolce sardo | dry, hard shepherd's cheese, often going into sandwiches | fiore sardo | sheep's cheese frequently used in cooking |

gorgonzola	soft, strong, blue-veined cheese	pecorino	strong-tasting hard sheep's cheese, either *romano* or *sardo*, both from Sardinia
grana	hard cheese often used instead of *parmigiano* on pastas and soups	provolone	cheese with grooved rind, either mild or strong
mozzarella	soft white cheese, traditionally made from buffalo's milk	ricotta	soft white cheese made from ewe's milk, used in sweet or savoury dishes
parmigiano	parmesan cheese		

Fruit and nuts

albicocche	apricots	limone	lemon
ananas	pineapple	mándorle	almonds
anguria/coccómero	water melon	mele	apples
arance	oranges	melone	melon
banane	bananas	néspole	medlars
cacchi	persimmons	pere	pears
ciliegie	cherries	pesche	peaches
fichi	figs	pignoli	pine nuts
fichi d'India	prickly pears	pistacchio	pistachio nut
frágole	strawberries	uva	grapes

Cooking terms and useful words

affumicato	smoked	al marsala	cooked with Marsala wine
alla brace	barbecued	milanese	fried in egg and breadcrumbs
arrosto	roast		
ben cotto	well done	pizzaiola	cooked with tomato sauce
bollito/lesso	boiled	ripieno	stuffed
brasato	cooked in wine	sangue	rare
cotto	cooked (not raw)	allo spiedo	on the spit
crudo	raw	stracotto	braised, stewed
al dente	firm, not overcooked	surgelato	frozen
ferri	grilled without oil	in úmido	stewed
al forno	baked	al vapore	steamed
fritto	fried		
grattugiato	grated		
alla griglia	grilled		

Sardinian specialities: starters, breads and cheeses

sa burrida — bits of dogfish boiled and marinated in garlic, parsley, walnuts and vinegar

culurgiones — ravioli stuffed with potato, cheese, garlic and mint

malloreddus — gnocchetti, or pasta shaped in little shells, with various toppings, for example, *alla campidanese*, a spicy sausage sauce

fainè — chickpea pizza to a Genoan recipe served plain, or with onion, sausage or anchovy (not usually available in summer)

sa fregula — couscous-type pasta, either in a meat stock or dry with mussels or clams

pane carasau — crisp wafer bread, often served with olive oil and salt to add flavour

pane frattau — carasau bread soaked in tomato sauce with pecorino and an egg, typically from Mamoiada

spianadas — soft round bread from the Logudoro district, often served with sausages

zuppa/suppa cuata — bread, cheese and tomato soup

Sardinian specialities: main courses

aragosta catalana — lobster in sauce as served in Alghero

cashcà — couscous-type wheat semolina steamed with meat, vegetables or fish, as prepared in Carloforte on San Pietro

sa còrdula — roasted or barbecued sheep's entrails

cuscus — a version of north African couscous, a speciality of the island of San Pietro, usually served with a fish and vegetable sauce

fritto misto — a standard seafood dish; deep-fried prawns and calamari rings in batter

fritto di pesce — as above but also with other fried fish, like sardines and whitebait

giogghe — snails boiled and then fried with garlic, parsley and paprika

gran premio — horsemeat steak

grigliata di pesce — a mixed fish grill, usually quite substantial and expensive

sa merca — salted mullet from the Cabras lagoon, cooked in herbs

monzette — small snails roasted with salt, a speciality of Sássari; the rarer *giogghe* are boiled, then fried slowly with garlic, parsley and paprika

panadas — pastry rolls filled with meat, fish and vegetables, or all three, originating in Assémini, near Cágliari

pécora in capotta — mutton boiled with vegetables, garlic and rosemary, typical of the Nuoro area

porceddu/ porcheddu — young pig roasted whole on a spit with myrtle leaves

stufato di capretto	chunks of kid casseroled with wine, artichokes and saffron	zuppa gallurese	"Galluran soup" made from layers of bread and fresh cheese, soaked with meat broth and baked in the oven until golden and fluffy
zuppa di pesce	a big dish of mixed fish in rich wine-based soup		

Sweets and desserts

aranciatte/ aranzada	very sweet confection, available from Nuoro, made with almonds, oranges and honey	seadas/sebadas	fried ricotta-filled pastry bubbles soaked in honey
pardulas/ casadinas	cheese-based pastries flavoured with saffron, vanilla and the peel of citrus fruit	torrone	crystallized almonds and honey, the best from the Barbagia villages of Tonara and Aritzo

Drinks

acqua minerale	mineral water	succo di frutta	concentrated fruit juice, sometimes sugared
aranciata	orangeade		
bicchiere	glass		
birra	beer	tè	tea
bottiglia	bottle	tónico	tonic water
caffè	coffee	vino	wine
cioccolata calda	hot chocolate	rosso	red
ghiaccio	ice	bianco	white
granita	iced coffee/fruit drink	rosato	rosé
latte	milk	secco	dry
limonata	lemonade	dolce	sweet
selz	soda water	litro	litre
spremuta	fresh fruit juice	mezzo	half litre
spumante	sparkling wine	quarto	quarter litre
		Salute!	Cheers!

Glossary

agriturismo rural B&B, usually with restaurant

anfiteatro amphitheatre

autostazione bus station

belvedere a look-out point

cappella chapel

castello castle

cattedrale cathedral

centro centre

chiesa church (*chiesa matrice/madre*, main "mother" church)

comune an administrative area; also, the local council or the town hall

corso avenue/boulevard

duomo cathedral

entrata entrance

festa festival, carnival

fiume river

golfo gulf

lago lake

largo square (like piazza)

lungomare seafront promenade or road

macchia *maquis*, or Mediterranean scrub

mare sea

mercato market

mezzo veloce high-speed ferry

Municipio town hall

palazzo palace, mansion or block (of flats)

parco park

passeggiata the customary early evening walk

piano plain (also "slowly", "gently")

piazza square

pineta pinewood

Pro Loco a local tourist office, usually run by the town hall and with limited hours

santuario sanctuary

spiaggia beach

stazione station (train station, stazione ferroviaria; bus station, autostazione; ferry terminal, stazione maríttima)

strada road/street

teatro theatre

tempio temple

torre tower

traghetto ferry

uscita exit

via road (always used with name; as Via Roma)

zona zone

Art and architecture

apse domed recess at the altar end of a church

architrave the lowest part of the entablature

atrium forecourt, usually of a Roman house

campanile bell tower

capital top of a column

Catalan-gothic hybrid form of architecture, mixing elements from fifteenth-century Spanish and Northern European building styles

cavea the seating section in a theatre

cella sanctuary of a temple

cupola a dome

decumanus the main street in a Roman town

entablature the part of the building above the capital on a classical building

ex-voto decorated tablet designed as thanksgiving to a saint

hypogeum underground vault, often used as an early Christian church

loggia roofed gallery or balcony

nave central space in a church, usually flanked by aisles

polyptych painting or carving on several joined wooden panels

portico the covered entrance to a building

Punic Carthaginian/Phoenician

stelae inscribed stone slabs

thermae baths, usually elaborate buildings in Roman villas

tholos a dome-shaped tomb, usually associated with the Greek Mycenaean period

triptych painting or carving on three joined wooden panels

Acronyms

AAST Azienda Autónoma di Soggiorno e Turismo (local tourist office)

ACI Italian Automobile Club

APT Azienda Provinciale di Turismo: provincial tourist office

CAI Club Alpino Italiano: Italian climbing club

EPT Ente Provinciale per il Turismo: provincial tourist office

ESIT Ente Sardo Indústrie Turístiche: regional tourist office

FdS Ferrovie della Sardegna

FMS Ferrovie Meridionali Sarde

FS Italian state railways, now also called Trenitalia

IVA Imposta Valore Aggiunto: VAT

PDS Partito Democrático della Sinistra: the former Italian Communist Party

PS d'Az Partito Sardo d'Azione: Sardinian Action Party

PSI Partito Socialista d'Italia: the Italian Socialist Party

RAI the Italian state TV and radio network

SP Strada Provinciale: a minor road, eg SP70

SS Strada Statale: a main highway, eg SS195

Index

and small print

Index

Entries in colour indicate a map

INDEX

V

W

Y

A Rough Guide to Rough Guides

In the summer of 1981, Mark Ellingham, a recent graduate from Bristol University, was travelling round Greece and couldn't find a guidebook that really met his needs. On the one hand there were the student guides, insistent on saving every last cent, and on the other the heavyweight cultural tomes whose authors seemed to have spent more time in a research library than lounging away the afternoon at a taverna or on the beach.

In a bid to avoid getting a job, Mark and a small group of writers set about creating their own guidebook. It was a guide to Greece that aimed to combine a journalistic approach to description with a thoroughly practical approach to travellers' needs – a guide that would incorporate culture, history and contemporary insights with a critical edge, together with up-to-date, value-for-money listings. Back in London, Mark and the team finished their Rough Guide, as they called it, and talked Routledge into publishing the book.

That first *Rough Guide to Greece*, published in 1982, was a student scheme that became a publishing phenomenon. The immediate success of the book – with numerous reprints and a Thomas Cook prize shortlisting – spawned a series that rapidly covered dozens of destinations. Rough Guides had a ready market among low-budget backpackers, but soon also acquired a much broader and older readership that relished Rough Guides' wit and inquisitiveness as much as their enthusiastic, critical approach. Everyone wants value for money, but not at any price.

Rough Guides soon began supplementing the "rougher" information about hostels and low-budget listings with the kind of detail on restaurants and quality hotels that independent-minded visitors on any budget might expect, whether on business in New York or trekking in Thailand.

These days the guides – distributed worldwide by the Penguin group – offer recommendations from shoestring to luxury and cover more than 200 destinations around the globe, including almost every country in the Americas and Europe, more than half of Africa and most of Asia and Australasia. Our ever-growing team of authors and photographers is spread all over the world, particularly in Europe, the USA and Australia.

In 1994, we published the *Rough Guide to World Music* and *Rough Guide to Classical Music*; and a year later the *Rough Guide to the Internet*. All three books have become benchmark titles in their fields – which encouraged us to expand into other areas of publishing, mainly around popular culture. Rough Guides now publish:

* Travel guides to more than 200 worldwide destinations
* Dictionary phrasebooks to 22 major languages
* History guides ranging from Ireland to Islam
* Maps printed on rip-proof and waterproof Polyart™ paper
* Music guides running the gamut from Opera to Elvis
* Restaurant guides to London, New York and San Francisco
* Reference books on topics as diverse as the Weather and Shakespeare
* Sports guides from Formula 1 to Man Utd
* Pop culture books from Lord of the Rings to Cult TV
* World Music CDs in association with World Music Network.

Visit www.roughguides.com to see our latest publications.

Rough Guide Credits

Text editor: Fran Sandham
Layout: Umesh Aggarwal
Cartography: Manish Chandra, Ashutosh Bharti, Rajesh Mishra, Animesh Pathak
Picture research: Jj Luck
Proofreader: Madhulita Mohapatra
Editorial: **London** Martin Dunford, Kate Berens, Helena Smith, Claire Saunders, Geoff Howard, Ruth Blackmore, Ann-Marie Shaw, Gavin Thomas, Polly Thomas, Richard Lim, Lucy Ratcliffe, Clifton Wilkinson, Alison Murchie, Fran Sandham, Sally Schafer, Alexander Mark Rogers, Karoline Densley, Andy Turner, Ella O'Donnell, Andrew Lockett, Joe Staines, Duncan Clark, Peter Buckley, Matthew Milton; **New York** Andrew Rosenberg, Richard Koss, Yuki Takagaki, Hunter Slaton, Chris Barsanti, Thomas Kohnstamm, Steven Horak
Design & Layout: **London** Helen Prior, Dan May, Diana Jarvis; **Delhi** Madhulita Mohapatra, Umesh Aggarwal, Ajay Verma

Production: Julia Bovis, John McKay, Sophie Hewat
Cartography: **London** Maxine Repath, Ed Wright, Katie Lloyd-Jones; **Delhi** Manish Chandra, Rajesh Chhibber, Jai Prakash Mishra, Ashutosh Bharti, Rajesh Mishra, Animesh Pathak
Cover art direction: Louise Boulton
Picture research: Sharon Martins, Mark Thomas, Jj Luck
Online: **New York** Jennifer Gold, Cree Lawson, Suzanne Welles; **Delhi** Manik Chauhan, Amarjyoti Dutta, Narender Kumar
Marketing & Publicity: **London** Richard Trillo, Niki Smith, David Wearn, Chloë Roberts, Demelza Dallow; **New York** Geoff Colquitt, David Wechsler, Megan Kennedy
Finance: Gary Singh
Manager India: Punita Singh
Series editor: Mark Ellingham
PA to Managing Director: Julie Sanderson
Managing Director: Kevin Fitzgerald

Publishing Information

This second edition published January 2004 by **Rough Guides Ltd**,
80 Strand, London WC2R 0RL.
345 Hudson St, 4th Floor,
New York, NY 10014, USA.
Distributed by the Penguin Group
Penguin Books Ltd,
80 Strand, London WC2R 0RL
Penguin Putnam, Inc.
375 Hudson Street, NY 10014, USA
Penguin Books Australia Ltd,
487 Maroondah Highway, PO Box 257,
Ringwood, Victoria 3134, Australia
Penguin Books Canada Ltd,
10 Alcorn Avenue, Toronto, Ontario,
Canada M4V 1E4
Penguin Books (NZ) Ltd,
182–190 Wairau Road, Auckland 10,
New Zealand
Typeset in Bembo and Helvetica to an original design by Henry Iles.

Printed in Italy by LegoPrint S.p.A

© Robert Andrews 2004

No part of this book may be reproduced in any form without permission from the publisher except for the quotation of brief passages in reviews.

400pp includes index
A catalogue record for this book is available from the British Library

ISBN 1-85828-2379

The publishers and authors have done their best to ensure the accuracy and currency of all the information in **The Rough Guide to Sardinia**, however, they can accept no responsibility for any loss, injury, or inconvenience sustained by any traveller as a result of information or advice contained in the guide.

1 3 5 7 9 8 6 4 2

Help us update

We've gone to a lot of effort to ensure that the second edition of **The Rough Guide to Sardinia** is accurate and up-to-date. However, things change – places get "discovered", opening hours are notoriously fickle, restaurants and rooms raise prices or lower standards. If you feel we've got it wrong or left something out, we'd like to know, and if you can remember the address, the price, the time, the phone number, so much the better.

We'll credit all contributions, and send a copy of the next edition (or any other Rough Guide if you prefer) for the best letters. Everyone who writes to us and isn't already a subscriber will receive a copy of our full-colour thrice-yearly newsletter. Please mark letters: **"Rough Guide to Sardinia Update"** and send to: Rough Guides, 80 Strand, London WC2R 0RL, or Rough Guides, 4th Floor, 345 Hudson St, New York, NY 10014. Or send an email to **mail@roughguides.com**

Have your questions answered and tell others about your trip at **www.roughguides.atinfopop.com**

SMALL PRINT

Acknowledgements

Thanks are due to the many enthusiastic and well-informed guides who shared their knowledge of and passion for Sardinia with me; to Luigi Colli for a great adventure and to Philip Lewis, my walking and driving companion who also snoozed. In Britain, the input of Peter Hack and Kate Hughes was greatly appreciated – thanks. At Rough Guides, Fran Sandham was an exemplary editor, patient beyond the call of duty; thanks also to Umesh Aggarwal for typesetting, Manish Chandra, Ashutosh Bharti, Rajesh Mishra, Animesh Pathak, Maxine Repath and Ed Wright for cartography, Jj Luck for picture research and Madhulita Mohapatra for proofreading.

This book is dedicated to my favourite holiday companions: Jo, Quin and Evelina.

Readers' letters

Thanks to all the readers who took the trouble to write in with their comments and suggestions (and apologies to anyone whose name we've misspelt or omitted):

Huge thanks to all the readers who contributed comments and information, often at great length and with a scrupulous eye: Finn Brandt, Catherine Bruzzone, Iola Bunting, Alison Cameron, Rosemary Catling, Naomi Caruso, Patrick Crofton and Sinead O'Dwyer, Gary Elflett, Chris Gale, Anita Gilles, Jum Glendinning, Alan Grieve, Paul Hagger, Els Hendrix, Ian Hill, Charles Holtom, Noel Jackson, Peter Kennedy, Martin Klopstock, Garry Lee, Benjamin Liebelt, Herman Meilak, Alex Metcalfe, Julie Moley, Harry M.F. Morten, Dick Newson, Luisa Pece, Anne Gerd Petersen, Daniel Philpott, M.A. Redmond, Anna Richman, Isis Rowan, Sue Taylor, Vaughan Webb, David Wechsler, Trevor and Helena Wright, and Rodney Yoder.

Photo Credits

Cover Credits

Main front: Smeralda coast © Robert Harding
Small top front picture: Cagliari © John Miller
Small front lower picture: Tharos
© Robert Harding
Back top picture: Santa Margherita di Pula
© Robert Harding
Back lower picture: Porto Cervo
© John Miller

Colour introduction

Castelsardo © Rob Andrews
Cathedral, Sassari © Rob Andrews
Market © Rob Andrews
Nuraghe Mannu, Cala Gonone
© Rob Andrews
Pisan Church © Rob Andrews
Elephant Rock, Castelsardo
© Rob Andrews
Musicians at festival © ESIT-Cagliari
Festival/Costume © Rob Andrews
Mouflon © Picture Library Waldhäusl/Alamy
Images
Mural, Orgosolo © Rob Andrews
Beach, Costa Rei © Rob Andrews

Things not to miss

01 Horses © ESIT-Cagliari
02 Tavolara © Rob Andrews
03 Nuraghe Santu Antine © Rob Andrews
04 San Gavino © Rob Andrews
05 Bosa © Rob Andrews
06 Walk to Tiscali © Rob Andrews
07 Museo Archeologico © Gianni Dagli
Orti/Corbis
08 Inland Gallura © Rob Andrews

09 La Pelosa © Robert Harding Picture
Library
10 Alghero: Grotta di Nettuno © ESIT-Cagliari
11 Castelsardo: the old town © Rob Andrews
12 Cágliari © Rob Andrews
13 Lobster Dish/Alghero © Sandro
Vannini/Corbis
14 Nora © Rob Andrews
15 Sa Sartiglia © Rob Andrews
16 Santissima Trinità di Saccargia
© Rob Andrews
17 Tharros © Rob Andrews
18 Costa del Sud © Ken Gibson/Travel Ink
19 Ethnographic Museum © Rob Andrews
20 Sássari Old Town © Rob Andrews
21 Santa Cristina © Rob Andrews
22 Easter Celebrations © Rob Andrews

Black and white pictures

Cagliari © ESIT-Cagliari (p.66)
Torre dell'Elefante © Rob Andrews (p.80)
Chia Beach © Rob Andrews (p.96)
Las Plassas Castle © Rob Andrews (p.130)
Nuraghe Su Nuraxi © Rob Andrews (p.145)
Nuraghe Losa © Rob Andrews (p.156)
Oristano Cathedral © Rob Andrews (p.178)
Miniature Donkeys © ESIT-Cagliari (p.190)
River Temo at Bosa © Rob Andrews (p.219)
San Pietro delle Immagine, Bulzi
© Rob Andrews (p.226)
Giants' tomb, near Arzachena
© Rob Andrews (p.260)
Yachts © ESIT-Cagliari (p.303)
Festival costumes © ESIT-Cagliari (p.306)
Valle Lanaittu, near Tíscali © Rob Andrews
(p.321)

Rough Guides travel...

Rough Guides are available from good bookstores worldwide. New titles are published every month. Check www.roughguides.com for the latest news.

...music & reference

Africa & Middle East
Cape Town
Egypt
The Gambia
Jerusalem
Jordan
Kenya
Morocco
South Africa, Lesotho & Swaziland
Syria
Tanzania
Tunisia
West Africa
Zanzibar
Zimbabwe

Travel Theme guides
First-Time Around the World
First-Time Asia
First-Time Europe
First-Time Latin America
Gay & Lesbian Australia
Skiing & Snowboarding in North America
Travel Online
Travel Health
Walks in London & SE England
Women Travel

Restaurant guides
French Hotels & Restaurants
London
New York
San Francisco

Maps
Algarve
Amsterdam
Andalucia & Costa del Sol
Argentina
Athens

Australia
Baja California
Barcelona
Boston
Brittany
Brussels
Chicago
Crete
Croatia
Cuba
Cyprus
Czech Republic
Dominican Republic
Dublin
Egypt
Florence & Siena
Frankfurt
Greece
Guatemala & Belize
Iceland
Ireland
Lisbon
London
Los Angeles
Mexico
Miami & Key West
Morocco
New York City
New Zealand
Northern Spain
Paris
Portugal
Prague
Rome
San Francisco
Sicily
South Africa
Sri Lanka
Tenerife
Thailand
Toronto
Trinidad & Tobago
Tuscany
Venice
Washington DC
Yucatán Peninsula

Dictionary Phrasebooks
Czech
Dutch
Egyptian Arabic
European
French
German
Greek
Hindi & Urdu
Hungarian
Indonesian
Italian
Japanese
Mandarin Chinese
Mexican Spanish
Polish
Portuguese
Russian
Spanish
Swahili
Thai
Turkish
Vietnamese

Music Guides
The Beatles
Cult Pop
Classical Music
Country Music
Cuban Music
Drum'n'bass
Elvis
House
Irish Music
Jazz
Music USA
Opera
Reggae
Rock
Techno
World Music (2 vols)

100 Essential CDs series
Country
Latin

Opera
Rock
Soul
World Music

History Guides
China
Egypt
England
France
Greece
India
Ireland
Islam
Italy
Spain
USA

Reference Guides
Books for Teenagers
Children's Books, 0–5
Children's Books, 5–11
Cult Football
Cult Movies
Cult TV
Digital Stuff
Formula 1
The Internet
Internet Radio
James Bond
Lord of the Rings
Man Utd
Personal Computers
Pregnancy & Birth
Shopping Online
Travel Health
Travel Online
Unexplained Phenomena
The Universe
Videogaming
Weather
Website Directory

Also! More than 120 Rough Guide music CDs are available from all good book and record stores. Listen in at www.worldmusic.net

Don't bury your head in the sand!

Take cover!

with Rough Guide Travel Insurance

Worldwide cover, for Rough Guide readers worldwide

UK Freefone **0800 015 09 06**
Worldwide **(+44) 1392 314 665**
Check the web at
www.roughguides.com/insurance

ROUGH GUIDES

Insurance organized by Torribles Insurance Brokers Ltd, 21 Prince Street, Bristol, BS1 4PH, England